DECOLONIZING THE ENGL
CURRICULUM

George Floyd's death on May 25, 2020, marked a watershed in reactions to anti-Black racism in the United States and elsewhere. Intense demonstrations around the world followed. Within literary studies, the demonstrations accelerated the scrutiny of the literary curriculum, the need to diversify the curriculum, and the need to incorporate more Black writers. *Decolonizing the English Literary Curriculum* is a major collection that aims to address these issues from a global perspective. An international team of leading scholars illustrates the necessity and advantages of reform from specific decolonial perspectives, with evidence-based arguments from classroom contexts, as well as establishing new critical agendas. The significance of *Decolonizing the English Literary Curriculum* lies in the complete overhaul it proposes for the study of English literature. It reconnects English studies, the humanities, and the modern, international university to issues of racial and social justice. This book is also available as Open Access on Cambridge Core.

ATO QUAYSON is the Jean G. and Morris M. Professor of Interdisciplinary Studies and Chair of the Department of English at Stanford University. His books include the two-volume edited *Cambridge History of Postcolonial Literature*, *Tragedy and Postcolonial Literature*, which won the Warren-Brooks Prize for Literary Criticism and *Oxford Street, Accra: City Life and the Itineraries of Transnationalism*, which won the Urban History Association Prize. He is Editor of the *Cambridge Journal of Postcolonial Literary Inquiry* and host of Cambridge Contours: The Cambridge Literary Studies Hour. He has also curated Critic.Reading.Writing, a YouTube channel dedicated to themes in the interdisciplinary literary humanities. He is elected Fellow of the Ghana Academy of Arts and Sciences, the Royal Society of Canada, the British Academy, and the American Academy of Arts and Sciences.

ANKHI MUKHERJEE is Professor of English and World Literatures at the University of Oxford and Fellow of Wadham College. Her books include *Unseen City: The Psychic Lives of the Urban Poor* (2021), which won Columbia University's Robert S. Liebert Award, and *What Is a Classic? Postcolonial Rewriting and Invention of the Canon* (2014), which won the British Academy's Rose Mary Crawshay Prize for English Literature. She has coedited *A Concise Companion to Psychoanalysis, Literature, and Culture* (2014) and edited *After Lacan* (2018). She is currently writing *A Very Short Introduction to Postcolonial Literature* (Oxford University Press, 2024).

DECOLONIZING THE ENGLISH LITERARY CURRICULUM

EDITED BY

ATO QUAYSON

Stanford University

ANKHI MUKHERJEE

University of Oxford

CAMBRIDGE
UNIVERSITY PRESS

Shaftesbury Road, Cambridge CB2 8EA, United Kingdom

One Liberty Plaza, 20th Floor, New York, NY 10006, USA

477 Williamstown Road, Port Melbourne, VIC 3207, Australia

314–321, 3rd Floor, Plot 3, Splendor Forum, Jasola District Centre,
New Delhi – 110025, India

103 Penang Road, #05–06/07, Visioncrest Commercial, Singapore 238467

Cambridge University Press is part of Cambridge University Press & Assessment,
a department of the University of Cambridge.

We share the University's mission to contribute to society through the pursuit of
education, learning and research at the highest international levels of excellence.

www.cambridge.org
Information on this title: www.cambridge.org/9781009299954

DOI: 10.1017/9781009299985

First published 2024

Printed in the United Kingdom by TJ Books Limited, Padstow Cornwall

A catalogue record for this publication is available from the British Library

A Cataloging-in-Publication data record for this book is available from the Library of Congress

ISBN 978-1-009-29995-4 Hardback
ISBN 978-1-009-29996-1 Paperback

Contents

v

Contributors

BRINDA BOSE is Associate Professor at the Centre for English Studies, Jawaharlal Nehru University.

RONALD CHARLES is Associate Professor in the Department for the Study of Religion at the University of Toronto.

JOE CLEARY is Professor of English at Yale University.

MARGERY FEE is Professor Emeritus of English at the University of British Columbia.

DEBJANI GANGULY is Professor of English and Director of the Institute of the Humanities and Global Cultures at the University of Virginia.

WILLIAM GHOSH is Associate Professor of World Literature at the University of Oxford and Fellow of Christ Church College.

PAUL GILES is Professor of English at the University of Sydney.

KATHERINE GILLEN is Associate Professor of English at Texas A&M University.

STEFAN HELGESSON is Professor of English at Stockholm University.

GERALDINE HENG is Mildred Hajek Vacek and John Roman Vacek Chair at the Department of English at the University of Texas at Austin.

JEANNE-MARIE JACKSON is Associate Professor of English at Johns Hopkins University.

CHRISTOPHER KRENTZ is Associate Professor in the Department of English at the University of Virginia.

NIGEL LEASK is Regius Chair of English Language and Literature at the University of Glasgow.

JOANNE LEOW is Associate Professor of English at Simon Fraser University.

SLOAN MAHONE is Associate Professor of the History of Medicine in the Faculty of History at the University of Oxford.

ELIZABETH MCMAHON is a professor in the School of Arts and Media at the University of New South Wales (UNSW).

NASSER MUFTI is Associate Professor of English at University of Illinois Chicago.

ANKHI MUKHERJEE is Professor of English and World Literatures at the University of Oxford and Fellow of Wadham College.

JAMES OGUDE is Director and Senior Research Fellow at the Centre for the Advancement of Scholarship, University of Pretoria.

KWABENA OPOKU-AGYEMANG is Lecturer in English at the University of Ghana and Academic Director of SIT, School for International Training.

SANDEEP PARMAR is Professor of English Literature at the University of Liverpool.

ATO QUAYSON is Jean G. and Morris M. Doyle Professor of Interdisciplinary Studies and Chair of the Department of English at Stanford University.

DEANNA REDER is Associate Professor in the Departments of Indigenous Studies and English at Simon Fraser University.

AKSHYA SAXENA is Assistant Professor of English at Vanderbilt University.

JOSEPH R. SLAUGHTER is Associate Professor of English and Comparative Literature at Columbia University.

NATHAN SUHR-SYTSMA is Associate Professor at the Department of English at Emory University.

AARTHI VADDE is Associate Professor of English at Duke University.

Acknowledgments

Ato Quayson wants to thank Gabriella Safran, Associate Dean of Humanities and Debra Satz, Dean of Humanities and Social Sciences at Stanford University for providing the funds to make this volume free and Open Access to the general public worldwide in perpetuity.

The editors wish to thank Ray Ryan, Edgar Mendez, Bethany Johnson, Kathleen Fearn, and the production team at CUP who helped bring this book to fruition. We thank each other for this journey, which has galvanised our pedagogy and research in unforeseen ways, and in a spirit of collaborative learning with all the contributors.

Introduction

Ankhi Mukherjee and Ato Quayson

In "Hope Gardens," Lorna Goodison writes wistfully about the famous botanical garden in Kingston, Jamaica.

> Seated now in a seminar, you're perplexed
> as this post-colonial scholar unearths plot
> after heinous imperial plot buried behind
>
> our botanical gardens; and you think pity
> the people never knew this as we posed
> for Brownie camera captured photographs
>
> *(Supplying Salt and Light* 53)

The self-identification of the poetic persona in "Hope Gardens" is split between a Joycean mobility figure who will forge in the smithy of their soul the uncreated reality of fleeting experience – "You write to immortalize the long-gone / Sunday afternoons" – and the general reader and public, "We the ignorant, the uneducated," strolling in the garden or scrolling its poetic namesake.[1] Presumably, the seminar attendee is "perplexed" not just by the data dump of postcolonial research but that this establishment, originally a sugar plantation, and a relic of the successive Spanish and British Atlantic empires in Jamaica, should become an anachronistic space for visitors "lost in daydreams of owning own / places with lawns the square of a kerchief" (53). A bellicosity creeps into the tone of the poem. The Hope Gardens loyalists may be "unaware" and "unenlightened" about the English provenance of the roses blooming, the very roses that lend themselves freely as ciphers in assignations, but "so what?" (53, 54). Who cares about the "colonial design" – out of sight and mind in the Hope Gardens of today – when the "two-leaved wrought iron double gates" had been flung open to one and all (54)? The colonial estate was now a public park: supplementing the work of "*this* post-colonial scholar," the claimants of "*our* botanical gardens" had indeed ushered in a new and enabling form of public engagement with the country's colonial and slaveholding past.

I

Goodison's nuanced poem about the Hope Royal Botanical Gardens sheds light on the often-unbridgeable gap between the classroom and the world outside. The "post-colonial scholar" is often considered the killjoy whose knowledge of the history and aftermaths of colonialism subsumes the complex lived experiences of postcolonial societies. In this respect, she is not different than the critical race scholar, who in the United States is accused of a range of sins, including the distortion of American history, if they want to teach the roots of slavery. In his essay "Muse of History," Derek Walcott had cautioned against a petrifying of colonial history into myth, with its unchangeable binary of perpetrator and victim: "In the New World, servitude to the muse of history has produced a literature of recrimination and despair, a literature of revenge written by the descendants of slaves or a literature of remorse written by the descendants of masters. Because this literature serves historic truth, it yellows into polemic or evaporates in pathos" (*What the Twilight Says* 37). What Walcott evokes instead is a "tough aesthetic" that "neither explains nor forgives history" (37). The civilian stakeholders in the hope and beauty offered by the Hope Gardens in Goodison's eponymous poem are not champions of what Patrick Wright, a staunch critic of the heritage industry in the UK, described as an "ethereal kind of holding company for the dead spirit of the nation" (51). As we see in Walcott's classic extrapolations, where characters with slave names such as "Helen" or "Achille" (in *Omeros*) are untroubled by the archetypes associated with their canonical counterparts in Homer's epics, Goodison marks a cultural forgetting and overcoming that is not willed cultural amnesia. However, this "tough aesthetic" of neither explaining nor forgiving history comes under pressure when decolonization itself has been thwarted and rendered incomplete.

Social ferment must be adjudged the ultimate progenitor of calls for decolonizing the literary curriculum or any curriculum for that matter. At a time when disciplines are scrambling to keep up with *both* the accelerations and upheavals of a global informational economy *and* radical geopolitical shifts away from Euro-American dominance, how might the literary curriculum be reconfigured even while paying attention to the views of writers such as Goodison, Walcott, Soyinka, and others like them who ask for the tough aesthetic love of critique? Since the turn of the century and well before that, we have witnessed genuine shifts in world literary flows brought on by proliferating information technology and translation networks; by transformed territorial and economic alignments in a post-Soviet era; and by the emergence of multiple war zones and new ethnic and religious conflagrations. Large-scale humanitarian crises wrought by wars and catastrophic climate change have brought new subalterns into our moral economy – asylum seekers, climate refugees, illegal migrants, and even large swathes of the Muslim populace demonized as a consequence of the ghoulish global visibility of fundamentalist versions of political Islam. A critical response to these developments on the part of literary scholars is that they ought not to ignore emergent literary topographies that can no longer be circumscribed by the classical postcolonial geographies of Europe and its others. The developments demand new modes of analysis that are at once conceptual, philological, translational, textual, generic, and more specifically decolonizing.

The term decolonization is often used interchangeably with "decoloniality" or "decolonial." "Decoloniality," in a general sense of the term, has many implications: the aftereffects of colonialism; a period of restoration and reparation; a questioning of Western modernity; an interrogation of and resistance to the colluding forces of capitalism, racism, and imperialism that structured colonial domination. The more specific – and prevalent – sense of "decoloniality" was developed by scholars from Latin and South America. One of the proponents of decolonial studies is Walter Mignolo, who, with Catherine E. Walsh, articulates the strongest position on the matter in *On Decoloniality: Concepts, Analytics, Praxis* (2018). As Mignolo and Walsh state clearly in the introduction, the legacies of decolonization – associated with the Bandung conference or the Conference of the Non-Aligned countries – are not the foundation of the decolonial project.

> For us, the horizon is not the political independence of nation-states (as it was for decolonization), nor is it only – or primarily – the confrontation with capitalism and the West (though both are central components of the modern/colonial matrix of power). Our interest and concern . . . are with the habits that modernity/coloniality implanted in all of us; with how modernity/coloniality has worked and continues to work to negate, disavow, distort and deny knowledges, subjectivities, world senses, and life visions. (4)

When the editors or contributors of *Decolonizing the English Literary Curriculum* use the term "decoloniality" or "decolonial," it is not marked by this absolute rejection of and break from the Western episteme or modernity. This volume is on the English literary curriculum after all, and our writers are well immersed in and even admiring of aspects of the tradition. We have already mentioned Lorna Goodison's and Derek Walcott's negotiations of European legacy; Ngũgĩ's writing was heavily steeped in the Bible; Wole Soyinka wrote his theory of tragedy drawing on and critiquing Nietzsche. Therefore, despite significant overlaps between postcolonial and decolonial thought – their critical attention to alternative epistemologies and marginalized spaces, for instance – we prefer the term "decoloniality" to denote the ongoing process of reevaluation of the literary curriculum.

It is vitally important to question why the discourse on decolonization has come *after* postcolonial thought and theory sprang fully formed from the brow of imperial history in the 1980s and 1990s. The "post" of post-colonialism literally means the period after colonialism has ended; it also refers to the contesting and supplanting of legacies for nation states and subjugated cultures to achieve self-sufficiency after the transfer of govern-ance. It therefore seems strange to return to the time of decolonization in what, strictly speaking, is the postcolonial era. The answer to the question of why calls for decolonization continue after the end of formal colonialism lies in a hard-won understanding of the temporality of formal decoloniza-tion, which Simon Gikandi describes as an "interregnum": "the lives of subjects stranded in time as it were" (1). Gikandi cites Hannah Arendt to understand this problem of time as a "scission or rupture in what is no longer simply an after or a before" (2).

Chinua Achebe's *Arrow of God*, written after the end of formal colonial-ism in 1960, is not usually read as a classic work of decolonization, as Gikandi points out. It offers neither a scathing critique nor a poetics of disillusionment about the initial promise of the postcolonial state, now descending rapidly into communal conflict and a civil war. Gikandi inter-prets *Arrow of God* as a definitive work of the crisis of decolonization, which shows how late colonialism haunts the culture of the modern "even as it sought to reconstitute African society as an impoverished version of identities and histories that had already been questioned in Europe" (2). What makes it a narrative of decolonization is its depiction of the failed postcolonial present. "Rather than present the problematic of colonialism as the opposition between two temporalities, between the past and the present, the novel is often bogged down by a present that it cannot name," Gikandi observes (4). Decolonization, in this definition, is not an agon between tradition and modernity but a disease of modern colonial time: the subject can neither seek redemption in a primordial past nor imagine a postcolonial future.

The very moment that the English colonial agent, Winterbottom, calls the old priest "the only witness of truth" (7), Ezeulu is deauthorized and made a stooge. As Achebe has shown in *Things Fall Apart*, imperialist axiomatics will always replace African tradition with its own invented tradition: the power imbalance is such that the two could not possibly coexist. The unique feature of *Arrow of God* is that Ezeulu is thwarted not by colonial agency alone but his own will to address – and we quote Gikandi again – "something lacking or missing in the hermeneutics of culture" (5). Ezeulu is torn between his nostalgia for a ruined past and his own zeal to create a space for the project of colonial modernity, one that sees him hand over a son to the missionary education system to act as his eyes and ears among them. His is a time of confusion, wedded as he is to the authority of the gods and communitarian traditions but at the same time disenchanted with the narratives of modernity. His crisis is not accelerated by a perceived superiority of the colonizer – Mr. Winterbottom is portrayed as sick and weak, his narrative of the internecine conflict between Umuaro and Okperi meant to be laughed at by the reader – nor is it the case that *Arrow of God* cannot imagine an African world before colonialism. Decolonization, instead, is that time after colonialism which makes Ezeulu, trapped between the anachronistic temporality of the past and unknowable futures, feel impermanent, like a placeholder:

> He was merely a watchman. His power was no more than the power of a child over a goat that was said to be his. As long as the goat was alive it could be his; he would find it food and take care of it. But the day it was slaughtered he would know soon enough who the real owner was. (3)

The materiality of this in-between time hyphenating the change of regimes is psychic, not just physical or even political. And the English literary curriculum has a part to play in this change of psychic regimes. Ngũgĩ wa Thiong'o published "On the Abolition of the English Department" in 1972, in which he made a special case for decommissioning an unexamined idea of English literary study that he thought was a form of continuing colonialism in his country Kenya and elsewhere in the postcolonial world. The general implications of Ngũgĩ's argument have continued to ramify in the design of the English literary curriculum in many parts of the world, but nowhere more insistently in recent times than in the Euro-American academy, whose doors, unlike the doors of Hope Gardens, have not been flung wide open.

All calls to decolonize the curriculum are also bound to be context-specific, such that in Australia, Aotearoa New Zealand, and Canada, decolonizing typically involves the two categories of Indigenous literatures and the literature written by immigrants. As Elizabeth McMahon notes in this volume (Chapter 4), the harsh historical processes of settler colonialism in Australia and Aotearoa New Zealand have led to ingrained social inequalities that have both shaped the study of English literature in the two countries and triggered the movement for the decolonization of the literary curriculum. In Ghana or South Africa, as both Kwabena Opoku-Agyemang (Chapter 11) and James Ogude (Chapter 26) also illustrate for us in the volume, decolonizing the curriculum involves not just countering the traditional English menu of Shakespeare, Milton, or Chaucer with Black writers from each country, it also involves the introduction of new methodologies for reading literacy alongside orality and the breaking of ingrained habits of thought that had been inculcated during the colonial and apartheid period and that continue to persist in the postcolonial era. At the heart of any context for decolonizing the curriculum then are critical social questions about changes in society that are tied to the rising voices of those minorities that had hitherto been marginalized.

While such calls are context-specific, they all share the central impulse of being tied to the correction of social anomalies specifically linked to the situation of oppressed or underrepresented minorities. In other words, the point is not just to detail the gaps in the curriculum but in using the curriculum as a way of changing society itself. If the echo of Marx's maxim of the relationship between describing the world and the active effort to change it for the better is detected here, it is not entirely accidental.[2] For the term decolonizing itself must be referred to the agendas of the newly decolonized world that was born in the second half of the twentieth century through various processes of struggle in India, Africa, Southeast Asia, and other places. These struggles may be described as only one installment of the decolonizing process, earlier ones having occurred in the processes that led to Latin American independence in the early 1800s. And, as Robert Young instructs us in *Empire, Colony, Postcolony*, all accounts of decolonization must also reflect upon the fact that internal struggles for decolonization have been continually taking place in the settler colonies of Australia, Aotearoa New Zealand, Canada, and the USA, especially in relation to the historical and continuing struggles of their Indigenous populations. This realization then serves to complicate what we might understand under the rubric of decolonizing.

A shift in the perception of what constitutes the decolonizing context for understanding the writing that emerged from the Global South had first been suggested in the work of Albert Memmi, Aimé Césaire, Frantz Fanon, and other postcolonial liberationist thinkers from the 1950s. Thus in 1955, Aimé Césaire outlined the earliest form of colonial discourse analysis in his monumental *Discours sur le colonialisme*, which was followed in rapid succession by Albert Memmi and Frantz Fanon setting out a mode of analysis that was rhetorically highly sophisticated as well as refracting revolutionary, political, and cultural ideals. C. L. R James, George Lamming, and V. S. Naipaul also each raised key questions about nation and narration, the struggle between universalism and localism in the literature of the newly independent nations, and the fraught intersections of the aesthetic, the ethical, and the political dimensions of these new forms of writing. A major return to these writers has taken place in the past twenty years or so, aimed at finding the right modes for grasping the practical background to the processes for decolonizing the curriculum. In her influential essay "On Decolonisation and the University," Priyamvada Gopal argues that anticolonialism "is the missing term, a pivotal absence, in academic discussions of decolonization today" (886). Anticolonial resistance varied "according to historical exigencies" (886), and took the form of a wide range of activities which cannot be subsumed under nationalism, as Gopal points out.

"Reframing discussions of decolonisation in the light of anticolonial thought – as the theory and practice of anticolonialism rather than a mere theoretical variant of postcolonialism – gives grounding and historical heft to them. It also enables a discussion of decolonisation as necessarily dialogical, and a process with a horizon of aspiration," states Gopal (886). Positing anticolonialism as an ideality and a futurity – a process rather than a destination that is reached – Gopal argues for an anticolonial university that "pushes to the horizon of decolonisation" rather than a decolonized one (889). The anticolonial university, instead of seeing education as redemptive of the very colonial histories that has shaped it, seeks instead to interrogate and eventually abolish the coercive knowledge systems that have continued to haunt it.

Few texts on decolonization are as powerful as Ngũgĩ wa Thiong'o *Decolonising the Mind*, which began its life as the 1984 Robb Lectures in honor of a former chancellor of Auckland University. Acknowledging the Māori people who had extended him a warm welcome inside and outside the university, Ngũgĩ is happy to note in the introduction that his lectures on the politics of language in African literature had coincided with Māori language week: as if in a gesture of solidarity with the "beauty of resistance" he had seen in Māori culture, Ngũgĩ declares this book as his farewell to English (ix). *Decolonising the Mind* starts with a discussion of imperialism, or what Ngũgĩ terms "the rule of consolidated finance capital" (2). Its yoke is total, spelling "economic, political, military, cultural and psychological consequences for the people of the world" (2). Not only are countries in the

Global South mortgaged to the IMF, the wretched and the dispossessed of the earth are decimated by what Ngũgĩ calls the "cultural bomb," whose task is to discredit a people's belief in their languages, epistemologies, heritage, and environment (3). "Amidst this wasteland which it has created, imperialism presents itself as the cure," Ngũgĩ states, forcing its victims to collude with the theft of their languages and treasures of the mind (3).

Imperialism is embedded in universities, its foundations built into language and literary studies: these institutions were set up in the colonies to produce yes-men, mimic men, and the "cool, level-headed servant of the Empire celebrated in Kipling's poem 'If'," as Ngũgĩ scathingly comments (93). This agenda continues to manifest in the way in which English (language and literature) is taught at university level across the globe, in the institutional imbalance in the teaching of indigenous versus imported languages and literatures, and in the lack of contextualizing of imported languages, intellectual traditions, theory, and philosophy. For the post-colonial or metropolitan university to not become neoimperial, for it to proclaim "liberty from theft," as Ngũgĩ puts it, it must unflinchingly confront colonial legacies through an ongoing scrutiny of unexamined course content and curricula as well as teaching, learning, and assessment methods (3). Decolonization, especially where it was granted rather than won, did not necessarily force the formerly colonized to self-decolonize and think for themselves, Achille Mbembe states in *Out of the Dark Night*: "rather than being the site of a renewed genesis of meaning, [decoloniza-tion] took on the appearance of an encounter with oneself through effrac-tion" (4). If we note that the word "effraction" means "breaking and entering, burglary," then what Mbembe seems to be saying here is that historical decolonization simply continued a mode of violent theft against the formerly colonized. We can see here echoes of Ngũgĩ's comments on the effects of the curriculum on the psyches of the people as far apart as the Māori and his own Kikuyu.

Decolonizing Orientations

Every so often demands for reform of the English literature curriculum are made from equity-seeking groups, either for the overhauling of the curriculum or for its complete replacement with something that appears more equitable to such equity-seeking groups. Thus, the term decolonizing must be understood as having historically specific as well as metaphorical implications. While it has come to define actions that seek autonomy from the legacies of colonization, slavery, White supremacy, sexism, and

Eurocentrism in a rapidly changing yet interconnected world, decolonization also provides a vocabulary by which new demands for social equity may help to reshape the literary curriculum in the direction of greater sensitivity to urgent racial and social justice issues in the world itself. The term "equity-seeking groups" stands for all those who feel themselves politically and socially marginalized by the lived systems in which they exist. At a minimal level, a list of equity-seeking groups would include the following: people of color and racial minorities, persons with disabilities, persons with non-heteronormative sexual orientations, formerly colonized people, Native peoples (pertaining specifically to the settler communities of Australia, Canada, and the USA), women, Jews, and Muslims, among others. The extreme racial and social injustice manifested in the killing of George Floyd (to which we shall return) has served to magnify the other injuries suffered by different equity-seeking groups, thus necessitating the linking of the quest for racial justice to that of social justice as its necessary corollary. The demands of equity-seeking groups have turned as much on calls for statistical representation on the curriculum as on how literary texts are interpreted from the perspective of the marginalized in the first place.

A second set of arguments for reform has also come from theoretical perspectives that do not necessarily attach themselves to any particular equity-seeking group. Thus, the canon wars of the 1980s centered on questions of meaning-making and interpretation and came from theoretical perspectives that sought to decenter long-held reading practices in general and to show that these were complicit with forms of hegemony and oppression in the world at large. Marxism, deconstruction, and psychoanalysis were the most coherent of such models adduced for decentering existing reading practices, and they in their turn inspired models of interpretation such as postcolonialism, feminism, disability studies, and critical race studies, among various others.

The third category of calls for reforms of the literary curriculum has come from interdisciplinary or intersectional perspectives. Such interdisciplinary calls typically arise due to the recognition that the problems in the real world are much too complex for any one disciplinary perspective to be able to deal with and that the urgency of such problems requires the necessary breaking down of standard disciplinary protocols. Thus, arguments from the perspectives of the Anthropocene and of environmental studies tend to by pass all monodisciplinary straitjackets to insist on the urgency of the questions that face humanity as a justification for ignoring disciplinary boundaries altogether. For us, these three decolonizing orientations must be seen as converging on the question of social justice, made particularly urgent by the fact that the impetus for curriculum reform in 2020 came from the transatlantic civil rights, Abolitionist, and anti-racist Black Lives Matter movement today. We intend in *Decolonizing the English Literary Curriculum* to include all three decolonizing orientations described above and will be using the term decolonizing as an umbrella concept to index the interests of different types of calls for fundamental curricular reform. Each chapter in the collection will be explicitly tasked with illustrating the necessity and advantages of reform from specific decolonial perspectives, with evidence-based arguments from classroom contexts as a matter of principle. The significance of this volume lies in the complete overhaul of how we think about the study of literature and its relationship to issues of racial and social justice in the world.

Black Lives Matter and Calls for Decolonizing the Curriculum

The death of George Floyd at the hands of Minneapolis police on May 25, 2020, marked a watershed in reactions to anti-Black racism in the USA and elsewhere and indeed triggered intense debates about the pressing need to decolonize the curriculum. The calls since 2020 strike a different note from similar calls that have taken place in English departments starting in the 1960s following the Civil Rights Movement. Now, these calls appear tied also to the politics of social address and the claims to public space both in the USA and the UK, but arguably even more intensely joined in South Africa, where the Rhodes Must Fall movement started, as we shall see presently. The intensity of demonstrations all over the world in response to the killing of George Floyd extended to places previously not known as being much concerned with questions of Blackness, such as Japan, Argentina, and Australia, among various others. The African Union, the European Union, the United Nations Commission on Human Rights, and several countries across the world put out statements expressing their horror at the manner of George Floyd's death and expressing support for the Black Lives Matter movement.

The demonstrations have also forced serious soul-searching regarding the literary curriculum. Bernadine Evaristo, cowinner of the 2019 Booker Prize, used the platform offered by the 2020 New Statesman/Goldsmiths Lecture to speak eloquently about the need for diversifying the curriculum in the UK not only to incorporate more Black writers, but also more writing by women and other people of color. It is a shock to learn, for example, that the AQA (formerly Assessments and Qualifications Alliance), the largest examining board in the UK, does not "feature a single book by a black author among set texts for its GCSE English Literature syllabus and has only two novels by non-white authors – Meera Syal's *Anita and Me* and Kazuo Ishiguro's *Never Let me Go*."[3] Elsewhere, calls from the Black Curriculum's founder Lavinya Stennett for Black history to be taught in British schools systematically throughout the education system and not just during Black History Month have increased pressure on the UK government, which has in its turn issued a statement decrying the use of critical race theory in schools. As its Equalities Minister Kemi Badenoch asserted in Parliament: "We do not want teachers to teach their white pupils about white privilege and inherited racial guilt."[4] This echoed Donald Trump's attack on critical race theory some weeks prior to the UK minister's statement. In the case of Trump, a presidential edict toward the end of his term in 2020 threatened to withhold federal funding from any government department that held diversity training for its staff.[5] That the subject matter of critical race studies has been fundamentally misunderstood by both governments is not as significant as the fact that both feel compelled to issue such statements after the rise of the strong coalition against racial injustice in the two countries following George Floyd's death. The battle lines for hearts and minds seems to have been drawn, with the stakes very high on both governmental and popular fronts.

Debates about the English curriculum have also been energized in English departments across the USA, which historically has always had intense arguments on race and racism given its history of racial oppression and the battles against these from the eras of Jim Crow, the Civil Rights Movement, and now Black Lives Matter. The leader in the debates on reform of the English literary curriculum has without a doubt been the English Department at the University of Chicago, whose statement on Black Lives Matter posted on their website shortly after the death of George Floyd set the tone for other such statements in English departments across the USA. In their revised statement of July 2020, the Chicago English Department noted among other things that "English as a discipline has a long history of providing aesthetic rationalizations for colonization, exploitation, extraction, and anti-Blackness. Our discipline is responsible for developing hierarchies of cultural production that have contributed directly to social and systematic determinations of whose lives matter and why."[6] While Chicago's clarion call was much applauded, their decision to devote all graduate places in the 2020/2021 cycle exclusively to students interested in working in Black Studies or with faculty of color was met with bewilderment and some disdain on social media. There are currently seventy-seven students studying for their PhDs in the English Department at Chicago, but all the ire on social media was reserved for the five entry places in question for 2020. While several English departments in both the USA and the UK have made similar pronouncements in support of Black Lives Matter, none has been as bold as Chicago's to declare a special focus on Black Studies.

Rhodes Must Fall

Ankhi grew up in a small town in West Bengal, its anglicized name, Burdwan, dating from its history as a district capital during the Raj. The Bengali name, Bardhaman, which means "expanding," commemorates Mahavira or Vardhamana (599–521 BCE), the twenty-fourth Tirthankara of Jainism, who consecrated the ground on his travels. A beloved land-mark here is a coronation arch that was originally called Bijay Toran, after the erstwhile ruler Bijay Chand Mahtab, but was informally renamed Curzon Gate after the Viceroy of India's grand visit in 1904. The name Curzon Gate (Karjon, in Bengali pronunciation) has stuck, its provenance forgotten every day by the townspeople and pigeons defiling it. This is one of countless examples of the selective amnesia of erstwhile colonies, as vividly depicted in the Lorna Goodison poem with which the chapter starts. When Rhodes Must Fall (RMF) arrived in Oxford from Cape Town in 2015, Ankhi notes that her iconoclasm toward dirty history's artifacts was tempered by the instability of signs she had known, where what sounds like a triumphalist Bengali moniker befitting a thriving agrarian economy ("Bardhaman") is actually the name of an unworldly transient and where fondness for a name-relic (Curzon) doesn't imply that the terrible repercussions of Lord Curzon's 1905 partition of Bengal have been forgiven.[7] RMF redux, a debate reignited by the #BlackLivesMatter protests in the aftermaths of George Floyd's murder, occasioned no such dithering.

The Rhodes Must Fall (RMF) movement returned to Oxford in May 2020, a debate that was itself reignited worldwide by the Black Lives Matter protests in the aftermath of George Floyd's murder in the United States in the same month. Liberation movements such as Rhodes Must Fall constitute the critical move of toppling acquiescence to redress incomplete emancipation and a failed postcolonial project: decolonization is the very name we give the process of disaggregating the present from a future overdetermined by the colonial past. This reckoning, revived by the killing of George Floyd, came during a pandemic which was also racial, impacting communities of color disproportionately, and the chilling realization that Floyd's death was preventable if a mass mobilization of the scale of that year's protests had demanded Abolition earlier. When Oriel College, where the Rhodes statue is lodged, declared in May 2021 that despite the wishes of the college's governing body – and the sympathetic recommendations of an independent commission (comprised of academics, city councillors, alumni, administrators, and journalists) – Rhodes wouldn't fall after all, Simukai Chigudu lamented the missed opportunity for utilizing this symbolic action as a harbinger of real change. Associate Professor of African Politics at Oxford, Chigudu has been at the forefront of the RMF campaign since 2015. His article in the *Guardian* unconsciously echoes Simon Gikandi's depiction of decolonization as a crisis of the present: "Arguments over statues are always about the present and not the past. They are about which aspects of our cultural heritage we choose to honour in public space and why. They are about what values we wish to promote and who has a voice in these matters."[8]

Decolonization brings with it, Frantz Fanon writes in *Wretched of the Earth*, "a new language and a new humanity" (30). One of the rallying cries of RMF redux, that of decolonizing the curriculum, shows, as had the previous Fallist movements at the Universities of Cape Town, Wits, and Oxford, a radical disenchantment with an education system unable to shake off the yoke of a tyrannical past and engender a viable decolonized future.[9] For campuses to become inclusive environments, courses should not be dominated by White, male, Eurocentric perspectives, a review from Universities UK stated in 2019. Baroness Amos, the first Black woman to serve as a minister in the British cabinet and in the House of Lords, said this applies to science subjects as much as it does to the arts and humanities.[10] "There are things like who is on the reading lists, how much are you enabling a critique of different approaches to subjects, who is being recognized as being someone who can make a valuable contribution on this?"[11] Decolonizing the curriculum necessitates the hiring of academic staff with relevant expertise and attracting and retaining more Black scholars to correct the original, majoritarian quota system. Iyiola Solanke, Professor of EU Law and Social Justice, compiled data for the Runnymede Trust (2017) that showed Black women constituting less than 2 percent of the professoriate.[12] According to HESA (the Higher Education Statistics Agency), there are 350 Black female professors in the UK out of a total of 18,000 professors. Solanke, founder of the "Black Professors Forum" uses "Black" politically to indicate not only African and Caribbean women, but also women of Asian and Arab descent. She states that the term Black is used to empower these communities of women, who are ethnic minorities in the UK despite being global majorities. "Allyship," a neologism forged by the virulence of racism, is applicable to the aims of the Black Professors Forum, which seeks to address a higher education system where only a handful of universities have more than five Black female professors.[13]

Universities, especially those in the Old World, are unlikely to have hair-trigger responses to student unrest, as change involves structural revisions – not just superficial curriculum revision and expansion but acquiring funding for new hires, coupled with new hiring strategies. In departments of English, where we teach the history of literature and language from Anglo-Saxon to World Literature, chronology is Eurochronology to a large extent, and to situate oneself in literary tradition is to inhabit structures that are historically Eurocentric, patriarchal, classist, xenophobic, or racist. We can, where relevant, read literature as a textual as well as a territorial inscription and remain vigilant of its implication in a given culture's criteria and contestation of value. Decolonizing the English literary curriculum would also entail a concerted effort to retrieve forgotten and discredited literary forms and figures, proletariat and women's voices, and such projects have been gathering momentum since the last quarter of the twentieth century.

So, how can one teach the canon in the mode of decolonizing? Let's take a literary history paper that extends from 1760–1830, for instance. Here, students can learn about postcolonial Austen and about Byron, Shelley, or Coleridge's self-situation as English poets and cultural arbiters in the mediated landscapes of an empire which included the near and far East. We can look at Romantic women writers (Anna Laetitia Barbauld, Hannah More, or Phillis Wheatley) and the antislavery movements they supported. We could examine the politics of Thomas de Quincey's anxiety about cancerous kisses from Nilotic crocodiles, reading it with reference to Charles Nicholas Sigisbert Sonnini's "Travels in Lower and Upper Egypt," which moves from crocodiles to the "unexampled depravation and brutality" of bestial Upper Egypt men with alacrity quoted in Lindop, p. 136. This could be studied alongside Richard Burton's *Arabian Nights*, where he deploys the metonymic meanings of the crocodile in Sonnini's work. These are some of the lessons on the period to be taken from Nigel Leask's chapter in this volume (Chapter 20).

Substantive canon expansion, however, is nothing without an informed critique of the canonical method. Acknowledging a certain complexion of literary genealogy, we need to be mindful about not perpetuating its politics by perversely denying the diversity of literatures in English in the postcolonial, global world. The impetus for the "world-ing" of literature – treating it as embedded and embodied – has largely come from humanities scholarship, through the emergence of equity-seeking feminist, postcolonial, gender, queer, race, disability, and eco-critical studies, which also have vital activist dimensions. We need to translate innovation in scholarship into renovated teaching practices, working not against the grain of institutions but with their financial, administrative, and moral support.

Aesthetic and Sentimental Education

One thing we might take from the current debates about the English curriculum is how they now centralize literature as the source of senti-mental and aesthetic education. But the aesthetic domain must be defined not just as pertaining to the beautiful or arts-related matters but as having to do with the distribution of the sensible, as Jacques Rancière notes in *The Politics of Aesthetics* (2004). The distribution of the sensible implies varying processes of validation and exclusion that are both policed and enforced in the ways in which English literature is taught. The aesthetic domain must also be understood in the sense in which Spivak uses it in *An Aesthetic Education in the Era of Globalization*, where it is the last possible means of yoking education to the goals of democracy and social justice. Given that literature does provide a form of sentimental and aesthetic education, but that such education cannot be divorced from the contexts and ways in which literature is studied, it means that the literary curriculum must be examined for the part it plays in the change of social and psychic regimes. It is also a well-known fact that literary texts are used in a variety of disciplinary contexts, such as in history, anthropology, criminology, cognitive studies, disability studies, cin-ema studies, psychology, philosophy, classics, law, medicine, and urban studies programs among others. Therefore, what passes for sentimental education in the teaching and research on English has additional impact in other disciplinary contexts. What is taught and how it is taught is of fundamental concern for how we think about both racial and social justice well beyond the discipline.

The Western canon of literature around which such a sentimental educa-tion may be imagined, however, is a colonial relic itself, enmired in its hierarchies and colluding in its exclusions and occlusions. In the introductory pages of *Playing in the Dark*, Toni Morrison describes canon revision cartographically, as her project of extending the study of American literature into a wider landscape: "I want to draw a map, so to speak, of a critical geography, and use that map to open as much space for discovery, intellectual adventure, and close exploration as did the original charting of the New World – without the mandate of conquest" (3). The primary incentive for Morrison's undertaking is the abiding yet not fully acknowledged African presence in American literature, a corollary to 400 years of Africans and African Americans in the United States. The coherence of American literature, Morrison states, exists because of this "unsettled and unsettling" population (6). While national literature presented itself as emanating from a singular Americanness, the Africanist presence was deliberately separated from and made unaccountable to it. "It is possible, for example, to read Henry James scholarship exhaustively and never arrive at a nodding mention, much less a satisfactory treatment, of a black woman who lubricates the turn of the plot and becomes the agency of moral choice and meaning in *What Maisie Knew*" (13). Decolonizing the curriculum, in this reckoning, is about confronting the codes and restrictions around omissions and contradictions, omissions which guarantee the false coherence of national and paranational entities such as "American literature." Furthermore, the contemplation of these excluded bodies, voices, and influences, Morrison states, "should not be permitted to hover at the margins of the literary imagination" (5). In fact, they should be brought to the foreground to start unravelling the very technology through which nationalist literature in the USA has shaped itself in a reactive mode to "a real or fabricated Africanist presence" (6).

The curatorial task of retrieving subaltern voices and spaces is key to preparing for a future of institutional change where student and teacher can participate in what bell hooks, in *Teaching Community*, calls "a liberating mutuality" in the classroom (xv). The report prepared by UUK and the NUS (National Union of Students) in 2019, titled "#ClosingTheGap," which Baroness Amos led, showed a 13 percent attainment gap between White students and their BAME (Black, Asian and Minority Ethnic) counterparts.[14] Expressing her shock at this statistic, Baroness Amos stated plainly that for universities to become junctions of "opportunity and aspiration," the fight for change must equally address curriculum, representation, pedagogy, and student experience. *Decolonizing the English Literary Curriculum* is an international and interdisciplinary undertaking, involving scholars across generations and with a wide variety of expertise, which demonstrates that looking awry at the English literary curriculum can provide material and psychic assistance to the ongoing campaign against structural inequality in universities.

Structure of the Volume

The essays in *Decolonizing the English Literary Curriculum* have been divided into four parts: Identities, Methodologies, Interdisciplinarity and Literary Studies, and Canon Revisions. The chapters in each part focus on specific problems in the English literary curriculum and also suggest some pedagogical points for consideration. No two chapters are the same, either in approach or examples, making the volume overall a wide-ranging reflection on the literary curriculum in general from a diverse set of perspectives.

In the "Identities" section, the first four chapters focus on specific national or cultural contexts. Joe Cleary writes about the unique challenge of decolonizing the English department in the context of the complex colonial history of Ireland (Chapter 2); Elizabeth McMahon adopts an intersectional approach to strategize about decolonizing pedagogies in Australia and Aotearoa New Zealand (Chapter 4). Margery Fee and Deanna Reder turn to Indigenous epistemes to reimagine the human connection with land and nature in Canada (Chapter 3). Two of the chapters in this section focus the discussion from the perspective of specific equity-seeking groups. Ankhi Mukherjee (Chapter 6) argues that Black British literature should not be treated as an isomorphism of Black culture and society: despite their immersion the realities of Black life, works such as Zadie Smith's reclaim the aesthetic autonomy denied to writers of color. Brinda Bose finds the possibility of decolonization in matching pluralities of methodology to the pluralities of genders and sexualities (Chapter 5). Paul Giles's chapter attempts a more wide-ranging discussion of how to decolonize the university that, alongside this Introduction, serves to lay out some key questions that are then picked up in the various chapters (Chapter 1).

"Methodologies" carries chapters that focus on specific topics ranging from broadly conceptual and theoretical questions to singular peda-gogical challenges. Aarthi Vadde's chapter explores ways of decolonizing the value and selection criteria guiding anthologies (Chapter 7). Stefan Helgesson examines the role of Marxism in historical contexts of and contemporary debates in decolonization (Chapter 9). Ato Quayson's chapter asks what reading for justice might entail, and how this project of decolonizing the English literary curriculum can go beyond the limits of postcolonial or critical race studies (Chapter 13). Akshya Saxena proposes a mode of reworlding the English literary curriculum that begins by examining the relationship of English to other language worlds and literary cultures (Chapter 12). Three of the chapters dwell on specific pedagogical contexts in different parts of the world: Jeanne-Marie Jackson proposes a "culturally minimalist" approach to teaching African literature in the US academy (Chapter 10); Joanne Leow traces the decolonizing tactics of confabulation in contemporary Singaporean literature (Chapter 8); Kwabena Opoku-Agyemang writes creative and critical interventions in decolonizing the teaching of African literature at the University of Ghana (Chapter 11).

"Interdisciplinary and Literary Studies" explores different modes of interdisciplinarity and how these may shape a decolonizing agenda. Joseph R. Slaughter explores how human rights, international law, and world literature may be revised in tandem so that "the empire's preferred prefabricated forms" do not continue in perpetuity (Chapter 14). Christopher Krentz's chapter brings disability studies into conversation with the challenges of decolonizing literary studies (Chapter 15). Ronald Charles argues that decolonizing the English literary curriculum could start with the Christian Bible (Chapter 16), while Sloan Mahone demonstrates how insights gleaned from literary works – and literary and cultural criticism – have been used in the field of history of medicine to rethink the colonial legacies and structures of knowledge production (Chapter 17).

The final cluster of chapters in "Canon Revisions" goes directly to the canon and what Nigel Leask calls the "monoglot regime of Global English," arguing for modes of critical teaching when it comes to the staples of the English literary curriculum. These range from reflections and recommendations on specific literary history papers (Geraldine Heng on medieval literature [Chapter 18]; Leask on Romanticism [Chapter 20]; Nasser Mufti on Victorian literature [Chapter 21]; Debjani Ganguly on World Literature [Chapter 22]) and key authors (Katherine Gillen on Shakespeare through a Latin American perspective [Chapter 19]) to those that focus on areas of specialist study within the curriculum (Sandeep Parmar on English Diasporic women's poetry [Chapter 23]; William Ghosh on Caribbean literature [Chapter 25]; Nathan Suhr-Sytsma on postcolonial poetry [Chapter 24]). James Ogude's chapter on the Rhodes Must Fall movement (Chapter 26) sets the question of methods and pedagogy firmly within the particular case of postapartheid South Africa and the calls for curricular reform that were made in that heady moment of collective action and social critique.

Notes

1. The famous line from James Joyce's *A Portrait of the Artist as a Young Man* is as follows: "I go to encounter for the millionth time the reality of experience and to forge in the smithy of my soul the uncreated conscience of my race" (Joyce 213).

2. The original quotation is: "The philosophers have only *interpreted* the world, in various ways. The point, however, is to *change* it," and is the eleventh of the "Theses on Feuerbach." See Karl Marx with Friedrich Engels, *The German Ideology* (Guilford, CT: Prometheus Books), 571.

3. See Alison Flood, "Bernadine Evaristo Slams Literature Teaching Bias for 'Whiteness and Maleness'," *The Guardian*, October 2, 2020, www .theguardian.com/books/2020/oct/02/bernardine-evaristo-slams-english-academic-for-bias-to-whiteness-and-maleness.

4. See Daniel Trilling, "Why Is the UK Government Suddenly Targeting 'Critical Race Theory'?" *The Guardian*, October 23, 2020, www .theguardian.com/commentisfree/2020/oct/23/uk-critical-race-theory-trump-conservatives-structural-inequality.

5. See Fabiola Cineas, "Critical Race Theory, and Trump's War on It, Explained," *Vox*, September 24, 2020, www.vox.com/2020/9/24/21451220/critical-race-theory-diversity-training-trump.

6. See https://english.uchicago.edu/.

7. www.indiatoday.in/education-today/gk-current-affairs/story/partition-of-bengal-1905-divide-and-rule-protests-1368958-2018-10-16.

8. The Oriel College website addresses the reasons for the non-removal of the controversial statue here, adding that "the Governing Body of the College, as charity trustees and following the receipt of regulatory and legal advice, took the decision to utilise funds to focus on the contextualisation of the statue in the immediate term, rather than pursue a course of action that was almost certain to result in failure." www.oriel.ox.ac.uk/about/the-rhodes-legacy/. Chigudu's *Guardian* piece, "More than just a statue" can be found here: www .theguardian.com/commentisfree/2021/may/24/oriel-college-rhodes-statue-anti-racist-anger.

9. See Sanders for an account and analysis of the South African hashtag campus movements of 2015–16.

10. Amos became the ninth Director of SOAS in 2015. She has been Master of University College, Oxford, since 2020.

11. www.telegraph.co.uk/education/2019/05/01/universities-must-decolonise-curriculum-boost-black-students/.

12. Solanke is the founder of Black Female Professors Forum: https://blackfemaleprofessorsforum.org/about/about/.

13. "Allyship" signifies solidarities between and within marginalized groups, as well advocacy for inclusion and equality by those who are not themselves marginalized.

14. The report can be found here: www.universitiesuk.ac.uk/latest/insights-and-analysis/closing-gap-how-can-university-leaders.

WORKS CITED

Achebe, Chinua. *Arrow of God*. Harmondsworth: Penguin Modern Classics, 2010.

Fanon, Frantz. *The Wretched of the Earth*. Trans. Constance Farrington. Harmondsworth: Penguin Modern Classics, 2001.

Goodison, Lorna. *Supplying Salt and Light*. Toronto: McClelland & Stewart, 2013.

Gopal, Priyamvada. "On Decolonisation and the University." *Textual Practice* 35.6 (2021): 873–99.

Gikandi, Simon. "*Arrow of God*: The Novel and the Problem of Time." *Research in African Literatures* 49.4 (Winter 2018): 1–13.

hooks, bell. *Teaching Community: A Pedagogy of Hope*. London: Routledge, 2003.

Joyce, James. *A Portrait of the Artist as a Young Man*, ed. Jeri Johnson. Oxford: Oxford University Press, 2000.

Lindop, Grevel. "De Quincey and the Cursed Crocodile." Essays in Criticism Volume XLV:2 (April 1995). Pp: 121–140.

Marx, Karl with Friedrich Engels. *The German Ideology*. Guilford, CT: Prometheus Books, 1998.

Mbembe, Achille. *Out of the Dark Night: Essays on Decolonization*. Durham, NC: Duke University Press, 2021.

Mignolo, Walter. *On Decoloniality: Concepts, Analytics, Praxis*. Durham, NC: Duke University Press, 2018.

Morrison, Toni. *Playing in the Dark: Whiteness and the Literary Imagination*. Cambridge, MA: Harvard University Press, 1992.

Ngũgĩwa Thiong'o. *Decolonising the Mind: The Politics of Language in African Literature*. London: James Currey, 1981.

"On the Abolition of the English Department." In Bill Ashcroft, Gareth Griffiths, and Helen Tiffin, eds., *The Post-Colonial Studies Reader*. London: Routledge, 1995, 438–42.

Rancière, Jacques. *The Politics of Aesthetics: The Distribution of the Sensible,* ed. Gabriel Rockhill. London: Bloomsbury, 2004.

Sanders, Mark. "The Space of the University: Time, and Time Again." *The Cambridge Journal of Postcolonial Literary Inquiry* 6.2 (2019): 257–71.

Spivak, Gayatri Chakravorty. *An Aesthetic Education in the Era of Globalization*. Cambridge, MA: Harvard University Press, 2013.

Walcott, Derek. *What the Twilight Says: Essays*. London: Faber, 1998.

Wright, Patrick. *On Living in an Old Country*. Oxford: Oxford University Press, 2009.

Young, Robert J. C. *Empire, Colony, Postcolony*. Chichester: Wiley-Blackwell, 2015.

PART I

Identities

CHAPTER I

Decolonizing the University

Paul Giles

The relationship between colonization and academia is a vast topic going back many centuries, but the more particular issue of decolonizing the university was brought into sharp focus in 2015 by protests against statues of Cecil Rhodes at the University of Cape Town and then at Oxford the following year. South African scholar Grant Parker commented on the apparent anomaly of how the "offending Rhodes statue at UCT famously received little notice for ... many years" (257), with these demonstrations taking place "nearly a generation after the establishment of democracy in the country" (256), long after the statue of Hendrick Verwoerd, architect of apartheid, had been removed from the South African parliament in 1994. But the more recent literal as well as metaphorical deconstructions of statues in many countries were spectacular visual events given heightened public impact by social media networks that did not exist twenty years earlier, and in South Africa this movement also became conflated with issues of student access through a "Fees Must Fall" movement. Within "the Oxford context," according to organizers of "Rhodes Must Fall," their "three principal tenets for decolonisation" were "decolonising the iconography, curriculum and racial representation at the university" (Nkopo and Chantiluke 137), with the movement being "intersectional" in identifying places where racial injustice overlapped with, and was exacerbated by, similar forms of inequity in class or gender.

Decolonization itself was defined by historian John Springhall as "the surrender of external political sovereignty, largely Western European, over colonized non-European peoples, plus the emergence of independent territories where once the West had ruled, or the transfer of power from empire to nation-state" (2). Geoffrey Barraclough, formerly Chichele Professor of Modern History at Oxford, observed that between 1945 and 1960 forty countries with a total population of 800 million, a quarter of the entire world's population, achieved political independence by rejecting colonial authority, and as far back as 1964 he argued that too many twentieth-century historians had focused their attention on European wars, even though when this history "comes to be written in a longer perspective, there is little doubt that no single theme will prove to be of greater importance than the revolt against the west" (154). It is hardly surprising that such a massive historical shift has carried reverberations in the academic world, nor that much influential decolonial theory and activism have been generated from outside more traditional universities in Europe and North America, often from the Southern Hemisphere.

Walter D. Mignolo, for example, though now based at Duke University, is a native of Argentina who has collaborated extensively with Peruvian sociologist Anibal Quijano and Colombian anthropologist Arturo Escobar to develop models of collective well-being that represent an emphatic break with assumptions of liberal society and a shift to embedding Indigenous and environmental perspectives within political systems. Mignolo's strategy of "de-linking" is directed "to de-naturalize concepts and conceptual fields that totalize A reality" ("Delinking" 459), thus dissolving purportedly universal systems into more "pluri-versal" variants ("Delinking" 499). In Latin America this outlook was interwoven in complex ways with liberation theology and given legal expression in 2008 through the valorization of nature as a subject with rights within the constitution of Ecuador (Escobar 396), and then by the ratification of Bolivia in 2009 under the leadership of Evo Morales as a "Plurinational State," one explicitly recognizing Indigenous communities (Cheyfitz 143). Working from Oceania, Epeli Hau'ofa emphasized oral fiction, local knowledge, and an experiential proximity that effectively deconstructed what Mignolo called the epistemic "hubris" associated with a mythical "zeropoint" of colonial knowledge ("Introduction" 5), thereby underlining how every angle of vision necessarily derives from somewhere specific. In Africa, struggles over apartheid and Rhodes were foreshadowed by Ngũgĩ wa Thiong'o's 1972 essay "On the Abolition of the English Department," which discussed a proposal at the University of Nairobi to replace English with a Department of African Literature and Languages, and by his 1986 book *Decolonizing the Mind*, which analyzed more comprehensively the intellectual relation between African and European languages.

It is important to recognize the subtlety of Ngũgĩ's argument in the latter work. He does not suggest English or European culture is simply redundant, but that there should be a realignment of epistemological assumptions in line with geographical reorientations. "What was interesting," noted Ngũgĩ, "was that ... all sides were agreed on the need to include African, European and other literatures. But what would be the centre? And what would be the periphery, so to speak? How would the centre relate to the periphery?" (89–90). As with Edward Said, whose critical work similarly invokes heterodox geographies to interrogate Western culture's hegemonic assumptions, Ngũgĩ's thinking was significantly shaped by Joseph Conrad, whom Simon Gikandi described as having a "substantive" influence on the Kenyan scholar's work (106).[1] Though one of the enduring benefits of decolonizing the university world has been to integrate Africa, Latin America, and Oceania more fully into discursive intellectual frameworks, this has involved more a repositioning than a discarding of Western cultural traditions. Nevertheless, there are important shifts of emphasis associated with this decolonial impetus. Mignolo defined it "as a particular kind of critical theory and the decolonial option as a specific orientation of doing" ("Introduction" 1), and these differentiate it in his eyes from the postcolonial theory that became very popular in English departments from the 1990s onward, which tended to leave familiar hierarchies in place. In a harsh critique of Homi Bhabha's work, Priyamvada Gopal suggested the readings of "psychic ambivalence" (15) Bhabha attributes to postcolonial texts modulate too comfortably into the kinds of equivocation associated with "Whig imperial history's own rendering of imperialism as a self-correcting system that arrives at emancipation or decolonization without regard to the resistance of its subjects" (19). For Gopal, the forms of structural hybridity foregrounded in the work of Bhabha or Gayatri Spivak were readily absorbed into a liberal system of academia where it became easy to carry on business as usual.

As with Ngũgĩ's analysis of how African literature relates to European, these are complicated (and interesting) debates, and it would seem more useful for any English department to provide the space for such ideas to be interrogated, rather than trying to impose any curriculum predicated upon the impossibility of trying to settle all such questions in advance. One of the historical advantages of Cambridge University, where Gopal is now based, is its relatively decentered structure, organized around some thirty colleges, which makes it difficult for centralized administrative authority of any kind to enjoy unobstructed sway. Salman Rushdie complained in 1983 about Cambridge's institutional use of "Commonwealth Literature," which he described as a "strange term" that "places Eng. Lit. at the centre and the rest of the world at the periphery," a notion he described as "unhelpful and even a little distasteful" ("Commonwealth" 61). However, that did not prevent him from pursuing his interest in Islamic culture during his History degree at Cambridge, with Rushdie recalling it was while studying for a special paper on the rise of Islam that he "came across the story of the so-called 'satanic verses' or temptation of the Prophet Muhammad" ("From an Address" 249), a story he subsequently embellished in his controversial novel *The Satanic Verses* (1988).

Following a similarly contrapuntal pattern, Caryl Phillips, who was born on the Caribbean island of Saint Lucia and grew up in Leeds before reading English at Oxford in the late 1970s, chose in his final year an optional paper on American Literature, since this gave him the opportunity to study for the first time Black writers: Richard Wright, Ralph Ellison, James Baldwin. Though Britain at this time "was being torn apart by 'race riots,'" Phillips later recalled, "there was no discourse about race in British society and certainly no black writers" on the mainstream Oxford English curriculum ("Marvin Gaye" 35). Under the aegis of Warton Professor John Bayley and his wife Iris Murdoch, the Oxford English Faculty at that time promoted a soft Anglican ideology based around the belief that idiosyncratic "human" qualities necessarily trumped any theory of social circulation. There are, of course, respectable intellectual rationales for this approach, involving a privileging of biography and what Murdoch, a former Oxford philosophy tutor turned novelist, called in her polemical rejection of existential abstraction a stance "against dryness." But this meant that undergraduates studying American literature tended to be uncomfortable discussing questions of race, with a special paper on William Faulkner when I taught there in the first decade of the twenty-first century attracting essays that made him appear to resemble Virginia Woolf, as the students focused more confidently on stylistic streams of consciousness than on representations of racial tension in Faulkner's fiction. The same thing was true at Cambridge, where I worked between 1999 and 2002 after the early death of Tony Tanner. Tanner's inventive and courageous work had helped to establish American Literature as a viable option on the highly traditional Cambridge English syllabus, but his own emphasis on the legacy of transcendentalism, and his critical understanding of American writing as an exploration of new worlds of "wonder," had led to a synchronic understanding of the field as synonymous with a mythic quest for freedom. Many students in the third-year American Literature seminar did not know or care about the dates of the US Civil War, nor did they see distinctions between antebellum and postbellum periods as relevant to their textual close readings.

None of these pedagogical issues was insuperable, and part of the pleasure in university teaching involves encouraging students to reconsider familiar authors from a more informed perspective. Moreover, the polycentricity of both Oxford and Cambridge helped ensure these intellectual agendas were driven largely by productive academic debates and disagreements, rather than, as at some other places I have worked, by deans or vice chancellors who fancy themselves as charismatic leaders and wish to impose "a future vision" of their own on the university. Phillips's own novels involve, in his words, "a radical rethinking of what constitutes British history" (Bragg), while avoiding "the restrictive noose of race" ("Introduction" 131), which as a category Phillips takes to be inherently reductive, and in this sense his fiction might be said to have internalized in paradoxical ways aspects of the Oxford idiom, even in resisting its ideological narrowness.

Mark Twain, who in *Following the Equator* (1897) directly addressed Cecil Rhodes's legacy in South Africa, also retained a guarded attitude toward questions of race and colonization, one that combined a sense of outrage at Rhodes's depredations with a darker fatalism shaped by Twain's sense of Social Darwinism as an inevitable force. Twain's presentation of Rhodes is consequently bifurcated, in line with the structural twinning that runs through much of his writing: "I know quite well that whether Mr. Rhodes is the lofty and worshipful patriot and statesman that multitudes believe him to be, or Satan come again, as the rest of the world account him, he is still the most imposing figure in the British empire outside of England" (708). Even critics who highlight Twain's radical aspects acknowledge these contradictions: "I confess," remarked John Carlos Rowe of *Following the Equator*, "that my representation of Twain's anti-imperialist critique of the British in India does not account for Twain's vigorous defense of the military conduct of the British in suppressing the Sepoy Mutiny of 1857" (132). Such ambivalence does not, of course, invalidate Twain's engagement with colonial cultures but makes it more thought-provoking. It does no favor to either literary studies or decolonial praxis to circumscribe such writers within restrictive interpretative grooves, and Kerry Driscoll's work on Twain and "Indigenous Peoples" perhaps misjudges the tone of *Following the Equator* in its claim Twain here "rages against the unjust dispossession of Australian Aboriginals and the genocidal efforts of colonial settlers who left arsenic-laced flour in the bush for them to eat" (11). It is true that foregrounding Twain's darker facets can generate more pointed discussions than were customary during the heyday of *Huckleberry Finn*'s "hypercanonization," when the novel was celebrated unproblematically as a fictional epitome of the free American spirit, and Driscoll illuminatingly expands scholarship on Twain and race to encompass questions of dispossession and Indigeneity as well as "African Americans and slavery" (4), with the latter having now become more familiar in critical discussions of the author.[2] There has of course been much valuable work since the 1970s to recover American writers who had been excluded from traditional canonical formations, but one of the most productive aspects of such inclusiveness has been a shift in the analytical relation between Black authors and established White figures such as Twain, Poe, or Henry James, a reorientation outlined most influentially by Toni Morrison in her Harvard lectures published as *Playing in the Dark* (1992). But Morrison's treatment of these issues is characteristically oblique, indicating how racist assumptions in these classic texts often circulate in underhand ways, and Twain's black comedy tends similarly to avoid narrative closure or polemic.[3]

The point here is simply that racial representations in literature are necessarily multifaceted and variegated. One of the qualities distinguishing the humanities from the social sciences, according to Helen Small, is their greater "tolerance for ambiguity" (50), with Roland Barthes declaring "nuance" to be synonymous with "literature" itself (11). Nevertheless, one clear benefit of decolonization for literary studies has been to demystify myths about the "universality" of American or European value systems and to interrogate subject positions whose implicit hierarchies have remained unacknowledged. James D. Le Sueur remarked on how one enduring legacy of the French–Algerian War (1954–62) was the way it generated a "fundamental reconsideration" (167) of French culture's place in the world, just as Dipesh Chakrabarty has argued for "provincializing Europe" more generally. In her account of the development of English departments in Australian universities, Leigh Dale described how old-style professors in the earlier part of the twentieth century tended to promote Anglophile ideas, with Donald Horne recalling how E. R. Holme, McCaughey Chair of Early English Literature at the University of Sydney until 1941, would use Sweet's *Anglo-Saxon Primer* "as a text for a series of sermons on the virtues of Empire" (67), with any interest in Australian literature being counted until the 1970s as, in Dale's words, "equivalent to an intellectual disability" (143). But the advent of postcolonial theory in the last decades of the twentieth century comprehensively changed these power dynamics, and conceptual intersections between different parts of the world are now an established feature of literature courses everywhere. Oxford at the beginning of the twenty-first century changed the title of its various undergraduate period papers from "English Literature" to "Literature in English," an apparently minor emendation that seemed to pass unnoticed by many college tutors, but one that resolved the previous ambiguity about whether the adjective "English" referred to language or nation and so allowed the possibility of studying, say, Les Murray or Adrienne Rich alongside Ted Hughes. Cambridge has retained the traditional nomenclature of "English Literature" but specifies in its outline that "the course embraces all literature written in the English language, which means that you can study American and post-colonial literatures alongside British literatures throughout." This did not necessarily mean that Oxbridge tutors who had spent half their lives teaching Dickens and George Eliot jumped at the opportunity to teach Indian or Australian literature instead, but it did allow for the possibility for the curriculum to evolve as new academic interests and priorities emerge. Decolonizing any university in substantive terms is always a long-term process rather than one accomplished by apocalyptic cleansing.

Recognition of the wide variety of colonial contexts also allows greater flexibility in understanding how a program of decolonization might be addressed. Australian anthropologist Nicholas Thomas, who now works at Cambridge, emphasizes the manifold dissimilarities of colonial situations, rejecting a "unitary and essentialist" version of "colonial discourse" (3) as "global ideology" (60) in favor of its "historicization" (19), where particular situations in, say, the Solomon Islands or Māori New Zealand are scrutinized for their "conflicted character" (3). This also leads Thomas to be skeptical about the claims of Australian Indigenous culture to any "primordial" purity (28), an idea he suggests has too often been appropriated for strategic or sentimental purposes. Concomitantly, the notion that decolonial politics should turn exclusively on a restitution of stolen lands might be said misleadingly to conflate pragmatism with philosophy. In complaining that "decolonization is not a metaphor," American Indigenous scholars Eve Tuck and K. Wayne Tang argued that "when metaphor invades decolonization, it kills the very possibility of decolonization; it recenters Whiteness, it resettles theory, it extends innocence to the settler, it entertains a settler future" (3). Such an emphasis does carry significant purchase in the Indian domain of land restitution that Tuck and Wang prioritize, but it is important to recognize that while land might constitute a form of "knowledge" (14) for some peoples, it certainly did not for those enslaved on American plantations, where they were not able to own land either legally or economically, nor for Jewish people who were banned from holding land in medieval Europe. To inflate a "spiritual" relation to land into an "ontology," as does Indigenous Australian academic and activist Aileen Moreton-Robinson (15), thus risks aggrandizing the legitimate praxis of specific claims grounded on the issue of territorial "sovereignty" (125) into an unsustainable universalist design.

Such political tensions have been particularly prevalent within Australian academia, where attempts to introduce Indigenous perspectives have often led to controversies around the definition of the subject and the question of who is empowered to articulate the field. At the University of Sydney, for example, an "Aborginal Education Centre" was established in 1989 and renamed in 1992 as the "Koori Centre," providing a focus for teaching and research led by Indigenous scholars as well as support for students; but this Centre was dissolved in 2012 in an attempt to embed Indigenous knowledge more fully within regular university curricula, with individual academics being redistributed across different departments. The problem here arises not so much from these organizational structures, for which advantages and disadvantages might be adduced on both sides: a separate Koori Centre always risked being intellectually isolationist, but attempts to integrate Indigenous knowledge across the curriculum risk such specificity becoming vitiated, particularly in an era of financial stringency and dwindling appointments. But the more fundamental difficulty turns on a potential displacement of complicated intellectual questions to rigid administrative blueprints within which such theoretical issues might find themselves prematurely foreclosed. There have, for instance, been many debates around the work of Alexis Wright, an astonishing novelist from the Waanyi people, but the reception of her fiction has often become locked within institutional tugs of war linked to proprietorial concerns, with some identifying her work specifically with Indigenous politics and language, while others have sought to associate it with global environmentalism and magical realism. Some Indigenous scholars regard the "mainstreaming" of their field as inherently hazardous, on the grounds that any "reconciliation" fundamentally involves "rescuing settler normalcy" and "ensuring a settler future" (Smith, Tuck, and Yang 15); others emphasize "the importance of relationality," with Sandra Styres suggesting that "decolonizing pedagogies and practices open up spaces ... where students can question their own positionalities, prior knowledge, biases, and taken-for-granted assumptions" (33). These arguments will inevitably continue, but it is crucial they are allowed a viable academic framework within which to evolve over time, perhaps in ways that are currently difficult to predict.

One indisputable contribution of Australian cultural theory to literary studies over the past decade has been to make debates around settler-colonial paradigms more prominent. The work of Patrick Wolfe, Lorenzo Veracini, and others, which had heretofore been regarded as relevant largely within an Australian or Pacific Island context, is now deployed to elucidate settler formations in Europe, the Middle East, and Africa as well as the United States, with Phillip Round in a 2019 essay on nineteenth-century US literature describing settler colonialism as "the foundational principle of all American sovereignty discourse" (62). Tamara S. Wagner similarly wrote in 2015 of how "in the last few years, new interest in settler colonialism has helped us see what postcolonial criticism has traditionally left out" (224), while Tracey Banivanua Mar observed a year later that although the Pacific had generally been seen as "an afterthought in most overviews of decolonization," this has changed "productively" in recent times (8). However, such perspectival expansiveness has introduced concurrent anxieties about a loss of traction for Australian Literature as a discrete field, along with concern that what Russell McDougall called "transnational reading practices" might lead to "deteriorating interest in Australian Literature" and its supersession by a generic model of "world literary space" (10), in which settler colonialism manifests itself as a more amorphous phenomenon. There are no easy answers to these questions, but they are complex equations that literary studies should always be thinking through: relations between hegemony and decolonization, the promise but also potentially illusory capacity of regional autonomy, the perennial liability to cultural appropriation through economic and political incorporation.

*

The third of the "principal tenets" for Rhodes Must Fall, "racial representation at the university" (Nkopo and Chantiluke 137), is in many ways more difficult to address than decolonizing its iconography or curriculum, since this necessarily involves confronting the kind of systematic racism that has long been endemic to British as well as most Western societies. The statistics in themselves are shocking: in 2016, 27 percent of pupils who attended state schools in Britain were Black, but there were only a handful of Black undergraduates at Oxford, with Patricia Daley, a contributor to *Rhodes Must Fall*, being the first Black academic to be appointed as a university lecturer at Oxford as late as 1991. The reasons for such anomalies are complex, involving what can be seen in retrospect as excessive trust during the second half of the twentieth century in the meritocratic model promoted by UK government policies after 1945, where applicants for admission were judged solely on their academic performance according to supposedly objective criteria.[4] British universities were slower than those in the United States to calibrate for different social and educational contexts, and apart from the overall inequity of this process it also involved a significant loss of scholarly capacity, as if professional football clubs were to base recruitment only on the number of goals students had scored for their high-school team rather than their overall playing potential.

Equal access to higher education is crucial to the health as well as integrity of any academic system, but often resistance to change was linked to forms of unconscious bias that the Black Lives Matter movement has effectively highlighted. As Chakrabarty noted, while "racism" as a theoretical concept may no longer be viable, subtler forms of racial profiling and discrimination have nevertheless proliferated (*Crises* 142).[5] Sara Ahmed has written about how ubiquitous university offices of "Institutional Diversity" remain blind to what she called "kinship logic: a way of 'being related' and 'staying related,' a way of keeping certain bodies in place. Institutional whiteness," Ahmed concluded, "is about the reproduction of likeness" (38). Again, this emphasis on "kinship" is by no means a recent or exclusively British phenomenon, nor one arising solely from the idiosyncrasies of the English class system; in 1666 at the University of Basle, for instance, all but one of the professors were related to each other, while in the 1790s at Edinburgh six chairs in the medical faculty changed hands, with five of them going to sons of former professors (Vandermeersk 228). Less blatantly, however, Oxbridge often accepted students with whom it felt "comfortable" through the narrowness of its own perspective about what constituted academic value. Since this is an issue embedded historically within the social structures of British life, it is not readily susceptible to amelioration simply through educational reform. In his chapter on university life in *English Traits* (1856), Ralph Waldo Emerson described Oxford and Cambridge as "finishing schools for the upper classes, and not for the poor," with England regarding "the flower of its national life" as "a well-educated gentleman" (117). It was this emphasis on individual character and manners as the epitome of cultural value that contributed for so long to social and racial circumscriptions of the student population.

Such pressures toward conformity can also be attributed in part to the notion, common since medieval times, that the academic world should properly be subservient to the jurisdiction of a secular state. Conflicts between the papacy and the Holy Roman Empire were famously replicated in England in 1535, when Henry VIII sent royal visitors to scrutinize the Oxford and Cambridge curricula, with a view to realigning it in accordance with new state priorities by eliminating the teaching of systematic theology and abolishing degrees in canon law (Logan). In this light, more recent political moves to make universities serve what Bill Readings called "the force of market capitalism" (38) have a venerable antecedence. Back in the twelfth century, as R. W. Southern observed, the great majority of students went on to become "men of affairs" (199), and for most students, then as now, university was more important as an opportunity for enhanced social and economic status rather than intellectual inquiry. This, of course, is one reason the middle classes have been so desperate to protect university space in order to benefit their own children's future, with class mobility in academic environments being no less a source of potential friction than racial equity, and Matt Brim describing "top schools" in the United States as "unambiguous drivers of class stratification" (86).

Since national economies started to become increasingly dependent on information technology in the 1990s, there has been exponential pressure from national bodies for universities to produce graduates adept at gathering and organizing data, with all developed nations rapidly expanding their student populations in the interests of supporting their economies. In 2013 there were some 160 million students enrolled globally (Schreuder xxxiv), and this has led to even more pressure for higher education to serve the interests of the state. This in turn has produced a more *dirigiste* version of academia as comprising "managed professionals" (Slaughter and Rhoades 77) employed to execute research agendas often dictated by a university's upper administration, in line with government funding priorities. Symbiotically intertwined with these systematic pressures toward conformity has been the fear among some observers "in every generation," as Collini commented, that the university world "was all going to the dogs" (33). John Henry Newman in 1852 declared: "A University, I should lay down, by its very name professes to teach universal knowledge" (33); but this etymological link between universities and universalism has always been fractious and contested, particularly given the perennially tense relations between academic and political worlds. In the Middle Ages, *universitas* was a term derived from Roman law that described a union of people bound together by a common occupation, an arrangement that gave it immunity from local systems of justice under the merchant code; but in 1205 Pope Innocent III cannily expanded this corporate meaning to embrace his vision of the *universitas* as engaged in universal learning, addressing a papal letter to "universis magistris et scholaribus Parisiensis," to all masters and students in Paris (Pedersen 101, 151). Nevertheless, medieval universities always had to fight to retain some measure of freedom, with their leaders often attempting to play off civic and religious authorities against each other.

In this sense, Immanuel Wallerstein's view that the model of the medieval university "essentially disappeared with the onset of the modern world-system" (59) seems doubtful, since universities have always been forced to negotiate uneasily with political and economic pressures. Southern commented on how the growth of scholasticism in the twelfth century heralded a "striving towards universality," with lecturers subsuming all "local peculiarities" of time and place within universal systems of knowledge (211), but competing claims of local and global have fluctuated over time and place. Many intellectual developments occurred when scholars working in universities challenged social or academic conventions: Peter Abelard's dialectical theology, for example, was seen as heretical in the twelfth century, even though two of his students eventually went on to become pope, while in the 1790s Immanuel Kant was reproved by a Prussian superintendent for his dissemination of unorthodox ideas (Ruegg 7). There has thus been a long and distinguished tradition in universities of dodging the bullets, of exploiting university infrastructures and resources to evade institutional authorities. Such transgressive practices are common across all disciplines, from Galileo's work on astronomy at the University of Padua between 1592 and 1610, to John Locke in the seventeenth century revising the basis of empirical philosophy, to Adrienne Rich in the twentieth century recasting formal poetic traditions in feminist, emancipationist styles, a project she undertook while working in a challenging urban environment at the City University of New York. In disagreeing with Eric Ashby's claim that the scientific revolution in the seventeenth century gained its momentum from outside academia, Roy Porter pointed to how universities "provided the livings" and "posts" (545) for most of the radical figures who advanced principles of physiology, medicine, and mathematical logic during this era: Carl Linnaeus, William Harvey, Isaac Newton.

From a historical perspective, then, Claire Gallien's assertion that "decolonial studies are not soluble in the neo-liberal university" (9) would appear dubious. It is not clear why a "neo-liberal" academic framework, for all its obvious reifications and follies, should be more of an impediment to innovative work than the scholastic environment of the Middle Ages, or the gentlemanly codes of conduct that predominated in the universities of eighteenth-century Germany, when professors and students liked to don the clothes of aristocrats and knights to display their social standing (Simone 316). As Porter remarked, despite all the pressures toward standardization, universities have proved over time to be "immensely durable" sites for the pursuit and dissemination of new knowledge (560). One of the reasons Peter Lombard's *Four Books of Sentences* was so popular among students in twelfth-century Paris was because it was a sourcebook of excerpts assembled "so that the enquirer in future will not need to turn over an immense quantity of books, since he will find here offered to him without his labour, briefly collected together, what he needs" (Southern 198), and a similarly instrumental view of higher education is readily apparent in academic marketplaces today. Nevertheless, universities still offer scope for productive work, even if indirectly rather than programmatically, since in academia chains of cause and effect, investment and outcome, tend to be linked together more obliquely than administrators and politicians would prefer.

In humanities, Stuart Hall, who played a major role in incorporating racial questions into university curricula during the final decades of the twentieth century, moved as a Rhodes Scholar in 1951 from Jamaica to Oxford, where he stayed until 1957. Hall later found continuities between his understanding of the "always hybrid" nature of "cultural identity" ("Formation" 204), linked to a "diasporic way of seeing the world," and the "diasporic imagination" of Henry James ("At Home" 273), on whom he started but never completed a doctoral thesis at Oxford. "I wanted my PhD to be on American literature," said Hall, "because it's somewhat tangential. I'm always circling from the outside. I'm interested in the complexities of the marginal position on the center, which, I suppose, is my experience of Oxford . . . I thought, I'm a Rhodes Scholar – the whole point of Rhodes was to send these potential troublemakers to the center, to learn." Given Hall's recollection of how his pioneering Cultural Studies department at Birmingham in the 1960s was accomplished by "stealth" and "double-dealing," it is not difficult to see the circuitous influence of this Oxford experience on the development of Cultural Studies in the UK, especially as Hall described the field as initially posing "some key questions about the Americanization of British culture and where English culture was going after the War" (Phillips, "Stuart Hall"). While decolonization has been associated more explicitly with Cultural Studies, it has also been linked to the English literary curriculum in roundabout ways. Hall's contributions, like those of Rushdie and Phillips, indicate how even the most conservative academic frameworks can engender heterodox styles of progressive thought that cannot be reduced simply to the expectations of funders or the often narcissistic visions of founders. Rhodes would never have approved of Hall, but Hall was nevertheless a product of the Rhodes legacy.

The opening up of the world to what Cameroonian scholar Achille Mbembe called "new cognitive assemblages" (244) – the pluriverse, the posthuman, the Anthropocene – consequently allows for "new, *hybrid thought styles*" (243), where traditional horizons can be reconceptualized. Mbembe, who has influenced the work of Judith Butler, described Africa as "a planetary laboratory at a time when history itself is being recast as an integrated history of the Earth system" (252), and the same thing is true of Oceania and Latin America, whose new visibility within the world of global scholarship effectively interrogates more calcified Western models.[6] Mignolo wrote of how "decolonial liberation implies epistemic disobedience" ("On Decoloniality" 114), implying again crossovers between decolonization and transgression. Similarly, it would be possible to recognize analogies between Hall's realignment of the epistemological foundation of White British culture by recalibrating it in relation to Black migration and an equivalent displacement of Euroamerican centers of gravity through such a "planetary laboratory."

Exactly how such global reorientations might manifest themselves will always be open to debate, as the many critical disagreements today about how to define "World Literature" amply demonstrate. Nevertheless, we should not underestimate the long-term social "impact" of the humanities. It is unlikely, for example, that Barack Obama would have been elected president of the United States in 2004 had it not been for the scholarship from the 1970s onward that worked successfully to elucidate blind spots in the American literary canon, sparking revisionist reassessments in the popular fiction of Toni Morrison and many others of how racialist assumptions had become entrenched within society. The recent exponential growth in college student numbers, rising in the United States in 2018 to around 69 percent of high-school graduates, means that university curricula now exert more influence throughout society than during the twentieth century, and the decolonization of the English literary curriculum has played an integral part in this process.

Writing from within Oxford, Patricia Daley argued: "Decolonisation is not about replacing Western epistemologies with non-Western ones, nor is it about prioritising one racialised group over another. It is to create a more open 'critical cosmopolitan pluriversalism' – where instead of Eurocentric thought being seen as universal, there is a recognition and acceptance of multiple ways of interpreting and understanding the world" (85). Such "pluriversalism" is categorically different from traditional versions of liberal pluralism, since its focus is not just on authorizing difference per se, but on how geopolitical and environmental variables frame the "pursuit of restitutive justice" that Robbie Shilliam regards as crucial to "the imperial world map" (19). While there are different ways of approaching questions of decolonization, they all involve, as Shilliam suggested, a "cultivation of different spatialities and relationalities" (22), a decentering of racial hierarchies that runs in parallel to a decentering of geographical hierarchies. To decolonize the university is to restore a sense of its etymological universalism and resist acquiescing in local conventions, whether political, social, or racial; yet this should involve what Wallerstein glossed as a "universal universalism," rather than a "partial and distorted universalism" (xiv) extrapolated merely from Western centers of power. While such a planetary universalism might be an evasive and infinitely receding concept, it is nevertheless one to which the idea of a university should always aspire.

Notes

1. On Ngũgĩ and Conrad, see Sewlall. Conrad was the subject of Said's PhD, which formed the basis of his first book, *Joseph Conrad and the Fiction of Autobiography* (1966).
2. On Twain's "hypercanonization," see Arac (133). On "the contradictory nature of Twain's racial and colonial discourse," see Messent (67).
3. On the complex links between black humor and slavery, see Carpio.
4. For the history of meritocracy in Britain, see Woolridge.
5. Chakrabarty was drawing here on a lecture given by Etienne Balibar at the University of Chicago in 2006.
6. In her 2021 *Time* article on dismantling "our egos and identities," Butler cites Mbembe on how "the political in our time must start from the imperative to reconstruct the world in common."

WORKS CITED

Ahmed, Sara. *On Being Included: Racism and Diversity in Institutional Life*. Durham, NC: Duke University Press, 2012.

Arac, Jonathan. Huckleberry Finn *as Idol and Target: The Functions of Criticism in Our Time*. Madison: University of Wisconsin Press, 1997.

Barraclough, Geoffrey. *An Introduction to Contemporary History*. 1964. London: Penguin, 1967.

Barthes, Roland. *The Neutral: Lecture Course at the Collège de France (1977–1978)*. 2002. Trans. Rosalind E. Krauss and Denis Hollier. New York: Columbia University Press, 2005.

Bell, C. Rosalind. "Worlds Within: An Interview with Caryl Phillips." *Callaloo* 14.3 (1991): 578–606.

Bragg, Melvyn. "Caryl Phillips." *The South Bank Show*, ITV, April 13, 2003.

Kwoba, Brian, Roseanne Chantiluke, and Athinangamso Nkopo, eds. *Rhodes Must Fall: The Struggle to Decolonise the Racist Heart of Empire*. London: Zed Books, 2018.

Brim, Matt. *Poor Queer Studies: Confronting Elitism in the Universities*. Durham, NC: Duke University Press, 2020.

Butler, Judith. "Creating an Inhabitable World for Humans Means Dismantling Rigid Forms of Individuality." *Time*, April 21, 2021, https://time.com/59533 96/judith-butler-safe-world-individuality.

Carpio, Glenda. *Laughing Fit to Kill: Black Humor in the Fictions of Slavery*. New York: Oxford University Press, 2008.

Chakrabarty, Dipesh. *The Crises of Civilization: Exploring Global and Planetary Histories*. New Delhi: Oxford University Press, 2018.

    Provincializing Europe: Postcolonial Thought and Historical Difference. Princeton, NJ: Princeton University Press, 2000.

Cheyfitz, Eric. "Resisting the Anthropocene: Linda Hogan's *Dwellings: A Spiritual History of the Living World*." *PMLA* 136.1 (Jan. 2021): 139–45.

Collini, Stefan. *Speaking of Universities*. London: Verso, 2017.

Dale, Leigh. *The English Men: Professing Literature in Australian Universities*. Toowoomba: Association for the Study of Australian Literature, 1997.

Daley, Patricia. "Reparations in the Space of the University in the Wake of Rhodes Must Fall." In Nkopo and Chantiluke, 74–89.

Driscoll, Kerry. *Mark Twain among the Indians and Other Indigenous Peoples*. Berkeley: University of California Press, 2018.

Emerson, Ralph Waldo. *English Traits*. 1856. In *The Collected Works, V*, ed. Douglas Emory Wilson. Cambridge, MA: Harvard University Press, 1994.

Escobar, Atruro. "Afterword." In Mignolo and Escobar, 391–99.

Gallien, Claire. "Is Decolonial Thought Soluble in the Neo-Liberal Academia?" *Postcolonial Studies Association Newsletter* 25 (June 2020): 7–10.

Gikandi, Simon. *Ngugi wa Thiong'o*. Cambridge: Cambridge University Press, 2000.

Gopal, Priyamvada. *Insurgent Empire: Anticolonial Resistance and British Dissent*. London: Verso, 2019.

Hall, Stuart. *Essential Essays, Vol. II: Identity and Diaspora*, ed. David Morly. Durham, NC: Duke University Press, 2019.

    "The Formation of a Diasporic Intellectual: An Interview with Stuart Hall by Kuan-Hsing Chen." In *Essential Essays, Vol. II*, 185–205.

    "At Home and Not at Home: Stuart Hall in Conversation with Les Back." 2008. In *Essential Essays, Vol. II*, 263–300.

Hau'ofa, Epeli. "Our Sea of Islands." In Eric Waddell, Vijay Naidu, and Epeli Hau'ofa, eds., *A New Oceania: Rediscovering Our Sea of Islands*. Suva: University of the South Pacific, 2–16.

Jansen, Jonathan, Ed., Decolonisation in Universities: The Politics of Knowledge. Johannesburg: Wits University Press, 2009. Pp: 239–54.

Le Sueur, James D. "Decolonising 'French Universalism': Reconsidering the Impact of the Algerian War on French Intellectuals." *Journal of North African Studies* 6.1 (Jan. 2011): 167–86.

Logan, F. Donald. "The First Royal Visitation of the English Universities, 1535." *English Historical Review* 106.421 (Oct. 1991): 861–88.

Mar, Tracey Banivanua. *Decolonisation and the Pacific: Indigenous Globalisation and the Ends of Empire.* Cambridge: Cambridge University Press, 2016.

Mbembe, Achille. "Future Knowledges and Their Implications for the Decolonisation Project." In Jansen, 239–54.

McDougall, Russell. "The 'New World' Literature: A Review Essay." *Transnational Literature* 6.2 (May 2014): 1–10.

Messent, Peter. "Racial and Colonial Discourse in Mark Twain's *Following the Equator.*" *Essays in Arts and Sciences* 22 (Oct. 1993): 67–84.

Mignolo, Walter D. "Delinking: The Rhetoric of Modernity, the Logic of Coloniality and the Grammar of De-Coloniality." *Cultural Studies* 21.2–3 (2007): 449–514.

"Introduction: Coloniality of Power and De-Colonial Thinking." In Mignolo and Escobar, 1–21.

Mignolo, Walter D., and Arturo Escobar, eds. *Globalization and the Decolonial Option.* Abingdon: Routledge, 2010.

Mignolo, Walter D., and Catherine E. Walsh. *On Decoloniality: Concepts, Analytics, Praxis.* Durham, NC: Duke University Press, 2018.

Moreton-Robinson, Aileen. *The White Possessive: Property, Power, and Indigenous Sovereignty.* Minneapolis: University of Minnesota Press, 2015.

Morrison, Toni. *Playing in the Dark: Whiteness and the Literary Imagination.* Cambridge, MA: Harvard University Press, 1992.

Murdoch, Iris. "Against Dryness: A Polemical Sketch." *Encounter* 16 (Jan. 1961): 16–20.

Newman, John Henry. *The Idea of a University: Defined and Illustrated.* 1852, ed. Ian T. Ker. Oxford: Oxford University Press, 1976.

Ngũgĩ wa Thiong'o,. *Decolonising the Mind: The Politics of Language in African Literature.* London: James Currey, 1986.

"On the Abolition of the English Department." 1972. In Bill Ashcroft, Gareth Griffiths, and Helen Tiffin, eds., *The Post-Colonial Studies Reader.* London: Routledge, 1995, 438–42.

Nkopo, Athinangamso, and Roseanne Chantiluke. "Anti-Blackness, Intersectionality and People of Colour Politics." In Kwoba, Chantiluke, and Nkopo 136–43.

Parker, Grant. "Decolonising Minds via Curricula?" In Jansen, 255–64.

Pedersen, Olaf. *The First Universities: Studium Generale and the Origins of University Education in Europe.* Trans. Richard North. Cambridge: Cambridge University Press, 1997.

Phillips, Caryl. "Introduction: The Gift of Displacement." In *A New World Order,* 129–34.

"Marvin Gaye." 2000. In *A New World Order*, 35–59.

A New World Order: Selected Essays. London: Secker and Warburg, 2001.

"Stuart Hall." *Bomb Magazine*, Jan. 1, 1997, https://bombmagazine.org/articles/stuart-hall/.

Porter, Roy. "The Scientific Revolution and Universities." In Ridder-Symoens, 531–62.

Readings, Bill. *The University in Ruins*. Cambridge, MA: Harvard University Press, 1996.

Ridder-Symoens, Hilde de, ed. *A History of the University in Europe, Vol. II: Universities in Early Modern Europe (1500–1800)*. Cambridge: Cambridge University Press, 1996.

Round, Phillip. "1830–1924: The Literatures of Sovereignty." In Cody Marrs and Christopher Hager, eds., *Timelines of American Literature*. Baltimore, MD: Johns Hopkins University Press, 2019, 53–66.

Rowe, John Carlos. "Mark Twain's Critique of Globalization (Old and New) in *Following the Equator, A Journey Around the World* (1897)." *Arizona Quarterly* 61.1 (Spring 2005): 109–35.

Ruegg, Walter. "Themes." In Ridder-Symoens, 3–42.

Rushdie, Salman. "'Commonwealth Literature' Does Not Exist." 1983. In *Imaginary Homelands: Essays and Criticism, 1981–91*. London: Granta-Penguin, 1991, 61–70.

"From an Address Delivered in King's College Chapel, Cambridge, on the Morning of Sunday 14 February 1993." In *Step Across This Line: Collected Non-Fiction 1992–2002*. London: Jonathan Cape, 2002, 249–52.

The Satanic Verses. London: Viking Penguin, 1988.

Said, Edward. *Joseph Conrad and the Fiction of Autobiography*. Cambridge, MA: Harvard University Press, 1966.

Schreuder, Deryck M. "Introduction: Why Universities? Anatomy of Global Change for Old and New Universities." In Deryck M. Schreuder, ed., *Universities for a New World: Making a Global Network in International Higher Education, 1913–2013*. New Delhi: Sage Publications, 2013, xxi–lii.

Sewlall, Harry. "Writing from the Periphery: The Case of Ngũgĩ and Conrad." *English in Africa* 30.1 (May 2003): 55–69.

Shilliam, Robbie. *The Black Pacific: Anti-Colonial Struggles and Oceanic Connections*. London: Bloomsbury, 2015.

Simone, Maria Rosa di. "Admission." In Ridder-Symoens, 285–325.

Slaughter, Sheila, and Gary Rhoades. "The Neo-Liberal University." *New Labor Forum* 6 (2000): 73–79.

Small, Helen. *The Value of the Humanities*. Oxford: Oxford University Press, 2013.

Smith, Linda Tuhiwai, Eve Tuck, and K. Wayne Yang, eds. *Indigenous and Decolonizing Studies in Education: Mapping the Long View*. New York: Routledge, 2019.

"Introduction." In Smith, Tuck, and Yang, 1–23.

Southern, R. W. *The Making of the Middle Ages*. 1953. London: Cresset-Century Hutchinson, 1987.

Springhall, John. *Decolonization since 1945: The Collapse of European Overseas Empires*. Basingstoke: Palgrave Macmillan, 2001.

Styres, Sandra. "Literacies of Land: Decolonizing Narratives, Storying, and Literature." In Smith, Tuck, and Yang, 24–37.

Tanner, Tony. *The Reign of Wonder: Naivety and Reality in American Literature*. Cambridge: Cambridge University Press, 1965.

Thomas, Nicholas. *Colonialism's Culture: Anthropology, Travel and Government*. Princeton, NJ: Princeton University Press, 1994.

Tuck, Eve, and K. Wayne Yang. "Decolonization Is Not a Metaphor." *Decolonization: Indigeneity, Education and Society* 1.1 (2012): 1–40.

Twain, Mark. *Following the Equator and Anti-Imperialist Essays*. New York: Oxford University Press, 1996.

Vandermeersk, Peter A. "Teachers." In Ridder-Symoens, 210–55.

Wagner, Tamara S. "The Nineteenth-Century Pacific Rim: Victorian Transoceanic Studies Beyond the Postcolonial Matrix." *Victorian Literature and Culture* 43 (2015): 223–34.

Wallerstein, Immanuel. *European Universalism: The Rhetoric of Power*. New York: The New Press, 2006.

Woolridge, Adrian. *The Aristocracy of Talent: How Meritocracy Made the Modern World*. London: Allen Lane, 2021.

CHAPTER 2

Decolonizing the English Department in Ireland

Joe Cleary

The university English department in Ireland has a long history, but of that history we have no history. This might appear paradoxical because for much of its existence the English department in Ireland as elsewhere conceived of itself in broadly historicist terms – offering curricula that generally ran from Anglo-Saxon and medieval to modern British literature – and cultivated critical models that can be described as historicist and contextualist in character (North). Nevertheless, while the history of education in Ireland is a well-established field, there are no histories of the formation of English departments in Ireland, of the curricula they offered, the agendas they hoped to serve, or of their reconfigurations in the changing world of the university more generally. In this sense, English departments in Ireland can be said to have little substantial historical memory and without such memory attempts to "decolonize" departments run the risk of being uninformed and unsystematic.

That the modern education system in Ireland generally was colonial and imperial in intent and function seems indisputable. In the period after the Tudor, Stuart, and Cromwellian plantations, the English state dismantled the remaining structures of Gaelic society in Ireland and enacted penal laws designed to consolidate the new Protestant Ascendancy, to limit access to land and the higher professions to Catholics, and to anglicize Irish subjects and culture. In 1695, "An act to restrain foreign education" was legislated to limit contact between Irish Catholics and possible continental allies, to which was added a domestic provision forbidding any "person whatsoever of the popish religion to publicly teach school or instruct youth in learning" (McManus 15). These laws were designed to discourage Catholicism and to encourage Catholics to have their children educated in the available Protestant schools to become loyal subjects of the United Kingdom.

The disenfranchised Catholic population did not readily comply. Instead, Catholic schoolmasters continued to teach surreptitiously in provisional schools often conducted out of doors and in the shelter of hedges, this giving rise to a "hedge school" system that continued until the end of the penal laws in the late eighteenth and early nineteenth centuries. Historians of these schools conceive of them as "a kind of guerrilla war in education," in which teachers were obliged constantly to evade law officers and were often prosecuted, especially in times of social unrest. In her account of the hedge schools, Antonia McManus notes, "a school master who contravened penal laws was liable to three months' imprisonment and a fine of twenty pounds. He could be banished to the Barbados, and if he returned to Ireland, the death penalty awaited him. A ten pound award was offered for his arrest and a reward of ten pounds for information against anyone harbouring him" (17). Despite such strictures, the hedge schools managed to provide education for students intended for the priesthood, for foreign military service, and for those going into business and trading enterprises domestically and overseas. In an increasingly British-dominated world, English was required for social advancement, and the hedge schools provided English instruction. As instruments of both anticolonial resistance and adaption, they probably prefigured in function the more state-sponsored forms of institutional education later developed in the nineteenth century.

Despite the turmoil created by the plantations and the insurrections protesting the new colonial system, the Irish population had grown to 8 million by the 1840s, at a time when that of the rest of the United Kingdom was approximately 18.5 million. By this time, the poorer Irish had become for many in England a byword for papism and poverty, squalor and sedition. Many had also become a ragged and unskilled migratory labor force pouring into England's and Scotland's industrial cities. The United Irish Rebellion of 1798, Daniel O'Connell's mass campaigns for Catholic Emancipation (achieved in 1828) and then for repeal of the Anglo-Irish Union of 1800, and the prominence of several Irish figures in the Chartist movement in England demonstrated that the Irish could be a formidable force for political unrest and rebellion in the United Kingdom as a whole.

Commentators as diverse as Thomas Carlyle and Marx and Engels observed as much. Mixing Biblical-style fulmination with social analysis, Carlyle's *Chartism* (1840) deals at length with Irish migration to England and its consequences. Referring mockingly to the Irish migrants as "Sanspotatoes," an obvious reference to the Parisian "sansculottes," Carlyle complains that:

> Crowds of miserable Irish darken all our towns. The wild Milesian features, looking false ingenuity, restlessness, unreason, misery and mockery, salute

you on all highways and by-ways. . . . He is the sorest evil this country has to strive with. In his rags and laughing savagery, he is there to undertake all work that can be done by mere strength of hand and back; for wages that will purchase him potatoes. . . . The Saxon man if he cannot work on these terms, finds no work. He too may be ignorant; but he has not sunk from decent manhood to squalid apehood; he cannot continue there. American forests lie untilled across the ocean; the uncivilized Irishman, not by his strength but by the opposite of strength, drives out the Saxon native, takes possession in his room. (28)

Here, colonial clichés and stereotypes agglutinate. They include: the dark simian qualities; the sly civility that combines "misery and mockery" or "laughing savagery"; the degenerate Celtic weakness that is nevertheless stealthy enough to expropriate the more manly Saxon and compel him to emigrate to "untilled" American forests while the slovenly migrant usurps "his room" at home.

Yet though he fulminates, Carlyle does not wholly blame the Irish for their own condition:

And yet these poor Celtiberian Irish brothers, what can *they* help it? They cannot stay at home and starve. It is just and natural that they come hither as a curse to us. Alas, for them too it is not a luxury. It is not a straight or joyful way of avenging their sore wrongs this; but a most sad circuitous one. Yet a way it is, and an effectual way. The time has come when the Irish population must be improved a little, or else exterminated. Plausible management, adapted to this hollow outcry or that will no longer do: it must be management, grounded on sincerity and fact, to which the truth of things will respond – by an actual beginning of improvement to these wretched brother-men. In a state of perpetual ultra-savage famine, they cannot continue. For that the Saxon British will ever submit to sink along with them to such a state, we assume as impossible. (29–30; italics in the original)

It is the Kurtz-like reference that what cannot be "improved" must be "exterminated" that catches the eye here. When the Great Famine came later in the same decade, the Irish really did become "Sanspotatoes," 2 million of them dying of hunger, a further 2 million emigrating. Following that catastrophe, the more militant Irish, at home and in the United States, would also think "extermination" and attribute the British government's weak and often contemptuous response to Irish starvation and disease as state-sanctioned genocide.

Nevertheless, both in the passage cited here, and in the treatise as a whole, Carlyle's stress falls on "improvement," not "extermination." In place of an ad hoc "plausible management" of what Carlyle represents as a chronic domestic British crisis, what *Chartism* calls for is the "beginning of an improvement" that will confront what will soon be called "the Irish problem" more systematically. When he is done railing on the inadequacies of English parliamentary reform and bourgeois complacency, what Carlyle finally advocates in *Chartism*'s closing chapter as the solution to the social unrest unleashed by the industrial revolution comes down to two Es, or really three Es: Education and Emigration, Empire serving as the bridge that connects the first two Es. Education is advocated for the English workers and slatternly Irish, "who speak a partially intelligible dialect of English" (28), so both constituencies may be disciplined out of their unruliness and into proper respect for order and authority. Emigration is offered as a response to Malthusian doomsayers; it is a valve that will allow this "swelling, simmering, never-resting Europe of ours" that stands "on the verge of an expansion without parallel" to make verdant the whole earth (112).

"Universal Education is the first great thing we mean, general Emigration is the second" (Carlyle 98). Education and emigration, in many cases education for emigration, would remain closely imbricated in Irish life throughout the nineteenth and twentieth centuries, but the approaches Carlyle called for in *Chartism* were in many respects already underway before 1840. The Act of Union passed in 1800 abolished Dublin's Ascendancy parliament and afterward Westminster directly governed Ireland. The shocks caused by the 1798 Rebellion and O'Connell's mass campaigns together with rapid transformations brought about by the industrial revolution in England forced a dramatic expansion in British state power and social controls, economic *laissez faire* notwithstanding. Experiments that were more difficult to implement in the United Kingdom proper were attempted in colonial Ireland, and by the mid-nineteenth century the smaller island possessed a complex of centrally administered social institutions. These included an extensive network of police stations and gaols, workhouses, hospitals, asylums, and, not least, a national education system.

In 1831, the establishment of the Commission of National Education steered Irish education away from Protestant conversion agendas and led to the formation of a state-centralized national education system. Though the Irish clergy of all denominations were mostly initially hostile to a centralized education system, they were nevertheless encouraged to participate as patrons of the new school system. Thus, as Kevin Lougheed comments, "the national school system quickly established itself in Ireland, such that it was one of the dominant suppliers of education in the country by the onset of the Famine in 1845, with close to 3500 national schools educating over 430,000 children" (3). By comparison, Lougheed adds, "the state emerged into the English education field much later than in Ireland, only becoming directly involved in education provision from 1870" (4). Though the two countries were officially parts of the same state, then, national education took different courses in Ireland and England. In Ireland, the state developed a centralized system earlier and attempted to attach the various clerical denominations to the state by way of school patronage; in England, state involvement was more gradual and there was ultimately less emphasis on religious involvement (Lougheed 5).

Educational innovations in Ireland had consequences that reached well beyond Ireland. In the White settler colonies especially, colonial authorities looked to the imperial center for models as to how to develop their own fledgling educational systems, and Ireland often served as a template. Canada and Australia also had settler populations divided by religion and nationality, and the Irish national school system appeared to offer a model by which to overcome such division and to create self-disciplined subjects loyal to the British Empire. Missions by the various churches to tend to the emigrant communities in the settler colonies brought Irish experience and knowledge to these regions, and this in turn further encouraged a tendency to emulate Irish examples. Akenson, Lougheed, and others note that the basic textbooks introduced for instruction in the Irish national schools remained for thirty years after their introduction what Akenson calls "probably the best schoolbooks produced in the British Isles" (229). "It can be said that, from the 1840s," Lougheed observes, "the textbooks published in Ireland became the standard textbooks throughout the British Empire" (10).

These textbooks did not contain detailed information on the geography, history, or culture of Ireland and instead presented the United Kingdom as a homogenous society and culture with a superior form of governance from which Ireland particularly and the colonies generally benefitted. As Lougheed remarks:

> The importance of the British Empire, with Ireland as a key part, and the "civilising mission" of imperialism were highlighted, especially in the geography sections [of the textbooks]. This emphasised the size and importance of the Empire and also served to inform individuals of opportunities for emigration. ... Throughout the publications, racial and cultural views were constructed which privileged European customs. For example, the description of the geography of Africa states that it was a barren region "both as respects to the nature of the soil, and the moral conditions of the inhabitants." (8–9)

When a century later Australian, Canadian, Nigerian, Kenyan, or Trinidadian writers would remark that their colonial educations had familiarized them with English landscapes or misty autumns to the exclusion of the ecologies or climates of their own regions, they were probably legatees to an educational and textbook culture initially pioneered in Ireland in the early 1800s.

The emergence of the modern university system and the English department in Ireland must be viewed in these wider national and imperial contexts. Trinity College, which remains Ireland's most internationally prestigious university, was founded in 1592 at the time of the Tudor plantations and would remain well into the twentieth century what David Dickson has called "the 'central fortress' of *ancien regime* values and Anglican power" (187). Protestant dominance of the professions in Ireland was, Dickson notes, at its apogee in the 1850s, and in the mid-nineteenth century Trinity competed strongly with other British universities in terms of securing clerkships in the Indian Civil Service (ICS), coming second only to Oxford in competitions for imperial opportunity. When in the 1850s it was decided that recruitment to the ICS should be by competitive examination, Trinity responded promptly and in 1855 appointed William Wright to the chair of Arabic and in 1859 a lecturer, later in 1862 professor, of Sanskrit, Rudolf Thomas Siegfried. R. B. McDowell and D. A. Webb comment that Trinity "was quick to see that the new category of 'competition-wallah,' even if looked down on at first by old hands nominated by personal influence, provided a new outlet for Dublin graduates seeking an employment that was at once adventurous and commensurate with their abilities and social status." As a result, "Trinity sent a steady stream of graduates to India as long as British rule lasted" (232–34).

Against the opposition of the Catholic episcopacy, secular nondenominational colleges were opened in Belfast, Cork, and Galway in 1845, which commenced teaching as associative members of the Queens University of Ireland in 1849, as the country was devastated by famine. A separate Catholic university was opened in Dublin in 1854, but without a royal charter to endorse its degrees and suffering from serious underfunding it fared poorly with government-sponsored rivals. In 1882, it was reorganized to become University College Dublin (UCD) and became a constituent member of the Royal University of Ireland, a revised version of the Queens University system. If the Famine devastated the poorest classes in Ireland especially and accelerated chronic migration outward for decades to follow, the same epoch also consolidated Irish Catholic middle-class professional formation. Soon, the new Queens and later Royal colleges were also competing to take advantage of imperial opportunity, turning out graduates to secure ICS clerkships or to work in the Indian medical service or as engineers to meet the demands of Irish and Indian railway booms. S. B. Cook argues that after 1870 Irish competitiveness in ICS exams suffered when Sir Charles Wood and Lord Salisbury reformed the recruitment process to improve the quality of Indian administration. Both men, Cook argues, were sincere in their improving intentions, but nevertheless "they shared the mid-Victorian belief that English gentlemen were the best conceivable imperial guardians. Both men loathed what they regarded as the tradesmen's instincts and infinite insecurities of youth. But they also doubted the ability of the Irish either to rule themselves or govern others" (514). The reduction in Irish recruitment for Indian positions coincided, then, with a period of increased domestic agitation in Ireland – the Land Wars, the Home Rule crises – and the same universities that contributed to training Irishmen for empire also educated an emergent Irish middle class that would rule the Irish Free State after 1921.

The emergence of English literature as a distinct subject of university study coincided with the appointment of Edward Dowden to the post of Chair of English in Trinity College in 1867. As histories of the discipline make clear, this development represented a wider secular and modernizing turn in Western university education, one that would eventually see the previously dominant Classics become in time a relatively minor discipline and which brought the study of national literatures to the fore. Though part of its mission might be to afford a humanist corrective to the competitive individualism of *laissez faire* capitalism, in universities committed to securing British national and imperial greatness the study of English inevitably meant that the new discipline acquired its own ideological cast.[1]

Dowden, for example, was a committed Irish unionist and devotee of the British Empire. Franklin Court claims "Dowden was an outspoken political conservative who distrusted and feared democracy as a great class leveler, but in Dublin particularly, the spectre of Paddy with a torch standing on his doorstep could seem real." Nevertheless, he adds, "Dowden was not alone among late-century English professors in his ethnocentric support for an idealized historical continuum and in his desire to curtail democratic reform efforts. Although the heritage of Burkean conservatism was more evident in Dowden than in other late-century English professors, the mainstream tradition of literary study in England generally had become tacitly more nationalistic and conservative" (154–55).

Dowden had written an authoritative *Life of Shelley* (1886) before his Trinity appointment and would later write *Robert Browning* (1904), but his reputation rests primarily on his many studies of Shakespeare, especially *Shakespeare: His Mind and Art* (1875). Dowden's Shakespeare offers the playwright as an epitome of Protestant manliness, sound business sense, and liberal tolerance, the antithesis to the mercurial Celtic flightiness then popularized in Celtic and Saxon racial discourses. Though receptive to international intellectual currents, Dowden was stubbornly hostile to the later nineteenth-century Irish Literary Revival, viewing with suspicion anything Irish that would distinguish itself from a common Britishness.[2] He was on friendly terms with William Butler Yeats's family and an admirer of the young Yeats's poems, but refused to write on Irish writers or subjects and refused permission for his own poetry to be published in a "specially Irish anthology" (Longley 30). In his later years, Dowden campaigned for the Irish Unionist Alliance against Irish Home Rule and in 1908 took charge of the Irish branch of the British Empire Shakespeare Society (BESS) that had previously been presided over by John Pentland Mahaffy, the distinguished Trinity classicist and onetime tutor to Oscar Wilde. The importance of the English Renaissance period – then celebrated as the "Golden Age" of empire, Shakespeare, and the Globe Theatre – was reflected also in the works of other early chairs of English (or History and English Literature as several were titled) in Irish universities. Frederick S. Boas, Chair of History and English in Queens University Belfast, published many books on Renaissance drama, and Thomas William Moffitt, who became chair of History and English in Queen's College Galway in 1863, published *Selections from the Works of Lord Bacon* (1847).

James Joyce was born in 1882, the same year that the Catholic university became University College Dublin. He received his early education in Clongowes Wood College, Co. Kildare, a Jesuit private boarding school opened in 1814 and one of Ireland's premier elite Catholic schools modeled on English equivalents such as Eton and Harrow. Clongowes had a strong record in training its students for imperial and missionary service and cultivated an English-style sporting ethos that included cricket, association football, lawn tennis, and cycling. Thanks to his father's improvidence, Joyce's education differed from that of this elite because he had later to transfer to Belvedere College, Dublin, another elite though somewhat less prestigious Jesuit school. In A *Portrait of the Artist as a Young Man* (1916), the young Stephen Dedalus's alienation from Clongowes's muscularly Catholic and imperial ethos is everywhere evident. Stephen is physically timid and lacks interest in sports; his father has Fenian and Home Rule sympathies; his family fortunes are in decline; he loses his religious faith and becomes sexually dissolute: all these things bring the young Dedalus into intellectual conflict with the Clongowes mission to educate cultivated Irish Catholic "gentlemen" with the social poise and assurance to match their Etonian English counterparts. Joyce's self-exile from Ireland after 1904 meant that he became an émigré distanced from the Home Rule Catholic elite with which he was educated or from the more militant Sinn Féin nationalist middle class as it assumed state power after the War of Independence and the establishment of the Free State in 1921. Nevertheless, *Ulysses* clearly reflects much of the historical resentment of England and indeed the high ambition of this Catholic bourgeoisie in the era of its radical self-assertion; Joyce worked on that novelistic epic throughout the violent years that led up to the foundation of the Irish Free State.

In the final section of *Portrait*, as Stephen makes his way toward his university lectures in Earlsfort Terrace, he passes "the grey block of Trinity on his left, set heavily in the city's ignorance like a great dull stone set in a cumbrous ring" and feels it pull his "mind downward" (Joyce 194). Passing the Trinity entrance, Stephen feels himself "striving this way and that to free his feet from the fetters of the reformed conscience" and observes the "the droll statue of the national poet of Ireland" (194). To Stephen, the monument to Thomas Moore positioned just outside Trinity College is pitiable, but he regards the edifice with more sorrow than anger because "though sloth of the body and the soul crept over it like unseen vermin," the statue "seemed humbly conscious of its indignity." As Stephen enters Earlsfort Terrace, site of University College Dublin, he reflects, "it was too late to go upstairs to the French class" (199). This lateness for French conveys his sense of being severed from the European continent, and Stephen sighs that his own poor knowledge of Latin and his nation's tardiness would always render him "a shy guest at the feast of the world's culture" (194).

Too late for French instruction, he makes his way to meet the Dean of Studies in one of *Portrait*'s much-cited set pieces. Listening to the English Jesuit dean speak, Stephen reflects:

> The language in which we are speaking is his before it is mine. How different are the words *home, Christ, ale, master,* on his lips and on mine! I cannot speak or write these words without unrest of spirit. His language so

familiar and so foreign, will always be for me an acquired speech. I have not made or accepted its words. My voice holds them at bay. My soul frets in the shadow of his language. (205)

In these passages, Joyce deploys Dublin's topography to illustrate a history of Irish educational and aesthetic formation that has shaped Stephen but which he must overcome if he is to liberate himself as an artist and "to forge in the smithy of my soul the uncreated conscience of my race" (276). The "dull grey stone" of Trinity College pulls Stephen's "mind downwards." Protestantism's "reformed conscience" does not represent for him the claims for individual freethinking and tolerance, which it claimed for itself, but merely another foot-fetter on his own people. Moore's statue with its "shuffling feet" and "servile head" symbolizes not some monumental Irish poetic achievement but a subservient sloth. However, because it is "humbly conscious of its indignity," the monument also painfully registers the centuries of oppression that bred this abased condition. If French culture is beyond his reach, English culture, "so familiar and so foreign," Stephen admits only as "an acquired speech," a colonially imposed language his voice "holds at bay" and within which "his soul frets" like a captured thing.

As is now widely recognized, in *Portrait* Joyce expresses a colonial and postcolonial predicament. Others elsewhere – Chinua Achebe in Nigeria, Ngũgĩ wa' Thiong'o in Kenya, C. L. R. James and V. S. Naipaul in Trinidad, Derek Walcott in Saint Lucia, Jamaica Kincaid in Antigua – would describe their own childhood schoolroom encounters with the English language and literature in British-centric education systems. These formative experiences usually nurtured lifelong affections for English literature but also the sense of an early indenture into an inheritance not merely not one's own but that of one's imperial master. The language options open to these writers varied but a sense of the English language and English literature as both franchise and fetter to self-expression pulsates through the works they created.

Still, there is reason not to overplay Foucauldian or Althusserian conceptions of disciplinary technologies or subject interpellations that control subjectivity so completely as to leave little room for resistance. There are distinctions between constriction and complete constructivism. The importance of the national school system and of university education to the anglicization of Ireland and the cultivation of imperialist mentalities cannot be doubted. However, as Joyce's situation illustrates, Irish subjects could obviously bring a critical consciousness to bear on the institutions that inculcated such subject formation and many of Joyce's predecessors and contemporaries responded to their colonial situations more militantly than Joyce did. Wolfe Tone and Robert Emmett, founding figures for militant republicanism, Thomas Davis and John Mitchel, leaders of the Young Ireland cultural nationalist movement, and Isaac Butt and John Redmond, leaders of the Home Rule movement, were all Trinity College students. Leading Catholic republican or nationalist figures including James Fintan Lawlor, a radical Young Irelander, James Stephens, a founder of Fenian Brotherhood, Frank Hugh O'Donnell, MP and anti-imperialist, and Patrick Pearse and Thomas McDonagh, leaders of the Easter 1916 insurrection, all attended Catholic-associated private schools or universities. Many of the most prominent figures in Irish political movements had very little formal schooling. Jeremiah O'Donovan Rossa, a prominent Fenian, spoke Irish only at home, learned English in a local school, saw his father die of fever in the Famine and his mother and siblings emigrate to America, and found early employment in a relative's hardware store. Michael Davitt's Irish-speaking parents were evicted from their Mayo tenant farm in 1850 and then emigrated to Lancashire, where Michael was homeschooled but lost an arm in a factory accident, aged eleven. Born to Irish emigrant parents in a slum district of Edinburgh, James Connolly, founder of the Irish Citizen Army, received minimal formal education at a local Catholic school. He went to work early before joining the British Army, where he may have served in India and did in Ireland, later becoming a trade unionist, socialist, and Irish separatist. Fanny and Anna Parnell, sisters to the charismatic Home Rule leader Charles Stewart Parnell, were born on a landlord's estate in Wicklow and enjoyed a comfortable upbringing but had very little formal education beyond what they obtained from the family library. The struggles against a colonial educational formation of which Joyce writes so searchingly in *Portrait* would speak to many young colonized subjects across the British Empire. However, until the universities became somewhat more accessible to women and the working classes after World War II, the educational experiences described by Joyce in *Portrait* applied only to a tiny percentage of such subjects.

How much did the establishment of the Irish Free State in 1921 do to decolonize the Irish university system or the subject of English more specifically? In the absence of proper departmental histories, the question is impossible to answer in any real detail, though one can hazard broad observations. The partition of Ireland after 1921 meant that the decolonization was partial, and the two new states compounded some of the less progressive features of the colonial system. In the new Northern Irish state especially, where a majoritarian Protestant unionist establishment took power against the backdrop of a slowly contracting British Empire and the emergence of anticolonial national movements on many continents, the colonial and imperial dimensions of higher education may have hardened rather than softened. In both states, primary and secondary education largely remained divided, as it had in nineteenth-century Ireland, along sectarian Catholic and Protestant lines. In the words of recent scholars, the new Ministry for Education in Northern Ireland sponsored "a very clear determination to create a system which would ensure allegiance to the Empire and protect against dissention (e.g. the explicit promotion of elements of Irish culture, history and language)" (O'Toole, McClelland, Forde, et al. 1030). In a subsection titled "Loyalty," the Lynn Committee report of 1923 commissioned to establish Northern Irish educational policy stipulated that all state-funded teachers were to take an oath of allegiance to the British Crown and "no books were to be used in the classroom 'to which reasonable objection might be entertained on political grounds'" (O'Toole, McClelland, Forde, et al. 1030). The report found no justification for any special status for the Irish language and "decided to treat it like any other language, precluding its teaching henceforth below standard five (11 years old) in line with the practice of other 'foreign' languages" (1030). In this repressive context, the Catholic church refused in the 1920s to transfer their schools to the authority of the Northern state and retained patronage of them, a decision which, the same authors conclude, "proved crucial in sustaining the identity of a coherent Catholic community through to the present day" (1030).[3]

South of the border, the Irish Free State deemed schools and schoolchildren crucial to the cultivation and consolidation of a new national identity. By the 1920s, Ireland was a much-anglicized society, and the new government viewed itself as striving to create or restore a strong sense of "Irishness" in the teeth of a far more powerful British culture in an era of wide-reaching media technologies and culture industries. Thus, the new state established the revival of the Irish language and culture as a priority. Southern policy stipulated that schools were to devote a minimum of one hour every day to instruction in Irish, while no time stipulations applied to other subjects. The Catholic church had already secured considerable control over the southern Irish education system in the post-Famine era, and partition further consolidated this. "The State-Church alliance in education was largely a pragmatic and symbiotic relationship, with the Free State benefitting from the financial resources and reputational legitimacy of the Catholic Church in the provision of educational and other services" (O'Toole, McClelland, Forde, et al. 1023).

Leah O'Toole et al. also note that the national school curriculum devised in 1900, before partition, was clearly gendered and specified that "the average primary schoolgirl, when she assumes the position of housewife" ought to be able to "perform the ordinary culinary and washing operations that may appertain to her position" (1028). The Victorian conception of girls as miniwives and mothers-to-be persisted after partition. In the 1922 and 1926 curricula in the South, cookery and laundry work were placed center stage for girls only, and every girl was to receive three hours of needlework instruction per week. In the North, too, the 1923 Lynn Report stressed that girls be taught practical skills such as cookery, laundry-work, and household management and that boys learn woodwork (O'Toole, McClelland, Forde, et al. 1028–29).

One of the more famous school poems of the era, William Butler Yeats's "Among School Children," opens with the poetic persona ruminatively visiting a Catholic girls' school and ruefully pondering the children's youth, his own aging, and the mysteries of beauty:

> I walk through the long schoolroom questioning;
> A kind old nun in a white hood replies;
> The children learn to cipher and to sing,
> To study reading books and history,
> To cut and sew, be neat in everything
> In the best modern way – the children's eyes
> In momentary wonder stare upon
> A sixty-year-old public smiling man.
>
> (Yeats 122)

Yeats may ponder whether "the best modern way" can produce the natural beauty of the aristocratic Maud Gonne, and he self-deprecatingly presents his own senatorial role in the Free State as he imagines the children might view him. However, the poem's detached patrician voice contemplating the idea of beauty among nuns and schoolgirls – described in passing as lower class "paddlers" to Maud Gonne's "swan" (122) – probably reflects something also of the wider hauteur of the new elites in both Irish states with regard to the children of the poorer sort and their education. In other words, the Yeats figure in "Among School Children" is much more preoccupied with his own memoires and cultural ideals than with the actualities of the schoolgirls' lives or aspirations. The Irish Free State, later Republic, might be accused of a like form of detached idealism, one that prioritized education as nation-building at the expense of any real consideration of the realities of the poor, most destined for manual labor at home or the emigrant boat to Britain or the United States.

Himself deemed only a moderate student in his schooldays, and someone who never attended university, Yeats's "Among School Children" was written after the poet-senator's visit in 1926 to St. Otteran's in Waterford City, a Sisters of Mercy convent founded only a few years earlier in 1920. The school practiced Montessori methods that stress a unity of intellectual and practical activities and creative self-expression. Yeats's poem conveys a like ideal when it rounds off with a final swerve stanza that favors an organicist mode of cultivation where: "The body is not bruised to pleasure soul, / Nor beauty born out of its own despair, / Nor blear-eyed wisdom out of midnight oil" (123). These are admirable sentiments, but the realities of Irish education at all levels were mostly remarkably different. For much of the twentieth century, in both the more religious and secular schools, discipline, especially for the lower classes, was harsh or openly violent, educational achievement was determined by rigid exam systems, class and gender stratifications were institutionalized, and university remained restricted, until the 1970s and 1980s, to small minorities. In recent years, commissions to investigate the "industrial schools," a euphemism for reformatory institutions for juveniles, have attested to an extraordinary history of physical, mental, and sexual abuse of minors. Yeats's views on education may have been more enlightened than those of many of his contemporaries, but his views on modern democracy, gender, class, and elite rule were mostly, like those of the new elites more widely, very nineteenth-century.[4] The more authoritarian, eugenicist, and fascistic notes sounded in his social and poetical works from the 1930s onward caution against any simple notion of linear social or educational progress as modern Ireland transitioned from Dowden's world of Victorian Ascendancy domination into the turbulence of the mid-twentieth century.

The brief history of the English department's place in the wider colonial history of Irish education roughly sketched here can in some respects be considered typical. In all regions of the British Empire, the teaching of English literature cultivated a sense of "Britishness" that was always classed, racialized, and gendered. In Ireland, as elsewhere, that process produced mixed results, and the state education systems that emerged out of the anti-imperial independence struggles retained many assumptions and features that had informed the colonial-era system even if they "decolonized" others. It would be interesting to know in more detail to what extent and in what ways university English departments in Ireland, north and south, changed – in terms of ambitions, personnel, curriculum, and modes of teaching – in the decades after the 1920s but, as remarked at the outset of this essay, there are few studies that document such changes.

Nevertheless, if the Irish experience resembles that of other regions of the British Empire in some general respects, in others it is clearly different. The racial, religious, political, and economic histories of particular colonies, and the different types of nationalist movements that assumed power in the aftermath of independence, suggest that the fortunes and dispositions of the English department will differ considerably from one country to another in the era after empire. University English departments in Ireland, Britain, the United States, India, South Africa, Nigeria, Ghana, Egypt, Trinidad, or Canada may all look rather alike in appearance, and their faculties may have broadly similar histories of professionalization and credentialing. Nevertheless, those departments clearly operate in quite distinctive circumstances and there are reasons, then, not to assume that the metropolitan histories of the English department in the United States or Britain, about which we have more extensive studies than of their counterparts elsewhere, can serve as standard models for English departments everywhere. By extension, the "decolonization of English" in Oxford or Cambridge, Harvard or Yale, will inevitably mean something quite different to what it might mean in Dublin or Delhi, Mumbai or Melbourne, Seoul or Singapore.

As English departments in North America and the United Kingdom institutionalized what we now call "postcolonial literatures" or "studies" from the late 1980s or 1990s onward, many academics and administrators in Ireland, north and south, regarded such developments nervously. In the context of the long-running conflict in Northern Ireland euphemistically known as "The Troubles," postcolonial readings of Irish literature seemed to some a reanimation of militant nationalist conceptions of Irish history and literature, or a subordination of literature to political ideology, or an unwarranted conflation of Irish history with that of the colonies proper. This hostility was not confined to conservatives; many liberals shared such views. They held that as Ireland was becoming increasingly integrated into the European Union, Irish culture might better be regarded in "European" rather than in "Third World" terms. Postcolonial studies, some liberal feminists argued, was too closely attached to national paradigms of oppression that attended too much to issues of British imperialism, too little to those of Irish Catholicism or nationalism, or to sexual and gender oppressions. These are simplifications of what were sometimes more complex positions, but they describe the broader contours of the debates that shaped the reception and tentative institutionalization of postcolonial studies in Ireland.

Even as these contentions over "postcolonial studies" animated English studies in Ireland, the transformation of Irish society continued apace. With the economic boom commonly described as the "Celtic Tiger" era, the Republic of Ireland especially underwent one of the most rapid demographic changes in Western Europe and in the island's modern history. Between the eighteenth and nineteenth centuries, Ireland's population had increased dramatically, rising from fewer than 3 million in 1700 to over 8 million by the 1841 census. A decade later, as the great Famine was ending in 1851, that population had dropped to 6.5 million. Thanks to chronic rural poverty and the huge diasporic outmigration that continued for decades after the Famine, that figure had dropped to 5 million by 1891 and by 1931 to over 4 million. The island's population did not rise again until the 1960s. In 2021, the Republic of Ireland's population topped 5 million for the first time since the 1851 census. However, the economic boom that commenced in the 1990s and lasted until the international banking crisis of 2008 transformed the Republic from a state with a chronic history of outward migration into a country that started to receive a steady flow of immigration. Today, it is estimated that over 17 percent of the population of the Republic of Ireland is foreign born, certainly one of the most dramatic transformations in the society's history since independence.

Given the size and speed of this transformation, and the fact that some of the new population hails from other former regions of the British Empire or Global South, and much of it thanks to European Union enlargement, from "Eastern Europe," where the word "colonization" may semaphore the Soviet Union or contemporary Russia rather than Great Britain, the usage "decolonization" will almost certainly be at least as contested and controversial as was the usage "postcolonial" from the 1980s onward. In the current moment, these rapid demographic changes have not yet significantly changed the literary or intellectual fields in Ireland, and the changing composition of the larger population is for now much more evident in the student cohorts taking "English" as a subject than in the teaching cohorts offering such study. This, too, will surely change in time. Though recent migrant populations often veer more toward STEM than to humanities subjects, the literary disciplines will see major changes also.

In the context of this complex colonial history, what might it mean to "decolonize" the English department in Ireland in the second quarter of the twenty-first century? Recent discussions of such matters typically proffer ready proposals such as diversification of teaching curricula and faculty, critiques of eurocentrism, critical histories of the discipline (of a kind, as mentioned at the outset, lacking in Ireland), and greater attention to matters of racial and other oppressions. In an era of rampant neoliberalism that has witnessed the creation of widening cleavages of wealth across classes and the privatization of all sorts of public goods, including education, one wonders whether such strategies, valuable though they be, can be adequate to meet the general challenge. Moreover, in a time when the humanities disciplines especially feel increasingly marginalized by governments and university authorities, some will argue that English literary studies can ill afford analyses of its grimmer historical entanglements and that scholars should articulate positive agendas for the future rather than raking over the past. It does seem imperative that English departments must discover new visions and new institutional structures that would support such visions, but some fuller reckoning with the past seems not so much an impediment as an essential first step toward the discovery and realization of such future visions.

Notes

1. On this history of English departments, see Baldick; Doyle; Court; Miller.
2. On Dowden's career generally, see Ludwigson.
3. The view cited here is that of Michael McGrath's *The Catholic Church and Catholic Schools in Northern Ireland: The Price of Faith.*
4. See *Report of the Commission to Inquire into Child Abuse, 2009* and the widespread media coverage of these and related Magdalen Laundry scandals. For an authoritative study that deals with these institutional histories and their social and cultural contexts, see Smith.

WORKS CITED

Akenson, Donald K. *The Irish Education Experiment: The National System of Education in the Nineteenth Century.* London: Routledge, 1970.

Baldick, Chris. *The Social Mission of English Criticism 1848–1932.* Oxford: Oxford University Press, 1983.

Carlyle, Thomas. *Chartism.* London: James Fraser, 1840.

Cook, S. B. "The Irish Raj: Social Origins and Careers of Irishmen in the Indian Civil Service 1855–1914." *Journal of Social History* 20.3 (1987): 507–528.

Court, Franklin E. *The Culture and Politics of Literary Study, 1750–1900.* Stanford, CA: Stanford University Press, 1992.

Dickson, David. "1857 and 1908: Two Moments in the Transformation of Irish Universities." In David Dickson, Justyna Pyz, and Christopher Shephard, eds., *Irish Classrooms and British Empire: Imperial Contexts in the Origins of Modern Education.* Dublin: Four Courts Press, 2012.

Doyle, Brian. *English and Englishness*. London: Routledge, 1989.

Joyce, James. *A Portrait of the Artist as a Young Man*, ed. Seamus Deane. London: Penguin, 1992.

Longley, Edna. "'A Foreign Oasis'? English Literature, Irish Studies and Queen's University." *The Irish Review* 17/18 (1995): 26–39.

Lougheed, Kevin. "'After the Manner of the Irish Schools': The Influence of Irish National Education in the British Empire." *Journal of Historical Geography* 60 (2018): 1–10.

Ludwigson, Kathryn R. *Edward Dowden*. New York: Twayne Publishers, 1973.

McDowell, R. B. and D. A. Webb. *Trinity College Dublin: An Academic History*. Dublin: Trinity College Dublin Press in association with Environmental Publications, 2004.

McGrath, Michael. *The Catholic Church and Catholic Schools in Northern Ireland: The Price of Faith*. Dublin: Irish Academic Press, 2000.

McManus, Antonia. *The Irish Hedge School and Its Books, 1695–1831*. Dublin: Four Courts, 2002.

Miller, Thomas P. *The Formation of College English: Rhetoric and Belles Lettres in the English Cultural Provinces*. Edinburgh: University of Edinburgh Press, 1997.

North, Joseph. *Literary Criticism: A Concise Political History*. Cambridge, MA: Harvard University Press, 2017.

O'Toole, Leah, Diane McClelland, Deirdre Forde, et al. "Contested Childhoods across Borders and Boundaries: Insights from Curriculum Provisions in Northern Ireland and the Irish Free State in the 1920s." *British Educational Research Journal* 47.4 (2021): 1021–38.

Smith, James M. *Ireland's Magdalen Laundries and the Nation's Architecture of Containment*. South Bend, IN: University of Notre Dame Press, 2007.

Yeats, W. B. "Among School Children." In M. L. Rosenthal, ed., *William Butler Yeats: Selected Poems and Four Plays*. New York: Scribner Paperback Poetry, 1996, 121–23.

CHAPTER 3

First Peoples, Indigeneity, and Teaching Indigenous Writing in Canada

Margery Fee and Deanna Reder

When I looked at education from an Indigenous perspective, I saw everything was a problem. ... I could not escape the discursive Eurocentric lens that measured everything against itself, and therefore, Indigenous peoples were always found lacking and ultimately to be acted upon by some government initiative.

Marie Battiste, *Decolonizing Education: Nourishing the Learning Spirit* (35)

Within the colonizing university also exists a decolonizing education.

K. Wayne Yang, "Decolonial Desires" (60)

Must all Native writing be reduced to a singular narrative of colonization and resistance?

Helen Hoy, *How Should I Read These?* (164)

Standing on Stolen Land: Where Is Here (Now)?

We respectfully acknowledge that we live and work on the unceded territories of the Coast Salish peoples: the xʷməθkʷəẏəm (Musqueam), Sḵwx̱wú7mesh (Squamish), səlilẇətaʔł (Tsleil-Waututh), q̓íc̓əẏ (Katzie), kʷikʷəƛ̓əm (Kwikwetlem), qiqéyt (Qayqayt), q'ʷa:n̓ƛ'ən̓ (Kwantlen), Səmyámə (Semiahmoo), sc̓əwaθən (Tsawwassen), and Stó:lō Nations.[1] It's not enough, clearly, just to say these words. These territories were never legally ceded to the Crown, although the Crown pretends to own them (see Erin Hanson, "Aboriginal Title"). And the Crown is the basis of Canadian law, which until recently did not acknowledge other laws and sovereignties. Land acknowledgments aim to inspire speakers to discover the history of the land on which they are standing and to inculcate a sense of responsibility to the place and its peoples. However, in Enlightenment thinking, land and all of nature are represented as material objects outside of us to be exploited, used, transformed, and known through observation, analysis, and experiment.

In Enlightenment thinking, Nature is opposed to Culture; people can only come to know nature by separating themselves from it.

In contrast, Indigenous epistemes give land an ontological and epistemological importance that is absent in Western culture. Nature is an animate teacher intertwined with culture; animals precede humans and have more power than we do; humans are entangled in a web of relationships that entail reciprocal responsibilities if everyone is to keep on living. And these epistemes have not vanished despite 500 years of colonization.

Even in the anthropological record, Indigenous critique of Western worldviews can be found. For example, in a 1976 article, anthropologist Madronna Holden analyzed some early satirical portraits of the White man popular with the Coast Salish peoples on whose territories Deanna and Margery live. She includes a story written down at the end of the nineteenth century by Boas-trained Livingston Farrand, later the president of Cornell University. Some of the stories Holden examines feature a character called "Jesus Christ," whose mission, "making all the crooked ways straight," comes from the Bible: "I will go before thee, and make the crooked places straight" (Isaiah 45:2):

> The man who first made the people came from the North and went south. In those days people were upside down and on all fours and crooked and they heard there was a man coming from the North who would make people straight and the man came to Neah Bay . . . the people were walking on their hands upside down and he straightened them up and made them straight . . . he went to Quillayute and they were crooked in the same way and he straightened them up . . . then he reached Hoh and turned and called them to come out . . . He went to the Quinalt and called them and said "I am the one who is straightening everybody out." (273–74)[2]

This busy Straightener keeps going until Farrand's notes "trail off in midsentence" (274). In this story, the White missionary takes on a familiar role, that of Transformer or Changer, but the repetition signals the satire. The storyteller uses few of the usual ways of engaging the listener. Except for the humor. Everyone is changed to be the same, over and over. And over.

This storyteller mocks the obsessive and repetitive work of straightening. One target of mockery could be the perspective that sees a fixed and essentialized object, category, canon, definition, interpretation, story, or self as the goal of analysis. (Plato's Idea, for example, which went so well with Christianity.) Raven, Coyote, and the other beings like them, however, are continually traveling, meddling, eating, seducing, thieving, destroying. and restoring. (Did Raven steal the light for all earth-beings, or because it was the brightest of bright shiny objects? Who can say?)[3] By relying on West Coast epistemes, the storyteller points out that more than one thought-world exists.

Our colleague Jeannette Armstrong (Okanagan/Syilx) explains her people's relationship to land in the interior of British Columbia:

> All my Elders say that it is land that holds all knowledge of life and death and is a constant teacher. It is said in Okanagan that the land constantly speaks. . . . Not to learn its language is to die. We have survived and thrived by listening intently to its teachings – to its language – and then inventing human words to retell its stories to our succeeding generations. ("Land Speaking" 178)

What would it mean for us as scholars of literary studies to read and teach literature as if our central social ethic, our most important value, was that there was no separation between people and nature? What if we felt responsibility for all earth-beings as kin, including a "sentient land"? (Cruikshank 142). The rapid adoption of land acknowledgments has not noticeably reduced the contested "development" of Indigenous lands; it seems fair to say that "until actual land is returned, and the terms of some treaties renegotiated or abrogated entirely," we have not fulfilled the responsibilities of good guests (Wilkes, Duong, Kesler, and Ramos 19). The coauthors of the 2014 publication "Learning from the Land" write: "We begin with the premise that if colonization is fundamentally about dispossessing Indigenous peoples from land, decolonization must involve forms of education that reconnect Indigenous peoples to land and the social relations, knowledges and languages that arise from the land" (Wilkes, Duong, Kesler, and Ramos, abstract). Those of us who teach literature in the standard low-context classroom, which could be anywhere, need to rethink the idea of "setting." How to do this will come from those who know the land intimately and can draw on its deep history. For example, Naxaxalhts'i Albert "Sonny" McHalsie provides tours of Stó:lō territory that show visitors that they are standing in a valley that is a library of stories (see Carlson). But we must not "reify back-to-the-land schools" either, if that risks overlooking or discounting the work of the Indigenous faculty, staff, and students in the urban university (Chambers 40).

In Canadian law, the Indigenous right to land is a unique legal right, *sui generis* Aboriginal title based on collective ownership prior to contact (Erin Hanson, "Aboriginal Title"). In Canadian practice, things are not so clear. As Thomas King notes in *The Inconvenient Indian*, "the issue has always been land" (228), but what land means remains quite different for settlers and Indigenous peoples. Indigenous literature provides a way to bring these different meanings into classrooms for generative conversations. Where you are in what is now called Canada makes a great difference not only to whose land you are on, but when settlement began, whether and how treaties were made and kept, how Indigenous oral narratives were written down and who wrote them, how Indigenous people became literate in their own languages or in English, what they chose to write and how it was preserved.[4] Thus, how we teach Indigenous literatures depends on where we are. Even the Straightener could not float over an abstract landscape, but traveled to real villages, their names providing the only variety in an otherwise repetitive story.

Who Are We (Now)? Introducing Ourselves

On the territories where we live, local protocols instruct us to introduce ourselves by name, family, and nation. This emphasizes that people have different standpoints and these are to be respected. Margery's British settler ancestors all took up land in Ontario. She spent childhood summers on Little Lake Panache, which bordered on the Whitefish Indian Reserve (Anishinaabe). Her decolonial education began while picking blueberries, when her aunt said, "No, we can't go further, because the berries that way belong to the Indians." When she arrived at UBC, a course on Indigenous literatures in the calendar had never been taught. After consulting Jo-ann Archibald, then the Director of the First Nations House of Learning, and others, she began to teach it in 1997.

While Deanna's dad was born in Canada, his German-speaking parents left Poland after World War I and ended up in Manitoba; her mom was born in Northern Saskatchewan, into a family of English- and Cree-speaking Cree and Métis people. Raised on or near Canadian military bases, she learned about her relatives through her mother's stories and summer visits. Despite her interest, the universities she attended offered no courses in Indigenous literatures. She took her first formal course with Margery in 2000, just before she applied to the PhD program.

While there are many purposes for the position statements embedded in Indigenous protocols and land acknowledgments, they highlight the variety of vantage points from which each of us speak and emphasize that an unbiased and neutral position is neither possible nor desirable. This aligns with Foucault's notion of power/knowledge and feminist standpoint theory, developed to undermine the notion of one universal and objective truth, a truth regarded as self-evident rather than constructed by (power-ful) men (Harding; Moreton-Robinson). What we know, what we can know, comes first from where we stand, not alone, but with those who have raised and taught us. To position oneself encourages reflection on one's roles, gifts, limitations, and responsibilities.

The Limitations of Our Discipline

Applied linguist Suresh Canagarajah summarizes Euro-Western monomania: "The graphocentric tradition is a monolingual (one language per text), monosemiotic (alphabets preferred over other sign systems such as icons, symbols, or images), and monomodal (visual preferred over oral, aural, and other multimodal channels). European modernity developed the idea that words were the most accurate and objective representation of ideas" (44). And in British settler colonies, these words are usually English words. English professor Siraj Ahmed examines how British orientalist philology appropri-ated prior oral and written narrative: "Colonialism involved the conquest of an epistemic space, by means of which the physical experience of language was turned . . . into 'abstract legality.' The human sciences have rewritten this act of conquest as the gift of historical sensibility" (324).

Our discipline's very name privileges the printed text. Critics who question the unqualified use of English terms for Indigenous oral genres propose alternatives, among them orature, oraliture, verbal art, and storywork.[5] They avoid folding oral narratives into written ones, which obscures how oral narratives proliferate in multiple versions within collect-ives, are performed for various audiences, pass knowledge ranging from the practical to the esoteric down the generations, and nurture both people and land. Because the study of spoken narrative has been taken up by other disciplines (anthropology, cultural studies, linguistics, performance stud-ies, rhetoric), our ability to teach literatures rooted in a living oral matrix is constrained. More interdisciplinarity and lines of communication with knowledge keepers outside the university would help. But however we tackle this limitation, we need to teach the colonial work done by the fetishization of the English written word.

"School Way" and Academic Rhetoric

As anthropologists Charles L. Briggs and Richard Bauman note, "Ways of speaking and writing make social classes, genders, races, and nations seem real and enable them to elicit feelings and justify relations of power, making subalterns seem to speak in ways that necessitate their subordination" (17). Since you are reading this, you are, as Mabel Mackay told Greg Sarris, "school way" (quoted in Sarris 48) and like fish in water, swim in print and academic rhetoric, barely able to recognize other good ways of keeping knowledge alive. We fish need to have – and teach – humility in the face of the difference between what is taken in dominant culture as fact or truth – and what dominant culture classifies as (implicitly unbelievable) "beliefs." Our field deals with products of the human imagination classified as untrue, leaving truth to science. What might happen if we saw Indigenous worldviews as true, rather than discounting them as primitive, superstitious, unsophisticated, unscientific? Many Indigenous scholars put their worldviews into dialogue with the dominant one, using metaphors like weaving, braiding, or "two-eyed seeing."[6] As articles, books, and dissertations by Indigenous scholars mount up, these worldviews challenge the status quo. For example, Métis scholar Warren Cariou, in his 2021 article, "On Critical Humility," insists that Indigenous literary analysis ought to be "like visiting a friend or relation, [which] would mean showing up without an agenda, without a preconceived notion of what we want to gain from this encounter"; it would be uninterested in establishing mastery and "more responsible to the Indigenous communities and people it is discussing" (11). Key to Cariou's ideas is that the responsibilities embedded in relationships should come first.

Following Cariou's advice leads us to rethink the relationship of the critic to language and languages: "Documentary practices focus on language as a code that needs to be preserved. This renders language as a science object that can be taken out of context and dismembered into its constituent parts: phonemes, morphemes, syntactic structures, and semantic analyses. This strategy also ignores the collateral extinctions that accompany language extinction, such as 'education, religion, knowledge, everyday social interactions, and identity'" (Baldwin, Noodin, and Perley 217). As Maya Odehamik Chacaby points out, "language resources are important, but often the translations without the high-context relationships with Anishinaabe worldview result in a shelf full of language resources and no reason to use them" (7). As she points out, these languages contain concept-words central to Indigenous philosophy.[7] The myth of the "vanishing Indian" supported "salvage" of the culture in the assumption that the people and their lived relationships were vanishing. We continue such extinction discourses by promoting the "definitive," the "canonical," and the "authoritative."

One strategy used by Indigenous authors to avoid always being drawn into the concerns of the canon is to "imagine otherwise," as championed by Cherokee scholar Daniel Heath Justice; to work within the speculative genres of science fiction, fantasy, and alternate history gives literary scholars the opportunity to "teach otherwise." Perhaps our familiarity with the "what if?" will help us appreciate the gift that we have already received. Sami scholar Rauna Kuokkanen writes: "Without waiting to be invited, Indigenous epistemes are already 'in' the academy. The problem is not how to bring Indigenous knowledge to the university, since it is already there. The problem is the epistemic ignorance that prevails because the gift of Indigenous epistemes remains impossible in the academy" (108). Traditional oral narratives should not be used without appropriate permission,[8] but the one about the Straightener was clearly intended for Farrand, and thus, for most of us. Bringing Indigenous ways of knowing, ways of teaching, and ways of writing into the academy, however, must be an ongoing Indigenous-led collective endeavor. Leanne Betasamosake Simpson writes that:

> We cannot carry out the kind of decolonization our Ancestors set in motion if we don't create a generation of land-based, community-based intellectuals and cultural producers who are accountable to our nations and whose life work is concerned with the regeneration of these systems rather than meeting the overwhelming needs of the Western academic industrial complex or attempting to "Indigenize the academy" by bringing Indigenous Knowledge into the academy on the terms of the academy itself. (159)

Despite Kuokkanen's and Simpson's justified wariness about indigenizing the academy, they are writing – helpfully – for those who are "school way." Many others have done the same: we need to engage with their work. To decolonize, we must explicitly teach how the discipline of English literature was developed to justify empire and how its teaching masked the conquest of Indigenous land and sovereignty (Viswanathan). We also need to teach how "epistemic ignorance" is continually reinforced by mainstream discourses. For example, every announcement of Indigenous students' drop-out rates shifts the responsibility for educational success onto individual students rather than onto a system designed for "students who are white, cismale, heterosexual, middle-to-upper class, lacking dis/abilities, and without children. If a student deviates from these categories, they are more likely to experience oppressive obstructions in the completion of their degree" (Gaudry and Lorenz 167). And they are likely to blame themselves for failing, too.

Literary Studies in English Canada

The Straightener certainly came to North American universities, producing a literary curriculum with a backbone formed by historical British literature. Indigenous peoples, defined as without writing, without history, and without literature, could not be nations. In Canada, in 1864, Edward Hartley Dewart published *Selections from the Canadian Poets* as evidence of "the subtle but powerful cement of a national literature" (ix). Nonetheless, W. J. Alexander's 1889 professorship at the University of Toronto instituted a British period-based curriculum as the national model; his anthologies promoted the British canon (Casteel; Hubert; Murray). Canadian literature courses became common only in the 1970s, a nationalist move crystallized by Northrop Frye's *The Bush Garden* (1971) and Margaret Atwood's *Survival* (1972). In the context of Canada's centennial, the anti-Americanism inspired by the Vietnam War, and the rise of Quebec sovereignist movements, Frye and Atwood regarded literature as the powerful cement needed to bond diverse and multilingual citizens. Frye writes: "to feel Canadian was to feel part of a no-man's land with huge rivers, lakes, and islands that few Canadians had ever seen" (222). His expression, "no-man's land," resonates with a powerful narrative: the legal concept of *terra nullius*, which underpins the doctrine of discovery (see Lindberg). In *Survival*, Atwood writes "Literature is . . . a map, a geography of the mind. . . . We need such a map desperately because we need to know about here because here is where we live" (18–19). This "we" excludes Indigenous peoples. Frye and Atwood imagine an empty territory, not the one that had, in fact, been emptied by disease, violence, and British law. Slowly, the publication of Indigenous memoirs, novels, plays, and poetry began to rework this hallucinated Great White North. Writers and critics, many of them racialized and classified as multicultural "immigrants" rather than proper (White, settler) Canadians, began to chip the façade off the sepulchre. Revisionist literary histories appeared. Daniel Coleman's *White Civility: The Literary Project of English Canada* discusses the "construction of White, English Canadian privilege" in popular literature between 1850 and 1950, a narrative that hid the "undead" history of slavery, racist immigration policies, and Indigenous oppression under the scrim of Canadian civility (3).

Indigenous literature courses first appeared in the 1990s, marked by the publication of the first teaching anthology, *An Anthology of Native Canadian Literature in English* (1992), edited by postcolonial scholar Terry Goldie and Delaware poet Daniel David Moses.[9] The shift to

Indigenous-content courses has accelerated since the publication of the final report of the Indian Residential Schools Truth and Reconciliation Commission in 2015 (Truth and Reconciliation Commission). Adam Gaudry and Danielle Lorenz survey Indigenous instructors' diverse responses to making such courses mandatory, a thrust that might "displac[e] a more ambitious goal of decolonizing education that aspires to more fundamentally transform relations of power beyond the academy" (162). Like the "New" World, Indigenous and ethnic minority literatures are often seen as new, although they are rooted in long-standing traditions. Courses in Indigenous literatures, comprised of genres recognizable as "literature," have often simply been bolted on to the existing British period-based curriculum, reinforcing an aesthetic and generic hierarchy, a center–periphery model of space and a linear model of "progressive" time. In response, Indigenous intellectuals, nations, and political organizations founded Indigenous-controlled literary-critical institutions and resources. To name only a few, they established writing schools (the En'owkin International School of Writing), presses (Theytus, Kegedonce), book series, journals (*Gatherings*; *Kivioq*; *Nesika*), anthologies (Hodgson; King; Armstrong and Grauer; McCall, Reder, Gaertner, and L'Hirondelle Hill), and collections of literary criticism (Armstrong, *Looking at the Words of our People*; Ruffo; McLeod, *Indigenous Poetics*; McFarlane and Ruffo; Reder and Morra). Overviews of nation-specific thought and writing appeared (e.g., Armstrong, *Constructing Indigeneity*; McLeod, *Cree Narrative Memory*; Monture). Additional resource material included overviews (Justice) and bibliographical databases (*Books to Build On: Indigenous Literatures for Learning*; *The People and the Text: Indigenous Writing in Northern North America to 1992*) and even an editor's style guide (Younging). These initiatives can be used to challenge the dominant approach to knowledge and pedagogy.

Start Local: Rethinking the University from Here

How could a literature class become a field school? Given that all universities sit on what once were actual fields, forests, or even waterways, getting into the field is simple. But how is our field connected to theirs? Individual instructors cannot get to know or teach all of the diverse cultural output of the many peoples crammed into categories such as First Nations, Inuit, and Métis. Our primary responsibility is to those on whose territories we live and work, especially if we are uninvited guests. Eber Hampton, the Chickasaw educator who presided over the transition of the Saskatchewan

Indian Federated College, founded in 1976, into the First Nations University in 2003, pointed out that "local control is a defining characteristic of Indian education, not just a philosophical or political good. There can be no true Indian education without Indian control. Anything else is white education applied to Indians" (quoted in Taner 307). And the local includes both the original landholders and the many Indigenous people who have moved to cities as a result of colonization.[10] Thus, literary scholars should look to the local, where it is more likely that they can connect with writers, Elders, and knowledge keepers, and where they may find, after appropriate consultation, that they or their students might be able to learn from and contribute to community.

Our discipline, founded as it was on the study of dead White male British writers, has to broaden its horizons to include methods we ourselves never learned.[11] We now deal not only with a diverse group of living writers, but also with their people's narrative belongings, both oral and written. The three major Canadian academic research agencies have instituted guidelines for research "developed with the participation and consent of Indigenous scholars and Elders in Canada," which includes this statement: "Indigenous knowledge belongs to specific peoples rather than to the public domain, creating specific laws about who can use, teach, know, and continue to use certain parts of that knowledge" (Canada, Tricouncil). The University of Manitoba Press series, First Voices, First Texts, for example, publishes first or new editions of works by Indigenous writers: "The editors strive to indigenize the editing process by involving communities, by respecting traditional protocols, and by providing critical introductions that give readers new insights into the cultural contexts of these unjustly neglected classics." One outcome can be the refusal of families to agree to publication, even if the work is in the "public" domain. How can we put notions of academic freedom into conversation with Indigenous "refusal as an analytic practice that addresses forms of inquiry as invasion"? (Tuck and Yang, abstract).

Reading on the Edges, Reading from Here

Everywhere in North America with a college or university is also the site of Indigenous narrative production. Our universities have campuses on Coast Salish and Interior Salish territories. We can quickly name Indigenous writers of mainstream genres with strong connections to these lands. Although poet and performer E. Pauline Johnson (1861–1913) was Mohawk, she retired to Vancouver. She was befriended by Joe (Sapluk)

and Mary Agnes (Lixwelut) Capilano, (Skwxwú7mesh), who told her
stories, most collected as *Legends of Vancouver* (1911).[12] As an Okanagan
woman, Mourning Dove (Christine Quintasket), author of *Cogewea, The
Half-Blood: A Depiction of the Great Montana Cattle Range* (1927), belonged
to one of several cross-border nations and moved back and forth across that
constructed divide. Jeannette Armstrong (Okanagan/Syilx) and Lee
Maracle (Stó:lō) have mothered creativity, mentoring Indigenous writers
and bolstering the publication and teaching of Indigenous literatures, as
well as writing their own multigenre works.

To restrict curricula to those Indigenous writers whose ancestors lived
here for thousands of years risks a straightening purism – Vancouver is
now home to many Indigenous people from far and wide. Some of them
write out of that dislocation, from seeing themselves or being seen as
"not authentic." As a result, lived experience as an Indigenous person
can be discounted and lost. Shirley Sterling attended the notorious
Kamloops Indian Residential School, writing about the experience in
her award-winning autobiographical children's novel, *My Name Is
Seepeetza* (1992). She wrote, "I have never thought of myself as
a particularly traditional or spiritual Nlaka'pamux person. In fact,
I delayed writing in the First Nations voice for many years, because
I thought I was not raised traditionally enough." Her experiences as
a graduate student and instructor led her to call the academy an "adver-
sarial arena" ("Seepeetza Revisited" n. pag.) Writing for many in the
next generation, Jordan Abel's multi-genre *NISHGA* (2020), explains
how the trauma from those schools has reverberated, leading many
Indigenous peoples living in cities to struggle to create identifications
that represent their experiences away from home territory and original
family and community.

Indigenous Interpretation and Pedagogy

Indigenous peoples preserve stories by telling and retelling them, not
through authorized interpretation or canonization. Storytellers do not
explain stories" (Brundige 291). Margery was both shocked and intrigued
when she read Maracle's "You Become the Trickster" in 1990, when she
had just begun teaching Indigenous students. Explaining Indigenous
stories, Maracle writes:

> The difference is that the reader is as much a part of the story as the
> teller. Most of our stories don't have orthodox "conclusions"; that is

left to the listeners, who we trust will draw useful lessons from the story – not necessarily the lessons we wish them to draw, but all conclusions are considered valid. The listeners are drawn into the dilemmas and are expected at some point to work themselves out of it. . . . When our orators get up to tell a story, there is no explanation, no set-up to guide the listener – just the poetic terseness of the dilemma is presented. (11–12)

So, Indigenous peoples did not have literary critics? Indeed, Maracle "wonder[s] about the necessity for the door-closing practice currently known as literary criticism" (*Memory Serves* 197–98). Why would story-tellers allow such interpretative autonomy? Keith Basso, an anthropologist who worked with the Western Apache, explains: "persons who speak too much insult the imaginative capabilities of other people, 'blocking their thinking,' as one of my consultants said in English, and 'holding down their minds'" (85). Neal McLeod (Cree) remembers that his father "never said what the points of his stories were; he forced the listeners to discover this for themselves" (*Cree Narrative Memory* 13). Keavy Martin writes about taking her students to the Arctic: "Younger Inuit also taught us the appropriate ways of learning from elders and this did not involve peppering them with enthusiastic questions" (54). Direct instruction is seen as disrespectful; a story is an acceptable way to warn, advise, instruct, reprove, or support someone else. This isn't to say that listeners are free to interpret by disregarding the stories, the storytellers, and the culture. Instead, interpretation needs to be based on respect and on the quality of relationships with the stories and their tellers.

An early staple of Indigenous literature curricula was Thomas King's *Green Grass, Running Water* (1993), which taught a huge swath of Indigenous knowledge by being funny enough and puzzling enough that readers spent a lot of time trying (in a pre-internet era) to understand the gnomic statements of the wise characters. The novel's way of working is exemplified by the chapter headings in Cherokee syllabics. Students were thinking and investigating for themselves, rather than waiting for the prof to explain – but of course, explain one of us did (see Fee and Flick). Although we cherish our own academic freedom, we don't always support the curiosity and cognitive autonomy of our students. Navajo scholar Gregory Cajete insists that "Indigenous teachings view each student as unique, each with a unique path of learning to travel during his or her lifetime. . . . each person is, fundamentally, his or her own teacher and that learning is connected to the individual's life process" (xv). Nonetheless, our discipline does foster such autonomy. English professor Ruth Felski notes, "while students nowadays are likely to be informed about critical debates and literary theories, they are still expected to find their own way into a literary work, not to parrot the interpretations of others" (11). This pedagogy is common in our interactions with graduate students when we begin to make knowledge together, rather than asking for or doling out information.

Indigenous young people are expected to observe how their Elders conduct themselves and how they carry out tasks, "watch-then-do" pedagogy (Donaldson). Youth sometimes visit an Elder and carry out chores for them or give them gifts of tobacco or sweetgrass in order to be apprenticed to a specific skill (see Wheeler on Cree). A course designed by Lorna Williams (Lil'wat) led a participant to express her first reactions to Indigenous pedagogy: "I grew frustrated and discouraged when I was not handed the answer on a platter. ... I chastised myself for not being able to wait, slow down, and just listen. All I was after was a quick fix, and that fact upset me" (Williams, Tanaka, Leik, and Riecken 245–47). Historian Katrina Srigley describes the drive for quick solutions to systemic inequities consolidated over centuries. She writes of her interactions with knowledge keepers and Elders, "Each time I hoped for a ten-point plan, a how-to guide; I never received one. Instead, I was given stories about reciprocity, developing ideas in partnership, ownership of knowledge, status, belonging, and identity" (20). Indigenous teachers focus on values rather than content.[13] Dwayne Donald calls the difference between mainstream and Indigenous teaching methods as the difference between "fort pedagogy" and "ethical relationality" (45).

We need to slow down, listen, and do our homework. Fortunately, Indigenous historians, writers, and critics are actively producing a decolonizing and heterogeneous narrative studies attentive to interconnected nation-specific, urban, diasporic, national, and global intellectual currents.

Aubrey Hanson (Métis) hails non-Indigenous Canadians to begin working to understand and dismantle the social systems that produced the residential schools so as "to make way for Indigenous resurgence," which is "people in their own communities nourishing their own traditions, languages, worldviews, stories, knowledges and ways of being" ("Reading for Reconciliation?" 75). At this juncture, given the gap between worldviews, conversations over tea are more likely to change things for the better than any checklist or ten-point plan.

Notes

We thank Aubrey Hanson for helpful comments on a draft of this paper.

1. Section 35 of the Canadian Constitution Act, 1982, recognizes three "Aboriginal" peoples – Indians, Métis, and Inuit (see Erin Hanson, "Constitution Act"). "First Nations," after the founding of the Assembly of First Nations in 1982, usually means "Status Indians," those registered with the federal government. The shift to "Indigenous" as an umbrella term derives from the importance of the UN Declaration on the Rights of Indigenous Peoples to Indigenous activists. "Native" was commonly used up to the passage of the Act. "First Peoples" includes those who were refused or involuntarily deprived of status. For Canada-wide land acknowledgments, see Canadian Association of University Teachers; see Wilkes, Duong, Kesler, and Ramos for an overview.

2. This story is set on the Olympic Peninsula in Washington State, just south of Vancouver Island. It is a stripped-down version of an origin story. In the official version of the Hoh Indian Tribe (Quileute), the change helps the people catch fish better, and thus, Changer feeds the people (Hoh Indian Tribe).

3. Boas found this story most common in the north with the Tlingit, and extending south as far as the nations that compose the Coast Salish (637).

4. For overviews, see Edwards, *Paper Talk*; Maud.

5. "Orature" (Gingell and Roy 6–8); "oraliture" (Armstrong); "verbal art" (Clement); "storywork" (Archibald 3–4).

6. See, for example, Powell; Dion; Iwama, Marshall, Marshall, and Bartlett.

7. See Williams, Tanaka, Leik, and Riecken for Lil'wat words relating to pedagogy (239–40); see Reder for the Cree word wâhkôhtowin and "the moral responsibility to remember" (179); for the nsyilxcən word en'owkin, see Armstrong, "Literature of the Land."

8. On permission, see Archibald; Canada, Tricouncil. On appropriation, see Keeshig-Tobias; Fee, "The Trickster Moment"; McCall 17–42. Ironically, the Hoh (Quileute) people of the opening story had their traditions plundered for the *Twilight* series of books and films (Dartt-Newton and Endo).

9. Anishinaabe poet and scholar Armand Garnet Ruffo joined the coeditors for the 4th edition, 2013; then Ruffo and Métis author Katherena Vermette coedited the 5th edition, 2020; the title is now *An Anthology of Indigenous Literatures in English: Voices from Canada*.

10. See Peters and Andersen. Over half of the Indigenous people in Canada now live in cities (Census Canada, 2016).

11. Tuhiwai Smith's path-breaking *Decolonizing Methodologies* (1999) inspired many nation-specific models for research.

12. Settler scholar Alix Shield has worked with family members of Joe and Mary Capilano from Skwxwú7mesh Nation to reissue *Legends of Vancouver* with additional stories and other material as *Legends of the Capilano*.

13. The UBC First Nations House of Learning propagates a mantra: Respect, Relevance, Reciprocity, Responsibility (Kirkness and Barnhardt).

WORKS CITED

Abel, Jordan. *NISHGA*. [Toronto]: McClelland & Stewart, 2020.

Ahmed, Siraj. *Archaeology of Babel: The Colonial Foundation of the Humanities*. Stanford, CA: Stanford University Press, 2017.

Archibald, Jo-ann (Q'um Q'um Xiiem). *Indigenous Storywork: Educating the Heart, Mind, Body, and Spirit*. Vancouver: UBC Press, 2008.

Armstrong, Jeannette. "Constructing Indigeneity: Syilx Okanagan Oraliture and tmixʷcentrism." 2009. PhD diss., University of Greifswald. https://d-nb.info/1027188737/34

"Land Speaking." In Simon Ortiz, ed., *Speaking for the Generations: Native Writers on Writing*. Tucson: University of Arizona Press, 1998, 175–94.

"Literature of the Land – An Ethos for These Times." In Bill Ashcroft, Ranjini Medis, Julie McGonegal, and Arun Mukherjee, eds., *Literature for Our Times: Postcolonial Studies in the Twenty-First Century*. Amsterdam: Rodopi, 2012, 345–56.

Armstrong, Jeannette, ed. *Looking at the Words of Our People: First Nations Analysis of Literature*. Penticton: Theytus Books, 1993.

Armstrong, Jeannette and Lally Grauer, eds. *Native Poetry in Canada: A Contemporary Anthology*. Peterborough: Broadview Press, 2001.

Atwood, Margaret. *Survival: A Thematic Guide to Canadian Literature*. Toronto: House of Anansi Press, 1972.

Baldwin, Daryl, Margaret Noodin, and Bernard C. Perley. "Surviving the Sixth Extinction: American Indian Strategies for Life in the New World." In Richard Grusin, ed., *After Extinction*. Minneapolis: University of Minnesota Press, 2018, 201–34.

Basso, Keith H. *Wisdom Sits in Places: Landscape and Language among the Western Apache*. Albuquerque: University of New Mexico Press, 1996.

Battiste, Marie. *Decolonizing Education: Nourishing the Learning Spirit*. Saskatoon: Purich Publishing, 2017.

Boas, Franz. *Indian Myths and Legends from the North Pacific Coast of North America*, edited and annotated by Randy Bouchard and Dorothy Kennedy. Translated by Dietrich Bertz. Vancouver: Talonbooks, 2002.

Briggs, Charles L., and Richard Bauman. *Voices of Modernity: Language Ideologies and the Politics of Inequality*. Cambridge: Cambridge University Press, 2003.

Brundige, Lorraine F. [now Meyer]. "Native Values: Cree and Ojibwa." Master's thesis, Lakehead University, 1997.

Cajete, Greg. "Foreword." In Michele T. D. Tanaka, *Learning and Teaching Together: Weaving Indigenous Ways of Knowing into Education*. Vancouver: UBC Press, 2016, xi–xvi.

Canada. Tricouncil. Tri-Council Policy Statement: Ethical Conduct for Research Involving Humans. 2018. ethics.gc.ca/eng/policy-politique_tcps2-eptc2_2018.html.

Canadian Association of University Teachers. "Acknowledging First Peoples' Traditional Territory." www.caut.ca/content/guide-acknowledging-first-peoples-traditional-territory#_ftn1.

Canagarajah, Suresh. *Transnational Identities and Practices in English Language Teaching*. Bristol: Multilingual Matters, 2021.

Cariou, Warren. "On Critical Humility." *Studies in American Indian Literatures* 32.3–4 (2020): 1–12.

Carlson, Keith, ed. *A Stó:lō Coast Salish Historical Atlas*. Vancouver: Douglas & McIntyre, 2001.

Casteel, Sarah Phillips. "The Dream of Empire: The Scottish Roots of English Studies in Canada." *Ariel* 31.1–2 (2000): 127–52.

Chacaby, Maya Odehamik. "Crippled Two-Tongue and the Myth of Benign Translatability." *Tusaaji: A Translation Review* 4.1 (2016): 1–11. doi.org/10 .25071/1925–5624.40315.

Chambers, Treena. "Unsettled Learning in Colonial Spaces." In Sabine Witter and Helmut Weber, eds., *Unsettling Educational Modernism*. Vancouver: adocs Publishing, 2021, 33–43.

Clement, William M. *Native American Verbal Arts: Texts and Contexts*. Tucson: University of Arizona Press, 1996.

Coleman, Daniel. *White Civility: The Literary Project of English Canada*. Toronto: University of Toronto Press, 2006.

Cruikshank, Julie. *Do Glaciers Listen? Local Knowledge, Colonial Encounters, and Social Imagination*. Vancouver: UBC Press, 2005.

Dartt-Newton, Deanna, and Tasio Endo. "Adjusting the Focus on *Twilight's* Misconceptions." Burke Museum of Natural History and Culture, 2010. www.burkemuseum.org/static/truth_vs_twilight/.

Dewart, Edward Hartley. "Introduction." In *Selections from Canadian Poets*. Toronto: University of Toronto Press, 1864, ix–xix. Early Canadiana Online, www.canadiana.ca/view/oocihm.05265/3?r=0&s=1.

Dion, Susan. *Braiding Histories*. Vancouver: UBC Press, 2009.

Donald, Dwayne. "Forts, Curriculum, and Ethical Relationality." In Nicholas Ng-A-Fook and Jennifer Rottmann, eds., *Reconsidering Canadian Curriculum Studies: Provoking Historical, Present and Future Perspectives*. New York: Palgrave Macmillan, 2012, 39–46.

Donaldson, Laura E. "Writing the Talking Stick: Alphabetic Literacy as Colonial Technology and Postcolonial Appropriation." *American Indian Quarterly* 22.1/2, (1998): 46–62. www.jstor.org/stable/1185107.

Edwards, Brendan Frederick R. *Paper Talk: A History of Libraries, Print Culture and Aboriginal Peoples in Canada before 1960*. Lanham, MD: Scarecrow Press, 2005.

Fee, Margery. "The Trickster Moment, Cultural Appropriation and the Liberal Imagination in Canada." In Deanna Reder and Linda Morra, eds., *Troubling Tricksters: Revisioning Critical Conversations*. Waterloo: Wilfrid Laurier University Press, 2010, 59–76.

Fee, Margery, and Jane Flick. "Coyote Pedagogy: Knowing Where the Borders Are in Thomas King's *Green Grass, Running Water*." *Canadian Literature* 161/162 (1999): 131–39. https://canlit.ca/article/coyote-pedagogy/.

Felski, Rita. *Uses of Literature*. Malden, MA: Blackwell Publishing, 2008.

Frye, Northrop. *The Bush Garden: Essays on the Canadian Imagination.* 1971. Intro. Linda Hutcheon. Toronto:House of Anansi, 1995.

Gaudry, Adam and Danielle E. Lorenz. "Decolonization for the Masses? Grappling with Indigenous Content Requirements in the Changing Canadian Post-Secondary Environment." In Linda Tuhiwai Smith, Eve Tuck, and K. Wayne Yang, eds., *Indigenous and Decolonization Studies in Education: Mapping the Long View.* New York: Routledge, 2018, 159–74.

Gingell, Susan, and Wendy Roy. "Introduction." In Susan Gingell and Wendy Roy, eds., *Listening Up, Writing Down and Looking Beyond: Interfaces of the Oral, Written and Visual.* Waterloo: Wilfrid Laurier University Press, 2012, 1–50.

Hanson, Aubrey Jean. "Reading for Reconciliation? Indigenous Literatures in a Post-TRC Canada." *English Studies in Canada* 43.2–3 (2017): 69–90. https://doi.org/10.1353/esc.2017.0022.

Hanson, Erin. "Aboriginal Title." Indigenous Foundations, First Nations and Indigenous Studies, University of British Columbia. https://indigenousfoundations.arts.ubc.ca/aboriginal_title/.

——. "Constitution Act, 1982." Indigenous Foundations, First Nations and Indigenous Studies, University of British Columbia. https://indigenousfoundations.arts.ubc.ca/constitution_act_1982_section_35/.

Harding, Sandra, ed. *The Feminist Standpoint Theory Reader: Intellectual and Political Controversies.* New York: Routledge, 2004.

Hodgson, Heather, ed. *Seventh Generation: Contemporary Native Writing.* Penticton: Theytus Books, 1989.

Hoh Indian Tribe. "Origin of the Hoh Tribe." https://hohtribe-nsn.org/culture/.

Holden, Madronna. "'Making All the Crooked Ways Straight': The Satirical Portrait of Whites in Coast Salish Folklore." *The Journal of American Folklore* 89.353 (1976): 271–93. https://doi.org/10.2307/53944.

Hoy, Helen. *How Should I Read These? Native Women Writers in Canada.* Toronto: University of Toronto Press, 2001.

Hubert, Henry A. *Harmonious Perfection: The Development of English Studies in Nineteenth-century Anglo-Canadian Colleges.* East Lansing: Michigan State University Press, 1994.

Iwama, Marilyn, Murdena Marshall, Albert Marshall, and Cheryl Bartlett. "Two-Eyed Seeing and the Language of Healing in Community-Based Research." *Canadian Journal of Native Education* 32.2 (2009): 3–23.

Johnson, E. Pauline. *Legends of Vancouver.* 1911. Revised as *Legends of the Capilano,* by E. Pauline Johnson, Joe Capilano, and Mary Agnes Capilano, edited by Alix Shield. Winnipeg: University of Manitoba Press, 2022.

Justice, Daniel Heath. *Why Indigenous Literatures Matter.* Waterloo: Wilfrid Laurier University Press, 2018.

Keeshig-Tobias, Lenore. "Stop Stealing Native Stories." 1990. In Bruce Ziff and Pratima V. Rao, eds., *Borrowed Power: Essays on Cultural Appropriation.* New Brunswick, NJ: Rutgers University Press, 1997, 71–73.

King, Thomas, ed. *All My Relations: An Anthology of Contemporary Canadian Native Fiction.* Toronto: McClelland & Stewart, 1990.

King, Thomas. *Green Grass, Running Water.* Toronto: HarperCollins, 1993.

 The Inconvenient Indian: A Curious Account of Native People in North America. Toronto: Doubleday Canada, 2012.

Kirkness, Verna J. and Roy Barnhardt. "The Four R's: Respect, Relevance, Reciprocity, Responsibility." *Journal of American Indian Education* 30.3 (1991): 1–15. www.jstor.org/stable/24397980.

Lindberg, Tracey. "The Doctrine of Discovery in Canada." In Robert. J. Miller, Jacinta Ruru, Larissa Behrendt, and Tracey Lindberg, eds., *Discovering Indigenous Lands: The Doctrine of Discovery in the English Colonies.* Oxford: Oxford University Press, 2010, 89–170.

Maracle, Lee. "You Become the Trickster." In *Sojourner's Truth and Other Stories.* Vancouver: Press Gang, 1990, 1–13.

Memory Serves: Oratories, ed. Smaro Kamboureli. Edmonton: NeWest Press, 2015.

Martin, Keavy. *Stories in a New Skin: Approaches to Inuit Literature.* Winnipeg: University of Manitoba Press, 2012.

Maud, Ralph *A Guide to BC Indian Myth and Legend: A Short History of Myth-Collecting and a Survey of Published Texts.* Vancouver: Talonbooks, 1982.

McCall, Sophie. *First Person Plural: Aboriginal Storytelling and the Ethics of Collaborative Authorship.* Vancouver: UBC Press, 2011.

McCall, Sophie, Deanna Reder, David Gaertner, and Gabrielle L'Hirondelle Hill, eds. *Read, Listen, Tell: Indigenous Stories from Turtle Island.* Waterloo: Wilfrid Laurier University Press, 2017.

McFarlane, Heather, and Armand Garnet Ruffo, eds. *Introduction to Indigenous Literary Criticism in Canada.* Peterborough: Broadview Press, 2016.

McLeod, Neal. *Cree Narrative Memory: From Treaties to Contemporary Times.* Saskatoon: Purich Publishing, 2007.

 "Introduction." In Neal McLeod, ed., *Indigenous Poetics in Canada.* Waterloo: Wilfrid Laurier University Press, 2014, 1–14.

Monture, Rick. *We Share Our Matters: Two Centuries of Writing and Resistance at Six Nations of the Grand River.* Winnipeg: University of Manitoba Press, 2014.

Moreton-Robinson, Aileen. "Towards an Australian Indigenous Women's Standpoint Theory." *Australian Feminist Studies* 28.78 (2013): 331–47. https://doi.org/10.1080/08164649.2013.876664.

Mourning Dove [Christine Quintasket]. *Cogewea, The Half-Blood: A Depiction of the Great Montana Cattle Range.* Boston: Four Seas, 1927.

Murray, Heather. "Alexander and After: Browning, Culture, Natural Method, and National Education, 1889–1914." *Modern Language Quarterly* 75.2 (2014): 149–70. https://doi-org.eu1.proxy.openathens.net/10.1215/00267929-2416581.

Peters, Evelyn and Chris Andersen, eds. *Indigenous in the City: Contemporary Identities and Cultural Innovation.* Vancouver: UBC Press, 2013.

Powell, Malea. "A Basket Is a Basket because . . .: Telling a Native Rhetorics Story." In James H. Cox and Daniel Heath Justice, eds., *The Oxford*

Handbook of Indigenous American Literature. New York: Oxford University Press, 2014, 471–88.

Reder, Deanna. "Indigenous Autobiography in Canada." In Cynthia Sugars, ed., *The Oxford Handbook of Canadian Literature*. New York: Oxford University Press, 2016, 170–90.

Reder, Deanna, and Linda M. Morra, eds. *Learn, Teach, Challenge: Approaching Indigenous Literatures*. Waterloo: Wilfrid Laurier University Press, 2016.

Ruffo, Armand Garnet, ed. *(Ad)dressing Our Words: Aboriginal Perspectives on Aboriginal Literatures*. Penticton: Theytus Books, 2001.

Sarris, Greg. *Keeping Slug Woman Alive: A Holistic Approach to American Indian Texts*. Berkeley: University of California Press, 1993.

Simpson, Leanne Betasamosake. *As We Have Always Done: Indigenous Freedom through Radical Resistance*. Minneapolis: University of Minnesota Press, 2017.

Srigley, Katrina and Lorraine Sutherland. "Decolonizing, Indigenizing, and Learning *Biskaaybiiyang* in the Field: Our Oral History Journey." *Oral History Review* 45.1 (2018): 7–28. https://doi.org/10.1093/ohr/ohy001.

Sterling, Shirley. *My Name Is Seepeetza*. Toronto: Groundwood Books, 1992.

"Seepeetza Revisited: An Introduction to Six Voices." *On-line Issues* 3.1 (1995). https://einsights.ogpr.educ.ubc.ca/archives/v03n01/sterling.html.

Taner, Shona. "The Evolution of Native Studies in Canada: Descending from the Ivory Tower." *The Canadian Journal of Native Studies* 19.2 (1999): 289–319.

The People and the Text: Indigenous Writing in Northern North America to 1992. Canadian Writing Research Collaboratory (CWRC), https://thepeopleandthetext.ca/.

Truth and Reconciliation Commission of Canada. Final Report. Canada's Residential Schools: The Final Report of the Truth and Reconciliation Commission of Canada, 6 vols. 2015.

Tuck, Eve and K. Wayne Yang. "Unbecoming Claims: Pedagogies of Refusal in Qualitative Research." *Qualitative Inquiry* 20.6 (2014): 811–18. https://doi.org/10.1177/1077800414530265.

Tuhiwai Smith, Linda. *Decolonizing Methodologies: Research and Indigenous Peoples*. London: Zed Books, 1999.

United Nations. Declaration on the Rights of Indigenous Peoples. 2007. www.un.org/development/desa/indigenouspeoples/declaration-on-the-rights-of-indigenous-peoples.html.

Viswanathan, Gauri. *Masks of Conquest: Literary Study and British Rule in India*. London: Faber and Faber, 1989.

Wheeler, Winona. "Reflections on the Social Relations of Indigenous Oral Histories." In Ute Lischke and David T. McNab, eds., *Walking a Tightrope: Aboriginal People and Their Representations*. Waterloo: Wilfrid Laurier University Press, 2005, 189–213.

Wildcat, Matthew, Mandee McDonald, Stephanie Irlbacher-Fox, and Glen Coulthard. "Learning from the Land: Indigenous Land Based Pedagogy and Decolonization." *Decolonization: Indigeneity, Education &*

Society 3.3 (2014): i–xv. jps.library.utoronto.ca/index.php/des/article/view/ 22248.

Wilkes, Rima, Aaron Duong, Linc Kesler, and Howard Ramos. "Canadian University Acknowledgment of Indigenous Lands, Treaties, and Peoples: Canadian University Acknowledgment." *Canadian Review of Sociology* 54.1 (2017): 89–120. https://doi.org/10.1111/cars.12140.

Williams, Lorna, Michele Tanaka, Vivian Leik, and Ted Riecken. "Walking Side by Side: Living Indigenous Ways in the Academy." In Catherine Etmanski, Budd L. Hall, and Teresa Dawson, eds., *Learning and Teaching Community Based Research: Linking Pedagogy to Practice*. Toronto: University of Toronto Press, 2014, 229–52.

Yang, K. Wayne. "Decolonial Desires: Is a Third University Possible? A Webinar Conversation with K. Wayne Yang." Interview by Jack Tchen, Erica Kohl-Arenas, and Eric Hartman, *Ethnic Studies Review* 43.3 (2020): 57–72. https:// doi.org/10.1525/esr.2020.43.3.57.

Younging, Gregory. *Elements of Indigenous Style: A Guide for Writing by and about Indigenous Peoples*. Edmonton: Brush Education, 2018.

CHAPTER 4

Decolonizing Literary Pedagogies in Australia and Aotearoa New Zealand

Elizabeth McMahon

> You have to navigate the space between the borders
> of your skin and the intelligence of the tongueless horizon
>
> and learn the language of touch   of signs and pain
> of what isn't and what may be in the circle of the tides
>
> that will stretch until you understand the permanent silence
> at the end of your voyage
>
> Albert Wendt, "Stepping Stones"

This chapter sets out some of the complexities and strategies regarding processes of decolonizing literary pedagogies in two proximate sites of the Global South: Australia and Aotearoa New Zealand. In this project, I advocate an intersectional approach and method that defetishizes the literary object and enables students to engage with various forms of literary creativity in their varied and shifting positions within place, history, and culture. Ben Etherington and Jarad Zimbler argue:

> A decolonized literary studies does not come off-the-peg, and making decisions about what or who we read requires that we think concertedly about the colonial legacies and entanglements of particular places and literary communities at particular historical junctures. It requires, in other words, that we think seriously about what exactly "context" means. (229)

So, too, as Wiradjuri[1] writer, teacher and academic Jeanine Leane writes, "history and literature are inseparable" (Leane, "Aboriginal Literature" 238) and, as Samoan writer Albert Wendt claims, "all creative writers are historians" ("Insider" 6, quoted and discussed in Sharrad, "Albert Wendt"). Accordingly, the ensuing discussion devotes a great deal of space to particularities of "context" and moves between specific and shared experiences of Australia and Aotearoa New Zealand and includes some comparison. This essay was researched and written on the unceded, sovereign lands of the Bedegal people of the Eora Nation of what is also called

Sydney, Australia. In this project, I have consulted First Nations writers and academics from both countries and, amongst a range of responses, I have met with some (depersonalized) resistance to my authorship of this chapter around issues of the ongoing authority accorded and exercised by non-Indigenous academics. I am a senior settler academic in a country, Australia, that only recognized the citizenship of its First Nations peoples in 1967 and which is only now debating whether the constitution should include recognition of First Nations primacy.[2] Also, I am neither a Māori nor a Pākehā[3] (European non-Māori) citizen of Aotearoa New Zealand so there are colonizing issues about me speaking of that context. This occurs in a long history of Australia commandeering debate in the Australasian context. The issue of decolonization, including the decolonization of literary pedagogies, is immediate, fraught, and painful in both places.

The points of connection and distinctiveness between Australia and Aotearoa New Zealand are clarifying relative to broad issues of decolonizing literary pedagogies as well as each of these two places. The key sites of these correlations and divergences concern their respective First Nations peoples, their particular British colonial histories, positions in the (colonized) region, scales of territory and population, the patterns of regional and global immigration, and their attendant demographics and literatures. Australia and Aotearoa New Zealand are close neighbors, and the bonds between them are deep, but they are also relatively recent. There was no relationship between the First Nations peoples of the two territories before British colonization, and they became more distant when the colonial structure of "Australasia" – which embraced the many British colonies in Oceania – was dismantled in 1901 when Australia federated to become a nation state (Denoon).

There has been little critical work on the literatures of both places. If they are grouped together at all, it is most often for bibliographic purposes, and from distant perspectives they seem to appear as a kind of duo. However, the actual links have been tenuous. In 2012, a proposal to expand the Association for the Study of Australian Literature (ASAL) to include the literature of Aotearoa New Zealand – where there is no equivalent scholarly society – was rejected by the Australian members (Brennan). The reasons for this decision were largely nationalist and partly logistical. There was also the view that the South Pacific Association for Commonwealth Literature and Language Studies (SPACLALS) fulfilled this function.[4] Resistance also reflected an anxiety connected to being a largely invisible national literature of the Global South at a time when the category of national literatures was contested (Dixon, "National Literatures"). At this time, Australia and Aotearoa New Zealand were encountering new – and ongoing – threats to copyright law that would decimate local publishing houses, which are vital to literary cultures in both places (Loukakis; Nagle). Finally, wider Australian culture including government, does not display much interest or support for its literary cultures (Meyrick). So there was an understandable motivation to protect ASAL from diffusion or increased opacity.

Nonetheless, in the view of this author, the decision not to expand the Association to include Aotearoa New Zealand was a missed opportunity that significantly slowed the pace of the decolonization of literary research and pedagogies in Australia, and perhaps Aotearoa New Zealand as well. In particular, it would have provided a forum for the First Nations peoples of both places, who have too often been in radical minority in such organizations, and it would have meaningfully complicated the power binary of the First Nations and settler cultures in each place. Moreover, ASAL missed the opportunity to provide this intellectual space and undertake the education and critique this process would have required.

Over the past decade, there has been increased contact between the First Nations writers of both places, including the biannual conventions of the First Nations Australia Writers Network (FNAWN) from 2013 (First Nations Australia Writers Network), in artistic practices such as Spoken Word Poetry, and in collections such as *Sold Air* (Stavanger and Te Whiu). I note also that *Black Marks on the White Page*, a collection of "Oceanic stories for the twenty-first century," edited by Witi Ihimaera and Tina Makereti, includes work from Wanyi Australian writer Alexis Wright, as the editors extend the category of the Pacific to its furthest western point in an explicit gesture of inclusion of Australia's First Nations.

These connections are an inchoate force gaining momentum. So, too, as Alice Te Punga Somerville recently showed, these links are not new (Te Punga Somerville). In "Reading as Cousins: Indigenous Texts, Pacific Bookshelves," Te Punga Somerville focuses on an "impossible photograph" that shows First Nations writer and activist Oodgeroo Noonuccal with Pasifika writers at the 1980 SPACLALS conference. SPACLALS, structured by the comparative practices of postcolonialism, now has far fewer members – there are far fewer academic staff in English literary studies – and the upsurge of First Nations activism and literatures in the last three decades has focused attention on the redress of specific histories. However, perusal of the programs of mainstream writers' festivals in either place over the last decade shows very little interaction or interest in either settler culture or First Nations writers between neighbors, with both countries preferring to select their international guests from farther afield rather than connecting with their own region.[5]

As this lack of interaction suggests, Australians and Aotearoa New Zealanders have a poor record of reading and teaching each other's litera- ture. This is, in large part, a legacy of colonial publishing structures, by which books were generally published in Britain until the mid-twentieth century. Most Australians would not ever have read any literature of Aotearoa New Zealand and vice versa.[6] There have been very few excep- tions to this mutual and structural aversion. Its most visible exception, Lydia Wevers, describes the situation: "I am an Aotearoa New Zealand reader of Australian literature. That makes me just about a category of one. The reverse category, an Australian reader of Aotearoa New Zealand literature, is also a rare beast, though perhaps there is a breeding pair in existence" ("The View from Here" 1). Wevers made this observation in her keynote address at the 2008 conference of the Association for the Study of Australian Literature (ASAL), an annual event she traveled across the Tasman Sea to attend for two decades – the only Aotearoa New Zealander to do so.

Australian First Nations writers and critics lead the decolonization of Australian literary studies and include the highly influential interventions of The First Nations Writers Network, Jeanine Leane, Kim Scott, Alexis Wright, Ali Cobby Eckermann, Lionel Fogarty, Jim Everett, Melissa Lucashenko, Evelyn Araluen, and Yvette Holt amongst many others. Wevers's perspective as a non-Australian and as Pākehā New Zealander also assisted in patterning modes of decolonization for Australian literary studies through comparison of the two contexts. She achieved this by her persistent and productive criticism of Australian scholarship's unconscious colonialism. Her 2006 essay, "Being Pakeha: The Politics of Location" provided a model for theorizing localized complexities and responsibilities of settler-culture standpoint (Wevers, "Being Pakeha"). She also convened the 2012 annual ASAL conference in Wellington, Aotearoa New Zealand – the only ASAL conference ever held offshore – where Australian delegates encountered the standard protocols of Māori recognition, including the extensive welcome onto the Te Herenga Waka Marae (Victoria University's tribal meeting ground), which went far beyond the tokenism of Australian settler-culture practices of the time. Wevers understood her position as the director of the Stout Research Centre for New Zealand Studies at Wellington University as an opportunity to effect decolonizing change and expected or imagined that we Australians shared that objective.[7] Her influence alone is evidence of the potential benefits of trans-Tasman interaction regarding the decolonization of literary studies in the region.

There has been some change. The Association of the Australian University Heads of English (AUHE), the peak body for university English education and research, amended its mission statement in 2021 to identify the necessity of "decolonising and indigenising the field of English education and research" and harvests information and strategies from across the country for use in teaching and research ("Mission Statement"). In 2022, all keynote papers at the ASAL conference were given by First Nations writers and critics from across Australia and from Aotearoa New Zealand. So, too, the conference was framed by local community members from nipaluna/Hobart and palawa writers from lutrawita/Tasmania, and many of the conference sessions were focused on the decolonization of Australian literary studies including research, curricula, and pedagogies ("Coming to Terms"). Of course, these shifts do not signal the achievement of a decolonized field, but they do mark a significant moment in the process of decolonizing literary studies research and teaching.

This mutual ignorance of Australia and Aotearoa New Zealand's literature is true also of educational institutions where, with only a couple of exceptions, neither place teaches the literature of the other. In researching this chapter, I located one course in Aotearoa New Zealand that includes Australian literature (Victoria University, Wellington, which was originally set up by Wevers) and one course in Australia (University of Adelaide), framed as a "Trans-Tasman" study, which engages with the literatures of both places as an interaction. One other, Australia and Oceania in Literature (University of New England), conceives of these literatures regionally. The Postcolonial Literatures course at my own university, the University of New South Wales (UNSW Sydney), opens with the verse novel *Ruby Moonlight* by Yankunytjatjara/Kokatha poet Ali Cobby Eckermann. It is a first-contact narrative set in mid-north South Australia in the 1880s. The course also includes a module that groups together Pacific, Aotearoa New Zealand, and Australian literatures relative to First Nations Spoken Word poetry. If there are any more courses in either country, they are well hidden. It is more common for the postcolonial courses in each place to develop curricula that span diverse and far-flung contexts of the former empire: Africa, South Asia, Canada, the Caribbean. Moreover, when Aotearoa New Zealand thinks regionally in this context it is far more commonly in relation to its Pacific neighbors rather than Australia.

The main reason for this is the deep connections between Pasifika peoples and Māori and the number of Pasifika people settled in Aotearoa New Zealand.[8] Aotearoa New Zealand is a Pacific country with a Pacific history, populations, and imaginary. Australia is not, though the state of Queensland in northeastern Australia has some strong identifications.[9] There are increasing numbers of Pasifika peoples migrating to Australia permanently or on extended fly-in–fly-out working visas, but Australia's imaginaries are of the interior and the littoral. When Australia federated in 1901 and separated from Britain's other Pacific colonies, it become more insular in this respect (Denoon; Perera; McMahon, "Gilded Cage"; McMahon, "Encapsulated Space").

Both Australia and Aotearoa New Zealand are what Alan Lawson first termed "second world" societies, so named to emphasize their "secondariness" and "second-ness." They share, with Canada and South Africa, the ambiguous status of being "both imperialised and colonising" (Lawson).[10] Together with Canada – but not South Africa – these second-world settler cultures now constitute significant majorities of the populations of each place. Australia's population as at 31 December 2021 was 25,766,605. Of this number, Aboriginal and Torres Strait Islander people represent 3.2% of the population; 26% of the population were born overseas, and Aotearoa New Zealanders ranked as the fourth-highest immigrant group. As of March 2022, the population of Aotearoa New Zealand was 5,124,100, of which 17.1% are Māori and a further 8.1% are Pasifika ("New Zealand Country Brief"). Just over 27% of the population of Aotearoa New Zealand were born overseas, and Australians have historically comprised one of the top three immigrant groups.[11]

The development of literary studies as part of the expansion of Australian universities is clarified by Catherine Manathunga's 2016 comparative study, "The Role of Universities in Nation-Building in 1950s Australia and Aotearoa New Zealand." Manathunga identifies three major differences between the two reports commissioned by Australia (1957) and Aotearoa New Zealand (1959) respectively to assess the need for the expansion of their university sectors. Manathunga's first finding underscores the well-known difference in attitudes to Britain. As a former penal colony, one of the ur-narratives of settler Australia is the need to cut ties with the "mother country." Accordingly, the Australian report included little about British universities. The Aotearoa New Zealand report, on the other hand, based its recommendations on a British educational ideal. The second finding points to the greater gender bias of Australia – no surprises there. Australia has a long history of settler-culture misogyny.[12] The third issue relates to the composition of disciplines and faculties. The Aotearoa New Zealand report considers the modern university in terms of cultural benefit, which it links institutionally to the arts and humanities. The Australian recommendations, on the other hand, in keeping with mainstream Australia's ongoing suspicion of the arts, view the arts and humanities as addenda for the main business of science and technology.[13] The three distinctions Manathunga identifies in the reports of the 1950s may well still hold in 2022, especially in relation to the respective institutional commitments to cultural benefit.

In 2023, policies of the governing bodies of Australian and Aotearoa New Zealand universities, Universities Australia and Universities New Zealand – Te Pōkai Tara respectively, indicate that Australia lags behind its neighbor in many aspects of decolonizing policies including literary pedagogies.[14] While not fully accounting for this lag, it is true that Australia is a much larger and more complex context: it has forty-three universities, spread over a vast continent that is homeland to 250 First Nations with as many languages. Its population is also far more multicultural. Aotearoa New Zealand has eight universities that cover the two main islands which are home to thirty-five Iwi (Māori community) groups, who, with variations, share(d) the same language, te reo Māori. This small number of universities and the shared understanding of te reo Māori has enabled Universities New Zealand – Te Pōkai Tara to implement the "Te Kāhui Amokura Strategic Work Plan" across all universities in the country.

However, even with the differences of scale and diversity noted, Universities Australia's actions regarding the decolonization of governance, research, and pedagogy are long overdue, which it admits in its Indigenous Strategy Paper 2022–2025. As with Aotearoa New Zealand, several Australian universities have now appointed First Nations deputy vice chancellors or pro vice chancellors onto their senior leadership teams. Most universities now include centers or departments to support First Nations staff and students. Increasingly, these centers also provide training for non-Indigenous staff in how to decolonize their research and pedagogies. My own faculty at UNSW Sydney houses Nura Gili (Place of Fire and Light), the Centre for Indigenous Programs, which devised and designed an extensive, two-stage "Cultural Reflexivity" course, mandated for all academic and professional staff in the faculty in 2021 and 2022. The course, like others across the country, was developed by First Nations staff and students and addresses many issues of pedagogy, including content and delivery, the potential complexities of tutorial discussion, and standpoint theory. Courses such as these across the country undergird current decisions regarding the decolonization of English literary studies and creative writing courses and inform the discussion here (Collins-Gearing, Brooke and Smith).

Colonization to Decolonization

For Australia and Aotearoa New Zealand, the timing and context of their discovery and invasion by the British established "the colonial legacies and entanglements of particular places and literary communities at particular historical junctures" (Etherington and Zimbler 229). As Paul Sharrad notes, Australia was the last of the "new worlds" discovered by Europeans, bookending the Columban discoveries of the Americas ("Countering Encounter"). Australia's First Nations peoples comprise the oldest continuing culture on earth, having occupied the full land area of 7,692,024 km^2 and surrounding waters for approximately 60,000 years. The documentary *First Australians* describes the 1788 invasion as the event when "the oldest living culture in the world [was] overrun by the world's greatest empire" (Blackfella Films, 2008). At the time of invasion, there were approximately 250 different First Nations language groups across the country, with many additional dialectical variations (Leane, "Teaching"). It is estimated that 120 languages were spoken in 2016, and a 2019 study estimated that 90 percent of the languages are endangered.[15]

The terms of the Australian invasion and occupation were/are unique. As Stuart Macintyre summarizes: "In striking contrast to its practices elsewhere, the British Government took possession of eastern Australia (and later the rest of the continent), by a simple proclamation of sovereignty" (34). This occurred according to the Roman law of *res nullius*, that is, the assessment that the land was not properly owned (cultivated) by the First Nations peoples (Fitzmaurice). The attendant assumption was that the Aboriginal peoples were not sufficiently civilized to enter into trade agreements or treaties. The terms of this proclamation and the denial of Aboriginal sovereignty and humanity continues to ravage Australia, especially its First Nations peoples. This shameful distinction is not widely understood by non-Indigenous peoples in Australia and needs to be discussed in teaching First Nations literatures. As Mununjali Yugambeh poet Ellen van Neerven writes in their poem "Invisible Spears" (74):

> you don't want us protecting
> our land like the Māori
> that means it was our land to protect

> we don't need
> a haka of whitefullas
> just let us resist

And so, in their 2020 collection *Throat*, van Neerven addresses the absence of a treaty in terms of authorship, publication, and reading (62):

> Who is the custodian of this book?
>> How do we co-exist on this page?
>> How can we re-imagine custodianship?
>> Is this an agreement or a series of
> unanswered questions?
>> Are you willing to enter an agreement that is
> incomplete and subject to change?

The British invasion and usurpation of Australia in 1788 marks the beginning of Britain's second empire, which paved the way for its "Imperial Century" (1815–1914) (Parsons). It was motivated by the perceived need to establish a penal colony after the loss of American colonies in 1783. Hence, from the outset, colonies in New South Wales and Van Diemen's Land (now lutrawita/Tasmania) and later Queensland and Western Australia were based on forced migration, harsh conditions, unfree labor, and imprisonment. These beginnings instilled a great and continuing distrust of (British but also general) authority amongst large elements of the settler population, which marks a significant cultural difference between the cultures of Australia and Aotearoa New Zealand.

The First Nations people of Aotearoa New Zealand, the Māori, first settled the country between 1320 and 1350, having navigated the Pacific tides west from Polynesia (Mafile'o and Walsh-Tapiata). This makes Aotearoa New Zealand the youngest country on earth. While English is the lingua franca, te reo Māori was recognized as one of the nation's two official languages in 1987. There are dialects within te reo Māori, but the one language is understood by Māori speakers across the country. Perhaps the greatest distinction between Australia and Aotearoa New Zealand in terms of decolonizing imperatives is the Treaty of Waitangi. The British colonization of Aotearoa New Zealand, which began in the early nineteenth century, was formalized by the Treaty of Waitangi in 1840, signed by the British Crown and Māori chiefs (rangatira) from Aotearoa New Zealand's North Island. This agreement, which is bilingual, contains some key differences between the English and te reo Māori versions. It grants governance rights to the Crown while Māori retain full chieftainship of their lands. It also gives Māori full rights and protection as British subjects.

However, disagreements regarding the respective claims of sovereignty caused wars and hostility between Māori and Pākehā for the next 150 years. This legacy remains highly problematic.

The Treaty of Waitangi – despite its many problems and ambiguous status – established a contractual relationship between colonizers and colonized that recognized Māori priority and, with contention, ongoing sovereignty. Aotearoa New Zealand was conceived of as a bi-cultural society. This is not to deny the genocidal policies inflicted on Māori. None of the Australian colonies, nor the federated nation of Australia from 1901, have ever developed such treaties. Those Australians who are not Aboriginal or Torres Strait Islanders are, therefore, living on lands that were never ceded to Britain. There have been numerous calls for a treaty in the last three decades ("The Barunga Statement"). The Treaty of Waitangi is often invoked as a possible model for Australia as it negotiates the instantiation of a formal recognition of First Nations' primacy, called "the Voice," into the federal constitution (O'Sullivan). This was a charged issue in Australia's federal election in May 2022, and there may be a national referendum to decide on the Voice in 2023. The Voice is a predicate of decolonizing the Australian polity.

Decolonizing Whiteness

The colonial regimes of both Australia and Aotearoa New Zealand effectively implemented immigration policies to ensure the dominance of White populations. The impact of these policies is still current and a vital issue in the decolonizing of literary studies. The White Australia Policy, formalized at Federation in 1901, was not fully dismantled until 1973, and Australia followed Canada in formally adopting a multicultural policy in 1978, the terms of which constitute a concerted "repudiation" of former policies. Aotearoa New Zealand's colonial government also implemented policies to ensure White immigration, including legislation that limited Asian immigration and inhibited Asian peoples' capacity to naturalize as citizens ("Chinese Portraits"). These racist policies have diminished since the 1970s, and many Pasifika peoples in particular have migrated to Aotearoa New Zealand from that time, as well as an increasing number from more diverse homelands. This "Whiteness" excluded all but Anglo-Celts and some northern Europeans. Its legacy also creates tensions between the postcoloniality and multiculturality of these places (Gunew). Any decolonization needs to negotiate this complexity, which is integral to addressing historical and current racism.

Pedagogical Strategy 1: Decolonizing History

The dates of Australian and New Zealand's colonization coincide, *inter alia*, with the development of a new historical consciousness in Western thought, including Kant's thesis on Universal History and Herder's theory of historical equilibrium, both published in 1784 (Kant; Herder). The encompassing, advancing sweep of Universal History authorized the "civilizing mission" of colonialism and relegated First Nations peoples to prehistory and/or the genocidal implications of universal progress. Jeanine Leane writes: "I am a creative writer of poetry and prose and am driven to write, as I believe many Aboriginal authors are, because I have always been positioned on the other side of history" (Leane, "Teaching"). Leane's guidelines for decolonized and Indigenized pedagogies in Australian literature include addressing the multiple problematics of history.

One of the main strategies Leane advocates is the reinclusion of the histories and experiences of First Nations peoples, whether we are teaching Australian texts by First Nations writers, settler-culture writers, or newer migrant writers. In all these contexts, Leane argues, the continuing presence of First Nations needs to be reinserted.[16] When there are no First Nations characters in the fiction or poetry, which is common, she directs us to identify the lands on which the texts are set, immediately identifying the erasures that provide the ground for settler writing. Instancing narratives of the nineteenth-century gold rushes, she asks: "On which Aboriginal lands did the many Australian goldfields lie? Who were the traditional custodians before the lands were mined for profit from which Aboriginal and Torres Strait Islander people never benefitted?" (Leane, "Teaching" 7). Discussing texts published more recently, Leane directs teachers to "familiarise students with the historical context of the Royal Commission into Aboriginal Deaths in Custody (1987) and the High Court's decision on the Mabo case (1992)" ("The Mabo Case") as crucial historical events in the colonized history of First Nations peoples.

Finally, Leane points out the need to teach the different experiences of colonization across the country. Some areas of the central Australian desert were deemed uninhabitable by Europeans until the 1920s – an irony given that the Arrernte people have lived there for tens of thousands of years. From the 1920s, miners and pastoralists made further ingressions into the Australian continental center, effectively staging a second era of colonization (Robin). This experience contrasts starkly with the experience of the Palawa people of lutruwita (the island state of Tasmania), who were killed en masse in the 1820s and 1830s. Given such a vast land area and so many First Nations peoples, history across Australia is not synchronous or consistent.

A number of the novels of Noongar[17] writer Kim Scott engage with archives: both the cultural heritage of the Noongar people and the archives of government records. Scott's essay, "A Noongar Voice: An Anomalous History," provides an account of the difficulties and pain of these processes. Specifically, he documents the difficulties of locating any "voice" of First Nations peoples in official records alongside the erasure of Noongar modes of memorializing experience. The latter was accomplished through government policies of cultural destruction, including the removal of children from their families. Hence, he finds a double erasure; there is little history in either archive. However, he persists with both processes and continues to see the value in conventional research for its capacity to affect the present and future: "that was my concern, researching a novel: not what was, but what might have been, and even what might yet be" (Scott 103).

One of the most striking aspects of contemporary First Nations writing for non-Indigenous Australians is the manner in which the texts sustain people's simultaneous histories in the constructions of world and being: the ontologies and deep time of traditional culture and country and those of European modernity and colonization. The decolonizing of Australian literature requires acknowledgment of this complexity, by which First Nations peoples have negotiated two vastly different, even incompatible realities. Chapter 1, "From Time Immemorial," of Alexis Wright's award-winning novel *Carpentaria* (2006) juxtaposes these histories.

> A NATION CHANTS, BUT WE KNOW YOUR STORY ALREADY. THE CHURCH BELLS PEAL EVERYWHERE. CHURCH BELLS CALLING THE FAITHFUL TO THE TABERNACLE WHERE THE GATES OF HEAVEN WILL OPEN, BUT NOT FOR THE WICKED. CALLING INNOCENT LITTLE BLACK GIRLS FROM A DISTANT COMMUNITY WHERE THE WHITE DOVE BEARING AN OLIVE BRANCH NEVER LANDS. LITTLE GIRLS WHO COME BACK HOME AFTER CHURCH ON SUNDAY, WHO LOOK AROUND THEMSELVES AT THE HUMAN FALLOUT AND ANNOUNCE MATTER-OF-FACTLY, *ARMAGEDDON BEGINS HERE.* (1; capitalization in original)

And then the text shifts from the time of the nation state to time immemorial: "The ancestral serpent, a creature larger than storm clouds, came down from the stars, laden with its own creative enormity" (1). The collision of these ontologies is intolerable for the traditional owners of the Gulf country, as the narrative starkly rehearses. However, the novel also shows how colonization – a glitch within time immemorial – is comprehended and eclipsed by this deeper history and understanding. Any deficit resides with the settler culture whose understanding is limited to the confinements of Western modernity and World History.

The first published novel by a Māori woman, Patricia Grace's *Mutuwhenua: The Moon Sleeps* (1978), follows the narrator's negotiation of these conflicting histories, temporalities, and their attendant ontologies. Throughout the narrative, Ripeka's literal touchstone is the shared meaning of a sacred and valuable stone, which she and others find as children and which is returned by her family to the gully of the ancestors as its right and proper place. The collective belief in the rightness of this action organizes the coordinates of time that Ripeka sustains alongside those of White Western New Zealand. Ultimately, she decides that her new baby will not be raised by her and her Pākehā husband but by her extended Māori family. Her husband needs to accept the rightness of what he cannot fully share or understand.

Pedagogical Strategy 2: Decolonizing Literary Histories

In the entanglement of literary and political history, the time of the colonization of Australia and Aotearoa New Zealand also coincides with the publication of the first *Bildungsroman*, Goethe's *Wilhelm Meister's Apprenticeship*, which was begun in the 1770s and published in 1796 (Goethe). As Peter Pierce claims, the account of Australia's literary maturation came to be seen as inseparable from Australia's political, national maturation according to this literary-historical *Bildung* (82). It is a connection that is rehearsed throughout Australian fiction from the first novel by the convict Henry Savery in 1830 to the present.[18] This network of progress narratives affects much if not all of the English literary curriculum but is of particular significance to Australian literature and its literary histories, given the enduring compaction of narratives and events, including colonial invasion and narratives of individual (and corrective penal) transformation.

Historically – for the purposes of this discussion, at least – English literary studies in Australia and Aotearoa New Zealand can be viewed in four stages. First is the establishment of "English" as part of the broader process of the rise of English literary studies, and as a strategy and effect of British colonialism. The first New Zealand Professor of Classics and English Literature and Language was one of the first three appointments upon the founding of the University of Otago in 1869, Aotearoa New

Zealand's first university. The first Australian Chair of English Literature and Language and Moral Philosophy was created in 1874 when the University of Adelaide was established (Dale 42–44). The second stage marks nationalist turns to the settler literatures, or what Robert Dixon refers to as "periods of nation-centrism." Regarding Australia, Dixon writes:

> In Australian literary history, there have been two periods dominated by the epistemology of nation-centrism: the period of Federation, from 1880–1920, and the period from the second world war to the Bicentenary, from 1945 to 1988, when Australian literature was established as a discipline. (Dixon, "National Literatures")

This latter period produced many histories of Australian literature, and the first Chair of Australian literature was established at the University of Sydney (1962), in response to public advocacy. (This Chair was not filled after the retirement of Professor Robert Dixon in 2019.) The Association for the Study of Australian Literature was established in 1977, an offshoot of SPACLALS discussed above, "to encourage and stimulate the writing and reading of Australian literature and the study of and research into Australian literature and Australian literary culture."[19]

In his 2007 history of Aotearoa New Zealand literature, *The Long Forgetting*, Patrick Evans recounts the formation of a similar period of nation-centrism in the 1930s.[20] The accepted account is that New Zealand literary cultural nationalism can be historicized around *The Phoenix*, a small four-issue Auckland University College student journal published 1932–33, whose contributors, James Bertram, R. A. K. Mason, Allen Curnow, Charles Brasch, J. C. Beaglehole, and A. R. D. Fairburn, together with Frank Sargeson, went on to dominate New Zealand literature until the 1970s (Schrader). The first journal dedicated to the "criticism and scholarship" of Aotearoa New Zealand literature, *Journal of New Zealand Literature (JNZL)*, was published in 1983. In his editorial for the first issue, Frank McKay justifies the publication on the basis of an increasing awareness of the national literature. He notes that all six (at that time) universities teach the national literature "as a distinct and significant area of study" (MacKay 1). The journal includes two parts: the first provides summaries of new poetry, fiction, criticism and drama, and the second comprises five critical essays. Sebastian Black's summary of new drama for 1983 is significant in relation to the current discussion in that he notes that many New Zealanders in 1983 were outraged at the very idea of a national theater (as opposed to performances of British and North

American plays) (Black). However, he also records that there were also those "who struggled to create a theatrical environment in which indigenous work might flourish" (Black 1). The five critical essays are notable in that three engage with work by Pasifika and Māori writers (Alistair Campbell and Witi Ihimarea and waiata aroha [Māori love poems]).

It is this stage of nation-centrism that most clearly announces the connection between Australia and Aotearoa New Zealand as "second-world" societies, as each exhibits their ambiguous status of being "both imperialised and colonising" (Lawson). For the desire to speak of local experience and to record the difference from Britain was championed as an anticolonial development. However, very few First Nations writers were included in the constitution of this difference. What appears clear from 2023 is that the ongoing need for settler cultures to attest maturity and attainment was enacted along the White mythologies of colonialism.

Māori/Pākehā writer and academic Tina Makereti illustrates the effects of this thinking. Her first diagram (Table 4.1) sets out how Māori literature is positioned in syllabi according to colonial periodizations and nation-centrism. She proceeds by offering two alternatives, in which she sets out a "Whakapapa [genealogy] of Māori Literature." Her final diagram

Table 4.1 *Māori literature in a conventional syllabus of Aotearoa New Zealand literature*

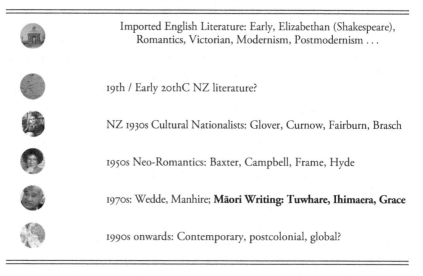

	Imported English Literature: Early, Elizabethan (Shakespeare), Romantics, Victorian, Modernism, Postmodernism . . .
	19th / Early 20thC NZ literature?
	NZ 1930s Cultural Nationalists: Glover, Curnow, Fairburn, Brasch
	1950s Neo-Romantics: Baxter, Campbell, Frame, Hyde
	1970s: Wedde, Manhire; **Māori Writing: Tuwhare, Ihimaera, Grace**
	1990s onwards: Contemporary, postcolonial, global?

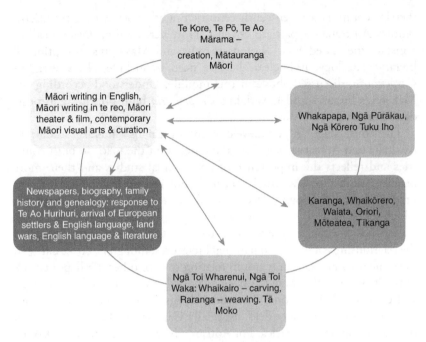

Figure 4.1 Whakapapa [genealogy] of Māori literature

(Figure 4.1) recognizes the linearity of generation but also captures inter-relationality, for – as she writes – "culture is always in flux, and colonisation – and the ongoing process of colonisation – shapes, limits, distorts and shifts how we know and tell our own stories. We are constantly spiralling back to reconnect and re-enact that whakapapa."

Makereti's reconfiguration highlights the profound differences between Western and Māori conceptions of time and history, especially the telos of modernity and "universal history" by which Māori people only come into (literary) being in the 1970s and then only according to the criteria of conventional canonicity.

Makereti's alternative whakapapa offers tangible ways of decolonizing the problem of linearity, history, and literature. A colleague and I who teach an Honours Year module on writing the world will alter the offering according to her model. We have taught the course as a dialogue between John Donne's poetics of discovery relative to European colonialism and Shirley Hazzard's 1980 novel of the post-War globe, *Transit of Venus*, whose title links the narrative to Cook's discovery of Australia. The course thereby connects a seventeenth-century English poet with a twentieth-century Australian expatriate novelist. However, heeding Leane's call to reinstate the erased First Nations peoples and Makereti's disruption of literary genealogy, it is clear that we need to include Alexis Wright's *Carpentaria*, discussed above in this module. Understood according the Makereti's literary model, Wright's *Carpentaria* both predates and post-dates Donne and Hazzard.

The third stage in the development of English literary studies in Australia and Aotearoa New Zealand dates from the 1980s in both coun-tries and reflects the importance of postcolonial studies and then, more problematically, of "World Literature" and multicultural literatures to literary studies. Deploying Dixon's useful schematization of literary scale, which he bases on the location of each text and the various spaces of its readerships, we can see the ways postcolonialism expanded or multiplied the relationships of these two national literatures, though not necessarily in the same ways and certainly not in relation to each other. Perhaps because of the issues of scale, there has been a consistent tendency of each to read and compare their national literatures alongside other postcolonial con-texts from much further afield, especially Canada, the Caribbean, South Asia, and Anglophone Africa. For Aotearoa New Zealand, there is also the additional sense of their interconnections with Pasifika countries. The focus and scales proposed by "World Literature" claim very little interest in the Global South and certainly not in Oceania.

The category of "postcolonial" can be fraught in "second-world" soci-eties such as Australia and Aotearoa New Zealand for First Nations peoples because of its perceived potential to erase the ongoing practices of the "second" or *ongoing* settler colonization and to merge the First Nations with settler subjects as fellow "colonials." The concept and practices of decolonization, the fourth and current stage, have the potential to clarify the perceived problematics of the "postcolonial" in three main ways. The first is the identification of colonizing practices as ongoing and active rather than as historical occurrences. Secondly, the active element signaled by the prefix *de* in *decolonization*, stresses the active intervention into and against an identified reality. In Australia and Aotearoa New Zealand, this means that the researcher or teacher must declare their own standpoint and its implications. The third shift relates to the reach of the term, which extends from the structures that underpin social and cultural institutions to every-day activities and interactions (Elkington, Jackson, Kiddle, et al.). Most literary studies students in Australia and Aotearoa New Zealand under-stand the decolonization of literary courses as part of this larger sociopolitical movement, which is tangibly supported by their institution of study – which is not to deny ongoing inequities. Nor is it a metaphorization of decolonization, though its potential diffuseness needs to be addressed and discussed with students so that its specific histories and contexts are not lost (Tuck and Yang).

In disciplinary terms, too, the initiative of decolonization functions as a more comprehensive imperative. While some institutions in both Australia and Aotearoa New Zealand included multiple courses framed by postcolonial perspectives in the 1990s and early 2000s, most faculties usually only had one or two courses dedicated to literature in English outside the canon of English and (White) North American writing: one on the national literature and one on Anglophone postcolonial literature. In the majority of institutions, the postcolonial intervention, along with the literature of settler "national" intervention, which promoted courses on the literature of Australia and Aotearoa New Zealand, was introduced into the curriculum without significant disruption to the canon. Courses on Shakespearean drama, Romanticism, or Modernism remained largely unchanged. Decolonization, however, comprehends the entire curriculum. In Australia and Aotearoa New Zealand, the decolonizing process is understood as necessary for all courses and all pedagogies.

Pedagogical Strategy 3: Rethinking Written and Spoken Languages

One of the most basic issues for decolonizing literary studies in Australia and Aotearoa New Zealand is the relationship between written and spoken language. As Rosemary Salomone observes in *The Rise of English*, colonization was driven by the ethos of "one nation, one language," or one empire, one language (15). The great number of Indigenous languages in Australia, spoken by small groups of people, stands in contrast to the shared language of te reo Māori, though R. M. W. Dixon's research identifies common features across many of Australia's original languages (Australian Languages). In both countries, however, language, culture, and country are equally inseparable.

All 250 of the languages of First Nations Australians and the various versions of te reo Māori were oral rather than written languages. The original transcription of languages into Latin script was undertaken by early colonials and missionaries in these countries and many others across Oceania. A solely oral language is not an inherent cultural deficit. Rather, language did/does operate within the interrelationship and immanence of country and culture, past and present. The Meriam linguist Bua Benjamin

Mabo, from Australia's Torres Strait Islands, writes: "Keriba gesep agiakar dikwarda keriba mir. Ableglam keriba Mir pako Tonar nole atakemurkak" (The land actually gave birth to our language. Language and culture are inseparable). So, too, recent studies reinforce the particular relationship between land, language, and well-being for Māori people (Matika, Manuela, Houkamau, and Sibley). Dispossession, forced removal, and colonization have had profound and particular consequences for the interconnections of language and culture. Decolonizing approaches to the fundamental issue of language include the contextualization of written and oral literatures and their respective capacities and intensities through the inclusion of spoken, sung, and performed texts alongside written texts. Tina Makereti's critique of conventional literary periodizations (above, p. 000) highlights the misconceptions that arise from a solely scriptal criterion, which presents First Nations peoples of Australia, Aotearoa New Zealand, and the Pacific as having no poetry, drama, or storytelling prior to colonization and their induction into Western modes of representation. As this is clearly untrue, the criteria must be rethought and expanded to include *inter alia* the particular forms of immanence that connect country and culture and cultural expression. This perspective also casts light on the separation and disembodiment that occurs with scriptal records and representations and enables comparison of ontologies of memorial continuance and the archival memory-shelf of the written text.

This defetishization of the written text needs to be kept in balance with the achievements of First Nations writing in more recent times, so that questions of the flow between ancient and modern modes are considered while the leap into the scriptal mode and, most often, into the language and forms of the colonizers, is also recognized and traced. These discussions are usefully mapped according to the range of continuities and discontinuities of history and of the individual writer and consider the range of work up to contemporary experimentalism and narratives focused on contemporary urban life.

There is also an expanding body of collaborative work that involves translations from First Nations languages into English and vice versa. The Australian Institute of Aboriginal and Torres Strait Islander Studies (AIATSIS) provides a detailed list of many of these texts, as does the National Library of New Zealand.[21] It is also possible to access recordings of singing with text in both the original language and English, with some also including performances. The official recordings of the glorious Yolngu musician Gurrumul are available on the Internet.[22] Also, the contemporary singer, Gamilaraay and Birri Gubba man Mitch Tambo, has recorded one of

Australia's unofficial national anthems, "You're the Voice," in Gamilaraay language and including the wide diversity of Australia's people.[23] Ngā Hinepūkōrero, the Spoken Word Collective, moves between English and te reo Maori.[24]

Students respond very well to song and performance poetry, and it is a form that sets up traditions and connections outside the English literary canon. They also have access to the work via the popularity of slam poetry more generally. Throughout Aotearoa New Zealand and the Pacific, and increasingly in Australia, performance poetry has become a powerful form where traditional performance meets contemporary poetics of critique (Stavanger and Te Whiu). The spoken word poetry of Selina Tusitala Marsh, the first Poet Laureate of New Zealand (2017–19), is a great exemplar of these interconnections. Her performance of her poem "Unity" at Westminster Abbey for Commonwealth Day in 2016 harnesses this raft of traditions and techniques to deliver a stinging critique of Pacific colonization.[25] This newly animated genre is also thriving in Australia amongst First Nations poets including Djapu social activist and writer from Yirrkala in East Arnhem Land Melanie Mununggurr-Williams, who won the 2018 Australian Poetry Slam National Final with a poem "I Run" that articulates the dilemma of being caught "between a Western white man's world and ancient Aboriginal antiquity."[26] So, too, the renowned comedian Steven Oliver, of Kuku-Yalanji, Waanyi, Gangalidda, Woppaburra, Bundjalung, and Biripi heritage, has produced performances pieces that invite conversation across communities and also claim a First Nations queer identity.[27]

Pedagogical Strategy 4: Formalist Analysis and the Question of Value

Ironically, enough, the raft of rhetorical tools within conventional literaryanalysis has a powerful role to play in the decolonizing of critical practices in the classroom when they are harnessed as one mode amongst others for reading First Nations texts. Close readings and formal literary analysis open up many First Nations texts, though its modes may be unfamiliar to some students. Relative to the performance poetry discussed above, for example, a formalist analysis could provide one vocabulary for mapping the networks between speaker, text, and reader/audience that are created by the dynamics of these texts. How does the call to the addressee articulated in a spoken word poem relate to that of, say, oratorical and lyrical apostrophe and their emphasis of the "circulation or situation of communication itself" (Culler 59). To what extent does the

Western rhetorical tradition enable ways of engaging with these new Spoken Word texts, and what are the limits of this mode of analysis?

The deployment of rhetorical analysis can be productive also in that it enacts formality, in its other sense of that word, as in ceremony and protocol. It is an act of respect across cultures and traditions and, by the terms of that tradition, accords the work aesthetic value in the conventional terms the discipline (see below, for a discussion of value). In the Western tradition also, the study of rhetoric predates English, as its origins are ancient Greece and Rome, thereby complicating temporality and tradition in productive ways. Of course, the mirror process is also necessary. How might our study of a contemporary spoken word poem about being-in-place alter how we read voice, persuasion, and nature in a canonical text such as Shelley's "Ode to the West Wind"? How might a spoken word poem of expressive intensity shift our reading of the lyric, or of the dramatic monologue?

Teaching Spoken Word poetry often leads students to question the political potential of poetry or of literature and art more generally. How can a poetic act, shared between a limited group of people, bring about social change, which is an integral aim to much of this work? Can words affect "the decision of the judge," as is the aim of oratorical apostrophe? Did Selina Tusitala Marsh's performance change the British Commonwealth's attitudes or policies regarding the South Pacific? These questions are necessary and productive as a decolonizing method. They focus on the diversity of investments from the creators, public performances, audiences, and feedback, building community and resilience and connecting our work in the classroom to these various contexts. These questions of investment, motivation, and effects relate in part to those of literary value. The teaching of Australian and Aotearoa New Zealand literary studies and postcolonial literatures that were based on a canon-forming "nation-centrism" model necessitated frameworks that opened up multiple value systems, which were often new to students and sometimes met with resistance. Students educated via New Critical universalism and an aesthetics of literary afflatus, are ill prepared to approach reading practices that trace cultures coming to writing. Much of the literature of "second-world" societies is not aurified. Students have not heard of the writers or the texts, so they are, at best, considered to be unproven and open for judgment as well as criticism.

In discussions of literary value, it is useful to work with students on mapping the range of values at work across the fields of literary and visual cultures prior to focusing on First Nations texts specifically. The first question might ask what texts warrant inclusion in any literary study. Students can list the range of their own reading and viewing and their different expectations from popular fiction and genre fiction, television series and films, and university syllabi. The list might also include family discourses, text chains, and graffiti. In diverse classrooms such as those of Australia and Aotearoa New Zealand, these lists will include texts from non-English sources. They will also be accessed and experienced in various forms. How do students assess the value of this amalgam? What is the experience of moving across the range of styles and the genres and levels of complexity? How does engagement with one form or mode affect the experience of another? To what extent do they consume and/or create these texts. How does this map read them?

Disagreement is welcome in this discussion as a way for students to experience shared and divergent values according to relative functions and purpose. Students coming to the diversity of First Nations literatures need to respect this range and learn how to articulate its particular location in the literary field. A final note on the question of value, which can be raised in light of the recognition that all literature has demographics and target audiences, is that they may not be the primary readership for the text they are reading or hearing or viewing. First Nations writing in English presumes a settler audience to some extent, but there is, from the outset, a displacement of the primacy of the Western reader. First Nations students will have a very different – and primary – position.

Pedagogical Strategy 5: Research and Citations for Essays

Students often find the limited number of resources about many First Nations writers – or any writers from Australia and Aotearoa New Zealand, for that matter – very challenging, as there is often little critical material. There are key reference books that are readily available, including literary histories and "companions" (Heiss and Minter; Williams; see also *BlackWords (Teaching)* in the AustLit database), and First Nations scholars such as Martin Nakata[28] and Linda Tuhiwai Smith (*Decolonizing Methodologies*). These need to be historicized, but those from the last decade are generally very useful. Jeanine Leane's pointer toward historical discourses (discussed above,) provides one methodology by which students can contextualize their essays and arguments. The reach of trans-Indigenous approaches may be helpful in this context too, as they assist in breaking down the binary that still privileges settler-culture writing. Chadwick Allen's foundational text *Trans-Indigenous: Methodologies for Global Native Literary Studies* is very useful here, and it has been strongly endorsed by Māori scholar Alice Te Punga Somerville. Allen's more recent essay, "Indigenous Juxtapositions: Teaching Maori and Aboriginal Texts in Global Contexts," is also very insightful, especially for teachers beyond Australia and Aotearoa New Zealand.

The particular challenges of researching in this field need to be discussed with the students as a particular aspect of decolonized study. Whatever decisions students adopt regarding their approach, it is imperative that they engage with secondary material from First Nations readers and writers. Finally, there may be First Nations students who are confident to follow pathways that may be unfamiliar to the teacher or to other students but will create meaningful and transformative knowledge and methods to literary studies.

Conclusion: Present and Future Challenges

One of the many challenges of decolonizing literary pedagogies in Australia and Aotearoa New Zealand is the maintenance of substantive practices in environments where "decolonization" is often adopted as a veneer of rightful thinking within the endless double-speak which plagues our universities. Right thinking, including decolonization, has been compromised in Australia – and to a lesser extent in Aotearoa New Zealand – by its deployment as empty rhetoric, an item on the checklist for global university rankings. In Australia specifically, this performance of virtue has operated as a blind to obscure the systematic dismantling of Australian working conditions in the academy, the induction of universities into the global labor market, and a reversion to colonial-era class systems.

A second challenge, in the context of the Anthropocene, is the turn to Indigeneity as a solution to the disasters of the environmental destruction and late-modern disenchantment. Non-Indigenous readers and scholars – and I include myself in this reminder – need to approach First Nations literatures, and model for our students, the value of this work on its own terms. To do this, we need to be guided by First Nations writers, academics, and students. Decolonization requires the decentering of authority and accepting the invitation to participate on the limited, partial terms that are yet available. Hopefully, literary studies provides some guidance for this process.

Notes

1. The Wiradjuri Nation is located in central western New South Wales. See *Murray Lower Darling Rivers Indigenous Nations.*

2. The resistance from First Nations writers and academics relates to the long history of being spoken for and about by White settler culture (a "whitefella" in Australia) and a Pākehā in the language of Māori, Te re Māori.

3. See Higgins and Terruhn; McKibbin; Wevers, "Being Pakeha."

4. SPACLALS, founded in 1977 was the inspiration for ASAL. It does great work but is a small organization and the Association's journal, *SPAN*, stopped publishing in 2016. Currently ten of its twelve-member executive are from Australia.

5. There are many annual writers' festivals in Australia and Aotearoa New Zealand: each state and territory of Australia holds an annual writers' festival, and there are many also held in the regions. There are annual writers' festivals in all the major cities across Aotearoa New Zealand. A study of past festival programs indicates increasing inclusion of First Nations writers in the last decade. Many of these writers routinely appear at international festivals and events. However, there is little to no programming of First Nations or settler-culture writers between Australia and Aotearoa New Zealand. I note that Selina Tusitala Marsh, the first Poet Laureate of Aotearoa New Zealand (discussed below, 000), has been invited to a number of Australian festivals including the 2023 Brisbane Writers Festival. The 2022 Sydney Writers Festival included a panel on Pacific writers drawn from Pasifika writers living in Sydney.

6. A notable exception is Mark Williams's *Patrick White*. Macmillan, 1983. Expatriate New Zealander Simon During has also written a study on White, *Patrick White.*

7. Many Māori scholars have attested to the decolonizing work achieved by Wevers. The month-long lecture series held in her memory in 2022, "Reading Aotearoa New Zealand in the company of Lydia Wevers' Work" included discussion and tributes by Māori writers and academics. https://cms .wgtn.ac.nz/stout-centre/about/events/seminar-series-reading-aotearoa-new-zealand-in-the-company-of-lydia-wevers-work.

8. See, for example, Ihimaera and Makereti.

9. For example, the Queensland Art Gallery has hosted the Asia Pacific Triennial in Contemporary Art since 1993: www.qagoma.qld.gov.au/about/asia-pacific-triennial.

10. For a contextualizing discussion of Lawson's paradigm, see Prentice and Devadas.

11. For a more detailed and predictive analysis, see also Smits 107.

12. One of the most iconic studies on this topic is Anne Summers, *Damned Whores and God's Police* (1975) – a 780-page analysis of sexism in Australia. Germaine Greer, the author of one of the most significant books of second-wave feminism, *The Female Eunuch* (1970) is an Australian who also writes scathingly of sex and gender structures in Australia.

13. The attack upon all artistic endeavor as inessential and subversive has been even more intense since the Conservative governments of John Howard (1996–2007) and Tony Abbott and his successors from 2013. See Meyrick.

14. See Universities Australia, www.universitiesaustralia.edu.au/ and Universities New Zealand – Te Pōkai Tara, www.universitiesnz.ac.nz/about-universities-new-zealand.

15. Australian Institute of Aboriginal and Torres Strait Islander Studies, https://collection.aiatsis.gov.au/austlang/search.

16. Leane, "Teaching with BlackWords." AustLit is the database of Australian literature and also includes a range of teaching resources. Within AustLit, BlackWords is the record of "Aboriginal and Torres Strait Islander publications mapping stories through a time when writing emerged as a practice of cultural significance." "About BlackWords." *AustLit*, www.austlit.edu.au/austlit/page/15517760.

17. Noongar Country covers the entire southwest corner of Western Australia. See Noongar Boodjar Language Cultural Aboriginal Corporation. https://noongarboodjar.com.au/history/?doing_Fwp_cron=1671760583.698678970 3369140625000.

18. For a fuller discussion, see McMahon, Islands Identity, 67–79.

19. "About ASAL." Association for the Study of Australian Literature, https://asal2022.org/about-asal/.

20. See also Simon During's reading of Evans's history, "Remembering, Resisting." See my review of the most recent literary history, McMahon, "A History of New Zealand Literature."

21. The Australian Institute of Aboriginal and Torres Strait Islander Studies https://aiatsis.library.link/resource/luqdJTCRrx8/; The National Library of New Zealand https://natlib.govt.nz/records/22619217.

22. Gurrumul: see "Wyathul," www.youtube.com/watch?v=7lmZXAdSMQI.

23. www.youtube.com/watch?v=tEdweyPh-N8.

24. www.youtube.com/watch?v=duBFm4eEq-c.

25. Selina Tusitala Marsh, "Unity," www.youtube.com/watch?v=DHWFl54jEg4. See also the Tusiata Avia, www.youtube.com/watch?v=TEvQviUtNFY.

26. Melanie Mununggurr-Williams, "I Run." Australian Poetry Slam, Word Travels, 2018, www.youtube.com/watch?v=xo3nIylz4Hg.

27. Steven Oliver, "Hate, He Said," www.youtube.com/watch?v=xurO_YulJ4c, and "I'm a blackfella," www.youtube.com/watch?v=dSnayKPFiBo.

28. To access Martin Nakata's extensive publications, see https://research.jcu.edu.au/portfolio/martin.nakata.

WORKS CITED

Allen, Chadwick. "Indigenous Juxtapositions: Teaching Maori and Aboriginal Texts in Global Contexts." In Nicholas Birns, Nicole Moore, and Sarah Shieff (eds.), *Teaching Australian and New Zealand Literature*. New York: The Modern Language Association of America, 2017, 179–89.

Trans-Indigenous: Methodologies for Global Native Literary Studies. Minneapolis: University of Minnesota Press, 2012.

Australian University Heads of English. "The Australian University Heads of English, Mission Statement." n.d. https://auhe555190908.wordpress.com/m ission-statement-and-values-statement/.

"The Barunga Statement." Australian Institute of Aboriginal and Torres Strait Islander Studies. October 10, 2022. https://aiatsis.gov.au/explore/barunga-statement.

Black, Sebastian. "New Zealand Plays, Playwrights and Theaters: First Productions, January-October 1982." *Journal of New Zealand Literature* 1 (1983): 5–15.

Brennan, Bernadette. "President's Report to the 2013 AGM." n.d. *Association for the Study of Australian Literature.*

"Chinese Portraits." Archives of Aotearoa – New Zealand. n.d. www.archives.govt.nz /discover-our-stories/chinese-portraits.

Collins-Gearing, Brooke and Rosalind Smith. "Burning Off: Indigenising the Discipline of English." *The Australian Journal of Indigenous Education* 45.2 (2016): 159–69. https://doi.org/10.1017/jie.2016.6.

"Coming to Terms 30 Years on: The Mabo Legacy in Australian Writing." Association for the Study of the Australian Literature Conference, 4–8 July 2022. https://asal2022.org/.

Culler, Jonathan. "Apostrophe." *Diacritics* 7.4 (1977): 59–69. https://doi.org/10 .2307/464857.

Dale, Leigh. *The Enchantment of English.* Sydney: Sydney University Press, 2012.

Denoon, Donald. "Re-Membering Australasia: A Repressed Memory." *Australian Historical Studies* 34.122 (2003): 290–304. https://doi.org/10.1080/ 10314610308596256.

"New Zealand Country Brief." Department of Foreign Affairs and Trade, Australian Government. 2022. www.dfat.gov.au/geo/new-zealand/new-zealand-country-brief.

Dixon, R. M. W. *Australian Languages: Their Nature and Development.* 2nd ed. Cambridge: Cambridge University Press, 2004.

Dixon, Robert. "National Literatures, Scale, and the Problem of the World." *Journal of the Association for the Study of Australian Literature* 15.3 (2015). https://openjournals.library.sydney.edu.au/index.php/JASAL/article/view/ 10577.

During, Simon. *Patrick White.* Melbourne: Oxford University Press, 1996.

"Remembering, Resisting, Repeating." *Journal of New Zealand Literature* 26 (2008): 172–77.

Eckermann, Ali Cobby. *Ruby Moonlight.* Broome: Magabala Books, 2012.

Elkington, Bianca, Moana Jackson, Rebecca Kiddle, et al., *Imagining Decolonisation.* Wellington: Bridget Williams Books, 2020.

Etherington, Ben and Jarad Zimbler. "Decolonize Practical Criticism?" *English: Journal of the English Association* 70.270 (2021): 227–36. https://doi.org/10 .1093/english/efab017.

Evans, Patrick. *History of New Zealand Literature*. 2007.

First Australians. Directed by Darren Dale and Rachel Perkins. Blackfella Films. 2008.

Fitzmaurice, Andrew. "Classical Rhetoric and the Promotion of the New World." *Journal of the History of Ideas* 58.2 (1997): 221–43.

Goethe, Johann Von. *Wilhelm Meister's Apprenticeship*. New York: P.F. Collier & Son, 1917.

Greer, Germaine. *The Female Eunuch*. London: HarperPerennial, 1970.

Gunew, Sneja. "Postcolonialism and Multiculturalism: Between Race and Ethnicity." *The Yearbook of English Studies* 27 (1997): 22–39.

Heiss, Anita and Peter Minter. *The PEN Anthology of Aboriginal Literature*. Crows Nest: Allen and Unwin, 2014.

Herder, Johann. *Outlines of a Philosophy of the History of Man*. Translated by T. Churchill. London: J. Johnson, 1800.

Higgins, Katie and Terruhn, Jessica. "Kinship, Whiteness, and the Politics of Belonging Among White British Migrants and Pākchā in Aotearoa/New Zealand." *Journal of Ethnic and Migration Studies* 47.15(2021): 3564–82. https://doi.org/10.1080/1369183X.2020.1766353.

Ihimaera, Witi and Tina Makereti, eds. *Black Marks on the White Page*. Auckland: Random House New Zealand, 2017.

Kant, Immanuel. "Idea for a Universal History with a Cosmopolitan Intent." In Hans Reiss, ed., *Kant: Political Writings*. Cambridge: Cambridge University Press, 1991, 41–53.

Koch, Harold and Rachel Nordinger. "The Languages of Australia in Linguistic Research: Context and Issues." In Harold Koch and Rachel Nordinger, eds., *The Languages and Linguistics of Australia: A Comprehensive Guide*. Berlin: De Gruyter Mouton, 2014, 3–6.

Lawson, Alan. "A Cultural Paradigm for the Second World." *Australian-Canadian Studies* 9.1–2 (1991): 67–79.

Leane, Jeanine. "Aboriginal Literature in the Classroom." In Nicholas Birns, Nicole Moore, and Sarah Shieff, eds., *Teaching Australian and New Zealand Literature*. New York: The Modern Language Association of America, 2017, 237–46.

"Teaching with Black Words: Aboriginal and Torres Strait Islander Writers and Storytellers." AustLit, www.austlit.edu.au/austlit/page/14121988.

Loukakis, Angelo. "Ignoring the Creators." 23 September 2014. *Arts Hub*. www.artshub.com.au/news/opinions-analysis/ignoring-the'-creators-245914-2339810/.

Mabo, Bua Benjamin. "Living Languages." Australian Institute of Aboriginal and Torres Strait Islander Studies. https://aiatsis.gov.au/explore/living-languages.

"The Mabo Case." Australian Institute of Aboriginal and Torres Strait Islander Studies. n.d. https://aiatsis.gov.au/explore/mabo-case.

Macintyre, Stuart. *A Concise History of Australia*. Cambridge: Cambridge University Press, 2016.

Mafile'o, Tracie and Wheturangi Walsh-Tapiata. "Māori and Pasifika Indigenous Connections: Tensions and Possibilities." *AfterNative: An International Journal of Indigenous Peoples* 3.2 (2007): 128–45. https://doi.org/10.1177/117718010700300209.

Makereti, Tina. "Māori Writing: Speaking with Two Mouths." *Journal of New Zealand Studies* NS 26 (2018): 60–2. https://doi.org/10.26686/jnzs.voiNS26.4842.

Manathunga, Catherine. "The Role of Universities in Nation-Building in 1950s Australia and Aotearoa New Zealand." *History of Education Review* 35.1 (2016): 2–15. https://doi.org/10.1108/HER-05-2014-0033.

Matika, Correna M., Sam Manuela, Carla A. Houkamau, and Chris G. Sibley. "Māori and Pasifika Language, Identity, and Wellbeing in Aotearoa New Zealand." *Kōtuitui: New Zealand Journal of Social Sciences Online* 16.2(2021): 396–418. https://doi.org/10.1080/1177083X.2021.1900298.

McKay, Frank. "Editorial." *Journal of New Zealand Literature* 1 (1983): 1.

McKibbin, Philip. "In Today's New Zealand, It's Not about Being Just Māori or Pākchā – Everyone Must Belong." *The Guardian.* 10 January 2022. www.theguardian.com/world/commentisfree/2022/jan/11/in-todays-new-zealand-its-not-about-being-just-Māori-or-Pākehā-everyone-must-belong.

McMahon, Elizabeth. "A History of New Zealand Literature edited by Mark Williams." *Australian Book Review,* April 2017. www.australianbookreview.com.au/abr-online/archive/2017/3978-elizabeth-mcmahon-reviews-a-history-of-new-zealand-literature-edited-by-mark-williams.

"Encapsulated Space: The Paradise-Prison of Australia's Island Imaginary." *Southerly* 66.5 (2005): 20–30.

"The Gilded Cage: From Utopia to Monad in Australia's Island Imaginary." In Rod Edmond and Vanessa Smith, eds., *Islands in History and Representation.* London: Routledge, 2002, 190–202.

Islands Identity and the Literary Imagination. London: Anthem, 2019.

Meyrick, Julian. "Arts and Culture under the Coalition: A Lurch between Aggression and Apathy." 10 April 2019. *The Conversation.* https://theconversation.com/arts-and-culture-under-the-coalition-a-lurch-between-aggression-and-apathy-114434.

Murray Lower Darling Rivers Indigenous Nations. n.d. www.mldrin.org.au/membership/.

Nagle, Jenny. "Submission on Review of the Copyright Act 1994: Issues Paper, New Zealand Society of Authors." April 2019. https://authors.org.nz/wp-content/uploads/2019/04/Issues-Paper-April-2019-review-of-copyright-act-1994-submission-NZ-Society-of-Authors.pdf.

Neerven, Ellen van. "Invisible Spears." *Overland* 220 (2015): 74.

Throat. Queensland: University of Queensland Press, 2020.

O'Sullivan, Dominic. "Treaties and Re-setting the Colonial Relationship: Lessons for Australia from the Treaty of Waitangi." *Ethnicities* 21.6 (2021): 1070–92.

Parsons, Timothy H. *The British Imperial Century, 1815–1914: A World History Perspective.* Lanham, MD: Rowman & Littlefield, 2019

Perera, Suvendrini. *Australia and the Insular Imagination: Beaches, Borders, Boats, and Bodies*. New York: Palgrave Macmillan, 2009.

Pierce, Peter. "Forms of Australian Literary History." In Laurie Hergenhan, ed., *The Penguin New Literary History of Australia*. Ringwood: Penguin, 1988, 77–90.

Prentice, Christine and Vijay Devadas. "Postcolonial Studies and the Cultural Politics of Everyday Life." *Sites: A Journal of Social Anthropology and Cultural Studies* 5.1 (2008): 1–19.

Robin, Libby. *How a Continent Created a Nation*. Sydney: UNSW Press, 2007.

Salomone, Rosemary. *The Rise of English: Global Politics and the Power of Language*. Oxford: Oxford University Press, 2021.

Savery, Henry. *Quintus Servinton*. Hobart: Henry Melville, 1830.

Schrader, Ben. "Magazines and Periodicals – Art and Literary Magazines, 1930 to 1950." n.d. *Te Ara - the Encyclopedia of New Zealand*. www.TeAra.govt.nz/en/magazines-and-periodicals/page-4.

Scott, Kim. "A Noongar Voice: An Anomalous History." *Westerly* 53 (2008): 93–106.

Sharrad, Paul. "Albert Wendt and the Problem of History." *The Journal of Pacific History* 37.1 (2002): 109–16. https://doi.org/10.1080/00223340220139315.

"Countering Encounter: Black Voyaging after Columbus in Australia and the Caribbean." *Kunapipi: Journal of Postcolonial Writing* 15.3 (1993): 58–72.

Smith, Linda Tuhiwai. *Decolonizing Methodologies: Research and Indigenous Peoples*. London: Bloomsbury Academic, 2012.

Smits, Katherine. "Multiculturalism, Biculturalism, and National Identity in Aotearoa/New Zealand." In Richard T. Ashcroft and Mark Bevir, eds., *Multiculturalism in the British Commonwealth: Comparative Perspectives on Theory and Practice*. Berkeley: University of California Press, 2019, 104–24. https://library.oapen.org/handle/20.500.12657/43719.

Stavanger, David and Anne-Marie Te Whiu. *Sold Air: Australian and New Zealand Spoken Word*. St. Lucia: University of Queensland Press, 2019.

Summers, Anne. *Damned Whores and God's Police* [1975]. Coogee: New South, 2016.

Te Punga Somerville, Alice. "Reading as Cousins: Indigenous Texts, Pacific Bookshelves." Dorothy Green Memorial Lecture: Association for the Study of Australian Literature Congress, 4–8 July 2022.

Tuck, E. and K. Wayne Yang. "Decolonization Is Not a METAPHOR." *Decolonization: Indigeneity, Education & Society* 1.1 (2012): 1–40.

Universities Australia. "Indigenous Strategy 2022–2025." n.d. www.universitiesaustralia.edu.au/publication/indigenous-strategy-2022-25/.

Universities New Zealand. "Te Kāhui Amokura Strategic Work Plan." n.d. www.universitiesnz.ac.nz/latest-news-and-publications/te-k%C4%81hui-amokura-strategic-work-plan.

Wendt, Albert. "Inside 'outsider' Wendt." *New Zealand Bookworld* 8 (Feb.–Mar. 1974): 6.

"Stepping Stones." *Poetry Magazine*, February 2018.

www.poetryfoundation.org/poetrymagazine/poems/145486/stepping-stones.

Wevers, Lydia. "Being Pakeha: The Politics of Location." *The Journal of New Zealand Studies* 4.5 (2006). https://doi.org/10.26686/jnzs.voi4/5.104.

"The View from Here: Readers and Australian Literature." *Journal of the Association for the Study of Australian Literature: JASAL*, special issue, *Australian Literature in a Global World* (2009): 1–10.

Williams, Mark. *A History of New Zealand Literature*. Cambridge: Cambridge University Press, 2016.

Wright, Alexis. *Carpentaria*. Artarmon: Giramondo, 2006.

CHAPTER 5

Genders, Sexualities, and Decolonial Methodologies

Brinda Bose

A Fistful of Critical Lineages

The words I use shift from desire to explore to reflect to question to deconstruct to interrogate to contest to disrupt to hope to decolonise. They are deployed for a specific purpose: to tangle up and tangle down what it means to live and work in-between: on the borders, on the edge, across, through and with difference: alongside knowing, being and doing I describe as intersubjective, intercorporeal, and intercultural. I think these words give me a way into, to *inter*.

Elizabeth Mackinlay, *Autoethnography, Feminism and Decoloniality*

To restore passion to the classroom or to excite it in classrooms where it has never been, professors must find again the place of eros within ourselves and together allow the mind and body to feel and know desire.

bell hooks, "Eros, Eroticism and the Pedagogical Process," *Teaching to Transgress*

There is no "object of study" that decoloniality can exhaust. Objects or events will always exceed decoloniality; there is no single method that will exhaust the objects or events. Decoloniality is an option among others.

Walter D. Mignolo, "On Decoloniality: Second Thoughts"

This book is an amorous gesture, a dedication to another kind of sexual future. It is an episode of language that reaches for the possibility that something else awaits us. This gesture is a kind of touching, a way of sensing what might flow between us. It is sexual in the queerest of ways, meant to inspire intense feeling rather than reproduction; it is multisensory, asynchronic, polysemous, perverse, and full of promise.

Juana María Rodríguez, *Sexual Futures, Queer Gestures, and Other Latina Longings*

a decolonial perspective on gender means conceptualizing the
category of gender as always already trans.

Alyosxa Tudor, "Decolonizing Trans/Gender Studies?"

Literatures, like Genders and Sexualities, Are a Palimpsest

I wish to take from Walter D. Mignolo the call for deconstructing in
decolonial mode – "decoloniality shall focus on changing the terms of the
conversation that would change the content" (Mignolo and Walsh 144) –
and run with it via genders and sexualities to think about multiple,
daring, trans/gressive methodologies for the English literary curriculum.
I am not invested in cancel cultures, and my brief therefore is not to
throw out (fictional or theoretical) texts of the West to replace them with
those of the non-West; the decolonial method offers possibilities,
I believe, to engage with literature historically and geopolitically as well
as critically, and in those spaces to attempt to change the terms of
interrogation, discourse, and discussion. In giving this essay its title,
I wanted to emphasize the plurals – gender*s*, sexualitie*s*, methodologie*s* –
as I consider plurality the first and necessary expansion that decolonization invites: a sense of breaking open boundaries imposed by the (once)
institutionalized and therefore more powerful critical praxis to let in
multifarious, conflicted ideas that kaleidoscopically create new and
recalibrated patterns of reading and writing.

I take what Walter Mignolo and Catherine Walsh formulate as "*pluriversal decoloniality* and *decolonial pluriversality*" (2), a sense of spaciousness
in investigating and engaging with all that has been inherited from modernity and coloniality. I distance myself from those understandings of
decolonial practice that seek to discard and replace: for literatures, like
genders and sexualities, are a palimpsest, they build on waves of what is
experienced and encountered through lineages; there are deaths and memories as well as traces and continuities, and I would want that they all be
folded in, for the reading, teaching, and writing experience to be, as bell
hooks outlines, exciting and passionate – and as Mignolo insists, exceeding
the "object of study." A palimpsest, to me, does not have a goal of
betterment: it is simply a layering of innocence with experience, in
which the most recent layer is lost yet again through a covering, but in
which all layers can be exposed again to be encountered afresh when
unpeeled: there is a telos, but it can also be overturned.

Octavio Paz, in an essay on Jean-Paul Sartre upon his death, writes: "much that he said, even when he erred, seems to me essential. Let me state it differently: essential *for us*, his contemporaries. Sartre lived the ideas, the battles and tragedies of our age with the intensity with which others live out their private dramas. He was a conscience and a passion" ("Memento"). Paz is as forthright about Sartre as he says Sartre was about his ideas and opinions: he does not dismiss Sartre for his erring words but embraces them as essential, and he does not dismiss "passion" in contradistinction to "conscience" but weighs them in together. Paz was an exemplar of the Mexican avant-garde in his poetry and essays and continually engaged with many artists (of the Global North) who are easily dismissed from within fixed frames of sexual morality and aesthetics, such as the Marquis de Sade and Marcel Duchamp. Instead, he retrieved them and held them up to critical light and insight. I would wish to work with this as a decolonial method, to revisit old and new frameworks of genders and sexualities for literary studies via avant-garde modernisms – in themselves an exemplar of the excessively nonconformist. Keeping many thinkers and poets as unruly talismans thrown together in an unruly manner, I want to look at paradigms of gendered/sexual signs to rethink pedagogies and research methodologies for English literature in the Global South: what could be a template to read historically, critically, and imaginatively across and between Western and non-Western texts with an incisive, generous, difficult passion that marks all erotic pursuit as errant and explosive, even the intellectual?

Sukanta Chaudhuri writes in *The Metaphysics of Text*, "We read texts in more or less stable states captured in time . . . We can cite those stable states to oppose a more problematized notion of the text, as Dr Johnson refuted Berkeley's idealism by kicking at a stone. But the text, like the stone, was not always in that state; and its formation can only be explained in terms of other forces and other orders of being" (4). Indeed, one cannot hope to penetrate any text with some reasonable understanding without the penumbra that surrounds it, an understanding of where it drew its layers of being from, metaphysically as well as physically, and what makes it lodge itself in the present moment with the possibility of dislodgement always already imminent. Alongside I may place Marjorie Perloff's recent study, *Infrathin: An Experiment in Micropoetics*, in which she draws from Marcel Duchamp's *Notes* on *infrathin/inframince* (1980), a method of reading where one reads minutely, through marking *difference* which is "*infrathin*": as Perloff interprets it, Duchamp iterates "that the same is never the same, and that hence every word, every morpheme and phoneme, and every rhythmic form chosen makes a difference" (6). The poet creates relationships – between words, images, contexts – that have *infrathin* possibilities of difference, and the reader comes to poetry with an eye to telling this difference.

Strung between the vastness of metaphysical forces and orders of being that surround a text (Chaudhuri) and the *infrathin* difference of micro-poetics as a method of reading/writing (Perloff) lie, I suggest, multiple possibilities of a different, decolonial practice, erotic for being quick with uncontained and turbulent promise. If these two methods – of studying the penumbra, and of diving into the text with a pointed eye that exposes shifting meanings of words and sounds and offers new insights – appear to be contradistinctive, they are meant to be so: somewhere in the chasm that yawns between metaphysics (penumbra) and physics (*infrathin*) the shadow may lift, if only momentarily, to light up a third possibility of reading.

Walter Mignolo talks of the centrality of knowledge creation, and its locations: "it is composed of actors, languages, and institutions. The institutions involved are mainly colleges, universities, museums, research centers (think tanks), institutes, foundations, and religious organizations" (Mignolo and Walsh 143). We are particularly concerned here with insti-tutions of higher education, and pedagogies and curricula for English literary studies – that which is at base a colonial practice. It would be easiest to wish to decolonize it by stripping it of its existence in the Global South, and to replace it with whatever is at the other end of the spectrum, untouched by the experience of the colonial. Is this possible? Can any knowledge be divested of its traces of the past? Should all literatures in English – not to mention critical writing – from the once and future colonizing territories be expunged, and a tabula rasa decolonial script be inscribed solely in noncolonizer/once-colonized tongues? Will the erasure of content erase the terms of the conversation – and how would conver-sation ensue, from nothing? If literature, and the teaching-learning of literature in the classroom, "must find again the place of eros within ourselves" as hooks sharply admonishes (199), would a homogeneous, secure, shared sense of origin with no fraught histories, located in the comfort zone of the familiar and acceptable, be the best impulse for the erotic?

Mignolo acknowledges three thinkers whose formulations on freedom and coloniality helped him construct his own theory of the decolonial – Gloria Anzaldúa (*Borderlands/La Frontera*, 1987), Aníbal Quijano ("Coloniality and Modernity/Rationality," 2007), and Rodolfo Kusch

(*Buenos Aires*, 1962) – to explain why he does not merely discard Western philosophers to replace them with the non-Western ("On Decoloniality" 1). Of Kusch, who studied Indigenous thinking of the Aymara population of northern Argentina and Bolivia, he sums up succinctly: "He reversed the geography of reasoning: instead of 'studying' Aymara's thoughts from Heidegger, he interrogated Heidegger through Aymara's thought" (1). In this traffic, Heidegger is not *replaced* but *displaced*. To me, this is far edgier in its politics, more erotic if one will, not to bluntly discard the enemy but to insinuate a wedge of suspicion, discomfort, and disentitlement that rocks the boat of power (what Mignolo calls the "colonial matrix of power," or the "CMP"). And this sharply political displacement can be pushed further, into conversation with both Mackinlay's living desire in-between, the "inter" – "intersubjective, intercorporeal, and intercultural" (155) – and Tudor's "category of gender as always already trans" (238).

Of Being Adrift and Reckless among Many Unknowns

Between *inter* and *trans* may fall the shadow: of hanging between, of bridging, or of shifting. There is always a strange tautness, for example, in poetry of the gendered body, about the sexed body – as if the body of the poem is exceeded by the shape of its words, always greater in the imagination before it is confined to a page. Poems of the body in particular seem to speak to each other across distances of space, time, and culture, often at counterpoint, sometimes throwing up uncanny echoes: creating conversations interspersed by shifts and fractures. I was struck by a concretization of this sense while browsing poetry: in an online competition inviting illustrations of poetry, three poems were listed from an eclectic collection of love poems selected and edited by Imtiaz Dharker. The poems, each electric, seemed to shoot sparks at each other when placed in conjunction: John Donne's "The Good-Morrow," Emily Dickinson's "Wild Nights – Wild Nights!," and Dharker's own "The Trick." Competing illustrators vied to come up with visuals for this set of poems, imaging assonances and dissonances, critical and creative minds coming together and pulling apart in this exercise. So much learning and expansion of thought, along with a sense of being adrift and reckless among many unknowns: both are achieved at the same time. This is a livewire method of exploring sexualities – throwing selected writings from varied sources together which exhibit some echoes and overlaps, and reading them closely for all that one may glean of and from them, together and separately, in their expressions and transgressions as well as their histories and geopolitics – and would work

well in the literature classroom to shake the teaching-learning experience
out of routine explicatory exercises.

From the three poems, I pick some lines to place against each other:

> Let maps to other, worlds on worlds have shown,
> Let us possess one world, each hath one, and is one.
> My face in thine eye, thine in mine appears
>
> Donne, "The Good-Morrow"

> Done with the Compass –
> Done with the Chart!
> Rowing in Eden –
> Ah – the Sea!
> Might I but moor – tonight –
> In thee!
>
> Dickinson, "Wild Nights – Wild Nights!"

> In a wasted time, it's only when I sleep
> that all my senses come awake. In the wake
> of you, let day not break. Let me keep
> the scent, the weight, the bright of you, take
> the countless hours and count them all night through
>
> Dharker, "The Trick"

A fascinating map of love, sex, time, space, exploration, dream, and
longing emerges from the poems when read with and against each other,
in their entirety of course – but even in extracts. From this map, multiple
senses of history, geography, knowledge, culture, gender, form, and the
imaginations of the three poets – completely distinct in location and age –
are extracted, and a cross-section of ideas and expressions around lovers'
bodies across oceans and time derived. Donne, English Metaphysical poet
of the seventeenth century, envisions love and the lover's body in the
wonder of exploration and the ultimate discovery of "worlds" in each
other. Dickinson, young, isolated American poet of the nineteenth century
who was herself "discovered" posthumously, is still communing with the
charts and compasses of exploration – a central preoccupation of the
Western world from the fifteenth to the twentieth centuries – but rejects
them in favor of mooring in the haven of a lover's body. Dickinson's
distinctive poetic style and form, comprising staccato phrases and hung
sentences, exclamation points, capitalization, and the liberal use of the dash
that identifies her like no other, puts the similarity with Donne's immersion in the lovers' bodies out to sea, marking difference. Dickinson, writing
in secret, can afford an abandon in her utterances (even as a young woman

reared in conservative New England and schooled in a seminary) that Donne, a scholar-poet, a worldly man of many pursuits, including women, who finally became a dean of the Church of England, would hardly have been inclined toward. Dharker, a British poet of South Asian descent writing from the late twentieth century into the present, returns to the image of lovers at night with a distinct shift in mood and visualities, though the focus still hovers on the body and its sexual gratification. The cadence is more akin to prose conversation, the sexualized images more graphically daring – and yet the echoes with Donne and Dickinson reverberate.

Goaded by the dialogic possibilities of grouping a set of poems to read between and across, I offer three more poems from distant locations and tongues, which are, however, from poets broadly analogous in time. These may seem like collations common enough to world literature courses or anthologies, but my emphasis is on an unworlding rather than a worlding, and it works outside of marking specificities of location, culture, and time to explore forms and shapes of language and meanings that meet and splinter at once; the "penumbra" and the "*infrathin*" of the text as word. These poems are slotted under modernist to postmodernist/postcolonial in literary histories to provide rich material for a decolonial investigation into poems of/on the body speaking from diverse locations: "Corona" by Paul Celan, "Counterparts" by Octavio Paz, and "The Prisoner" by Kamala Das. While "Corona" is a slightly longer poem, "Counterparts" and "The Prisoner" are four and six lines each; all three focus on a single moment of intense physical togetherness, when the mind strays to hope, longing, fear – despite, or because of, bodily proximity. The first lines of each of the three poems set up the dramatic scenes of encounter:

> Autumn eats its leaf out of my hand: we are friends.
>
> Paul Celan, "Corona"

> In my body you search the mountain
>
> Octavio Paz, "Counterparts"

> As the convict studies
> his prison's geography
>
> Kamala Das, "The Prisoner"

I shall read a single image from each, to then expand into a larger understanding and critical knowledge of each poet's literary being and oeuvre.

> My eye goes down to my lover's sex:
> we gaze at each other,
> we speak of dark things
>
> Celan, "Corona"

> In your body I search for the boat
> adrift in the middle of the night.
>
> Paz, "Counterparts"

> I study the trappings
> of your body, dear love,
> for I must some day find
> an escape from its snare.
>
> Das, "The Prisoner"

In immense intimacy, a shadow descends: this is the bare, perhaps incomparable truth of sexual love and longing. Celan, Paz, and Das are avant-garde modernist poets from distant continents, each groping to find words in their own languages of poetry to make sense of this shadow that is an inevitable corollary to desire's immersion in the body of a lover. The Romanian-born poet in German Celan is known for speaking "of dark things" in the history and politics of the Western world; here it is remaindered to the quietest act of intimate speech, when there is almost no physical space between lovers. Paradoxically enough, this possibility of speaking – especially of "dark things" – when physically intimate or imagining/anticipating intimacy, is what makes such moments memorable, difficult, exquisite. Paz, Mexican poet, diplomat, and literary scholar, steered his poetry around politics and/of sexualities, searching not for moorings but for "the boat adrift in the middle of the night" in the lover's body: for desire is to lose, rather than find, oneself in the other. A boat adrift invokes the impossibility of language, poignant too for those reading in translation: however close a translation is in letter and spirit, it can only approximate the original.

Searching for a boat adrift in the dark is to search for meaning in what cannot be apprehended; as T. S. Eliot (whom Paz admired greatly) has it in "Little Gidding,"

> Not known, because not looked for
> But heard, half-heard, in the stillness
> Between two waves of the sea.

Fellow Mexican critic Ramón Xirau has a sharp comment on Paz's poetic play: "The poetry of Octavio Paz does not hesitate between language and silence; it leads into the realm of silence where true language lives" (219). One could propel it further along to think about what Paz does with a lover's longing to find in the body of the beloved "a boat adrift in the middle of the night": what, then, is the equivalence of being adrift in a body one is intimate with, if not to be continually lost and searching, continually distanced and desiring? And what does it mean, in the poem, for two lovers' desire for each other to be couched in two seemingly apposite metaphors from nature – a sun hidden in mountain forests, a boat adrift in the middle of the night – both evocative of a search, perhaps a futile one?

Kamala Das, fiery feminist Indian poet who wrote with equal felicity in her vernacular tongue Malayalam and in English, drives the knife of antagonism deep into the wedge between lovers' bodies in her short and succinct poem, "The Prisoner," where she imagines the beloved as a jailer, both from whose confinement and in whose body she must seek escape. The contradiction is as inescapable as the lover's predicament as "the prisoner": she must "study the trappings" of her lover's body closely – seek and find greater intimacy and knowledge in her explorations – so that she can plot her escape from its "snare." The poem is centered on the line "I study the trappings of your body, dear love" following on "As the convict studies / his prison's geography": the extended metaphor of a map (of her prison) runs through the entire six-line poem, a prison that is her lover's body, which she scrutinizes minutely in order to map a path for getting out. Or so she says. The trap is in the endearment, "dear love," carelessly appended to an apparently dire pronouncement; it balances the "snare" as Celan balances speaking of "dark things" with the line that follows it in "Corona" – "we love each other like poppy and memory" – and Paz has two perfect images for the two lovers, of traveling the body in four lines: one searching "the mountain / for the sun buried in its forest" and the other for a boat adrift on the water in the middle of the night.

This journey across poetic triads in languages, time, space, silences, and images that echo and separate, takes us around again to Elizabeth Mackinlay when she talks (quoted in the chapter epigraph) of finding "a way in, to *inter*" via decoloniality – albeit in the discipline of ethnomusicology – as the route she traces is one that can well be borrowed or stolen for literature: "to tangle up and tangle down what it means to live and work in-between: on the borders, on the edge, across, through and with difference" (155). A singular way to decolonize is clearly to upset the applecart of established teaching-learning frameworks that categorize and separate writers into boxes that cannot be messed with or tangled up. The politics of genders/sexualities point us to a very basic principle of deconstructing immovable frames: that they must be tangled up and tangled down and shifted around so that their paradigms are shaken and stirred, to fall into new and changing patterns of perception and knowledge. To be decolonial, one must not be afraid to sail into territories marked different – for difference, as Mackinlay quotes French feminist thinker and theorist Hélène Cixous, is the word that everything comes back to, in the end (156). To decolonize is to *inter*, to find one's way into established and bounded texts and categories, and as genders are and sexualities do, tie them up and tie them down, into and out of knots of one's own intricate making. What emerges at the end is an untying and an unknotting that disinters and discombobulates even as it produces new substances of wonder and curiosity.

Queer Method: "Sexual in the Queerest of Ways"

My interest in the decolonial is located in the boiler room of methodologies, where ideas about approaches bubble and steam – in Mignolo's *pluriversal* mode, as claiming a single efficacious method to "do" decoloniality would overturn the premise of heterogeneity and difference in which I have a critical stake – what one could call, in shorthand, genderqueer methods of doing the humanities. In a warm and generous call for new "sexual futures" spun by "Latina longings," Juana María Rodríguez opens her book by defining it as "an amorous gesture," and a queer one: "This gesture is a kind of touching, a way of sensing what might flow between us. It is sexual in the queerest of ways, meant to inspire intense feeling rather than reproduction; it is multisensory, asynchronic, polysemous, perverse, and full of promise" (1). There is little that can be stable and conserved amid such immense fluidity, polysemy, perversity: it can only upend and turn the expected around, and then around again, till one's known universe is trembling on the verge of endlessly new births. Suniti Namjoshi, feminist fabulist, had mocked our known universes thus:

> "And then, of course,"
> she was saying,
> "we have grown so great
> that now we dream
> only of the possible."
>
> "Altitudes"

Namjoshi was among the first known queer poets to venture into impossible territories for her poetic form, and her feminist fables opened up a new vista for poetry and prose from the then fairly young stables of Indian English writing in the late decades of the twentieth century.

It is necessary and important to distinguish between queer methods for the social sciences and the humanities, as queer aesthetics have a playing field that is quite unique, allowing im/possibilities of form and content that are factored in by the freedom of creative imagination and impelled by the need, if not demand, to be always already different. In a special issue of the *WSQ: Women's Studies Quarterly* in 2016 titled "Queer Methods," its editors Matt Brim and Amin Ghaziani begin their introduction by claiming a space for method over theory ("Queer studies is experiencing a methodological renaissance. In both the humanities and the social sciences, scholars have begun to identify research protocols and practices that have been largely overshadowed by dramatic advances in queer theory" [14]) and then go on to trace the reluctant recognition of "queer methods" in the broad disciplines, together and separately. As Brim and Ghaziani posit, it was not as if the early scholars who worked toward establishing gay and lesbian studies were not using queer methods, but that they were chary of delineating them as such as "that might have threatened queer theory's constitutional claims to inter/antidisciplinarity" (15). Along with a nascent queer method, there appeared to be an "overriding queer suspicion of method . . . Framed as a watershed . . . queer theory could then do new intellectual work: work unrestrained by identities, disciplinarities, and traditional methods" (16). However, as they note, this was an overwhelming paradox, for queer theory's use of self-narration/self-invention was nothing if not a methodological intervention and inquiry.

More recently, this wariness about claiming a method for queer academic work has waned, and along with this, perhaps, the distinction between methods for the social sciences and the humanities has become clearer. In the social sciences, queer methods reject empiricism as ultimate knowledge and generalizations as unviable, giving space to subjective narratives and embracing "multiplicity, misalignments, and silences" (Brim and Ghaziani 17). In the humanities, Brim and Ghaziani write, the changes have been manifold, coming from multiple quarters – feminist/queer, trans, non-White and non-Western – introducing distinctly resistant and intimate archival/imaginative methods of doing queer scholarship to the Anglo-American origins of LGBTQ studies. Juana María

Rodríguez offers a felt account of these, and also other, winds of change in her book that explores sexual futures and queer gestures:

> Thinking about queerness through gesture animates how bodies move in the world, and how we assign meaning in ways that are always already infused with cultural modes of knowing. The gestures that I take up in this book are about the social and the sexual: the social as that force of connection and communion that binds us to friends and strangers, and the sexual as that tangled enactment of psychic encounters that promise ecstasy and abjection. (2)

The humanities, in not being tied to empirical data and analytics, allows for expansions and contractions beyond the categories of identity catalogued by Brim and Ghaziani – along with agreements and disagreements, shock, surprise, horror, pain, and joy – that can fold into itself what Rodríguez's gestures call for, multiple entanglements "that promise ecstasy and abjection," flying above and below singularities of color and community. Many of these entanglements call for comparison, contradiction, resistance, and rejection, along with abjection, hurt, and sadness – through to the other end of the spectrum: ecstasy, wonder, thrill, love, passion, beauty. The humanities is capacious enough to hold these in changing shapes, to examine them and interrogate them, to embrace them or discard them, but always to engage – which is why they do not need to reject any of their pasts or antecedents, but keep them in necessary and critical circulation as they enlarge or shrink their ambit at will, much like the social encounters and sexual entanglements one sieves in the course of living. Brim and Ghaziani reference a range of new critical queer thinking in the humanities, in which Phillip Brian Harper argues for "speculative rumination" making space for "guesswork and conjecture"; Peter Coviello for "long exposure" to texts; Heather Love for "close reading and thin description"; Paisley Currah for a "provisional and generative" transgender feminist methodology that is modeled on gender asymmetry rather than neutrality or plurality (18–19). Drawing upon these queer methods for literature will mean upending traditional methodologies: not by replacing them, but by accepting the path of "complex returns" to intellectual, social, and political inheritances, and by creating a space of interaction with them for new methods to emerge that will propel conversations forward.

Alyosxa Tudor in "Decolonising Trans/Gender Studies?" makes a brief but remarkable statement that invites the decolonial project for genders/sexualities to recognize gender's inherent and sustained characteristic of shape-shifting – "a decolonial perspective on gender means conceptualizing

the category of gender as always already trans" (238) – which finds
a promising equivalence in literary studies. To conceptualize – understand,
recognize, and imagine – the shape of a category of identification as changing, shifting, chameleon-like, is to question the essential nature of that
identity, expected to be always already stable. What does this mean for
a method of study? It means at base that a queer method should neither seek
stability in the representations or discussions of gender that it studies, nor
aspire to be stable and unchanging in its ways of apprehending them.
"Always already trans" then opens up possibilities not just for the present
and future, but also for the past: this is to me particularly significant, for it
allows revisits to stubborn pasts that can also now be seen as "always already"
shifting and uncertain.

While the dismissal of radical positions that use "a simplistic understanding of sexual violence to legitimize feminist transphobia" (Tudor 244)
in the West, and some strains of antigender debates in the Global South
(Tudor 245), are well taken, Tudor clarifies that "trans-ing gender"
involves the crucial practice of *criticizing* and *interrupting* (249) dominant
Western scripts and methods for doing trans/gender studies – and therefore, not *dismissing* them to cater to neoliberal academia's fetishes:

> I see the endeavor of decolonizing higher education as a necessarily
> multilayered and collective process that pays attention to gaps, complex
> contradictions, and differently positioned complicities. In my view, any
> decolonization must bridge diaspora approaches with approaches from
> the global South, connect indigenous studies with migration studies,
> and question the paradigm of the nation-state. Moreover, feminist,
> queer, and trans perspectives and their deconstructions of gender and
> sexuality are crucial for decolonizing epistemologies and spaces. (250)

The assimilation of a new literary curriculum anywhere in the world
must be a similar process, accruing to itself multiplicities of content and
method, both of which come naturally to gender and sexuality studies. If
far more destabilizing queer/trans methods of critical interrogation can be
imported into literary studies – those that begin and continue with a strong
and clear sense of the various layers that constitute a text, its changing
histories, its assonances and dissonances, its own shifts in shape as well as
critical and/or resistant responses to it – then a more contemporary and
political approach to literary studies via trans-ing is possible. This will be
distinct from other methods – such as feminist, Marxist – that also seek to
destabilize established structures of power in narratives, by focusing on the
body, or shape, of the text, in how words carry (or fail to carry, as Jack

Halberstam claims movingly and eruditely in *The Queer Art of Failure*, 2011) the brunt of its meanings, and how the text itself is never rigid for its masses of readers across time and space. It is crucial to see instability and uncertainty as richness and depth rather than as shortcomings, in order to embrace the shape-and-color-shifting nature of a text as a characteristic that gives and gives.

Heather Love in her short, succinct essay "Queer Messes," in the *WSQ* Special issue on "Queer Methods," cautions: "Because it is not merely an epistemological conflict, the tension between *queer* and *method* can never be resolved. Rather, this tension is material – and here to stay" (347). This, I would think, is especially felicitous for a transhistorical, transnational, and difficult matter such as a curriculum for literature, that the tension between identity and method is irresolvable, material, and here to stay. It is the only way into, and "to *inter*," as Mackinlay had it, the unruly, transforming realities and fantasies that make up literature, wedging one's gaze in the "*infrathin*" difference between uncertain knowledges of the gendered material body that is "always already trans," and the shifting, textured, layered materiality of the text.

Coda

This essay – this text – wishes to be a shape-shifter: to constrict and expand, to engorge and contract, changing through its encounters with various other words and texts, poetic and critical, as it meanders toward this coda – to end by reaching out to touch the symbolic and the elemental. It attempts to challenge the governmental/colonial/institutional/academic sense of how a reading must proceed, how it should set out all parameters of its argument at the start, how it should contain the number of poets it alludes to, how it should explain each line it quotes and reference its referent in the argument – by spilling over its edges, repeating, constricting, layering (like the palimpsest I claimed as a metaphor for literatures and genders/sexualities at the start) – hoping that some thought here, some idea or poetry there, will echo like a footfall in the reader's vast repertoire of conscious and unconscious readings and experiences. That the exploration of "trans-ing" appears as a late thought in the sequence of writing in this essay about trans/gressive erotic methods of critical reading is deliberate: it wants to be that layer in this essay that is discovered only to uncover those that lie beneath it (of feminist theories of the social, for example), to revisit and revise even as one reads or writes. Trans-ing brings us closer to the body like no other – the body of the self, the lover, the parent, the child, the other, the poem, the word – and keeps us there insistently in its discomfiting materiality of presence, reaching out to nudge and touch us into confronting all that shakes us out of ease. I cannot emphasize enough how capacious and enriching this unease is and must be, and how its failures are as illuminative as its successes: for opening up, for striking down, for unbuilding, for unworlding, for decolonizing those seemingly large boxes within which we are told we must operate in our critical forays into literatures, genders, sexualities.

I will end by lighting a path through a few texts that excavate this body and this touch. Henri Cole, contemporary American poet, writes of sycamores and the burning human body that emerges from and melts into its limbs, "touching across some new barrier of touchability":

> I came from a place with a hole in it,
> my body once its body, behind a beard of hair.
> And after I emerged, all dripping wet,
> little drops came out of my eyes, touching its face.
> I kissed its mouth; I bit it with my gums.
>
> "Sycamores"

Cole makes a series of astonishingly erotic moves between and beyond the human and natural worlds, "I lay on it like a snail on a cup, / my body, whatever its nature was, / revealed to me by its body": we are not sure what "it" is, but there "was a hard, gemlike feeling . . . like limbs of burning sycamores." The approximation, the signifier, the measure of everything that is experienced as bodily sensation, is this liquid and fiery thing, *the limbs of burning sycamores*. The body *inters* and *trans*-es in this one fluid movement. Its beauty is, and shrivels, simultaneously – "I did not know I was powerless before a strange force. / I did not know life cheats us" – but this intensely erotic contradiction is still "touching/across some new barrier of touchability."

In a study "on touching and not touching" across (old, constructed) barriers of un/touchability between humans alone in a specific historical and cultural context, Aniket Jaaware reads carefully between elements and forms of touch and notes that while elements of touch are common to all touch, "touch, however, has only one *form*, which is that of contact. It can be seen, we believe, that contact itself is of a two-fold nature: It is the *form* of touch, and at the same time, the *content*" (21). In social realities, the form and content of touch may diverge to create disturbances and dislocations, while in the philosophical and creative imagination, it is possible for these barriers and fissures to dissolve, engendering new and changing patterns of touch that rarely ossify.

Octavio Paz, in reading the Marquis de Sade philosophically and aesthetically in *An Erotic Beyond: Sade*, talks of the necessary and "universal dissolution" of erotic barriers between the living and nonliving if one is not to live as an automaton: "There is nothing more concrete than this table, that tree, that mountain . . . they only become abstract through the force of a will that uses them or a consciousness that thinks them. Turned into instruments or concepts, they abandon their reality; they cease to be these things, but they continue to be things" (*Erotic Beyond*, 53). Paz demurs that the psyche of the libertine treats fellow humans as "erotic objects": he "does not desire the disappearance of the other consciousness. He conceives of it as a negative reality: neither concrete existence nor abstract instrument . . . The erotic object is neither a consciousness or a tool, but rather a relation, or more exactly, a function: something that lacks autonomy and that changes in accordance with the changes of the terms that determine it" (*Erotic Beyond*, 54–55).

The changing literary erotic object finally comes to rest in language: language that is inherited and tussled with, like the poet's inspiration, and language that is elusive and transforming, like the beloved's, which the poet both touches and cannot ever fully touch. In Kashmiri-American poet Agha Shahid Ali's lyrics that give a new embodiment to the *ghazal* form, the veins of the poet imprison the blood of his poetic ancestor; in turn he transforms his inspiration into another language, trapping form and lineage even while transgressing tongues. In a succession of bodies, poetry enacts a bloodline and its exile at once:

> Your lines were measured
> so carefully to become in our veins
> the blood of prisoners. In the free verse
> of another language I imprisoned
> each line – but I touched my own exile.
>
> "Homage to Faiz Ahmed Faiz," 58

WORKS CITED

Ali, Agha Shahid. "Homage to Faiz Ahmed Faiz." In *The Veiled Suite: The Collected Poems*. New York: Penguin, 2009.

Brim, Matt and Amin Ghaziani. "Introduction." *WSQ: Women's Studies Quarterly*, special issue, "Queer Methods," 44.3/4 (2016): 3–27.

Celan, Paul. *Memory Rose into Threshold Speech: The Collected Earlier Poetry*. Translated by Pierre Joris. New York: Farrar, Straus and Giroux, 2020.

"Corona." https://poets.org/poem/corona.

Chaudhuri, Sukanta. *The Metaphysics of Text*. Cambridge: Cambridge University Press, 2010.

Cole, Henri. "Sycamores." www.theparisreview.org/poetry/7255/sycamores-henri-cole.

Das, Kamala. *Kamala Das: Selected Poems*, ed. with an Introduction by Devindra Kohli. Gurgaon: Penguin, 2014.

Dharker, Imtiaz. *Love Poems Selected and Edited by Imtiaz Dharker*. www.behance.net/gallery/92338701/Love-Poems-Selected-And-Edited-By-Imtiaz-Dharker.

Eliot, T. S. "Little Gidding." www.columbia.edu/itc/history/winter/w3206/edit/tseliotlittlegidding.html.

Halberstam, Jack. *The Queer Art of Failure*. Durham, NC: Duke University Press, 2011.

hooks, bell. *Teaching to Transgress: Education as the Practice of Freedom*. Delhi: Taylor & Francis, 2017.

Jaaware, Aniket. *Practicing Caste: On Touching and Not Touching*. Hyderabad: Orient Blackswan, 2019.

Love, Heather. "Queer Messes." *WSQ: Women's Studies Quarterly* 44.3/4 (2016): 345–49.

Mackinlay, Elizabeth. *Critical Writing for Embodied Approaches: Autoethnography, Feminism and Decoloniality*. Cham: Palgrave Macmillan, 2019.

Mignolo, Walter D. "On Decoloniality: Second Thoughts." *Postcolonial Studies* 23.4 (2020): 612–18. https://doi.org/10.1080/13688790.2020.1751436.

Mignolo, Walter D. and Catherine E. Walsh. *On Decoloniality: Concepts, Analytics, Praxis*. Durham, NC: Duke University Press, 2018.

Namjoshi, Suniti. *The Jackass and the Lady*. Writers Workshop, 1980. www.poemist.com/suniti-namjoshi/altitudes.

Paz, Octavio. *An Erotic Beyond: Sade*. Translated by Eliot Weinberger. New York: Harcourt, Brace and Company, 1998.

"Memento: Jean-Paul Sartre." *PN Review* 35: 10.3 (1984). www.pnreview.co.uk/cgi-bin/scribe?item_Fid=8112.

The Poems of Octavio Paz. 1973. Ed. and translated by Eliot Weinberger. New York: New Directions, 2012.

Perloff, Marjorie. *Infrathin: An Experiment in Micropoetics*. Chicago: University of Chicago Press, 2021.

Rodríguez, Juana María. *Sexual Futures, Queer Gestures, and Other Latina Longings*. New York: New York University Press, 2014.

Tudor, Alyosxa. "Decolonizing Trans/Gender Studies? Teaching Gender, Race, and Sexuality in Times of the Rise of the Global Right." *TSQ: Transgender Studies Quarterly* 8.2 (2021): 238–56.

Xirau, Ramón. *Entre la poesia y el conocimiento: Antologia de ensayos criticos sobre poetas y poesia iberoamericanos*. Mexico City: Fondo de Cultura Económica, 2004.

CHAPTER 6

Black British Literature Decolonizing the Curriculum

Ankhi Mukherjee

The pioneering cultural theorist and sociologist Stuart Hall saw in the works of Frantz Fanon, a "re-epidermalisation, an auto-graphy," a new politics of the Black signifier (27). Fanon's *Black Skin, White Masks* turns the mechanisms of fixed racial signification against themselves in order to begin to constitute new subjectivities, new positions of identification and enunciation. Speaking at a conference on film, performance, and visual arts work by contemporary Black artists at the Institute of Contemporary Arts (ICA), Hall dwells on the "spectral effect," the ghost of Fanon, the colonial man who wrote for his people. "Rather than trying to recapture the true Fanon, we must try to engage the after-life of Frantz Fanon . . . in ways that do not simply restore the past in a cycle of the eternal return, but which will bring the enigma of Fanon, as Benjamin said of history, flashing up before us at a moment of danger" (14).

As is widely known, Fanon wrote *Peau noire, masques blancs* (translated into English in 1967) while preparing for the exams that would enable him to join the august ranks of France's psychiatric health system. The book came together in Lyon between 1951 and 1952, a period marked by, as his biographer Alice Cherki puts it, "a triple junction" of encounters and experiences (24). These were psychiatry, his chosen vocation; his discovery of phenomenology, existentialism, and psychoanalysis; and finally, the encounter with a racist White French society and the ways in which Fanon assimilated this experience, both in the army and during his years in Lyon, as a minority and a Black man. The doubt and trepidations of the introduction – "Why write the book? No one has asked me for it" (7) – juxtapose with the author's quiet determination that the book will be a "mirror with a progressive infrastructure, in which it will be possible to discern the Negro on the road to disalienation" (184). Fanon situates the man of color in a world where he is seen, is heard, and is for others. The look of the other, rather than confirming oneself back to oneself, fixes one in a lethal epidermal scheme. Trapped in their respective "Whiteness" and

"Blackness," White settler and Black native create one another without reciprocity. Critics have long noted that Fanon's reinvention as a Black West Indian occurred only when he arrived in the French capital.[1] Here, Fanon had come to realize that volunteerism on behalf of the abstract principles of "freedom," "France," or "antifascism," counted for nothing in the eyes of the majority of French citizens, for whom he remained inferior, inassimilable, nothing but an interloper. At the intersection of colony and the imperial metropolis, Fanon lost the "honorary citizenship" his facility with the French language had accorded him and became an "Antilles Negro" (*Black Skin* 38).

Stuart Hall, with whose homage to Fanon this chapter begins, is considered the founder of British multiculturalism, Hall was also the first editor of *New Left Review* and the long-time director of the Birmingham Centre for Contemporary Cultural Studies, the flagship institution of cultural studies in the world (until administrators closed it down in 2002). Born in Kingston, Jamaica, in 1932, he came to Oxford as a Rhodes Scholar in 1951, ditching it – and his thesis on Henry James – in 1956 to plunge into activism, supporting himself by teaching part-time in the working-class neighborhoods of London. Echoing Fanon in France, Hall liked to say that he realized he was Black only when he arrived in England.[2] Like Fanon, he too never went back to the Caribbean after being confirmed in a constituted Blackness. Despite his relatively privileged position as a middle-class Jamaican and Black European, Hall's lifelong struggle to redress the plight of populations suffering the simultaneous effects of race, gender, class, and migration in multicultural Britain stemmed from the painful realization that race was a great leveler. "There's not much respect for black PhDs from Oxford," he said jokingly to the novelist Caryl Phillips in an interview. "People looked at me as an immigrant, they couldn't tell me apart from another boy just knocking around Notting Hill" ("Stuart Hall by Caryl Phillips").

While this chapter is not on Fanon, it examines the related dynamic of learning and unlearning – learning to unlearn biased and compromised intellectual formations – in novels of growth or social initiation in African and Caribbean diasporic modernity. I evoke the spectral Fanonism Stuart Hall commemorates to examine Zadie Smith's negotiations of what Fanon called a "dark and unarguable blackness" (*Black Skin*, 117). In his influential essay, "Critical Fanonism," Henry Louis Gates Jr. posits Fanon "as an agon between ... ontogeny and sociogeny," supplementing Sigmund Freud's conception of human development at the intersection of ontogeny and phylogeny (469). Gates enjoins that we read Fanon, not simply treat him as an icon or screen memory: "It means not to elevate him above his localities of discourse as a transcultural, transhistorical Global Theorist, nor simply to cast him into battle, but to recognize him as a battlefield in himself" (470). Zadie Smith's corpus testifies to a similar agon between the writer's prerogative of impersonality and elective affinities and the "dark and unarguable blackness" that relentlessly attaches to raced bodies. The novels and nonfiction ask to be read not as global theory or interventionist polemic but as battlefields in themselves. Reading Zadie Smith according to the terms set up by Fanon and Hall could also be crucial for decolonizing hard-bitten reading habits in the classroom that treat Black literature as interchangeable with Black culture and society. While Smith's writing of this culture and society is immersive, she routinely and systematically problematizes the category of Blackness itself, as we shall see in what follows.

Unlike Hall and Fanon, Zadie Smith is a girl from the Athelstan Gardens Council Estate in Willesden (northwest London). Born to an English father and a Jamaican mother, she said of her first visit to Jamaica that "I was allergic to everything . . . I didn't want to belong to the place" (Eugenides). Years later, when she traveled to West Africa, she felt unassimilated in an opposite, if equally tragicomic, way. "I was in the middle of what I thought was some kind of spiritual experience in West Africa, this search for my identity. It became clear after the end of quite a long trip that everybody I had been with thought I was white" (Eugenides). "When I was fourteen I was given *Their Eyes Were Watching God* by my mother," Smith writes in the introductory essay of *Changing My Mind*. "I knew what she meant by giving it to me, and I resented the inference" (3). When her mother prods her to read the book lying unopened on the bedside table, the teenager asks if she is meant to like it just because Zora Neale Hurston is Black. "No – because it's really good writing," her mother insists (3). The budding author grows to love Hurston but does so furtively: "I wanted to be an objective aesthete and not a sentimental fool. I disliked the idea of 'identifying' with the fiction I read: I wanted to like Hurston because she represented 'good writing,' not because she represented me" (7). Zadie can finally out herself as a Hurston reader two decades later, when the world has woken up to the genius of Hurston thanks to biographies, films, and Oprah, and African American literature departments and the publishing industry are invested in reclaiming and constructing the "Black Female Literary Tradition" (8).

Just as it is ideologically flawed to think of literary writing and criticism as universal and isotemporal – this, Smith confirms, is a prerogative of the privileged, a White mythology – she baulks at the fetishization of Black women writers. Hurston had a very difficult life and died in poverty, but Smith would still like to make a case for her greatness that supersedes crude identity politics, including the notion that Black women are the privileged readers of a Black woman writer. "I want . . . to be able to say that Hurston is my sister and Baldwin is my brother, and so is Kafka my brother, and Nabokov, and Woolf my sister, and Eliot and Ozick," states Smith, albeit with ambivalence and self-doubt (*Changing My Mind*, 10). While it is hard-won progress that Hurston is no longer a well-kept secret among educated Black women such as the author's mother, the point Smith forcefully makes in this essay is that overcompensating by splashing her now across curricula needs to lead eventually to a concomitant correction and revision of the very modes of literary and aesthetic reception. In an ideal world, one should have the creative freedom, as readers or literary critics, to gravitate to Kafka, Nabokov, Woolf, Eliot, and Ozick while stating, in the same breath, that Hurston "makes 'black woman-ness' appear a real, tangible quality, an essence I can almost believe I share" (13). This chapter dwells on two of Smith's novels, *On Beauty* and *Swing Time*, to elaborate on some of the themes encapsulated in the example from *Changing My Mind* above: the curriculum and its occlusions and amnesia; Black British writing pitted against a writing that is not delimited by the qualifier "White"; aesthetics versus politics; normative literary criticism and its mistrust of what it perceives to be the narcissism of identity politics; Anglo-American traditions of critique and the civilizational and temporal lag it posits between itself and "black women talking about a black book" (12).

Speaking of the difficulty of establishing a diasporic order of things, Samantha Pinto describes diasporic epistemologies as a "difficult play" between "recognizable forms of being, knowing, belonging, and acting in the world and the new forms that emerge as we try to understand its shifts" (7). Pinto's use of "order" refers to Foucault's 1966 work, *The Order of Things: An Archaeology of the Human Sciences*, where he excavates the bases and systematic frameworks of a series of representations in philosophy, natural history, and economics.[3] Whether her novels are rooted in Kilburn or they cross continents, it could be argued that Smith is a proponent of dis-ordered writing, one that examines the diasporic phenomenology of being out of place on a temporal, and not just spatial, axis. In this interruption, a belated correction of what Matti Bunzl calls "the enabling temporal formations" of colonial discourse, lies the decolonizing potential of Zadie Smith's work (vii).[4] In the *New York Times* interview with Jeffrey

Eugenides conducted soon after the publication of *Swing Time* (2016), Smith says that:

> what was done to black people, historically, was to take them out of the time of their life. . . . We had a life in one place and it would have continued and who knows what would have happened – nobody knows. But it would've gone a certain way, and we were removed from that timeline, placed somewhere entirely different, and radically disrupted. And the consequences of that are pretty much unending. Every people have their trauma. It's not a competition of traumas. But they're different in nature. And this one is about having been removed from time.

The "swing" in *Swing Time*, Eugenides observes, is both noun and verb. It refers to the 1936 musical and swing music, seemingly, but enjoins also that we interpret swing not as an adjective defining time but a verb acting on it. Nowhere is this more evident than in Smith's novels of displacement and disorder, which circle around the twinned foci of social mobility and (higher) learning, in school classrooms and on the university campus.

Class, Classroom, Race Mobility

In *Swing Time*, the unnamed narrator describes a mad playground game that erupted in her school when she was nine:

> It was like tag, but a girl was never "It," only boys were "It," girls simply ran and ran until we found ourselves cornered in some quiet spot, away from the eyes of dinner ladies and playground monitors, at which point our knickers were pulled aside and a little hand shot into our vaginas, we were roughly, frantically tickled, and then the boy ran away, and the whole thing started up again from the top. (65)

At first, this seems to be a form of prelapsarian sex play. But as the game continues, and moves into the classroom, a sinister change can be observed.

> The random element was now gone: only the original three boys played and they only visited those girls who were both close to their own desks and whom they assumed would not complain. Tracey was one of these girls, as was I, and a girl from my corridor called Sasha Richards. The white girls – who had generally been included in the playground mania – were now mysteriously no longer included: it was as if they had never been involved in the first place. (66)

This is how colonialism enters the novel, not by the narrator's reanimating its remnants in Africa or the Caribbean but, frighteningly, in her finding its deformations and hierarchies still operative in her classroom in London in the early eighties. The sexual experiments of children are informed by a racial pecking order and undergo a perceptible "blackening" of the game in the shift from playground to the classroom. Somehow her male class-mates have understood that it is the brown girls whose knickers can be pulled aside; and it is the brown girls who accept this as a natural order of things, all at an age before sexual role play has become conscious, culti-vated, or coerced.

The low educational attainment of Black pupils has been a feature of policy debates and a concern for Black families for several decades. However, as scholars of education such as Nicola Rollock point out in *The Colour of Class*, there is scant British empirical work that explicitly explores how race and social class *jointly* shape their experiences. The example from *Swing Time* enjoins that we add gender to this mix. Policy debate positions Black British families as a homogenous working-class entity, deficient, uninterested, and uninvolved in their children's educa-tion. It is, in other words, the "deficit model" of thinking about education, entertained on both sides of the Atlantic, which presumes, as Robbie Shilliam has argued, that Black families and communities have no cultural capital to gift their children as an inheritance and can only transmit pathological behavior. Shilliam reflects on the low acceptance rates of Black students in "prestigious universities"; the negative experience of university faced by this ethnicity; and the relatively low attainment levels of those who do enter the student population. "Some have explained away these disparities by presuming that Black students arrive at the gates of the university with pronounced social and cultural deficits garnered from their familial and community upbringing – that is, their blackness. I would direct their assumptions back to the image of Stuart Hall studying at Oxford," Shilliam states ("Black/Academia" 59). The racial differentials are produced within the British academy, itself an isomorphism of the society which had created Blackness, as inhering to the Windrush gener-ation and their descendants in Britain, as a negatively defined identity, not-English and not-White. What is missed out in Eugenicist reports of underachievement in British secondary education is what Shilliam calls the "educational maltreatment of . . . children" pointed out painstakingly by citizens' groups such as the Black Parents Movement, established in 1975 ("Black/Academia" 59). Both entities in the decolonization debate – those clamoring for decolonization and those jealously guarding their elite cultural privilege – err in not connecting the pinnacle of higher studies at university with the base of the population pyramid, "growing relentlessly blacker, browner, poorer" ("Black/Academia" 59).

Studies on the education of the middle classes, on the other hand, focus exclusively on the White middle class, and the ways in which it mobilizes cultural capital strategically for the betterment of offspring. In the *Colour of Class*, the authors – Rollock, David Gilborn, Carol Vincent, and Stephen Ball – recommend that instead of focusing solely on schools and education policy, we analyze the educational experiences of Black children in the context of their homes, focusing on how Black parents view and interact with schools. Political theorists like Shilliam recommend also that we penalize the monocultural university environment and the raciological thinking behind the conventional curriculum for making deficits where there are none. They point out spaces outside academia where non-White activists, not academics themselves, have chosen to situate their dissent. Smith's *Swing Time*, more so than the other sociological fiction she has written, looks at the promise of social betterment as it galvanizes the Black Caribbean middle classes, even as they continue to be positioned as outsiders and imposters in the apartheid of a wealthy neocolonial metropolis. She elegizes the neutralization of this promise beyond the tertiary level and also dispassionately questions the curious self-hatred and social animosity that attaches to the survivor figure of African continental heritage who makes it in predominantly White and white-collar professions.

The most spectacular mobility figure in Smith's *Swing Time* is the mother of the nameless narrator. The story revolves around two mixed-race families, converging on the figures of two little tan girls, both living in the council estates of northwest London in the 1980s, one (the narrator's home) relatively gentrified compared to the other. Neither family is on benefits, despite Tracey's mother's numerous attempts to "get on the disability" (10). The narrator's father is an unwitting poster child of the enervated White working classes; her friend Tracey's father is absconding, polygamous, and criminalized, a dangerously charismatic man-child, the unlived-out life of whose kinetic energy is expressed in Tracey's own prodigious enjoyment of dance. Tracey's mother is "white, obese, afflicted with acne," her thin blond hair pulled back in a "Kilburn facelift": the narrator's mother is a feminist autodidact, a copy of *Black Jacobins* under her arm (10).

Describing her mother's plain white linen trousers, her blue-and-white-striped Breton T-shirt, her frayed espadrilles, her beautiful Nefertiti head, the narrator says:

> She dressed for a future not yet with us but which she expected to arrive . . . everything so plain, so understated, completely out of step with the spirit of

the time, and with the place. One day we would "get out of here," and she would complete her studies, become truly radical chic, perhaps even spoken of in the same breath as Angela Davis and Gloria Steinem ... Straw-soled shoes were all part of this bold vision, they pointed subtly at the higher concepts. (10)

The mother actualizes the vision only partially, educating herself long-distance and immersing herself in socialist activism before consolidating her considerable rhetorical prowess and populist politics as an MP. She enjoys the incorporation into the socially exclusive meritocracy, but, unlike her daughter, who remains ambivalent till the end about Black Power and White liberal guilt alike, the world remains Manichaean to her. While her mother sanctimoniously talks about "our people," the narrator hears the "overlapping quack and babble of those birds," repeating again and again, "I am a duck! I am a duck!" (311). While the mother reads Marx and Frankfurt school, sociology and politics, Hughes and Robeson, the narra-tor dreams of MGM idols of dance such as the Nicholas Brothers – Fayard and Harold – in midair, doing the splits. She finds, in the school library, *The History of Dance*, "a different kind of history from my mother's, the kind that is barely written down – that is felt" (101). She mines the performative transmission of history in dance and music for postpolitical biopolitics, where Tracey's dad got *it* – his ability to leapfrog into a split – from Michael Jackson, Michael Jackson got *it* from Prince, and maybe James Brown, and they all got *it* from the African American tap-dancing duo, the Nicholas brothers. And Fred Astaire got *it* from the Nicholas brothers too, blacking up his face to perform the "Bojangles" number in "Swing Time."

As Taiye Selasi put it in her review of *Swing Time*, her friend Tracey "is the narrator's abiding point of reference, the one with the talent, the clarity and the fire." The narrator's success, happiness, and her precarious self-situation in the world, whether in relation to the carnal networks of global capitalism or the surveillant networks of new media, are all relative to Tracey. It is Tracey who is the foe of the narrator's mother, soma to her psyche, village life to her city ambitions, Dionysus to her Apollo. Tracey is the obscure, sidelined genius to the mother's considerable, if also cultivated and derivative, talent. At the receiving end of a lecture by the narrator's mother on the history of racial epithets – Tracey had used the word "Paki" at Lily Bingham's tenth birthday party – she shuts her up with the devastating logic of an upturned chin and "It's just a word" (82). In a disjointed world, with the grown-ups particularly unaligned with its time signatures, Tracey as dancer "knew the right time to do everything"

(26). As in dance, so in storytelling. The girls write stories about ballet dancers in peril, Tracey dictating and the narrator transcribing. "Just as you thought the happy ending had arrived, Tracey found some wonderful new way to destroy or divert it, so that the moment of consummation . . . never seemed to arrive" (32). The theories of "secular salvation," as Ashis Nandy terms it, shaping social knowledge in the West – anarchism, Christian socialism, communism, for instance – have little appeal for Tracey.[5] Unlike the narrator's mother, who goes out in a fug of bravery, denial, and delusion, Tracey ends where she begins – in a familiar place and an obdurately unchangeable time.

The narrative unraveling of the Black woman who seemingly *has it all* is something we have seen in Smith's 2012 novel *NW*. I am referring to Keisha, who has survived a childhood in the projects, Kilburn Pentecostal, and Brayton Comprehensive – "some schools you 'attended.' Brayton you 'went' to" (9) – to rename herself Natalie and become a barrister. Her narrative is the most disjointed of the four parts of the novel, broken into 185 staccato sections, the confessional flow repeatedly thwarted by quiz answers, menu items, and Instant Messaging (IM) chats. "Natalie Blake had become a person unsuited to self-reflection" (252). Natalie's psychic life suffers equally from the narrative control over it of which she is justifiably proud (her word for it is "time management") and the panic and rage that is related, no doubt, to her friend Leah's growing hatred (Leah has stayed much where she was), the emotional abandonment of the natal family that she has left far behind (a professional hazard for the mobility hero), her uncomprehending and infantilized banker husband, and the baffling fullness of motherhood into which she finds herself coerced.

In "Two Directions for the Novel," Zadie Smith reads Joseph O'Neill's *Netherland* and Tom McCarthy's *Remainder*, an unusual pairing that she herself identifies as "antipodal" and mutually cancelling (71). She contemplates the "extraordinary persistence" of realist fiction of the Balzac-Flaubert model, "a literary form in long-term crisis" (73, 72), and wonders why American metafiction, once touted as an antidote to realism, has been relegated to a corner of literary history. It is evident in the essay that between the lyric realism of *Netherland* and the postmodern play of *Remainder*, Smith would personally authenticate the latter. "If *Netherland* is a novel only partially aware of the ideas that underpin it, *Remainder* if fully conscious of its own" (82). However, despite her sharp critique, in essays such as "Two Directions for the Novel," of the "essential fullness and continuity of the self" (73) that Smith sees as an unexamined credo of traditional realism, her novels *NW* and *Swing Time* see closure and completion in uncannily similar terms (namely, the fullness and continuity of the self).

Enraged though she is at the psychological torture her dying mother has incurred in the hands of Tracey, whose barrage of abusive emails to this local politician is also a catalog of pain – child-support woes, rent arrears, skirmishes with social workers, fears of losing child custody – the narrator of *Swing Time* claims responsibility, not retribution.

> There is no case I can make that will change the fact that I was her only witness, the only person who knows all that she has in her, all that's been ignored and wasted, and yet I still left her back there, in the ranks of the unwitnessed, where you have to scream to get heard. (448)

In both *NW* and *Swing Time*, Smith posits individual development as autogenous, while also subsuming its brute solipsistic force in linked chapters, an epic narrative arc, and dreams of the common weal. The seemingly *sui generis* nature of characters in *Swing Time* is downplayed by revelations of their fractal nature. The novel throws up new assemblages at every turn: Tracey and the narrator, Tracey and Jeni LeGon, the narrator and Hawa, even the mother and Aimee. Individualism itself is seen as an imported American secular ideology, a hodgepodge of Social Darwinist capitalism, New Age spirituality, and a relentless desire for self-improvement. The "notorious narcissism" (Jennifer Egan's term) of the *Bildung* narrative is replaced here by new forms of connectivity, collectivity, cellularity (when each small group in the cell only knows the identities of the people in their cell).[6] It seems to say, as Robbie Shilliam argues in "Austere Curricula," that "the deficit does not lie with Black heritages – familial and community – but in the racist structures that devalue, demean and exclude the sources of cultural capital that Black children carry with them into the classroom" (98). It would therefore be simplistic to read in the worldly protagonist's return to childish certainties and the council estate, in both *Swing Time* and *NW*, a regressive compulsion. If anything, it is a rewriting of the novel of formation as an interminable gestational process, and an acknowledgment of the village that it takes to raise a gifted child.

The Campus Cosmopolis

Zadie Smith's *On Beauty* (2005), which a staff writer at the *Harvard Crimson* said could have been titled "On Harvard,"[7] is also about assemblages and a dreamed-for connectedness between the assembled but nonidentical actors. An avowed *hommage* to E. M. Forster's *Howards End*, what draws Smith to the precursor novel of 1910 is, as Christian Moraru observes, Forster's "relational imagination and, behind it, his uniquely cosmopolitan mindset" (134). True to this legacy, *On Beauty* seems to aspire to a world where interpersonal connection is not restricted to the ties of blood, culture, or nation but is overlaid instead with elective affinities, disinterested friendships, or professional loyalties. Forsterian liberalism is layered further in the novel with insights from Elaine Scarry's *On Beauty and Being Just*, a philosophical treatise which gives Smith the title of her novel. In a nutshell, Scarry's argument is that beauty is a "compact, or contract between the beautiful being (a person or thing) and the perceiver" (90). The perceiver and the object perceived bestow on each other the gift of life. "Beauty is pacific," Scarry goes on to say, its live-giving pact with participants one that bestows peace and justice "in reciprocal salute to continued existence" (107). Smith's *On Beauty* examines the connection between beauty and distributive justice in a campus novel where not all bodies can be cosmopolitan alike even in the liberal haven of a twenty-first-century college town, and beauty, instead of repairing existing injuries, as promised by Scarry, becomes an ally of the perpetrators of social and racial injustice.

Dorothy Hale has astutely identified in Smith's revisionism of Scarry the gap between a philosopher's treatment of beauty and the novelist's:

> Whereas Scarry seeks primarily to describe "the felt experience of cognition" (3) that unites all human beings of every culture in their experience of beauty, Smith portrays the particularity and contingency of each individual's apprehension of beauty. And while Scarry aims to enumerate the fundamental qualities of beauty, Smith stresses its relativity and social constructedness. (815)

The relativity and discursive formation of beauty is explored through the vicissitudes of the characters in *On Beauty* and their individual attempts to comprehend beauty "through private contemplation as well as through acts of social exchange" (Hale 815). The "felt experience of cognition" (Scarry's term) is indissociable from one's educational advantage and sociocultural location, the novel seems to say. Hale's phrase "aesthetics of alterity" encapsulates *On Beauty*'s work of demystifying autotelic responses to beauty; it refers also to the capaciousness and capacity of the novel form itself in representing the lives of others, or the "variety and autonomy of social perspectivalism" (Hale 817).

However, while I agree about the Forsterian strain of self-othering and estrangement Smith injects into identity politics in *On Beauty*, it is limiting and reductive to describe her contribution to the philosophy and phenomenology of beauty as a "novelistic aesthetics of alterity," as Hale does (816). The allusive and citational structure of *On Beauty* – Smith extrapolates from a variety of literary and academic genres – troubles the extant distinctions between the anthropological novel, autofiction, cultural criticism, and lyric poetry. The novel posits beauty as socially constructed but undercuts its own truth claims with personal experiences of beauty that are immediate, overwhelming, and too unique or accidental to be reified. This inherent dichotomy is key to understanding the mutually cancelling impulses of Black British writing such as Zadie Smith's: this fiction may do the work of ideology critique or represent the lives of others, but it jealously reserves the right to be abstract and nonmimetic art, not a communicative form, at times. The work generates its own terms of exegesis, enjoining readers to treat it as literature, not autoethnography, and thereby ushering a process of decolonizing the reading and reception of Black British writers.

Zadie Smith has said in interviews that she came to the undergraduate English degree at Cambridge from a non-academic background. Her adolescent self had immediately associated the university with a salvation narrative that wasn't dashed to the ground because her college, King's, was unique in the Cambridge system: "King's was a real intellectual community; I knew nothing about drinking societies or Blues or banking. Maybe it went on, but I never saw it. To me King's was one long, invigorating conversation" ("An Interview with Zadie Smith"). She mentioned in the same interview that without the Cambridge English course, which "started at the beginning and ended near-ish the end," and the great breadth of novels she read there, she would not have become a novelist: the literary theory and philosophy she studied on the course, in particular, helped develop critical skills lacking from her school education. The fictional institution of Wellington is no King's College, Cambridge, but we could read Smith's campus novel as a dreamed-for conversation between outsiders and insiders where the cultural and literary heritage shared between colonial history's winners and losers assumes recombinant forms.

Ideally, there would be space for deliberate reflection and critical evaluation even in the neoliberal and corporate university, and the principles and aims of higher education would be attuned, not opposed, to liberation and social justice movements gathering momentum outside the classroom. However, as Kanika Batra has persuasively argued, Smith's treatment of institutionalized Black Studies at Wellington marks a failure, in the micro-cosm of *On Beauty*, of aspirations of inclusivity and widening access. "The discipline is presented as disconnected to social reality and actively partici-pating in the perpetuation of social inequality" (1080). Batra disagrees with this skeptical depiction of Black Studies, which occupies a marginalized position in the Anglo-American academy and White liberal arts institu-tions. She points out that in Britain, especially – and she has in mind Stuart Hall's monumental contribution to Birmingham's School of Cultural Criticism and his pioneering of cultural studies in general – the theoretical space of academic discourse was not only coterminous with the vernacular space of Black cultural life, but it actively enabled these elaborations of the vernacular. In fact, Batra implies that a novel such as *On Beauty* is itself a beneficiary of the legacies of Black Studies and that it showcases some of its ongoing debates: "Smith's representation of the class specific dimension of the black diaspora through Haitian migration to the US brings to the fore cultural identity, race relations, and economic stratifications – key concerns explored by Black Studies from its inception" (1085).

While Batra's reading defends the impetus of Black Studies as intellec-tual and pedagogical as well as political, it also sounds a cautionary note about the limits of "progressive racial politics" such programs stand for (1090). What brings the tenuous link between academic and the social to breaking point in *On Beauty* is the treatment of Carl, the "street poet" embraced by the Belsey family after they meet him at a free performance of Mozart's *Requiem* on the Boston Common. Carl's inclusion in faculty parties – and his involvement as discretionary student in English professor Claire Malcolm's class – reveal the savior complexes masquerading as inclusive gestures, even when some of the actors in this campus circus, such as Kiki Belsey or Erskine Jegede, are Black, diasporic, or cosmopolitan themselves. "Are you interested in refining what you have?" Claire asks Carl after his spoken word performance at the Bus Stop, a hub for local artists in Wellington (232). A professor of Creative Writing, Claire is a poet herself, and a teacher and talent scout par excellence. She initiates her students into a dynamic interaction with the canon, not reinstating the hierarchy between the immortals and wannabes but discussing dead poets side by side with student work. She is adept at impressing on her wards the magic of commuting intimate thoughts through the stylized language of poetry, "through rhyme and metre, images and ideas" (259).

Carl's refinement in her hands is there for the class to see. He had attended his first session with an affected slouch, mumbling his lyrics and reacting in a hostile way to the implication that the rap he was chanting was a poem: "rap ain't no art form. It's just *rap*" (259).

> The first thing Claire did with Carl's rap that day was show him of what it was made. Iambs, spondees, trochees, anapaests. Passionately Carl denied any knowledge of the arcane arts. He was used to being fêted at the Bus Stop but not in a classroom. Large sections of Carl's personality had been constructed on the founding principle that classrooms were not for Carl. (259)

His historical mistrust of White and elite civic institutions is not unfounded, and we, as readers, had anticipated this. Carl lowers his guard despite his unease with the wave of attention from Claire and her pupils, and in the full knowledge that there was no mobility story unfolding at this institution, where he was not even a registered student. Perhaps it was not a sick joke after all; she wanted him to do well, and he wanted to do well for her. Carl writes the sonnet Claire had repeatedly asked for. He doesn't think it is great but "everybody in the class made a big fuss like he'd just split the atom" (260). Overwhelmed, he looks at the sonnet on the crumpled sheet of paper where his rap would normally be scribbled, resolving to type the thing out next time if he could get his hands on a keyboard. True to Deleuze and Guattari's reading of the encoding function of relations of power in capitalism, Claire has decoded Carl – freed him from established codes – only to rebind that energy into "factitious" and self-serving codes.[8] *On Beauty* would suggest that this process of progressive unfixing, rapidly followed by re-inscription into new forms of production and consumption, marks the self-expansion of capital and the capitalist university alike.

Just as Carl is easing into a timid feeling of affiliation to this community of aspiring writers, Claire embarrasses him in front of the whole class by asking if he was serious about the opportunity. "I mean, do you want to stay in this class? Even if it gets difficult?" (261). Carl is tempted to angrily retort but relents to Claire's conviction that *he* needed the class. Soon after, Claire would appoint Zora, daughter of art historian Howard Belsey, to speak at a faculty meeting on behalf of Carl and the other unregistered students. The self-styled "communist loony-tune anti-war poetess" Claire Malcolm tells Zora unabashedly that she would ideally send Carl to make his case, but "the truth is these people won't respond to an appeal to their consciences in any language other than Wellington language" (263). Zora Belsey, who is indeed fluent in Wellington language – and who has long harbored the fantasy of addressing Wellington College faculty with an impassioned speech – falls into step with Claire's prejudice that Carl doesn't have a voice and needs someone like Zora, Black but with an enviable pedigree and a level of cultural distinction, "to speak for him" (263). These moments of class differentiation even in Black writing are key to the process of decolonizing the interpretation of Black literature: there is no room for a sanctimonious reading here, and Smith provokes critical thinking on the interrelated issues of race and class or economic and social factors. Carl is betrayed and banished from the diegetic space not by White racism alone but the very proponents of Black meritocracy and a Black public sphere, including the Foucault-reading Zora and her brother Levi, with his faux Brooklyn accent and his hankering after authentic racial identity 200 miles north of Brooklyn.

The Zadie Smith novels discussed in this chapter imagine counter-hegemonic spaces of education and Black reading publics transversally, through compromised and corruptible classroom and campus politics. The novels are particularly valuable for questions of decolonizing the English literary curriculum because of the nuanced and ambivalent way in which they use literary lineage to claim a postcolonial literature and culture to come. The themes of these works have a history of mobilizing both sides in the decolonization debate: multiculturalism, equality and diversity, widening access, canon revision, value criteria and aesthetic judgment, aesthetics and ethics. These are novels of ideas punctuated by doubt and guilt surrounding the learned exposition of ideas, an elite prerogative; it is imaginative writing that strays into imaginative activism.

In my interpretation, the implied reader of this body of work is both Carlene Kipps and Kiki Belsey of *On Beauty*, with their polarity of responses to the painting, "Maîtresse Erzulie," by the Haitian artist Hector Hyppolite. Kiki is wife of the "Empson Lecturer in Aesthetics" at Wellington College; Carlene is married to Howard Belsey's nemesis, the right-wing Black Christian Monty, a Rembrandt scholar at the same institution. At the start of this scene, the women act as cartoonish opposites of the academics they are married to. Kiki's response to art, unlike that of her husband's, is subjective, wilfully naïve, and blunt. She declares that they have no paintings in the house, "at least none of human beings," although this is because Howard mistrusts representational art (175). Carlene, on the other hand, offers a feminist deconstructive reading of the Voodoo goddess Erzulie, calling her "the *mystère* of jealousy, vengeance and discord, *and*, on the other hand, of love, perpetual help, goodwill, health, beauty and fortune" (175). The naked Black woman in the Hyppolite painting, her "fantastical white space" surrounded by tropical branches, flowers, and birds, functions as a contingency, unexpectedly providing common ground (175). When Kiki trots out a thesis of Howard's about binaries in metaphysics to impress Carlene, Carlene puts an end to this nonsense by simply and kindly saying to Kiki that she likes Erzulie's parrots. This momentary truce is a triumph of Forsterian cosmopolitanism, Randi Saloman argues, which makes "connection the endpoint rather than the condition of moving forward" (690). The university and the university adjacent, Smith implies, could be a transformative space in its openness to difference and the play of the signifier. To quote Saloman again, "vast possibilities ... emerge from the simple joining together of different individuals in unexpected combinations" (690).

"By reducing the body and the living being to matters of appearance, skin, and color ... the Euro-American world in particular has made Blackness and race two sides of a single coin, two sides of a codified madness," writes Achille Mbembe in *Critique of Black Reason* (5). Zadie Smith corrects the madness of making Blackness stand for racial difference exclusively, implicating Whiteness with Blackness every step of the way. The novels are vibrant with the chatter of the English literary canon. "I want ... to be able to say that Hurston is my sister and Baldwin is my brother, and so is Kafka my brother, and Nabokov, and Woolf my sister, and Eliot and Ozick," Smith has stated. There is an identical moment of double consciousness in Toni Morrison's *Playing in the Dark*, where she expresses her awe of the prodigious imaginations behind "Faulkner's Benjy, James's Maisie, Flaubert's Emma, Melville's Pip, Mary Shelley's Frankenstein" (4). As a reader, she can freely inhabit the canon that she is historically estranged from, while as an African American woman writer she is just as unfree in "my genderized, sexualized, wholly racialized world" (4).

There are no pieties associated with the fact of Blackness. In Smith's short story, "Sentimental Education," Monica, who, like Zora Belsey in *On Beauty* is obtusely "on the side of law and order" (13), wants her boyfriend's childhood best friend to stop lodging furtively in their Oxbridge college. Monica and Darryl are Black, the tracksuited friend Leon White, working class, and a drug dealer. "I don't like the idea of a young white man dragging a young black man into the mud," Monica sanctimoniously states, before reporting Leon anonymously to the provost (15). As with Monty Kipps in *On Beauty*, the vaunted ideal of meritocracy upheld by Monica is unmitigated by self-reflection on her privilege. Zadie Smith can be taught to decolonize the English literary curriculum not only because second-generation Caribbean literature has arrived, the derisive trope of arrival itself a colonial inheritance. Novels such as *On Beauty* and *Swing Time* do not err on the side of essentialism, demonstrating instead that beauty or rhythm are extracultural and transhistorical forces, but they can also be individual and personal in the Fanonesque ambivalences of identification.

Notes

1. See Macey. Henry Louis Gates Jr. points out that Fanon, "whose mother was of Alsatian descent, grew up in Martinique thinking of himself as white and French," and that his "painful reconstitution" as Black West Indian occurred only when he arrived in Paris (468).

2. The biographical information on Stuart Hall can be found here: www .runnymedetrust.org/blog/black-history-legacies-stuart-hall. The biographical details also come up in Stuart Hall's interviews. See, for instance, the conversation with Les Back: https://research.gold.ac.uk/id/eprint/2321/2/At_Home_and_Not_at_Home-1.pdf.

3. Pinto is also alluding to the Guadeloupian author Maryse Condé's "disorder" of gendered writing. Disorder, evoked by Condé in relation to what she describes as the "forgotten, out of print, misunderstood" Caribbean women writers, is a synonym for creativity, which breaks free from the constraining decrees on West Indian writing issued by male writers (161). Condé's powerful essay "Order, Disorder, Freedom, and the West Indian Writer," is a valorization of an antipodal realist feminist tradition whose seemingly "pessimistic, negative, and fatalistic" elements – its antimessianism, frank sexuality, and unsparing look at domestic discontent – she finds preferable to the "conventional revolutionary bric à brac" (164).

4. This phrase appears in Matti Bunzl's foreword to Johannes Fabian's *Time and the Other: How Anthropology Makes Its Object*, a highly influential work of critical anthropology where Fabian has interrogated the role of time in the constitution of Anglo-American and French anthropology and the production of ethnographic knowledge.

5. The idea of secular salvation theories or narratives cropping up at the time of modern colonialism occurs repeatedly in Ashis Nandy's writings. An elucidation can be found here, in the text of Nandy's Ambedkar Memorial Lecture delivered in 2012: https://kafila.online/2013/02/06/theories-of-oppression-and-another-dialogue-of-cultures-ashis-nandy/.

6. Jennifer Egan, "Black Box," a Twitter-formatted short story, appeared in the New Yorker: www.newyorker.com/magazine/2012/06/04/black-box.

7. www.thecrimson.com/article/2005/10/7/beautiful-zadies-novel-disappointingly-dense-on/.

8. These concepts of decoding and recoding appear in Deleuze and Guattari's *Anti-Oedipus*. Eugene Holland describes "decoding" as a positive moment which "frees desire from the constraints and distortions of codification." Recoding, however, consists of opposing processes which reverse the emancipatory charge of decoding. These tie "freed libidinal energy back into factitious codes . . . so as to extract and realize privately appropriable surplus-value" (80).

WORKS CITED

Batra, Kanika. "Kipps, Belsey, and Jegede: Cosmopolitanism, Transnationalism, and Black Studies in Zadie Smith's *On Beauty*." *Callaloo* 3.4 (2010): 1079–92.

Brenkman, John. "Race Publics." *Transition* 66 (1995): 4–36.

Bunzl, Matti. "Foreword: Syntheses of a Critical Anthropology." In Johannes Fabian, *Time and the Other: How Anthropology Makes Its Object*. New York: Columbia University Press, 2014, vii–xxxii.

Cherki, Alice. *Frantz Fanon: A Portrait*. Trans. Nadia Benabid. Ithaca, NY: Cornell University Press, 2006.

Condé, Maryse. "Order, Disorder, Freedom and the Caribbean Writer." *Yale French Studies* 97, *50 Years of Yale French Studies: A Commemorative Anthology*. Part 2: 1980–1998 (2000): 151–65.

Eugenides, Jeffrey. "The Pieces of Zadie Smith": www.nytimes.com/2016/10/17/t-magazine/zadie-smith-swing-time-jeffrey-eugenides.html.

Fanon, Frantz. *Black Skin, White Masks*. Translated by Charles Lam Markmann. New York: Grove Press, 1967.

Gates, Henry Louis, Jr. "Critical Fanonism." *Critical Inquiry* 17.3 (1991): 457–70.

Hale, Dorothy. "'On Beauty' as Beautiful? The Problem of Novelistic Aesthetics by Way of Zadie Smith." *Contemporary Literature* 53.4 (2012): 814–44.

Hall, Stuart. "The After-Life of Frantz Fanon: Why Fanon? Why Now? Why Black Skin, White Masks?" In Alan Read, ed., *Fact of Blackness: Frantz Fanon and Visual Representation*. Seattle, WA: Bay Press, 1996, 12–31.

Holland, Eugene. *Deleuze and Guattari's Anti-Oedipus: Introduction to Schizoanalysis*. London: Routledge, 1999.

Macey, David. *Frantz Fanon: A Biography*. n.p.: Verso Books, 2012.

Mbembe, Achille. *Critique of Black Reason*. Trans. Laurent Dubois. Durham, NC: Duke University Press, 2017.

Moraru, Christian. "The Forster Connection or, Cosmopolitanism Redux: Zadie Smith's *On Beauty, Howards End*, and the Schlegels," *The Comparatist* 35 (2011): 133–47.

Morrison, Toni. *Playing in the Dark: Whiteness and the Literary Imagination*. Cambridge, MA: Harvard University Press, 1992.

Pinto, Samantha. *Difficult Diasporas: The Transnational Feminist Aesthetic of the Black Atlantic*. New York: NYU Press, 2013.

Rollock, Nicola, David Gillborn, Carol Vincent, and Stephen J. Ball. *The Colour of Class: The Educational Strategies of the Black Middle Classes*. London: Routledge, 2014.

Saloman, Randi. "'The Battle against Sameness': Zadie Smith's Rewriting of E. M. Forster's Liberalism." *Textual Practice* 35.4 (2021): 687–705.

Scarry, Elaine. *On Beauty and Being Just*. Princeton, NJ: Princeton University Press, 2001.

Selasi, Taiye. "*Swing Time* by Zadie Smith: A Classic Story of Betterment": www.theguardian.com/books/2016/nov/13/swing-time-zadie-smith-review.

Shilliam, Robbie. "Austere Curricula: Multicultural Education and Black Students." In Stefan Jonsson and Julia Willén, eds., *Austere Histories in European Societies: Social Exclusion and the Contest of Colonial Memories.* London: Routledge, 2017, 92–112.

"Black/Academia." In Gurminder K. Bhambra, Dalia Gebrial, and Kerem Nişancıoğlu, eds., *Decolonising the University.* London: Pluto Press, 2018, 52–63.

Smith, Zadie. "An Interview with Zadie Smith." www.english.cam.ac.uk/cambrid geauthors/smith-interview/.

Changing My Mind: Occasional Essays. London: Penguin Books, 2009.

NW. London: Penguin Books, 2012.

On Beauty. London: Penguin Books, 2005.

"Sentimental Education." In Zadie Smith, *Grand Union: Stories.* London: Penguin Books, 2020, 5–23.

Swing Time. London: Penguin Books, 2016.

"Two Directions for the Novel." In Zadie Smith, *Changing My Mind: Occasional Essays.* London: Penguin Books, 2009, 71–96.

"Stuart Hall by Caryl Phillips," *BOMB* (January 1, 1997): https://bombmagazine .org/articles/stuart-hall/.

PART II

Methodologies

CHAPTER 7

Theories of Anthologizing and Decolonization

Aarthi Vadde

Decolonizing the English literary curriculum is a necessary and yet impossible task. It requires more than overcoming institutional inertia within the university; it requires much more than having a series of difficult conversations at the departmental level regarding the purpose and scope of an English literary education today. Decolonizing the literary curriculum in the United States, the location from which I write, demands nothing short of revolutionizing an entire educational apparatus where the university is only the tip of the iceberg. Add to it Kindergarten–12 schools, the textbook industry, and state legislatures, eight of which as of 2021 have banned the discussion of structural racism, sexism, and White privilege in the classroom (Ray and Gibbons).

I begin with the enormity of the challenge not to be defeatist, but to acknowledge that colonialism suffuses the infrastructure of humanities education. Its tentacular reach is what makes decolonization an unfinishable project (Vadde 21). Parting ways with Jurgen Habermas's characterization of modernity as an unfinished project, proponents of decolonization have learned to question the philosophical optimism implied by a telos of accomplishment. To think in terms of the unfinishable rather than the unfinished is to take into account the persistence of neocolonial institutions and debt structures as well as the continuation of settler colonialism across continents despite the official demise of territorial empires. Within this framework, decolonizing the curriculum functions less as an apogee and more as an ongoing check on the institutional power of educators and educational administrators.

In the field of English literary studies, a primary vector of such institutional power is the canon. Theoretically, the canon and the curriculum should reinforce one another as part of the wider apparatus of academic literary study, but practically speaking, the Canon with a capital "C" has come under fire for its assimilationist and depoliticizing connotations, while smaller canons organized around minoritized or historically

underrepresented identities have proliferated. Even as courses on major
authors such as William Shakespeare, John Milton, and James Joyce
persist, disciplinary self-definition has responded to the splintering of
canonicity by turning away from core texts to core methodologies. If
English professors cannot agree on which authors and texts should anchor
the curriculum, many still believe that close reading should remain the
primary pedagogy of a discipline attentive to the global circulation of
English and the plurality of literary Englishes.[1] The turn from adjudicating
canonical texts to promoting signature methods might seem like an abdication of aesthetic judgment, but it has shifted the terms of curricular
debate away from matters of gatekeeping (i.e. are these texts literary), an
obviously polarizing and often racially and ethnically coded question,
toward matters of cultural transmission and social reproduction (i.e. how
should an English major regard literary tradition).

Gauri Viswanathan's landmark study *Masks of Conquest* precedes the
turn to transnationalism within English literary studies, but it is foundational to contextualizing global English literary traditions within the
matrices of imperial power. In it, she argues that no serious account of
the disciplinary origins of English Literature can ignore the strategic role
literary study played in the consolidation of the British Empire. Published
through a book series entitled "The Social Foundations of Aesthetic
Forms," *Masks* historicized the birth of the English literary curriculum in
colonial India as an "instrument of Western hegemony in concert with
commercial expansion and military action" (167). Conceptually, she
approached curriculum formation "not in the perennialist sense of an
objective, essentialized entity but rather as discourse, activity, process, as
one of the mechanisms through which knowledge is socially distributed and
culturally validated" (3).

When *Masks of Conquest* was first published in 1989, Viswanathan was
wary of generalizing her study of disciplinary English beyond nineteenth-
century colonial India. However, in her preface to the twenty-fifth-
anniversary edition, she is more willing to think in comparatively colonial
terms. She finds her understanding of the curriculum as an instrument of
social control reflected in Isabel Hofmeyr's work on the circulation of John
Bunyan's *Pilgrim's Progress* in Africa. Viswanathan describes how the text
only became part of the English literary canon after it had served as an
international tool of conversion for Christian missionaries (vii). Ironically,
the canonization of *Pilgrim's Progress* within England itself depended on
muting its prior evangelical role in African education campaigns.
Hofmeyr's attention to the domestication and racialization of Bunyan

lends insight into the nationalist underpinnings of the discipline of English under formation in England in the late nineteenth and early twentieth centuries (222). Her meticulous study of the international and multilingual itinerary of a single work joins Viswanathan's study of colonial archives in decolonizing the category of Englishness. Both show how the literary curriculums of the colonies provide shadow contexts for decisions made about literary curriculums at the seat of the British Empire.

Twenty-first-century movements to decolonize the university have drawn on the historical work of scholars such as Viswanathan and Hofmeyr, but their leaders have set their sights firmly on the here and now. Simukai Chigudu, a Zimbabwean-born scholar and one of the leaders of the Oxford chapter of the Rhodes Must Fall (RMF) movement, argues that the Foucauldian approach to knowledge for which Viswanathan calls is heralded in the university as long as its insights apply elsewhere to another time and place. The struggle lies in bringing a critical approach to knowledge and self-fashioning to metropolitan centers of power and wealth: "But Oxford, Britain, and the west must be decolonized, too. Essential to this is advancing a richer, more complex view of the imperial past and its bearing on the present. Zimbabwe is not England's troubled colony – it is its mirror." Kehinde Andrews puts the matter more polemically when he writes of the RMF-Oxford movement: "In the heart of whiteness, students mobilized to reject not only their colonial schooling but the hidden curriculum embodied by the statue of racist Cecil Rhodes" (ix). Both assert that a colonial education is not solely a product of geography but also a matter of mentality. The hidden curriculum embodied in the statue of Rhodes reflects the ways in which diversity does not guarantee inclusivity or equity. In predominantly White institutions, Andrews asserts, Black, Asian, and Minority Ethnic (BAME) students occupy the edges of the university; their success relies on learning the unspoken rules of assimilation.

Chigudu is a professor of African politics, and Andrews is a cultural sociologist, but both ground their arguments in rhetorical reversals that are distinctly Conradian. Andrews dubs Oxford the "heart of whiteness," while Chigudu calls Zimbabwe (known as Rhodesia until 1980) a "mirror" of Britain. Neither mention *Heart of Darkness* by name, but Chigudu quotes Chinua Achebe's unsparing critique of *Heart of Darkness* when he implores British citizens to do away with a curriculum that reproduces old prejudices, distortions, and mystifications of Africa. Reading Chigudu's and Andrews's essays, I could not help but wonder where *Heart of Darkness*, like *Pilgrim's Progress*, fit into "the hidden

curriculum" embodied in the statue of Cecil Rhodes. Was the hypercano-
nical novel, like the statue, now an emblem of White supremacy, imperial
nostalgia, and the vested interests of an old donor class who remain as
committed to the ideology of the Great Books as they do to the ideology
of Great Britain? Or did the novel, first published in 1898, remain
a powerful if unspoken touchstone for advocates of decolonization as
they explained the contemporary institutional configurations of colonial
power?

I ask these questions not only as a scholar of English literature but as one
of the editors of the upcoming 11th edition of the *Norton Anthology of English
Literature* (hereafter *NAEL*). First published in 1962 under the general
editorship of M. H. Abrams, the *NAEL* was the brainchild of Abrams and
George Brockway, president of W.W. Norton and Company from 1958 to
1976. Brockway recruited Abrams to create an anthology of British literature
that would parallel the anthology *The American Tradition in Literature*. The
NAEL sought to compete with two preexisting anthologies, namely *The
College Survey of English Literature* (1942) and *Major British Writers* (1959),
both published by Harcourt Brace. Within a few years of its publication, the
NAEL captured 85 to 90 percent of the market for English literature
textbooks (Shesgreen 305).

Given its market dominance over the last sixty years, the *NAEL* has been
described as "the sine qua non of college textbooks, setting the agenda for
the study of English literature in this country [the United States] and
beyond" (Donadio). The prominence of the anthology within the North
American literary educational system has made it a lightning rod
for critique in the intervening decades as feminist, multicultural, and
postcolonial critics questioned not only the maleness and Whiteness of
the anthology but also the narrative of literary history underpinning its
organization. Such conflicts over the diversity of authors represented in the
NAEL have also yielded more extreme positions among United States-
based scholars against anthologizing itself.

For some, the core processes of anthology editing – selection, excerp-
tion, arrangement, and framing – too closely replicate the decontextual-
izing and objectifying practices of colonial epistemologies. World
literature anthologies, by this definition, are an irredeemable "technology
of appropriation" that center themselves by establishing dominion over
literatures from elsewhere (Slaughter 54). For others, anthologies are
simply incapable of relinquishing colonial categories of value. The consolidation of the category of literariness, for example, has historically
excluded and diminished the importance of expressive forms that do not

fit into European genres of poetry, prose, and drama. When anthologies become arbiters of literary merit and discriminating tastes, they do so by obscuring discrimination against peoples and disavowing the "unequal social relations" that remain the "scaffolding" of English as a field of study (Alemán 473). Such antianthology positions show the degree to which pessimism toward the genre has become interchangeable with pessimism toward the discipline of English.

Theories pointing to the colonial underpinnings of the anthology bring up vital truths about the enterprise. Yes, anthologists have historically treated the cultural production of the colonies as raw materials to be turned into property and profit. The practice is memorably enshrined in *Ulysses* when Stephen Dedalus bitterly imagines his best lines ending up in an English visitor's book of Irish folklore: "For Haines' chapbook . . . A jester at the court of his master, indulged and disesteemed, winning a clement master's praise" (Joyce 25). Yes, anthologies inevitably center themselves and their narratives as definitive of a literary tradition. Noting these unsavory elements within the history of genre, however, should not culminate in throwing the baby out with the bathwater.

Critical theories of anthologizing lay the groundwork for decolonizing actually existing anthologies. This is crucial editorial work given the popularity of anthologies for introductory survey courses particularly at large state schools and community colleges, if not in the elite bastions of the Ivy League and private liberal arts colleges. Anthologies are assigned more often in less elite educational spaces, and they are the practical medium through which many teachers first expose students to the premises, objects, and methods of English as a discipline. Without interrogating the organizational principles of anthologies in light of real-world use, we cannot mount a decolonized approach to English literary history that triangulates the canon, the curriculum, and the classroom.

Theorizing the English Literary Anthology

Critiques of anthologies, grounded in postcolonial theory and ethnic studies, treat the genre as representative of and implicated in a power structure much larger than itself. Given their general suspicion and rejection of the anthological project, it is unsurprising that these critiques have little to say about the anthology as an everyday teaching tool. For all their limitations, anthologies remain appealing to instructors and students because they are a relatively affordable one-stop shop for an entire course. To think about the anthology as a classroom text is to contextualize more abstract questions about the politics of its construction within the concrete demands of its adopters.

In 2001, as part of its inaugural issue, the journal *Pedagogy* did just that. Its editor, Christine Chaney, convened a roundtable of professors who regularly teach with anthologies and asked them to compare the 7th edition of the *NAEL* with the *Longman Anthology of British Literature*. The premise of the discussion was simple: anthologies are widely used in the teaching of college English, yet rarely theorized as such (Chaney 192). This was a problem because, as the comparisons of the Norton and Longman anthologies revealed, ideological convictions shaped not just the construction of anthologies but also instructor preferences for the disciplinary visions on offer. Although the editors of English literature anthologies rarely position themselves as promoting a grand narrative of literary history, anthological paratexts (the preface, introduction, table of contents, headnotes, and illustrations) and scope (six centuries of literary history packed into a hefty tome or tomes) all contribute to one. As one respondent put it, drawing on Nietzsche, anthology editors face a choice between presenting their collated canons as forms of "monumental" history or "critical" history (Drake 199). And college instructors, upon adopting an anthology for a survey course, are essentially deciding whether the literary history they teach will be monumental or critical as well.

Of course, the answer in most classrooms will be somewhere in the middle of these two poles, but how to negotiate that middle is something that anthology editors do *with* classroom instructors and not *for* them. Norton commissions surveys from all its adopters asking them to evaluate the selections they deem essential and to offer feedback on the framework and presentation of selections. In preparation for editing the 11th edition, I reviewed the surveys based on the 10th edition of the *NAEL* and found that many instructors recognized and wanted redress for the racialized and gendered exclusions forged by previous iterations of the canon. In practical terms, such redress called for the inclusion of more women and writers of color, but as a whole these writers were less commonly taught than the traditionally canonical figures who respondents considered essential (Joseph Conrad and T. S. Eliot foremost among them). In thinking about how to meet the needs of college instructors, I found a diversity model of anthologizing insufficient; we needed to rethink our presentation of essential works and canonical authors through a decolonizing frame.

I thought again of Nietzsche's lexicon of monumental and critical histories as it might organize a survey course on English literature. These terms, introduced in his 1874 essay "On the Uses and Disadvantages of

History for Life," formed part of Nietzsche's larger meditation on educational culture at his own historical moment. They reflect his turn away from the disinterested scientific mode of knowledge, enshrined in the Germany university system that employed him, toward a more philosophical engagement with history as a life-enhancing activity. Nietzsche was concerned with the interests different models of history perpetuate in the present. A survey of English literature tilted toward his concept of monumental history would resemble a Great Books course, while one tilted toward critical history would likely be grounded in cultural-studies methodologies. For Nietzsche, monumental histories unify and beautify the past into a series of high points that dull attention to their animating causes in the name of producing "effects in themselves" (70). Such effects are totems of inspiration and are described mystically as "something the brave wear over their hearts like an amulet" (70). Critical histories on the other hand emphasize the power of human beings to resist idealizing the past and instead to "break up and dissolve a part of the past" (75). Critical histories, like monumental histories, serve the living, but in different ways. Whereas monumental histories offer the encapsulation of an immemorial greatness, critical histories in their irreverence offer liberation from the conditioning of our forefathers.

Although unshackling ourselves from the values of the past is at the heart of progressivism, Nietzsche warns against mistaking liberation for exoneration. He posits that the danger of critical history lies in the eagerness of its adherents to distance themselves from those aspects of their inheritance that would seem to merit destruction. For Nietzsche, we are the products of earlier generations, that is, "of their aberrations, passions, mistakes, and indeed of their crimes ... If we condemn these aberrations and regard ourselves as free of them, this does not alter the fact that we originate in them" (76). Nietzsche does not specify who this "we" is, but it certainly seems like he is talking about the beneficiaries of the past, for whom turning a critical eye upon previous generations seems one way of rectifying complicity with them.

A "we" limited to the beneficiaries is not the "we" conjured by RMF and various other decolonization movements across multiple universities on multiple continents. The "we" of these movements is as internally fissured as the "we" of the university populations to which they belong. While it is tempting to accuse student activists of an us-versus-them mentality, what essays like Chigudu's clarify are attempts to change the conditions under which shared space in the university is forged. The campaign to remove monuments whose primary purpose is to *glorify* figures whose complicated and often violent legacies should not be obscured is part of a larger call for the recontextualization of monumental histories within their contested legacies across various lines (color, class, and continent being the most visible).

Literary anthologies as taught in the classroom have an important role to play in reappraising the past and reconceptualizing common ground in the university. Today's decolonization movements embrace critique for its associations with structural analysis and revolutionary politics, but they also share Nietzsche's rejection of "critical history" as a form of self-purification from the shameful dimensions of lineage. The English literary anthology, precisely because of its long historical and geographical span, is an essential locus for telling the global story of English lineage anew. Rather than putting its multicentury narrative of literary history to assimi-lationist ends (for example, framing writers of color as indebted to a tradition defined by William Shakespeare and T. S. Eliot), an anthology such as the *NAEL* can draw on the insights of postcolonial and minority writers to offer a much more complex rendition of how classic forms were put to use in colonial educational contexts to eradicate pride in or connection to local culture. When instructors teach the anthology in the classroom, they can use its selections and paratextual matter to address the canon as a cultural institution buoyed by the economic might of the British Empire but also upended by those subjects who felt both initiated into and alienated by English literary tradition.

To offer but one example, Caribbean poet Kamau Brathwaite coined the term "nation language" to denote the aesthetic and political task of breaking out of the "entire pentametric model" defined by the English poetic tradition from Chaucer onward ("Nation Language" 864). Iambic pentameter represents the sound of English as an "imposed language," whereas its deformation through African folk song and syncopated rhythms enabled Brathwaite to dislocate and indigenize English through the sound and meter of his Caribbean milieu. Brathwaite's deep attention to the components of language led him to focus on the relationship between the sound of poetry and the visual appearance of poems on the page. His later poetry supplemented nation language with what he called "Sycorax video style," that is a style that emphasized typographical experi-mentation and the use of word-processing tools to retrieve a version of the written word that "could still *hear itself speak*" (*ConVERSations* 167). Brathwaite may have rejected the pentameter of Chaucer, but he uses the affordances of the computer, its selection of fonts and the scroll function of the screen, to return to another, less Christian, account of the Middle Ages defined by the illuminated manuscript and the historical interactions between Europe, the Mediterranean, and the Middle East.

As the name implies, Sycorax video style also sent Brathwaite back to Shakespeare's *The Tempest*. In his poem "Letter to Sycorax," he reimagined Sycorax, mother to Caliban, as a ghost living inside his computer and inspiring his reclamation of the tools of literacy from a colonial print culture. Writing in light, as Brathwaite would call the practice of composing on a computer, countered the symbolic weight of Prospero's book and guided his poetic return to various points of origination: the birth of English literary tradition, the slave trade, the genocide of Indigenous peoples in the Caribbean, and the spoils that resulted from those conquests.

Brathwaite made his *NAEL* debut in the 8th edition in a section entitled "Nation and Language." This section, which appeared in "Volume 2: The Twentieth Century and After" under the editorships of Jahan Ramazani and Jon Stallworthy and the general editorship of Stephen Greenblatt, was the first to address directly territorial decolonization and the migration of Brown and Black peoples from the former colonies to Britain. "Nation and Language" arrayed writers of color alongside White working-class, Scottish, and Irish writers. In addition to Brathwaite, it featured Claude McKay, Hugh MacDiarmid, Brian Friel, Louise Bennett, Ngũgĩ wa Thiong'o, Salman Rushdie, Wole Soyinka, Tony Harrison, and John Agard. In the 9th edition, the section would be revised as "Nation, Race, and Language," and Hanif Kureishi, Grace Nichols, and M. NourbeSe Philip would replace MacDiarmid, Friel, Harrison, and Agard. In the 10th edition, the section continued to diversify the writers represented in the anthology by broaching historical and political conditions through the linguistic question of "which English?" (853). The choice of whether to abandon English for Indigenous languages, to write in a vernacular or creole, or to adopt Standard English carried within it the need to balance the marks left by the British Empire with the marks its former subjects could leave on the English language.

As the *NAEL* editorial team prepared the 11th edition, matters of nation, race, and language suffused every period of literary history. The editorial team thought comprehensively about how the perspectives of postcolonial and immigrant writers might alter the selections and normative framework of the anthology as a whole. Period editors, while respectful of one another's specialist knowledge, also engaged in conversations across period boundaries to determine how older literary works signify differently across centuries and political geographies. We debated whether the profoundly complicated legacy of *The Tempest* in the Caribbean should exert retrospective pressure on which Shakespeare plays were included in "Volume B: The Sixteenth Century and Early Seventeenth Century" and how those plays should be paratextually framed through headnotes, footnotes, and bibliographies. As we finalized our selections for the 11th edition, period editors decolonized our principles of selection by recognizing how the global diffusion of English literature was grounded in the power dynamics of territorial, educational, and cultural imperialism. The colonial legacy of English in the twentieth and twenty-first centuries alters our choice of representative and significant texts from previous centuries.

And yet to say that a shared interest in decolonization guides changes to our organizing principles is not to suggest that *NAEL* editors are simply plucking concepts of racial or linguistic difference from the present and applying them to the past. In their revisions to "Volume A: The Middle Ages," editors Julie Orlemanski and James Simpson find that a period-specific engagement with race demands following notions of racial identity into older discourses of bodily, religious, and cultural difference. Following the lead of premodern critical race studies, they aim to pluralize the genealogies of race as a literary and cultural lens by including texts that stage European fantasies of Islam and Judaism and explore geographic alterity. For instance, the 11th edition features a romance known as *The King of Tars* in which religious difference is written on the body when the conversion of a character from Islam to Christianity results in the apparent whitening of his skin. Selections from the *Book of John Mandeville*, a popular travel narrative, survey the wonders supposedly witnessed on a journey as far east as India and thus give a sense of how cultural distance and foreignness were figured by writers of the time. The editors also include texts in translation such as a poem originally written in Hebrew by Meir ben Elijah of Norwich, ruminating on the painful experiences of Jewish persecution leading up to the expulsion of Jews from England in 1290.[2]

Brathwaite's rejection of one powerful strand of English poetic tradition, the iambic pentameter, led him back to other strands of English literary tradition and textual culture, namely scrolls and illuminated manuscripts. It also led him to a version of the Middle Ages that privileged points of intercultural contact rather than autochthonous culture. We see this version of the Middle Ages emerging from revised editions of the *NAEL* as Orlemanski and Simpson draw attention to the imagining of cultural difference within the period. They also explain the salience of medieval literature to recognizing the religious and iconographic dimensions of modern racisms. Such an editorial strategy builds on the specific interventions of contemporary scholars of color who have worked tirelessly to render race a legible category within earlier periods of literary history. These same scholars have also had to fight against their own persistent marginalization within the profession of English literature and were among the first to denounce misinformed appropriations of medieval symbols by alt-right and White nationalist groups.

Kimberly Anne Coles, Kim F. Hall, and Ayanna Thompson have argued that remaining studiously neutral in the face of White supremacist myth-ologizing results in cultural histories of early literatures that unwittingly "assist far-right fictions." They call upon fellow scholars in the early periods (where scholars of color are less likely to be represented) to confront how the colonial project is woven into canonical texts, and they advocate for editorial and teaching approaches that transmit the political complexities of early literatures. For medievalist Mary Rambaran-Olm, disabling racist fantasies of a glorified Anglo-Saxon past also demands decentering Eurocentric narratives of ancient literary history and doing the work of historical recovery. She foregrounds figures such as Hadrian and Theodore – late seventh- and early eighth-century monks and "refugees from Asia Minor" who brought Greek Christian traditions to England by way of Syria and Palestine. The Bigger 6 Collective, started by a group of scholars dedicated to fighting structural racism in the field of Romantic literature, takes its name from the shared mission to promote scholarly and creative work by historically marginalized people and to give a wider view of the Romantic period than the one on offer through figures such as Wordsworth, Coleridge, Blake, Byron, Shelley, and Keats (the Big Six).

The periodic revision processes of anthologies like the *NAEL* respond to the latest developments in scholarship and to the work of antiracist academic collectives such as Bigger 6, Medievalists of Color, and Shakerace. These groups have been at the vanguard of decolonizing work in the North American academy, and they have explicitly tied research innovation (or the lack thereof) to hiring and recruitment practices within the profession. Their interrogation of the English literary tradition yields not a convenient revision-ism but a compelling need for renewal in ways that connect literary research to the bodies doing and teaching the research. The suspension of a literary dominant, for example a canonical meter or set of writers, engenders a return to the historical and cultural milieu from which it emerged. I have come to think of the suspension that is also a reinvigoration as central to a decolonized theory of anthologizing. Such a theory uses the exigencies of the contemporary moment to exact new forms of recognition and amplification from the narratives we develop about literature in the English language.

Reimagining Literariness

Certainly, critics of English as a discipline might respond that the *NAEL*, by virtue of its scope and mission, can never go far enough in dismantling a Eurocentric canon or displacing traditional curricular categories built on the paradigms of major authors and genres (poetry, drama, fiction). Anthologies organized around parallel traditions (for example, Caribbean literature or postcolonial poetry) or a more capacious category of textuality (for example, Black British writing) play a vital role in the formation of distinct collective identities.[3] In turn, the publication of identity-based anthologies creates the strategic groundwork for the recognition and consolidation of fields and can serve as a prerequisite to the curricular accommodation of in-depth courses on minority or diasporic literatures.

While I welcome anthologies dedicated to raising the visibility and accessibility of less-taught literary cultures, I do not want to underestimate the power of changing the story a dominant literary culture tells about itself. Rethinking the contours of the *NAEL* leverages the influence of a historically powerful publishing enterprise in universities and classrooms where decolonizing methodologies are not always incompatible with notions of canonicity. The most faithful adopters of the *NAEL* teach at large state institutions in the southern United States, in particular Texas and Alabama, where introductory survey courses are changing but the category of "Great Books" has not fallen out of fashion. Working with these instructors demands meeting them where they are and introducing changes to the anthology that recognize progress made on the ground.

When Martin Puchner, the general editor of the *Norton Anthology of World Literature* (*NAWL*), met with instructors in Alabama, he found that their curricular understanding of "greatness" had evolved from an emphasis on Western civilization to a more comparatively religious and civilizational approach. These anthology users strove to give their students access to "the foundational texts of foreign cultures" and to address an increasingly large cohort of students from China, India, Saudi Arabia, and South Korea (the four largest groups reflected in the internationalization of United States higher education). Learning more about the changing constituencies and continuing values of Southern universities spurred Puchner to revise the operative definition of literature at work in the *NAWL*. No longer grounded in modern categories like the novel or even ancient ones like poetry, the anthological category of world literature now encompasses religious scripture, orature, and philosophical writing.

The move to deprovincialize Great Books courses and world literature anthologies overlaps with the aims of decolonizing the English departments that house such courses. For Caroline Levine, a member of the *NAWL* editorial team and a scholar originally trained in nineteenth-century British literature, the political potential of anthologizing world literature lies in foregrounding "literature's role in a large-scale story of global inequality" (218). As Levine argues, literature presupposes literacy in the written word, with the consequence that world literature anthologies reproduce a European progress narrative in which mass literacy becomes an index of civilizational superiority and orality becomes an index of civilizational simplicity. Given that 90 percent of the world "could not read as recently as 1850," Levine pleads for the category of world literature to make room for orature (226). By recognizing and granting prestige to complex oral works and to the oral performances of written works, the world literature anthology decolonizes its own standards of cultural achievement. It makes room for the complex verbal artistry of modern African and Asian cultures while also granting pride of place to the songs, folktales, and legends of Indigenous and enslaved peoples in colonial and nineteenth-century American literature – groups historically given short shrift by the yardstick of literacy.

The *NAWL* approach mitigates the historically exclusionary and misleading effects of the category of "literariness" without dispensing with the commitment to honor aesthetic achievement in the verbal arts. Its reckoning with literacy as an instrument of power, discipline, and indoctrination recalls Brathwaite's stance in his essays on nation language and Sycorax video style. It also raises the question of whether a Norton anthology can meaningfully evolve beyond the format of the printed book to make use of digital platforms in a decolonizing fashion. Can we connect transcriptions of oral poetry with recordings or performances of it? The 10th edition of the *NAEL* includes poetry by Black British poets Linton Kwesi Johnson and Patience Agbabi in addition to Bennett and Brathwaite. While the linguistic ingenuity of each of these poets is amply available on the page, sound and performance are indelible elements of their work and are not reproducible within the limits set by the printed book.

Yet if we can marshal the resources of the e-book format, we can create a literary anthology across print and digital formats that allows teachers and students to access literature – that is, read, hear, and experience it – as the multimedia category that it is. Reimagining the anthology across book formats means thinking of it as a transmedia genre. This is essential for multiple reasons, not least that electronic literature is unable to be anthologized satisfactorily in the codex form. The kinetic poetry of bpNichol, the Flash animations of Young-Hae Change Heavy Industries, and the Twitter fiction of Teju Cole show that twenty-first-century literature is evolving in ways that demand anthologizers think with and beyond the printed book. These forward-looking examples provide opportunities to reappraise how past entries have been anthologized and whether they could be anthologized differently.

Take Agbabi for example. Although she identifies primarily as a poet, as opposed to a spoken-word poet, she has talked about the centrality of the "voice with its cadences" (Novak and Fischer 361) to her body of work: "For me it is about trying to get to the emotional truth of a poem through the sound of it" (358). While the poet laureate of Canterbury, she began composing *Telling Tales*, a rewriting of Chaucer's *Canterbury Tales* in the voices of diverse members of British society who would mirror the nation's twenty-first-century demographics. The Wife of Bath becomes a Nigerian immigrant, the wife of Bafa, who speaks in rhyming couplets and in the cadences of a Nigerian English that irregularly follows iambic pentameter. Agbabi describes the project as "retelling the stories that Chaucer himself retold from those circulating around medieval Europe." *Telling Tales* draws on a variety of poetic forms from Chaucer's rime royale to the sonnet corona. Into these forms, Agbabi blends the sounds of regional accents garnered from audio recordings and transcriptions available through the *Sounds Familiar?* website of the British Library. Her collection hails Chaucer's by emphasizing the conjunctures of oral and written cultures in ways that represent ordinary speakers from across all levels of society.

I would like to anthologize Agbabi's poems from *Telling Tales* on the printed page and through recordings of their oral performance. The same goes for Bennett's "dialect" poetry, which she performed for mass audiences in the Caribbean under the stage name of Miss Lou. Bennett's "Jamaica Language," which currently appears in the *NAEL*, is a radio monologue that begins "Listen, na!" (856); yet the anthology does not yet give readers the ability to do so. Norton publishers and users have understandably prioritized the printed book since the inception of the anthology in 1962, but it is high time to make theoretically informed use of the e-book format for texts that were written for stage and page, ear and eye.[4] The e-book presents an opportunity for decolonizing the operative notion of literariness in the *NAEL* so that it encompasses more than the written word and speaks to constituents who have experienced print culture as a tool of cultural alienation and subordination. If we as editors of the 11th edition can rise to the challenge of creating a multimedia anthology, the next step will be convincing anthology adopters that recordings of performances are not supplements to the written poem but essential versions of the literary work.

An Anthology Is Not a Monument

The decolonizing of the *NAEL* will proceed in tandem with the decolonizing of college English pedagogy. As survey courses become more diverse, comparative, and ideally multimediated, the histories professors offer about literatures in the English language should also become more inclusive of the varied and entangled literacies of the anglophone world. When discussing the *NAEL*, Abrams insisted that the anthology not become "a monument" (Donadio). The refusal of the analogy between anthologies and monuments seems especially prescient in the wake of the global RMF movements. Monuments in these movements have become symbols of institutional ossification and recalcitrance in the face of social progress.

Anthologies collect great, some might say monumental, works of literature, but how editors frame and revisit these works over updated editions cannot remain the same. The continued value of anthologies of English literature and for that matter world literature is not a foregone conclusion; indeed, the historical association of anthologies with the cultural arm of imperialism cannot be ignored. For the anthology to be a genre with a bright future, its publishers and editors will have to acknowledge and redress its dark past. An anthology is not a monument, but it is a balancing act. The task is to balance the project of literary and cultural custodianship with a responsiveness to historical change writ large and to demographic change within universities. Anthology makers serve teachers and students who likely do not share the same cultural and social norms even if they are sharing classroom space. The more we can ground our theories of anthologizing in an awareness of that diversity, the more capable we will be of thinking concretely about the revision, transmission, and decolonization of literary tradition.

Notes

1. For literary histories that both model and defend close reading within the expanded framework of global English, see Wai Chee Dimock's *Through Other Continents: American Literature Across Deep Time*; Jahan Ramazani's *Transnational Poetics*, and Rebecca Walkowitz's *Born Translated: The Contemporary Novel in an Age of World Literature*.
2. My thanks to Julie Orlemanski for discussing specific texts as well as the broader editorial strategy for Volume A with me.
3. Yet these identities can come at a cost. Barbara Christian has written about the double bind facing editors of anthologies dedicated to more particular identity groups, for example Caribbean women's writing. While strategically essential to rendering these groups legible within literary curriculums, such anthologies participate in a consolidation of identity that is fundamentally at odds with the irreducibility of literary expression and authorial freedom. Hence, anthologists of ethnic literature must contend with the limitations of the category of ethnicity on the reception of the writers and works they aggregate (Christian 258). For accounts of experimental anthologies of Black writing that attempt to assert identity while also eluding it, see Edwards.
4. Janet Neigh argues that staging poetry is an important avenue by which to decolonize collective memory (170). Performing in pubs, clubs, and music halls allows poets to reshape the internalized scripts of their colonial education and to reach audiences who would not access their works through the traditionally literary means of the chapbook or the anthology.

WORKS CITED

Agbabi, Patience. "Stories in Stanz'd English: A Cross-Cultural Canterbury Tales." *Literature Compass* 15.1 (2018). https://compass.onlinelibrary.wiley.com/doi/abs/10.1111/lic3.12455.

Alemán, Jesse. "The End of English." *PMLA* 136.3 (2021): 470–74.

Andrews, Kehinde. "Preface." In Brian Kwoba, Roseanne Chantiluke, and Athinangamso Nkopo, eds., *Rhodes Must Fall: The Struggle to Decolonize the Racist Heart of Empire*. London: Bloomsbury Academic, 2018, ix–xiv.

Brathwaite, Kamau. *ConVERSations with Nathaniel Mackey*. Staten Island: We Press, 1999.

"Nation Language." In *Norton Anthology of English Literature*, Gen. ed. Stephen Greenblatt. 10th ed. Vol. F. New York: W.W. Norton and Company, 2018, 861–66.

Chaney, Christine. "Editor's Introduction." *Pedagogy* 1.1 (2001): 191–94.

Chigudu, Simukai. "Colonialism Has Never Really Ended: My Life in the Shadow of Cecil Rhodes." *The Guardian*. Jan. 14, 2021. www.theguardian.com/news/2021/jan/14/rhodes-must-fall-oxford-colonialism-zimbabwe-simukai-chigudu.

Christian, Barbara. "A Rough Terrain: The Case of Shaping an Anthology of Caribbean Women Writers." In David Palumbo-Liu, ed., *The Ethnic*

Canon: Histories, Institutions, and Interventions. Minneapolis: University of Minnesota Press, 1995, 241–59.

Coles, Kimberly Anne, Kim F. Hall, and Ayanna Thompson. "BlacKKKShakespearean: A Call to Action for Medieval and Early Modern Studies." *Profession*. Nov. 2019. https://profession.mla.org/blackkkshake spearean-a-call-to-action-for-medieval-and-early-modern-studies/.

Dimock, Wai Chee. *Through Other Continents: American Literature across Deep Time*. Princeton: Princeton University Press, 2006.

Donadio, Rachel. "Keeper of the Canon." *The New York Times*. Jan. 8, 2006. www .nytimes.com/2006/01/08/books/review/keeper-of-the-canon.html.

Drake, George. "Placing the Canon: Literary History and *The Longman Anthology of British Literature*." *Pedagogy* 1.1 (2001): 197–201.

Edwards, Brent. *The Practice of Diaspora: Literature, Translation, and the Rise of Black Internationalism*. Cambridge, MA: Harvard University Press, 2003.

Greenblatt, Stephen, Gen ed. *Norton Anthology of English Literature*, 10th ed., Vol. F New York: W.W. Norton and Company, 2018.

Hofmeyr, Isabel. *The Portable Bunyan: A Transnational History of The Pilgrim's Progress*. Princeton: Princeton University Press, 2003.

Joyce, James. *Ulysses*. 1922. New York: Vintage, 1986.

Levine, Caroline. "The Great Unwritten: World Literature and the Effacement of Orality." *Modern Language Quarterly* 74.2 (2013): 217–37.

Mission Statement, *The Bigger 6 Collective*. https://www.bigger6.com

Neigh, Janet. "Orality, Creoles, and Postcolonial Poetry in Performance." In Jahan Ramazani, ed., *The Cambridge Companion to Postcolonial Poetry*. Cambridge: Cambridge University Press, 2017, 167–79.

Nietzsche, Friedrich. "On the Uses and Disadvantages of History for Life." In Daniel Breazeale, ed., *Untimely Meditations*, trans. R. J. Hollingdale. Cambridge: Cambridge University Press, 1997, 59–123.

Novak, Julia and Pascal Fischer. "On the Interface between Page and Stage: Interview with Patience Agbabi." *Zeitschrift für Anglistik und Amerikanistik* 64.3 (2016): 353–63.

Puchner, Martin. "Learning from World Literature in the South." *Inside Higher Ed*. Dec. 13, 2017. www.insidehighered.com/views/2017/12/13/scholar-changes-his-view-about-literary-marketplace-and-what-literature-can-do.

Ramazani, Jahan. *A Transnational Poetics*. Chicago: Chicago University Press, 2009.

Rambaran-Olm, Mary. "Anglo-Saxon Studies [Early English Studies], Academia, and White Supremacy." *Medium*. Jun. 27, 2018. https://mrambaranolm .medium.com/anglo-saxon-studies-academia-and-white-supremacy-17c87b36obf3.

Ray, Rashawn and Alexandra Gibbons, "Why Are States Banning Critical Race Theory?" *Brookings Institute*. Jul. 2, 2021. www.brookings.edu/blog/fixgov/2021/07/02/why-are-states-banning-critical-race-theory/.

Shesgreen, Sean. "Canonizing the Canonizer: A Short History of *The Norton Anthology of English Literature*." *Critical Inquiry* 35 (2009): 293–318.

Slaughter, Joseph. "World Literature as Property." *Alif: Journal of Comparative Poetics* 34 (2014): 39–73.

Vadde, Aarthi. *Chimeras of Form: Modernist Internationalism beyond Europe, 1914–2016*. New York: Columbia University Press, 2016.

Viswanathan, Gauri. *Masks of Conquest: Literary Study and British Rule in India*. New York: Columbia University Press, 1989.

Walkowitz, Rebecca. *Born Translated: The Contemporary Novel in an Age of World Literature*. New York: Columbia University Press, 2015.

CHAPTER 8

Confabulation as Decolonial Pedagogy in Singapore Literature

Joanne Leow

it seemed to us that during such times, no fiction could be stranger, or
more exciting, than the truth

Sonny Liew, *The Art of Charlie Chan Hock Chye*

LIYANA: So we can't imagine ourselves outside of imperial history?
SIEW: That would be indulging in counterfactuals.
LIYANA: Then why are we even here?

Alfian Sa'at and Neo Hai Bin, *Merdeka / 獨立 /சுதந்திரம்*

The Singapore Bicentennial and the Work of State Pedagogy

In 2019, the Singapore state unironically commenced a year-long commemoration of the bicentennial of the country's colonial founding with
"SG200," a series of art exhibitions, interactive audiovisual productions,
talks, community engagement projects, and other events. The first commissioned work was unveiled with great fanfare on January 2, 2019: the
usually white polymarble statue of Singapore's colonial founder Sir
Stamford Raffles had been papere.d over by the artist Teng Kai Wei to
enable it to blend into the city skyline. Making Raffles invisible through
this optical illusion, this symbolic gesture was ostensibly meant to question
the colonizer's centrality to Singapore's modern mythmaking. The dis-
appearing act of the statue was, however, merely a temporary publicity
stunt. Quoting Kwame Nkrumah, online commentator Paul Jerusalem's
humorous meme pointed out that Teng's work could be read subversively
as a commentary on the neocolonial reality of Singapore's urban spaces,
where the influence and legacy of the coloniality remain firmly entrenched
even as they have become invisible or unremarkable to most.[1]

The momentary erasure of Singapore's most famous colonial figure at the
start of the Bicentennial wrapped up in his legacy reflects the contradictory

167

ways Singapore has begun to wrestle with its postindependence decision to overtly retain much of the material, symbolic, and political legacies of the British Empire. Indeed, two days after Teng's initial alteration of the Raffles statue, a new intervention entitled "The Arrivals" appeared, with the statues of Sang Nila Utama, Tan Tock Seng, Munshi Abdullah, and Naraina Pillai being placed alongside Raffles. Not only were non-European migrants being celebrated, the Srivijayan prince from Palembang Sang Nila Utama was placed in front of Raffles and the others as a precolonial founder of Singapore in 1299.[2]

While other decolonizing and anticolonial movements have sought, in recent years, to destroy and remove statues of colonizers and slave-owners, the Singapore state's most recent approach appears to be to camouflage the centrality of its colonial history with the cosmetic addition of other marginal narratives. Minister Josephine Teo, cochair of the Singapore Bicentennial Ministerial Steering Committee, noted that the purpose of the Bicentennial was to uncover new materials and stories about Singapore's past and to develop "immersive and interactive techniques" to tell these stories (quoted in Kwa 475). More extensively, SG200 and its events functioned as a state-wide curriculum that enforced Singapore's neocolonial nation-building. Aware that solely focusing on colonialism might be out of step with the times, the organizers insisted that they were instead cognizant of the 700-year *longue durée* of Singapore's history, seemingly redefining the word "bicentennial" with nary a thought.

Nevertheless, the beginning of British colonial rule continued to be the undeniable fulcrum around which the national narrative was construed. In his speech for the launch of these commemorations, Prime Minister Lee Hsien Loong was frank about the story he wanted to tell regarding the country's British colonial legacy:

> 1819 marked the beginning of a modern, outward-looking and multicultural Singapore. Without 1819, we may never have launched on the path to nationhood as we know it today. Without 1819, we would not have 1965, and we would certainly not have celebrated the success of SG50. 1819 made these possible. And this is why the Singapore Bicentennial is worth commemorating. ("Speech by PM Lee Hsien Loong")

Lee credits colonialism with the birth of modernity, globalization, multiculturalism, and indeed, the independent Singaporean state. He further predicates the existence of the postcolonial nation on its colonial predecessor. As the official website puts it, it was a "sequel" to SG50, a state celebration in 2015 of the jubilee of Singapore's independence. In constructing the *event* of the Singapore Bicentennial, the state attempted to control what colonialism signified for the postcolonial state.

Even though this may seem retrograde, it is perhaps not inaccurate in summing up Singapore's self-narration of postcolonial exceptionalism and continuity. As Philip Holden rightly posits, Raffles's arrival is seen as "an imposition of certain forms of necessary modern rationality – town planning, good governance, a commitment to free trade – that the postcolonial nation-state would realise in the fullness of time" (Holden 639). This discourse is an integral part of the dominant narrative of an orderly handover of power from the British colonial authorities to an elite English-educated ruling class. Aside from the more obvious visual markers of colonial architecture that were preserved in its central business district, the legal frameworks (including legislation retained from emergency colonial laws regarding detention without trial and restrictions on freedoms of assembly and expression), civil service, language, and systems of justice and governance are all deeply indebted to colonial legacies. Singapore's education policies and curricula continue to be intimately tied to colonial standards, with thousands of exam scripts for the standardized General Certificate of Education (GCE) level exams being assessed annually by the UK-based Cambridge Assessments. Celebrating the Bicentennial in these contexts becomes a logical pedagogical exercise, one that attempts to create coherence in the everyday lived experience of Singaporeans surrounded by these material and structural legacies.

In this chapter, I examine two highly successful and popular contemporary Singaporean texts that are not only exemplars of this growing contemporary literary and filmic archive but further evince a counter-pedagogical awareness that hinges upon what I theorize as dissident tactics of confabulation. The *Oxford English Dictionary* defines to confabulate as "to fabricate imaginary experiences as compensation for loss of memory" (*OED*, 2017). In the Singaporean context, my theorization of the term points to the role of the fictional in the face of wilful state-sponsored amnesia and suppression. Both Sonny Liew's Eisner award-winning graphic novel *The Art of Charlie Chan Hock Chye* (2015) and Alfian Sa'at and Neo Hai Bin's play *Merdeka* / 獨立 /சுதந்திரம் (2019) directly confront the state's self-narration. Both texts self-reflexively collate and examine historical documents, events, and artifacts by reenacting, reimagining, and crucially, inventing stories and characters. Liew's imaginary cartoonist and satirist Charlie Chan Hock Chye provides an artistic, visual, and narrational counterpoint to dominant state narratives. Told in a pastiche-driven style, the *Künstlerroman* twines the artist's ultimate failure with his vividly imagined alternate pasts and futures, all tied to an instructive history of comic styles through the latter half of the twentieth century. Alfian and Neo's multilingual play follows a study group, Raffles Must Fall, who come together to investigate lesser-known anticolonial stories from Singapore's history. Using historical documents and speeches, the multiracial cast of actors create plays within the play: hyperdramatic, metatheatrical reenactments that ultimately employ the theater as a processual space of learning and unlearning. In the absence of formal curriculum reform toward the work of decolonization, I argue that con-fabulation is a crucial literary and pedagogical mode in these attempts toward creating and disseminating truly decolonial narratives of Singapore. It functions in the absence of a decolonizing literary curriculum in the country and of free and open space for artistic expression. It carefully sidesteps the state's desire for a "factual," fixed history, singular modes of narration, and its censorious instincts.

Thus, these texts stand in pointed contrast to the Singapore Bicentennial's "signature event": "From Singapore to Singaporean: The Bicentennial Experience @ Fort Canning." This audiovisual, theatrical, and filmic extravaganza was set, seemingly without irony, in a former British military installation. In an echo of how many colonial buildings in the city center have been gutted and repurposed, the creators of this multimedia exhibit remodeled the interior of the spaces to create purpose-built sets and produce a carefully scripted, immersive version of Singapore's history. Helmed by Michael Chiang, a playwright, and Beatrice Chia-Richmond, a theater director, who both have experience directing the annual National Day Parade, the two-part experience had a familiar arc of mystical beginnings, colonial vision, war-time suffering, and manifest destiny. "The Time Traveller" was divided into five acts (Beginnings, Arrival, Connectivity, Occupation, Destiny) like a classic play, while the accompanying "Pathfinder" was a series of nonguided exhibits set in a park, featuring maps, artifacts, and other more static objects. "The Time Traveller" employed live actors, surround screens and sound, and elaborate water and light features to provide what Gene Tan, the executive director of the Singapore Bicentennial Office, called *a history lesson* translated "to the mainstream audience in an emotional way" ("Creating the Bicentennial Experience"). Tellingly, the British Occupation is subsumed under the acts "Arrival" and "Connectivity," while – consistent with the dominant narrative – the Japanese Occupation during the World War II is depicted as the pivotal and violent conflict in this history. Decolonization from British rule, on the other hand, is glossed over as part of Singapore's continuing trajectory as a successful global port city. The show represented an intensification of the cooptation of meaningful personal and collective narratives in service of the state's larger goal of affective nation-building. It was held up as a great success, with the official metrics recording over 760,000 visitors and their 97.3% approval rating. For the majority of its population, the Singapore state's power to shape its foundational myths through mass pedagogy is far-reaching.

The desire of the postcolonial nation-state or any nation-state to script its historical narratives is, of course, nothing new. The earnest tone adopted in the accompanying behind-the-scenes documentary about this lavish exhibit amply illustrates what Homi Bhabha notes in "Nation and Narration": that the nation-space is processual and "meanings may be partial because they are *in medias res*; and history may be half-made because it is in the process of being made; and the image of cultural authority may be ambivalent because it is caught, uncertainly, in the act of 'composing' its powerful image" (Bhabha 3). Chiang, Chia-Richmond, and Tan repeatedly reiterate their desire to "create ... emotion" in this "history lesson" and to construct "a very intimate encounter with Singapore," and further to define "what it means to be Singaporean" ("Creating the Bicentennial Experience"). The need for the state to constantly revise, revisit, and repeat the enduring narrative of Singapore's vulnerability and exceptionalism post-Empire reached a fever pitch during SG200.

But the tensions inherent in nation-building on a foundation of colonial development pose interesting conundrums. In their introduction to the seminal critical anthology *The Scripting of a National History: Singapore and Its Pasts* (2008), Lysa Hong and Jianli Huang note how the country's history has been reverse engineered to "shape and disseminate a sense of national identity which privileges political identification at the level of the nation-state – a product of negotiations with historical identities" (Hong and Huang 1). Most crucially, they argue, "the history that the state tells of itself, and the degree of its success in getting its citizens to embrace that history as their own, are thus central to the process of its nation-building" (1). The use of a powerfully emotive and manipulative, multimedia-enhanced state storytelling apparatus represents an obvious manifestation of insecurity about the incoherence of a bicentennial narrative that purports to cover 700 years of history. In her analysis of more recent state attempts at storytelling during the Bicentennial, Cheng Nien Yuan cautions against accepting state-sanctioned plurality without skepticism: "unlike the relatively straightforward top-down approach of Rajaratnam's era ('this is the past and we say so'), the storytelling state gives an illusion of democratic engagement and inclusivity of voices" (Cheng).

Ragini Tharoor Srinivasan points out, in her critique of Bhabha's "DissemiNation": "The problem posed by the nation was never simply power. The problem is whose" (Srinivasan). In calling for "less subversion and more persuasion. Less disruption, more renewed solidarity. Less repetition with a difference and more pedagogy of difference," Srinivasan turns our attention to what Bhabha labels as "the unspoken tradition[s]" of "colonials, postcolonials, migrants, minorities . . . who will not be contained" (Bhabha, quoted by Srinivasan) by the state's singular narration. She posits that it is overdue for these traditions to be spoken and to be heard. A similar impetus toward decolonizing redress has meant that Singapore's lavish emphasis of its colonial histories during the Bicentennial led a new generation of scholars, activists, and artists to critique the accepted state pedagogy, asking the fraught and complex questions about what a decolonial Singapore might mean. In fact, the state's own extravagant and multifaceted attempts at consolidating the event of the Bicentennial led paradoxically to a slew of theatrical, artistic, and academic explorations of alternative modes of grappling with colonial and postcolonial history and historiography. This included a special inter-disciplinary issue of the *Journal of Southeast Asian Studies* and an edited collection of critical essays, interviews, and historical documents entitled *Raffles Renounced: Towards a Merdeka History* (2021). Numerous plays were also written and performed in 2019, including The Necessary Stage's *Civilised*, Drama Box's *Tanah•Air* 水•土, and The Art of Strangers' *Miss British*.

These efforts have joined an increasing number of texts in the past decade – including Tan Pin Pin's banned documentary *To Singapore with Love* (2013), Jeremy Tiang's novel *State of Emergency* (2017), Alfian Sa'at's flash fictions *Malay Sketches* (2013), Alfian and Marcia Vanderstraaten's play *Hotel* (2015), Wong Souk Yee's novel *Death of A Perm Sec* (2017), Jason's Soo's documentary *Untracing the Conspiracy* (2015), and Suratman Markasan's novel *Penghulu* (2012) – that have reexamined suppressed episodes in Singapore's history. Collectively, this body of work offers a much-needed alternate national literary canon and remedial historiography that emphasizes anticolonial movements, Indigenous communities displaced by state development and control, and the loss of political rights such as a free press, the freedom to organize and assemble, and unfettered artistic expression.

"Of My Country, That Is Yet to Be": The Multiplicity of National Narratives in *The Art of Charlie Chan Hock Chye*

In its first impulse, Sonny Liew's graphic novel *The Art of Charlie Chan Hock Chye* is a text that seeks to educate the reader. On the surface, it is an introduction to "the art" of a neglected but vital comics artist in Singapore. The imaginary life and artistic tribulations of Charlie Chan Hock Chye, however, are pedagogical strategies that allow Liew to twine a primer on historic cartooning styles and genres with a self-reflexive accounting of Singapore's repressed histories of anticolonial student uprisings, detentions, and exiles of political dissidents. Through the confabulated, fictional character of Charlie, the text not only delineates the vulnerable status of the artist and student in the authoritarian state but also presents alternate, confabulated histories and futures in Charlie's unpublished, antiestablishment oeuvre. Crucially, Liew represents himself in the comic as an interlocuter drawn into the framing narrative of this work, asking questions of Charlie, presenting his work with commentary and research, and ultimately acting as both student and teacher. Much of the text has explanatory captions and, in one chapter, even footnotes in the form of a separate comic strip, where the comic-book rendition of Liew himself attempts to engage a skeptical, child-like Singaporean.

By interpolating himself into the narrative, Liew creates complex systems of meaning-making in *The Art of Charlie Chan Hock Chye* that force the reader to engage with the story on multiple registers with critical distance and skepticism. We are learning from Charlie but also about his frailties, hubris, and failures through his art. Similarly, we are learning about various episodes from Singapore's history as they are entwined with Charlie's life story, his historical research, his artistic process, and his (and Liew's) ambivalence. The confabulation of Charlie's life is a satire of a nationalist *Bildungsroman*, since he ultimately fails in his ambition to be Singapore's greatest comics artist. Yet it is also a failure that allows us to consider the grave tragedies hidden beneath Singapore's glossy postcolonial success. The text poses a simple question: if Charlie is meant to be a forgotten artist, discovered and presented by Liew, then what else in the story of Singapore has been similarly neglected, buried, and censored?

Read all together in a dizzying palimpsest of historical documents, sketches, drafts, and comic strips of incredibly diverse styles, Liew's book acts as an alternate literary curriculum that pairs Singapore's political history with a transnational, cosmopolitan set of artistic influences. The tropes of learning and questioning continue as a through thread in all the chapters. In the first two, we begin our education at the start of Charlie's journey as an artist where he privileges the "five foot way libraries" or "pavement libraries" of comic books (Liew 6–7) over the English language school system that he has been enrolled in. The very medium of drawing itself is seen as an act of studying (Liew 19). This archive of material provides a rich fodder for Charlie to create his confabulated, allegorical political cartoons. They also provide the opportunity of the text to illustrate the gaps and absences in Singapore's dominant history.

Each chapter of the text pairs a controversial episode in Singapore's modern history with Charlie's life and art. Liew's text weaves the confabulatory web of Charlie's life around crucial events such as anticolonial student protests the end of the Japanese Occupation and Malayan Emergency, Singapore's separation from Malaysia and the detention without trial of opposition politicians, and the censorship and suppression of a free press. Each unpublished or obscure comic that Charlie produces in response to the historical events happening around him holds up these events through the prisms of science fiction, satire, allegory, and counterfactual narratives. They refract the uncertainty that undercuts the official versions and the manipulation inherent in all storytelling. For instance, Charlie recounts the story of the sixteen-year-old student Chong Lon Chong, who was struck by a stray bullet during labor unrest in 1955 and later died of his wounds. The official version of events blames his death on the procommunist students who paraded him around to inflame the crowd, but Charlie pinpoints the unknowns in the actual reports of the incident. He notes, "not having been there to *see* and *hear* for ourselves, perhaps we can never really know the truth, asking 'what exactly is the story being told?'" (Liew 55). In doing so, the text reveals the confabulatory nature of the state's narratives themselves, even as they purport to be the factual accounting of events.

In the final chapter of Liew's text, Singapore's possible futures and presents intersect in a counterfactual version of its present in Charlie's comic "Days of August." In this version of Singapore, the skyline remains iconic and unchanged, yet Lee Kuan Yew's rival Lim Chin Siong is in power, and the former has taken himself into self-exile in Cambodia. In the subsequent narration, the text rewrites Singapore's history, in part as a homage to Philip K. Dick's *The Man in High Castle*, to create a Singapore where the ruling party's crackdowns and detentions of its socialist rivals had never happened, and the latter had won the elections in 1963. Jini Kim Watson argues that Liew's text "knowingly plays on the fact that it is almost impossible to imagine the future of Singapore otherwise even *had* its political history turned out differently," pointing out that "the very task of *imagining*, from the present, the postcolonial state as vehicle of emancipative, redemptive futurity is at once absolute necessary and almost impossible" (Watson 182). Charlie makes a cameo as a successful artist in this alternate universe, who even has a gallery dedicated to his work. In other ways, Lim Chin Siong and Lee Kuan Yew's similarities are highlighted. In another interview depicted in the comic, Lim fends off questions about a "cult of personality" (Liew 277) that has arisen around his name. Liew's alternate history in "Days of August" thus reveals the official narrative of People's Action Party (PAP) dominance and inevitability as one that is arbitrary.

Liew's text seeks to flesh out these other possible paths and to confabulate alternate narratives of Singapore's history. In effect, this opens up the possibilities of how Singapore might have achieved decolonization in ways that did not leave power in the hands of an English educated elite, which was aligned with the British colonial project. Predictably, the Singapore state, with its unyielding pedagogical narrative of the birth of the nation, has been less than enthusiastic about *The Art of Charlie Chan Hock Chye*. While the text initially benefited from a National Arts Council grant, this was quickly withdrawn due to what were deemed politically sensitive reasons.[3] This grant withdrawal signaled the government's tacit disapproval of having the text taught in public schools or other state institutions of higher learning. The state thus foreclosed an opportunity to use the space of the literary classroom and curriculum to grapple with counterfactual speculative fiction that might challenge the dominant narrative.

This is not to say that the text is simply harboring a fantasy of paths not taken. What it is equally interested in is how storytelling comes to affect accepted realities and histories – what it calls "the power of the word, the image" (Liew 282). In "Days of August," the alternate world breaks down due to a specter that resembles a "man in white" – a young Lee Kuan Yew. Charlie's cameo is central to the action, since he is the artist who is writing an alternate history comic within the alternate Singapore. In a dizzying turn of events, the doubly fictional Charlie Chan is writing a comic of Singapore's actual history with Lee Kuan Yew in power. This Charlie sees this as a mission to assuage the anger of the alternate reality, his comic within a comic is one where "every panel [is] a prayer, a shot in the dark"

(Liew 282). The power of the "true" reality eventually triumphs, destroying the alternate Singapore and sending Charlie and Lim back into the past to preindependence Singapore in 1955. Only now, they have an awareness of their doomed futures – Charlie to a life of invisibility and Lim Chin Siong to one of persecution and ignominy. In this final section of the chapter, we return to the realist visual style that began *The Art of Charlie Chan Hock Chye*, which documents preindependence Singapore. It is a careful graphic echo of the earlier part of the text that lends unity to the work but with one crucial alteration: a complex temporal and narrative awareness that suffuses these historical street scenes with greater weight and importance. Instead of the nostalgic reworking of the past that the graphic novel begins with, this historic version of Singapore is invested with a paradoxical sense of both inevitability and possibility.

If artistic confabulation in Singapore means to imagine otherwise in compensation for the amnesia of a state-driven narrative and urban landscape, Liew's final challenge to the instrumentalization of nostalgia and Singapore's preindependence past in official propaganda could not be more bittersweet. Lim and Charlie have returned to 1955 on the day of the Hock Lee Bus Incident, which was a conflict between the British colonial authorities and students and unionized workers. Charlie, now newly young again in his own comic, knows that he *would* "be a fool to go down that road again" (Liew 289). He says this in reference to both himself and Lim Chin Siong, since, as he tells him, "everything you were. Or are working towards . . . it all fails in the end. The P.A.P. and Lee Kuan Yew will win . . . and **nothing** we do now can alter the course of this history" (Liew 286). Surrounded by the sights and sounds of preindependence Singapore, Lim replies with the belief that "these things that we're fighting for . . . the **welfare** of the workers, our **freedom**, our dignity . . . whatever the costs they're still worth the while, are they not?" (Liew 287). Lim's idealism and conviction are balanced by superimposed text boxes in the voice of the fictional Charlie, who sees the fixed path of Lim's future even as his young self walks away from Charlie, literally down a street in 1950s Singapore. Forced to relive their choices and lives in "Days of August," the characters move from the complexities of past conditional temporality, *what could have been*, to an incomplete present modality. Charlie knows that he will have to contend with the "harsh reality" of trying to make a living as an artist in Singapore but seeks instead in this final moment to dwell on the comics that he has "yet to draw," a life he has "yet to live," and of a Singapore "that is yet to be" (Liew 292–93).

"That Would Be Indulging in Counterfactuals": Metatheatrical Reenactments in *Merdeka* / 獨立 /சுதந்திரம்

A similar desire to relive, reenact, and retell the nation's narrative through self-reflexive and literary confabulations infuses Alfian Sa'at and Neo Hai Bin's play *Merdeka* / 獨立 /சுதந்திரம். The starting premise of the play is that the six characters belong to a reading group called "Raffles Must Fall." They meet to share their research on anticolonial figures and stories from Singapore's history, reenacting these little-known narratives and debating their significance to the body politic. The decolonizing pedagogical significance of this theatrical piece cannot be overstated. Indeed, numerous critics have cited its similarity to a "lecture" or "lesson," with its long passages of direct quotation from historical texts, speeches, and documents (Kuttan; Bakchormeeboy). The play was written in response to the Bicentennial and directly troubles the centrality of the date of Singapore's colonial founding. It reveals the arbitrary nature of 1819 as a defining moment in the founding of modern Singapore. Instead, through an alternate curriculum and a pedagogy of performative re-enactment, *Merdeka* / 獨立 /சுதந்திரம் provides a messy and complex lineage between colonial power and the contemporary authoritarian state.

Staged by the theater company W!ld Rice on Singapore's only thrust stage, *Merdeka* / 獨立 /சுதந்திரம் begins with a set where its actors are, according to the stage directions, "*seated, as if in a classroom*" (Alfian and Neo, Sc. 1). The trilingual title (Malay, Mandarin, and Tamil) signals the play's reclamation of non-English forms of storytelling and concepts of decolonization and self-determination. In particular, the Malay word "Merdeka" is fraught with the history of its usage during the Malayan quest for independence from the British, as will be seen in the latter part of my analysis.

In the lively and fraught discussions that ensue amongst the characters about race, language, and history, the play creates a pedagogical space in Singapore that only exists in the theater. It is a space that is free from state-sponsored national education and is one where histories are contested and performed. Each of the characters brings up a particular historical episode or personage that they have been researching, and the group proceed to reenact the events in an exaggerated manner. This is followed by a metatheatrical analysis by the characters of each reenactment and its biases, constructions, imperfections, and lacunae. As the actors reenact scenes from suppressed histories, they begin to question whether decolonization and freedom are truly possible from such a fraught and compromised colonial past.

It is precisely from an attention to the gaps in the "facts," the so-called "counterfactuals," that *Merdeka* / 獨立 / சுதந்திரம் draws its confabulatory power. Its often campy reenactments allow us to hear the songs and speeches of the past and reevaluate visual signifiers such as the Raffles statue and other historical artifacts, and thus gives us an opportunity to experience these visual and aural signs in the flesh. In its curation of alternate moments of Singapore's precolonial, colonial, and (post)colonial histories, it is doubly self-conscious as it performs history, quoting directly from archival and source materials and highlighting numerous possible interpretations of these accounts. In its eleven scenes, the production eschews a linear timeline, skipping 100 years back to Singapore's Centenary celebrations, then sixty-five years ahead to S. Rajaratnam's seminal speech, before moving at breakneck speed to 1812, and so on. The play continues in this vein, bypassing most of the officially emphasized dates and years with aplomb, enacting a new national canon.

Thus, if the state has control over the mainstream historical narrative discourse outside the stage-world, and further within the theater scene through censorship, the play-within-the-play in *Merdeka* / 獨立 / சுதந்திரம் opens up an alternative space in the mode of the self-conscious, sometimes melodramatic historical reenactment. In Singapore's censorious context, the actors play characters who are acting as other characters and in doing so heighten the sense of theatricality, while questioning the ways in which histories are told and retold. The use of metatheater, a technique that highlights the theatricality of a piece of drama to critique the performance of history and to allow for skepticism at the framing of these narratives, stands in direct contrast to the state's dominant narratives that brook no dissent. Unlike the state's account, however, the play, in its historiographic metatheatrical way, remains conscious and suspicious of the national narrative and its literary conventions.

This is theater that is highly aware of the unforgiving regime it exists in. It repeatedly uses the structure of the play-within-the-play as a means to confabulate narratives in the face of suppressed histories, and to do so in a way that foregrounds the idea of history as performance. As Alexander Feldman argues:

> There is always a power imbalance between those who inhabit the stage-world and those above, beyond and outside it. Within this authoritarian structure, however, the play-within-the-play creates a potentially subversive space, permitting the assertion and enactment of truths, through the mechanism of theatre, that challenge the status quo. (Feldman 14)

The playful, hyperdramatic nature of the historical reenactments of *Merdeka* / 獨立 /சுதந்திரம் allow it to literally "play" with history, to interrogate, parody, satirize, and give it a fluidity that is absent in the Singaporean context. It provides a knowing space in which the actors can challenge the orthodox histories that have been promoted and reclaim the suppressed histories that were inconvenient.

The conceit of a history reading group called "Raffles Must Fall" reenacting historical scenes and figures chosen for their affective, familial, political, and personal significance forces the audience to consider an alternate historiographical method. This is a way of narrating the nation that suggests echoes and resonances while resisting the desire for strict structures of cause and effect. It also enlarges Singapore's erstwhile national borders, giving us important insights into the complexities of kinship in the precolonial Malay Archipelago, Raffles's invasion and humiliation of the city and court of Yogyakarta, and the close ties between other anti-colonial movements and Singaporean activists.

The play acts as well as a form of close reading through its confabulation of some of the key anticolonial texts of the period. Here is where the political and the theatrical are brought together to suggest that both are performances to a certain extent and must be interrogated as such. Toward the end of the performance, it places two famous speeches almost side by side to weigh their words within and without their context. The first is a fiery speech given by the young Lee Kuan Yew on August 31, 1963 at a Malaysia Solidarity Day Mass Rally where he declares Singapore's allegiance to its union with Malaysia and its independence from the colonial British authorities. The second is a quiet recitation of the Indonesian President Soekarno's speech from the Bandung Conference of 1955. Lee's speech recognizes the performativity of his own proclamation for the people of Singapore:

JARED (LEE KUAN YEW): We have the will to be a nation in our own right. That is
    the right that we the people of Singapore today proclaim.
    Our act follows the traditions of the great anti-colonial revolutions in Asia . . .
    If we live up to our convictions, we will stand the test and judgment of history.
    On the 16th we go on with Malaysia and we will survive, and prosper and
    flourish.
    Merdeka! (*Audience follows*)
    Merdeka! (*Audience follows*)
    Merdeka! (*Audience follows*) (Alfian and Neo, Sc. 11)

Lee's words attempt to will independent Singapore into being. It is an "act," theatrical, performative, proclamatory, and political all at once.

The moment replayed here is a crucial one that blurs the lines between the aspirational dream and strategic reality of seeking decolonization. It is a moment where the fiction and theater of Singapore as a postcolonial nation begins as an utterance and ends as a speech act as the crowd joins in his call for freedom. But it is also an incredibly fraught moment – for all the freedom that Lee calls for, it is clear that the play *Merdeka* / 獨立 / சுதந்திரம் exists only because there is so little in terms of narrating a different tale of Singapore. Indeed, Lee had just managed to arrest and detain many of his political rivals without trial just six months earlier in Operation Coldstore.

True to its metatheatrical form, the actors have already set the audience up to understand their complicity in this troubled yet compelling moment. Breaking the fourth wall, the character Siew addresses the audience directly and asks them to rehearse repeating the word "Merdeka" in preparation for their involvement in the play. Collapsing the boundaries again between past and present, Siew asserts:

> It is 1963. All of you, all of *us*, are at the Padang right now. We are attending a Malaysia Solidarity Day Mass Rally. Lee Kuan Yew is delivering a speech at the Padang. He is 39 years old. (Alfian and Neo, Sc. 11)

By switching deliberately to the present tense and to the first-person plural, Siew implicates and imbricates the audience in the play and in the country's collective history. As the theatrical performance reenacts Lee's speech, so does the audience step into the shoes of the audience in the Padang – to the point that their bodies and voices are coopted into the moment, into the utterance of Singapore's independence. As the reenactment ends, the characters immediately begin analyzing the significance of this 1963 scene to the construction of the Singapore Story. Unlike most postcolonies that celebrate an Independence Day, Liyana points out, Singapore commemorates a National Day (August 9, 1965) that also marks the failure of its merger with Malaysia and its consequent vulnerability. The word that the audience were made to repeat so enthusiastically just a moment before takes on a quality of even greater hollowness.

By contrast, the actors read Soekarno's Bandung Conference speech "as if it's *not* a speech" (Alfian and Neo, Sc. 11). Taking his words out of the context of the highly politicized gathering, the actors focus only on the surface meaning of the words which note how "for us, colonialism is not something far and distant. We have known it in all of its ruthlessness. We have seen the immense human wastage it causes, the poverty it causes, and the heritage it leaves behind" (Alfian and Neo, Sc. 11). The actors take turn to read portions of the speech, producing a polyphony of ordinary citizens who at the end quietly repeat "Merdeka," a Malay word that means independence or freedom. The stage directions call for the final iteration of the word to be "*almost a whisper*" (Alfian and Neo, Sc. 11). Even as it was a rallying cry at the point of Singapore's uncoupling from the British Empire, by the end of the text, it takes on a wistful resonance in the face of the postcolonial state's continued authoritarian ways.

"Past Conditional Temporality"

In the epilogue to his memoir *From Third World to First* (2000), Lee Kuan Yew reflects on the sweep of history and what he views as Singapore's improbable existence. To follow Lee's account, every decision taken by him was one that was completely pragmatic, toward the goal of Singapore's continued survival. Lee's story, meant to echo the planned success of the city-state, is of the full triumph of twentieth-century high modernist ideology coupled with authoritarian determination. He locates Singapore's success as part of the industrial revolution and European colonialism, "their inventions, technology, enterprise ... the story of man's search for new fields to increase his wealth and well-being" (Lee 689). He begins his story with the usual recourse to British colonialism and then ties Singapore's progress to technological advancements and a calculative investment in human capital.

The single exception to this certainty lies in the last pages of his book. Here Lee allows himself a moment of retrospeculation, as he muses, "would I have been a different person if I had remained a lawyer and not gone into politics?" (Lee 688). He describes "the swirling currents of political changes" (Lee 685) that swept him along and rhetorically asks himself whether he *would have* continued on the path to Singapore's founding leader if he had known the tribulations that lay ahead of him. This is a strange use of the past conditional tense in a relentless memoir full of confident and fateful anecdotes that purports to be a guide, a book that tells you "how to build a nation" (3). Indeed, without prior knowledge of what was to come, Lee says that he and his colleagues "pressed on, oblivious of the dangers ahead" (686). Yet the note of uncertainty that Lee strikes here at the end, his musing about alternate paths that might have lain in front of him, crucially stops short of the alternate histories and futures that Singapore might have had.

These suppressed histories are the starting point of the literary texts that I have read in this chapter, what Lisa Lowe calls "the *past conditional temporality* of the 'what could have been'" (Lowe 40). For the most part, Lee's worldview had no time or space for what Lowe sees as the essential power of this temporality. He was only really interested in condemning "what could have been" as potential failure without the strict governance of the ruling party. In Lowe's view, however, the past conditional temporality allows "a different kind of thinking, a space of productive attention to the scene of loss, a thinking with twofold attention that seeks to encompass at once the positive objects and methods of history and social science, and also the matters absent, entangled, and unavailable by its methods" (Lowe 40–41). Unlike the myriad catastrophic endings for Singapore that Lee often holds up as warnings, Lowe emphasizes the critical openness of this temporal mode and its important representation in literary fictions. Indeed, she writes, we must turn to what could have been "in order to reckon with the violence of affirmation and forgetting, in order to recognize that this particular violence continues to be reproduced in liberal humanist institutions, discourses, and practices today" (Lowe 41). In other words, "what could have been" is singularly crucial for examining the truths and paths *not* taken that underpin our current moment, since understanding them is the key to shaping what might be to come and preventing the inexorable drift of colonial legacies.

Both Liew's graphic novel and Alfian and Neo's play function as consciously decolonial pedagogies arising within a state where postcolonial national narratives are tightly restricted. Where the state seeks an orderly, completist narrative in five conventional acts with carefully managed affect, artistic practitioners such as Liew, Alfian, and Neo seek the confabulated, unfinished, and counterfactual. Alfian, Faris Joraimi, and Sai Siew Min write in the introduction to *Raffles Renounced: Towards a Merdeka History* that a "Merdeka history" is one that "not only untangles us from colonial narratives" but is also an approach to understanding Singapore's history through an "emancipatory" approach that involves "empowering the plural, the non-elite and the oblique" (15). In the face of a controlled and controlling state pedagogy, it offers artistic and theatrical spaces for collective learning, contemplation, lacunae, and possibility. It demands of its students a commitment to uncertainty and ambivalence.

Notes

1. See www.facebook.com/photo?fbid=976056375921980&set=pb.10000552
   8806960.-2207520000.
2. Philip Holden questions the official impetus of this work, since "the display concealed paradoxes: in its racialised divisions, it still followed the contours of

colonial governance of subject peoples the British introduced, and it erased colonial violence" (Holden 632).

3. See https://cbldf.org/2015/06/censorship-by-financial-sabotage-cartoonist-sonny-liew-loses-singapore-arts-grant/.

WORKS CITED

Alfian Sa'at and Neo Hai Bin. *Merdeka / 獨立 /சுதந்திரம்*. 2019. Theatrical script.

Alfian Sa'at, Faris Joraimi, and Sai Siew Min. "Introduction." In Alfian Sa'at, Faris Joraimi, and Sai Siew Min, eds., *Raffles Renounced: Towards a Merdeka History*. Singapore: Ethos Books, 2021.

Bakchormeeboy. "Review: Merdeka / 獨立 /சுதந்திரம்" by W!ld Rice." *Bakchormeeboy*, October 17, 2019. https://bakchormeeboy.com/2019/10/17/review-merdeka-獨立-சுதந்திரம்-by-wld-rice/.

Bhabha, Homi K. *Nation and Narration*. London: Routledge, 1990.

Cheng, Nien Yuan. "The Singapore Bicentennial: It Was Never Going to Work." *new mandala: New Perspectives on Southeast* Asia, March 6, 2019. www .newmandala.org/the-singapore-bicentennial-it-was-never-going-to-work. Accessed January 15, 2022.

"Creating the Bicentennial Experience." Mediacorp, 2019. *Channel NewsAsia*. www.channelnewsasia.com/watch/creating-bicentennial-experience-1487411.

Feldman, Alexander. *Dramas of the Past on the Twentieth-Century Stage: In History's Wings*. Abingdon: Routledge, 2013.

Holden, Philip. "Colonialism with Benefits? Singaporean Peoplehood and Colonial Contradiction." *Journal of Southeast Asian Studies* 50.4 (2019):632–44. https://doi.org/10.1017/S0022463420000090.

Hong, Lysa and Jianli Huang. *The Scripting of a National History: Singapore and Its Pasts*. Singapore: NUS Press, 2008.

Kuttan, Sharaad. "Another Merdeka Is Possible." *apublicsquare.sg*, October 31, 2019. www.substation.org/blog/another-merdeka-is-possible.

Kwa, Chong Guan. "Editorial Foreword: The Singapore Bicentennial as Public History." *Journal of Southeast Asian Studies* 50.4 (2019): 469–75. https://doi .org/10.1017/S0022463420000120.

Lee, Kuan Yew. *From Third World to First: Singapore and the Asian Economic Boom*. New York: Harper Collins, 2000.

Liew, Sonny. *The Art of Charlie Chan Hock Chye*. Singapore: Epigram Books, 2015.

Liu, Vanessa. "Statue of Sir Stamford Raffles in Boat Quay 'disappears' for Singapore Bicentennial." *The Straits Times*, January 2, 2019. www.straitstimes.com/singa pore/statue-of-sir-stamford-raffles-at-boat-quay-disappears-for-singapore-bicentennial.

Lowe, Lisa. *The Intimacies of the Four Continents*. Durham, NC: Duke University Press, 2015.

"Speech by PM Lee Hsien Loong at the launch of the Singapore Bicentennial on 28 January 2019," *Prime Minister's Office*, January 28, 2019. www.pmo.gov.sg/

Newsroom/PM-Lee-Hsien-Loong-at-the-launch-of-the-Singapore-Bicentennial-Jan-2019.

Srinivasan, Ragini Tharoor. "The Nation We Knew: After Homi Bhabha's 'DissemiNation,'" *Post45*, May 19, 2020. https://post45.org/2020/05/the-nation-we-knew-after-homi-bhabhas-dissemination/.

Watson, Jini Kim. "Separate Futures: Cold War Decolonization in Mohamed Latiff Mohamed's *Confrontation* and Sonny Liew's *The Art of Charlie Chan Hock-Chye*." *Discourse (Berkeley, Calif.)* 40.2 (2018): 165–87.

CHAPTER 9

Marxism, Postcolonialism, and the Decolonization of Literary Studies

Stefan Helgesson

In the June 1949 issue of *Nouvelle Critique*, a Paris-based journal promoting "militant Marxism," the Senegalese-French intellectual Gabriel d'Arboussier launched a furious attack on negritude. His *casus belli* was the recently published *Anthologie de la nouvelle poésie nègre et malgache de langue française*, a landmark volume of francophone poetry by Black writers edited by Léopold Sédar Senghor and prefaced by Jean-Paul Sartre. D'Arboussier's main target was in fact Sartre's preface, "Black Orpheus," which soon would become the single most influential account of negritude. Despite Sartre's use of a Marxist vocabulary, d'Arboussier took him to task for mystifying negritude as an "antiracist racism" (Sartre xl).[1] By recoding the epiphenomenon of race as a metaphysical category that would underwrite an emancipatory humanism, Sartre was seen here as obfuscating the material particularities of imperialism. Without denying that race could be an aspect of oppression, d'Arboussier questioned the assumption of a unified black identity. What exists, he said, "are different *groups [peuples]* . . . who are dominated and exploited not by another *race*, but by other groups, or, to be precise, by the *ruling classes of other groups*" (d'Arboussier 39).[2]

With remarkable precision, this polemic from 1949 puts the spotlight on the tight yet troubled relationship between Marxism and decolonization within the ambit of literature. D'Arboussier's claims on behalf of an historical materialism that subsumes "race" under "class" have been repeated with variations through the decades. And so have the counter-claims that the colonial predicament undercuts central Marxist tenets. Frantz Fanon's words in *The Wretched of the Earth* that in the colonial context "what parcels out the world is to begin with the fact of belonging or not belonging to a given race, a given species" (30–31) continue to resonate as a challenge to doctrinaire Marxism, with its privileging of political economy over questions of race.

What needs to be noted from the outset is that Marxists can credibly lay claim to being the *original* decolonialists, at least from a Western epistemic horizon. Vladimir Lenin and Rosa Luxemburg offered thorough critiques of imperialism as a stage of capitalism, and in the colonial experience of the early twentieth century – as registered by, among others, Aimé Césaire, Doris Lessing, and C. L. R. James – Marxism was the only established branch of political theory and practice that steadfastly rejected colonialism and racism. With reference to James, W. E. B. Du Bois, and Richard Wright, Cedric Robinson notes that Marxism was their "first encompassing and conscious experience of organized opposition to racism, exploitation, and domination" (5). In Lessing's case, a novel such as *A Ripple from the Storm* shows how her protagonist Martha Quest's only reprieve from the colonial claustrophobia of 1940s South Rhodesia was to be found in Marxism – Martha's (and Lessing's) later rejection of communism notwithstanding. As we follow the ups and downs of Martha's communist faction in Salisbury – with its one African member, Elias Phiri – the anticolonial inflection of Marxism becomes clear. It is largely an intellectual exercise, buoyed by an almost religious faith in the imminence of world revolution and fueled by reading. As Anton, the leading figure in the group says: "If we are to be serious, we must study. We must study hard" (Lessing 67).

Although one might imagine that a historical-materialist politics always privileges "factory floor" mobilization, the example of Lessing shows how literature – and the culture of letters more broadly – has been of central importance to the anticolonial history of Marxism. Indeed, in the era after the World War II many (or even most) of the leading public intellectuals – in a wide range of settings – have been Marxists of one kind or another. Besides names already mentioned, one could add Amílcar Cabral of Guinea-Bissau, the Kenyan writer Ngũgĩ wa Thiong'o, South Africans such as Alex la Guma and Ruth First, the Brazilian critic Roberto Schwarz, the Swedish writers Sara Lidman and Jan Myrdal, and so on.

And yet the relationship between Marxism and anticolonialism or postcolonialism has not been straightforward. D'Arboussier's attack can be read as a template for subsequent battles between competing schools of thought, especially on the cultural arena. With regard to the decolonization of reading, it goes without saying that Anton Hesse's admonition in Lessing's novel to "study hard" referred to a European and Western archive of knowledge. As this chapter will show, there have since then been clusters of debates in different parts of the world whose common denominator has been disagreements over the extent to which Marxist analysis should be privileged epistemologically and whether it can be combined with other, often culturally embedded, explanatory frameworks. When pushed to the limit, the stakes of these debates are exceptionally high: they concern nothing less than what counts as reality. Karl Marx, after all, was a philosopher with the highest ambitions. His sprawling, voluminous writings were not merely an exercise in economic theory but intended to provide an all-encompassing philosophical framework that could analyze, explain, and even change the nature of human reality. Famously, he adopted the dialectical method of Georg Friedrich Hegel, but set Hegel "on his feet" by viewing material conditions, and not the so-called Spirit (*das Geist*), as the foundational element of history and being. Materialism itself, then, as a mode of analysis, springs forth dialectically as a negation of Hegelian idealism. This is where we can locate the beginnings of many later rifts between Marxism and other schools of philosophy – including post-colonial and decolonial theory.

After exploring how Marxism fared in two contexts of decolonization, this chapter will focus briefly on one recent *literary* mode of Marxist analysis with far-reaching implications for our discussion: the Warwick Research Collective's (WReC) notion of "world-literature" with a hyphen. How does their take on "combined and uneven development" square with the current push for decolonization? What are the pedagogical implica-tions of juxtaposing, as WReC does, literatures from discrete spaces and traditions under the umbrella of materialist theory? Taking its cue from those questions, the conclusion contrasts WReC with some of Walter Mignolo's claims on behalf of "decoloniality" to illustrate the sharp differ-ence between their presuppositions. Rather than falsely trying to harmon-ize theoretical paradigms, this chapter will propose that the *specific* contribution of Marxism to contemporary decolonization might be – as d'Arboussier already suggested – to question tendencies to reify concepts such as "race," "culture," or the "West" as metaphysical categories. That contribution, in turn, is best received on the understanding that there are experiential dimensions relating to aesthetics, language, race, gender, sexu-ality, or indeed religion that the Marxist framework is ill equipped to account for in a nonreductive fashion. Ultimately, I argue that the dialect-ical *method* is the enduring lesson of Marxism – a method that may, by turns, bracket and then reintroduce the Marxist optic in the unending labor of making sense of the world.

Two different historical developments are illustrative of the depth and complexity of the matters I sketch out above. One is the parallel emergence in South Africa, in the 1970s, of Black Consciousness and a materialist school of historiography. The other is the more famous formation of the Subaltern Studies Group (SSG) of Indian historians, also beginning in the late 1970s. Both cases need to be approached in a highly context-sensitive manner.

In the 1960s, South Africa reached the nadir of the oppressive legal and economic system known as apartheid. Following the Sharpeville massacre in 1960, virtually all political opposition had been silenced. Organizations such as the African National Congress (ANC) and the Pan-African Congress (PAC) had been banned, their leaders had been persecuted and imprisoned, rigorous censorship laws had been imposed, and much of the country's intelligentsia had gone into exile. A compelling portrayal of the period's political atmosphere can be found in Nadine Gordimer's novel *The Late Bourgeois World* (1966), which conveys a sense of a crippling stasis that could not last. Nor did it. The budding generation of both Black and White intellectuals and scholars who came of age around 1970 took it upon themselves to craft a renewed critical analysis of South African society. The role Marxism played in this process is intriguing and not entirely predictable. It is nevertheless clear that just how these young intellectuals engaged their task was predicated on their racial positioning.

With Steve Biko and Barney Pityana as leading figures, what became known as Black Consciousness (BC) started not as a political movement, but as a profoundly existential and even theological exercise in reconstructing a sense of self. Famously, BC first entered the limelight in 1969 when the South African Students' Organisation (SASO) broke off from the multiracial National Union of South African Students (NUSAS). SASO was an all-Black student group who refused in this way to continue under what they saw as White tutelage. Instead, the guiding principle of BC was for the oppressed to take responsibility for their own liberation – and this entailed not least an internalized labor of affirming one's dignity and worth. The analysis undergirding such a project was that the strongest instrument of oppression was the minds of the oppressed.

The subsequent successes of BC and its merging with the objectives of a broader antiapartheid movement are well known. (As is the apartheid state's obscene confirmation of its significance in the heinous murder of Steve Biko in 1977.) The interesting point here is that BC created a dilemma for oppositional White intellectuals in South Africa at the time. When the BC activists refused on principle – if not always in practice – to collaborate with Whites, a certain category of White dissidents lost their political footing. If the "liberal" analysis had been that the pathology of apartheid could be resisted through a programmatically colorblind approach that promoted the cause of representative democracy, BC rejected colorblindness and challenged "the legitimacy of oppositional politics by whites" (Ally 79). Its main target was precisely the White liberals in South Africa who were seen as hypocritically accepting the racial hierarchy, but the charge of irrelevance was keenly felt also by more radical Whites.

It was for this reason, then, that Marxism presented an alternative to many young White writers and academics at the time, not least through the History Workshop at Witwatersrand University that started running in 1977. With recourse to the work of the "New Left" in Britain, the Frankfurt school, and the 1968 Paris philosophers, a thoroughly revised analysis of apartheid emerged. As Ally explains, "Marxism refuted the liberal claim that industrial capitalism would erode the apartheid system in South Africa, by arguing that race was only an ideological justification for the class project of apartheid" (74). No longer seen as an atavistic aberration, apartheid was theorized as a particular mode of "racial capitalism" and "internal colonialism" in which the rigorous policy of segregation ensured the consent of the White working class, who benefited hugely from the system. In this way, White academics put a theoretical spin to the problem of race that moved beyond the immediate problem of how groups and individuals were identified or identified themselves.

There is in hindsight a striking complementarity to BC and Marxist revisionism in 1970s South Africa. If BC focused on the subjectivity of the oppressed, the Marxists privileged an "objective," materialist account of society. But inversely, BC's definition of Blackness, as it evolved in Biko's thinking, became increasingly compatible with the Marxist analysis. In BC circles, "Black" eventually became an inclusive category, covering all those groups systemically excluded and divided by apartheid laws. "Coloureds" and "Indians," who had different legal status, could therefore also claim Blackness, understood as a distinctly *political* identity constructed by the apartheid system. More than that, Magaziner even argues that Biko's take on race was closer to Sartre's dialectical understanding in "Black Orpheus" than to Frantz Fanon's ontological position in *Black Skin, White Masks*. "Black selfhood," as Magaziner writes, was seen as "contingent, topical, and limited" and could in principle yield to a nonracial "true humanity" under another political order (Magaziner 44). In this way, BC's subjective focus led ultimately to a confrontation with the material conditions underpinning South African apartheid.

There are two distinctly literary interventions that illustrate this complementarity of BC and Marxism in South Africa: Mike Kirkwood's early essay "The Colonizer: A Critique of the English South African Culture Theory," first delivered at a poetry conference in 1974, and Njabulo Ndebele's influential collection of essays *Rediscovery of the Ordinary*, published in 1991 but written over a number of years in the 1980s. Kirkwood's sharp materialist analysis of a cultural "Anglo" identity was presented in a spirit of "White consciousness," which aimed at an appraisal of the deep entanglement of race and power in South Africa. "The racial oligarchy," Kirkwood insisted, was "not the creation of the Afrikaner alone. Our mining interests and our industries created the system of cheap contractual and migrant labour, and our White working class demanded, and got, a privileged stake in the maintenance of a prosperity dependent on that labour" (108). In its undermining of sentimental self-conceptions, this could be read as a mirror image of Njabulo Ndebele's critique, which from a Black perspective aimed at cultivating a poetics of deep social analysis. It was only through "an honest rendering of the subjective experience," Ndebele argued (*Rediscovery* 53), that writers could move beyond a focus on the surface effects of racial oppression. In this way, by engaging the full register of experience and the "dialectic between the personal and public," literature could "provide an occasion within which vistas of inner capacity are opened up" (*Rediscovery* 55, 56). The wording is reminiscent of the BC movement, from which Ndebele had emerged in the 1970s, yet its compatibility with, for example, the Marxist realism of a critic such as Georg Lukács should be evident.

The South African example, which of course does not end with the 1980s, is one instance where theory and praxis converge dynamically, leading to a significantly renewed understanding of society and, by extension, to a "decolonization" of literary practice – although that particular word was not used in South Africa at the time. My other example, the SSG in India, is a more strictly academic development. In addition, it relates primarily to the discipline of history rather than literature. Its importance is such, however, that it has been regarded by some as the main Global South context where Marxism was (supposedly) displaced by a more diffuse theoretical agenda that attempted to account for the historical conditions prevailing in South Asia. With the historian Ranajit Guha as its early leading figure, "subaltern studies" became known when the book series by that name started publishing in 1982. Drawing on the Italian Marxist Antonio Gramsci's use of the word "subaltern" to identify diverse subordinate groups, the intention here was to excavate histories of political contestation in India from "below," that is, the histories that had been silenced and suppressed in the dominant narrative of India's transition to national independence.

With the participation of well-placed Indian scholars in the Western academy – such as Gayatri Chakravorty Spivak, Dipesh Chakrabarty, and indeed Guha himself – subaltern studies rapidly gained a high global profile at precisely the moment when poststructuralism reached its peak in the 1980s. Spivak's exceptionally influential essay "Can the Subaltern Speak?," first presented at a conference in Illinois in 1983 (but published in its final version as late as 1999), offered perhaps the most consequential critical account of subaltern studies. By way of dense readings of Foucault, Deleuze, Marx, and the British colonial prohibition of Sati, or widow burning, Spivak focused on the equivocations of "speaking for" the subaltern. Even within the most radical Western iterations (and critiques) of Enlightenment thinking, Spivak concluded, the subaltern could never speak *as* a subaltern. She derided Deleuze's invocation of "*the* workers' struggle" as "incapable of dealing with global capitalism" (Spivak 250; emphasis in the original). Instead of assuming that there could be what she called "undivided subjectivity" (248) in such struggles, subaltern subjectivity would remain an "irretrievably heterogeneous" (270) cipher even as it was transposed, through an act of epistemic violence, to the type of speaking position that Enlightenment discourse acknowledged. In other words, the radical historians' wish to vindicate the rights-bearing citizen dwelling on the margins of society was itself an exercise of power.

As we can see, Spivak's argument was as critical of Foucault's and Deleuze's Eurocentrism as it was of the presuppositions of Guha's project. Moreover, it proceeded through a careful reading of Marx and insisted on the centrality of capital as an analytical concept. Indeed, the very theme of the 1983 conference was nothing less than "Marxism and the interpretation of culture" (Nelson and Grossberg). Even so, "Can the Subaltern Speak?" is justly known as a pivotal moment in the formation of "postcolonial theory," a label that normally refers to *poststructuralist* postcolonial theory. Spivak had already contributed an earlier piece to subaltern studies in a similar vein, but it was here – on the back of Edward Said's *Orientalism*, published in 1978 – that a significantly different, largely non-Marxist, approach to colonialism and imperialism gathered strength.

One of the most thorough and succinct statements of this *theoretical* difference is found in Dipesh Chakrabarty's widely cited *Provincializing Europe*. In the second chapter, Chakrabarty offers a careful reading of Marx's conception of history in *Capital*. Rather than subsume history wholesale under the history of capital, Marx suggested in fact that history was split between a history that led to the formation of capital, and a history that did not belong to capital's "own life-process" (quoted in Chakrabarty 63). For pedagogical reasons, Chakrabarty dubbed these two "histories" History 1 and History 2. His philosophical account is detailed and too extensive to summarize here, yet the central point is clear: the history of capital, and hence of modernity, isn't all there is to history. But it would be wrong, Chakrabarty writes, to think of History 2 "as necessarily precapitalist or feudal, or even inherently incompatible with capital. If that were the case, there would be no way humans could be at home – dwell – in the rule of capital, no room for enjoyment, no play of desires, no seduction of the commodity" (67).

What we see in Chakrabarty's formulation is a more theoretical variant of the previously discussed subject–object tension between Black Consciousness and South African Marxism. Again, the subjective dimension, or what Chakrabarty with phenomenological vocabulary calls "life-worlds," is juxtaposed with the objectivist and totalizing aspects of Marxist analysis. This tendency is evident already in Ranajit Guha's *Elementary Aspects of Peasant Insurgency in Colonial India* – arguably the foundational text of subaltern studies – which places strong emphasis on the study of "negative class consciousness" (Guha 20). An important difference indicated in this phrase, however, is that subaltern studies tended to downplay race. It is not entirely absent, but class, caste, and ethnicity are more prominent categories. One should also observe that the ambitions of a work such as *Provincializing Europe* were far grander than anything to have come out of South Africa at the time. In his critique of what he called "historicism" (best understood as the ideology of progress), Chakrabarty implicated *all* of the formerly colonized world. To the extent that Europe was seen as offering a universally valid template for a transition to modernity, this relegated societies in the Global South to a status of "lack," or incompleteness. On a discursive, epistemological level, Chakrabarty was arguing, the historical and political analysis of a country such as India remained straitjacketed by the notion of "a certain 'Europe' as the primary habitus of the modern" (43). Hence his project to "provincialize" Europe and develop alternative conceptions of modernity.

The turn in subaltern studies toward incommensurability and multiple modernities failed to convince dedicated Marxists. There is in fact an entire genealogy of materialist criticism that has shadowed the poststructuralist tendency in postcolonialism from the word go, with notable interventions such as Benita Parry's numerous critiques beginning in the 1980s ("Problems"; "Signs"; "The Postcolonial"), Aijaz Ahmad's *In Theory*,

Neil Lazarus's two books *Nationalism and Cultural Practice in the Postcolonial World* and *The Postcolonial Unconscious*, and, somewhat controversially, Vivek Chibber's *Postcolonial Theory and the Specter of Capital* (reviewed negatively by Lazarus, one might note, see "Vivek Chibber"). The volume *Marxism, Modernity, Postcolonial Studies* edited by Crystal Bartolovich and Lazarus is perhaps the most productive engagement between the two fields on record, with the intention to further a distinctly "*Marxist* postcolonial studies" (Bartolovich and Lazarus 1; emphasis in the original). More recently, a highly consequential literary result of the Marxist critique of postcolonialism is to be found in the WReC's *Combined and Uneven Development: Towards a New Theory of World-Literature*. With Parry and Lazarus as two of the seven listed authors of the book (the collective has expanded since then, but Parry passed away in 2020), the link to the long sequence of debates spurred by "postcolonial theory" is clear.

The underlying premise of *Combined and Uneven Development* is that literature in the modern era needs to be theorized not in relation to colonialism, which is a secondary phenomenon, but in relation to the global rule of capital. The forceful formula of the main title is derived from Leon Trotsky's analysis of Russia's supposedly anomalous revolutionary conditions when compared to western Europe. Being in the early twentieth century largely a nation of peasants, Russia was an unlikely candidate for revolution, at least if one considered the implications of Marx's *Capital*, which rather indicated that the most thoroughly capitalist and industrialized societies (such as Britain) would be the first to undergo revolution. Instead of assuming, however, that capitalism imposed itself on the world uniformly and comprehensively, Trotsky recognized that the old and the new coexisted. Peasants would be "thrown into the factory cauldron snatched directly from the plow," leading to an "amalgam of archaic with more contemporary forms" (quoted in WReC 11). In the lineage of Marxist literary theory, this conception of differentiated social time has then been further developed by Fredric Jameson (building on Ernst Bloch) in terms of the "synchronicity of the non-synchronous" (Jameson 307).

The attraction of such a perspective to scholars wishing to devise a globally applicable method of reading should be obvious. It allows them to have their cake and eat it too – both History 1 and History 2, to use Chakrabarty's terms, but with clear precedence given to History 1, or the history of capital. Or rather, they see everything as being absorbed into History 1. Rather than move toward a pluralized conception of modernity, as does Chakrabarty, WReC insists on understanding modernity as a singular, complex phenomenon: "Modernity is to be understood as governed always – that is to say, definitionally – by *unevenness*" (12). It is from such an understanding of an all-encompassing but endlessly differentiated and unbalanced world-system that WReC can take the next step to theorizing what they call "world-literature" (with a hyphen), understood precisely as the literature of the world-system of capitalism. Their assumption is that literature can be read as a "registration" of the world-system, and that the "effectivity" of this system "will *necessarily* be discernible in any modern literary work" (WReC 20).

A reflection one might make here is that WReC (as they explain on pages 28–48) ultimately is attempting to supplant the colonizer/colonized or West/rest binary that governs the paradigm of postcolonial studies. This is not because they deny colonial power relations – on the contrary – but because they see this as simply one form of the dominance of capital. There are some interesting methodological advantages to this view. One is, as *Combined and Uneven Development* demonstrates, that writers as diverse as Tayeb Salih, Halldór Laxness, and Victor Pelevin can be juxtaposed unapologetically within a comparative framework that looks at "discrepant literary subunits and social formations of the world-system" (WReC 68). Another is that in the contemporary capitalist order, where countries such as China, Saudi Arabia, and Turkey have become key players, the explanatory value of a world-system analysis is clearly superior to the more restricted colonizer/colonized optic. A third is that the peripheries of wealthy societies (such as rural Louisiana) can be compared meaningfully to the peripheries of the Global South.

The challenge, of course, is to make this work as a *literary* methodology. It is one thing to provide a broad theory of capitalism as an economic system, and quite another to connect it to practices of reading – which has been a perennial challenge for Marxist literary critics. For some empirically minded scholars, systemic postulates such as those proposed by WReC have the effect of effacing the uncontainable heterogeneity of the actual textual material at hand. In a cowritten article, Karima Laachir, Sara Marzagora, and Francesca Orsini bluntly state that "deterministic models like the Warwick Research Collective's or Moretti's use frameworks derived from the social sciences like world system theory to explain literary phenomena, including stylistic choices, in a way that becomes flat and reductionist" (292). Not unlike Spivak's "irretrievably heterogeneous" subaltern, we seem to be faced once again with a methodological aporia: for all its flexibility, the optic of combined and uneven development hardwires aesthetic production to the economic model of capitalism.

This premise works to the extent that one *believes* in it, but there is a point beyond which the assumption of causality between capital and literature may seem to have explanatory value, yet without being able to ground itself in anything outside of itself. If we revisit the WReC quotation above about literary "registration," this happens "necessarily" because "the world-system exists unforgoably as the matrix within which all modern literature takes shape and comes into being" (20). This is circular reasoning, pure and simple. Textual analysis proves what is already assumed by the theory, and whatever does not fit – such as the deep time of literary traditions – is suppressed.

This should not be taken as a blanket rejection of this mode of reading – it is just an indication of its perils and limitations. With, say, the Brazilian critic Roberto Schwarz's magnificent work on the nineteenth-century novelist Machado de Assis, we encounter a "decolonizing" Marxist interpretation at its level best, and it is for a good reason that WReC identifies Schwarz as a key inspiration. This, however, is scholarship of the most demanding kind, where Schwarz mined the Brazilian archives for years to arrive at a wholly original and unexpected understanding of the novelist's ironic style. It is, in other words, not the kind of work that lends itself to easy polemical points but is an outcome of engaging with the full complexity and internal contradictions of a particular Brazilian and European cultural legacy.

On a slightly different tack, WReC could also be accused of privileging just one line of capitalist history – the one we normally think of as Western – whereas current world-system analyses tend to emphasize the plural origins of capitalism itself. Janet Abu-Lughod and Kenneth Pomeranz belong to the forerunners in this line of debate. In their more recent work on capitalisms in the plural, Kaveh Yazdani and Dilip Menon discuss the complexity of tracing multiple economic and historical trajectories of what might credibly be called "capitalism" – without turning the term into an abstract historical constant. They not only point out that "political economy in Western Europe cannot be disentangled from developments in and encounters with Asia and Asians" (Yazdani and Menon 8) but also that Ibn Khaldun already in the fourteenth century developed "a labour theory of surplus production" (9). The former point is entirely compatible with WReC's global vistas, but the latter definitely challenges their narrow historical timeframe.

There is of course yet another branch of contemporary critical theory that apparently undercuts much of WReC's brand of Marxism, even as it nominally adheres to some version of Marxism. I am thinking of the so-called "decolonial" variety of theory with its main grounding in Latin America. If by decoloniality we mean its most encompassing formulations by Aníbal Quijano, Walter Mignolo, Maria Lugones, and other Latin American thinkers, then Marxism is embraced but also absorbed into a theory of the "coloniality of power" (Quijano) – a formulation which already tips the balance toward a more Foucauldian mode of analysis and is also, arguably, more flexible than the metropole–colony model of mainly anglophone postcolonialism.

Sociologically, decoloniality resembles the other regional groupings of scholars discussed in this chapter, the historical materialists in South Africa and the SSG, insofar as it emerges from a distinct regional context – Latin America – but has achieved a global presence, thanks not least to scholars placed at US universities (such as Mignolo and Lugones). Its theoretical claims are less easy to pinpoint, although there clearly is some overlap with tendencies in the other two groupings. A difficulty with decoloniality, however, is that it tends to place a tremendous rhetorical premium on a few, totalizing concepts – notably the triad modernity/coloniality/decoloniality and the colonial matrix of power (CMP) – while at the same time, again on a rhetorical level, downplaying the importance of conceptual thinking and stressing the unfathomable "pluriversality" of decolonial praxis.

It is highly instructive in this regard to juxtapose WReC and the account Walter Mignolo gives of decolonial theory in *On Decoloniality* (cowritten with Catherine Walsh). If WReC is entirely committed to Marxist world-system theory and the ways in which literature can "articulate powerful critiques of *actually existing reality*" (WReC 83; emphasis added), Mignolo turns this assumption on its head. What matters, he writes, "is not economics, or politics, or history, but knowledge" (Mignolo and Walsh 135). From a decolonial perspective, "it is epistemology that institutes ontology, that prescribes the ontology of the world" (147). It is not that Mignolo is anti-Marx. On the contrary, he sees him as a leading figure among the "internal critiques" of Western thought (3), yet the claim that no reality exists outside of its discursive articulation is – strictly speaking – incompatible with Marxist materialism.

Once again, it would seem that decoloniality rehearses the subject–object antinomy I have been tracing throughout this chapter, albeit with a vocabulary of its own. The lesson I draw from the archives of Marxist studies and decolonization is however not to rigidly choose sides, but to consider the antinomy dialectically. Any attempt to articulate the "actually existing reality" of our material existence must inevitably confront the limitations of its own language and methods of investigation. There are, so to speak, turtles all the way down, and knowledge becomes that Nietzschean abyss that stares back at the knower. Yet, conversely, the struggles motivating the full range of "decolonizing" practices and discourses today, even as they find anchorage in other languages and conceptions of social being (among Andean peasants, say), will just as inevitably have to reckon with the material deprivations (as well as affordances) produced by the long and always-localized histories of contemporary political economy. On such an understanding, it is the flexibility of the dialectical method itself, rather than any specific Marxist doctrine, that holds the greatest promise for decolonial modes of reading.

In closing, I will exemplify this open-ended methodological stance by turning to the aforementioned Njabulo Ndebele's much-loved short story "The Prophetess." Focalized through a young boy in a township in apartheid South Africa, it recounts the boy's encounter with the local prophetess, who is said to possess awe-inspiring magical powers. The boy's mother, who is ill, has sent him there to ask the prophetess to bless a bottle of water on her behalf. In anticipation, the ritual fills the boy with amazement: "She would then lay her hands on the bottle and pray. And the water would be holy" (*Fools* 31). On his way back with the precious water, the boy drops and breaks the bottle. In his anguish and shame, rather than admit what happened, he quickly fills another bottle that he hands over to his mother – who visibly improves as she drinks the water. The boy's sense of devastation transforms into triumph: "He had healed his mother" (*Fools* 52).

In "The Prophetess," Ndebele strikes a fine balance between an ironic and earnest mode of narration. The ironic reading is constantly latent and even explicitly articulated when the boy overhears a group of commuters debating whether to believe in what was said about the prophetess's powers. Indeed, the outcome of the story, with the boy getting away with his deception, apparently supports the ironic – and hence secular and knowing – reading: it made no difference whether or not the prophetess blessed the water. In that interpretation, the "objective" antithesis of human bodies and plain water prevail over the "subjective" cultural beliefs entertained by some of the township inhabitants.

But is the boy really deceiving his mother? And who is the woman known as the prophetess? There are the rumors, but then there is also the boy's encounter with her, which shows us a different person. She speaks to him warmly about his mother. She sings him a song, allegorically prophesying the downfall of White power. "Always listen to new things," she tells him. "Then try to create too" (*Fools* 40). She is in other words a counsellor and a teacher and an artist, not a magician, and her power is only equal to the strength of the communal relations that she helps to maintain. This, of course, is the key to how we may read the redemptive ending, where the boy himself contributes to those communal bonds: "He had healed her" (*Fools* 52). The phrase is not a mockery of the boy's false consciousness, but on the contrary an affirmation of how a locally grounded and internally differentiated set of cultural practices can contribute to making the world new. Out of the story's subject–object dialectic – which, at a stretch, could also be read as an Africa–West or Black–White dialectic – something unprecedented springs forth, intimating a decolonized future. The subsequent realization that the story's implied future, in contemporary South Africa, has turned out to be troublingly different to the horizon of struggle and hope in the 1980s hardly detracts from Ndebele's story. It shows, rather, the unceasing need to provide renewed dialectical accounts of our social worlds as they unfold in time.

Notes

1. "un racisme antiraciste."
2. "il y a des *peuples* divers ... soumis dans leur ensemble à l'oppression et à l'exploitation non pas d'une autre *race*, mais d'autres peuples, ou, plus exactement, des *classes dominantes d'autres peuples*."

WORKS CITED

Ahmad, Aijaz. *In Theory: Classes, Nations, Literatures.* London: Verso, 1992.

Ally, Shireen. "Oppositional Intellectualism as Reflection, Not Rejection, of Power: Wits Sociology, 1975–1989." *Transformation: Critical Perspectives on Southern Africa* 59 (2005): 66–97.

Bartolovich, Crystal and Neil Lazarus, eds. *Marxism, Modernity, and Postcolonial Studies.* Cambridge: Cambridge University Press, 2002.

Chakrabarty, Dipesh. *Provincializing Europe: Postcolonial Thought and Historical Difference.* Princeton, NJ: Princeton University Press, 2000.

Chibber, Vivek. *Postcolonial Theory and the Specter of Capital.* London: Verso, 2013.

D'Arboussier, Gabriel. "Une dangereuse mystification: la théorie de la 'négritude'." *Nouvelle Critique* 7 (1949): 34–47.

Fanon, Frantz. *The Wretched of the Earth*, translated by Constance Farrington. London: Penguin, 2001.

Guha, Ranajit. *Elementary Aspects of Peasant Insurgency in Colonial India.* Delhi: Oxford University Press, 1983.

Jameson, Fredric. *Postmodernism, or, the Cultural Logic of Late Capitalism.* Durham, NC: Duke University Press, 1995.

Kirkwood, Mike. "The Colonizer: A Critique of the English South African Culture Theory." In Peter Wilhelm and James A. Polley, eds., *Poetry South Africa: Selected Papers from Poetry '74.* Johannesburg: Ad Donker, 1976, 102–33.

Laachir, Karima, Sara Marzagora, and Francesca Orsini. "Significant Geographies: In Lieu of World Literature." *Journal of World Literature* 3.3 (2018): 290–310.

Lazarus, Neil. *Nationalism and Cultural Practice in the Postcolonial World.* Cambridge: Cambridge University Press, 1999.

The Postcolonial Unconscious. Cambridge: Cambridge University Press, 2011.

"Vivek Chibber and the Spectre of Postcolonial Theory." *Race and Class* 57.3 (2016): 88–106.

Lessing, Doris. *A Ripple from the Storm.* Bristol: MacGibbon and Kee, 1965.

Magaziner, Daniel R. *The Law and the Prophets: Black Consciousness in South Africa, 1968–77.* Athens: Ohio University Press, 2010.

Nelson, Cary and Lawrence Grossberg, eds. *Marxism and the Interpretation of Culture.* Houndmills: Macmillan, 1988.

Ndebele, Njabulo. *Fools and Other Stories.* Braamfontein: Ravan Press, 1983.

Rediscovery of the Ordinary: Essay on South African Literature and Culture. Johannesburg: COSAW, 1991.

Parry, Benita. "The Postcolonial: Conceptual Category or Chimera?" *The Yearbook of English Studies* 27 (1997): 3–21.

"Problems in Current Theories of Colonial Discourse." *Oxford Literary Review* 9.1–2, (1987): 27–58.

"Signs of Our Times: Discussion of Homi Bhabha's *The Location of Culture.*" *Third Text* 8.28–29 (1994): 5–24.

Mignolo, Walter and Catherine Walsh. *On Decoloniality: Concepts, Analytics, Praxis.* Durham, NC: Duke University Press, 2018.

Quijano, Aníbal. *Colonialidad del poder, eurocentrismo y América Latina.* Buenos Aires: CLACSO, 2000.

Robinson, Cedric. *Black Marxism: The Making of a Black Radical Tradition*, 2nd ed. Chapel Hill: University of North Carolina Press, 2000.

Sartre, Jean-Paul. "Orphée noir." In Léopold Sédar Senghor, ed., *Anthologie de la nouvelle poésie nègre et malgache de langue française.* Paris: Presses Universitaires de France, 1948, ix–xliv.

Schwarz, Roberto. *Um mestre na periferia do capitalismo: Machado de Assis.* São Paulo: Duas Cidades, 1990.

Spivak, Gayatri Chakravorty. *A Critique of Postcolonial Reason: Toward a History of the Vanishing Present.* Cambridge, MA: Harvard University Press, 1999.

Warwick Research Collective (WReC). *Combined and Uneven Development: Towards a New Theory of World-Literature.* Liverpool: Liverpool University Press, 2015.

Yazdani, Kaveh, and Dilip M. Menon. "Introduction." In Kaveh Yazdani and Dilip M. Menon, eds., *Capitalisms: Towards a Global History.* Oxford: Oxford University Press, 2020, 1–32.

CHAPTER 10

Against Ethnography
On Teaching Minority Literature

Jeanne-Marie Jackson

If people who write about African literature were to agree on one thing, it would be the inadequacy – or just flat-out wrongness – of every larger category into which African literature has been subsumed across its entwined academic and publishing histories. This includes even the seemingly basic designation "African," which, like more obvious offenders such as "postcolonial," "Third World," and "global anglophone," has often been accused of effacing heterogeneity of all kinds in the name of tokenistic inclusion.[1] Some of these critiques have been more hard-hitting than others, and the terms of complaint have evolved, broadly speaking, across the past half century or so from advocacy *for* "Otherness" to frustration with its lingering reinforcement. What all such categorical chafing tends to share is a difficulty positing what African literature *is*, or at least how it should be presented given the practical constraints of selling books and building university curricula. With the aim of beginning to fill this gap, this chapter suggests that a culturally minimalist approach to teaching African literature in the American university offers one way of furthering a culturally maximalist conception of intellectual decolonization. By teaching African works that wear their cultural locations lightly, that is, in order to foreground their cosmic and/or existential engagements, we may get closer to disinvesting from the persistent and often racist cause of fictional representativeness.

It is important to set a few contextual parameters at the outset, given the broad reach of this volume's concerns. First, the "we" I refer to here includes scholars and teachers of African literature in American and British universities, as well as others in the Anglosphere where "African" signifies a minority position. While some of my observations will be applicable to academies where that is not the case (parts of South Africa's, for example), I will leave it to the reader to make those connections. Second, the pedagogical tack I propose here should be taken as one piece in a larger toolkit for decolonizing non-Africa-based students' African literature curricula; it is not meant to be exclusive of teaching or scholarship that takes texts' cultural or historical dimensions as their main point of entry. And, finally, I see the politics of the English literature classroom in this setting as being in variable and unfixed relation to politics of a more concrete sort. By this I mean that I do not assume a fluid translation between concepts as they are mobilized for reading and teaching – including signal terms such as "identity" or "liberation" – and concepts as they anchor adjacent social and institutional debates. This distinction bears repeating in the present context because African literature has been so foundationally and explicitly conjoined to the goal of cultural restitution, for better and worse. Indeed, the history of the field can be powerfully narrated as a series of assertions and rejections of African literature's value as a proxy for "culture," a back-and-forth from which I hope here to break free.

To do this I will start with a discussion of "representativeness" and its strictures. Then, I turn to a Ghanaian short story collection whose critical reception has been tellingly sparse: Martin Egblewogbe's *Mr. Happy and the Hammer of God & Other Stories* (2012). The text features stories whose Ghanaian origins are identifiable but not definitive; their "Africanness," while by no means disavowed, is simply taken for granted as they home in on essential experiences of disorientation. A far cry from earlier, more culturally assertive approaches to literary decolonization, this strategy also departs from what has become a common brand of *opposition* to cultural representativeness that privileges (usually realist) world-building and immersion. Instead, Egblewogbe rebuffs representative readings with his choice of socially dislocative content conveyed by the marginal form of the short story. These are profoundly and existentially self-minoritizing rather than only social-minoritarian works, in the sense that they do not speak for any position that finds commonality through culture or even location. Instead, Egblewogbe's stories serve as a useful example of cultural transcendence achieved not through individual complexity but through cosmic anonymity, thereby confounding both ethnographic and limitingly counterethnographic pedagogical approaches to African writing.

The Same Not-Single Story

Many of the most-cited figures and venues in the recent African cultural landscape have, with good reason, focused on transforming Africa in the global imaginary from an abstract signifier to a complex set of particulars.

Chimamanda Adichie's 2009 TED talk "The Danger of a Single Story" has reached legendary status, with tens of millions of views on YouTube alone. Adichie, like the cheeky name of the popular African commentary website *Africa Is a Country*, links Africa's economic disempowerment in the world to the long-standing flatness of its image in Western literature and media. Their pique is with single Africans and African situations being made to stand in for the continent writ large, often with pernicious implications. "It would never have occurred to me to think that just because I had read a novel in which a character was a serial killer that he was somehow representative of all Americans," Adichie says. And then, famously, "to insist on [only negative] stories is to flatten my experience and to overlook the many other stories that formed me. The single story creates stereotypes, and the problem with stereotypes is not that they are untrue, but that they are incomplete." Literary discourse on Africa is united across popular and academic registers by its wariness of an African orientalism of sorts, whereby tropes like "the White savior" and "the starving African" drive genres such as "poverty porn." Binyavanga Wainaina's *Granta Magazine* piece "How to Write about Africa" has driven countless classroom conversations about such cliches since its 2005 publication, satirically goading students to acknowledge that Africa is in fact a complex place.

Such rejections of reductiveness have been intimately linked to a frustration with African literary texts being read for their ethnographic (or really, pseudoethnographic) insights in particular. As the literary scholar and *Brittle Paper* website founder Ainehi Edoro attests in a 2016 essay for the *Guardian*, this implicit bias has a long history rooted in the explicit practice of reading African novels as anthropological texts. After summarizing the would-be "scientific" reception of Thomas Mofolo's novel *Chaka* around the time of its English publication in 1931, she bemoans the fact that "African fiction is invisible except when it is reflected on a mirror of social ills, cultural themes and political concerns." This sense of being deaestheticized has been widely echoed by contemporary African writers. Taiye Selasi, the "Afropolitan" novelist partly responsible for the popularization of that term, leveled the charge in the same paper that African writers were evaluated not in terms of craft but rather "assumed to be or accused of writing for the west, producing explanatory ethnographic texts dolled up as literary fiction." In this way, the accusation of writing merely to convey a cultural perspective has become as loaded (and as common) as the accusation of reading for one. Suspicion of the term "African writer" is now a critical trope in its own right, surfacing in nearly every discussion of the field. A recent interview with the debut novelist Ayo Tamakloe-Garr is a strong case in point. The first question that the website *Flash Fiction Ghana* asks him is, "Do you have a conception of who a Ghanaian writer is? Would you accept being categorized as a Ghanaian writer?" Tamakloe-Garr responds that while he does not personally mind the label, he finds it a "limiting" way to imagine himself.[2]

Some of this reluctance to identify as an African writer is an understandable reaction against decades of not only Western critics', but also some African writers' and intellectuals' postcolonial attachment to African literature's culturally restitutive value. As Biodun Jeyifo described the field in 1990, the works first institutionalized as "African" in, especially, British and American universities were lauded as "powerful, exemplary texts of nationalist contestation of colonialist myths and distortions of Africa and Africans" (51). He places Chinua Achebe and Wole Soyinka within a postindependence wave of literary "demythologization" (52), whereby "the writer or critic speaks to, or for, or in the name of the post-independence nation-state, the regional or continental community, the pan-ethnic, racial or cultural agglomeration of homelands and diasporas" (53). Achebe here is on what we might call the softer end of such cultural reassertion; elsewhere, Jeyifo takes issue with the dubious ontologization of culture by early decolonial critics such as Chinweizu, author of books such as *Decolonising the African Mind* from 1987.[3] Regardless of the vigor or exclusivity of any given African writer's "reassertion or reinvention of traditions which colonialism ... had sought to destroy or devalue" (53), cultural representation by default performed a representative role when the field of African literature was in its institutional infancy. The postcolonial African writer was thus faced with what seems like a binary choice between accepting or refusing that role, with Dambudzo Marechera standing as the best-known example of the latter position. His self-styling as the photo negative of the "African writer" as cultural arbiter entails an insistently abject and disarrayed subjectivity, what his most recent biographer Tinashe Mushakavanhu calls alternately his "black heretic," "dissident," and "outsider" standing (8–9).

In this way, an interesting tension begins to emerge within the idea of the minority as it pertains to African writing making its way through the world. One version disaggregates "Africa" into its constituent cultural parts, and in theory could achieve a kind of curricular decolonization through the liberal-adjacent means of finding representative writers and/or texts for all of them. Another version (the Marechera one, what Edoro calls the "anarchic" tradition in her blurb for Mushakavanhu's book) foregrounds the individual writer's principled refusal of cultural ambassa-dorship. A decolonized curricular ideal from this vantage point might see Marechera taught alongside other experimental writers from all over. We might think of these alternatives, presented here in exaggerated form, as representative and antirepresentative minoritarianism. The representative path to a more equitable curriculum quickly becomes untenable on a practical level, over and above any criticism of its merits. Bibi Bakare-Yusuf, a cofounder of Nigeria's independent Cassava Press, argues point-edly that her work in helping to build up Nigeria's literary field will not be done until "The day we can speak of more than ten Nnedi Okorafors (speculative/fantasy fiction), ten Zaynad Alkalis (oft-cited female writer from the north), ten Olumide Popoolas (writing queer humanity), ten Yemisi Aribisalas (food writer and polemical non-fiction), ten Noo Saro-Wiwas (travel writing), and ten Zulu Sofolas (playwright)" (Mang). By this logic, the unstated goal of more representation is to make representative*ness* untenable. It is an admirable objective, but even on the single national scale proposed here it quickly exceeds the capacity of a semester-long course, or for that matter of many universities' whole English curriculum.

There has to be *some* basis of selection, or African literature risks being squeezed out of the picture as it contends with other minoritized (which is not always to say minority) traditions for space within what are, these days, often-struggling English departments. That underrepresented groups are often implicitly pitted against one another is not a novel or difficult point, but it is worth restating. As Bhakti Shringarpure and Lily Saint demon-strate with their recent survey of African literature professors mainly in the United States and Europe, this often means that writers pushing back against their reduction to a culture or place end up assuming representative roles in their own right. After breaking down the most commonly taught African texts by country and author, they bemoan "the overreliance on a handful of representative canonical writers who are themselves often opposed to having their work deployed in this way," Adichie chief among them. Often this bolsters an aesthetic premium on realism as it nurtures readerly attachments to psychologically robust individual characters, and by extension, advances an underdeveloped commitment to personal uniqueness as literature's guiding force.

Aminatta Forna claims, for example, that "writers do not write about places, they write about people who happen to live in those places." Selasi goes still further. She counters her sense that Afro-diasporic writing "is subjected to a particular kind of scrutiny; it is forced to play the role of anthropology" by championing Adichie for having "immersed herself fully in the world and the work of her fiction, attending with such care and wisdom to her characters that they cannot possibly be read as representations." This is an odd line of argument because at its core, realism works precisely along the lines of social representativeness. Virtually every major theorist of realism from Georg Lukács onward has reflected on these mechanics, including the interplay of character and setting to engender an illusion of singularity that distills a social whole.[4] And as Yoon Sun Lee notes aptly in a 2012 essay for *Modern Language Quarterly*, "minor" or lesser-taught literatures are often the most deeply marked by the tension *between* "the standard of truthful representation" and "[defenses of] the autonomy of the artistic work" (416).

The dynamics of asserting and rebuffing African literature's presumed "Africanness" are, moreover, complicated by the fact that many current debates about literary decolonization take place as a conversation between Western and African locales; most of the writer-theorists mentioned thus far argue against cultural pigeonholing on the basis of their own culturally hybrid biographies. As is so often true in addressing majority–minority dynamics as they evolve across disparate but conversant settings, African literature in the English curriculum finds itself between a rock and a hard place. Slickly packaged versions of cultural fluidity only go so far to issue a substantive challenge to a Euro- and US-centric curriculum, and yet to teach specific writers and texts solely to showcase their minoritization risks reinforcing an unevenly distributed burden of representativeness. It is also difficult to know when decolonization in an American (or other western anglophone) classroom best entails a focus on particular African literary contents, and when it is more a matter of a general effect of disruption or surprise. As the Cambridge anthropologist Adam Branch likewise suggests, "At some UK universities, to simply affirm the existence of African intellectual production against long-standing historical silences, to affirm that the rest of the world has writing and thinkers that should be studied in any curriculum that claims general or global relevance – this can still be a radical idea when students can complete entire classes without reading non-white scholars" (74). As such I often feel in my own university like I am balancing on a seesaw, demanding a larger presence for Africa in our institution's intellectual life at the same time as I refuse from intellectual wariness to commit to any clear account of what that means.

Riffing on Jeyifo's term "arrested decolonization," the overarching challenge in my current position is to keep African literature from getting stuck in the critique of African literature as a category. The heavy weight of past essentialisms means that it is easy to stall out by repeating a series of metadiscursive negations and reassertions. Teaching cultural fluidity to counter cultural cliches invites criticism for overinscribing a certain sort of elite heterogeneity, one that, as many have argued, tends to elevate diasporic narratives of African literature over more emplaced and politically pointed continental versions. By the same token, it is easy to overcorrect this correction by limiting African literature's decolonizing potential to an overt "decolonial" message. And if African texts are wielded as tools exclusively to decolonize Western curricula in a narrow sense, it seems to me that little has been gained in a broader one. One example of how this tactic falters – and how widely it *has*, at earlier moments in the discipline – can be found in a 1991 essay from *New Literary History*, in which Georg M. Gugelberger argues that, "The issue then is not to integrate Third World literary works into the canon but to identify with 'the wretched of the earth' and to learn from them – to learn from the Third World writer how to look into what is *really* going on in the world and why it has been going on and thus to learn about our own limitations" (506). I do not mean to single Gugelberger out but rather to uphold his position in this piece as distillatory of its Third Worldist moment in American English departments, a moment still reeling from furious debates over Fredric Jameson's 1986 essay "Third-World Literature in the Era of Multinational Capitalism."[5] Whereas Jameson moved to read all literature from the so-called Third World as registering "a life-and-death struggle with first-world cultural imperialism" (68), Gugelberger allows that not all literature from the Third World is "Third World Literature" in any identifiable sense. In this account, Third World writing is an opt-in genre, or perhaps mode, that exists in the geopolitically designated Third World alongside "the literature we associate with the established [Western] canon" (508). The valorization of the former over the latter – a still-familiar preference for *really* Third World Third World writing – anticipates what I will call the "Adichie fatigue" strain of our present discourse. It is common, on this front, to hear African and other postcolonial literary scholars agitate for what amounts to decolonizing tepid forms of decolonization.[6]

Each of the turns outlined thus far has something to offer the Anglo-American African literature classroom as it retires ethnographic reading practices once and for all: there is still value in reinforcing students' understanding of African complexity and difference, and there is also value in pointing out the limitations of that gesture by introducing more politically forceful material. All the same, these debates can sometimes feel like a dog chasing its own tail. "Difference" undoes cultural essentialism, radicalism takes aim at the implicit liberalism of difference, and heterogeneity contends with solidarity as the guiding principle of African literature and literary pedagogy. To be "against ethnography" in how African literature is framed and discussed thus raises the question of what one can be *for* that is both distinctive of literary study and still has the power to redress entrenched curricular injustices. How can African writing be part of decolonizing the English literature curriculum without being reduced in yet another way, to the role of decolonial shock troops? What might *really* feel different, forcing students to question clichés and counterclichés, easy complexity and political hardship alike? I turn now to some carefully nonrepresentative African short stories in search of an answer.

Egblewogbe's Ghanaian Cosmicism

Critics have not known quite what to do with Martin Egblewogbe's debut story collection *Mr. Happy and the Hammer of God & Other Stories* (2012). An admired presence in the Ghanaian literary community as a cofounder of the Writers Project of Ghana, recognition has nonetheless eluded him in the lucrative ranks of "global" African writers. *Mr. Happy* was originally self-published and then later reissued by the small press Ayebia Clarke Publishing; Egblewogbe's second collection, *The Waiting*, was released in 2020 by flipped eye publishing, both founded by Ghanaians in England. The palpable influence of Egblewogbe's background in physics (he is a senior lecturer in the subject at the University of Ghana), along with his often-nameless characters and abstract reveries, make his work difficult to place within African literary debates about culture and representation. The stories, in a word, are weird. Synopses of the work all seem to stop just shy of the term – the back cover of *Mr. Happy* includes "surreal" and "unsettling" – and some readers have expressed outright hostility to its off-kilter tone. Silindiwe Sibanda, for example, in his review of *Mr. Happy* calls its "literary exploration of the tangential nature of being" a "clumsy and artless" philosophical exercise (146).

Egblewogbe's stories do not develop characters or relationships, and their Ghanaian settings, while sometimes highly specified with street names and the like, are largely incidental to the repeated "action" of communicative failure. So what *do* they offer, exactly? Sibanda's criticism hints at a certain existential bluntness that makes it difficult to find a pedagogical angle on them. With the longer context of African literature in mind, however, I want to suggest that such ostensibly "pointless" stories are an undervalued kind of classroom material. Egblewogbe's work often narrates moments of unresolved frustration that could in theory occur almost anywhere, and whose setting is thus meaningful more for its part in generating atmosphere than as a purveyor of cultural information. And while it would be a mistake to completely overlook African literary influences on his writing, he invites readers to foreground historically (and geographically) remote sources of inspiration. When asked about his favorite writers and those he most relates to, Egblewogbe routinely cites European absurdists.[7] "Let's put it this way," he acknowledges to Geoff Ryman in *Strange Horizons* magazine, "Kafka and Beckett have been very strong influences on me. More than I would say any African writer because of the extent of their imaginings." His attraction to far-flung traditions of profound existential questioning also recalls many descriptions of "weird" writing. As Kate Marshall argues, that genre depicts human disorientation by minimizing agency and, to some degree, subjectivity itself. By favoring "the modalities of indifference, the cosmic, and external or object agencies" (634), she writes, weirdness foregrounds the inscription of human interiority by an exterior universe that is apathetic at best, hostile at worst.

The second story in *Mr. Happy*, "Coffee at the Hilltop Café," is a good case in point. Its first paragraph introduces a cast of characters known only by the pronouns "she" and "I" and the label "the man" before describing two transparent details: the "large glass window" of the titular café and a woman's laughter rendered as "peals like jewels falling from her lips" (7). Right from the start, the story emphasizes the unelaborated perception of discrete sense objects over the organic intermingling of character and scene. The reader's focus is then drawn similarly to what at first seem like a clear and precise set of objects that take up the whole of the narrator's awareness – "the woman," a "cup of coffee," and "the view" (7) – but about which Egblewogbe in fact reveals nothing distinctive. This procession of vacant details is punctuated by a pair of localized inflections *if* one knows where to look. First, the narrator notes that the café "has a tradition for excellence" (7), which we might read as a wry comment on Ghanaian metropolitan achievement culture. Finally, we get a quintessentially but generically Ghanaian description of the businesses occupying the same street as the cafe: a jewelry store, a beauty shop, and a tailor. In a page full of spatial particularization, Egblewogbe grants close to no insight into socio-cultural particulars.

Part of this story's minimalism in situating itself in a culturally "thick" as opposed to spatially immediate sense can be explained by the fact that Egblewogbe has a mainly Ghanaian audience. He likely feels no pressure to "seem African" in a way that will register to a broad transnational readership looking to expand its multicultural bona fides, but nor does he expend effort on resisting Africanity. His market nonrepresentativeness works in concert with, not simply as an explanation for, the cultural nonrepresentativeness of his prose: both his readership and his style take his location as given, using it as a springboard to a geographically transposable *sense* of not quite apprehending life's purpose. As "Coffee at the Hilltop Café" continues for two more pages, the narrator grows more and more focused on maintaining existential equilibrium in the face of a minor disturbance to his routine: usually he (or perhaps she) drinks coffee alone, and the presence of the unnamed couple at the cafe threatens this anonymity. To the degree that the story is "about" anything, then, it is the precariousness of atmosphere itself, with even the narrator playing a supporting role. The story charts the restoration of perceptual peace by turning its narratorial gaze to "The whole western horizon ... tainted a mellow, mature purple, with the sun, a purple-gold orb, sinking majestically behind the tree-crowned hills" (8). Brief mention of "an evangelist from another town" (9) visiting the narrator's nearby church might again offer some cultural context to students who know how heavy the evangelical Christian presence is in much of Ghana. But it is neither here nor there in terms of the story's development from a steady existential rhythm, through reckoning with its disruption, and finally toward a state of carefully calibrated sensory repose. "I open my Bible but I do not read," it concludes. "I close my eyes and listen to the music. It is beautiful" (9).

Even this brief example conveys Egblewogbe's interest in narrating the experience of moving intentionally through life when life might go askew at any moment. In the case of "Coffee at the Hilltop Café," beauty is restored by a focus on universal atmospheric effects: light interacting with shadows, or pavement illuminated by lamps (9). In other stories, the luster revealed by disturbance to shine beneath the surface of routine is replaced by a grimmer kind of estrangement from habitual observation. In "Pharmaceutical Intervention," an unwanted pregnancy is depicted but not named as foreboding embryonic development, "a clot steadily thickening, thickening at an astonishing speed" (11). That story, too, forgoes nuanced representation in favor of cosmic-cum-religious sensation: Egblewogbe renders a medically induced abortion through a dialogue between the patient and "voices crossed over from the other side" (15), which may or may not be psychological projections. The book's fourth story, the cryptic and evocative "Down Wind," begins with a man calling his doctor from a phone booth to describe a vague feeling of pain. It quickly escalates through a series of frantic phone calls with anonymous speakers during which the caller is accused of some unnamed transgression, at the same time as the phone booth starts to stink and an epic storm gathers outside. Communication comes in fits and starts across the unreliable phone line until it finally fails altogether (28). Again, the story concludes by invoking the unknowable part of life – be it heaven or void – as experienced by the lonely people groping their way through it. "Behind him the telephone booth stood," we read, "yellow, solitary, dark and deserted: a strange aural terminal to the rest of the world" (29). It is difficult to have any idea what has happened in "Down Wind," other than the gathering of tension through panicked, erratic speech and then its eerie release into light.

The stories in *Mr. Happy and the Hammer of God* are disorienting and rich with a cosmic suggestiveness that goes largely unfulfilled as anything more concrete. Brought into an American literature classroom full of students who are interested mainly in learning about African cultures either for personal or professional reasons (their parents are from Lagos, say, or they plan to spend a summer volunteering abroad), the fact that Egblewogbe's work is so heavy on atmosphere and so light on ethnographic content is a good thing. It offers something approaching a blank slate for discussion of African writing; teaching such material asks students to build their understanding of that term's possibilities from the ground up, regardless of what stereotypes or counterstereotypes they may have brought into the room. In this way, cosmic or existential stories such as Egblewogbe's (or Mohammed Naseehu Ali's collection *The Prophet of Zongo Street*, or the South African Henrietta Rose Innes's *Homing*, to name just two more examples) estrange on both a metadisciplinary and formally local level. Rather than baptize students into an unrelenting chain of reactivity, nonrepresentative texts ask them to start from a place of terminological suspension. They then face the task, elemental in the best sense, of trying to describe the *how* of their unsettlement: the rhythm, mood, and instrumentation of its source. Minority literature can be a beginning to many ends, finally permitted to mark its own time.

Notes

1. For what remains a forceful and perhaps uneasily relevant overview of the various controversies surrounding these terms, "none of which has ever been acceptable across a wide spectrum of scholars" (745), see Tejumola Olaniyan's 1993 essay "On 'Post-Colonial Discourse': An Introduction" from *Callaloo*. Much of Olaniyan's analysis of postcolonialism's advantages and limitations as

a category would, now, apply to decolonial as well, including his summary of the former as "an open warrant to rifle through the history of Empire – before, during, and after – *from the perspective of the victims*" (744). Olaniyan's effort to taxonomize the postcolonial is also instructive in a different way for those of us working under a decolonial imperative. Rather than trying to define rapidly expanding terms such as "postcolonial" and "decolonial," often by distinguishing between their authentic and bad-faith versions, we might, following Olaniyan, focus not on such "[crises] of naming" but on the "relevant work [being] done in [these terms'] name" (745).

2. See also Aminatta Forna's 2015 *Guardian* piece "Don't Judge a Book by Its Author," in which she opines, "All this classifying, it seems to me, is the very antithesis of literature. The way of literature is to seek universality. Writers try to reach beyond those things that divide us: culture, class, gender, race. Given the chance, we would resist classification. I have never met a writer who wishes to be described as a female writer, gay writer, black writer, Asian writer or African writer. We hyphenated writers complain about the privilege accorded to the white male writer, he who dominates the western canon and is the only one called simply 'writer'."

3. See Jeyifo's powerful 1990 essay "The Nature of Things: Arrested Decolonization and Critical Theory," where he states that, "What is anomalous, and problematic is that this point [of nations having claims on their own traditions], which in most other cases is taken for granted and silently passed over in the criticism of specific works or authors, becomes, in this [African] instance, a grounding, foundational critical rubric, a norm of evaluation and commentary. Pushed to the limits of its expression, it becomes a veritable ontologization of the critical enterprise: only Africans must criticize or evaluate African literature, or slightly rephrased, only Africans can give a 'true' evaluation of African literary works. . . . Among the most clamorous advocates of this viewpoint, Chinweizu is exemplary in his constant deployment of the collective, proprietary pronoun 'we', which he invariably uses in a supremely untroubled fashion as if he were absolutely certain of its axiomatic representativeness" (37).

4. The best-known example of this approach to realist criticism is probably Marshall Brown's 1981 *PMLA* essay "The Logic of Realism: A Hegelian Approach."

5. For a generous overview of this essay's field-shaping contributions and reverberations, see Imre Szeman's "Who's Afraid of National Allegory? Jameson, Literary Criticism, Globalization" in *The South Atlantic Quarterly* (2001).

6. See, for example, Shringarpure's *Africa Is a Country* piece "Notes on Fake Decolonization," a companion piece of sorts to her analysis of African literary curricula with Saint.

7. Also see Egblewogbe's interview with Nana Fredua-Agyemang on the latter's personal blog.

WORKS CITED

Adichie, Chimamanda Ngozi. "The Danger of a Single Story." Lecture delivered at TEDGlobal 2009. Archived online with transcript at: www.ted.com/talks/chimamanda_ngozi_adichie_the_danger_of_a_single_story?language=en.

Ali, Mohammed Naseehu. *The Prophet of Zongo Street: Stories*. New York: HarperCollins, 2005.

Branch, Adam. "Decolonizing the African Studies Center." *The Cambridge Journal of Anthropology* 36.2 (2018): 73–91.

Brown, Marshall. "The Logic of Realism: A Hegelian Approach." *PMLA* 96.2 (1981): 224–41.

Edoro, Ainehi. "How Not to Talk about African Fiction." *The Guardian*. April 6, 2016. www.theguardian.com/books/2016/apr/06/how-not-to-talk-about-african-fiction.

Egblewogbe, Martin. *Mr. Happy and the Hammer of God & Other Stories*. Banbury: Ayebia Clarke Publishing, 2012.

Fredua-Agyemang, Nana and Martin Egblewogbe. Interview with Martin Egblewogbe on Fredua-Agyemang's personal blog. August 31, 2009. Web. https://freduagyeman.blogspot.com/2009/08/interview-with-author-martin-egblewogbe.html.

Forna, Aminatta. "Don't Judge a Book by Its Author." *The Guardian*. February 13, 2015. www.theguardian.com/books/2015/feb/13/aminatta-forna-dont-judge-book-by-cover.

Gugelberger, Georg M. "Decolonizing the Canon: Considerations of Third World Literature." *New Literary History* 22.3 (1991): 505–24.

Jameson, Fredric. "Third-World Literature in the Era of Multinational Capitalism." *Social Text* 15 (1986): 65–88.

Jeyifo, Biodun. "For Chinua Achebe: The Resilience and the Predicament of Obierika." *Kunapipi* 12.2 (1990): 51–70.

"The Nature of Things: Arrested Decolonization and Critical Theory." *Research in African Literatures* 21.1 (1990): 33–48.

Lee, Yoon Sun. "Type, Totality, and the Realism of Asian American Literature." *Modern Language Quarterly* 73.3 (2012): 415–32.

Mang, Riley. Interview with Bibi Bakare-Yusuf. *Los Angeles Review*. 2014. https://losangelesreview.org/interview-with-bibi-bakare-yusuf/.

Marshall, Kate. "The Old Weird." *Modernism/modernity* 23.3 (2016): 631–49.

Mushakavanhu, Tinashe. *Reincarnating Marechera: Notes on a Speculative Archive*. Brooklyn: Ugly Duckling Presse, 2020.

Olaniyan, Tejumola. "On 'Post-Colonial Discourse': An Introduction." *Callaloo* 16.4 (1993): 743–49.

Rose-Innes, Henrietta. *Homing*. Cape Town: Umuzi, 2011.

Ryman, Geoff and Martin Egblewogbe. Interview with Martin Egblewogbe. *Strange Horizons*. March 2020. http://strangehorizons.com/non-fiction/martin-egblewogbe/.

Selasi, Taiye. "Stop Pigeonholing African Writers." *The Guardian*. July 4, 2015. www.theguardian.com/books/2015/jul/04/taiye-selasi-stop-pigeonholing-african-writers.

Shklovsky, Viktor. *Theory of Prose*. Translated by Benjamin Sher. Normal, IL: Dalkey Archive Press, 1991.

Shringarpure, Bhakti. "Notes on Fake Decolonization." *Africa Is a Country*. December 18, 2021. https://africasacountry.com/2020/12/notes-on-fake-decolonization.

Shringarpure, Bhakti and Lily Saint. "African Literature Is a Country." *Africa Is a Country*. August 8, 2020. https://africasacountry.com/2020/08/african-literature-is-a-country.

Shringarpure, Bhakti and Priyamvada Gopal. "A Demanding Relationship with History: An Interview with Priyamvada Gopal." *The Los Angeles Review of Books*. August 30, 2021. https://lareviewofbooks.org/article/a-demanding-relationship-with-history-a-conversation-with-priyamvada-gopal/.

Sibanda, Silindiwe. Review of *Mr. Happy and the Hammer of God and Other Stories* by Martin Egblewogbe. *English Academy Review* 33.1 (2016): 145–47.

Szeman, Imre. "'Who's Afraid of National Allegory? Jameson, Literary Criticism, Globalization." *The South Atlantic Quarterly* 100.3 (2001): 803–27.

Tamakloe-Garr, Ayo. Interview with *Flash Fiction Ghana*. July 20, 2020. https://flashfictionghana.com/2020/07/20/interview-with-ayo-tamakloe-garr/.

Wainana, Binyavanga. "How to Write about Africa." *Granta* 92 (2005). Republished online May 2, 2019. https://granta.com/how-to-write-about-africa/.

CHAPTER 11

Orality, Experiential Learning, and Decolonizing African Literature

Kwabena Opoku-Agyemang

Introduction

The expression "dead White men" has become hackneyed in decolonial conversations. It is a given that there is a pressing need to diversify academia: this obligation involves questioning, dismantling, and reconstructing canons in their most old-fashioned forms on the one hand, while gravitating toward practices that promote a more equitable redistribution (if not diffusion) of power on the other hand. These actions are required all over the world, not least in Africa, where colonialism was experienced in some of its worst forms. And yet, even in the twenty-first century, the phrase "dead White men" takes on a visually and conceptually poignant pertinence at the Department of English in the University of Ghana, Legon.

Prominent on the walls of this two-floor department are thirty-seven portraits of poets, writers, and playwrights – as well as Queen Elizabeth I (see Figure 11.1). Of this number, only five – Ngũgĩ wa Thiong'o, Ama Ata Aidoo, Ousmane Sembène, Kofi Anyidoho, and Kofi Awoonor – are of African descent (see Figure 11.2). Perhaps equally striking is the fact that out of the total, Aidoo is the only other woman author apart from Jane Austen. The remaining twenty-nine personalities are British and American White male literary artists, including well-known giants such as Shakespeare, Milton, and Conrad and others such as Thomas Wyatt the Elder, Aldous Huxley, Henry Howard, and Joseph Addison; none of the latter group, among other authors hanging on the walls, has featured in either undergraduate- or graduate-level syllabi or faculty-level research for decades. In other words, this visual greeting to students, staff, and visitors at the department is overwhelmingly by dead and somewhat obscure White men who, what is more, have little bearing on their immediate audience.

Figure 11.1 Portraits of dead White men, Jane Austen, and Queen Elizabeth I at the Department of English, University of Ghana. Photograph by author

This means that after more than seven decades of existence, a founding department of the oldest university in the first African country south of the Sahara to gain political independence from Western colonialism grapples with a situation that presents a twofold challenge to educators: first, many of those writers being held up as the standard have direct ties to colonial and neocolonial cultures whose presence looms over local/African output.[1] Secondly, the prominent presence of these personalities is sharply belied by their remoteness in terms of cultural and academic relevance.[2] In addition to the familiar nationally embraced social, economic, and political challenges that are presented by the colonial accident and filter into African universities, it is within this paradoxical context that the department functions.

Figure 11.2 Portraits of Ama Ata Aidoo and Ngũgĩ wa Thiong'o at the Department of English, University of Ghana. Photograph by author

And even if this situation at Legon is not visualized as dramatically at other African universities, the curricula of English and Literature departments in many institutions across the continent are similarly encumbered by obstacles that demand the addressing of pedagogical structures to decolonial ends. A casual sampling of syllabi in African literature courses from other universities in Ghana as well as universities in Senegal, the Gambia, Nigeria, South Africa, Cameroon, Malawi, and Botswana reveals methods of teaching and textual choices that are steeped in conservative modes and gravitate toward conservative tendencies.[3] For example, courses privilege written texts (over oral and digital texts), while the traditional classroom space continues to be idealized as the sole learning environment. A more carefully done formal survey by Bhakti Shringarpure corroborated this situation but also found that other African universities, especially in Kenya and Uganda, allow students to "gain a deep knowledge of African literary traditions with emphasis placed on orature and orality."[4] In other words, different universities adopt practices that have varying degrees of success in being decolonial in nature and application.

This chapter is not intended to unduly criticize universities in Africa, which have collectively made impressive strides despite astonishing difficulties. Apart from unacceptably high student–teacher ratios for instance, finance is a big challenge: access to local funding for African universities remains chronically low, while a handful of Africa-based researchers occasionally win grants usually from foreign sources.[5] Even worse, political interference occurs in many institutions. In Ghana, for example, there were multiple government-sponsored attacks and attempts to destabilize universities and university systems between 2017 and 2020.[6] More specifically to literature, it must not be forgotten that hardly anyone researched into or taught African literature up until the middle of the twentieth century (Lindfors vii). In fact, Tejumola Olaniyan and Ato Quayson's *African Literature: An Anthology of Criticism and Theory*, which is the first ever critical anthology to focus exclusively on African literature, came as late as 2007.[7] The progress that has been made despite these challenges can still be extended by suggestions that are informed by my experience gained from teaching an English course at the University of Ghana.

I use ENGL 314: Introduction to African Literature, taught in three different semesters (between 2020 and 2022), to highlight decolonial pedagogical techniques that ultimately tackle two concerns. The first is this most classic of questions that can be traced to the colonial encounter: how does one find a "balance" between the imposition of "untouchable" and "Western" standards in the literary canon and African creative expression in a postcolonial country such as Ghana? Secondly, in an age where the humanities faces various crises, including questions of finance and relevance, how is the significance of literature to aspects of students' life, including the political, sociocultural, and ethical, to be highlighted by relevant pedagogical strategies? These questions are contextualized within a brief history of the university as well as in the evolution of the department.

Legon: The History of an African University

According to its website, the University of Ghana "was founded as the University College of the Gold Coast by Ordinance on August 11, 1948, for the purpose of providing and promoting university education, learning and research."[8] What is missing from this condensed history is that the university was set up after sustained agitation from different colonized subjects, including farmers and the educated elite, who demanded the establishment of a tertiary institution in the Gold Coast territory. Obviously there existed (and continue to exist) African forms of education (typically called "informal education") (Adeyemi and Adeyinka 425). Still, the establishment of the University of Ghana marked the beginning of

Western-style tertiary education in the Gold Coast, which had ended at the secondary-school level prior to these developments. Money from cocoa farmers formed the bulk of funds that were used to set up the University College of the Gold Coast.

The colonial administration modeled this new institution on the University of London, thus giving the institution a British identity from the beginning.[9] Francis Agbodeka notes that documents call this association a "special relationship" (18), but for all intents and purposes, the new university was under the tutelage of its British counterpart, which exercised absolute control: the University of London approved courses, had a major hand in recruiting staff through an interuniversities committee in London, and had to approve syllabi and reading lists prepared by faculty at Legon. Additionally, examination questions were sent to the British counterpart for approval, while Legon faculty regularly traveled to London for examiners' meetings. The university was purely European in idea and practice – explained further by the fact that the first staff recruits were Europeans who were trained in European universities. They brought with them wholesale what they had learnt from Europe, with little to no African input. The curriculum therefore remained exclusively Eurocentric from the beginning.

To the credit of the European staff, there was a coordinated movement to Africanize courses, especially after Ghana gained independence in 1957. Resident faculty, including Polly Hill, Ivor Wilks, and E. F. Collins, started to produce research that was relevant to their immediate environments; they then brought their work to the classroom. Hill, for example, explored the migratory and capitalist practices of cocoa farmers, while Wilks researched the history of the Asante kingdom.[10] This Africanization push was supplemented by a decision in 1953 to increase the recruitment of qualified Ghanaians, as the university began a staff development program which involved identifying promising students and awarding them scholarships to pursue graduate studies. Beneficiaries of this policy included Alexander Adum Kwapong (who later became the first Ghanaian vice chancellor of the university), while J. H. Nketia had joined the university as a research fellow in Traditional Music, Folklore, and Festivals in West Africa in 1952. Most of these graduates traveled to universities in the United Kingdom, although a few went to the United States.

While undertaking their graduate studies, this first group of Ghanaian graduates typically wrote dissertations that focused on Western research. However, as their numbers started to increase, newer cohorts, including scholars such as George Benneh, John K. Fynn, L. A. Boadi, Florence Dolphyne, and G. K. Nukunya, invariably produced doctoral theses on African studies topics while abroad.[11] They started returning to Legon from the early 1960s and, because they had Africanist backgrounds, establishing African courses was relatively straightforward. Accordingly, through new syllabi and reading lists, disciplines such as Music, History, Anthropology (which increasingly adopted a Sociology character), Linguistics, Geography, Archeology, and Philosophy started to assume identities that moved further away from their exclusively Eurocentric origins. An even stronger effort at Africanization commenced with Nkrumah's establishment of the Institute of African Studies in 1961, and scholars further Africanized the curriculum at the pretertiary level by writing textbooks on African Studies subjects.[12] With these efforts, high-school graduates who entered university had a fairly decent background in terms of formally taught African content.

In the midst of this transformation, English lagged in embracing Africanization, mainly due to the faculty's lack of belief in the quality of African writers (Anyidoho 9).[13] Influenced by his Nigerian colleague Ikide, faculty member K. E. Senanu introduced the department's first course on African literature in the 1970s, which was open only to English majors in their final year; all other courses remained a spillover from the colonial period.[14] Disagreements between Sey and Senanu over introducing new African-centered courses at the department led to the departure of the latter to Kenya in the 1970s. Senanu had earlier played a crucial role in attempting to dismantle conservative structures at the department after spending a sabbatical at the University of Ibadan, which was set up in the same year as Legon. Ibadan at the time was a site for radical decolonial efforts, with scholars such as Biodun Jeyifo spearheading the charge.[15] Added to the famous efforts of Ngũgĩ in Kenya (reflected in his seminal essay "On the Abolition of the English Department") and others across the continent, African scholars had been bringing progressive developments to English departments in Africa. In East Africa, the name "English" was replaced by Literature or its equivalents, signaling an ideological shift. This was not reflected at Legon's English Department anywhere as intensely.

The Africanization of the Department of English also lagged in terms of research at both faculty and student levels. In an interview, Kofi Anyidoho, who was an undergraduate student in the 1970s and a former head of department from 2004 to 2006, recalls being forced to move to the Linguistics department to write a long essay on oral literature because department faculty strongly discouraged his decision to do so at the English Department.[16] Needless to say, the change at the department was gradual. Up until the 1970s, there was still a substantial number of British faculty at the department and at the university as a whole.[17] However, in the late 1970s, the British government withdrew the British University Grants Committee (UGC) subsidies for lecturers overseas, which had been set up in 1919 and was crucial to them staying.[18] This withdrawal led to an exodus of British lecturers from Ghana, clearing the way for more African faculty.[19] By the time the university survived the economic crisis that plagued Ghana in the early 1980s, there was a majority African presence in terms of staff, which has remained the case until today.[20]

Still, as late as 1986, Bernth Lindfors had surveyed 194 courses from thirty universities in fourteen African countries, finding that while the "most radical reorientations" in the curriculum had occurred in Kenyan and Tanzanian universities, the "staunchest conservatism" was the case at the English Departments at the University of Ghana and the neighboring University of Cape Coast, both of which had only affected "minor alterations of the old colonial curriculum" (48). The department's history of being slow to embrace decolonial endeavors has meant that it has taken monumental efforts to chip away at its conservative nature.

Shifts in curriculum development in the 1990s led by such faculty as Anyidoho, Awoonor, Dako, and Mensah helped the English department make significant strides at decolonial efforts. By the turn of the millennium, and under the tenure of Anyidoho as head of department, the first two doctoral dissertations in African oral literature were passed in the department, with an increase in numbers since then.[21] In the last two decades, more African-centered courses have been introduced to the department at both undergraduate and graduate levels, including Oral Literature, Ghanaian Literature, Postcolonial Literature, and Literature of the Black Diaspora, all of which expanded the curriculum to decolonial ends. These courses, like most other literature courses at African universities, privilege written text and do not typically require students to go outside the classroom. Grappling with these legacies, I argue the need to do more than just revising the text of the curriculum, by introducing new modes of pedagogical engagement that foreground relevance while utilizing the resources immediately available. In times when African Studies must evolve, it is important especially for African universities to utilize Indigenous forms of knowledge and reconceptualize the environment to benefit students and optimize pedagogical potential.[22]

Orality and Experiential Learning at Legon

The following section expands upon this proposal to recollect and subsequently reflect on the treatment of the ENGL 314: Introduction to African Literature course at the University of Ghana, taught during the second semesters of the 2019/2020, 2020/21, and 2021/22 academic years. This course is required for all third-year students of English and has been taught in different forms for at least forty years. During the scope of study for this chapter, the class size has ranged from 75 to 110, including foreign students in all iterations apart from the last one (due to a nationwide university strike among faculty that shifted the calendar). The class size is one of the limitations that will be discussed later in the chapter, even though it is important to note here that the different semesters had a similar syllabus. Historically, the course is usually taught neither with recourse to optimal usage of the physical environment nor by harnessing nonwritten texts in a central manner.[23] A marked departure from previous offerings of the course thus involved implementing an interplay of oral and experiential learning strategies, away from centering a syllabus around conventional understandings of text and writing that in turn privilege Eurocentric offerings.[24]

What Karin Barber terms as investigating "the very constitution of the text itself" (67) helped to further understand what a text is. Barber further states "what a text is considered to be, how it is considered to have meaning, varies from one culture to another. We need to ask what kinds of interpretation texts are set up to expect, and how they are considered to enter the lives of those who produce, receive and transmit them" (67). Varied interpretations of text are not intended to create a hierarchy that privileges some interpretations over others; the intention is to place them on a horizontal scale from which to make relevant choices. Additionally, the fact that one culture accepts certain interpretations does not prevent that culture from adopting and accepting alternatives from other cultures. In a globalized world where cultures have always borrowed and lent themselves despite tension and appropriation, cross-cultural exchange allows an instructor to pick and choose from a wide selection. Following from Barber, then, it is important to underline that for this course, text and writing were thus seen as both embodied and geographical due to the relationship that exists in African literature between orality and creative expression.

On all three occasions, the first few class sessions involved helping students unlearn the regular understanding of texts and writing as absolute in Western/colonial terms. The students subsequently imbibed the concept of decentering these meanings to incorporate forms that they had not immediately considered as acceptable texts.[25] As Uzoma Esonwanne explains, treating oral discourses as literary devices does not trigger repetition; it rather causes the former to be spoken in a new context that creates a non-pre-discursively new utterance (142).[26] By deconstructing orality and text, the intention was to put pressure on their elasticity, thereby allowing students to rethink their natural environment as a text that was ripe for intellectual engagement. They were able to then understand their lived experiences in Accra as a series of learning moments.

In a time when African cities are increasingly the focus of mainstream research, it is incumbent upon teachers to utilize their environments for pedagogical purposes.[27] The basic logic underpinning this move was that if learning about African literature was taking place at an African university, then it was important to engage with the host African city in productively relevant ways. Accra (and by extension both Ghana and Africa) is written and spoken simultaneously – addressing only the former side of this equation through conventional learning practices leads to an incomplete understanding of the city.

One way of approaching a fuller understanding of the city was to introduce a research assignment that involved investigating the makeup of Accra through oral histories. Oral histories are the major source of both official and unofficial knowledge, and on a continent with a relative dearth in written research, oral information is a crucial source. Again, a significant amount of research on places in Africa is done through Eurocentric framings. For example, foundational texts in African studies are Eurocentric in authorship and origin, as European missionaries, soldiers, administrators, and other scholars wrote about the continent in various disciplines. V. Y. Mudimbe argues in his seminal *The Invention of Africa* that "Africa" is a constructed culmination of centuries of discourses and practices – largely starting from the fourteenth century by Europeans and responded to from the nineteenth century by Africans. In their attempts to question this invention, African scholars have not escaped the Eurocentric invention of Africa. Even though African studies aims at reclaiming the voice that was taken away from African subjects, there has been a tendency to maintain the West as the subject of history.[28] In contemporary times, Akosua Adomako Ampofo points out how Western scholarly outlets are prized, influencing African researchers to gravitate toward such destinations (17). Even though (or maybe because) the students in the ENGL 314 class do not have formally extensive training in research methods, it was important for them to appreciate that oral sources are as legitimate as published articles and monographs.[29]

Different student groups were to choose suburbs in Accra from a list and were tasked with investigating the history of the origin of the place. They were to accomplish this assignment by identifying and speaking to people who would have knowledge of its history. They were at liberty to complement this research by looking for documented evidence, even though this was to be a secondary strategy. After minimal training – involving introduction and observational skills – the students were to create a set of questions that would serve as a springboard for finding out the needed information. The purpose of this exercise was to let the students realize the consequence of considering people as recognized sources of information. Oral sources of information on the same issue are notorious for differing in terms of accounts; this feature was to help the students to think through authoritative sources while looking out for inconsistencies in competing accounts. In cases where histories of places were readily available – such as Jamestown and Labone – the information obtained was sometimes different from what was documented and available in libraries and archives, again allowing for an understanding of contested sources.[30]

By approaching and interviewing people about the histories of different places in Accra, the students were again able to define knowledge as embodied in the people they spoke to.[31] Often, students would find that older people were walking history libraries who had an admirable understanding of how the place in question had evolved. Additionally, knowledge was circumscribed by specific places in the suburbs they were to investigate. For instance, churches and mosques were usually the places where students found origin stories of the various suburbs. In subsequent discussions, students appreciated the fact that people, articles, and books could be placed on the same scale of credibility on the one hand; on the other hand, different people and different written sources could compete among each other for authenticity and authority. The tendency to not have a single authoritative source allowed for a questioning of what it means to diffuse authority and "truth" in a spectral sense. Learning through this experiential model of quasi-ethnographic research was therefore useful.

It is important to harness the creative and scholarly engagements with these cities through experiential learning to make the classroom space relevant to African students. Universities in Abuja or Abijan, or Khartoum or Kigali, for instance, can adapt this assignment to appreciate the importance of understanding the rapidly changing nature of their cities. Instead of drawing a dichotomy between the classroom and the street (Quayson, "Kóbóló Poetics" 428), the classroom becomes the street, and the street is the classroom, as students are constantly alert to finding out how to learn from their physical environment.

Another decolonial strategy involves provoking a sustained critique of conventional teaching modes by displacing agency to students, allowing for the interrogation of assumptions that underpin their lived experiences. This strategy was meant to avoid replicating colonialism in the classroom in the scenario where the instructor wielded undue levels of power. The course facilitator, namely the professor, is in the prime position to exercise judgment in shaping the course and content of research and study. We must also trust students with the ability to be responsible sharers of this power. This point for me was important because anecdotal experiences corroborate research that indicates that students do not feel empowered in the classroom.[32] Youth agency has to be amplified on a continent where more than two out of every three Africans south of the Sahara are younger than thirty years of age.[33]

Thematizing a Class

All three iterations of the course were themed around sound. This was done upon consultations with experienced faculty both in and outside the University of Ghana.[34] There was additional theoretical grounding in sound studies, with Jonathan Sterne, Igor Reyner, Gavin Steingo and Jim Sykes, and Marleen de Witte particularly helpful.[35] As mentioned in the course description of the syllabi, African literature is loud and full of sound: modern African literature such as novels and plays on the one hand, and African digital literature on the other hand, consistently emphasize noise, dialogue, and music. Written African literary texts such as Chinua Achebe's *Things Fall Apart*, Ayi Kwei Armah's *Fragments*, Noviolet Bulawayo's *We Need New Names*, and Fiston Mwanza Mujila's *Tram83* are full of both sounds and music. And Wole Soyinka's *Death and the King's Horseman* is famous for being structured around various forms of drumming in all parts of the play, even in scenes involving only the White characters. Oral literature is full of singing, dancing, and performance, while the acoustics and beats of contemporary music genres allow sound to permeate through creative expression all across the continent. The course was intended to introduce students to the uniqueness of African literature through a focus on sound in various ways: mythically, textually, politically, socially, culturally, and symbolically. Outside of the surrounding environment of Accra, the choice of conventional text and writing was therefore premised on understanding how to engage with sound centrally, tangentially, and indirectly.

As mentioned above (p. 000), even though the definition of text was elastic, there were still novels, plays, and short stories. Out of the selected texts, about half were authored by women, while there was a healthy mix of canonical authors such as Achebe and Aidoo, relatively newer well-known writers including Adichie and Bulawayo, and amateur writers from websites such as *Brittle Paper* and *Flash Fiction Ghana*. Writers came from countries that included Ghana, Nigeria, Algeria, Congo DR, Zambia, and Zimbabwe. The intention was for students to not expect a monolithic demographic with its attendant narrow implications for perspective formation and viewpoint shaping. Spreading the author choice around these various parameters was an obvious attempt to cover an appreciable amount, even if it must be immediately admitted that, as with any set of choices, many important aspects would be inevitably left out. It would be unconscionable to many lovers of African literature, for instance, that only three of the top five most-mentioned African writers featured on the syllabus.[36]

The Pandemic as Opportunity

In the first two times that the course was taught, the COVID-19 pandemic altered the mode of teaching. The pandemic first reached Ghana during the middle of the semester (March 2020), with attendant implications for the mode of delivery and experiential learning. In a country that has not kept up with digital advancements, there was a general difficulty in adapting to online teaching. Subsequent teaching of the course was informed by less face time and more virtual interaction. Considering the high cost of data to the average student and the lack of digital infrastructure in some places, this challenge hampered the pedagogical effectiveness of courses all over the country and continent.

COVID-19 still provided a ripe opportunity for digital technology to be an integral part of the class. There had been plans to invite creative artists to class to interact with students and do performances/readings of their work. Because of a lockdown in Accra and general social-distancing guidelines, students interacted with musicians, poets, and spoken word artists via Zoom calls and Instagram Live sessions. Through networking, I was able to have my students partake in interactive sessions with the hiplife musicians Reggie Rockstone and Kojo Cue, the poet Agyei Adjei Baah, and the spoken word artist Poetra Asantewa, mainly via Instagram (see Figure 11.3).

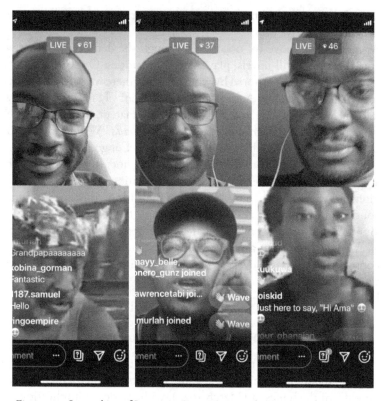

Figure 11.3 Screenshots of Instagram Live sessions with Reggie Rockstone, Kojo Cue, and Poetra Asantewa, respectively, in 2020. Photograph by author

African literature classes will benefit from finding ways of interacting with creative artists who are local to whichever space that the institution is located.

Creative artists are busy people, and securing their time was not always a success. During the second running of the course, no artist was able to make the time to join the class. This absence was also due to a shortened semester, the circumstances of which are explained in the conclusion of this chapter. For the third iteration, students had the pleasure of talking to the Ghanaian musicians Worlasi and Jupitar (see Figure 11.4), who physically came to class and fielded questions regarding inspiration, theme, character development, and other literary aspects of their songs. The amateur writer Fui Can-Tamakloe also visited the class on all three occasions (see Figure 11.5). His Pidgin-English stories, which appear on online portals, were intended to open the students' minds to the possibility of seeing

Figure 11.4 Respective class visits by the Ghanaian musicians Worlasi and Jupitar in 2022. Screenshot by author

Figure 11.5 Guest appearance from the Pidgin-English writer Fui Can-Tamakloe in 2020. Screenshot by author

Pidgin-English appear in mainstream spaces.[37] Listening to practitioners speak about their craft in nonscholarly ways was intended to complement class discussion and remind students of multifaceted engagements with texts.

While guest visits by practitioners are by no means a novel mode of pedagogy in African universities, having them interact with students is another way of fulfilling the call by Ato Quayson and Tejumola Olaniyan to ensure that African literary and critical production are not discrete entities but relate in a "supportive and critical, mutually affective intimacy" (1). The students on the one hand related up close with them; the creatives on the other hand saw their work through the eyes of their audiences in ways that made them rethink aspects of their work such as thematic and character development.

Conclusion: Limitations and Shortcomings

Apart from the litany of challenges that hamper teaching in a university in a postcolonial country such as Ghana, a new mode of pedagogical engagement that relied on learning on the go while dealing with unforeseen problems like COVID-19 would inevitably yield a series of omissions, mistakes, and limitations. Each iteration of the course had a set of unique and overlapping hurdles to cross: the first time was disrupted by the COVID-19 pandemic; the second time was limited by a compression of the semester due to logistical challenges that the university faced in trying to catch up after closing down for months – the semester was done exclusively online, with twice the number of classes per week in half the total semester time; the third iteration of the course witnessed a reversion to the regular semester, even though the period was also compressed into ten weeks instead of thirteen, due to the strike and aftereffects of the pandemic. Even after the university eventually manages to return to a regular schedule, the other challenges (class size, finances, etc.) will most likely remain.

In terms of the breadth of syllabus, the truth of the matter is that the beauty and force of African literature is too diverse to be captured in an undergraduate class that allows for ten to twelve weeks of teaching. Different authors, themes, and texts will inevitably be left out, while the intention to foreground student agency by allowing their perspectives to influence class discussion and direction also means that occasionally, lesson plans that intend to cover certain concerns might not always be fully realized. Focusing on the various realizations and utilizations of sound was one window through which to approach the texts; alternative approaches can appropriate place and space, the home, queerness, social relations, power dynamics, and the public sphere, to name a few. In other words, like many thematized classes in different disciplines, African literature courses are open to a multitude of angles from which an instructor can take the class. The choice of theme can inform the text selection, even though, as always, certain texts will always be left out.

There were other limitations. The architectural shortcomings of the classroom venue prevented the adoption of a seating style that redirected attention from the front of the class to an oral-style circular form. This form is proven to deemphasize attention on a sole speaker. Neil ten Kortenaar recalls a time in Canada when a First Nation elder required participants at a workshop to sit in a style that incorporated traditional meeting practices (236). According to the elder, thinking and acting differently required change, which would in turn "begin with the way we framed our questions and our discussion" (236). The diffusion of power dynamics due to the spatial relations engendered by such arrangements was unfortunately not possible in my class. One way of circumventing this obstacle was for me to move around the classroom and sit at different vantage points during discussion. In other words, instructors must use the tools at our disposal to improvise.

In this light, my suggestion is for African departments to continue the process toward decolonizing the literature curriculum by considering such methods. Institutions across the continent might not be able to compete with counterparts in the Global North in terms of resources and funding, but the key is to use the tools at our disposal to our advantage. In my opinion, the primary advantage is place, as the city in which the class is being held is already African. Place then lends to aspects of culture that engender experiential learning, as students learn by experiencing the environment around them through scholarly engagement, including interviews in this case. In other cases, surveys, case studies, archival research, and other methods of inquiry can enable students to realize firsthand the potential of their environment, causing a rethink of conventional modes of pedagogical engagement.

Arguably, these suggestions will not necessarily result in reaching the point of being fully decolonized or uncolonizable – if either state even exists. Universities are trapped within larger global contexts that are usually beyond their purview. Regardless, incorporating alternative methods of conceptualizing the natural environment and focusing more on iterations of orality are possible ways of making African Studies become more relevant to students, leading to positive outcomes for all stakeholders.

Notes

1. Some authors like Conrad have had a long history of pushback from African scholars, primary among whom is Chinua Achebe in his famous "An Image of Africa: Racism in Conrad's 'Heart of Darkness'" (1975).

2. These authors represent an imperial (and pedagogical) moment that privileges Eurocentrism, and by virtue of mere representation, their presence cannot be removed from the problematic literary history that is imparted through the teaching of English language and literature at the University of Ghana.

3. Thanks to colleagues from representative universities who sent syllabi that featured African literature.

4. Shringarpure sampled syllabi from 105 professors from all over the world; respondents were skewed toward Western countries, even though Africa-based faculty – this author included – responded.

5. The World Bank has a comprehensive report on the challenges facing higher education in Africa, including student–teacher ratios (131), funding (168), and foreign-sourced grants (106–107).

6. The government forcibly replaced the vice chancellor at the University of Education in 2017 and tried to do same at the Kwame Nkrumah University of Science and Technology in 2018, before attempting to introduce the Public Universities Bill in 2020, which was intended to wrest control of university policy and decision-making into the hands of the government.

7. Olaniyan and Quayson start the introduction to their groundbreaking anthology by acknowledging that there was "not a single anthology of African literary criticism and theory" until their volume (1).

8. www.ug.edu.gh/about/overview. I am indebted to archival sources from the University of Ghana's Institute of African Studies and Human Resources Department, Francis Agbodeka's *A History of University of Ghana: Half a Century of Higher Education*, and interviews with University of Ghana's Dr. Kofi Baku (History) and Prof. Albert Sackey and Prof. Kofi Anyidoho (English) for the historical information.

9. The Asquith Commission, with advice from the Inter-University Council for Higher Education in the Colonies, was responsible for the initial direction of the university (Richards 336), while there was supposed to be some Oxbridge influence (Shattock and Berdhal, "Idea" 613).

10. Whether this move was altruistic or informed by the fact that they could not further their Eurocentric research due to proximity constraints is a matter of debate.

11. These dissertations included Dolphyne's *The Phonetics and Phonology of the Verbal Piece in the Asante Dialect of Twi* in linguistics; Fynn's *Ashanti and Her Neighbours c. 1700–1807* in philosophy; and Nukunya's *Kinship and Marriage among the Anlo-Ewe* in sociology.

12. Adu Boahen of the History department wrote *Topics in West African History* (1966), while *A Selection of African Poetry* (1976) was edited by K. E. Senanu of the English department with his Nigerian colleague Theo Vincent.

13. Kofi Sey, who became the first Ghanaian head of department in 1973, famously complained about the lack of quality African writers, preferring to teach British and American writers at the department.

14. Prior to this new course, African literature had been taught only at the Institute of African Studies (IAS), from 1964, at the first-year level.

15. While at Ibadan, Jeyifo was the founding editor of the extant cyclostyle journal *Positive Review: Journal of Society and Culture in Black Africa*, one of several outlets through which he shared his views on radicalizing the English curriculum.

16. Personal interview with Kofi Anyidoho, September 15, 2021. Alec Hardy, who was head of department at the time (and the last British head of department), was so adamant about him doing conservative topics that he even tried to force him to do his graduate studies at Cambridge, rather than an American university, where he would specialize in oral literature and bring about monumental change to the department decades later.

17. In an interview (September 18, 2021), Albert Sackey, who was a student at the department in the mid-1960s and teaches at the department, recalls having only three Ghanaian lecturers – Senanu (who taught literature) and Sey and Kwami (who both taught language) – and eight British counterparts.

18. See Richards (336) and Shattock and Berdhal ("Grants Committee" 471; "Idea" 613).

19. Records from the University's Human Resources Department, although scanty, indicate that foreign/Western faculty numbers dropped from thirty-five to three after the subsidies were withdrawn.

20. The economic crisis included a famine in 1983–84, which caused many Ghanaian faculty to flee to Nigeria and other countries. Departments were severely understaffed during this period.

21. Mawuli Adzei wrote on Pan Africanism and Slavery with fieldwork where he documented related proverbs and oral texts in 2004. In the same year, Mabel Komasi's award-winning dissertation focused on African children's literature, based on fieldwork with exposure to storytelling. In his reports, Manthia Diawara of New York University, who was the external examiner, found both to be impressive.

22. While Frances Owusu Ansah and Gubela Mji define African Indigenous knowledge as "experiential knowledge based on a worldview and a culture that is basically relational" (1) and privileges oral tradition (2), Molefi Kete Asante advocates for the education of African-descended people to be "responsive" to African tradition and history ("Afrocentric Idea" 1), since Western thought should not be construed as universal (*Afrocentric Idea* 168). In other words, the education curriculum benefits from pedagogy that is informed by familiar cultural practices.

23. Previous syllabi consistently have written texts as the major source of readings, while interviews with past course instructors revealed their interest in letting students engage with texts in conventional ways.

24. Irele divided African literature into oral and modern, while Anyidoho (6) contends that oral literature forms the bedrock of African creative expression. This is not the case in absolute terms, as White South African and White Zimbabwean writing and some Black African writers such as Jean-Luc Raharimanana, Taiye Selasi, and Kossi Efoui have little or no relationship with oral literature forms.

25. This concept follows from Douglas Kellner, who draws on Deleuze, Guattari, and Foucault, who argue that decentering liberates from "the terror of fixed and unified identities," leading to freedom for dispersion and multiplicity, as well as the reconstitution "as new types of subjectivities and bodies." Accordingly, the art of developing a fuller envelope of significations to incorporate oral forms was intended to enable a "democratic" engagement with the surrounding environment.

26. Despite following from Esonwanne, I stay away from the debate of whether orality is or is not "Africa's true literature" (142). All forms of creative expression (including oral, written, and digital) in Africa contribute to the complexity of African literature.

27. While creative work has always imagined African cities, there is a steady increase in research on African cities, with monographs on Accra (Quayson, *Oxford Street*; Hart), Lagos (Newell; Whiteman), and many other African urban spaces.

28. See Opoku-Agyemang and Thiam 424–25 for further expatiation.

29. This assignment was not intended to make them experts in the field; rather, they were to embrace the multiple perspectives that they could find while engaging in this mini-field-research work.

30. For example, Kropp Dakubu finds that Labone was so named because oral tradition traces the origin of La people from a place in Nigeria called Bonnie and, via linguistic and historical analyses, doubts the validity of the argument that the name came to be due to the translation of Labone from the Akan – "La" and "bone," which means "bad" (5–6). However, a student group found this latter explanation to be dominant among church leaders, who opined that the pagan actions of people led to the name.

31. Apart from obvious financial and logistical advantages of making Accra the site of engagement, there were conceptual and pedagogical benefits. For example, the students were able to appreciate the multifaceted nature of the city and the differing depths of history associated with parts of Accra.

32. See Afful and Afful and Mwinlaaru, for example.

33. www.un.org/ohrlls/news/young-people's-potential-key-africa's-sustainable-development.

34. I especially appreciate the advice of scholars such as Kofi Anyidoho (University of Ghana) and Ato Quayson (Stanford University) in creating the course.

35. While both Sterne (12) and Reyner (133, 134, and 139) admit to western bias, their arguments are helpful in establishing the stakes in sound studies and linking the discipline to literature respectively. Steingo and Sykes on the other

hand are careful to avoid a neocolonial narrative that maintains the centrality of the west (7). De Witte's essay on sound in Accra, albeit in the context of religion, situated the class within a postcolonial context by deflecting from Western framings of the city.

36. Bhakti Shringarpure's survey found that the top five writers were Ngũgĩ, Achebe, Adichie, Coetzee, and Dangarembga, while Lindfors's similar research about two decades prior revealed the list to comprise Soyinka, Ngugi, Achebe, Armah, and Clark.

37. Dako notes that Pidgin-English has typically been frowned upon as an unacceptable and even invisible mode of communication in Ghana.

WORKS CITED

Achebe, Chinua. "An Image of Africa: Racism in Conrad's *Heart of Darkness.*" *Massachusetts Review* 18.4 (1977): 782–94. First given as a lecture in 1975.

Adeyemi, Michael B. and Augustus A. Adeyinka. "The Principles and Content of African Traditional Education." *Educational Philosophy and Theory* 35.4 (2003): 425–40.

Afful, Joseph. "Address Terms among University Students in Ghana: A Case Study." *Language and Intercultural Communication* 6.1 (2006): 76–91.

Afful, Joseph and Isaac Nuokyaa-Ire Mwinlaaru. "When 'Sir' and 'Madam' Are Not: Address Terms and Reference Terms Students Use for Faculty in a Ghanaian University." *Sociolinguistic Studies* 6.3 (2012): 491–517.

Agbodeka, Francis. *A History of University of Ghana: Half a Century of Higher Education (1948–1998).* Accra: Woeli Publishing Services, 1998.

Ampofo, Akosua Adomako. "Re-viewing Studies on Africa, #Black Lives Matter, and Envisioning the Future of African Studies." *African Studies Review* 59.2 (2016): 7–29.

Anyidoho, Kofi. "The Back without Which There Is No Front." *Africa Today* 50.2 (2003): 3–18.

Asante, Molefi Kete. *The Afrocentric Idea.* Philadelphia: Temple University Press, 1987.
    "The Afrocentric Idea in Education." *The Journal of Negro Education* 60.2 (1991): 170–80.

Barber, Karin. *The Anthropology of Texts, Persons and Publics.* Cambridge: Cambridge University Press, 2007.

Bryce, Jane. "Desperate Optimism: Biodun Jeyifo and Talakawa Journalism." *Journal of the African Literature Association* 12.1 (2018): 49–59.

Dako, Kari. "Student Pidgin (SP): The Language of the Educated Male Elite." *Institute of African Studies Research Review* 18.2 (2002): 53–62.

De Witte, Marleen. "Accra's Sounds and Sacred Spaces." *International Journal of Urban and Regional Research* 32.3 (2008): 690–709.

Esonwanne, Uzoma. "Orality and the Genres of African Writing." In Ato Quayson, ed., *The Cambridge History of Postcolonial Literature*, 2 vols. Cambridge: Cambridge University Press, 2012.

Hart, Jennifer. *Ghana on the Go: African Mobility in the Age of Motor Transportation*. Bloomington: Indiana University Press, 2016.

Irele, Abiola. *The African Imagination: Literature in Africa and the Black Diaspora*. Oxford: Oxford University Press, 2001.

Kellner, Douglas. "Postmodern Theory. Chapter 3: Deleuze and Guattari." https://pages.gseis.ucla.edu/faculty/kellner/pomo/ch3.html. n.d.

Kropp Dakubu, Mary Esther. *Korle Meets the Sea: A Sociolinguistic History of Accra*. New York: Oxford University Press, 1997.

Lindfors, Bernth. "The Teaching of African Literature in Anglophone African Universities: An Instructive Canon." *Wasafiri* 5.11 (1990): 13–16.

Mudimbe, Valentin Y. *The Invention of Africa: Gnosis, Philosophy, and the Order of Knowledge*. Bloomington: Indiana University Press, 1988.

Newell, Stephanie. *Histories of Dirt: Media and Urban Life in Colonial and Postcolonial Lagos*. Durham, NC: Duke University Press, 2019.

Olaniyan, Tejumola and Ato Quayson, eds. *African Literature: An Anthology of Criticism and Theory*. Malden, MA: Blackwell, 2007.

Opoku-Agyemang, Kwabena and Cheikh Thiam. "VY Mudimbe: The Philosopher-Poet." In Adekeye Adebajo, ed., *The Pan-African Pantheon: Prophets, Poets, and Philosophers*. Manchester: Manchester University Press, 2021, 422–33.

Owusu-Ansah, Frances E. and Gubela Mji. "African Indigenous Knowledge and Research." *African Journal of Disability* 2.1 (2013): 1–5.

Quayson, Ato. "Kóbóló Poetics: Urban Transcripts and Their Reading Publics in Africa." *New Literary History* 41.2 (2010): 413–38.

Oxford Street, Accra: City Life and the Itineraries of Transnationalism. Durham, NC: Duke University Press, 2014.

Reyner, Igor. "Fictional Narratives of Listening: Crossovers between Literature and Sound Studies." *Interference Journal* 6 (2018): 129–42.

Richards, Audrey I. "The Adaptation of Universities to the African Situation." *Minerva* 3.3 (1965): 336–42.

Shattock, Michael and Robert Berdahl. "The British University Grants Committee 1919–83: Changing Relationships with Government and the Universities." *Higher Education* 13.5 (1984): 471–99.

"The UGC Idea in International Perspective." *Higher Education* (1984): 613–18.

Shringarpure, Bhakti. "African Literature Is a Country." *Africa Is a Country*. https://africasacountry.com/2020/08/african-literature-is-a-country.

Steingo, Gavin and Jim Sykes. "Introduction: Remapping Sound Studies in the Global South." *Remapping Sound Studies*. Durham, NC: Duke University Press, 2019. 1–36.

Sterne, Jonathan. *The Sound Studies Reader*. New York: Routledge, 2012.

ten Kortenaar, Neil. "Introduction to Special Issue on Literature Pedagogy Confronting Colonialism." *Cambridge Journal of Postcolonial Literary Inquiry* 7.3 (2020): 235–37.

Whiteman, Kaye. *Lagos: A Cultural and Literary History.* Vol. 5. Luton: Andrews UK, 2013.

World Bank. "Financing Higher Education in Africa." 2010. https://openknow ledge.worldbank.org/handle/10986/2448.

"Young People's Potential, the Key to Africa's Sustainable Development." *Welcome to the United Nations,* www.un.org/ohrlls/news/young-people's-potential-key-africa's-sustainable-development.

CHAPTER 12

Vernacular English in the Classroom
A New Geopolitics of the English Language

Akshya Saxena

> It may be in English, but often it is in an English which is like a howl
> or a shout, or a machine-gun, or the wind, or a wave. It is also like the
> blues.
>
> Edward Kamau Braithwaite, *History of Voice*

Decolonize What? What's Decolonization?

Soon after enthusiastically agreeing to write this essay, I panicked at the
enormity of the task ahead: Decolonizing the English Literary Curriculum.
As a scholar of postcolonial studies, I read and write with a commitment to
the decolonial possibilities of comparative methodologies. Against the
parochialism of a racialized English literature, I work across south–south
political geographies and Hindi, English, and Urdu media. Of course,
I wanted the opportunity to reimagine the English curriculum.

I talked to colleagues and students about what the decolonization of an
English literary curriculum meant to them. A few people expressed cyni-
cism about the institution-speak of decolonizing, some others noted the
urgency of decolonial practice. In an email exchange, Bhakti Shringarpure,
scholar and series editor of *Decolonize That! Handbooks for the
Revolutionary Overthrow of Embedded Colonial Ideas* (OR Books) framed
decolonial practice in terms of "what we 'do' and how we 'behave,'
'interact' etc. and stage our particular positionalities in everyday life."[1] It
quickly became clear that to write about decolonization meant writing
about praxis and practice. In terms of literary studies, decolonial practice
calls attention to what we teach and how we teach it, as well as what and
how we choose to write in our scholarly and public work. This account-
ability from the daily – often unseen and unsung – work of being in our
culturally specific classrooms and the ongoing pursuit of our strongest
political beliefs was not something I had always stopped to consider.

Broadly, decolonization refers to the critical appraisal of the hierarchical and racialized logics of Western European cultures and institutions that organize knowledge. Referring to the literal end of colonial rule, Frantz Fanon in *The Wretched of the Earth* (1961) wrote that decolonization is necessarily violent. To decolonize is to unsettle. Thus, any institution that wishes to decolonize should return the land to Indigenous populations.

There were questions that needed answers: Could everything be decolonized? Which English literary curriculum did I wish to decolonize? Would decolonization demand different strategies in different parts of the world? I recalled discussing with Ato Quayson the largely sophisticated scholarship on the institution of English literary studies from India (one of my areas of study). But I had neglected to ask what we meant when we said the English literary curriculum. While there was a reasonable answer to this second question based on our professional locations in the United States, it nagged me that I had understood what the editors meant when they said *the* English literary curriculum. This was exactly the path from language to identity I hoped to disrupt in my scholarship.

At the same time as calls for decolonization have grown across scholarly fields, so have calls to caution. We know from Eve Tuck and K. Wayne Yang's foundational essay that decolonization is not a metaphor (Tuck and Wang). It is not possible to decolonize in culturally, historically, or geopolitically abstract ways. Thus, at the outset, it is important to acknowledge – in the spirit of decentering and decolonizing – that there is no one English literary curriculum. Today, English literature is not only taught or studied in the US American academy but in many anglophone and nonanglophone countries, where it can be a vehicle for language skills and taught with a wide variety of textual materials beyond a shared understanding of a literary canon (Ben-Yishai; Kuortti). Scholars of English literature in erstwhile colonies have also engaged with it with a keen understanding of the colonial foundations of the English literary curriculum. Well before institutions in the United States changed their departmental names to reflect the diversity of what can be studied under the sign of English, Indian universities were offering degrees in Literature in English (Flaherty).

Surveying the contemporary decolonization discourse, Roopika Risam argues that the verb "decolonize" often functions as "extractive currency," and "decolonization" itself becomes a metaphor for "diversity work" that "assuages white guilt and obfuscates institutional complicities with the structural violence of racism" (11). Less pessimistic about the possibility of decolonization, Christopher J. Lee nonetheless attributes a "cruel optimism" to the imagined revolutionary potential of decolonization movements and projects. Lee argues that decolonization is not necessarily revolutionary, as the calls to decolonize are bound doubly in the tragedy of the postcolonial and the eternal hope of a revolution.[2] Writing about political cul-de-sacs and fantasies of radical change that debilitatingly never arrive, Lee leaves the reader with more questions about the political objectives of decolonization. Is decolonization a resetting of the order to a prior moment before colonization or is it an end in pursuit of a future yet to come? That decolonization – literal, figurative – may not equal revolution or progress is amply illustrated by neocolonial postcolonial states and the ascendance of ethnic and religious nationalism across the world.

In the specific context of English literary curriculum, a generation of postcolonial scholars have shown that both the English language and English literature as a disciplinary field of study were first piloted as political and administrative projects in the colonies.[3] The translation of local cultures into the English language made governance efficient and English literature held up values of morality and civility for the colonial subjects. This well-known history – brought to bear upon English literary studies through postcolonial scholarship – prompted Gaurav Desai to write in his essay "Rethinking English Studies: Postcolonial English Studies" (2005) that "no aspect of English literary studies, whether it be concerned with the Medieval period or the Renaissance or the Romantics can ignore its own colonial conditions of possibility" (525).

How does one decolonize a field of study that was invented in and for the better control of British colonies? How does one decolonize when coloniality is not a bug but a feature? Briefly, these questions made me wonder if perhaps Ngũgĩ wa Thiong'o had the right idea when he called for the abolition of English departments, rejecting the primacy of English language and literature and turning instead to African literature (Ngũgĩ wa Thiong'o). He and Obiajunwa Wali before him both argued that African literature in English was a contradiction of terms. Instead, in "On the Abolition of the English Department" (1972), Ngũgĩ, along with Taban Li Liyong and Henry Owuor-Anyumba, proposed the possibility of imagining literary studies from the perspective of African cultures.

What is at stake in wanting to hold on to English departments and English literary curricula in the first place? Why decolonize, why not burn it all down?

A New Geopolitics of the English Literary Curriculum

These deliberately provocative questions are not meant to diminish our collective efforts in this volume or to cast doubt on them but to gather context. The political and intellectual challenges to the project of decolonization can clarify what is at stake and illuminate the path ahead. If English is the language of British colonialism and US American neoimperialism, it is also the language lived and made anew by the colonized every day. At stake in holding onto an English department is the potential to restage the encounter with a colonial language and to retell the story of English – as resistance, rebuttal, and regeneration. Decolonizing the English literary curriculum is an opportunity to reworld the sign of "English" from its historical and cultural others, where "reworlding" as "re-creating/remaking/reconstituting after centuries of de-constitution and destitution of other worlds and other lives of those who were subjected to genocide, enslavement, colonialism, imperialism, capitalism and heteropatriarchal sexism" (Ndlovu-Gatsheni).

My essay answers the call to decolonize the English literary curriculum by proposing what María Lugones has called a "new geopolitics" of the English language. In her essay, "Toward a Decolonial Feminism" (2010), Lugones wrote that the potential for decoloniality lies in a new geopolitics of "knowing and loving," calling decolonization a practice that is concerned with the politics of knowledge production and contesting the colonial world order established by European empires (756). Thinking between the colonial and neocolonial geopolitics of English cutting through my classroom in the US American South, I call attention to the embodied, multimedia, and multilingual mediations that bring something called English language and literature into the classroom. The pedagogical objective of decolonization is not simply to substitute and replace English literature with other language literatures. Instead, I understand decolonization as an active program of reading and critique – of reworlding – that traces the relations of an "English literary curriculum" with other languages and literary cultures. This program of reading implicates the reader in challenging the stable meanings of an ideological, historical, and geographical English.

To this end, I reprise the term "vernacular" which I proposed in *Vernacular English: Reading the Anglophone in Postcolonial India* (2022) to argue that the unmarked neutrality of English as a scholarly medium as well as its much remarked-upon expropriations as a global imperialist language both perpetuate the absorptive logic of English. In *Vernacular*

English, I examine the English language as part of the multilingual local
milieu of postcolonial India by turning to a transmedia archive of little-
known debates and practices that have shaped the meanings of the English
language in India – from English, Hindi, and Urdu literature to law, film,
visual art, and public protests. For instance, British colonial administration
in the eighteenth century advanced English as a translational vernacular
that could encode Indian languages. This functional administrative role of
English as a language of universal communicability takes on a new political
life as the Roman script becomes a vernacular writing system for numerous
Indian languages in digital media. At the same time, the English language
was adopted as postcolonial India's associate official language along with
Hindi. Low castes, Dalits, and tribal/Adivasi (Indigenous) groups have
routinely used the "elite" language of English – available in the Indian
Constitution – to protest the Hindu casteist Indian state. The representative power of English, its imagined and desired capacity to speak for
colonized and independent people, makes English a vernacular language
in India.

As it explores the vernacular registers of a global language, *Vernacular
English* challenges postcolonial and comparative literary studies' reliance
on the vernacular as something non-English – something common, native,
local, nondominant, and Indigenous. Vernacular is often used to refer to
a common – demotic, nonelite, nonstandard – experience of language. In
scholarship on India, vernacular is a term reserved for quotidian and local
registers of modern Indian languages, or *bhashas*. But reading across
medieval, early modern, and African American discussions of the vernacular shows that a vernacular is as much a political assertion as it is an
embattled position. Indeed, as much historically grounded scholarship
has shown, equating the vernacular with authenticity is historically
inaccurate and theoretically suspect, as it loses sight of how languages are
politically marshalled as expressions of cultural authenticity.[4] As Christina
Kullberg and David Watson write, "the vernacular is not only a language or
a thing such as an expression of the local, rather it refers to certain
potentiality of language to become something else; it is a pre-coded
language that may be politically, aesthetically, or culturally charged" (19).
Associating vernacular with only the minor misses how vernacular languages, literature, and knowledge brace religious fascism and anticaste
resistance in India.

Against the groundswell of discussions on global English, "vernacular" reframes the English language within multilingual landscapes
where it is often, in the words of Rebecca Walkowitz, "less than one

language" ("Less Than" 95). Vernacular English is a way of asking "what becomes intelligible as English and how does English become intelligible," questions that can be asked about any language. "Vernacular" surfaces a new geopolitics of English language and literature by convening literary production outside of metropolitan centers. At the same time, it also models a practice of reading that explores nontextual modes of languaging at the limits of ability, expertise, and literacy. To call English a vernacular is not to simply say that English is another Indian language or that English is suddenly not a language of power and dominance. Instead, vernacular is a way of naming the colonial and global power structures associated with English without reinscribing them each time we discuss the language.

In this pursuit of English as a vernacular, existing work by postcolonial scholars offers a starting point to think from. Postcolonial studies as a field has led the examination of the colonial foundations of English literature as a discipline (Ahmed; Bhattacharya). It has brought attention to literatures from the previously colonized parts of the world, showing that colonial Englishness is always tied with the subjectivity of the colonized (Bhabha). The comparative methods of postcolonial studies have centered translation as a critical practice and concept to examine transnational cultural flows. This scholarship offers us new perspectives – different ways of staging the colonial and capitalist encounters – on the compulsory global-ness of the English language and English literature. As Gauri Viswanathan argued in an interview with Michael Allan, "To regain the world through other imaginings that recapture texts from a point outside the institution offers a challenge to English studies that its postcolonial offshoot has considerably reinvigorated" (Allan 246).

Thus, in contrast to Lee's ambivalent conclusions about the objectives of decolonization, I find useful Debashree Mukherjee and Pavitra Sundar's special issue on decolonial feminist media studies. Mukherjee and Sundar present "decolonial" as a term to describe an active process, not the marker of a particular historical epoch that has passed but an active, evolving set of strategies. Like them, I see "the future not as an endpoint, the decolonial not as a goalpost, but rather as an ongoing struggle, a revolution that is not past or impending, failed or irretrievable, but continual" (13).

This ongoing nature of decolonization is not simply temporal or chronological. The call to decolonize is multidirectional and not just directed at the imperial center. Postcolonial scholars such as Rajeswari Sunder Rajan and Ania Loomba have shown how English literature "became the surrogate – and also the split – presence of the Englishman, or a repository of abstract and universal values freely available to the colonized as much as to the colonizer" (Rajan 12). It offered anticolonial and nationalist thinkers the epistemic grounds from which to critique the empire. As a scholar of South Asia, the imperative to decolonize English literary curriculum is meaningful both in the Anglo-American academic contexts and in India where "decoloniality" has given credence to casteist and majoritarian consolidation of what native or local culture should be. Aditya Nigam's *Decolonizing Theory: Thinking Across Traditions* argues that the idea of the nation demands a homogeneity of culture in anticolonial gestures and that the Hindu Right in India ironically relies on colonial knowledge production to claim a Brahminical Hindu past as Indigenous (Nigam). In the context of global modern and premodern histories of migration, the turn to Indigeneity can also justify a politics of exclusion.[5]

Indeed, the risks of romanticizing an unsullied precolonial past or elsewhere and the awareness of an enduring coloniality as the condition of our work make decoloniality an ongoing struggle. This is also what makes Ngũgĩ principled position unsustainable. In the context of the famous language debates between Chinua Achebe and Ngũgĩ, I often think of Ken Saro-Wiwa's essay "The Language of African Literature: A Writer's Testimony" (1992) in the special issue on the Language Question in *Research in African Literature*. Saro-Wiwa not only defended his decision to write in English, as British colonialism had rendered English education an integral experience in Nigeria; but Saro-Wiwa also framed colonialism as "not a matter only of British, French, or European dominance over Africans" but also the rule of the numerical majority over the numerical minority. "In African society, there is and has always been colonial oppression," wrote Saro-Wiwa, and he raised questions about "the implications of [Ngũgĩ's] decision for the minority ethnic groups in Kenya and for the future of Kenya as a multiethnic nation or, indeed, as a nation at all" (156).[6]

Or take the example of Thomas Babington Macaulay's "Minute on Indian Education." No story of postcolonial studies or English literary studies can begin without invoking this speech, which changed India and English education for ever. It highlights the complicity of English education with colonial expansion as well as the institutional marginalization of local linguistic and literary cultures in India in favor of English education. The Orientalist-Anglicist debates are important to teach students about the history of English education in the colonies. One way to build on the existing body of scholarship on the lasting impact of Macaulay's policies is to introduce the question of caste. For instance, the introduction of English language and literature did not simply create "a class of persons Indian in blood and colour, but English in tastes, in opinions, in morals and in intellect" (Macaulay 171). It also sharpened what Aatish Taseer has called the linguistic colorline in India. Historian Shefali Chandra's *The Sexual Life of English: Languages of Caste and Desire in India* (2012), for instance, discusses how English education presented a way of consolidating caste privilege in India even as it opened paths to mobility for those not privileged in terms of caste and gender.

It would be pedagogically productive in this context to pair Macaulay's "Minute on Indian Education" with Dalit writer Chandrabhan Prasad's short essay "The Impure Milk of Macaulay" and excerpts of Chandra's work (which includes poems of praise in English by feminist anticaste thinker Savitribai Phule). With libertarian leanings, Prasad has praised the English language for its potential to usher Dalits and other minoritized groups into circuits of global capitalism where the Brahminical dominance is contested and made irrelevant. Prasad specifically celebrates Macaulay's birthday publicly every year and has argued that Macaulay's proposal was not in itself wrong but just imperfectly executed. He draws attention to the lines after the oft-cited ones I have quoted above: "To that class we may leave it to refine the vernacular dialects of the country, to enrich those dialects with terms of science borrowed from the Western nomenclature, and to render them by degrees fit vehicles for conveying knowledge to the great mass of the population" (Macaulay 171). The problem with Macaulay's proposal, according to Prasad, was not the hierarchization and replacement of Sanskrit and Persian knowledge systems but the brahmins' abdication of their responsibilities to the castes below them.

While Prasad might be one of the most provocative and playful proponents of the English language in India – he has built a temple for the English goddess – he is far from the only one (Saxena). The English language continues to live in less identifiable ways as the Roman script for languages understood to be more "native" or as the language of choice for writers who may not have access to other linguistic and literary traditions (Misra). For instance, in his work on Santali language in *Graphic Politics in Eastern India: Script and the Quest for Autonomy* (2021), Nishaant Choksi shows that a Roman alphabet–based script devised by missionaries came to be the preferred script for Santali, an Austroasiatic language spoken in eastern India, Nepal, and Bangladesh largely by Adivasi (original inhabitants, "Indigenous") communities. A nonstandard Romanized Santali transcription, which was initially created to mediate between several other scripts of Santali, gained prominence as Santali speakers started using it in digital and online communication in the twenty-first century. Choksi calls this script a "trans-script" since the graphic choices involved in it invoke the knowledge of multiple scripts by people utilizing the script digitally and in print (62). Examples like these require that as literary critics and teachers, we keep in view what English – across modalities of sound and script – reveals and what it remakes. This objective also demands new reading practices that can take an expansive approach to reading and language.

Tracing my path toward decolonizing through the insights and work of postcolonial scholars, I find useful Mukherjee and Sundar's words that claim no newness for their pursuit of decolonial feminist approaches to media studies but see it as unfinished work that needs to be done. According to them, the challenge is to ask how to do this work – how to think decolonization – in the contemporary moment. They call for humility that traces different genealogies of their own efforts to decolonize. This means acknowledging the work of communities, practitioners, activists, and scholars before us. This collaborative and coalitional approach to literary history is necessarily comparative and interdisciplinary.

Decolonizing Language

The question of language – in all its forms – has been critical for scholars in postcolonial studies. Knowledge of "other languages" and language as such is foundational to challenge colonial projects. As Julietta Singh writes in *Unthinking Mastery* (2020), "across twentieth century anticolonial discourses, language repeatedly emerged as one of the most vital problems in the production and articulation of decolonized subjectivities" (69). But "the intellectual authority of literary and area studies, its 'credibility' and 'viability,' continuously relies on mastery as its target, as that which will produce authoritative, legitimate knowledge and in so doing resist the power of Eurocentrism" (8).

Such an approach to language, ironically, works with a monolingual model and loses sight of the diverse modes of languaging and subject formation. Today, these concerns with multilingualism and translation have come closer home as scholars reflect on the classroom space in the United States and how the global lives of languages challenge the monolingual logic of our institutions and critical methods. Yet, at the same time as language learning has become critical to thinking our classrooms and universities, the questions about *our* reading method are still less concerned with them.

Decolonizing English literary curriculum does not conclude with the curricular inclusion of languages besides English, whether in the original or in translation. Instead, we must interrogate how languages reveal and disappear a variety of linguistic experience. The corollary of the critique of the monolingual paradigm is that notions of multilingualism also rest on the countability/cohesion of languages. We cannot count without assuming languages to be discrete, and we cannot think linguistic discreteness without ascribing to some kind of monolingual logic.[7] By asking how we know what we know, we might take multilingualism as a decolonial method without counting languages and reinforcing colonial notions of language.

The vernacular lives of English language and literature outside of South Asia also emphasize the people who use the English language rather than any inherent colonial meanings. I will take just one example from Caribbean anglophone literature. Writing about the late eighteenth-century history of Creole "dialect" literature, Belinda Edmondson in *Creole Noise: Early Caribbean Dialect Literature and Performance* (2021) rejects the racialization of English as White and creole as Black as historically inaccurate. She shows the lived multiracial and transnational origins of literary dialect that counters its story as "mimicry" or merely as a political strategy. For conceptual purchase on Edmondson's arguments, I turn to perhaps the most foundational and memorable for vernacular English – Edward Kamau Braithwaite's idea of the "nation language." It frames English as a vernacular that is used by the people. The politics of English – whether the master's tools can ever destroy the master's house – depends on the people who bring the revolution. Nation language, thus, not only brings English closer to the bodies that speak and in whose name English is spoken, it also suggests that we take the different sensory experiences of Caribbean language users into account to understand its meaning. About Caribbean poetry, Braithwaite writes, "noise that it makes is part of the meaning, and if you ignore the noise (or what you would think of as noise, shall I say) then you lose part of the meaning" (17). Thus, as we read the English language in the classroom, we might also be alert to its sonic and phonic materiality.

Vernacular English – as a practice of reading in translation and transmediation – seeks to hold on to the part of the meaning that Braithwaite thought would be lost in language as written. It approaches multilingualism through relationality with other named languages and highlights different sensory engagements with language itself. In doing so, it also approaches the "bodies and experiences [that] have served as structuring absences" in our scholarly histories and attempt to remediate their absence (Mukherjee and Sundar 7).

As I have argued before, the term anglophone – with its emphasis on the heteronymic speakers (people and technologies) – can be a productive term to read the vernacular life of English. Anglophone as a term also centers practices of translation and transmediation. The argument that anglophone literature necessarily translates between different linguistic cultures also provides the opportunity to examine through what embodied and material mediations languages come into being (Walkowitz, *Born Translated*; Mufti Forget English!). Theorists and practitioners of translation in critical translation studies have thought how language becomes meaningful in relation to other languages. They have shown that translations bring languages into being, they do not just translate from one existing linguistic discourse to another. Attention to how language happens – how English become recognizable – can also center the people who make it and inflect the colonial logics of language imposition.

Literary studies have long been concerned with the liberal axiom of voice – who speaks – and have thus sought to bring new voices into the scholarly field. While this is an important step in decolonizing the English literary curriculum, it is not the only one. The next section asks the critic and teacher to situate themselves and their conceptual categories: who listens and how? Which English is legitimized as "English" and which as its "other"? How do we, as readers, make English speak on the page?

English lives contested politically and mediated across the world in South Asia (India, Sri Lanka, Bangladesh, and Pakistan), the Caribbean, Eastern Europe, and anglophone Africa. For instance, English is not only a formerly colonial language in South Asia or a language of the postcolonial state in India, Pakistan, Bangladesh, and Sri Lanka. As we saw in the brief survey above, it is also a populist language that mediates Dalit, racioethnic, and Indigenous assertion against the fascist logics of vernaculars such as Hindi, Urdu, and Sinhala. Here, English often lives outside literary works – on other media and in other languages – as "less than one language," as a sound, a sight, and materiality that inflects meanings on the page. We must make the diverse English practitioners in the Global South our interlocutors so that literatures of the anglophone world, for instance, are not just read through the language – English, theory – of the Global North.

Strategies in the Classroom

So how do we teach vernacular English in the classroom or teach in the shadow of vernacular English? This section answers the question with a multipronged approach. It makes suggestions for building a syllabus, an early classroom exercise, and a teachable literary text.

Syllabus In their essay "Twisted Tongues, Tied Hands: Translation Studies and the English Major" (2010), Emily O. Wittman and Katrina Windon model how translation history can be taught as English literary history. Translation makes visible voices and stories that disappear within a univocal and racialized understanding of what it means to be English and study English literature. Using translation as the organizing principle of literary survey courses or world literature courses can strengthen relations with other literary cultures and language departments. It can make space for the study of marginalized authors and texts and shore up affinities between the knowledge students bring from outside the classroom and the materials they encounter in it. It models a possible conceptual framework for students to situate literary fields such as early modern, American, and postcolonial studies. In doing so, translation also illuminates moments in time and space where – either by love or violence – discontinuous literary cultures become continuous.

For instance, in my world literature course, I often teach Okot p'Bitek's *Song of Lawino* to discuss how p'Bitek uses Acholi words and idiomatic expressions to construct a linguistically grounded literary world. *Song of Lawino* is modeled as an epic poem. The poem is addressed by Lawino to her clansmen and invokes an oral tradition. Lawino's husband, Ocol, has returned from England with a newfound distaste for his native customs. In each of the verse chapters of *Song of Lawino*, Lawino bitterly criticizes Ocol's now-preferred "Western" customs of food, clothing, and kinship and argues that these are not sensible ways for her to adopt within her cultural context. Given Lawino's investment in authenticity and her desire to persuade Ocol to see the wrongheadedness of his cultural mimicry, it is easy to read *Song of Lawino* as a literary text that claims authenticity for itself when, in fact, it stages the dangers of binary ethnocentric thinking in colonial and anticolonial positions.

The chapter "The Poet as 'Native Anthropologist': Ethnography and Antiethnography in Okot p'Bitek's *Songs*" in Jahan Ramazani's *The Hybrid Muse: Postcolonial Poetry in English* (2001) can be a valuable secondary resource to teach *Song of Lawino*. It brings together reviews of p'Bitek's poem to show how it was praised as a literary work that was quintessentially Ugandan. By showing p'Bitek's stylistic debts to Henry Wadsworth Longfellow's *Song of Hiawatha* and examining the relation of postcolonial studies and anthropology, Ramazani argues *Song of Lawino* reverses the ethnographic gaze often cast on postcolonial literature.

Building on Ramazani's work, I teach *Song of Lawino* with sections of Longfellow's *Song of Hiawatha* and Ojibwe poet Jane Johnston Schoolcraft's poems collected in Robert Dale Parker's *The Sounds the Stars Make Rushing through the Sky* (2008). This pairing complicates expectations of authenticity or cultural immediacy we might bring to a poem that features several Acholi "untranslatable" words and idioms. Jane Johnston Schoolcraft is perhaps the first known Native American poet. She wrote in Ojibwe and English. Her husband Henry Rowe Schoolcraft was an Indian agent who liaised between Indigenous communities and White settlers. As he collected Ojibwe stories and translated them to further his career as a writer, he erased the collaborative contribution and work of his wife, Jane. Teaching *Song of Lawino* through its longer history of literary influence and "cultural theft" (Parker 26) can help address anxieties of authenticity and create conditions for a coalitional thinking that reads Indigenous and African literature relationally.

Assignment A classroom exercise that can sharpen students' awareness of the uneven relation between language and identity is "Linguistic Autobiography." I borrowed this exercise from Pavitra Sundar to heighten students' awareness of their own linguistic and lingual experiences in a collaborative course on "accent." I have since found it useful to ask students to craft a linguistic biography at the beginning of most courses that deal specifically with language and power. The exercise also draws out for students their own latent multilingualism, which can destabilize the classroom as a monolingual space. We revisit the exercise at the end of the course to reflect on the way readings on translation and multilingualism may have transformed their own sense of themselves. Rather than further a straightforward relation between language and identity, this assignment turns attention to the students' lived experiences of language to answer the question, how do we know what we know?

> Write an essay 2–3 pages long outlining your history and relationship to language. What is the relationship between language and your identity, your personal and familial history? Your linguistic autobiography should address not only languages you've studied formally, but the accents, registers, and dialects (or varieties) that have come to mark your speech and your language

use more generally. How was language categorized for you in your growing years? What institutions have been linked to language? What people do you associate with different varieties of language that have been important in your life? Think also about how your understanding of language – your own and others' language – has shifted since arriving at [Vanderbilt]. What did you come to know about other people and their language use when you came to college?

In thinking about these questions, you may recall moments of linguistic stereotyping you've experienced or observed. Feel free to write about such moments of linguistic discrimination. But think also about moments that were (or seemed) less fraught. Think of moments when you have struggled with a language or when it came so easy you were told you have an "ear" for language. What assumptions about language (about particular languages, accents, or dialects) were embedded in those moments of learning and disciplining? How were you taught about language – how were you being taught language ideologies – even as you were learning to read, write, and speak?

Text Much has been written about the insufficiency of the frameworks of world literature and global anglophone because they eclipse other languages. I want to propose a lesser known text, *I Even Regret Night: Holi Songs of Demerara* (2019), which asks us to consider the latent multilingualism of one language in the spirit of the assignment above, the materiality of language in the spirit of Braithwaite's nation language, the question of translation as mediation, as well as the comparative grammars of caste and race that bring necessary nuance to discussions of decoloniality in the United States and the Indian subcontinent. This text could be taught in a postcolonial studies course, a world literature course, or a translation course for a presumed monolingual audience. As we teach translation, the English translation of *I Even Regret Night* challenges our relation to those translations. It complicates any expectation of an anticolonial or resistant politics from a writer of color or Bhojpuri and thwarts other marginalized languages and writers as essentialized identity positions from where to extract indigeneity.

I Even Regret Night: Holi Songs of Demerara was written by Lalbihari Shastri in the early twentieth century and published in 1916. Through it, translator Rajiv Mohabir offers us an example of recovery as well as of English as a translational vernacular. *I Even Regret Night* is the only known literary work written by an indentured laborer in the anglophone Caribbean. Sharma originally belonged to what is now the state of Bihar in India. He was bound to the Golden Fleece Plantation in British Guyana, and his poems describe his life on the island.

Originally published in the Bhojpuri dialect as a pamphlet of spiritual songs in the style of sixteenth-century devotional poetry, *I Even Regret*

Night became available in English only recently, in 2019, through the collaborative efforts of several different people, including Gaiutra Bahadur and Rajiv Mohabir. Bahadur is the author of *Coolie Woman* (2013). Her research in that book reveals that Shastri was likely an upper-caste director on the plantation in British Guyana. He wrote Hindu songs of devotion in Bhojpuri to celebrate the festival of Holi. Decades later, Mohabir, with the assistance of several different translators, translated this rare record of indentured diasporic experiences in the Indo-Caribbean. The act of translation and the constitution of the poems into a book form dramatizes a return to home promised by the unfulfilled indenture contract. English translation of Shastri's poetry is an act of historical recovery and literary discovery.

In her introduction to *I Even Regret Night*, Bahadur writes that she had really wanted to recover this "footnote" in history into English to bring it to the descendants of indenture. She understood the value of anglophone availability and wanted to render into English what she at the time thought must be a radical voice. The songs penned by Shastri were in, what Mohabir has called, a "broken" language – the Bhojpuri of the plantation, with few speakers in the world today – and had lived a flimsy textual life up until the publication. Bahadur writes poignantly about her desire for Shastri to be a politically radical figure but learns over the course of her research that he was indeed a man of conservative politics, who likely sided with the plantation owners rather than with the indentured workers on the land. Still, it is a story that gains importance as a document about identity as it is and disseminated by other Indo-Caribbean descendants.

Bahadur approached and entrusted this translational project to Rajiv Mohabir. For Mohabir, the translator, poetry and folk music are important poetic inspiration. He has written in the doubly broken language of the indentured laborers and their descendants in his other works such as *The Cowherd's Son* (2017) and also reflected beautifully on coming into language through idioms cast away by history in *Antiman* (2021). He writes:

> By reading and translating Sharma, I've learned to constantly engage with the materiality of sound as I attempt to reclaim what is lost to my generation. I have come to truly appreciate that in order to do so I must write in and out of all my languages: Guyanese Creole, English, and Bhojpuri. In Sharma's plantation Hindi, I hear echoes of my own ancestors singing for the spring of the soul, praying colors into play. (Mohabir 203)

In his "Translator's Note," Mohabir writes that his translation was itself a kind of activism and he hopes that readers will appreciate the texture of Caribbean political existence through its oral cultures:

> Given that South Asian languages rarely appear [in] the world of postcolonial Caribbean literature, it is my sincerest hope that people come to this text understanding what this tradition of oral language gives to the Caribbean landscape. Our particular mix of South Asian languages has been almost entirely extinguished by the cultural hegemony of English. (Mohabir 202)

Keeping these political resonances of different linguistic registers in play, the English translation of *I Even Regret Night* published by Kaya Press is bilingual. It places Bhojpuri and English verses *en face* and categorizes Shastri's songs into different traditions of song and poetry such as *Chautal*, *Kavitt*, *Chaupai*, and *Ulara*. Additionally, it includes Creole transliterations of the songs for contemporary users of the songbook, along with sounds of the early twentieth-century Golden Fleece through Shastri's poetry as in this song, "*Dimki dimki*/ on the damaru drum / *tananana* plays the bhrigi. / *Sararara sararara* / the bowed sarangi lilts / the solfa" (Shastri 63). This archive of sound, spirituality, image, orality, and music curated by Sharma is translated into English against English. The collection also features transliterations as Mohabir and others transform a text for music "originally intended to be worn in throats and ears, into one that belongs to an entirely different world" (Mohabir 197).[8] Different kinds of sounds ricochet across the pages of this small book and create a sonic effect quite different from Shastri's already polyvocal songs. Mohabir writes that his desire was to reproduce the materiality of sound in these poems, sounds that were lost to him as a descendant of indenture. Anglophone poetry in the works Mohabir is itself a migrant from different media forms and languages.

The translations highlight the wide and varied worlds that English lives in today and reminds us that English has always had plurilingual and polyvocal lives. From here, Mohabir's translation of *I Even Regret Night* demands a newer conceptualization of English as a language that is necessarily always in translation. Mohabir runs his fingers over the coordinates of political history to recover a personal history, conjuring the ghostly memories of ancestors passed. In this process, he also remakes and resounds the language of dominant power carving out a specifically resistant postlingual aesthetics that rises from the much-maligned racialized body that speaks English. Rebecca Walkowitz and Yasser Elhariry describe postlingual as a turn to the lingual (happening around the tongue) against the linguistic, that recognizes languages as necessarily learned and not natural. "No one is born speaking or writing a language. We all begin as language learners, and in that sense, there are no native languages. There are only foreign languages" (3).

The text is helpful to think about the oral cultures that have shaped the life of the English language. Reading the poems out loud in the classroom can recreate some of the sonic atmosphere of the anglophone. It is important to create a sense of how different languages exist together and through our breath suffuse the English language with the sounds of other languages.

Taking their English seriously and distinguishing it from hegemonic forms of language is crucial to decolonizing and not consolidating the authority of a global language. In this goal, historical scholarship and postcolonial studies are both our ally. Works such as Lalbihari Shastri's can help respond to the global hegemony of languages like English and Hindi as well as invite a critical eye on the Hindu diaspora's role in supporting Hindutva ascendancy in India. Decolonizing also means being critical about the nation as a category and a continuing commitment to antiracist and anticaste pedagogies.

Notes

1. Bhakti Shringarpure, email to the author, August 19, 2022.
2. See also Quayson.
3. This well-known history can be found in several works including Gauri Viswanathan, *Masks of Conquest* and Aamir Mufti, *Forget English!*
4. See Kullberg and Watson.
5. See for instance Parreñas.
6. "In my case, the Ogoni had never been conquered by their Igbo neighbors. But the fact of British colonialism brought both peoples together under a single administration for the first time. And when the British colonialists left, the numerically inferior Ogoni were consigned to the rule of the more numerous Igbos, who always won elections in the Region since ethnic loyalties and cultural habits were and continue to be strong throughout Nigeria. Biafra propaganda invariably claimed that the Biafrans were one. But this was a lie, hoax. I saw it as my responsibility to fight that lie" (155).
7. See also Sakai; Yildiz.
8. Mohabir, "Translator's Note," 197.

WORKS CITED

Ahmad, Siraj. *Archaeology of Babel: The Colonial Foundation of the Humanities.* Stanford, CA: Stanford University Press, 2017.

Allan, Michael. "Heterodox Philology: A Conversation." *Philological Encounters* 6.1–2 (2021): 243–64.

Ben-Yishai, Ayelet. "Through English, Densely: Partitions, Complicity, and the Anglophone Classroom." *Representations* 155 (2021): 263–64.

Bhabha, Homi. *The Location of Culture*. London: Routledge, 1994.

Bhattacharya, Baidik. "On Comparatism in the Colony: Archives, Methods, and the Project of Weltliteratur." *Critical Inquiry* 42.3 (2016): 677–711.

Braithwaite, Edward Kamau. *History of Voice: The Development of Nation Language in Anglophone Caribbean Poetry*. London: New Beacon, 1984.

Chandra, Shefali. *The Sexual Life of English: Languages of Caste and Desire in India*. Durham, NC: Duke University Press, 2012.

Choksi, Nishaant. "From Transcript to 'Trans-script': Romanized Santali Across Semiotic Media." Signs and Society 8.1 (2020): 62-92.

Choksi, Nishaant. *Graphic Politics in Eastern India: Script and the Quest for Autonomy*. London: Bloomsbury, 2021.

Desai, Gaurav. "Rethinking English Studies." In Henry Schwarz and Sangeeta Ray, eds., *A Companion to Postcolonial Studies*. Oxford: Blackwell, 2005, 523–39.

Edmondson, Belinda. *Creole Noise: Early Caribbean Dialect Literature and Performance*. Oxford: Oxford University Press, 2021.

Elhariry, Yasser and Rebecca Walkowitz. "The Postlingual Turn." *Substance* 50.1 (2021): 3–9.

Flaherty, Colleen. "Not the Queen's English Department." *Inside Higher Ed.* February 15, 2021. www.insidehighered.com/news/2021/02/15/english-departments-rethink-what-call-themselves.

Gikandi, Simon. *Maps of Englishness: Writing Identity in the Culture of Colonialism*. New York: Columbia University Press, 1997.

Kullberg, Christina and David Watson. *Vernaculars in an Age of World Literatures*. London: Bloomsbury Academic, 2022.

Kuortti, Joel. "Teaching South Asian Women's Writing in Finland." In Deepika Bahri and Filippo Menozzi, eds., *Teaching Anglophone South Asian Women Writers*. New York: Modern Language Association, 2021, 286–94.

Lee, Christopher J. "The Cruel Optimism of Decolonization." *Comparative Studies of South Asia, Africa and the Middle East* 42.2 (2022): 541–45.

Lugones, María. "Toward a Decolonial Feminism." *Hypatia* 25.4 (2010): 742–59.

Macaulay, Thomas Babington. "Minute on Indian Education." In Lynn Zastoupil and Martin Moir, eds., *The Great Indian Education Debate: Documents Relating to the Orientalist-Anglicist Controversy, 1781–1843*. London: Routledge, 1999, 161–73.

Misra, Tilottoma. "Crossing Linguistic Boundaries: Two Arunachali Writers in Search of Readers." *Economic and Political Weekly* 42.36 (2007): 3653–61.

Mohabir, Rajiv, "Translator's Note." In Lalbihari Shastri, *I Even Regret Night: Holi Songs of Demerara*. Los Angeles: Kaya Press, 2019, 190–203.

Mufti, Aamir. *Forget English! Orientalisms and World Literature*. Cambridge, MA: Harvard University Press, 2018.

Mukherjee, Debashree and Pavitra Sundar. "Editors' Introduction: Decolonial Feminisms In Medias Res." *Feminist Media Histories* 8.1 (2022): 13.

Ndlovu-Gatsheni, Sabelo J. "Beyond the Colonizer's Model of the World: Towards Reworlding from the Global South." *Third World Quarterly*, February 2, 2023. https://doi.org/10.1080/01436597.2023.2171389.

Ngũgĩ wa Thiong'o, Henry Owuor-Anyumba, and Taban Lo Liyong. "On the Abolition of the English Department (1968)." In Bill Ashcroft, Gareth Griffiths, and Helen Tiffin, eds., *The Postcolonial Studies Reader*. London: Routledge, 1995, 438–42.

Nigam, Aditya. *Decolonizing Theory: Thinking Across Traditions*. New Delhi: Bloomsbury India, 2020.

Parreñas, Juno Salazar. "From Decolonial Indigenous Knowledges to Vernacular Ideas in Southeast Asia." *History and Theory* 59.3 (2020): 413–20.

P'Bitek, Okot. *Song of Lawino and Song of Ocol* (1966). Long Grove: Waveland Press, 2013.

Prasad, Chandrabhan. "The Impure Milk of Macaulay." *Dalit Diary 1999– 2003: Reflections on Apartheid in India*. Pondicherry: Navayana Press, 2004.

Quayson, Ato. *Tragedy and Postcolonial Literature*. Cambridge: Cambridge University Press, 2021.

Rajan, Rajeswari Sunder. *The Lie of the Land: English Literary Studies in India*. Delhi: Oxford University Press, 1992.

Ramazani, Jahan. "The Poet as 'Native Anthropologist': Ethnography and Anti-ethnography in Okot p'Bitek's *Songs*." In *Hybrid Muse: Postcolonial Poetry in English*. Chicago: University of Chicago Press, 2001, 141–78.

Risam, Roopika. "Indigenizing Decolonial Media Theory: The Extractive and Redistributive Currencies of Media Activism." *Feminist Media Histories* 8.1 (2022): 134–64.

Sakai, Naoki. "How Do We Count a Language? Translation and Discontinuity." *Translation Studies* 2.1 (2009): 71–88.

Saro-Wiwa, Ken. "The Language of African Literature: A Writer's Testimony." *Research in African Literatures* 23.1 (1992): 153–57.

Saxena, Akshya. *Vernacular English: Reading the Anglophone in Postcolonial India*. Princeton, NJ: Princeton University Press, 2022.

Schoolcraft, Jane Johnston. *The Sound the Stars Make Rushing Through the Sky: The Writings of Jane Johnston Schoolcraft*, ed. Robert Dale Parker. Philadelphia: University of Pennsylvania Press, 2008.

Shastri, Lalbihari. *I Even Regret Night: Holi Songs of Demerara*. Los Angeles: Kaya Press, 2019.

Singh, Julietta. *Unthinking Mastery: Dehumanism and Decolonial Entanglements*. Durham, NC: Duke University Press, 2018.

Tuck, Eve, and K. Wayne Yang. "Decolonization Is Not a Metaphor." *Decolonization: Indigeneity, Education, and Society* 1.1 (2012): 1–40.

Viswanathan, Gauri. *Masks of Conquest: Literary Study and British Rule in India*. New York: Columbia University Press, 1989.

Walkowitz, Rebecca. *Born Translated: The Contemporary Novel in the Age of World Literature*. New York: Columbia University Press, 2015.

"Less Than One Language: Typographic Multilingualism and Post-Anglophone Fiction." *SubStance* 50.1 (2021): 95–115.

Wittman, Emily O. and Katrina Windon. "Twisted Tongues, Tied Hands: Translation Studies and the English Major." *College English* 72.5 (2010): 449–69.

Yildiz, Yasemin. *Beyond the Mother Tongue: The Postmonolingual Condition*. New York: Fordham University Press, 2012.

CHAPTER 13

Reading for Justice
On the Pleasures and Pitfalls of a Decolonizing Pedagogy

Ato Quayson

Like most people seeing the video clip of the police killing of George Floyd in May of 2020, I was viscerally shocked and inconsolable. While it is true that racial and social injustice have been commonplace throughout the entire history of the United States, the George Floyd moment seems to have intensified our consciousness of it in a way different than had been in the past.[1] In addition to this, my relatively recent arrival in the USA in 2017 meant that I was on an acute learning curve to understand such fraught race relations at very close quarters, something that my sojourns in the UK and Canada over the previous two decades had not quite prepared me for, despite the evident tensions in race relations in those countries too. The events around George Floyd's death also opened my eyes to the fact that my entire literary training, both personal and professional, had not pre-pared me for thinking about how to relate what I did as a professor of literature to what was unfolding around me in the outside world. I kept asking myself if what I did in the classroom had any bearing on the terrible conditions of racial and social injustice that were being persistently expressed around us. While I had myself grown up in a context of political turmoil in Ghana in the 1980s under the military junta of J. J. Rawlings, in which the study of literature was always done with an eye to the political turmoil of the outside world, I had never been personally disposed to connect the torn halves of my intellectual life in any coherent way. At any rate, the question of instrumentalist readings of literature had always remained anathema to me, and I insisted in my teaching and writing on first prioritizing close attention and respect for literary details within the texts themselves before any attempt was made to apply them in any way to the outside world. And it was not unusual for me to stop at the level of textual analysis itself, enacting what I thought was radical enough through different forms of close-reading inflected by Marxism, postcolonialism, or forms disruptive of what appeared to be predictable interpretations of the African postcolonial text, or indeed the canonical Western text. And the more I thought about these matters in the context of the United States, the more I felt that I needed to do a full and careful rethink of my most fundamental principles as a literary scholar and teacher. As I stated to various colleagues and friends in the months following George Floyd's killing, teaching literature anywhere in the United States is not like teaching it in Prague or Accra. If proof were needed of this truism, 2020 had amply provided it.

But then a major and recalcitrant question arises. What does it actually mean to read for justice and what might this entail? To read for justice each one of us has first to have a personal commitment to fighting against injustice. Now, depending on our particular interests, we will likely define injustice quite differently. But the point is to feel strongly that there is something not quite right with the world as it is, and to commit oneself to making it better. In other words, you cannot really read for justice if you think the world is just fine as it is. Something must bother you about the outside world to start with, and no matter how little it is, an irritating speck of sand in the eye even, you must want to do something about it. But the thing that is bothering you may be something that you see only by yourself. The important thing is that it should be bad enough to galvanize you to try and do something about it. Reading for justice will then be a constituent part of that larger set of concerns. This also means being comfortable with lifting your head out of the books you are reading and looking at the world outside with new, committed eyes.

One of the things that struck me most forcefully as Ankhi Mukherjee and I started working on the proposal for *Decolonizing the English Literary Curriculum* is how important it is to come to terms with the struggles for justice of other equity-seeking groups so that we can understand how to decolonize the literary curriculum more holistically and not just from the perspective of critical race theory or postcolonialism. As we note in the Introduction, demands for reform of the English literature curriculum are often made by equity-seeking groups seeking either the overhaul of the curriculum or its complete replacement with something that appears more equitable to such groups. The term "decolonizing" has historically specific as well as metaphorical implications. Thus, the term "equity-seeking groups" would minimally include at least the following: people of color and racial minorities, persons with disabilities, persons with nonheteronormative sexual orientations, formerly colonized people, Native peoples (pertaining specifically to Australia, Canada, and the United States), women, Jews, and Muslims, among others.

Here, I want to register a note of caution, which as you will quickly see, comes from my thoroughly engrained scholarly disposition. I do not think that reading for justice or attempting to decolonize our reading practices simply means reading for political positions inside of the literary text, whatever those political positions might be thought to be. And I do not think that reading for justice is merely reading literary content for the extent to which a particular text empowers or disempowers various communities of the dispossessed. Those are obviously important questions, but as I repeat at the start of all my African literature classes, to read Chinua Achebe's *Things Fall Apart* is not the same as reading the *New York Times*. We are obliged in reading the former to think of the ways in which Achebe mediates our access to nineteenth-century colonial relations between the Igbo of Eastern Nigeria and the colonial authorities depicted in his novel. And to do this, we are obliged to get a clear sense of what he is doing as a writer of literature primarily, and not as a journalist or indeed historian. I may have irreparably undermined my case for trying to set out some methods for reading for justice in what I have just said, but I think it is important to keep the distinctions between literature and other nonliterary writings in mind even as we intentionally try to bridge the gap between them.

Just Add Achebe (or Toni Morrison)!

In reading for justice, a preliminary distinction must be drawn between decolonizing the curriculum and decolonizing our reading of individual texts. The first is much more elusive and difficult than the other, especially as it touches on what is typically conceived of as the breadth requirements completing a degree in English literary studies. Steady criticisms of the literary curriculum from different interest groups since the late 1960s, rising in intensity in the 1980s, have led to progressive changes to the curriculum in many parts of the world, most critically in Europe and America. The changes have taken place on two fronts: first on that of adding writers to the curriculum from different cultural traditions – Achebe or Morrison or Head or Rushdie or Coetzee. But these additive changes often do not alter the way in which the literary texts themselves are taught. For while work by Shakespeare and Milton is often taught as literary texts, with all the rigorous apparatus of discursive proof that this requires, Achebe and others from the postcolonial and non-White world are merely viewed as ethnic sociologists and native informants. The problem then is not that students in most Euro-American university programs are required to study large period papers, but that when they are exposed to literatures from outside of mainstream White Euro-America, those are treated in a subliterary way, such that there is an implicit structural bias in how they are embedded into the curriculum in the first place. What is even more worrying is that in most English departments, breadth requirements are structured such that areas such as postcolonial or world literature are tagged on as electives rather than as core requirements, so that it is perfectly possible for a student to complete an entire English literature degree without having even the faintest acquaintance with anything beyond the Euro-American hegemonic White canon. And yet the corrective to this often-undisguised bias is not just to make acquaintance with writers from other traditions a core requirement of the degree, important though this is, but also to assess whether professors have made a commitment to evolving beyond their original areas of expertise to encompass and incorporate insights from other literary and cultural traditions. For most other literary specialists, there is no incentive to know anything beyond one's immediate area, the perfectly defensible position being that those things are best left to the specialists in those other areas. This, I think, is a serious mistake both in the ways in which we train our students and in our pedagogical dispositions. For the English literary curriculum ought to be thought of holistically and interconnected in all its parts, with each part able to speak to all the others. I will elaborate on some ideas for conceiving of this broader curricular purview later on in this chapter.

Context versus Contexture: Joseph Conrad's *Heart of Darkness*

As Edward Said has pointed out: "Every act of criticism is always literally tied to a set of social and historical circumstances; the problem is in specifying or characterizing the relationship, not merely in asserting that it exists" (*Reflections* 171). This applies both to the context of production, and as Michaela Bronstein adroitly argues in *Out of Context* (2018) with respect to modernist literature, in the transhistorical encounter between texts and readers across time and in different cultural contexts. This explains for example how Ngũgĩ rereads, critiques, and replicates formal and thematic details from Conrad's *Under Western Eyes* for his own *A Grain of Wheat* (see Bronstein 147–59). Achebe echoes similar principles in invoking the elemental character of the Umuofian forest at different points in *Things Fall Apart*. In various accounts of literary history, the literary text has been interpreted as a form of social chronicle, or as the expressive ensemble of a class or social fraction, and thus been made to yield direct insights into discrete sociological forms beyond the literary. As noted earlier (p. 258), this is especially true with respect to texts from the non-White Euro-American world, though not exclusively. This tendency has by no means remained uncontested, since it is also patently the case that literary form transcends its context or repeatedly refuses straightforward contextualization. This generates efforts to identify the particular syntax of such sociocultural forms, whether they are ultimately relatable to classes or other methodologically definable sociological entities. The social, on the other hand, has also been seen as produced by the referential relays within a discursive ensemble in which different fragments "speak" to each other across the interplay of knowledge, ideology, and power. This is essentially the view of Stephen Greenblatt and the New Historicists. Gallagher and Greenblatt note: "The interpreter must be able to select or to fashion, out of the confused continuum of social existence, units of social action small enough to hold within the fairly narrow boundaries of full analytical attention, and this attention must be unusually intense, nuanced and sustained" (26). The operational phrases in their formulation seem to be "confused continuum of social existence" and "units of social action." We might add the observation that every social context identified as providing the "background" to the literary representation is already processual, in motion and on the threshold of dissolving into something else. This then requires the careful bounding of the analytical field to which we give the name of context. As Valentin Daniel and Jeffrey M. Peck note in their introduction to *Culture/Contexture* (1996), from the many borrowings between literature and anthropology over the past several decades has come the realization that both disciplines are mutually alive to their extrinsic and intrinsic contextures. For them, contexture points in two directions at once: it is the historical, sociological, and political background to the text, but it is also what lies beyond the text that serves to manufacture certain modes of significance inside of it.

The difference between context and contexture is directly pertinent to a decolonialized reading of the literary curriculum. While there are many instances where this can be tried out, I shall focus here on Joseph Conrad's *Heart of Darkness*, which is a historical test case both for discussions of modernism and of postcolonialism, and also in its various afterlives in literature and in film. When I was first introduced to Conrad's novel in my undergraduate degree at university in Ghana, no mention whatsoever was made of colonialism or indeed of the real violence of the Congo Free State that had deeply informed its context. The interpretation provided us was steadfastly aimed at highlighting modernist devices. We studied *Heart of*

Darkness in a course that also included T. S. Eliot's "The Love Song of J. Alfred Prufrock," James Joyce's *Portrait of the Artist as a Young Man*, Virginia Woolf's *Mrs. Dalloway*, and F. Scott Fitzgerald's *The Great Gatsby*, and some stories from *Dubliners*, among others. Looking back now, I think the course could have been minimally augmented with the modernist poetry of Gabriel Okara and the inimitable Christopher Okigbo. Coetzee's *Waiting for the Barbarians*, Chinua Achebe's *Arrow of God*, Yvonne Vera's *Without a Name*, Bessie Head's *A Question of Power*, and Dambudzo Marechera's collection of stories in *The House of Hunger* could also have been thrown in for good measure from within the African literary tradition. But that is not what we were offered as undergraduate students of English at Legon. The focus was on modernism as a set of devices seemingly pertinent specifically to the English canon of the early twentieth century and completely separated from any other cultural context. And the course we took on African literature had all the usual suspects from that tradition but also made no reference to modernist or indeed formalist experimentation of any kind.

Rereading *Heart of Darkness* in 2020 following the killing of George Floyd and specifically in the context of an episode on the novel I prepared for Critic.Reading.Writing, the YouTube channel in which I started to explore the relationship between literature and other vectors of social life, the contexture of the novel suddenly gained extraordinary prominence as an essential part of my decolonized reading of it.[2] Conrad is famous for having depicted the Congo River and the forest around it as the sites of primal impulses and longings, thus converting them into the locations of various elusive epiphanies. And yet the problem of representation, couched by Conrad in terms of the contrast between narrative surfaces and their kernels, also allows *Heart of Darkness* to partially divest the historical Congo of the horror of its more sordid details and to render it the staging place of a different kind of crisis, namely that of representation itself.

The Congo Free State was given to Leopold II of Belgium (King of Belgium, 1865–1909) after the Berlin Conference in 1884–1885, and he run it as his personal property from 1885 to 1908. The Berlin Conference was assembled to decide on the terms of the European colonization and regulation of trade in Africa and is credited by historians to have formally started The Scramble for Africa, with the Congo as its epicenter. The Congo Free State at the time of King Leopold's ownership was a whopping 905,000 square miles in size. This is roughly the size of France, Spain, Germany, Italy, the UK, Ireland, Portugal, Belgium, The Netherlands, and Greece all put together, or Texas, California, Montana, New Mexico, Arizona, Nevada, and Colorado as a single continuous land mass.

Conrad's *Heart of Darkness* was first serialized as a three-part story in *Blackwood's Magazine* in 1899. The novella draws on material that Conrad wrote in his diary on a six-month trip to the Congo in 1890, when he worked as a ship's captain on a boat on the Congo River. His eyewitness observations of the atrocious methods of Belgian exploitation of the region and its natives were so upsetting that it led nine years later to one of the most famous representations of the violence of colonial extraction in all of world literature.

To understand how Conrad converts the scenes of near-apocalyptic devastation to those of supersubtle and elusive modernist narration, however, we must first come to grips with the real historical, geographical, and social context that informed his impressions. Here is where context gives way to contexture, that is to say, to the ways in which the historical period both provides the framing and insinuates itself in the modernist formal structure of elusiveness that Conrad used to capture his phenomenological sense (and not just the facts) of the events.

As we have noted already, the then-Congo Free State was privately owned by King Leopold II of Belgium from 1885 to 1908. King Leopold had managed to procure the Congo Free State by convincing other European states and the USA at the Berlin Conference that he was going to turn the region into a Free Trade zone and rid it of slavery, which at the time was dominated by Arab traders. What happened next was the direct opposite of what he had promised, and the region was subjected to systematic and rapacious plunder, with the most horrific violence being visited upon the people of the Congo in a bid to extract ivory, and after that rubber and other minerals, for sale on the international market. The extraction of the precious primary products was done through the granting of large concessions to various merchants and corporations that divided the country up into different fiefdoms, with the Belgians themselves forming a company with a skeletal bureaucracy that oversaw the entire region. They also set up a much-feared army.

The Congo Free State was the source of incredible wealth that serviced first the luxury tastes of Europeans and Americans through its ivory production, and then also the demands of the growing automobile industry and its dependence on rubber for tyres. As David Van Reybrouck tells us in his book *Congo: The Epic History of a People* (2014):

> In Antwerp there were warehouses packed full of tusks. In 1897, 245 metric
> tons of ivory were exported to Europe, almost half of the world's production

in that year. Antwerp outstripped Liverpool and London as the global distribution center for ivory. Pianos and organs everywhere in the West were outfitted with keys of Congolese ivory; in smoky salons the customers tapped billiard balls or arranged dominoes that were made from raw materials from its equatorial forest. The mantlepieces of middle-class homes sported statuettes made of "elfin wood" from Congo; on Sunday the people went out strolling with walking sticks and umbrellas whose handles had once been [elephant] tusks. (111)

The methods that the Belgians used in the Congo had a devastating effect on all the communities along the Congo River as well as in the hinterland. Girls as young as eleven and twelve were seized by European merchants to act as their concubines, sometimes even being incorporated into large harems for the merchants. This is the source of the image of Kurtz's "Intended" in Conrad's novella. More importantly, the extraction of ivory and rubber depended on various acts of wanton brutality upon the natives. Africans were routinely seized and held hostage until their chiefs or families delivered set cargos of ivory and rubber. If the cargo was not satisfactorily delivered, the hands of captives were chopped off as punishment. Sometimes, girls' hands were also chopped off for refusing to have sex with Belgian men, or simply as a show of unbridled lust and power. Every bullet shot by members of the *Force Publique*, the Belgian army in the Congo, had to be accounted for by bringing back either a dead body or cut-off limbs. In combination with disease epidemics and the social disruptions brought on by these violent colonial extraction atrocities, the local population was decimated, with an estimated 500,000 Congolese dying in 1901 alone.

The atrocities were finally exposed by the diplomat and Irish nationalist Roger Casement (1864–1916), who was asked by the British government in 1903 to investigate the rumors of atrocities in the Congo. He delivered the Congo Report to the British government in 1904. Casement had already been acting since 1901 as the British consul at Boma, a trade station on the Congo River. To write his Report Casement travelled for weeks interviewing people throughout the region, including overseers, mercenaries, and African workers. The revelations of the sordid reign of terror that had been unleashed on the people of the region led to an international outcry and universal condemnation of King Leopold's methods from all quarters, which in turn led to the termination of his private ownership of the Congo Free State. Leopold surrendered the region to the Belgian government in 1908, and Belgium ran the Congo until its independence in 1960. Casement and Conrad had briefly met in the Congo in 1890, and even though they were united in exposing the atrocities in the region, it is the differences in their depictions of the African natives in their two accounts that is most telling from the point of view of the question of the contexture behind the literary representation (see Armstrong xii).

To conduct his investigation, Roger Casement had by necessity spoken to many African natives. Even though he is credited with having spoken some African languages at the time, many of his interviews were conducted through translators. At various points in his report, Casement describes the demeanour and character of his African interlocutors, painting a picture of their fears, anxieties, and their humanity in the face of the Belgian-inflicted apocalypse. It is evident that in Conrad's own six-month stay in the Congo he too would have had to rely on Africans for a variety of services, including being taken care of when he was down with malarial fever and dysentery toward the end of his stay. In other words, even though unlike Casement, he did not speak any local languages, Conrad too must have communicated with African interlocutors of various social statuses through translators, thus gaining some familiarity with them over his six-month stay.[3]

And so, it is something of a surprise, as Chinua Achebe notes in his famous critical essay "An Image of Africa: Racism in Conrad's Heart of Darkness" (1977), that Conrad does not grant his African characters even a modicum of language. Achebe laments how Conrad refuses to grant speech to the Africans in his novella, simply reducing what they say to grunts, jabbering, and other strange and presumably incomprehensible nonlinguistic sounds. Conrad also refers to them as "savages" at various points in the work. When compared with the account in Casement's report, we find that not only is Achebe correct in his critique of Conrad, but that there is also an additional question that needs to be answered regarding the nature of the literary representation of colonial atrocity. Why did Conrad decide to pare down the Africans in his novella simply to elemental sounds, when he must have known full well that they not only had language, but also well-constituted forms of communication, which he most likely had himself been a beneficiary of?

However, an accusation of anti-Black racism on the part of the writer on its own does not quite reach the heart of the matter, for Conrad also produces an excoriating representation of the Belgians in the Congo, whom he ironically calls "pilgrims" throughout the novella. One way to address the troubling question of Conrad's obvious racism is to look at the ways in which *Heart of Darkness* harnesses the problematic question of literary representation to those of allegory rather than of realism. In this regard, we must recognize that the Africans in the novella are assimilated into the register of inscrutability encapsulated in the vital yet elusive backdrop of the Congo River and its forest themselves. The effect of this assimilation of the African human characters into the geographical landscape is to render both landscape and characters as equally incommensurable as representational objects. Collectively, they all thus offer an ever-elusive and recalcitrant problem for modernist literary representation, a problem, as Brian McHale notes in *Postmodernist Fiction* with respect to modernism in general, of the dominance of epistemological doubt in modernist representation (see McHale 3–21) . Conrad couches the problem of representation partly in the perceived contradictions between kernel and surface, between manifest and latent dream content, and between narrated form and described events. But for Conrad, as we shall see in a moment, the form or reality precedes the literary content, that is to say, it is the very structure of the real world that generates the dreamlike and elusive content that retains the content's persistent representational difficulty, thus making the two ultimately inseparable as two categories of representation. At one point in his storytelling, Marlow exclaims in exasperation to his listeners on the *Nellie* the difficulty he faces in conveying the dream-like sensation of what he has been describing to them:

> I became in an instant as much of a pretense as the rest of the bewitched pilgrims. This simply because I had a notion it somehow would be of help to that Kurtz whom at the time I did not see – you understand. He was just a word for me. I did not see the man in the name any more than you do. Do you see him? Do you see the story? Do you see anything? It seems to me I am trying to tell you a dream – making a vain attempt, because no relation of a dream can convey the dream-sensation, that commingling of absurdity, surprise, and bewilderment in a tremor of struggling revolt, that notion of being captured by the incredible which is of the very essence of dreams. . . . No, it is impossible; it is impossible to convey the life-sensation of any given epoch of one's existence. It is impossible. We live, as we dream – alone. (27)

Marlow is here making broad generalizations about the difference between dream fabric and dream sensations or between manifest and latent dream content, if we follow a Freudian analogy from *The Interpretation of Dreams* (1899). But the generalization needs to be questioned, because not all dreams we have are necessarily elusive in the way Conrad or indeed Freud describes them. There are many simple dreams we have for which the content and the sensation completely coincide and are easy to convey to a listener. Dreams of the satisfaction of primary bodily functions, for example, may sometimes appear garbled and confusing, but at other times appear exactly as what they point to, namely, as the satisfaction of the urge to eat, or pee, or have sex, or otherwise relieve oneself of some pressing physical need. What Marlow seems to be doing in the novella is actually transferring the sense of unreality about his experiences in the Congo, which he has already been struggling to describe to his listeners, into the description of elusive dreamscapes in general.[4] In other words, it is his experiences along the Congo River that create the sensation of elusiveness, for which he then casts about to find a narrative form and a descriptive metaphor. Thus, when he says it is like the difference between the dream and the dream sensation, he is really saying that the experience of the Congo explains the character of what he takes to be the dreamscape, rather than the other way round. Not only has the form of his experiences in the Congo preceded the analogy with the dreamscape, but it has also prefigured the elusive texture of the narrative of the novel itself. Marlow has created an affective leakage between experience and dreamscape in which it is experience that defines dreamscape but for which dreamscape stands as a metaphorical or indeed allegorical exemplar. This is what I mean by the form preceding the content of narration in the novella at all levels, even, as we see here, at the level of analogy. First, the elusive experiences in the Congo elicit a particular form of narration that has specific structural features, such as the novella's adjectival insistence first noted by F. R. Leavis (177–80), the reduction of majority of the characters to fleeting walk-on roles or locations in tableaux-like settings and without the attribution of names, and the description of landscape and background as always somehow containing something brooding and filled with indescribable sounds as if to overwhelm all the senses completely. We may argue that Conrad uses the metaphor of dreamscape to explain the experiences in the Congo that have always remained incommensurable to him. But because the experiences are so elusive and impossible to pin down, they distort what might be understood as the dreamscape and forces a generalization of the elusiveness of all dreams rather than of some dreams, and thus of the difficulty of conveying dream sensation as a general rule. We might say, then, that for Marlow and for Conrad beyond him, the form of experience in the Congo distorts the idea of dreamscape and makes the dreamscape into its own image. Thus, to understand the dreamscape in *Heart of Darkness* you must first explore the contexture of life in the Congo itself and not vice versa.

As we have already noted, what Conrad does in representing the African characters is to assimilate them to the depiction of the Congo River and its forest and to render all of them as somehow the source of primal realities that defy representation as such. They are taken to arouse the most subliminal cognitions of both infinite resemblances and infinite possibilities in the European mind, as if, in the face of such realities, anything can literally happen, including the recreation of the world and of all human relationships within it. This is what Marlow tells us about the journey up Congo on a steamer:

> Going up that river was like travelling back to the earliest beginnings of the world, when vegetation rioted on the earth and the big trees were kings. An empty stream, a great silence, an impenetrable forest. The air was warm, thick, heavy, sluggish. There was no joy in the brilliance of sunshine. The long stretches of the waterway ran on, deserted, into the gloom of over-shadowed distances. On silvery sandbanks hippos and alligators sunned themselves side by side. The broadening waters flowed through a mob of wooded islands; you lost your way on that river as you would in a desert, and butted all day long against shoals, trying to find the channel, till you thought yourself bewitched and cut off forever from everything you had known once – somewhere – far away in another existence perhaps. There were moments when one's past came back to one, as it will sometimes when you have not a moment to spare to yourself; but it came in the shape of an unrestful and noisy dream, remembered with wonder amongst the over-whelming realities of this strange world of plants, and water, and silence.

In literature, epiphanies often involve an intensification of the perspectival sensorium, that is to say, a heightening of all the senses of smell, touch, sight, color, sensation, and other aspects of feeling and perception. But along with these, epiphanies also sometimes involve the intensification of the sense of time, as though time reveals a primary eternal dimension that either obliterates immediate sense perception or ties it to something much larger than the moment of perception itself. This is what we see in this passage of Marlow going up the Congo River. Going back to the beginnings of the world implies not just the beginning of things, but that anything at all is possible. The thing to note, however, is that Marlow seems to be the only one to experience these sensations of epiphany on the Congo River. The other White pilgrims, being completely devoted to extracting ivory and thus making money, do not seem to experience the same perspectival intensifications. This also assigns to Marlow the contradictory location of an inside/outsider, as though he is both part of what he is observing and experiencing and yet somehow also separate from it, as if looking from some transcendental place beyond it.

In putting matters in this way, Conrad was breaking ranks fundamentally with the ways in which the world outside of Europe had been represented in the highly popular masculine adventure narratives of the eighteenth and nineteenth centuries. Starting with Daniel Defoe's

Robinson Crusoe (1719), R. L. Stevenson's *Treasure Island* (1883), and H. Rider Haggard's *King Solomon's Mines* (1885), as well as Rudyard Kipling's *Kim* (1901) and the novellas of A. G. Henty, among various others, young European boys and men were depicted in different parts of the Empire doing all manner of things, including conquering the natives and attempting to reveal the ways of God to them. Many of these novels were blockbusters when they were first published, with some running into several editions and selling 100,000 copies each. They were frequently given as presents to young boys. And at the same time, respected scholars such as the priest, historian, and social reformer Charles Kingsley at Cambridge and the famous art critic John Ruskin at Oxford delivered inaugural lectures in 1860 and 1870 respectively in which they extolled the virtues of young British men going out into the Empire to prove themselves. As Miranda Carter puts it in an article in *The Guardian*, these novels provided:

> a vast, exotic, canvas, far from increasingly safe and conventional Britain, on which to recast old familiar plots: quests, struggles with evil, tests of strength, [and] exciting encounters with the unfamiliar. Their protagonists were tested and came through. An energetic plot was vital – it is no accident that many of the most famous have spawned multiple film versions.

The question of the justification for why they would go to such places when they had not been invited was never raised in these masculine adventure narratives at all, for the White men (and these were typically men) asserted an inalienable right to be wherever they happened to be without needing to explain themselves to anyone, including the natives whose wealth they were happy to plunder. Conrad's *Heart of Darkness* was the first literary work to raise serious doubts about the White man's place in different parts of the New World and to seriously interrogate the relationship between the civilizing mission and the quest for profit. In his novella, self-assurance is replaced with doubt, and the justness of the European as an actor in other parts of the world is turned to a question of deep existential anguish. But Conrad did this by also linking the entire question of the White man's place in the Empire to that of literary representation, thus delivering insights that have continued to exercise generations of readers interested in colonialism and its aftermath. And it is by understanding the complex nature of the contexture in which it was set, and the ways in which this contexture puts pressure on the literary-aesthetic choices of the writer, that we are able to stop reading *Heart of Darkness* as simply a classic of modernist narration somehow insulated from the effects of the context it was trying to depict.[5] And the method relayed here can be extended to other kinds of texts that represent both violent encounters between races, or simply the privileging of one subject position over another.

If I have so far read *Heart of Darkness* in relation to a contexture that helps to explain the novels literary devices, I will now turn to a different kind of decolonized reading that also invokes context but this time sees in it important intersectional dimensions deriving from the sometimes-implicit discursive positions of equity-seeking groups that can be discerned in a literary text even in their absence.

Intersectionality: The Irruption of Blackness in Fitzgerald's *The Great Gatsby*

The term intersectionality was first introduced into academic discourse by Kimberlé Crenshaw from the perspective of legal studies to point out the multiple ways in which women of color are oppressed from different directions in terms of their race and class status, as well as their gender. For Crenshaw, intersectionality is a mode of critique as well as a practice, thus the starting point of critique is to grasp the simultaneity and conjunctural processes of oppression, and, even more importantly, to attempt to devise a collective means for ending that oppression. In terms of praxis and not simply critique the Combahee River Collective, the radical group of Black feminist lesbians in Boston who started working in the 1970s, may be considered to have modeled its main terms. They perceived themselves as dedicated to "struggling against racial, sexual, heterosexual, and class oppression, and see as our particular task the development of integrated analysis and practice based upon the fact that the major systems are interlocking" (9). In both Crenshaw and the Combahee River Collective usages, intersectionality is considered to be only the starting point of a longer process of linking perception to modes of action. It is in this spirit that I deploy the term here.

Despite Baz Luhrmann's best efforts at introducing Black figures in peripheral roles in his movie of *The Great Gatsby* (2013), readers of Fitzgerald's novel itself will know that, in spite of its being set in New York's Jazz Age, we see only one reference to Black characters. This is as Tom drives with Gatsby's car into New York from West Egg: "As we crossed Blackwell's Island a limousine passed us, driven by a white chauffeur, in which sat three modish negroes, two bucks and a girl. I laughed aloud as the yolks of their eyeballs rolled toward us in haughty rivalry" (69).

This single mention, as we can see, is met with a form of derisive or nervous laughter from Nick (but what is so funny about these modish Black folk, one might ask?). The absence of Blacks is most telling in the rumbunctious party scenes at Gatsby's mansion, to which we are told "People were not invited – they went there" (41). The list of names of partygoers that Nick gives us has no hint of any Black people among them:

> From East Egg, then, came the Chester Beckers and the Leeches, and a man named Bunsen, whom I knew at Yale, and Doctor Webster Civet, who was drowned last summer up in Maine. And the Hornbeams and the Willie Voltaires, and a whole clan named Blackbuck, who always gathered in a corner and flipped up their noses like goats at whosoever came near. And the Ismays and the Chrysties (or rather Hubert Auerbach and Mr. Chrystie's wife), and Edgar Beaver, whose hair, they say, turned cotton-white one winter afternoon for no good reason at all. (48)

While some might argue that you cannot necessarily tell simply from a name the race of its bearer, the point is that as a general rule in writings by White writers if a person is not specifically marked for race it can safely be assumed that they are White. And at no point does Nick in any of the descriptions he gives of the many people he meets both at the parties and in different settings (at the impromptu get-together at Myrtle's apartment; with Meyer Wolfsheim at the social club in New York City) give the faintest indication that any of them is Black. Nor do Tom, Daisy, and Jordan indicate at any point that in either their present lives in East Egg or earlier when they were in Chicago that they consorted with any but White folk.

And so, it comes as something of a surprise (a big one) when in the revelation scene at the Plaza Hotel, Tom goes as far as calling Gatsby the n-word, not directly, but by heavy imputation. To understand how this happens we must first reconstruct the scene and the conversation the main characters have there. This will be done in broad strokes, but the scene is worth attending to slowly. Tom, Daisy, Jordan, and Nick rent themselves a large suite on an upstairs floor of the Plaza Hotel on a sudden whim because of the oppressive summer temperature and the fact that they all experience a lot of awkwardness when Nick brings Gatsby to visit Tom and Daisy at their home for the first time. Directly below their hotel suite is a wedding ceremony and, as the scene unfolds, there wafts to them from time-to-time strains of Mendelssohn's Wedding March as well as sounds of other music and dancing from the celebrants. The spatial arrangement of the scene is significant, because it suggests a contrast between the revelations of marital infidelity that we are soon going to be privy to and the inception of a pristine marital relationship marked by marriage vows and the witnessing of others. It is not entirely accidental that at some point during the scene Tom, Daisy, and Jordan refer back to events when Tom and Daisy got married some five years earlier. They mention someone fainting, the strange case of a chap called Biloxi who made boxes, and Asa Bird. By this, the three friends invoke a social circle from their shared past of which Gatsby is not a part. This insulation of a social fraction is then scaled up and given a hard-edged racial (and not just social) articulation by Tom, shortly after it becomes unambiguously clear to him that Gatsby was having an affair with Daisy. After the unexpected disclosure that Gatsby did indeed go to Oxford, only not as a regular student but for three months as a veteran from the army, Tom is red-faced and clearly seriously upset. His wife tells him to "Please have a little self-control." To which he blurts out angrily:

> "Self-control!" repeated Tom incredulously. "I suppose the latest thing is to sit back and let Mr. Nobody from Nowhere make love to your wife. Well, if that's the idea you can count me out . . . Nowadays people begin by sneering at family life and family institutions, and next they'll throw everything overboard and have intermarriage between black and white." Flushed with his impassioned gibberish, he saw himself standing alone on the last barrier of civilization.

As though to underline the utter ridiculousness of what Tom has just said, Jordan murmurs plaintively: "We're all white here" (130).

The scene and Tom's outburst is nothing short of extraordinary because he has, even if not in so many words, practically called Gatsby the n-word. But why? When Nick first goes to visit Tom and Daisy early in the novel, Tom is extolling the virtues of *The Rise of the Colored Empires*, a book by one Goddard. The actual book that Fitzgerald is referring to here is the eugenicist Lothrop Stoddard's *The Rising Tide of Color* published in 1920, the subtitle of which was "The Threat Against White World-Supremacy." But Tom's mention of Goddard rather than Stoddard as author of the book also helps to invoke the eugenicist Herbert Goddard's *Human Efficiency and Levels of Human Intelligence*, also published in 1920, as another part of his mental makeup on the question of race relations. Both these texts predate *The Great Gatsby* by five years and so were part of the discursive backdrop to the novel. But if his outburst places Gatsby firmly amidst the colored threats to White supremacy, it is not simply because Tom has just had confirmation that Gatsby has been sleeping with his wife, or indeed that he is a crook who has even had something to do with fixing the World Series of 1919, but for another reason altogether, for understanding which we have to turn to the social context of bootlegging during the period of Prohibition. For among other unsavory things, Gatsby and Meyer Wolfsheim, whom we have met earlier in the novel, have made much of their money from bootlegging alcohol. Prohibition, which ran roughly from 1920 to 1933, coincided first with the nativist and anti-immigrant movement in the United States, and then with the Christian temperance movement, which was itself driven by strong anti-immigrant sentiment. This is partly because much of the illegal sale and distribution of alcohol in the period was done by newly arrived immigrants from Europe, specifically Poles, Italians, and Jews. What is more striking with specific reference to Gatsby, however, is that the period from the mid-nineteenth century also saw the ultimately unsuccessful attempt of Jews to settle as farmers on the East Coast and the Midwest. As Michael Pekarofski (2012) persuasively argues, Gatsby's fragmentary description of his background before his fateful meeting with Mr. Dan Cody, the owner of the yacht on which the seventeen-year-old James Gatz was to undergo his metamorphosis into Jay Gatsby, provides strong hints that his parents were unsuccessful Jewish farmers who had settled in the Midwest. The young James Gatz had been born in rural North Dakota and had himself worked along the shores of Lake Superior as a clam-digger and salmon-fisher before his encounter with Cody. That he is likely Jewish is entirely plausible from his deep association with Meyer Wolfsheim and his "gang." The central point to be noted here, however, is that when Tom Buchanan accuses him of being representative of the darker races that threaten to overrun the White race, he is seeing him as a prime example of a Jewish gambler, bootlegger, and all-round crook. In other words, the comment is both racist and anti-Semitic at one and the same time. But to get to its inherent anti-Semitism you must first interrogate its blatant racism. The question of why Tom practically calls Gatsby the n-word is the starting point for grasping how race is a placeholder for an intersectional form of otherness in the novel, in this case both Black and Jewish, both of which are only latent and not manifest in the narrative. An intersectional reading, in which we bring to bear on our interpretation as many interests and perspectives from different equity-seeking groups can also deliver a form of reading for justice, effectively decolonizing our interpretation by forcing us to complicate any simple monological reading of who or what group is the subject of microaggression or indeed oppression.

"Shall I Compare Thee to a Summer's Day": Pedagogy and the Politics of Comparison

One of the key problems with the English literary curriculum in most departments is the way in which the compulsory period papers do not necessarily speak to one another, and much less to the elective components of the curriculum. Some might say that this is because of the steady retreat from the large survey courses that start from Beowulf to say Sandra Cisneros or Nnedi Okorafor. I must admit to a slight sense of regret for the passing of the era of the Great Tradition of English literary studies. Harold Bloom's ambitious yet ultimately flawed *The Western Canon* (1994) when it first came out was no help in this respect, because it was mainly composed of piecemeal attention to various texts that he considered of canonical status, but with no real attempt at reading them contrapuntally, to invoke Edward Said's highly productive term for comparative reading that he exemplified to great effect in *Culture and Imperialism*. But both conceptual and methodological problems must be confronted in trying to establish a Great Books literary survey that is both inclusive and treats each text with equal critical attention. How is this to be achieved? I think there are two ways of doing this, the first is via what I describe elsewhere as interleafing, and the second is by following a particular cluster of questions that are incrementally taken up in each installment of the literary survey from beginning to end.

As I note with respect to the principle of interleafing in the final chapter of *Tragedy and Postcolonial Literature* (2021):

> The idea of an interleafed reading is best understood in terms of how we read well-known canonical texts from any tradition. Each well-known text you encounter is always read as if for the second time, even if it is your very first time of encountering the text in question. Or your second, or your third, or your fourth reading. Interleafing also means that to take any literary text seriously you have to read it with the subliminal or explicit knowledge of all the various ways in which it is impinged upon by other texts and may in its turn impinge upon others. This should be the preliminary starting point, even if you have no idea how these interrelations might be established. In other words, every text is to be read as a portal to other things of literary value and not simply to confirm already-established cultural experiences and dispositions. In this type of reading, attitude is incipient action, that is to say, to read as if what you are reading is part of a larger set of cross-cultural illuminations is to be open to finding out more about how such cross-cultural illuminations take place. (302)

Thus, an interleafed reading by definition takes seriously everything that has been read before or alongside the text being read. It is this that allows us to read Okonkwo's decision to walk off and commit suicide at the end of Achebe's *Things Fall Apart* as a gesture similar to Oedipus' act in taking out his eyes in Sophocles' *Oedipus Rex*. They are both acts of defiance against the inscrutability of what they consider their destinies. They are acts that humanize them and that assert a form of agency despite the their clear futility.[6] Or that the description that Gatsby gives Nick Carraway of the first time he kisses Daisy in *The Great Gatsby* is evocative of a form of epiphanic elementalism that puts it in the same frame of the perceived transcendence of time that we just saw in *Heart of Darkness* but that we also see more than once in Tayeb Saleh's *Season of Migration to the North*, and in Samuel Beckett's *Murphy*, among various others.

Which brings us to the second proposition for establishing transhistorical comparative frames for our teaching that help to elevate individual texts from their simple fixity within their respective periods. It seems to me worthwhile to think always in our teaching of clusters of ideas, concepts, and themes that might help to animate texts comparatively. The key question of course is whether the transhistorical is another name for thematized course offerings. The rationale behind many period courses, such as the Oxford Final Honour School 1760–1830 paper, is that students need to learn a wide range of literary forms, from polemics to novels to Romantic poetry, and not just the salvageable bits, of this period. What I am suggesting here is that the idea of "coverage" be thought of more creatively, and even while introducing students to a wide range of forms, it might still be possible to model the diversity of forms within the framework of transhistorical comparison.[7]

I have already mentioned two of them above, but it is entirely possible to find others that are both capacious and generative. Take for example the concept of doubt. How do we adopt doubt as a concept to animate different texts, genres, and features of the literary curriculum? While we can start from as far back as the Greeks, Shakespeare's *Hamlet* is a good place to begin for those without much patience or expertise with the *longue durée* of English literary history. And yet even in Shakespeare, Hamlet is not the only one subject to doubt: we have the examples of *Antony and Cleopatra, Richard II, King Lear,* and *Macbeth* to draw on. Each of these would deliver a different configuration of the problem of doubt. Once the terms of doubt are established, there are any number of texts that can be considered pertinent to the general question, including sacred texts such as the Bible, the Quran, the poetry of the Sufi mystics, and on to Virginia

Woolf, William Faulkner, Jorge Luis Borges, Toni Morrison, Tsitsi Dangaremgba, Wole Soyinka, J. M. Coetzee, and many others that readily spring to mind. Or, to take another broad and productive example, suffering. Where do we not see suffering in English literature, and why is it that we are not able to compare representations of suffering in different literary and cultural traditions? But what I am saying here has implications not just for the design of large survey courses, but also for the internal orchestration of echoes and resonances within individual courses. While it should be impossible to teach a survey course on the history of poetry at an American university without paying serious attention to the Harlem Renaissance or Native American poetry (amazingly, this has been known to happen!), it should also be impossible to teach any course without getting your students to realize explicit and implicit connections to the rest of the broad literary tradition. And thus, in my own classes on African literature, I resolutely refute any imputation, real or imagined, that my students are being inducted into a cultural enclave, namely, that this is a course strictly on African literature and nothing else. Rather, my students are required to attend systematically to all manner of other texts in the broader literary tradition. The point for me is to get my students to see the entailments of African literature in the rest of their literary training. This is also important for decolonizing the curriculum.

It is also important to acknowledge the essential difference between what I have described here so far as decolonizing the curriculum, and how Walter Mignolo and Catherine Walsh interpret the concept of the deco-lonial more specifically.[8] For Mignolo, the decolonial requires the complete jettisoning of Western models of thought and their replacement with Indigenous modes from Latin America, Africa, and India, among others. The problem with this idea for the English literary curriculum is that writers practice a form of interleafing in the way that I described it a moment ago, so that it would be practically impossible to completely parenthesize, say, Sophocles from our reading of Achebe (or vice versa), or Virginia Woolf and William Faulkner from our interpretations of Toni Morrison's novel. In the second instance, this is simply because we cannot discount the fact that Morrison wrote her MA thesis on the earlier writers. By the same token, it would be irresponsible to refer the meanings of Achebe and Morrison's writings exclusively to the Euro-American tradition without paying attention to the Igbo and African American traditions that inescapably infuse their works. The point, *contra* Mignolo, is to read contrapuntally or dialectically, paying as much attention to what originality these and other postcolonial or minority writers bring to bear on their work from their own traditions, but not discounting the inspiration that they also draw from the Euro-American one that is a central part of their education and literary aesthetics.

Conclusion: Articulating Principles

1. A preliminary approach to reading for justice is to focus on the manner of the text's representation of historical events, what I refer to as its contexture. Here, while we may be treading on slippery ground, what we are interested in are the representational choices that are made because of the background, the ways in which historical context might be seen as impinging determinedly upon the text. Another dimension to doing this is to see all historical (and cultural) details as thresholds rather than particularities, and thus as the means by which the relevant text deploys such details as fulcrums connecting other dimensions of the text. The manner in which we are able to do this would lend complexity to what might risk becoming the mere attempt at synchronizing literature with historical events, or as reading literature as the simple and unmediated mimesis of historical reality.

2. The second vector of reading for justice is in the broad shape of a holistic understanding of the curriculum and its constituent parts as in dialogue with one another. As I hope to have shown, reading for justice and indeed decolonizing the curriculum requires a broad grasp of all the literary curriculum simultaneously and as a matter of principle, even if it is manifest as individual instantiations in the first instance. The student, and indeed their instructors, must see the entire curriculum as interconnected and not just a collection of disparate parts. This may require a radical change in the way we undertake training in the profession, because the enclave mentality enjoined by strict specialisms actually undermines the prospect of decolonizing.

3. Related to the previous point, one of the important critical procedures in reading for justice is that to do it properly requires forms of intersectionality, and of reading from the perspectives of different equity-seeking groups simultaneously. Some of such intersectional readings have already been adroitly done by feminist, postcolonial, and critical race scholars. Two great recent examples of such intersectional reading are to be found in Ian Smith's *Black Shakespeare: Reading and Misreading Race* (2022), and in Geraldine Heng's *The Invention of Race in the European Middle Ages* (2018).

Neither of these is likely to escape controversy in their respective fields, but the point is that the intersectional readings that they deploy require us to see things from multiple equity-seeking perspectives at once. In the case of Smith's book, it is that of critical race theory and Shakespeare, while Heng's gives us situated intersectional readings of race, gender, and the vagaries of anti-Semitism in the period in question all at the same time.

Ultimately, however, we must convey to our students in the classroom the absolute passion of what we do, for it is the passion that may ignite their interest in encountering and reencountering the texts that we introduce them to, and, hopefully, to an understanding that literature is also a tool for dismantling befuddled forms of thinking. But first, you have to read it properly.

Notes

1. On my attempt to interpret the George Floyd incident in light of the principle of tragedy and *musuo*, the Akan concept of taboo, see Quayson, "On Postcolonial Suffering."
2. See Ato Quayson, "Joseph Conrad's *Heart of Darkness*: Representing Colonial Atrocity," https://youtu.be/qgYZEZvtQls.
3. On Casement's Congo Report, see the 5th Norton Critical Edition of Joseph Conrad's *Heart of Darkness*, ed. Paul B. Armstrong (Conrad 138–54).
4. What I am trying to describe here resonates somewhat with Ian Watt's concept of delayed decoding, except that in his case, the concept is explored with respect to *Lord Jim* and not *Heart of Darkness* and applies to the delay between a character's sensory impressions and what they understand as happening to them. My interest here is in how Conrad himself transfers what are the over-whelming sensory impressions he experienced in the Congo into the domain of his literary representation in *Heart of Darkness*. For his account, see Watt 269–85.
5. For different interpretations of *Heart of Darkness* that also insist on not reading it simply as a modernist classic separate from its postcolonial implications and to which my own reading is particularly indebted, see Said, "Two Visions" and Parry, *Conrad and Imperialism*, among various others. Achebe's essay on the racism in the novel that I have already cited is also critical to reading the novel.
6. This point is well articulated by Peter Szondi with respect to Schelling's views on the tragic. See his An Essay on the Tragic 7–10.
7. I want to thank Ankhi *Mukherjee* for this brief description of a period paper from Oxford English, which coincides with the way that period papers are structured in other universities I have worked at including Cambridge, Toronto, NYU, and Stanford.
8. For Walter Mignolo and Catherine E. Walsh's powerfully articulated position, see *On Decoloniality: Concepts, Analytics, Praxis*. See also Boaventura De Sousa Santos, *The End of the Cognitive Empire*.

WORKS CITED

Achebe, Chinua. "An Image of Africa: Racism in Conrad's *Heart of Darkness*." *The Massachusetts Review* 18 (1977): 782–94.

Armstrong, Paul B., "Introduction." In Joseph Conrad, *Heart of Darkness*, ed. Paul B. Armstrong. New York: Norton, 2017, ix–xxi.

Bloom, Harold. *The Western Canon: The Books and the School of Ages*. New York: Riverhead Books,1994.

Bronstein, Michaela. *Out of Context: The Uses of Modernist Fiction*. Oxford: Oxford University Press, 2018.

Carter, Miranda. "British Readers and Writers Need to Embrace Their Colonial Past." *The Guardian*, January 23, 2014. www.theguardian.com/books/2014/jan/23/british-readers-writers-embrace-colonial-past.

"Combahee River Collective Statement: Black Feminist Organizing in the Seventies and Eighties." Freedom Series #1. Kitchen Table: Women of Color Press, 1986.

Conrad, Joseph. *Heart of Darkness*, ed. Paul B. Armstrong. New York: Norton, 2017.

Crenshaw, Kimberlé. "Intersectionality, Identity Politics, and Violence Against Women of Color." *Stanford Law Review* 43.6 (1991): 1241–99.

Daniel, Valentin and Jeffrey M. Peck, eds. *Context/Contexture: Explorations in Anthropology and Literary Studies*. Berkeley: University of California Press,1996.

De Sousa Santos, Boaventura. *The End of the Cognitive Empire: The Coming of Age of Epistemologies of the South*. Durham, NC: Duke University Press,2018.

Fitzgerald, F. Scott. *The Great Gatsby*, ed. James L. W. West III. New York: Scribner, 2018.

Freud, Sigmund. *The Interpretation of Dreams*. Leipzig: Franz Deuticke, 1899.

Goddard, Henry Herbert. *Human Efficiency and Levels of Intelligence*. Ann Arbor: University of Michigan Library, 1920.

Greenblatt, Stephen and Catherine Gallagher. *Practicing New Historicism*. Chicago: Chicago University Press, 2000.

Heng, Geraldine. *The Invention of Race in the European Middle Ages*. Cambridge: Cambridge University Press, 2018.

Leavis, F. R. *The Great Tradition: George Eliot, Henry James, Joseph Conrad*. New York: George W. Stewart, 1948.

McHale, Brian. *Postmodernist Fiction*. London: Routledge, 1987.

Mignolo, Walter and Catherine E. Walsh. *On Decoloniality: Concepts, Analytics, Praxis*. Durham, NC: Duke University Press, 2018.

Parry, Benita. *Conrad and Imperialism: Ideological Boundaries and Visionary Frontiers*. London: Salem House Publishers, 1984.

Pekarofski, Michael. "The Passing of J. Gatsby: Class and Anti-Semitism in Fitzgerald's 1920s America." *The F. Scott Fitzgerald Review* 10 (2012): 52–72.

Quayson, Ato. "On Postcolonial Suffering: George Floyd and the Scene of Contamination," Introduction to special issue on postcolonial suffering, *The Cambridge Journal of Postcolonial Literary Inquiry* 8.2 (2021): 121–227.

Tragedy and Postcolonial Literature. Cambridge: Cambridge University Press, 2021.

Said, Edward. "Two Visions in Heart of Darkness." In *Culture and Imperialism*. New York: Alfred Knopf, 1993, 19–30

Reflections on Exile and Other Essays. Cambridge, MA: Harvard University Press, 2000.

Smith, Ian. *Black Shakespeare: Reading and Misreading Race*. Cambridge: Cambridge University Press, 2022.

Stoddard, Lothrop. *The Rising Tide of Color against White Supremacy*. New York: Charles Scribners and Sons,1920.

Szondi, Peter. *An Essay on the Tragic*. Stanford, CA: Stanford University Press, 2002.

Van Reybrouck, David. *Congo: The Epic History of a People*. Translated by Sam Garrett. New York: HarperCollins, 2014.

Watt, Ian. *Conrad in the Nineteenth Century*. Berkeley: University of California Press, 1979.

PART III

Interdisciplinarity and Literary Studies

CHAPTER 14

Literature, Human Rights Law, and the Return of Decolonization

Joseph R. Slaughter

Ousmane Sembène's 1974 film *Xala* opens with a tight focus on a beating drum amid an ecstatic celebration. The scene shifts between a jubilant crowd outside the *Chambre de Commerce* in Dakar and the postcolonial power drama taking place inside, as a voice-over, speaking in formal French tones reminiscent of Senegalese president Léopold Sédar Senghor, delivers a rousing declaration of independence: "Mr. Minister, Deputies, and honorable colleagues. Never before has an African occupied the presidency of our chamber. . . . We must take control of our industry, our commerce, our culture" (my translation). Seven men in chic West African dress enter the Chamber to confront three White French adminis-trators; they seize two alabaster busts of Marianne, placing them on the steps outside the building and then expel the Frenchmen, as the voiceover resumes: "Our march is irreversible. . . . We are businessmen. We must take control of all directorships, including the banks. . . . This is the culmination of our struggle for *true* independence." On the Chamber steps, the Senegalese men raise their arms in victory as the colonial administrators depart; drums beat; dancers whirl; decolonization is done!

And yet the farcical aspects of the scene already anticipate the hairpin turn in decolonization that follows the native bourgeoisie's occupation of the Chamber of Commerce. The old French administrators march back into the building carrying seven hefty briefcases. The independence speech voice-over returns as well: "We have chosen socialism, the only *true* socialism, the African path of socialism, socialism on a human scale. . . . Our independence is complete." The speech is undercut instantly as the camera finds the seven Senegalese "businessmen," now attired in full tuxedos, sitting silently as the former administrators place an attaché case before each of the new deputies, stepping back to assume the attentive position of ministerial advisors. With big smiles, the businessmen unlatch their briefcases to find stacks of West African CFA franc notes. The new

Chamber president rises to proclaim their revolution a success and to announce the wedding of one of their own to a much younger third wife. "Our modernity must not mean that we lose our *africainité*," the president insists, to enthusiastic shouts of "*Vive l'africainité!*"

Xala lampoons the hypocritical corruption of postcolonial Senegal's native bourgeoisie, whose affirmations of "*africainité*" preserve selfish political and patriarchal privileges. It vividly illustrates the pitfalls of decolonization coopted by a comprador elite whose "sole motto," in Frantz Fanon's words, is "Replace the foreigner" (158). Indeed, it reads like a satirical dramatization of the "Pitfalls of National Consciousness" chapter of *The Wretched of the Earth*: in the postcolony, "the national middle class constantly demands the nationalization of the economy and of the trading sectors. . . . To them, nationalization quite simply means the transfer into native hands of those unfair advantages which are a legacy of the colonial period" (152). In *Xala*, decolonization is a farce; the new postcolonial administrators put a Black mask on neocolonialism while the white-skinned former masters retain hold of the puppet strings. Instead of the revolutionary "disorder" that seeks "to change the order of the world" itself (Fanon 36), decolonization here looks more like interior decorating; the contents of the Chamber of Commerce have changed, but the institutional form and its colonial, predatory functions remain. Indeed, in Sembène's stinging caricature, formal decolonization, where the new state has "all the outward trappings of international sovereignty," is camouflage for neocolonialism as Kwame Nkrumah described it in 1965: the postcolonial state is "nominally independent" but, in fact, "its economic system and thus its political policy is directed from outside" (ix).

Sembène's comical depiction of neocolonialism's arrival on the heels of decolonization offers a *tableau vivant* for visualizing what Aníbal Quijano called "the coloniality of power" – "the European paradigm of modernity/ rationality" (172) that "is still the most general form of domination in the world today, once colonialism as an explicit political order was destroyed" (170). Sembène's vignette about the lingering coloniality of power exposes a divergence within decolonization between two versions of the process. The first, formal decolonization (or "flag independence") is construed as a relatively straightforward matter of filling colonial forms with native content – an act of simple substitution. The second entails the more challenging problem of decolonizing colonialism's residual forms – that is, of unmaking and remaking the political, legal, economic, social, cultural, and epistemological forms that colonialism leaves in its wake and through which the coloniality of power persists. Formal decolonization is generally treated as a political event completed when a colonial power returns territory and administrative authority to a native or postcolonial regime – celebrated when the new nation raises its flag. The second vision of decolonization is epistemic and cultural, with no attendant celebration; it insists that "*colonial forms* might need decolonizing themselves" (Gevers 384). In this processual version of decolonization, colonial institutions, economic systems, modes of production, educational programs and curricula, political structures, legal codes, social relations, patterns of thought, cultural modes, literary genres, and so on need to be dismantled and reconstructed in order to serve local realities and priorities. In historical practice, these two impulses of decolonization are rarely separable and not entirely differentiable from one another. Indeed, with every effort in the "unfinished project" of decolonization (Wenzel 449), the two impulses operate simultaneously, sustained in dynamic tension, sometimes one weighted more heavily than the other.

With the recent return of decolonization to the political and intellectual agenda, most conspicuously inside educational institutions of the old imperial powers, it is worth attending to the historical differences between formal decolonization and the decolonization of forms as they continue to shape today's debates. The problems of decolonization are not new, even if wider understanding of the pervasive perniciousness of things like institutional racism and systemic sexism (or the currency of the term "decolonial") might give them a renewed sense of urgency for a new generation of eager decolonizers. Likewise, the tension between the dual impulses for decolonization (sometimes dismissed too quickly as reformist or celebrated too easily as revolutionary) has been part of the problematics of decolonization whenever and wherever colonialism has landed. In practice, demands and projects for decolonization have historically (perhaps inevitably) entailed tacit acceptance, if not embrace, of some institutional and epistemological forms of colonial domination. This phenomenon reflects not only decolonization's double bind – that is, the tremendous difficulty (impossibility?) of trying to think and achieve decolonization wholly outside of terms legated by colonialism itself – but also the ontological fact that, as a historical matter of human liberation (or of liberating humanity), decolonization is never entirely done – that is, we can never be done with decolonization.

The first view of decolonization (formal decolonization) tends to treat the political, economic, and cultural forms of the colonizer (whether the nation-state, wage labor, the novel, etc.) as historically necessary or desirable, sometimes as "natural," "universal," or even "superior." These are, of course, the very terms in which European colonialism justified itself as the conveyor of universal norms and benefits. For such reasons, Walter Mignolo, a leading advocate of "decolonial thinking" today, describes the historical "political decolonization movements that existed approximately between 1947 and 1970" as "failed"; "they changed the content but not the terms of the conversation, and maintained the very idea of the state within a global capitalist economy" (50). For Mignolo, mid-century decolonization movements "failed" because they did not attempt to decolonize the political and economic forms of colonial modernity. However, such a blanket dismissal oversimplifies the heterogeneous forms of mid-century decolonization, failing to recognize (or ignoring) the facts that political independence was never the only agenda for decolonization and that political decolonization was, in any case, always shadowed (sometimes overshadowed) by comprehensive calls for economic, cultural, and epistemological decolonization.

In the "Cold War" context in which salt-water decolonization unfolded, differences between the two impulses of decolonization were often signaled in anticolonial discourse by the application of emphatic adjectives to articulate goals of "*true* independence," as the Senghorian voiceover in Sembène's film declares. In other words, desires for something more than the mere political independence of formal decolonization were often expressed by adding absolute adjectives ("true," "full," "complete") to intensify ideals of freedom, in which we might hear the echo of Aimé Césaire's famous adjectival indictment in *Discourse on Colonialism*: "the West has never been further from being able to live a *true* humanism – a humanism made to the measure of the world" (73; my emphasis). Those adamant adjectives can tell us much about the incomplete project and ever-receding horizon of decolonization.

It is true that, for the most part, mid-century decolonization movements were strongly marked by a "methodological nationalism" that naturalized the nation-state as the "necessary form of colonial emancipation" and treated decolonization as primarily a matter of filling its form with native administrators (Wilder 4). Both the Afro-Asian Conference of Bandung in 1955 and the Non-Aligned Movement meeting in Belgrade in 1961 generally reflect this approach. Instead of rejecting the founding principles of nation-statism or Eurocentric international law, the conference in fact doubled down on the standard principles and Westphalian promises of the international legal order, insisting that the basic package of international rights be extended to all peoples through the form of the nation-state. Indeed, the Final Communiqué of Bandung "declared its full support of the fundamental principles of Human Rights as set forth in the Charter of the United Nations" (3) and, like the later Non-Aligned Movement, decried the lack of a Marshall Plan for the Third World, calling on the World Bank (later cast as a chief villain of neocolonialism) to allocate "a greater part of its resources to Asian-African countries" (2).

In 1960, a high-water mark for national independence in Africa, the Bandung declaration served as the basis for UN General Assembly Resolution XVIV, "The Declaration on the Granting of Independence to Colonial Countries and Peoples," which expanded the compass of the "universal" principle in international law that "all peoples have the right to self-determination; by virtue of that right they freely determine their political status and freely pursue their economic, social and cultural development" (Article 2). Thus, recently independent postcolonial states managed to enshrine an implicit human right to formal decolonization within the text of international law under the rubric of self-determination in the form of the nation-state, construed as the ultimate (or at least historically necessary) vessel for fulfilling a people's desires for modernization, ethnonational aspirations for self-expression, development, and human freedom.

However, after a couple decades of collective experience with the pitfalls of formal decolonization and the betrayal of promises for state sovereignty and self-determination, attention turned to the coloniality of international law itself. Given the de facto subordination of postcolonial states within the international order (a situation that Algerian international lawyer and politician Mohamed Bedjaoui described as "nominal decolonization" or "fictitious independence" [81]), many anticolonial movements and thinkers knew that the nation-state could not be an end on its own; rather, they sought to use it as a means to decolonize the international order itself. As Antony Anghie has shown, many of the central doctrines of international law were forged in large part to manage and normalize "the colonial confrontation" (*Imperialism* 3). Thus, while still aspiring to occupy the form of the nation-state, they also wrestled with the colonial origins, imperial legacy, and neoimperial implications of the very international order that made such occupation necessary in the first place.

Anticolonial solidarity conferences throughout the 1960s and 70s gave increased urgency and expanded briefs to decolonization, which often found rhetorical expression in revolutionary adjectives interposed in the text of international law. The Tricontinental meeting in Havana (1966) is perhaps the most explicit example; the assembled African, Asian, and Latin American states and liberation movements proclaimed "the inalienable right of the peoples to *full* political independence and to resort to all forms of struggle that may be necessary, including armed struggle, to conquer that right" (106; my emphasis). The revolutionary assembly unfurled a series of amplifying militant adjectives to stress the unfinished business of decolonization: "In order to achieve *total* liberation it is necessary to eliminate *all forms* of imperialist oppression and exploitation, carry out profound changes in the social and economic structures . . . To political emancipation must be added economic liberation. Only in this way can social equality of all men and *true* independence of all states be insured" (106; my emphasis).

Against mere political independence is posed "true independence"; against mere national liberation is posed "full liberation." Relationally, the first term in each pair signifies an insufficient approach to decolonization (i.e. filling colonial forms with native content), while the adjectival insistence of the second term indicts the first by signaling the pressing need for more radical efforts to decolonize the incomplete forms of formal independence. Rhetorically, "true independence" always comes after independence alone has disappointed, redoubling the demand for emancipation (what Achille Mbembe calls "a second abolition" [50]) under the sign of revolution; historically, this corresponds with a shift in emphasis from formal decolonization to the decolonization of forms. This pattern, I suggest, continues today, with "decoloniality" presenting itself as the current champion of "true decolonization" in opposition to what it dismisses as false forms pursued by postcolonialism and Cold War anticolonial movements, inevitably (unwittingly?) repeating a historical pattern within decolonization discourse that wavers between prioritizing one of the two poles of decolonization, forever in search of a truer decolonization.

In principle, the universal needs no adjective, and it is, of course, not possible to make imperialism, international law, or capitalism blush at their venal hypocrisy simply by adding firm adjectives to liberationist ideals that purported to be universal all along. Moreover, what at first appears as wholesale rejection of "false" forms of decolonization is often articulated in pursuit of repossessing and renovating (that is, re-forming), with a difference, colonialism's pretended "universal" forms. Thus, although Fanon observed that, because decolonization takes many forms, "reason hesitates and refuses to say which is a true decolonization, and which a false" (59), he nonetheless famously asserted that decolonization is revolutionary disorder that brings "with it a new language and a new humanity" (36); "this new humanity cannot do otherwise than define a new humanism both for itself and for others" (246). With echoes in both Césaire and Sylvia Wynter, this "new humanity" and "new humanism" are implicitly counterposed to the old humanity and classic humanism that were historically complicit with colonialism, slavery, and genocide – called to the lower task of justifying the mass exclusion of most human beings from the real and symbolic benefits of "civilization," "modernity," and human liberation. From this perspective, Fanonian decolonization is a dialectical historical process for dismantling, remaking, and occupying the space of the universal itself.

For the Tricontinental, speaking in the name of "This Great Humanity," conquering the "inalienable right" to *true* self-determination meant taking the fight to cultural and epistemological dimensions in order "to expel from their cultural life the expressions of imperialist influence, thus enriching the lives of their peoples with *true* art and culture" (112), while demanding "access to the enormous material and intellectual wealth that the knowledge and the work of man have accumulated for centuries" (103). Claiming entitlement to the vast cultural heritage imperialism had amassed might look like acceptance of Eurocolonial constructions of the "universal." However, the radicalness of the Tricontinental's demand for decolonization and redistribution of humankind's cultural and intellectual "wealth" (a term that nonetheless seems to capitulate to a colonial-capitalist logic of property) perhaps resonates better if we read it in the same reparationist vein as Fanon's unequivocal insistence that "The wealth of the imperial countries is our wealth too. ... Europe is literally the creation of the Third World. The wealth which smothers her is that which was stolen from the underdeveloped peoples" (Fanon 102). In other words, the Tricontinental insisted that the cultural and intellectual wealth of the imperial countries was (always) already the wealth of colonized peoples too, with the inescapable implications that so-called European culture was the creation of the Third World and that colonialism created Europe. Thus, as Mbembe repeatedly insists, given the long "entanglement of histories and the concatenation of worlds" (112) – the fact that "as form and figure, act and relation, colonization was in many regards a coproduction of colonizers and colonized" (4) – decolonization could never be a simple matter of expelling imperialist influence or "decolonial delinking" (Mignolo 45), since what we think of as colonialism's forms (and our thinking about them) were themselves formed dialectically (albeit on unequal terms) in colonial contact zones across the globe.

Although the most immediate practical goal of mid-century decolonization was the occupation of the nation-state form, the new postcolonial majority of the UN also trained its sights on remaking the forms of international law. Thus, within the General Assembly, they tried collectively to leverage the relatively weak power of "Third World sovereignty" (Anghie, *Imperialism* 2) to change "the rules of the game" of an international order that emerged in large part to exploit their human and natural resources (Abi-Saab 30). That is, they sought to wring some of the coloniality (of power) out of the international legal order, to "reform an international system that had been created to subordinate it" (Anghie, "Legal Aspects" 149). In addition to strengthening (Westphalian) territorial doctrines of political sovereignty, the newly independent states produced twin proposals for decolonizing the international order on both economic and cultural fronts. In 1974, the General Assembly adopted the Declaration on the Establishment of a New International Economic Order (NIEO), which sought to clear away "the remaining vestiges of alien and colonial domination, foreign occupation, racial discrimination, apartheid and neo-colonialism *in all its forms* [that] continue to be among the greatest obstacles to the *full* emancipation and progress of the developing countries and all the peoples involved" (Article 1; my emphasis). In the late 1970s, Third World states also pressed the cultural/epistemological side of decolonization, proposing a New World Information and Communication Order (NWICO) that pursued the "decolonization of information" (International Commission 38) to help bring about "the abolition of the vestiges of domination as *full* national liberation becomes a reality" (6; my emphasis). As Sarah Brouillette has described it in more humanistic terms, postcolonial states "argued not just for the expansion of publishing industries but for the right to tell their own stories and be heard" (13). In Fanon's terms, these legal efforts to decolonize the international order express a new humanist desire for a revolutionary new humanities (a new arts and sciences) that might foster a new humanity – a "humanity" that cannot be taken for granted nor prescribed in advance.

Far from simply accepting the international order as colonialism bequeathed it (as Mignolo intimates), the Third World bloc instead dared to attempt to decolonize global capitalism itself, albeit by trying to leverage the nation-state (itself historically a creature of and for modern capitalism) against what the Tricontinental called "the world system of exploitation" (103). First step or last, the nation-state may well be the dead end of decolonization, but instead of viewing mid-century decolonization simply as "failed," it would be more accurate to say it was debilitated by neoimperial agents serving vested corporate interests of the most powerful states and elite class interests of the weaker ones. As I have argued elsewhere, the fates of the NIEO and NWICO are part of the more general history of the rise of neoliberalism in the 1970s and revanchist responses to

Third World challenges to Western hegemony, what Walden Bello called the "rollback" – "the structural resubordination of the [Global] South within a U.S.-dominated global economy" (Bello 3) – that entailed other reversals of radical efforts to decolonize the forms of the international order, including the Euro-American "hijacking of human rights" (Slaughter, "Hijacking").

When Fanon urged his readers to "rid ourselves of the habit ... of minimizing the action of our fathers," saying that "they fought as well as they could, with the arms that they possessed then," he did so while emphasizing the historical contingencies that conditioned mid-century decolonization. In particular, he stressed the international dimension of anticolonial struggle and the transformed character of the Cold War international order within which it unavoidably operated: "if the echoes of their struggle have not resounded in the international arena, we must realize that the reason for this silence lies less in their lack of heroism than in the fundamentally different international situation of our time" (206–7). Indeed, for Fanon, decolonization was the pursuit of resonance in the international arena. We, too, would do well to rid ourselves of the habit of minimizing mid-century decolonization movements, since like their forerunners (and ourselves today), they fought with the arms they possessed – or, in the case of the nation-state, with debilitated versions of a form they sought to occupy.

Calls for formal decolonization, by both anticolonial movements and colonizers alike, tend to imagine the nation (or "nation-ness," as Benedict Anderson described it) as a set of modular components that coordinate the "Westphalian unities of nation-time and nation-space" (Slaughter, *Human Rights* 92). In Anderson's influential account, the "cultural artefacts" of nation-ness created at the end of the eighteenth century in Europe and the Americas quickly became "capable of being transplanted" (4). Historically, colonialism and decolonization both served to transplant, normalize, and naturalize the form of the nation-state, with its liberal ideals of popular self-determination and rights-based citizenship as "the highest worldly forms of [human] expression of an abstract universalism" (Slaughter, *Human Rights* 120). Indeed, following mid-century decolonization, Anderson says, "the very idea of 'nation' is now nestled firmly in virtually all print-languages; and nation-ness is virtually inseparable from political consciousness" (135). Fanon himself operated and theorized from within this conceptual framework and understood well the international bind of decolonization – that, as a practical matter, both political and epistemological decolonization would inevitably have to unfold within a preestablished international system of states, and, therefore, to be undertaken historically they entailed a certain embrace of the nation-state as the near (or at least nearest appearing) horizon of decolonization. Thus, when Fanon writes that "national consciousness, which is not nationalism, is the only thing that will give us an international dimension" (247), he concedes to historical constraints on forms of emancipation and reinforces a formula for decolonization (mental, cultural, and political) that affirms the nation as the key conduit of a people's collective self-determination and self-expression – thus, his unwavering focus throughout the book on *national* consciousness, *national* liberation, *national* life, *national* culture, and so on. As Egyptian international lawyer George Abi-Saab observed, one of the "great handicaps" (34) of formal decolonization in the mid-twentieth century was the creation of many new states without nations, leaving the daunting task of "building the social and economic infrastructure necessary to support a modern State" (35) – in a word, "nation-building" (35). Culture was understood to be part of the required infrastructure for "translating independence into a social reality" (Abi-Saab, 34), and literature specifically was often tapped to serve the postcolonial cause of building nation-ness, as with Fanon's urgent appeal for "a fighting literature, a revolutionary literature, and a national literature" (223).

The problems of political decolonization in the legal arena are intertwined with parallel projects of cultural decolonization in literary studies, whether in the form of canon wars, curricular reform, revolutionary pedagogies, new field formations, or postcolonial proposals for "the abolition of the English Department" (Ngũgĩ). As Christopher Gevers has shown, Third World legal debates over decolonization followed the patterns of well-known debates among African authors in the 1960s about the legacy of colonial languages in developing and sustaining African national literatures and nation-ness. The literary debate is typically illustrated by the contrast between Chinua Achebe's famous assertion in "English and the African Writer" that the English language "will be able to carry the weight of my African experience. But it will have to be a new English . . . altered to suit its new African surroundings" (30) and Ngũgĩ wa Thiong'o's later insistence that "true decolonization required nothing less than abandoning the English novel altogether" (Gevers 384), which he theorized in *Decolonising the Mind*. As Gevers reads it, the debate hinged upon a dispute over the coloniality of forms – of languages and literary genres – and whether "colonial forms" could be repurposed "without residual colonial influences" (391). The genre of the novel has often been a privileged site for such literary debates over the dual approaches to decolonization, probably because of its close historical association with nation-ness, famously pinpointed by Anderson as a key modular technology of print-capitalism (along with the newspaper) involved in producing the "imagined political community" of the nation (6). In the context of mid-century decolonization, occupying the form of the novel can be understood as part of the greater effort to occupy the form of the nation itself.

These Third World approaches to international decolonization give real weight to the links between law and literature that are purely metaphorical in the dominant paradigms of world literature today, such as Pascale Casanova's influential account of "world literary space and the international laws that structure it" (94). Emerging from the same philosophical/philological tradition and ethical framework of liberal humanism (with its attendant pretenses to universality), international law, human rights, and comparative and world literature studies were assembled around the central unit of the nation. Historically, they all also share fundamental assumptions about the modularity of nation-ness. As regulatory regimes, international law, human rights, and world literature have functioned like empires, organizing and managing diversity and difference (e.g. national languages, literatures, and laws) under the sign of the universal and the principle of abstract formal equality; they provide institutionalized mechanisms (however limited) for expanding the scope of their own incumbent "universality" without fundamentally threatening the system or its forms of operation. In each, nation-ness and its ready-made forms are said to be ready for transport and for immediate occupation. Thus, they incentivize reformist approaches to decolonization that encourage the historically dispossessed to occupy the empire's preferred prefabricated forms – novels as much as nations.

Even in our putatively globalized world – that is, formally but still only nominally decolonized – the nation remains the most weighted category for entry into the catalog and canon of world literature. Indeed, deep assumptions about nation-ness and the modularity of modern literary forms underpin our most influential theories of world literature today. For example, in Casanova's account of "the formation of international literary space" (79), nations and authors (representing nations) compete for standing and privileges within a system of recognition where the so-called "independent [putatively universal] laws of literature" (86) were determined by the old and new imperial powers in Europe and the United States. Moreover, the generic rules of the international game for what counts as literature (more pointedly, as *national* literature) were largely formulated before the arrival of "the newly independent nations of Africa, Asia, and Latin America," who are obliged, she says, to "[obey] the same political and cultural mechanisms, moved to assert linguistic and literary claims of their own" (79). Thus, formal cultural decolonization in Casanova's account amounts to claiming the modular European literary forms of nation-ness as one's own, forgetting that so-called European literary forms were themselves formalized within the crucible of colonialism. Franco Moretti is even more explicit (and more forgetful) in this regard, claiming to have discovered what he calls a "law of literary evolution": "in cultures that belong to the periphery of the literary system (which means: almost all cultures, inside and outside Europe), the modern novel first arises ... as a compromise between a western formal influence (usually French or English) and local materials" (58). Moretti never asks after the colonial conditionality of his examples, or after the coloniality of power within either the world literary system or literary form itself. Instead, Moretti's law is absolute (universal): "when a culture starts moving towards the modern novel, it's *always* as a compromise between foreign form and local material" (60). Here the novelistic equivalent of formal decolonization features as the primary mechanism by which peripheral literature is worlded – and worlded in the image of literature that the colonizers insist is their own, having nothing to do with colonialism or the colonized. In other words, what we have been calling formal decolonization is, in both Moretti's and Casanova's models, the world literary system's own reformist mechanism for expanding access to the regime of the universal, extending its scope by pouring new "native" content into old colonial forms.

The imperative to decolonize the curriculum is nearly as old as the imperial curriculum itself, its impulses ranging from formal decolonization to the decolonization of curricular forms. I conclude with a particularly rich example from colonial West Africa, where desires and designs for decolonization might be especially difficult to appreciate viewed through today's decolonial lenses. More than a century ago, just a year after Conrad's *Heart of Darkness* consolidated the colonial image of Africa as a place without civilization, nations, or even "recognizable humanity" (Achebe, "Image" 9), Gold Coast lawyer, writer, and politician J. E. Casely Hayford published his anticolonial treatise, *Gold Coast Native Institutions* (1903). Hayford argued passionately that "the Native State itself has been disorganised by British aggression and interference" (27); the complexity of his vision of decolonization is announced in the book's subtitle *With Thoughts upon a Healthy Imperial Policy for the Gold*

Coast and Ashanti. Card-carrying member of the Gold Coast Aborigines' Rights Protection Society, Hayford was especially concerned about the destruction of native forms of social and political life, but his demand for decolonization is framed as a right to imperialism: "I have ventured to suggest a key to the solution of the problem. It is none other than the imperialisation of the Gold Coast and of Ashanti on purely aboriginal lines" (ix). Addressing British readers directly, Hayford insists that the "only way to remedy the past is to undo what wrong . . . has already been done; and the way to do so is by restoring [the] Native State System as nearly as may be" (100). Political decolonization for Hayford entailed repatriation (that is, restoration of what the author regards as a precolonial polity resembling, or nearly enough, a modern nation-state) and political self-determination, "the keynote of healthy imperialism" (126). For Hayford, a restored native state, within an international order of similar sovereign states under British Empire, is the only form that can secure the rights and interests of colonized peoples, giving access to a historical regime of the universal. Thus, Hayford stakes out a critical position that is at once anticolonial and proimperial, where political decolonization means imperialization: *Imperium in Imperio*.

Advocating formal decolonization, *Gold Coast Native Institutions* itself occupies the generic form of a rather conventional "customs and manners" ethnography like those British anthropologists produced in service of colonial administration. Hayford offers detailed policy recommendations for securing his "ideal of Imperial West Africa" (269) that, in outline and substance, resemble the framework for Indirect Rule that Frederick Lugard later famously formulated in *The Dual Mandate* (1922), which became the backbone for both official British colonial policy and the League of Nations' Mandate System that normalized colonial rule under modern international law. Indeed, Hayford clearly imagines decolonization and imperialism, or what he sometimes refers to as "true imperialism" (125), as coproductions. The generic conventionality of *Gold Coast Native Institutions* contrasts sharply with Hayford's more experimental and genre-bending novel, *Ethiopia Unbound* (1911), which, among many other things, lays out a program for decolonizing the native mind by remaking colonial institutions, in particular by establishing a national university with an Africa-centered curriculum. One of the earliest examples of the anglophone African novel, *Ethiopia Unbound*, subtitled *Studies in Race Emancipation*, is a marvelously disordered (in the revolutionary Fanonian sense) text that does not fit standard European generic conventions nor abide Moretti's "law of literary evolution" and, perhaps for that reason, has largely been ignored by both institutionalized World Literature and the dominant "global" histories of the novel. With a fictionalized version of Hayford himself acting as protagonist, the novel both imagines and performs cultural decolonization as it seeks "to learn to unlearn all that foreign sophistry has encrusted upon the intelligence of the African" (*Ethiopia* 164). Together, Hayford's two books form a diptych that epitomizes the dual mandate of decolonization, but both press the same polemical point: "the eternal verity remains that the natural line of development for the aborigines is racial and national, and that this is the only way to successful European intercourse and enterprise" (*Ethiopia* 69). For Hayford, decolonization is a dialectical process that entails both inhabiting and remaking colonialism's legated forms in the struggle to join empire and rewrite "universal history," a primary topic to be taught at his decolonized National University, "with particular reference to the part Ethiopia has played in the affairs of the world" (*Ethiopia* 194).

The tension between the two decolonizing impulses has intensified in recent calls to decolonize everything from hearts to minds to life, love, and land. In 2012, Eve Tuck and K. Wayne Yang famously rejected what they saw as the "colonization" of decolonization by "civil and human rights-based social justice projects" (2), especially curricular reform efforts in the settler-colonial context of the United States, insisting that decolonization is not a metaphor. For Tuck and Yang, decolonization is "unsettling work" (4) – where "unsettling" is also not a metaphor – that requires above all "the repatriation of [stolen] Indigenous land and life" (21). The legalistic Latinate word they use in their essay to describe the ultimate goal of decolonization – "repatriation" – seems to push the pendulum back in the direction of formal decolonization and to reaffirm classic (even colonial) linkages between territory, identity, and freedom that postcolonial studies often sought to delink. Indeed, unless "repatriation" is itself a metaphor in Tuck and Yang, the word seems anachronistic, implying a certain acquiescence to the coloniality of property and power, since it draws its usual meaning from the political framework and vocabulary of a modern international order in which the world's lands and peoples are already partitioned into nation-state units – a world order of territorialized ethnic identities presumably under contest by radical ("true") decolonization.

The decolonization of forms is no more metaphorical than formal decolonization, and literature (the traditional realm of metaphor) has never been merely metaphorical in relation to acts of possession, dispossession, and repossession. Fanon's sustained interest in matters of literary form in "On National Culture" attests to the important dialectical relations between forms of expression and the material forms that both domination and emancipation take. Indeed, the linguistic, legal, and cultural forms in which the dispossession of peoples and the possession of land and resources were claimed are inextricable from the material acts and facts of possession themselves, inflecting the real terms of colonialization and decolonization. Thus, the forms through which all claims of possession (colonial, native, or other) are made not only shape the material reality in which life and land are perceived, imagined, and lived, they also shape the historical possibilities for both formal decolonization and the decolonization of forms.

Both the modern nation-state and the classic English literary curriculum were forged with the project of European colonialism; but they are not simply or merely colonial constructions or impositions, at least not as we must reckon with them today. Both the nation as we know it now and literary studies in our current moment were also shaped by the energies and histories of mid-century decolonization and never-ending efforts by dominated groups to decolonize their forms. It does decolonization no good today to pretend otherwise, that is to pretend that we are simply dealing with colonial forms endlessly perpetuating the coloniality of power, or that we could as a practicable matter entirely wring coloniality out of power itself, when they are also forms forged in the crucible of multiple decolonizations. Given the centrality of colonialism in shaping our present – our modes of being, knowing, and feeling – decolonization can never be completely done once and for always. Indeed, the eternal return of desires for decolonization indicates (and not for the first time) the undying need for a second "true" decolonization that neither diminishes nor forgets previous efforts.

WORKS CITED

Abi-Saab, George. "The Third World and the Future of the International Legal Order." *Revue égyptienne de droit international* 29 (1973): 27–66.

Achebe, Chinua. "An Image of Africa." *Research in African Literatures* 9.1 (1978): 1–15.

"English and the African Writer." *Transition* 18 (1965): 27–30.

Anderson, Benedict. *Imagined Communities: Reflections on the Origin and Spread of Nationalism.* London: Verso, 1983.

Anghie, Antony. *Imperialism, Sovereignty, and the Making of International Law.* Cambridge: Cambridge University Press, 2004.

"Legal Aspects of the New International Economic Order." *Humanity: An International Journal of Human Rights, Humanitarianism, and Development* 6.1 (2015): 145–58.

Bedjaoui, Mohamed. *Towards a New International Economic Order*. New York: Holmes and Meier, 1979.

Bello, Walden. *Dark Victory: The United States, Structural Adjustment and Global Poverty*. London: Pluto Press, 1994.

Brouillette, Sarah. *UNESCO and the Fate of the Literary*. Stanford, CA: Stanford University Press, 2019.

Casanova, Pascale. *The World Republic of Letters*. Translated by M. B. DeBevoise. Cambridge, MA: Harvard University Press, 2004.

Césaire, Aimé. *Discourse on Colonialism*. Translated by Joan Pinkham. New York: Monthly Review Press, 1972.

Fanon, Frantz. *The Wretched of the Earth*. Translated by Constance Farrington. New York: Grove Press, 1963.

Final Communiqué of Bandung. *Asian-African Conference Bulletin* 9 (April 24, 1955): 2–6.

"General Declaration of the First Conference." *Tricontinental Bulletin* 1 (1966): 101–12.

Gevers, Christopher. "Literal 'Decolonization'." In Jochen von Bernstorff and Philipp Dann, eds., *The Battle for International Law: South–North Perspectives on the Decolonization Era*. Oxford: Oxford University Press, 2019, 383–403.

Hayford, Casely. *Ethiopia Unbound: Studies in Race Emancipation*. London: C. M. Phillips, 1911.

Hayford, J. E. Casely. *Gold Coast Native Institutions: With Thoughts upon a Healthy Imperial Policy for the Gold Coast and Ashanti*. London: Sweet and Maxwell, 1903.

International Commission for the Study of Communication Problems. *Many Voices, One World: Towards a New More Just and More Efficient World Information and Communication Order*. Paris: UNESCO, 1980.

Mbembe, Achille. *Out of the Dark Night: Essays on Decolonization*. New York: Columbia University Press, 2021.

Mignolo, Walter. "Epistemic Disobedience and the Decolonial Option: A Manifesto." *Transmodernity: Journal of Peripheral Cultural Production of the Luso-Hispanic World* 1.2 (2011): 44–66.

Moretti, Franco. "Conjectures on World Literature." *New Left Review* 1 (2000): 54–68.

Ngũgĩ wa Thiong'o, "On the Abolition of the English Department." In *Homecoming: Essays on African and Caribbean Literature, Culture and Politics*. London: Heinemann, 1972, 145–50.

Nkrumah, Kwame. *Neo-Colonialism: The Last Stage of Imperialism*. London: Nelson, 1965.

Quijano, Aníbal. "Coloniality and Modernity/Rationality." *Cultural Studies* 21:2–3 (2007): 168–78.

Slaughter, Joseph R. "Who Owns the Means of Expression? (Review of Sarah Brouillette's *UNESCO and the Fate of the Literary*)." *The b2o Review*, June 2020. www.boundary2.org/2020/06/joseph-slaughter-who-owns-the-means-of-expression-review-of-unesco-and-the-fate-of-the-literary/.

"Hijacking Human Rights: Neoliberalism, the New Historiography, and the End of the Third World." *Human Rights Quarterly* 40.4 (2018): 735–75.

Slaughter, Joseph R. *Human Rights, Inc.: The World Novel, Narrative Form, and International Law*. New York: Fordham University Press, 2007.

Tuck, Eve and K. Wayne Yang. "Decolonization Is Not a Metaphor." *Decolonization: Indigeneity, Education and Society* 1.1 (2012): 1–40.

Wenzel, Jennifer. "Decolonization." In Imre Szeman, Sarah Blacker, and Justin Sully, eds., *A Companion to Critical and Cultural Theory*. Hoboken: John Wiley & Sons, 2017, 449–64.

Wilder, Gary. *Freedom Time: Negritude, Decolonization, and the Future of the World*. Durham, NC: Duke University Press, 2015.

Wynter, Sylvia. "Unsettling the Coloniality of Being/Power/Truth/Freedom: Towards the Human, After Man, Its Overrepresentation: An Argument." *CR: The New Centennial Review* 3.3 (2003): 257–337.

CHAPTER 15

Decolonizing Literary Interpretation through Disability

Christopher Krentz

In a 2002 chapter called "Looking Awry: Tropes of Disability in Postcolonial Writing," Ato Quayson notes that figures of disability proliferate across postcolonial literature in English, identifying a fascinating aspect of the corpus and a productive area for future critical inquiry. Until then, disability in postcolonial literature had received little attention despite the rise of postcolonial studies and disability studies in the prior decades, and despite the fact that approximately 80 percent of the world's disabled people – more than half a billion people – live in the Global South, often in precarious situations.[1] In their introduction to *Relocating Postcolonialism*, Quayson and coeditor David Theo Goldberg further argue that postcolonial studies and disability studies share many concerns, not least about questions of power and oppressed identities. They call on postcolonial and disability critics "to pursue joint projects of agitation for justice that would embrace the disabled equally with the racially othered, gendered, and postcolonial subject" (xvii). With their words, they helped to initiate a period where a few other scholars explored the rich multilayered depictions of disability in anglophone postcolonial literature.[2] These critical contributions expanded the scope of postcolonial studies, uncovered exciting new dimensions of the literature in English from the Global South, made literary disability studies more global, and called attention to the relationship between literary representations and the millions of actual disabled people around the world, who often confront ableist prejudice and disenfranchisement. Within the larger interdisciplinary field of disability studies, literary disability studies has been an important thread, showing how disability has existed in the human imaginary in the past and how authors have used representations of disability to do cultural work that reflects and sometimes critiques their specific historical moments. In postcolonial literature, often depictions of disability go to the heart of the decolonization process. In my recent book *Elusive Kinship*,

I investigate how authors deploy disability to make more vivid not just the lives of disabled people in the Global South, but also such crucial issues as the effects of colonialism, global capitalism, racism and sexism, war, and environmental disaster. As we consider how to decolonize literary studies and to agitate for justice, we must include disability alongside other vulnerable identities, and strive for more North–South dialogue and collaboration in interpreting texts. Doing so will not just liberate literary studies, but also improve understanding of decolonization and liberation around the world.

Reading Disability in Postcolonial Literature

One does not have to look far to discern why disability in postcolonial literary works has been slow to receive attention. Both of the two likeliest fields to consider it, postcolonial studies and literary disability studies, emerged in the late twentieth century but at first had little contact with each other. In early decades, postcolonial scholars, like literary scholars in general, had little to say about disability, perhaps because they deemed it uninteresting compared to other pressing issues.[3] Such oversight recalls historian Paul Longmore's observation in the 1980s about disability in media and film; he asks, "Why do television and film so frequently screen disabled characters for us to see, and why do we usually screen them out of our consciousness even as we absorb those images?" (132). We might pose a similar question with regard to postcolonial literature. When postcolonial critics noted disability in the literature, they tended to see it as metaphorical, as emblems of the agonizing experience of colonialism, rather than realistic. Admittedly, many works invite such a figurative reading. For example, in Salman Rushdie's *Midnight's Children* (1981), the narrator Saleem is born with birthmarks and no sense of smell; as he grows, he acquires partial deafness, amnesia, and other disabilities. Because he was born at the moment of India's independence, he insists that he is "handcuffed to history" (3) and his life is entwined with postcolonial India's. Such a depiction encourages readers to interpret Saleem's body metaphorically. Along the same lines, in J. M. Coetzee's *Life & Times of Michael K* (1983), the significance of the cognitively disabled title character, who also has a cleft lip, consistently eludes others and himself. A medical officer in wartime South Africa imagines himself chasing Michael after he escapes from a rehabilitation camp and futilely calling out "your stay in the camp was merely an allegory [of] how outrageously a meaning can take up residence in a system without becoming a term in it. . . . Am I right?"

(166–67). The medical officer gives Michael larger meaning even while acknowledging the latter's essential elusiveness, just as many readers are tempted to do. Through such examples, one can see why Frederic Jameson (perhaps too easily) concluded that "all third-world texts are necessarily . . . allegorical" (69). Yet while suggestive, as Clare Barker has pointed out, readings that attend only to the metaphorical leave real-life material disability and disabled people's experience out of the equation, not to mention the relationship of disability to narrative structure: they create gaps in interpretation that prevent full understanding of the literature, of decolonization, and of justice.

For its part, disability studies arose out of the disability rights movement in the United States and United Kingdom in the 1970s and 80s as a small number of advocates sought to take the insights of the movement into classrooms and academic intellectual inquiry. The movement directed attention to how barriers in society, rather than in the body, stigmatized and excluded disabled people, so it turned attention from medical discourse to how societies are organized, including in areas such as architecture, social policy and attitudes, public transportation, and more. In addition, it brought together people with a variety of impairments, causing them to see themselves as part of larger group with common goals in a way they had not done before. Animated by the slogan "Nothing about Us without Us," activists protested for access and equity in all areas of life, leading to such landmark legislation as the Americans with Disabilities Act of 1990. Building on these successes, pioneering scholars in literary disability studies examined how well-known works in the Anglo-American canon deploy disability. In the 1990s, they offered groundbreaking readings, especially revealing how depictions of disability aid in the social formation of normalcy.[4] While such analyses were insightful, the focus on Anglo-American texts unfortunately left out other literature in English, other cultures, and by extension millions of disabled people in the world. Anglo-American scholars may have felt unqualified to analyze depictions of disability from the Global South, wary of trampling on Southern ways of knowing and apprehensive of being inadvertently racist, classist, or even in effect "colonizing" literary texts produced in the South. Such reluctance would be understandable, but this omission left a grievous lacuna.

With their call in 2002, Quayson, who is originally from Ghana and now has an academic position in the United States, and Goldberg, who grew up in South Africa but now also has an academic post in America, opened the way for collaboration and dialogue between not just scholars in postcolonial studies and those in disability studies, but also scholars in the

North and those in the South, who together have advanced the critical conversation about disability in this great literature. In the following years, scholars including Quayson, with Aesthetic *Nervousness* in 2007, the British literary critic Clare Barker, whose *Postcolonial Fiction and Disability* appeared in 2011, and the American scholar Michael Bérubé, with *Secret Life of Stories* in 2016, published books that explore disability in postcolonial texts. They investigate works by authors such as Wole Soyinka, J. M. Coetzee, Salman Rushdie, Tsitsi Dangaremba, Patricia Grace, Bapsi Sidhwa, and Ben Okri, sometimes alongside Anglo-American writers. Moreover, the *Journal of Literary & Cultural Disability Studies* and *Wagadu* devoted special issues to disability in postcolonial literature, while diverse scholars such as Nirmala Erevelles, Michael Davidson, Shaun Grech, Karen Soldatic, Jasbir Puar, and others have advanced global disability theory in the humanities.[5] Building on this exciting work, I published *Elusive Kinship: Disability and Human Rights in Postcolonial Literature* in 2022, taking on both established (and often-taught) authors like Chinua Achebe, Rushdie, Coetzee, and Anita Desai, and also younger contemporary writers such as Edwidge Danticat, Jhumpa Lahiri, Chris Abani, Indra Sinha, and Petina Gappah, seeking further to reveal the instructive presence of disabled characters in this literature.

Such scholarship has revealed that, far from being simple or straightforward, representations of disability regularly work on multiple levels simultaneously, signify on any number of matters, and reveal the deepest meanings of a text. In *Aesthetic Nervousness*, Quayson gives examples of a variety of compelling ways that disability shows up in literature, including as a test for the morals of other characters, as a marker of otherness, as epiphany, as a hermeneutical impasse preventing understanding, as giving tragic insight, and as normality. Such a preliminary typology gives a sense of the broad range of cultural significance disability can have in literature. Arguing that interactions between nondisabled and disabled characters, and disabled characters and readers, often produces anxiety, Quayson says such nervousness can lead to a crisis of representation. He concludes by calling for more rigorous reading practices "alive to the implications of disability," because representations of disability often help to illumine the "ethical core" of narratives that are otherwise easy to miss (*Aesthetic* 208). For example, in Coetzee's *Waiting for the Barbarians*, the Empire's sadistic Colonel Joll tortures an Indigenous girl, leaving her partially blind and with damaged ankles. Her physical impairments raise questions about the morality of the Empire's imperialism and prompt readers to pay close attention to the Empire's relationship to Indigenous people.

Others build on Quayson's lead. Although she agrees with Quayson's contention that depictions of disability are crucial, Barker disputes the idea of a narrative crisis. She argues that portrayals of child disabled characters in literature from Zimbabwe, Nigeria, India, Pakistan, and Aotearoa New Zealand serve as both metaphoric critiques of "dominant (post)colonial or national ideologies" and empathetic depictions of disabled experience (Barker 26). In other words, she maintains that disabled figures can be both figurative *and* realistic depictions at the same time, even in cases of magic realism. Meanwhile Bérubé calls attention to the way that ideas about cognitive disability can shape narratives through questions about time, self-reflexivity, and motive. All three scholars point to how, even when disabled figures are not present, disability can work at the level of language, metaphor, and shape of a narrative's plot, sometimes simultaneously. For my part, I connect some depictions of disability in postcolonial literature to the gradual emergence of global disability human rights, most prominently in the United Nation's landmark Convention on the Rights of Persons with Disabilities (CRPD, ratified 2008). Such work shows that literary deployments of disability are often both complex and meaningful, meriting our careful attention as we seek a fuller understanding of literature, decolonization, and global justice.

Peripheral Everywhere: The Marginalization of Disabled People

These matters do not just enrich our understanding of literature and any number of topics authors use disability to comment upon, but also relate to one of the most vulnerable groups in the world.[6] Despite encouraging signs such as increased activism, attention, and progress in disabled rights, disabled people everywhere often confront ableist prejudice and oppression. In a world beset by severe problems, from climate change to enormous inequity to the COVID-19 pandemic, it may seem especially daunting to focus on disabled people, but they are of course profoundly affected by larger crises and give us a useful perspective for approaching them. Scholars have long recognized the "vicious circle" that often connects disability and indigence, where disability leads to poverty and poverty leads to disability, reinforcing each other (Eide and Ingstad 1). Problems are amplified by the fact that disabled people are often perceived as useless and unable to reciprocate. In the Global South, they typically have limited access to health care, education, housing, and employment and are among the first to suffer during food shortages, natural disasters, and other emergencies. Disabled women and girls are disproportionately illiterate and victims of violence, including rape and domestic abuse. As the United Nations puts it, "girls and women of all ages with any form of disability are generally among the more vulnerable and marginalized of society" (UN "Women"). Matters are compounded by the legacies of colonialism, war, and neoliberal economic policies that leave some people behind.

Although these statements convey sobering realities, we should remember that they are broad generalizations that lack contextual detail; they may miss ways disabled people are proactive.[7] For example, in agrarian societies, disabled women often work, but their (unpaid) labor typically is not counted in development reports (Price and Goyal). The Global South contains tremendous variety among cultures, including Indigenous cultures, and practices, which serves as an important reminder to the need for specificity. For this reason, Barker and Stuart Murray call on scholars to practice situated readings when they examine disability in postcolonial literature rather than simply applying grand theories about disability developed in Europe and the United States. Rigorously attending to portrayals of disability in postcolonial literature offers a way for scholars to be precise and avoid generalization.

In world media, disabled people are usually faceless, making it easier for the public to ignore their plight or to assume it is unimportant, but by taking literary deployments of disability seriously, scholars can raise awareness and make a positive difference. Nirmala Erevelles decries how, in Northern media, disabled people in the Global South "face the social, political, and economic implications of being invisible" (133), implications that are almost uniformly negative, as they are cast to the margins or considered disposable. In the face of such invisibility, the attention of scholars to literary depictions of disability in postcolonial literature can raise awareness of ongoing ableism and injustice and make a significant difference. Representations of minority groups in literature, we see repeatedly, almost always reflect reality in some way and how literary scholars read and teach them have consequential real-world effects. Such a statement is as true of depictions of disabled people as it is of other minority groups.

Disability in Chris Abani's *Song for Night*

To illustrate a specific case of how attention to disability enriches our understanding of literature, decolonization, and questions of justice, I turn to Nigerian-American author Chris Abani's memorable novella, *Song for Night* (2007). The book us takes into a horrific war that is at first so unspecific as to almost seem universal, but gradually we get clues as to where we are. The narrator, a fifteen-year-old child soldier named My Luck, says we are reading his thoughts in Igbo that somehow – he says he does not have time to figure out how – are translated into English. That he speaks Igbo connects him to the cultural group of the same name in southeast Nigeria; later, we encounter references to the Yoruba and the Hausa, other large ethnic groups in Nigeria, to a divided nation, to pogroms, and to bloody strife between Muslims and Christians. Such ethnic and religious conflict historically took place in the years after Nigerian independence from British colonization in 1960. Later in the decade, it prompted Igbo people to try to secede and form their own country of Biafra, resulting in the Biafran War (as the calamitous Nigerian civil war in the late 1960s is known). My Luck's narration apparently occurs in the war's final stages. Early in the novella, he remembers encountering, with his platoon of child soldiers, a group of elderly women who are eating what proves to be a baby. The grisly scene relates to the debilitating famine that Igbo people suffered as the result of a blockade that federal forces put around their ports; hundreds of thousands of people died of starvation. In terror and disgust, My Luck instinctively shoots the women with his AK-47, one of many appalling incidents he recounts. To tell this nightmarish story about war in the aftermath of independence, Abani employs disability on a variety of levels that add complexity and even lyrical beauty to the spare narrative (which only runs to 146 pages).

Physical, sensory, and cognitive difference show up in many ways that add power to the novella. First, My Luck himself is physically disabled: he can't talk vocally. "What you hear is not my voice," he begins (19). We learn that three years before, at the end of training camp, My Luck and other child soldiers in his mine-defusing platoon had their vocal cords severed, apparently so they wouldn't frighten each other with screams if a mine exploded on them. The image of a platoon of voiceless child soldiers serves as a clear metaphor for how such children and many vulnerable others devastated by the violence of wars do not have a voice in public discourse. They ordinarily cannot represent themselves and remain largely invisible and forgotten. My Luck does not seem particularly upset by his severed vocal cords, perhaps because the whole group shares the same fate. They have invented a rudimentary sign language (which My Luck is quick to distinguish from the more sophisticated sign language his deaf cousin used at school) to communicate with each other. Abani makes that sign language stay at the forefront of readers' awareness, for each of the short chapters is titled with the description of a sign, such as "Dawn Is Two

Hands Parting before the Face," so disability remains a constant presence throughout the tale (45). In addition, My Luck's voicelessness gives his inner thoughts a certain eloquence. "There is a lot to be said for silence," he says, "[it] makes you deep beyond your years and familiar with death" (21). Through disability, Abani, a poet, is able to give his largely uneducated narrator (My Luck went to war at age twelve) thoughts that resonate. A gap exists between the ghastly circumstances My Luck relates and his lyrical language. In this way, disability makes his story more compelling and arguably even helps to humanize him.

In this violent setting, My Luck tries to come to terms with the gruesome events around him and his own self and actions. The narrative opens with him waking up alone after a mine blast; much of the story concerns My Luck's search for his lost platoon. Along the way, we get flashbacks that help us to understand the ghastly things he has experienced, from the murder of his parents to obscene depravity during the war, as when an officer forces a man to butcher his children with a knife before killing him. My Luck is honest about his own participation in the savagery. Near the beginning he appears a hardened soldier: he calls enemy combatants "scum" and admits that "deep down somewhere I enjoy [killing them], revel in it almost" (12). But increasingly as the narrative unfolds, he expresses weariness of all the hatred and questions his own morality. Near the end, he asks philosophically, referring to child soldiers, "If we are the great innocents in this war, then where did we learn all the evil we practice?" (143). He points to how the chaos around decolonization has led him to perform vile acts, and he goes on to lament his status as a child soldier: "I have never been a boy. That was stolen from me and I will never be a man – not this way. I am some kind of chimera who knows only the dreadful intimacy of killing" (143). In this manner, *Song for Night* gives expression to an orphan who has been forced into a brutal war and who has lost not only his family, but also in many ways his identity.

The novella shows how political decolonization almost always involves violence, especially in the early stages, and that violence in turn disables, orphans, and maims many people, who typically remain anonymous to the public. Drawing on his own experiences with the Franco-Algerian War, Frantz Fanon in *The Wretched of the Earth* asserted a few years before the start of the Biafran War that "decolonization is always a violent phenomenon," adding that it is also a "programme of complete disorder" (27). In presenting the move from colonialism to independence as invariably violent and turbulent, Fanon aptly describes turmoil that is distressingly familiar: the descriptors convey the shocking Hindu–Muslim violence of partition in 1947 after the British left India[8] and the brutal all-out war that surrounds the teenage My Luck.[9] In the case of Nigeria, the British colonizers artificially decided on the borders of the nation, putting many different ethnicities, who spoke different languages and had different religious and cultural traditions, together. When the colonizers left in 1960, conflict between the groups broke out. During decolonization, colonizers fade into the background, but as My Luck's experience shows, the remnants of imperial practices continue to be deeply felt after independence.

Northern countries beyond the former colonizer, Britain, have a subtle but strong effect in *Song for Night,* showing neocolonial forces after independence and how difficult true liberation is to achieve. For one thing, we learn that many of the weapons in the war come from the North. My Luck tells us of the remarkable guns, ammunition, and grenades that "U.S.-armed enemy soldiers" possessed (28). While the United States government did hope that one unified Nigeria could be preserved, it officially was neutral during the conflict, so it is unclear if My Luck is right here. Britain and the Soviet Union were more active backers of the Nigerian federal forces. Still, possibly US weapons made it to the federal army via the active black market. My Luck adds that France had promised the rebels weapons and that "since land mines are banned in civilized warfare, the West practically gives them away at cost" (47). My Luck's remarks indicate how the United States and Europe contribute to the devastation by providing weapons. In giving mines they deem too barbaric to use themselves, governments and companies in the North demonstrate their disregard for African lives like My Luck's.

Moreover, the strangely sadistic Nigerian commanding officer uses American symbols to get the children to follow his orders, hinting at how the North can even unwittingly enable warped postcolonial identities that complicate decolonization. In boot camp, the man claims to have been trained at West Point (the manual for proper soldierly protocol, he says, tapping his temple, is in his head). Because of his cowboy boots, the children come to call him John Wayne after the American film actor. Despite these elements of legitimacy, the Nigerian John Wayne turns out to be hideously corrupt. Without anesthesia or even explanation, he has a doctor sever the children's vocal cords. In the war, he compels the twelve-year-old My Luck to commit rape before killing the woman. When John Wayne holds a seven-year-old girl named Faith and implies he will have sex with her – "I will enjoy her," he says (40) – My Luck almost automatically kills him (and the little girl too, by accident), and the other children in the platoon make him their leader. That such depravity could come in the name of a popular American film hero is ironic and conveys both the prestige and haughty destructiveness of the North in My Luck's mind and how it can corrupt Nigerian identities.

Through disability, Abani is able even more forcefully to convey the destructive effects of Northern intrusion and the conflict itself. Along with his voicelessness, the structure of the book, and his interior eloquence, My Luck's disability also serves as material evidence of all the grievous injury and trauma that accompany the war. As ethnic tension escalated before the conflict, My Luck saw each of his parents brutally murdered, deaths that he emotionally struggles to recount. My Luck's pain causes him voluntarily to join the Biafran army, and he says that all the other child soldiers, after losing loved ones, similarly "wanted revenge" against the enemy (19). All the child soldiers and many of the adults, one infers, have been traumatized. In the pages that follow, we see awful mutilation, death, depravity, and hunger take place one after the other in this all-out war. One could say that My Luck's own disability epitomizes all such trauma, makes it personal, hard, and real.

Scholars in disability studies have pointed out how war produces more disability, which Abani abundantly dramatizes in the novella. The narrative illustrates Jasbir Puar's point that war and military occupations often serve as "circuitry" where "disability – or, rather, debility and debilitation – is an exported product of imperial aggression" (89). Puar directly links colonialism and its afterlives to violence that causes disability. For her part, Helen Meekosha cites a stunning estimate that 85 percent of major military conflicts since World War II have taken place in low-income countries, presumably mostly in the Global South (675). In 2008, Michael Davidson noted that there are more than 110 million land mines in sixty-four countries, including 1.5 mines per person in Angola (where 120 people per month become amputees) and one mine for every two people in Afghanistan (170–1). In Nigeria, decades later they are still uncovering landmines from the Biafran War (Durosomo).

Yet importantly, in *Song for Night* Abani does not just deploy disability as a negative entity but instead consistently points at the humanity and worth of disabled people. Such an idea, he shows, is not a contradiction. At one point, My Luck describes a group of disabled children dancing, a surprising scene in the midst of the devastation of the war. A young one-legged girl laughs at the dancers and, when challenged to do better, throws her crutch-like stick aside and joins the circle. My Luck says:

> Balanced on one leg, her waist began a fierce gyration and her upper body moved the opposite way. Then like a crazy heron she began to hop around,

> her waist and torso still shaking. She was an elemental force of nature.
> I couldn't take my eyes off her. I have never seen anything like it before or
> since – a small fire sprite shaking the world and reducing grown war-
> hardened onlookers to tears. (51)

In this episode, disability serves as an undeniable material sign; the trauma
and ravages of the gruesome war are inscribed on the bodies of the disabled
children. Yet at the same time and seemingly contradictorily, the girl is
a life-affirming figure of irrepressible joy. Rather than summarily relegating
disability to the margins or showing it as always bad, the novella presents it
as an integral part of people's lives. Disabled people are indisputably
human.

As the novella rushes to its surprising conclusion, My Luck slowly
realizes he might no longer be alive. As he explains:

> Here we believe that when a person dies in a sudden and hard way, their
> spirit wanders confused looking for its body. Confused, because they don't
> realize they are dead. I know this. Traditionally, a shaman would ease such
> a spirit across to the other world. Now, well, the land is crowded with
> confused spirits and all the shamans are soldiers. (109)

Without a shaman to help him, My Luck's journey proves to be him
revisiting sites of past trauma in order to come to terms with them before
moving to the next realm. He presumably dies at the beginning of the
novella in the mine blast and has been a spirit all along. We get clues along
the way: he has a seemingly endless supply of cigarettes; he is rarely hungry;
upon seeing him an elderly woman says "*Tufia!*," an "old word for
banishing spirits or bad things" (84); and when challenged to step across
a line if not a ghost, he cannot do it. In the final lines, he rides in a coffin
across a mystical river to find his mother, young and smiling. She hugs
him, calls him by name, and tells him he is home. My Luck concludes: "I
am trying to make sense of it, to think, but I can't focus. 'Mother,' I say,
and my voice has returned" (167).

It could be called an overly sentimental ending, and some readers may
have reservations to his disability being removed in a way that will satisfy
ableist assumptions, but after all the horror of the narrative it gives
undeniable peace and closure. Moreover, while the novella presents My
Luck's satisfying end, it also implicitly presents all of the other remaining
people still injured and traumatized by the conflict, including the other
voiceless child soldiers in the platoon and the dancing disabled girl. The
effects of decolonial violence will not quickly go away.

Abani's short novel may also demystify master narratives produced in the North, especially since he writes from personal experience. In his 2007 TED talk "Stories of Africa," he explains that he was born in 1966 (in Igbo territory), near the start of the war, and for a year during the hostilities his British mother traveled with five small children from refugee camp to refugee camp to get to a place where they could fly to England. At each camp, Abani says, his 5′2″ mother faced down military men who wanted to take his older brother, who was nine, and make him a boy soldier. For Abani, the subject is deeply personal, but it appears he added the severed vocal cord part to achieve his aesthetic vision and grasp readers' imaginations even more fully. The family did make it to England and then after the war returned to Nigeria, where they must have witnessed the destruction and trauma after the conflict first hand. The Biafran War happened during the American fight in Vietnam, and Abani wrote the novella during the United States' Iraq War, disastrous examples of American intervention abroad.

In these ways, disability in *Song for Night* serves as a focal point for many aspects of decolonization. With disability, Abani finds an unusual way to make My Luck's story unique and powerful. Readers care about his fate (despite the harrowing brutality in the story, college students respond well to the tale). My Luck's eloquence and severed vocal cords make him serve as an apt representative of all the voiceless people in the Global South harmed by colonialism and its violent afterlives. It humanizes disabled people, reminding us of their often-faceless presence throughout the Global South. It portrays the grievous situation of child soldiers, too; despite human rights interventions, Mia Bloom reports that the number of child soldiers has risen over the last twenty years, indicating how this dynamic is still a problem. Starting with disability, readers come to see that colonization does not simply end with independence. My Luck's narrative makes us aware of how decolonization can lead to violence, corruption, and vile acts and that Northern intrusion continues. Considering disability in *Song for Night* can thus yield numerous insights for how we understand anticolonial resistance, including that true decolonization is often violent and painful.

Other postcolonial novels also point to how attending to disability can deepen our understanding of the varied complications of decolonization. Some quick examples: Anita Desai's *Fasting, Feasting* presents Uma, a woman with learning disabilities and epilepsy in late twentieth-century small-town India, where "modern" (usually British) and traditional notions of gender coexist. Her parents allow Uma to try school, but she cannot leave home until she marries; as she struggles to find a place for herself, Desai implicitly asks readers to think about what decolonization means in terms of gender expectations and roles. On another continent, Zimbabwean author Tsitsi Dangarembga's *Nervous Conditions* presents Nyasha, a bright, independent girl who is the product of two worlds (Zimbabwean and British) that near the end of the novel drive her into mental illness and an eating disorder. Considering her fate forces readers to contemplate the complexities of decolonization in a global world. Meanwhile, in Indra Sinha's novel *Animal's People*, a boy in India named Animal has a bent spine and goes about on all fours due to a disaster at a nearby chemical plant owned by Americans. Based on the tragedy at Bhopal, Animal's disability and narrative raises questions about transnational neoliberalism and the continuing effects of global capitalism after formal colonization has ended. These examples are just a few to give a sense of the vast range of depictions of disability in postcolonial literature and the equally numerous ethical questions they raise.

As we seek to decolonize literary studies, we must attend to disability. Doing so will not only make readers more aware of the humanity and diversity of disabled people in the Global South, but also open up any number of pressing topics, from gender roles to neoliberalism, from war to racial relations, related to decolonization. That will cause readers to read more closely and carefully and to consider the complications of achieving decolonization in our current chaotic world. We need to give teachers the knowledge to be confident about helping students through the intricacies of these complex portrayals. Only by concerted dialogue and attention to literary deployments of disability, and more provocative works like *Song for Night*, will we continue to move toward true decolonization of literary studies and liberty for all people.

Notes

1. For a useful discussion of global disability statistics, see Arne H. Eide and Mitchell Loeb, "Counting Disabled People."
2. As I discuss more below, these scholars include Clare Barker, Michael Bérubé, and me.
3. Perhaps, too, they felt unsure of the language best used for such depictions.
4. I'm thinking here especially of Lennard J. Davis's *Enforcing Normalcy* (1995), Rosemarie Garland-Thomson's *Extraordinary Bodies* (1997), and David Mitchell and Sharon Snyder's *Narrative Prosthesis* (2000).
5. Because new work in this area is constantly appearing, any listing is partial and incomplete.

6. The phrase "Peripheral Everywhere" is from the title of a James Charlton essay that traces the marginalized status of disabled people around the world.
7. Not surprisingly, some literary representations of disability can reflect these stereotypes and be quite flat.
8. The 1947 partition of India left between 200,000 and 2 million people dead and another 14 million displaced (Doshi and Mehdi).
9. The Biafran War historically killed between 500,000 and 2 million civilians (many by starvation).

WORKS CITED

Abani, Chris. *Song for Night*. New York: Akashic Books, 2007.

"Stories of Africa." TED. 2007. www.ted.com/talks/chris_abani_telling_stories_from_africa.

Barker, Clare. *Postcolonial Fiction and Disability: Exceptional Children, Metaphor and Materiality*. New York: Palgrave Macmillan, 2011.

Barker, Clare and Stuart Murray. "Disabling Postcolonialism: Global Disability Cultures and Democratic Criticism." *Journal of Literary & Cultural Disability Studies* 4.3 (2010): 219–36.

Bérubé, Michael. *The Secret Life of Stories: From Don Quixote to Harry Potter, How Understanding Intellectual Disability Transforms the Way We Read*. New York: New York University Press, 2016.

Bloom, Mia. "Child Soldiers in Armed Conflict." *Armed Conflict Survey 2018*. International Institute for Strategic Studies, 36–50. www.iiss.org/publications/armed-conflict-survey/2018/armed-conflict-survey-2018/acs2018-03-essay-3.

Charlton, James. "Peripheral Everywhere." *Journal of Literary & Cultural Disability Studies* 4.2 (2010): 195–200.

Coetzee, J. M. *Life & Times of Michael K*. New York: Penguin, 1983.

Waiting for the Barbarians. New York: Penguin, 1980.

Dangarembga, Tsitsi. *Nervous Conditions*. London: Women's Press, 1988.

Davidson, Michael. *Concerto for the Left Hand: Disability and the Defamiliar Body*. Ann Arbor: University of Michigan Press, 2008.

Davis, Lennard J. *Enforcing Normalcy: Disability, Deafness, and the Body*. New York: Verso, 1995.

Desai, Anita. *Fasting, Feasting*. New York: Houghton Mifflin, 1999.

Doshi, Vidhi and Nisar Mehdi. "Seventy Years Later, Survivors Recall the Horrors of the India–Pakistan Partition." *Washington Post*. August 14, 2017. www.washingtonpost.com/world/asia-pacific/70-years-later-survivors-recall-the-horrors-of-india-pakistan-partition/2017/08/14/3b8c58e4-7de9-11e7-9026-4a0a64977c92%5Fstory.html.

Durosomo, Damola. "Nigerian Government to Pay $245 Million to Victims of Biafran War." *Okayafrica*. October 31, 2017. www.okayafrica.com/nigerian-government-to-pay-biafra-war-victims-245-million/.

Eide, Arne H. and Benedicte Ingstad, eds. *Disability and Poverty: A Global Challenge*. Bristol: Policy Press, 2011.

Eide, Arne H. and Mitchell Loeb. "Counting Disabled People: Historical Perspectives and the Challenges of Disability Statistics." In Shaun Grech and Karen Soldatic, eds., *Disability in the Global South: The Critical Handbook*. Cham: Springer, 2016, 51–68.

Erevelles, Nirmala. *Disability and Difference in Global Contexts: Enabling a Transformative Body Politic*. New York: Palgrave Macmillan, 2011.

Fanon, Frantz. *The Wretched of the Earth*. 1961. Translated by Constance Farrington. New York: Penguin, 1990.

Garland-Thomson, Rosemarie. *Extraordinary Bodies: Figuring Physical Disability in American Culture and Literature*. New York: Columbia University Press, 1997.

Grech, Shaun, and Karen Soldatic, eds. *Disability in the Global South: The Critical Handbook*. Cham: Springer, 2016.

Longmore, Paul. "Screening Stereotypes: Images of Disabled People in Television and Motion Pictures." 1985. In *Why I Burned My Book and Other Essays*. Philadelphia: Temple University Press, 2003, 131–46.

Jameson, Frederic. "Third-World Literature in the Era of Multinational Capitalism." *Social Text* 15 (1986): 65–88.

Krentz, Christopher. *Elusive Kinship: Disability and Human Rights in Postcolonial Literature*. Philadelphia: Temple University Press, 2022.

Meekosha, Helen. "Decolonising Disability: Thinking and Acting Globally." *Disability & Society* 26.6 (2011): 667–82.

Mitchell, David T. and Sharon L. Snyder. *Narrative Prosthesis: Disability and the Dependencies of Discourse*. Ann Arbor: University of Michigan Press, 2000.

Price, Janet, and Nidhi Goyal. "The Fluid Connections and Uncertain Spaces of Women with Disabilities: Making Links Across and Beyond the Global South." In Shaun Grech and Karen Soldatic, eds., *Disability in the Global South: The Critical Handbook*. Cham: Springer, 2016, 303–21.

Puar, Jasbir. *The Right to Maim: Debility, Capacity, Disability*. Durham, NC: Duke University Press, 2017.

Quayson, Ato. *Aesthetic Nervousness: Disability and the Crisis of Representation*. New York: Columbia University Press, 2007.

"Looking Awry: Tropes of Disability in Postcolonial Writing." In David Theo Goldberg and Ato Quayson, eds., *Relocating Postcolonialism*. Oxford: Blackwell Publishing, 2002, 217–30.

Quayson, Ato and David Theo Goldberg. "Introduction: Scale and Sensibility." David Theo Goldberg and Ato Quayson, eds., *Relocating Postcolonialism*. Oxford: Blackwell Publishing, 2002, xi–xxii.

Rushdie, Salman. *Midnight's Children*. 1981. New York: Random House, 2006.

Sinha, Indra. *Animal's People*. New York: Simon & Schuster, 2007.

United Nations. "Women with Disabilities Fact Sheet." www.un.org/develop ment/desa/disabilities/resources/women-with-disabilities-fact-sheet.html.

CHAPTER 16

Decolonizing the Bible as Literature

Ronald Charles

The Bible remains the book of empire. The liberal project of "the Bible as Literature" has engaged mostly in placing the Bible on a pedestal as an important cultural artifact of the Western imagination, worthy to be read and to be studied in schools or universities. The contention of my analysis is that the Bible should be understood as an ambiguous text in terms of its position vis-à-vis empires. In other words, there is a complex, equivocal, and problematic relationship between the Christian Bible and colonialism. The biblical text has been used, and continues to be used, to subjugate and to otherize. Conversely, the Bible has also been deployed in struggles for liberation and emancipation.[1] The Bible as a text is replete with both tendencies. Thus, studying the Bible cannot simply be a descriptive project. The Bible is and is not what we make of it. It is not a blueprint. Simply stating that the Bible is for or against colonialism diminishes the complexities of its various narratives. Instead, we must strive to understand how the Bible is constructed, how its discourse contains alienating elements, how it has been used as a tool of colonization, and how it also contains elements that can be used for more liberating projects.

In various regions of the world, the Bible, or interpretations of some of its texts, continues to be central in the colonial history and reality of the local populations. Several people in and outside the State of Israel, for example, continue to refer to a text such as Joshua 1:1–4, with its mandate to conquer the inhabitants of the land across the Jordan river, to justify a particular understanding of what should constitute the parameters of a modern Jewish polity. In many African nations, the Bible, both in Western languages and its translations in Indigenous African languages, has served as a major instrument of control. In the colonization of Africa, the Bible was used as a tool for obedience and for oppression (Dube, Mbuvi, and Mbuwayesango; Dube; Mbuwayesango). The biblical story of the curse of Ham has been foundational in the production of a specific discourse of inferiority attributed to sub-Saharan Africans. Missionaries,

315

anthropologists, army officers, and traders invoked the so-called Hamitic curse in establishing and supporting their colonial endeavors. Although the Bible does not mention skin color in Noah's curse of Ham for seeing his nakedness (Gen. 9:22–25), the association with black skin and slavery has been woven into the interpretation of this narrative early on, and such an association has had a devastating effect on the lives of millions of Blacks throughout history (Goldenberg).

The origins of the modern terms "White" or "White supremacy" can be found in Protestant missionary ideologies of the early seventeenth-century Protestant Caribbean milieu, which aimed to control the bodies and souls of African slaves.[2] In the early colonial period, Protestant slave owners in the English, Dutch, and Danish colonies did not want their slaves to convert to Christianity because they believed that their religion was for free people only. As slaves converted and were baptized into the Christian religion, slave owners developed ways to integrate race into their colonial discourse to justify the bondage of non-Europeans brought to the colonies to work as slaves (Gerbner). The emergence of Protestant supremacy was due to the lack of a legal framework as well as the absence of theological clarity concerning what to do with slaves who accepted Protestant baptism in the early modern Atlantic world. By redefining Christian to mean White, slave owners were able to exclude Black slaves from Christian rites. Protestant slave owners were not homogenous but adopted various stances regarding slavery and slaves. Some viewed conversion as a destabilizing and unpredictable force to the slave system, whereas others believed that slaves could become Christians and be taught how to read to understand the teachings of the Bible. Many slaves felt it beneficial to convert to Christianity so that they could gain access to reading lessons and books (Gerbner, especially chapter 8, "Defining True Conversion," 164–88). Many enslaved Africans in the Caribbean learned how to read the Bible, came to question some of the missionaries' interpretations of the Bible, and developed other, more liberative alternative interpretations of the biblical text. Many slave owners burned books, since they feared that literate slaves could ignite a rebellion against the slave system. And to appease the White slave owners, the missionaries conformed to the status quo and developed racialized/proslavery discourses that allowed the slave system to flourish unabated. More and more, missionaries rejected the importance of reading for the African slaves and followed the established institutional norm of slavery. For slaves, reading, and to a lesser extent writing, were important tools in the struggle for liberation. Two streams of Christianity surfaced in the Atlantic world, one that catered more and more to an unjust system based on a highly racialized discourse and rationale, and another fueled by the Black slaves' desire to find freedom through education and community.

African Americans read the Bible to find liberation, equality, and a shared experience (Smith; Bowens). A hermeneutic of trust was built around the biblical text, whereas a clear hermeneutic of suspicion was deployed against White interpreters and their preaching and reading of the Bible. African Americans saw parallels between Hebrew history and their own, which they understood in terms of a second Exodus. From their perspective, American slavery was like Hebrew slavery in Egypt, and the White slave master was the new Pharaoh. Hence, the motif of liberation persisted and was adapted to new social and political realities.

In Haiti, my native land, colonization came with the Bible. It came with a message of salvation and with a program of *mission civilisatrice* from the European Christians (Hurbon, *Comprendre*; Hurbon, *Religions*; Bellegarde-Smith; Farmer). It was a violent colonization program in the name of God. The first colonial gesture was to plant a cross at Môle-Saint-Nicolas on the northwest coast of Ayiti, or land of great mountains, as the island's first inhabitants called it. The colonizers changed the island's name to Hispaniola (little Spain), thus claiming the land for the throne of Spain. The extinction of the Indigenous Taino population of Haiti by the Spanish and the ensuing brutal oppression of the Africans brought to the island by the French remain a colonial legacy with traumatizing consequences for the future of the country.

The question of interest in this essay is, how can one approach the topic of decolonizing the Bible as literature? To answer this, I will parse the Book of Revelation to show how a particular biblical text may offer liberative ways of confronting empire and its economic aspects and at the same time also serve to recolonize. I will situate some of the decolonial impulses of the Book of Revelation in the specific social and political contexts of Haiti, a place where the Bible has been used and continues to be used mostly for colonizing effects. I will first situate the Book of Revelation in its own imperial context by showing how it served as a cautionary tale that urged marginalized Christian communities of the first century to be vigilant and to resist, warning them to expect harsher persecutions from the ambient Roman political regime in its brutality and threats against any group not willing to comply with its political posture. The text is written in coded language to offer the little communities on the margins of the power structure a subversive hope, while imagining a counterhegemony, that of Christ, displacing the Roman empire. The second methodological undertaking is to show how a text that evokes an imagined world set in opposition to a world perceived to be in crisis is used in later and different historical, social, and political milieus to subjugate and create Others. With its proposal of a savior in battle against the Roman empire (dubbed Satan), the final argument of the chapter is that the text contains seeds that will be developed to alienate and/or Satanize those deemed to be opposing particular theological interpretations of specific (powerful) groups. This type of reading, which colonizes by way of exclusion and by way of advocating transcendental truths at the cost of social reality, is what I will highlight as the usual and debilitating reading done in the specific context of Haiti.

Revelation in Its Socio-Historical Context

John the Seer is in exile on a remote island called Patmos. He is a "brother, and companion in tribulation" (1:9), and he is banished because of "the word of God, and the testimony of Jesus Christ" (1:9). John composed his text as a revelation or unveiling to offer a subversive resistance tract to comfort Christians in Asia Minor.[3] The Book of Revelation is an apocalyptic[4] work that evokes an imaginative world set in opposition to one perceived as chaotic. The Seer is cautioning his communities to hold fast, to be vigilant, to resist the Roman emperor's claims to divinity, and even to expect harsher persecutions for refusing to participate in imperial cults. The goal of public religion was to ensure the *pax deorum* ("the peace of the gods" or their goodwill), from which communal prosperity would flow. Not offering libation on behalf of the emperor was considered a refusal to do one's proper civic duties. Any group not willing to do their duties was seen as acting against state policy, the *Pax Romana* (the Roman Peace). The Seer wrote his Revelation at a time of political, social, and economic upheaval in a turbulent Judean context with different political/religious movements that seemed to be ready to take arms against Rome for liberation.[5]

John's message stands in opposition to a political system that is judged as subhuman and degrading and which pacifies through killing. John's message to these fearful and apprehensive communities on the margins of the power structure is one of hope amid despair, a message that is fundamentally structured around Jesus, the anointed one of God. John's message is a call to live and struggle in the present in light of what God has already done and of what is yet to come. The book starts with a series of messages sent to seven different communities scattered throughout the Mediterranean. The pattern of these missives follows the same composition pattern: they state that Jesus knows the work of the community; they identify the strengths and weaknesses of a specific Christ-group; and they conclude with an exhortation or encouragement.

John's overall purpose seems to be that God will bring the end of the present corruption and ensure the coming of a new era. Then, there will be judgment upon non-Jews and unfaithful Israelites alike. All Christ's enemies will be put to death, and the earth will be restored to health in a renewal as wide as the creation itself. The underlying motivation of the Book of Revelation was to justify the ways of God to the suffering Christian communities: though everything is bleak in the present, God, in the end, will vindicate the faithful and punish their oppressors.[6]

The messages in chapters 2 and 3 reflect antagonism toward a variety of Christ-followers' groups. John uses traditional images from Near Eastern myths such as sea dragons and holy war scenarios to interpret his situation and that of his community. He associates chaotic images with Rome as a new Babylon and the image of a sun-clad woman with the faithful people of God. He resorts to two symbols to represent different aspects of the empire: the beast and the sea monster. The beast represents the military and political power of the Roman emperors. The sea monster alludes to the economic order and hegemony of Rome dominating the Mediterranean Sea to develop its exploitative commerce.[7]

To empower his community, John invokes the combat myth. Thus, the Seer sets the coming kingdom of God in Christ in opposition to the kingdom of Caesar, depicting a struggle between two distinct and powerful forces, good and evil, for kingship. In this myth, evil is often represented by a pair of dragons or beasts waging war against another pair such as husband and wife, brother and sister, or mother and son. In the Book of Revelation, the combat myth is found in the story of a great dragon waging war against a woman and her son (Rev. 12). In the opening scene of the story, a pregnant woman is crying out in agonizing birth pangs. A great dragon is standing before the woman so that he might devour her child as soon as it is born. Suddenly, the reader/hearer is in the heavenly realm watching a war breaking out. Michael and his angels, representing the good, are fighting against the dragon/Satan and his angels, representing evil. The dragon and his angels fight back, but they are defeated, and there is no longer any place for them in heaven. The brutality of the Roman Empire is contrasted with a vision of Christ as the head of a great army of heavenly avengers dressed in white. This combat myth makes it possible to grasp complex realities more easily, and in the imagination of the Seer, it functions as a powerful cultural and sacred force. It is designed to displace fear in the small Christ-communities and to give them the strength to face persecution for their faith. They are offered visions of monsters and martyrs to articulate a position of domination against the threatening Other (Frilingos). In its original context, the combat myth was a powerful way of standing up against a totalitarian regime. However, as noted by Leif E. Vaage, "God and Jesus in Revelation are mirror-imitation of the Roman emperor," and because of this, "such language, originally of resistance, soon would serve equally well as the discourse of succession" (268). In other words, transposed from other times and culture, this same combat myth, this same anti-imperial text, had ingrained in it the possi-bilities of becoming a tool of domination, of colonization in the hands of powers who were intent on eradicating other groups who could be per-ceived as "the enemy."

Colonizing through the Book of Revelation

As described above, the text of Revelation is written out of the experience of a minority in the colonized Roman Empire. It speaks of struggles, sufferings, and nightmares, that is, of the everyday experience of people in many parts of the world. Many impoverished and marginalized com-munities today share with the Johannine communities the longing for justice, for peace, for security, and for their well-being. Several writers from the Global South have pointed out the liberating project of this text in their own context. In this vein, Tina Pippin notes, "the ethical choice in Revelation of either Christ or Caesar has been used by Daniel Berrigan, Ernesto Cardenal, and Alan Boesak to address the oppression of nuclear proliferation, the oppression of Nicaragua under Somoza's rule, and the apartheid system of South Africa, respectively. Revelation is a cathartic text for Christians in oppressive system" (115–16). The Book of Revelation is certainly close to the heart of various Christian communities located in so-called Third World countries, but because of its ambiguous nature, the same text is also used in ways that are devastating in various geographical and political contexts, such as Haiti.

The typical reading of the Book of Revelation in Haiti offers nothing that empowers people to change the present. The usual scenario for interpreting the Book of Revelation in Haiti is that we are literally living at the end of time in our devastated country (Charles). As Christians, we need to live a life pleasing to God and not miss the call of the last trumpets to be caught up in the sudden rapture of the Church. The rest who did not live up to the biblical standards will be left behind. As for those who did not make it to heaven at the rapture, they are to endure the Great Tribulation and wait until the battle of Armageddon for the final victory of God. Then, those who resisted the Antichrist during the terrible years will be rescued by God and be saved through fire. Afterward, a thousand years of worldwide peace and security will be ushered in under the lordship and authority of Christ before the final release of Satan and the final victory of God. Woven into this narrative is the fantastic idea of leaving the mess behind, of going to glory to live a life of security and of plenty. Life, it is reasoned, is extremely difficult, and the best way out is to project oneself into a blissful kind of future. For most Haitian Christians, the Book of Revelation clearly evokes the final days of the world, the coming Antichrist, and the beast already at work in the world. It instills in the hearts of the faithful the fear of the evil number 666, the number of the enemy *par excellence*, that is Satan.[8]

The combat myth in the Book of Revelation is deployed in Haiti to combat the religion of Vodou, which many Haitian Christians consider the main curse that prevents Haiti from receiving God's blessings. Violent language against Vodou and its practitioners is a constant staple of the sermons delivered by many preachers (mostly Protestants). Many Vodou priests or *ougan* have been lynched, stoned, or burned alive, mainly shortly after the departure of the dictator Baby Doc in 1986, and those horrible acts were perpetuated with the blessings of the Church at large in Haiti. The Catholic Church in Haiti organized, with the acquiescence of the state, the horrific antisuperstitious campaign of 1942–44, which destroyed many Vodou places of worship and sites of pilgrimage (Desmangles; Michel and Bellegarde-Smith).

Many Haitian Christians, especially the so-called evangelicals, take a certain pleasure in pointing to the cataclysmic destruction that will befall unbelievers. Earthquakes and natural disasters are believed to be divine judgment, and those with different theological understandings are seen as deserving to go to hell. The world is conceived in Manichaean terms,[9] whereby those anointed to act as agents of God are good and the hypocrites, degenerates, Vodou practitioners, and other agents of Satan are evil. In Haiti, the combat myth is performed and articulated by othering Christian groups perceived to be different and by diabolizing other religions by means of discourses of fear, hatred, exclusion, and apocalyptic violence borrowed from the Book of Revelation.

Criticizing the Colonizing Reading in the Haitian Context

In the context of Haiti, the Book of Revelation becomes a pacifying power in a situation where one is concerned only with one's survival against everybody else. Overwhelming and pressing issues such as environmental degradation, famine, cholera, COVID-19, proliferation of gangs controlling vast regions in the capital city and elsewhere, innumerable numbers of young Haitians fleeing the country, many of them to die during the perilous voyage or brutally arrested to be sent back to Haiti empty-handed to face the social, economic, and political nightmares, all these are understood through the lens of "end times" theology. White American fundamentalists, especially those of a Southern Baptist stripe and Pentecostal fervor who harbor no complex social and political insights, support many Haitian Christian institutions in their lethargy and discourage them from speaking up and seeking truth and justice.

A plethora of so-called prophets ceaselessly broadcast apocalyptic pronouncements, some more sinister and dire than others. In the meantime, the mercantile class (a conglomerate of six oligarchic families who immigrated to Haiti a few generations back, namely the Brandt, Acra, Madsen, Bigio, Apaid, and Mevs families) control everything from customs to drugs, from banking to security, from energy to gangs (Plummer; Casimir). They are also supported by their multinational friends and operate under the approving gaze of the foreign embassies in Port-au-Prince. Those families control the sea and the air. They tolerate or even encourage violence, destruction, kidnappings, the demolition of all democratic institutions, as long as it all accrues to a political system that maintains the status quo.

The apocalyptic nature of the Book of Revelation has been used to promote a dualistic perspective whereby violence against the forces or agents of evil is deemed acceptable and the fatalities among God's people are celebrated as martyrs for the faith. Such a dualistic perspective is particularly dangerous in the sort of social and political system that prevails in Haiti. Following a scenario whereby the marginal groups take on the rulers in an eschatological and cosmic battle, as portrayed in the combat myth, uncritical Haitian readers can engage and indeed have engaged in violence against other groups perceived as the enemy. But the biblical narratives, one must remember, are about how the writers, creators, and editors of these texts understood and imagined their worlds and the place their deity played in the process of forming their own identities vis-à-vis the identities of others. These texts are products of specific spaces, times, worldviews, prejudices, dreams, nightmares, and hopes. They cannot be uncritically adopted to suit one's time and space, which is very different from the space–time frameworks of the biblical narratives. Most needed now are critical voices that envision a more empowering message coming out of the struggles and tradition of revolutionary resistance of the Haitian people, with a fresh understanding of how to be in the world and for the world as a Haitian Christian (Casséus). One egregious colonizing effect of the previously discussed reading of the Book of Revelation in Haiti is that it fosters fear and not hope. The mystery of the book is played out as if one were captive to the fate of this present world, and as if the only way out was escapism, violence, and the belief that it is God's will to survive life as a constant nightmare.[10]

Decolonizing the Book of Revelation in the Haitian Context

Reading to decolonize means taking the ideas regarding the Book of Revelation's original context and transferring them to the Haitian context while resignifying the text for the social, economic, and political liberation of the Haitian people. John's little communities existed in the margins of the power structure, where they were experiencing fear and apprehension.[11] The overall message of the Book of Revelation is that imagination and faith inspire other ways of tackling the practical problems of these marginalized groups. By renewing his audience's imagination, John aims to create an alternative reality to help his communities cope with the uncertainties of the present. The Book of Revelation is, in this sense, a call to resistance, to perseverance in times of persecution, and to faithfulness to God and to Jesus Christ. The Book of Revelation presents a critique of imperial power. It is a call to stand up against economic exploitation and to resist any political system of domination and of subjugation. The book offers a vision of Jerusalem descending from above to dwell with humans. Heaven is joined to earth since "here is the tent of God among human beings. He will make his home among them; they will be his people" (21:13).[12]

Christian churches in Haiti are caught up in endless debates about the end times, about identifying who the Antichrist might be, and looking at world events to figure out if the time of the rapture is close or not (Rossing). The Book of Revelation, however, presents a different vision: it is God who descends instead of people going up. In the Book of Revelation, the coming of God's kingdom is the advent of a social, public, and visible act of God expressed in markedly political terms here in history, on earth. The Seer's critique is a call to challenge political arrangements that accept violence as "business as usual." With the destruction of Babylon/Rome, wealth and peace come (21:22–26). Babylon is presented as a mirage; it is an empire of illusions; it is the tyranny of a fallen empire. The Seer envisions people drawn from all nations, tongues, and ethnic groups who would come to worship the Lamb (Rev. 7:9).

In rereading/resignifying the Book of Revelation in the Haitian context, Haitians need to understand that the number 666 should not lead to fear but to understanding how utterly foolish an empire of illusions is. The number 666 signifies total imperfection in a human system, truly and merely human and deficient, which will never attain seven, which expresses fulfillment and divine perfection. The empire of old, as the empire of today, is beastly and incomplete. Today's empire is under the absolute rule of the market, with its prison industrial complex and military systems, multinational corporations and tech giants that exercise control over the lives of many. The great Beast today is the political, military, and economic systems that constitute a threat to life and to the sustainability of the whole planet.

The Seer presents a vision in which "the sea was no more" (21:1). Rome is understood as transient, hence faith in a sovereign God's victory and in his promise to support the faithful is at the heart of the book. The call is to hope amid hopelessness and to be confident that God, and not the imperial regime, has the last word. The challenge is to resist, even when one's act of resistance might seem foolish before the might of the powerful forces that are against the small communities and the voices standing up against injustices. The Seer takes the risk of speaking up against power by using coded language to point to the ugliness of the empire. The image of the beast is alluring, seductive, offering as it does spectacles of violence, might, and technologies. But the marginalized communities may also perceive the destructive reality of bowing to a system of exploitation and of annihilation that values market commodities and profits at the expense of life.

The goal of resignifying the text is to let it speak comfort to the people of faith in Haiti so they can imagine, as the text intended for its first recipients, a new reality in opposition to the world of the present in its crisis. It is a vision of hope for Haiti and not destruction; a future, another possible world, where no one is left behind. Resignifying the Book of Revelation in the Haitian context is to let the text serve as a prophetic denunciation of those groups who hold power in Haiti and anybody who cooperates with them, including any Christians in Haiti who seek to benefit from it. Thus, the Book of Revelation can help the Christian church in Haiti articulate a political-religious resistance to any pretention to divinization that modern neocolonial forces wish to impose on us. This rereading of the text appropriates the voice of John in denouncing the pretensions of any power or system which places terror, injustice, lies, and extermination at the forefront. It is most urgent to embrace this new reading that prods us to invest in and improve the lives of the wretched of the earth, such as peasants, slum-dwellers, and the uneducated who constitute the bulk of church members in Haiti.

Haitians can use the rich social and cultural fabric of *konbit* (collective work in Haitian Creole, which makes the toil of one's farmland less onerous with the help of others) to foster human flourishing. Haitians can resignify the Book of Revelation in the same spirit that inhabited the community of the Seer by doing what Haitians love to do: laughing, singing, and dancing in the face of oppression (Taylor). Haitians can also use the resources of songs that celebrate life, find resources in Haitian folktales that make fun of evil, and continue to be inspired by the use of the carnivalesque, as we have much of it in the Book of Revelation, to ridicule any oppressive system and create safe and healthy communities.

This reimagining/resignifying will, I hope, help marginalized groups, whose voices are seldom heard in the arena of the world's political gurus, find the possibility to create liberative readings and liberative communities. This kind of decolonizing reading is intended to inspire Haitian faith communities to decide for themselves what they want to do in their struggle for justice, basic human rights, dignity, and emancipation with a piece of early Christian literature they consider sacred Scripture. This reappropriation of the text may allow us to let the text speak to us within our specific cultural, social, and political context without the deafening drumming of the powerful. The reading of Revelation proposed here offers hope for the apocalyptic situation in Haiti, not just for tomorrow, but also for today. We can take this reading and be empowered by it for social, political, and economic change in the present.

Conclusion: Then and Now

The Seer wrote his Apocalypse at a volatile time and space similar enough to the turbulent present Haiti that a comparison between the two social situations does not seem too farfetched. Because of the fragile situation of his communities, John employs the combat-myth scenario, where the marginal groups take over the rulers in an eschatological and cosmic battle, in order to empower his audience. In a new reading of Revelation in the Haitian context, some of the language used by John can be reappropriated to create a new reality, where the imagination is renewed for social change and justice to deal with present issues while planning for future development in the interests of all. The Book of Revelation is an ambiguous text; along with its problematic scenes of violence and destruction aimed at the perceived "enemy," it proclaims a liberating message of comfort and protest against the imperial forces of death; it aims to renew the readers' imagination to create beauty and hope in the midst of ashes. One may, then, appreciate and/or embrace its liberating potential for faith communities in Haiti while rejecting the cycle of emperors and counteremperors that the book seems to propose in its Christian mythmaking.

In the Haitian context, the Book of Revelation has been perversely interpreted to keep Haitian Christians and others under oppression. The mythical hope of the Book of Revelation, with its mythical and futuristic space where there will be "no need of sun or moon to shine on it, for the glory of God is its light, and its lamp is the Lamb" (21:23–24), is not even a metaphor or image in a nation where electricity is a luxury. The culture of death, as opposed to the celebration of life, is what the new imperial forces and their minions offer the "little peoples" of the world. Death engulfs Haiti, although there are a few feeble lights and signs of life here and there in the resiliency of my people, in the many ways we resist and negotiate a nightmarish existence. The Book of Revelation offers hope for a new humanity where there "was a great multitude that no one could count, from every nation, tribe, people and language, standing before the throne and before the Lamb. They were wearing white robes and were holding palm branches in their hands" (7:9). It is a vision of celebration of life and of vindication that Haitians can incorporate. But we also need to be prudent in what we adopt from the Seer and how we adapt it to our own social and political realities.

Part of the process of decolonizing the Bible as literature may be in envisioning a future without the Bible (Petrella). That is, as long as the Bible remains central in the construction of identities, spaces, myths of origins, histories, and genealogies, the possibility for it to be used as tool of colonization and violence remains a real possibility. The plurality of beliefs and the complexities of our world may be best addressed by trying to understand this world and its variegated scriptures than by focusing on one book. Bibliolatry may well be passé. The collapse of many modern economies and worldviews may be a warning sign that no genuine solutions aimed at human flourishing and dignity will be coming from any new exodus thinking, apocalyptic understanding, a particular religious text and tradition, or arrogant humanistic programs. That means that, on the one hand, running to the Bible in the pursuit of liberation is problematic, because the biblical text is a complex compilation of narratives with various answers or with no solutions to the problems we face today. But, on the other hand, grand pronouncements and narratives, political systems right or left with agendas that exclude many in the world fighting for survival, will not lead to liberation either. Decolonizing the Bible is a program that consists in learning and unlearning, in criticizing and of taking what may be useful, in collaging scriptures and traditions, in combating ideologies that are put in place to kill mentally, intellectually, and physically. This program of deconstruction and dismantling should not limit itself to the Bible, but must be pursued in such fields as classics, archaeology, economics, sociology, political science, history, medicine, religious studies, and other disciplines.

Notes

1. To reiterate the point, while the Bible has been used to endorse colonial projects and wage colonial violence, it has also been used to resist these applications in various ways by a variety of peoples. A decolonizing account points to hybridity and the ways in which people have entered into complex negotiations with the Bible that includes uses of the Bible for colonialism but also alternative readings to resist and reject colonization.
2. A similar discursive development occurred as well in Catholic Spanish and French colonies in the same period.
3. It may be that the audience of the Book of Revelation consists also some members capitulating to certain features of the Roman Empire, specifically participating in religious rites for the sake of economic gain in various associations (civic, cultic, professional, and trade), and that the text uses apocalypse as a genre to convince those who are compromising their identity to take up a different stance. See Friesen, 23–131; Harland.
4. See the now-classic definition of what constitutes an apocalypse in Collins, *Apocalyptic Imagination*. Collins defines an apocalypse as "a genre of revelatory literature with a narrative framework, in which a revelation is mediated by an otherworldly being to a human recipient, disclosing a transcendent reality which is both temporal, insofar as it envisages eschatological salvation, and spatial insofar as it involves another, supernatural world" (5).
5. The discussion on the dating of the Book of Revelation is enormous. One of the reasons for these heated scholarly debates is that the interpretation of the work is contingent on its dating. The majority views seem to locate the work during either the reign of Nero (54–68 CE) or the reign of Domitian (81–96 CE). The last years of Nero's reign seem to make more sense of the conflict with the empire as portrayed in the book. See Marshall.

6. One may also see that the work is functioning as a rhetorical exhortation urging people too comfortable amidst the local sacrificial edifice of imperial cities (i.e. in trades associations, for example) to leave off their participation and remove themselves and thereby end their integration with society. It does so in a way that challenges the audience with the tropes drawn from the Hebrew scriptures of idolatrous outsiders who are subject to God's judgment. As a rhetorical device, it creates profiles of heroes and villains to shore up a resistance that the author sees is entirely lacking except in a couple of instances mentioned in the seven messages (namely the messages to Sardis and Philadelphia), the second and sixth messages. There alone do we see the kind of resistance and persecution John champions.

7. The reason why economics figures so large in Revelation (chapters 13 and 18, as well as 19) is because the text aims to curtail economic participation. In that regard, it is precisely decolonizing of an economic system that exploits, and in which exploitation some of its audience is participating. At the end of the story, the kings of the earth bring their "glory" into a city where there is water without price and where all of the things that were used in Rev. 18 to exploit people economically have been transformed into a new city of justice.

8. This kind of reading is commonplace in other Third World contexts as well. The sociopolitical context of the Seer is abstracted into an allegory of the end times. Satan is in the economic details and the details of moral deficit that Christians have to fight against in order to ascend into glory. This reading is also applied to entirely exclusionary ends, such as to attack strong women or to curtail sexual and gender rights.

9. Mani (216–76 CE) was a religious prophet of Persian origin and a self-described apostle of Jesus Christ. The core of Manichaean belief is a strict call to an ascetic way of life (no sex, no wine, and no meat) and a revulsion against the material world. Mani taught his followers that there is an ongoing and cosmic struggle between light and darkness, and between good and evil. Evil is conceived as an eternal and powerful presence in the world; without vigorous exertion, people are not able to escape the grip of evil. The Manichaeans are taught to disentangle the good and the evil in their own lives and to return the good to its rightful place. They need to live in and for what is good while shunning what is evil and those who continually sin because they are trapped in the sphere of evil. For a recent and scholarly treatment on the topic, see Teigen.

10. Aimé Césaire's observation on how the power of the colonizer is perceived as divine will in some colonized settings and religious traditions is a very pertinent one. See his *Discourse on Colonialism*, 39–42.

11. They might have had a perceived fear and tension, which could have been far from actual reality. See Collins, *Combat Myth*.

12. It is worth noticing, however, that the Heavenly Jerusalem of Rev. 21 is purged of idolaters and sorcerers. There is no room in this city for dissent. Thus, even while showing the potential for a more liberative alternative, the lack of room for dissent in the image of heaven on earth points to a colonizing gesture embedded in the text.

WORKS CITED

Bellegarde-Smith, Patrick. *Haiti: The Breached Citadel.* Boulder, CO: Westview Press, 1990.

Bowens, Lisa M. *African American Readings of Paul: Reception, Resistance & Transformation.* Grand Rapids, MI: Eerdmans, 2020.

Casimir, Jean. *Haiti: A Decolonial History.* Translated by Laurent Dubois. Chapel Hill: University of North Carolina Press, 2020.

Casséus, Jules. *Pour une église authentiquement haïtienne: Essai d'introduction à une théologie chrétienne haïtienne.* Limbé, Cap Haïtien: Séminaire théologique baptiste, 1987.

Césaire, Aimé. *Discourse on Colonialism.* Translated by Joan Pinkham. New York: Monthly Review Press, 1972.

Charles, Ronald. "Interpreting the Book of Revelation in the Haitian Context." *Black Theology: An International Journal* 9.2: 177–98.

Collins, Adela Yarbro. *The Combat Myth in the Book of Revelation.* Missoula, MT: Scholars, 1976.

Collins, J. J. *The Apocalyptic Imagination.* Grand Rapids, MI: W.B. Eerdmans, 1998.

Desmangles, Leslie. *Faces of the Gods: Vodou and Roman Catholicism in Haiti.* Chapel Hill: University of North Carolina Press, 1992.

Dube, Musa W. "Christianity and Translation in Colonial Context: Inventing Globalization." In Elias Kifon Bongmba, ed., *Companion to Christianity in Africa.* New York: Routledge, 2015, 156–72.

Dube, Musa W., Andrew M. Mbuvi, and Dora Mbuwayesango, eds., "Colonized Bibles: Re-Reading the Colonial Translated Bibles," Part 3 of *Postcolonial Perspectives in African Biblical Interpretations.* Atlanta: Society of Biblical Literature, 2012, 157–99.

Farmer, Paul. *The Uses of Haiti.* Monroe, ME: Common Courage Press, 2003.

Friesen, Steven J. *Imperial Cults and the Apocalypse of John: Reading Revelation in the Ruins.* Oxford: Oxford University Press, 2001.

Frilingos, Christopher A. *Spectacles of Empire: Monsters, Martyrs, and the Book of Revelation.* Philadelphia: University of Pennsylvania Press, 2004.

Gerbner, Katharine. *Christian Slavery: Conversion and Race in the Protestant Atlantic World.* Philadelphia: University of Pennsylvania Press, 2018.

Goldenberg, David M. *Black and Slave: The Origins and History of the Curse of Ham. Studies of the Bible and Its Reception.* Berlin: Walter de Gruyter, 2017.

Harland, Philip A. *Associations, Synagogues and Congregations: Claiming a Place in the Ancient World.* Minneapolis: Fortress Press, 2003.

Hurbon, Laennec. *Comprendre Haiti: Essai sur l'Etat, la nation, la culture.* Paris: Karthala, 1987.

Religions et lien social: l'Eglise et l'Etat moderne en Haïti. Paris: Cerf, 2004.

Marshall, John W. *Parables of War: Reading John's Jewish Apocalypse.* Waterloo: Wilfrid Laurier University, 2001.

Mbuwayesango, Dora R. "Bible Translation in the Colonial Project in Africa and Its Impact on African Languages and Cultures." In R. S. Sugirtharajah, ed.,

The Oxford Handbook of Postcolonial Biblical Criticism. New York: Oxford University Press, 2018, ebook, n.p.

Michel, Claudine and Patrick Bellegarde-Smith, eds., *Vodou in Haitian Life and Culture: Invisible Powers.* New York: Palgrave MacMillan, 2006.

Petrella, Ivan. "Without the Bible: A New Liberation Theology." In Tat-siong Benny Liew and Fernando F. Segovia, eds., *Colonialism and the Bible: Contemporary Reflections from the Global South.* New York: Lexington Books, 2018, 251–70.

Pippin, Tina. "The Book of Revelation." In Elisabeth Schüssler Fiorenza, ed., *Searching the Scriptures, Vol. 2: A Feminist Commentary.* New York: Crossroad Press, 1994.

Plummer, Brenda Gayle "Between Privilege and Opprobrium: The Arabs and Jews in Haiti." In Ignacio Klich and Jeffrey Lesser, eds., *Arab and Jewish Immigrants in Latin America: Images and Realities.* London: Frank Cass, 1998, 80–94.

Rossing, Barbara R. *The Rapture Exposed: The Message of Hope in the Book of Revelation.* Boulder, CO: Westview, 2004.

Smith, Mitzi. *Insights from African American Interpretation: Reading the Bible in the 21st Century.* Minneapolis: Fortress Press, 2017.

Taylor, Patrick, ed. *Nation Dance: Religion, Identity, and Cultural Difference in the Caribbean.* Bloomington: Indiana University Press, 2001.

Teigen, Håkon Fiane. *The Manichaean Church in Kellis: Social Networks and Religious Identity in Late Antique Egypt.* Leiden: Brill, 2021.

Vaage, Leif E. *Roman Empire and the Rise of Christianity.* Waterloo: Wilfrid Laurier University Press, 2006.

CHAPTER 17

Decolonizing Literature
A History of Medicine Perspective

Sloan Mahone

The truth is that there are no races: there is nothing in the world that can do all we ask "race" to do.

(Appiah, "Uncompleted Argument")

Introduction

Tasked with representing a history of medicine perspective for a discussion of the decolonizing turns that have emerged within academia in recent years, I am prompted to reflect on a wide spectrum of personal and scholarly identities we may hold close. Our editors suggest that such a preoccupation with *decolonizing this* and *decolonizing that* has arrived quite late to the party. The postcolony has long been here, whether or not its presence is felt acutely everywhere or by everyone. And as is often the case, the inspiration to act against colonial constructions and residues in the curricula was spearheaded not by the Academy's bright stars, but by activist students in the Global South. This was followed by legions more in the Global North's elite institutions, which paradoxically (and stubbornly) held fast in the protection of the very same imperial icon in the form of a statue of Cecil John Rhodes. The Rhodes statue in Oxford and other colonial tributes continue to be overlooked by many as simply part of Oxford University's architectural landscape with an acknowledged, but not necessarily critiqued, colonial past. To many others, however, walking past such laudatory symbols has not merely been intellectually taxing but serves as a reminder of an unapologetic institutionalization of the lived experience of racism felt within both the city and the university.

This essay aims to engage with decolonizing turns within the history of medicine as a set of sources and as a discipline and will consider how such readings and pedagogical choices might help us reflect upon a decolonizing turn within the English literary curriculum. Literary sources intersect seamlessly with histories of medicine, science, disability, and emotion. However, it is still possible that history and literature as complementary but starkly different methodologies rarely reflect adequately on one's disciplinary borrowings from the other. This essay is an attempt to facilitate such a conversation and knowledge exchange. For my purposes, I define "literature" for the historian in a way that incorporates a broader range of "creative" writing, including ethnography, memoir, psychological or psychoanalytic note-taking, and polemics. There is some value in the extension of the literary beyond, say, the novel, but we might also reflect upon the emotional content of fiction properly historicized so that it might serve multiple purposes.

This reflection will focus on three brief case studies where insights might be gleaned from a greater dialogue between two fields; teaching "race" within the history of science and medicine; colonialism and medicine (psychiatry); and the historical and intellectual legacy of Sarah Baartman, a seminal life history that has been reproduced on countless syllabi. These case studies reflect some of my own (imperfect) experiences in teaching postgraduate-level students.

In the introduction to her groundbreaking book, *Decolonizing Methodologies*, Linda Tuhiwai Smith speaks to the embeddedness of images, speech, and symbols not only as stories from a racist past, but also as deeply entrenched modes of research and knowledge production. While we recognize and object to easily identifiable racist and dehumanizing language, there are many other ways one might speak of other, often-marginalized, groups that do not give us a moment's pause (Tuhiwai Smith 9). It is still common to find references to a "native" or a "tribe," of course, but we inscribe our witnessing of such anachronisms with the inverted comma. When we engage with the history of medicine specifically, our sources may also attempt to represent a *type* of person with deeply racialized images of sickness – the "leper," the "epileptic," the "schizophrenic." Not all of this language has disappeared, and to Tuhiwai Smith's point, we perpetuate such dehumanizing erasures in our own research methodologies and in our teaching. This is not a simple dynamic explained by White privilege only. Tuhiwai Smith relates her own experiences as an Indigenous researcher working with Indigenous communities and the ways in which local or nonlocal, or Western-educated or not, may present additional categories of insider and outsider (Tuhiwai Smith 14).

Today's Class Is about Race . . .

In 2020, Mark Hinton and Meleisa Ono-George coauthored an article that I had long been looking for. Their reflections on coteaching a course on "race" and racism (aimed at the legacies felt within British communities) marries a difficult challenge (teaching "race") with an even bigger challenge, employing an informed, actively antiracist pedagogy within the classroom (Hinton and Ono-George). Perhaps most importantly, the authors, alongside their students, attempt to "move [themselves] and others from a place of trying to be 'non-racist' to a place of active anti-racism" (716).

Hinton and Ono-George, who identify themselves as a White middle-class British man and a Black working-class woman, were inspired in their course design in part by the Rhodes Must Fall movement and efforts within the United Kingdom to "decolonize the curriculum." Their approach was experimental in asking the question "is it possible for the history of race and racism to be taught in such a way that is academically rigorous and transformative for the students and teachers?" (Hinton and Ono-George 717). For my own part, I felt a first step in this process was to begin to imagine what this might look like and ask how such an environment might differ from teaching practices I have employed or encountered in the past. An additional and essential part of this would be to own up to what might be lacking in reflections about how the teaching has gone. For me, a minor innovation was to include Hinton and Ono-George's article on a short reading list for a single class on "Race and Racisms" that sits within an eight-week module on overarching themes in the History of Science and Medicine.

Prompting students to consider their own positionality when engaging with both literary and historical texts highlights an often-overlooked tension in classrooms and on the syllabus. I have long been bothered by the problem of "we," that is, the suggestion that "we" must incorporate more diverse and marginalized voices, which, although unintended, creates in the mind a normative syllabus where "we" signals predominantly White Western voices as the natural point of departure. What might it mean, for instance, to begin with a "White" syllabus and then add the requisite number of non-White perspectives to decolonize an already-skewed construction? In history writing, we engage with primary sources, and the role of these sources within the curricula is to represent a problem. Within the history of colonial medicine and science, for instance, this might be a problem of scientific racism and knowledge production, or ideology embedded into medical treatises. Our goal is to read the politics and the oppression through the lenses of medicine, psychology, and science and divert the gaze back to colonial or other dominant frameworks born of corruption.

The publication of *The Bell Curve* (1994) is a case in point. The book itself exists within scholarship today as an artifact, a piece of material culture, that serves to illustrate the intractability of racially deterministic arguments well beyond the era of eugenics. However, the book's success in penetrating mainstream discourse as "scientific" was alarming enough when it was first published that it instigated a counterscholarship that mobilized expressly to respond to its spurious claims. Steven Fraser's edited volume, *The Bell Curve Wars* (1995) followed quickly on from the book, but in the post-Trump era, newer volumes have appeared to respond to more recent reverberations of the pernicious debate about race and intelligence (Staub; Fischer et al.). Students find some fascination in the history of eugenic thought, but they are not always prepared to recognize the cyclical nature of popularized racist science recast in languages that attempt to mask resurgent racist ideologies.

Engaging with travel and exploration narratives is a useful exercise here. These historical and literary sources frequently present ideas about the tropics, and by extension, the "tropical races" that inhabited them. Explorers' prose is unsurprisingly littered with the language of disease and death. Stephen Donovan asserts that despite the hardship and danger, the Congo was an important site developed for adventure travelers. "Congo tourism," he writes, "has its origins in a dense matrix of travel, imperialism, and textual representations" (Donovan 39). He notes, however, that the greatest inspiration for amateur travelers was not the thick tomes of Henry Morton Stanley or Richard Burton, but Conrad's *Heart of Darkness*. The Congo as a site of darkness and disease, of moral corruption, and a fecund backwardness is reflected in Conradian references that continue to appear in myriad forms today. Anthropology has made use of the "diseased heart of Africa" metaphor in deconstructing racist depictions of the continent (Comaroff 305–29), Francis Ford Coppola's *Apocalypse Now* remains a film masterpiece transplanting the tropes of "darkest Africa" to the horror of the Vietnam War, and one disastrous exhibition at the Royal Ontario Museum in Toronto, *Into the Heart of Africa* (Cannizzo), sparked years of protest after the exhibit, curated to be "ironic," was found by the city's Black community to be an overwhelmingly uncritical display of racist imagery (Burrett). The failed exhibit has become such a well-known cautionary tale in museum practice that it has an associated scholarship documenting the show and its aftermath.

Returning to Hinton and Ono-George's pedagogical lessons, they caution that "one of the dangers of teaching histories of race, and in particular of racial violence, without considering contemporary racism is that you can easily end up detaching these historic acts from their legacies in contemporary society and in the lived experiences of those in the classroom" (Hinton and Ono-George 717). Students are not unaware of the need for some reflection about positionality, but it is easy enough to lose sight of what this might look like in practice. Reading nineteenth-century depictions of Africa or other colonized spaces through the genre of travel writing can feel like a safe distance from modern experiences of racism. When we periodize these texts too rigidly, however, we might ask if we are in danger of overlooking some of the same racist tropes that appear in other forms of writing and in more modern periods. The skill to impart to students is to question disciplinary authority (history, anthropology, literature) by utilizing the skill set from one to critique the other. For example, one might look for well-established literary tropes – dripping with references to tropical rottenness – within modern political science.

Writing about a "slum" called Chicago in Abidjan, prominent author Robert Kaplan employs a language that recreates the imaginary of the rotting, dangerous, disease-ridden tropics:

> Chicago, like more and more of Abidjan, is a slum in the bush: a checkerwork of corrugated zinc roofs and walls made of cardboard and black plastic wrap. It is located in a gully teeming with coconut palms and oil palms and is ravaged by flooding. Few residents have easy access to electricity, a sewage system, or a clean water supply. The crumbly red laterite earth crawls with foot-long lizards both inside and outside the shacks. Children defecate in a stream filled with garbage and pigs, droning with mosquitoes. In this stream women do the washing. Young unemployed men spend their time drinking beer, palm wine, and gin while gambling on pinball games constructed out of rotting wood and rusty nails. These are the same youths who rob houses and more prosperous Ivorian neighborhoods at night. One man I met, Damba Tesele, came to Chicago from Burkina Faso in 1963. A cook by profession, he has four wives and thirty-two children, not one of whom has made it to high school. (10–11)

To my mind, this is a medical, or rather a pathological text. With a few alterations, we might be reading a nineteenth-century explorer's log, a Conradian passage of misery, or a neo-Malthusian plea for resurgent eugenics. We are transported to a "slum," and yet we are in the "bush." The environment *teems*, *crawls*, or is *ravaged*. Mosquitoes drone. There is no irony here, but a warning – the "coming anarchy" of African garbage, and pigs, and mosquitoes, and children. The disciplines of History and Literature work in concert to expose twenty-first-century ways of imagining Africa.

Feminist Literatures and Masculine Anxieties

Literary scholar Marilyn Booth tells the story of nineteenth-century feminist writer and activist Zaynab Fawwaz's efforts to collect and disseminate women's perspectives and literary works both locally and globally. Booth shows how Fawwaz challenged Western representations of Arab women as either sexual objects or silent by sending her 500-page Arabic-language volume of historical biographies of great women for inclusion in the "much publicized" women's library at the 1893 Chicago World Exhibition. According to Booth, the inclusion of Fawwaz's *Scattered Pearls among the Generations of Mistresses of Seclusion*, whether comprehended by visitors to the space or not, upends the Western imaginings of Egyptian women as the exotic belly dancers they were presented to be in Chicago (Booth 275). With tireless drive and commitment, Fawwaz paid equal attention to local gender politics through essays published in the nationalist press as well as two historical novels, one of which Booth contends is a "gendered rewriting of local history" (275). The "coy" renaming of the novel's protagonists suggest that there is little to differentiate the "historical novel" from the "historical chronicle" (279). Arab women wrote fiction as a means of rewriting the histories that excluded or misrepresented them. Arab feminists began to write themselves into the dynamic spaces of nationalist newspapers, which saw women as sources of disruption, with pieces on women's troubling presence in urban spaces, girls' education, and most pointedly a preoccupation with prostitution (276). The novels that Zaynab Fawwaz either wrote or helped to promote can be seen as acts of exposure of Arab men's anxieties about wayward women losing their morals and traversing into respectable spaces. Booth notes that Fawwaz "rewrites the trope of 'women's wiles'," depicting instead the more truthful knowledge of women who "know how to resist and thwart the violent acts of men" (291).

Fawwaz's extraordinary activism in responding to antifeminist agendas in the press allowed for a unique visibility that provided a platform for her first historical novel, *Good Consequences, or The Lovely Maid of al-Zahira* (1899). The novel included a preface that, Booth writes, included a "plea for the moral utility of fiction that was, she insisted, proximate to historical 'truth'" (278). Zaynab Fawwaz's intellectual life and work might appear well outside of the disciplinary interests of the history of medicine and science, and her work, despite her most expansive ambitions, also sits outside of the English-speaking world. However, once found, it is hard to ignore Fawwaz within this important period for feminist creativity and participation. If we turn our perspective slightly, Fawwaz's intervention in the Chicago World Exhibition, if considered not by her actions but by what such exhibitions would have expected from her, is a direct assault on the fetishizing and pathologizing gaze that scientific disciplines either sought to establish or already asserted to be true. Such exhibitions and World Fairs popularized anthropological and medicoscientific representations of (gendered) ethnic and (gendered) racial types. The objects normally associated with the exhibitions were carefully curated to conform to how Western audiences understood non-Western people, whether Congolese or Navajo. The insertion of an object of literary import and scholarship from an Arab feminist runs counter to our usual interpretations of such exhibits and engages scholars with new questions about how subalterns subverted the intended purposes of such displays.

Another writer, a feminist sister and journalist from the English literary canon, was similarly staking an intellectual claim against the conventional thinking of her time. Charlotte Perkins Gilman's *The Yellow Wallpaper* (1890) is heralded both as feminist tract and a fictionalized autobiographical account of mental ill health, brought on in part by the oppressive environment imposed on creative (all) women, by the expectations of society, by doctors, and by husbands. However, reading Gilman's short story *only* as a metaphor for hysteria or as an illness narrative is far less interesting than reading it alongside the one-page explanation she published in her own magazine years later. In *Why I Wrote The Yellow Wallpaper* (1913), published in *The Forerunner*, Gilman responds to a physician critic who claimed the text should never have been written and that it "was enough to drive anyone mad to read it" (Perkins Gilman 19–20). Gilman continues to explain that her nervous breakdown and melancholia from years earlier had prompted the advice of the "rest cure" with a strict admonishment to "never touch a pen, brush or pencil again as long as I lived." However, Gilman did write again, casting such advice "to the winds," she said, to produce a fictionalized account of the mental distress and hallucinations of a woman intellectually constrained by the men around her. In the first pages of *The Yellow Wallpaper*, it is modern medicine, dominated by men, that is implicated in her sickness, and this includes the oversight of her physician husband. Perhaps, she muses (secretly, telling only the "dead paper" in front of her) that *this* is the reason she does not get well faster.

Fawwaz and Gilman together, writing as contemporaries, subverted the dominant narratives produced by the times and spaces they lived in. When we read Fawwaz, or about her, we discover a counterimage to the colonial and Western constructed Arab woman's body and capacity. While the ethnographically distorted depictions of Congolese "pygmies," "Eskimos," and "Indians" have been critiqued already in a well-developed historiography, we might now look beyond the obvious racism of these displays to look also for the subversion of these depictions as an alternative way of reading the historical moment presented by this period of scientific categorizations of imperial subjects.

Charlotte Perkins Gilman wrote in direct opposition to one of the most prominent physicians of her time, neurologist Silas Weir Mitchell. She wrote with authority about the illness experience, however dramatized, and about the degradation caused by the sexism of modern medicine. Gilman was well aware that the treatment prescribed to her was an assault on her autonomy as a woman. Fawwaz does not write about illness or medicine in the same way, but she does make an appearance that challenges the narrative at a World Exhibition that would have been rife with depictions of the stability or capacity of non-Western people. Like Gilman, Fawwaz also comes up against the constant erasure of womanhood, which is the instigation behind her writing and the need to compile a 500-page tome attesting to the greatness of women. Both women wrote pointed critiques of sensational newspaper practices, with Gilman taking on the Hearst newspapers for their attacks on her personally and for the stance that all women's writing was presumptuous, if not monstrous (Edelstein 73).

These two writers (could they possibly have known about each other?) complement each other in dismantling the oppressive authority of male-dominated scientific knowledge and its false narratives around womanhood. They could do this most effectively through literature in its various forms. For the English Literary Curriculum, there is something to be gained by engaging familiar literary motifs as they were enacted within other disciplines in the medical or social sciences. This moves beyond the mere documentation of racist symbols to actively seek out how to read the existence of feminist writing as a subversion of racist science.

Writing, History, and Colonialism

The history of colonial psychiatry, a robust subfield in the history of medicine, has produced an extensive range of work on institutional, political, social, and intellectual histories that seek to unpack the largely political landscape that is laid bare when an analysis of the uses of psychological language takes place. Psychological profiles of whole populations (the African, the Indian, the native) provided an additional layer of rationale for occupation, and signaled how such regimes could be characterized as logical by the languages of science and medicine. In short, all racist regimes and institutions stack the deck. Superior guns are one way to do this. But the presumed superiority of the ruler built into a medicalized rationale for occupation might be more palatable to government in the metropole.

Colonial administrators pathologized not only African dissenting behaviors, but also oral or written expressions of discontent. They also noted what, and more importantly *how*, Africans read. Missionary-translated Bibles and prayer books were scrutinized by colonial police in Kenya to see which parts of Scripture were underlined, annotated, or reinterpreted by local prophets (Mahone, "Psychology of Rebellion" 254). Africans coopting the sacrosanct written word of the colonizer and daring to rewrite it suggested a kind of madness. At the very least, such inscriptions spelled trouble. Derek Peterson's monograph on the "creative writing" of African writers, translators, and bookkeepers details how Ngũgĩ wa Thiong'o himself was a Bible translator, providing new phraseology and meaning for the political context of Gikuyu freedom fighters going to the forests during the Mau Mau war (Peterson 228).

While there remains a great deal of historical scholarship that contextualizes how colonial regimes played the long game by hijacking scientific understandings of colonized peoples, there is something to be gained from the careful handling of the actual primary source as textual artifacts. I have seen a remarkable and quite visceral response from students when handling the material culture of colonialism even when they are already familiar with its content and language. As I have in my possession the influential tract *The Psychology of Mau Mau* (Colonial Office, 1954), I have passed around the document in its original pamphlet form. This report, largely self-plagiarized from psychiatrist J. C. Carothers's equally troubling World Health Organization monograph *The African Mind in Health and Disease* (1953), helped to lay the groundwork of the medical rationale for the mass internment of Kenyan men and women. The unexpected materiality of

colonialism within a history of medicine discussion provoked surprise at
the "realness" of this moment in history, but also a more reflective response
than the scholarship alone could provoke. The document itself is unre-
markable-looking. It is pamphlet-size, laid out in book format, and printed
on thin off-white pages. It consists of thirty-five pages of small typeface
with no illustrations or photographs. The front cover is adorned only with
the title, author, and colonial crest from the Colony and Protectorate of
Kenya. Reading about J. C. Carothers is a first port of call for the niche
market of historians of colonial psychiatry. The doctor's notorious comparison of African "normal" brains with the brains of lobotomized
Europeans appears time and again in the literature as an exemplar of racist
pseudoscience from this period.

     Reading Carothers in tandem with Frantz Fanon, who explicitly took on
the psychiatrist and his influence, exposes what exactly is at stake when
only the most powerful institutions control scientific knowledge, or as
Fanon might put it, when corrupt institutions develop scientific knowledge. The Carothers case brings forward much more than a gratuitous
racist diatribe. The dynamics of a public health study, a government-
commissioned report, a series of both positive and negative book reviews,
all portray the ease with which extremist ideas may be produced and
circulated. Fanon's polemical writings pass a bit too quickly over the
specifics of Carothers's dehumanizing rhetoric; nonetheless, Carothers
does appear within *The Wretched of the Earth* with Fanon's explicit attack
on the rising influence of the "East African School" (of psychiatry) and its
coopting of medical education and politics, both of which asserted the
lesser humanity of colonized people (Mahone, "Three Psychologies").
While historians of medicine have engaged with the scientific racism of
colonial governments by illustrating how such language was used to
rationalize imperial interests, the absurdity of colonial representations are
perhaps best expressed by literary sources. Flora Veit-Wild has highlighted
how African writers have exposed the "violence of colonial and postcolonial oppression and the absurdity of power" with the opposing "power of
the written word" (Veit-Wild 5). Fanon's polemical writings allow us to
engage with a decolonizing literary canon, while also observing an explicit
dialogue between a revolutionary and a colonial psychiatrist.

     While the history of psychiatry is now well represented by studies from
myriad former colonial territories, there is less attention paid to Black
intellectual life apart from resistances or protest movements. One such
author, who ought to be read more widely, is Noel Chabani Manganyi,
South Africa's first Black psychologist and a prolific essayist on the

experience of apartheid (among many other things). I came to know this writer only because a student opted to write an undergraduate thesis about him (Dalzell). Manganyi's first groundbreaking work, *Being Black in the World* (1973), resonates like *The Souls of Black Folk* for our global modern times. A memoirist as well as a social commentator, Manganyi, like Fanon, is a clinician, whose witness and testimony were a crucial part of the antiapartheid movement's intellectual and material resistance. His later memoir, *Apartheid and the Making of a Black Psychologist* (2016), is a testament and an important historical document in its own right. However, Manganyi's forays into literary criticism, biography (of Es'kia Mphahlele and Gerard Sekoto), and social commentary, *as a clinical psychologist*, places him into historical conversation with, and also an ability to critique, the psychiatrists we know from both ends of the political spectrum during the period of decolonization. There are interesting parallels to be found between Fanon and other writers' accounts of the psychic trauma of living under colonialism and Manganyi's accounts of the psychology of living not only under apartheid, but also in exile. In a 2002 interview, Manganyi describes the synergy between writing biography (a "written narrative") and the therapist's intervention. "Psychotherapy is a verbal narrative reconstruction. Both are enriched by and brought to life by the interpretations of the biographer and psychotherapist" (Manganyi in Ngwenya and Maganyi). Perhaps within the decolonizing turns in both history writing and the English literary curriculum, it is time to privilege the textual contributions of these writers in order to highlight not only what they subverted, but also what they accomplished despite the colonizing structures that surrounded them.

(Mis)(re)interpretations of the Sarah Baartman Story

The tragic story of Sarah Baartman has been told and retold. It has been made visual and has been dramatized. I have long used Baartman's story in my own teaching as a way to expose how the historical racisms associated with Baartman's treatment are not frozen in time in the nineteenth century but still resonate deeply today. The continued relevance of Sarah Baartman is expressed in multiple historiographical and literary forms. More recent writing supplants the retelling of her biography with analysis of how the "theoretical industry" that has developed around her has created problems and misinterpretations anew.

For my own early engagement with Baartman, I was struck by a series of pertinent dates; 1810, 1974, 1985, 2002. In 1810, Sarah Baartman was brought to London to be exhibited as the "Hottentot Venus." More than a century-and-a-half later in 1974, her skeleton, long displayed with a body cast and her genitalia, was finally removed from public display at the Musée de l'Homme in Paris. In 1985, an influential essay by historian Sander Gilman gave a heavily psychological interpretation of the fascination with her sexualized body in the form of a lengthy article in *Critical Inquiry*. And in 2002, Sarah Baartman's remains were repatriated for burial and a memorial in her homeland, the result of years of activism and a formal request by Nelson Mandela.

Andrew P. Lyons refers to "much controversy" over the right to finally tell Baartman's story in his 2018 article in *Anthropologica*. His review is an attempt to disentangle why this contested narrative has unfolded in the way that it has. Lyons helpfully traces the multi-disciplinary "second life" of Baartman literature with (post Sander Gilman) studies from history, anthropology, sociology, creative writing, feminist studies, and filmmaking (Lyons 327–28). Lyons notes, as have others, that factual details about Baartman's early life (including her original name) and the nature of her physical appearance are either unknown or contested. He notes also that her personal agency and "who has the right to describe her career" also require contextualization, particularly in light of what has been termed an "ethnopornography" – the familiar body of literature that seeks to encapsulate whole ethnicities or cultures or peoples within a series of dehumanizing tropes, representations, and discourses (Lyons 328). The wealth of academic literature on Baartman's (and Khoisan) sexuality is perhaps matched only by the historiographical treatment of the creation of the "Hottentot Venus" caricature and the subsequent zeal to market her as a traveling exhibition. While Sarah Baartman, and Ota Benga, who was famously exhibited in a chimpanzee enclosure in the Bronx Zoo, exemplify the exploitation of notable individuals in sideshows and pseudoscientific colonial exhibitions, human displays remain a popular research topic in the history of science and medicine, particularly as a material culture engagement with the enormous volume of racist ephemera they produced in the form of exhibition posters, advertisements, and political cartoons.

The subject of Baartman's agency within the circumstances of her exploitation is harder to glean. Zine Magubane, a sociologist, takes on what she sees as the overreliance on historical sources that focus on Baartman's racialized body and sexuality. This turn, beginning with Gilman's broader interests in representations and difference, has become the dominant scholarly trope for Baartman studies over the years. Ironically, this discourse scholarship has become its own discursive trap and has in some ways perpetuated the dominance of the racist imagery attached to her, overshadowing more nuanced interpretations of Baartman's short life. Sander Gilman's interpretation of the symbolic import of Baartman's story has been, according to Magubane, the "genesis for a veritable theoretical industry" (Magubane 817). Magubane calls for a deeper reflection from scholars who, while uncovering the racism behind nineteenth-century depictions of Baartman's "difference," have themselves focused almost entirely on the very same bodily fascinations of pseudo-scientists and sideshow gawkers (Magubane 817). Magubane's most compelling insight is that the misplaced focus that conflates the life of Baartman with the reception of her imagery has failed to ask pertinent questions about politics, social relations, and geographic context, thus placing Baartman "outside history" and with a status as "theoretically fetishized" (Magubane 818).

Magubane asks "why this woman?" Why should Sarah Baartman become the scholarly icon for "racial and sexual alterity" when many thousands of men and women (and children) were exhibited in fashionable displays of European modernity in contrast to the primitive? The wealth of tantalizingly awful visual sources, from cartoons to plaster casts, have helped to obscure the nuances of Baartman's daily existence, her subjugations, resistances, and performances. It is far more surprising that Baartman appeared not in exhibitions, but in the courtroom. Baartman's biographies are rarely microhistories in themselves. Some creative attempts at depicting her agency in the form of theatrical productions have had to speculate on the finer details of her life and thought, but these depictions, while attempting to right a wrong, also have their own agendas and points of view.

When and how we might teach about Baartman's life and legacy has become the subject of reflection and debate. The emotional impact of the frequent reproduction of Baartman's imagery has brought to the fore new writing in history and literary criticism about positionality, perspective and privilege. Natasha Gordon-Chipembere and others have refused to display or republish the colonially produced images of Baartman that are so easily available and familiar (Lyons 335; Gordon-Chipembere, *Representation* 5). Baartman's image (or rather her exploitative and distorted image) appears in teaching slides and research presentations, the purpose of which is to highlight the scientific racism behind the creation of such illustrations. The end result is that these images remain in circulation and subvert efforts to point out how racist images circulated *in the past*. Gordon-Chipembere's analysis extends to literary attempts to retell Baartman's story through the novel, such as Barbara Chase-Riboud's *Hottentot Venus* (2003). However, this fictionalized reimagining depicts Baartman herself referring to her own "huge hips and buttocks," recreating the colonial narrative about Baartman's body and further diminishing her voice (Gordon-Chipembere, *Representation* 6).

My own use of a well-known cartoon illustration of Baartman in a teaching lecture on "race" within the history of medicine was intended to challenge the notion that nineteenth-century abuses may be neatly contained within an identifiable racist past. Assigned readings include critiques of earlier historiographical accounts of Baartman, but perhaps most important is the ensuing discussion about what it might mean that viciously racist displays of genitalia and body image should remain intact as late as the 1970s or that the request for a repatriation of Sarah Baartman's body for burial was the subject of any debate whatsoever. Zine Magubane asserts that Baartman's curious "theoretical odyssey" exemplifies the dangers of applying theory without historical specificity. In Gilman's case, this is an exercise in privileging an overriding human propensity to see the world in terms of iconography and stereotypes including those of sexualized Black women (Sander Gilman 204–42). In his *Critical Inquiry* piece, "Black Bodies, White Bodies: Toward an Iconography of Female Sexuality in Late Nineteenth-Century Art, Medicine, and Literature," Gilman reproduces six images of either a nearly nude Sarah Baartman or associated scientific drawings of "Hottentot" genitalia.

The sheer expanse of Baartman scholarship and creative output has prompted reflection and critiques from myriad perspectives and disciplines. Ayo Coly, writing in 2019, asks: "What is at stake in continuing to extend hospitality to the specter of Baartman, especially when she has been laid to rest and mourned properly?" (Coly 183). Coly's project engages with the many claims and debates about what is "at stake" in finally letting go when perhaps, as Natasha Gordon-Chipembere asserts, Baartman's story with all of its (even well-meaning) misreadings, speaks for itself, not as a symbol but as a tale of a Khoisan woman whose life was deeply marred by colonial intent (Gordon-Chipembere, "Intentions"). Within the History of Medicine, Baartman's story is still largely one of symbolism and display. The problems with some historical narratives of Baartman's life have been answered by fictional accounts, but these too have found it hard to know Baartman without a recreation of her bodily image. Two decades have now passed since Baartman has returned home for a proper burial. We may yet hope to reveal an end to the long story of a short life.

The melding of historical and literary voices in methodological partnership allows for a greater understanding of how to read through the symbols, silences, and absences that appear within the imperfect texts we work with. The symbols and stereotypes of race science, collective psychology, and ethnological and commercial exhibitions can be interrogated well beyond the images they conjure up. The literary curriculum might have something to gain by engaging with the historical specificities of the medical and psychological frames that would have governed historical actors' lives.

BIBLIOGRAPHY

Appiah, K. Anthony. "The Uncompleted Argument: Du Bois and the Illusion of Race." *Critical Inquiry* 12.1 (1985): 21–37.

Booth, Marilyn. "Fiction's Imaginative Archive and the Newspaper's Local Scandals: The Case of Nineteenth-Century Egypt." In Antoinette Burton, ed., *Archive Stories: Facts, Fictions, and the Writing of History*. Durham, NC: Duke University Press, 2006, 274–95.

Burrett, Deborah. "'Into the Heart of Africa': Curatorship, Controversy, and Situated Knowledges." In Barbara Gabriel and Suzan M. Ilcan, eds., *Post-Modernism and the Ethical Subject*. Montreal: McGill-Queen's University Press, 2004, 125–45.

Cannizzo, Jeanne. *Into the Heart of Africa: Exhibition Program*. Toronto: Royal Ontario Museum, 1989.

Carothers, J. C. "The African Mind in Health and Disease." World Health Organization, 1953.

Carothers, J. C. "The Psychology of Mau Mau." Colonial Office, 1954.

Chase-Riboud, Barbara. *Hottentot Venus*. New York: Doubleday, 2003.

Coly, Ayo A. "Haunted Silences: African Feminist Criticism and the Specter of Sarah Baartman." In Ayo A. Coly, ed., *Postcolonial Hauntologies: African Women's Discourses of the Female Body*. Lincoln: University of Nebraska Press, 2019.

Comaroff, Jean. "The Diseased Heart of Africa." In Shirley Lindenbaum and Margaret M. Lock, eds., *Knowledge, Power, and Practice: The Anthropology of Medicine and Everyday Life*. Berkeley: University of California Press, 1993, 305–29.

Dalzell, Sara. "The Psychology of Racial Oppression: Apartheid through the Writings of N. Chabani Manganyi." Undergraduate thesis, University of Oxford, 2021.

Donovan, Stephen. "Touring in Extremis: Travel and Adventure in the Congo." In T. Youngs, ed., *Travel Writing in the Nineteenth Century: Filling the Blank Spaces*. London: Anthem Press, 2006.

Edelstein, Sari. "Charlotte Perkins Gilman and the Yellow Newspaper." *Legacy* 24.1 (2007): 72–92.

Fanon, Frantz. *The Wretched of the Earth*. 1961. New York: Grove, 1963.

Fischer, Claude S., Michael Hout, Martín Sánchez Jankowski, Ann Swidler, and Kim Voss. *Inequality by Design: Cracking the Bell Curve Myth*. Princeton, NJ: Princeton University Press, 2021.

Fraser, Steve. *The Bell Curve Wars: Race, Intelligence, and the Future of America*. New York: Basic, 1995.

Gilman, Charlotte Perkins. "Why I Wrote The Yellow Wallpaper." *The Forerunner* (October 1913).

Gilman, Sander L. "Black Bodies, White Bodies: Toward an Iconography of Female Sexuality in Late Nineteenth-Century Art, Medicine, and Literature." *Critical Inquiry* 12.1 (1985): 204–42.

Gordon-Chipembere, Natasha. "'Even with the Best Intentions': The Misreading of Sarah Baartman's Life by African American Writers." *Agenda: Empowering Women for Gender Equity* 68 (2006): 54–62.

Gordon-Chipembere, Natasha. *Representation and Black Womanhood: The Legacy of Sarah Baartman*. Basingstoke: Palgrave Macmillan, 2011.

Hinton, Mark and Meleisa Ono-George. "Teaching a History of 'Race' and Anti-Racist Action in an Academic Classroom." *Area* 52.4 (2020): 716–21.

Kaplan, Robert D. *The Coming Anarchy: Shattering the Dreams of the Post-Cold War*. New York: Vintage Books, 2001.

Lyons, Andrew P. "The Two Lives of Sara Baartman: Gender, 'Race,' Politics and the Historiography of Mis/Representation." *Anthropologica* 60 (2018): 327–46.

Magubane, Zine. "Which Bodies Matter? Feminism, Poststructuralism, Race, and the Curious Theoretical Odyssey of the 'Hottentot Venus'." *Gender & Society* 15.6 (2001): 816–34.

Mahone, Sloan. "The Psychology of Rebellion: Colonial Medical Responses to Dissent in British East Africa." *The Journal of African History* 47.2 (2006): 241–58.

"Three Psychologies of Mau Mau." Africa Is a Country, June 10, 2021. https://africasacountry.com/.

Ngwenya, Thengani H. and N. Chabani Manganyi. "'Making History's Silences Speak': An Interview with N. C. Manganyi, 5 March 2002, University of Pretoria." *Biography* 26.3 (2003): 428–37.

Peterson, Derek R. *Creative Writing: Translation, Bookkeeping, and the Work of Imagination in Colonial Kenya*. Portsmouth, NH: Heinemann, 2004.

Staub, Michael E. *The Mismeasure of Minds: Debating Race and Intelligence between Brown and The Bell Curve*. Chapel Hill: University of North Carolina Press, 2019.

Tuhiwai Smith, Linda. *Decolonizing Methodologies: Research and Indigenous Peoples*. London: Zed Books, 2012.

Veit-Wild, Flora. *Writing Madness: Borderlines of the Body in African Literature*. Oxford: James Currey, 2006.

PART IV

Canon Revisions

CHAPTER 18

Decolonizing the Medieval Literary Curriculum

Geraldine Heng

> Not a single tea plantation exists within the United Kingdom. [Tea] is
> the symbolization of British identity – I mean, what does anybody in
> the world know about an English person except that they cannot get
> through the day without a cup of tea? Where does it come from?
> Ceylon/Sri Lanka, India. That is the outside history that is inside the
> history of the English. There is no English history without that other
> history.
>
> Stuart Hall, "Old and New Identities, Old and New Histories,"
> *Essential Essays: Identity and Diaspora*

The call to decolonize the teaching of premodernity – and especially the
European Middle Ages – has assumed increasing urgency lately. As everyone knows, White supremacist and alt-right groups in the United States
and Europe have in recent years aggressively weaponized the symbols,
histories, material culture, and expressive culture of the European
Middle Ages – so as to build a fantasied past of White racial purity and
superiority, prelapsarian Christian homogeneity and harmony, and
a religiopolitical supremacy that, for these extremists, characterized premodern Europe (Christendom/the Latin West) – in order to make their
version of the past the basis of authority for reproducing the past anew in
today's world (see, e.g., Kim, Miyashiro, Rambaran-Olm, Perry).

From the deployment of symbols such as the Nordic god Thor's
hammer and the imperial eagle of the Holy Roman Empire to the celebration of medieval Crusades (the crusader cry, "Deus Vult," or "God Wills
It," has found new popularity in the twenty-first century) and the eleventh-
century settler colonization of North America by Greenlanders and
Icelanders ("Hail Vinland!" has nearly replaced "Heil Hitler"), right-
wing extremist groups increasingly marshal the cultural legacies of premodern Europe to awaken a specific strain of fantasied nostalgia for the
past among majority-White populations, so as strategically to mobilize,
channel, and direct public emotions toward militancy and violence in their

drive to claim, and reenact, the putative glories and triumphs of the Christian West.

Christian extremist and White supremacist movements thus ironically parallel Islamist and Salafist groups such as Al-Qaeda, the so-called Islamic State, Al-Nusra Front, and others, who are themselves also strategically recalling the past, to urge a renewal of the early days of the Islamic empire under the Prophet Muhammad and the Rashidun (the first four rightly guided caliphs), in order to recreate the seventh-century Islamic Caliphate in the twenty-first century. Islamist nostalgia of this kind is equally alive and virulent in draconian state-sponsored sociopolitical cultures like Saudi Arabia's and Iran's, and that animates Turkey's Recep Tayyip Erdoğan's devout desire for an Islamist new Ottoman empire of the twenty-first century.

Concomitant with the resurgence of populist extremism, however, are important counterforces.

Among these are the changing population demographics of twenty-first-century societies in the West (these changes being themselves a trigger for White extremism) – transformations that are, in turn, responsible for new and transformed demographics of current and emerging cohorts of students in higher education. Like the societies in which they live, contemporary cohorts of students in higher learning have diversified substantially in terms of their race, class, countries of origin, sexualities and genders, and physical, cultural, and psychosocial composition. And students, more than faculty, are among those who have called for curricular transformations responsive to the exigencies of the day.[1]

Medieval studies, an academic field once considered sleepy and "ornamental" by some – a field that has been diagnosed as urgently requiring decolonization because of its entrenched conservatism – has thus been experiencing a wake-up call on several fronts.[2] In spring 2021, the University of Leicester in the United Kingdom announced an administrative decision to cut medieval authors from its English curriculum altogether, as part of an attempt to decolonize the university's curricular offerings – a process that renders the university's medievalists in English obsolete and jobless.[3] Suddenly, premodernists who were ignoring sociocultural and political exigencies in the societies where they live and work began to pay attention – because now, it seems, their jobs may be coming undone.

Some premodernists, however – primarily led by those who are part of the antiracist collective, the Medievalists of Color, and allied groups and individuals – have been undertaking the critical teaching of the past now for some years. I have taught a critical canon, and a countercanon, for nearly three decades. In 1994 – long before September 11, 2001 – I began the critical teaching of the so-called holy wars known as the Crusades, followed by premodern critical race courses, courses in critical early global studies, and courses aimed at countering anti-Semitism and Islamophobia. The work I undertake is, of course, contested (see Heng, "Why the Hate," "On Not Reading," and "Before *Race*").

Another example of such teaching is Dorothy Kim's "Toxic Chaucer," a course on the dead White male dubbed the Father of English Literature, and one that confronts head-on the racism, Islamophobia, misogyny, anti-Semitism, coloniality, and classism visible in the Chaucerian corpus.[4]

The pedagogical trajectories, strategies, and curricular offerings I focus on below are thus best seen as distillations and summaries of the kind of work undertaken today by a number of us in a dispersed community of largely premodernists of color working to teach a decolonizing curriculum, a community whose members are profoundly engaged in transforming how the deep past is taught and studied in the twenty-first century academy.

A *decolonizing curriculum* is a term that fittingly captures the *en procès* character of the evolving, unfinished pedagogy we undertake. Given that varieties of neocolonialism around the world today are coterminous with and comfortably complicit with postcolonial regimes and conditions, the lesson that decolonizing is a process *sans fin* – a process that of necessity remains open-ended, urgent, and unfinished – is a lesson that is rapidly, if grimly, learnt.

A decolonizing *medieval* curriculum is also necessarily *en procès* – in process and on trial, subject to testing, revision, adaptation, and transformation as needed. Keeping in mind the volume's focus on *English* literature, my essay will address the challenges of teaching a critical canon in a decolonizing curriculum that concentrates on English and a few European texts. It will conclude with a coda on countercanonical teaching that decenters Europe altogether by introducing students to a premodern globalism and its literatures that are scarcely cognizant of Europe's existence at all.

A Critical Canon: Teaching Race, Empire, Class, Gender, and Sexuality in English and European Medieval Literature

I have argued in *The Invention of Race in the European Middle Ages* and elsewhere that international wars and territorial invasions, slavery and human trafficking, transnational migrations, trade and commerce, pilgrimage, colonization, settlement, all bear witness to a medieval Europe that contained people from everywhere – Jews, Arabs, Turks, "Gypsies," Africans, Indians, Mongols, steppe peoples and others – and an encounter with the historical and cultural archives of the European Middle Ages refuses the fiction that a singular, homogenous, communally unified Caucasian ethnoracial population existed in an early Europe that was still Latin Christendom. The notion that an all-White Europe existed as a historical *fact* – and not as a *fiction* manufactured by centuries of assiduous identity construction – is thus a fantasy of contemporary politics and political factions in the West.

Bioarcheology attests that even in the far northwestern corner of the medieval Latin West, in insular England, there was a sizable population of non-White people. In their pathbreaking study "'Officially Absent, but Actually Present': Bioarcheological Evidence for Population Diversity in London during the Black Death, AD 1348–50," Rebecca Redfern and Joseph T. Hefner's meticulous analysis of genomic and biomorphic evidence from the graves of the interred in an East Smithfield cemetery in London during the plague years of 1348–1350 finds that fully 29 percent of those interred had African, Asian, or Afro-Eurasian ancestry.

Any teaching of race in texts from the long centuries of the European Middle Ages should thus begin by unmasking the fantasy of an all-White West in an early Europe that was supposedly the opposite of Europe today, a continent containing global populations from everywhere and a diversity of faiths. A variety of archives offer ample evidence.[5]

For instance, medieval archives attest that *Jewish communities* existed in virtually every country of Europe, intimately ensconced in cities and towns of the heartlands of Christendom (*Invention of Race*, chapter 2). *Islamicate settlements* in Andalusian Iberia and southern Italy and Sicily give the lie to the pretense that Muslims in Europe are a recent phenomenon (*Invention of Race*, chapter 3). *Black Saharan Africans* were seemingly everywhere in the European Middle Ages – in Roman Britain and medieval England, post-invasion Al-Andalus, in the Holy Roman Emperor Frederick II's Lucera in Italy, all around the Mediterranean, and according to the abbot of Nogent-sur-Coucy, the crusade historian Guibert, even in northern France (*Invention of Race*, chapter 4).

The diaspora of the *Romani* ("Gypsies") from northwestern India in the eleventh century spread a dark-skinned race of *Asians* across the face of western Europe. In southeastern Europe, especially Wallachia and Moldavia – territorial polities that later joined to become Romania in

1859 (with Transylvania added at a later date) – Romani became enslaved and supplied servile labor for the monasteries and the boyars, and "Gypsy" became the name of a slave race, till they were finally manumitted in the nineteenth century (*Invention of Race*, chapter 7).

Human trafficking, a flourishing trade undertaken by many medieval peoples, and at which the Italian republics particularly excelled, also ensured the dispersal of a variety of ethnoraces – Turks, Africans, Arabs, Mongols, Indians, and others – as domestic, military, and commercial labor around the Mediterranean. Reading the archive of slavery, we see that even so-called White Christian Europeans fail to be homogenously "White" people: because young female enslaved persons of all races, deployed predominantly as domestic labor and intruded into households – as historians have repeatedly demonstrated – furnished sexual recreation for their masters and bred new, mixed races.

Higher prices paid for young females of reproductive age, and their disproportionate representation in the slave markets and records of sale, over males, means that an unfathomable number of today's "White" Europeans (including those White supremacists themselves) have descended from inter-mixed human DNA, so that future generations of ostensibly White Europeans were less than White (*Invention of Race*, chapter 3).

Scientists have even discovered shared DNA between Native Americans and Icelanders. Among all the ethnoracial groups in the world, the C1e gene element is only shared by Icelanders and Native Americans, a discovery that will not surprise those who teach the *Saga of Eirik the Red* – one of two surviving Vinland sagas narrating the failed settler colonization of the North American continent half a millennium before Columbus – which tells of the abduction of two Native boys by Greenlanders and Icelanders who, after their defeat by the Native population, forcibly take the Indigenous children back to Europe, teach them Norse, and Christianize them (*Invention of Race*, chapter 5).

Any critical teaching of premodernity must needs recognize that *religion* forms the magisterial discourse and knowledge system of the medieval period – just as *science* forms the magisterial discourse and knowledge system of modern eras – and supplies the formative matrix of race-making in the long centuries of the European Middle Ages. The teaching of medieval literature thus needs an understanding of race that is apposite for the period, and a minimum working hypothesis such as this one:

> Race is one of the primary names we have – a name we retain for the epistemological, ethical, and political commitments it recognizes – for

a repeating tendency, of the gravest import, to demarcate human beings through differences among humans that are selectively essentialized as absolute and fundamental, so as to distribute positions and powers differentially to human groups. Because race is a structural relationship for the management of human differences – a mechanism of sorting, for purposes of prioritizing and hierarchizing – rather than a substantive content, the differences selected for essentialism will vary in the *longue durée* of human history, from the premodern eras well into late modernity and the twenty-first century: fastening on bodies, physiognomy, and somatic differences in some instances; on social practices, religion, or culture in other instances; or a multiplicity of interlocking discourses elsewhere.

Racial thinking, racial acts, racial laws, racial institutions, and racial phenomena emerge across a range of registers and crucibles of instantiation in the medieval period: invasion and occupation, nation formation and state formation, political theology, the imperatives of mercantile capitalism, holy war, settler colonization, economic adventurism, empire formation, contact and encounter, slavery, the consolidation of universal Christendom, and epistemological and epistemic change.

Eyewitness crusade chronicles, and accounts of Pope Urban II's address at the Council of Clermont in 1095, supply ample invasion-and-occupation narratives for in-class analysis of how Muslims were racialized. Robert the Monk's report of Urban's address offers up Muslims as an abominable, polluting, infernal race poisoning the Holy Land, torturing and eviscerating Christians, raping women, forcibly circumcising men, and defiling church altars and baptismal fonts with the blood of the victims. In fact, Robert's account is precisely where the rallying cry of the pilgrim militia of the First Crusade – and popularly parroted today by White extremists – is recorded: *Deus vult!* God wills it! (*Invention of Race* 114).

The late eleventh-century racialization of an enemy in the killing fields of war births a panoply of twelfth-century ways to dehumanize enemy combatants. St. Bernard of Clairvaux, who cowrote the Rule of the Knights Templar, reassured those who might feel ambivalence toward the killing of fellow humans – an act so contrary to the commandments and teaching of Christ – that to kill a Muslim was not, in fact, to kill a fellow human. Rather than constitute *homicide* – the murder of a person – slaughtering a Muslim was really *malicide*, the extermination of incarnated evil. Muslims were not only unspeakably vile, abominable, and accursed, as Urban had said; they were not to be seen as human at all, but as personified evil. In his tract *In Praise of the New Knighthood*, St. Bernard thus saw no difficulty in calling for genocide to extirpate from the earth these enemies of the Christian name (*Invention of Race* 115).

Religioracial strategies exercised against Muslims ingeniously herded a multiplicity of Near Eastern, Eurasian, and Asian peoples into a single collectivity defined by their religion, Islam, and characterized Islam as founded on lies, with its founding figure of the Prophet as the ultimate liar and heresiarch.

Although a number of names existed for the international enemy that Latin Christendom fought – Ishmaelites or Ismaelites, Agarenes or Hagarenes, Moors, Turks, Arabs, Persians, Ottomans, Mohammedans, or, more pejoratively, infidels, heathens, pagans, and even heretics – the preeminent name by which the enemy was known in the Latin West for centuries was *Saracens*.

A word of Greco-Roman origin that in late antiquity referred to pre-Islamic Arabs, *Saracens* streamlined a panorama of peoples – of diverse geographic origins, linguistic communities, and ethnoracial affiliations – into a single demographic defined by its adherence to Islam alone. To the Christian authors of the West, Islam thus became an essence-imparting machine that conferred essential identity. Made over into an instrument of essentialism, Islam raced all Muslim believers into a singular, homogenous whole.[6]

I point out to students – to show them how the past is never completely past but inhabits and troubles the present, rendering the present nonidentical to itself – how the medieval racialization of Islam rapidly reemerged in the twenty-first century, after 9/11, when airport security checkpoints, Western political leaders, and public discourse *again* began treating Muslims – of all races, nationalities, and linguistic communities – as a singular, undifferentiated whole once more.

The medieval racing of a heterogeneity of Muslims as *Saracens* also embedded a lie at the heart of the raced identity. The name *Saracens* is first used by St. Jerome (347–420 CE), the church father who says Arabs took for themselves the name of *Saracens* in order falsely to claim a genealogy from Sara, the legitimate wife of Abraham, to hide the shame that their true mother, Hagar, was a bondwoman. Islam's arrival in the seventh century and its rapid succession of territorial conquests then induced a ramification of the fake etymology: Muslims now, not just Arabs, became *Saracens*.

Attributing the name "Saracens" *to* the enemy, as a sly act of self-naming *by* the enemy, is thus not only an ingenious lie, but a lie that ingeniously names the enemy as wily liars, in the very act of naming them as enemies.

Herding diverse populations into a single race defined as originating a collective lie, Christian political theology turned on a panoply of lies that aggregated the racial character of Muslims as a collectivity of liars. Half a millennium later, in the nineteenth century, we see Muslims *still* bearing the name of liars, *Saracens*, in Walter Scott's *The Talisman*.

"Saracens" are everywhere in medieval literature. In English literature, they are depicted as bloody, ruthless, and homicidal, like the mother of the "Sultan of Syria" in Chaucer's *Man of Law's Tale* in the *Canterbury Tales*, who has everyone slaughtered because her son wants to marry a Christian princess (Heng, *Empire of Magic*, chapter 4). They are also monstrous Black giants who battle Charlemagne and his elite Twelve Peers in romances such as the Middle English *Sultan of Babylon*, and in the French epic genre known as the *chanson de geste*.[7]

Medieval romance, the foremost narrative genre of the European Middle Ages, is rife with "Saracens." If they are targets for eventual conversion to Christianity, they appear as fair and feisty princesses or martially skilled princes. If they are there to be killed, they appear as hideous, monstrous Black enemies (often giants). In 2003, I argued that the genealogical history of medieval romance is intricately intertwined with the colonial history of the Crusades, and romance is a narrative literature replete with depictions of race and crusader colonization (*Empire of Magic*, chapter 1).

Two Middle English crusade romances that are excellent to dissect with students are *Richard Coer de Lyon* and *The King of Tars*. In *Coer de Lyon*, the putative hero of the Third Crusade, the English king Richard Lionheart, becomes an unwitting cannibal when his men feed him the stewed head of a "Saracen" boy when he falls ill while on crusade. The narrative presents this as a kindly joke played on their king by his people when the English king's desire for pork cannot be met, since they are in the Near East.

Richard instantly grows well and strong from his salvific repast, and, on discovering the source of the delicious healing remedy, the English king gleefully decides to eat other Muslims too and hosts a feast where the ambassadors of Saladin (Salah ad-Din Yusuf ibn Ayyub) – the leader of the countercrusade who historically wrested Jerusalem back from the Latin West in 1187 – are served, piping hot, the cooked heads of their freshly killed and plucked relatives, while King Richard himself devours with relish and a hearty appetite his own Muslim head, before their horrified eyes. The Muslim heads are black, with grinning white teeth – a conventional color trope in medieval romances.

An unabashed racist-imperialist-cannibal, the King of England then boisterously announces that henceforth all English Christian men will be cannibals and will consume the territory of Muslims even as they consume Muslims themselves: jubilantly, literary fantasy thus solves a historical problem of supply for Christendom's invading armies. Literalizing a metaphor of colonization, the trope of cannibalism in this romance marshals the power and dynamics of the joke – first, in the form of a healing ruse visited by his men on Richard, then in Richard's immediate expansion of the joke into a collective racial-colonial aggression unleashed on the Muslim enemy, whose sons and youths are devoured by a cannibal-king who uses the occasion to define all Christian Englishmen as the cannibal-conquerors of the East.

Teaching *Richard Coer de Lyon* alongside postcolonial criticism and Freud on the politics of the joke – especially political jokes that draw tight the circle of group identity – and crusader chronicles and letters allows students to unravel intersecting weaves of race, imperialism, colonization, nationalism, and gender and sexual identity in the medieval literature of England. The Richard of *Coer de Lyon* is also hypermasculine, wielding gigantic phallic weapons, and the text positions sly jokes on how Richard thrusts into his enemy from the rear.[8]

Middle English romances are thus excellent to include in syllabi of colonial texts, since they supply ample examples of how religious conversion can function as cultural capture and cultural imperialism, at a time in Europe's history – the late fourteenth and fifteenth centuries – when it is clear, after one crusading army after another has failed to recapture Jerusalem, that military-territorial invasions are meeting with no success.

Accordingly, the late Middle English romance called *The King of Tars* fantasizes the successful conversion and cultural capture of a Black and "loathly" Sultan of Damascus by a fair, white-skinned Christian princess of Tars. The nuptial union of this Muslim sultan and Christian princess births a lump of flesh – without face, bone, or limbs – till, upon baptism, the shapeless lump transforms into the fairest child ever born.

This miraculous transformation arranged by a Christian sacrament persuades the sultan himself to be baptized, whereupon he instantly transforms from Black and "loathly" to White "without taint" – a spectacular performance of race-changing that amply demonstrates, for students, the politics of color in the European Middle Ages. The freshly whitened sultan then becomes a crusading king who slaughters any of his own people who refuse to become Christians too.

When religion is an essential defining factor of ethnoracial identity, successful conversion to Christianity signals racial death: the extinction of an earlier religioracial identity, upon entrance into a new religioracial formation. In literature, of course, a conversion can be confirmed as successful by a sensational miracle pivoting on color and somatic transformation.[9]

When the religious other is transformed into the same, a compensatory victory of sorts is snatched from the failure of geoterritorial military invasions; and, in literature, as in history, the conversion of kings and populations is seen to be best secured by key royal women. Evidently, there are gender-specific roles for women in cultural colonization, and medieval stories of conversion are useful to teach alongside modern colonial literatures thematizing the conversion of native others, and the role of native women subjects, under later, modern, imperial conditions.

That *white* is the color of Christian sanctity, and *black* the color of sin, the demonic, and the infernal – as *The King of Tars* resoundingly demonstrates – is commonplace in medieval theological understanding; and the politics of color are amply displayed in literature and art (*Invention of Race*, chapter 4). Beyond *English* literature, German, Dutch, French, and Scandinavian literatures treat with equal enthusiasm the politics of color, religion, and ethnoracial identity.

Wolfram von Eschenbach's *Parzival*, arguably the finest romance of the German Middle Ages, plumbs a nexus of economic feudalism, color, and religion, when an opportunistic White Arthurian knight seeks economic gain in Islamic lands, sires a piebald son on a Black queen in the land of the Blacks, Zazamanc, and returns to European Christendom decked in the opulent wealth of the Islamic and Black East, as Zazamanc's king.

The Middle Dutch *Roman van Moriaen* follows a Black knight from Moorland who has been Christianized but economically and sociopolitically disenfranchised because his White Arthurian father failed to marry his Black mother, so that the Black knight arrives in Europe seeking redress. In the Middle High German *King of Moorland*, Christian European knights travel the opposite route of conversionary politics depicted in *The King of Tars*, by becoming Black when they are seduced by Black women and converted to "heathenry."

These literary texts highlighting the politics of color can be supplemented in the classroom by medieval art. From the end of the twelfth century and all through the thirteenth – an era of intense anti-Black virulence – the portrayal of sinners, demons, and devils as black is joined by lifelike representations of Black Saharan Africans who are dramatically staged as torturers of Christ and killers of John the Baptist. Generations of Christians in Europe were thus conditioned to see Black African men torturing Christ and slaughtering his saints.

Beyond the Crusades, a course on colonization should also scrutinize what has been called England's first empire – accomplished with the invasion and occupation of Ireland, Wales, and, less successfully, Scotland. Undertaking the work of colonial ideology, Gerald of Wales's ethnographic *History and Topography of Ireland* features lengthy descriptions of the Irish as savage, barbaric, and quasi-human, situating a twelfth-century example of the logic of evolutionary racism wherein colonial masters must tutor conquered natives to enter a civilized future on a timeline with an ever-vanishing horizon (*Invention of Race*, chapter 1). Paired with Edmund Spenser's *A View of the Present State of Ireland*, students can see, in a transhistorical curriculum, England derisively lamenting its primitive, uncivilized, backward, savage Irish subjects across four centuries of English colonial tutelage.

Across centuries of English literature, then, the lesson imparted here to students is that evolutionary racism of the colonial kind pivots on a language of colonialism in which the "not-yet" of an evolutionary logic that seems to promise the attainment of civilizational maturity by a subject population that will guarantee equality with colonial masters becomes a perpetual deferment, a "not yet forever" (Ghosh and Chakrabarty 148, 152).

Across the Atlantic, the settler colonization of North America by Icelanders and Greenlanders narrated in two Vinland sagas – the *Greenlanders' Saga* and *Eirik the Red's Saga* – furnishes stories of Northern Europeans swindling the Natives of the Americas in trade half a millennium before Columbus. The colonists amass valuable furs, pelts, and skins from the Indigenous and offer in return sips of milk and ever more paltry strips of red cloth. Consequently, the leader of the foremost expedition – Thorfinn Karlsefni – returns to Europe a wealthy man, lionized by the elites of Norway, buys a farm and homestead in Iceland, and – *Eirik the Red's Saga* tells us – relates and controls the story of the incursions into Vinland (*Invention of Race*, chapter 5).

Despite the Vinland sagas' racing of Native North Americans as naive Stone Age savages with primitive weaponry, however (in pitched battles, Native arrowheads and catapults are up against the Norse colonists' swords and steel), what is important to emphasize to students is the *abject failure* of northern Europe's eleventh-century settler colonists, for all their trade swindles and Europe's so-called advanced metallurgy.

"Hail Vinland!" is thus a vacuous and hollow rallying cry if, unlike
White extremist groups in the United States, you are acutely aware that the
Natives thoroughly routed the settler colonists, forcing them to evacuate
their settlements and return to Europe with their tails between their legs.
Even the abduction and kidnap of the two Native boys, we see, is
a compensatory squib resulting from the settlers' failure to capture or kill
the adults who are with the children.

Moreover, when we pair the Vinland sagas with a twentieth-century
novella about this failed settler colonialism – *The Ice Hearts*, authored by
a Native American, Joseph Bruchac – or a twenty-first-century Young
Adult novel such as *Skraelings*, coauthored by a pair of Indigeous authors,
Rachel and Sean Qitsualik-Tinsley, students gain a countercanonical view
of medieval colonization that depicts what the standpoint of the
Indigenous themselves might look like.

The vantage point of the Indigenous can also be taught through resistant
reading of the dominant narratives in medieval texts. Just as
Shakespeareans have taught *The Tempest* not from the viewpoint of the
settler colonist Prospero, but from that of the displaced Indigenous –
Caliban and Sycorax – and the enslaved – Ariel – the Old English epic
Beowulf can be taught from the perspective of the Indigenous inhabitants
in the story, Grendel and his mother, who are portrayed by the text as
biblical descendants of the so-called accursed "line of Cain."

In *Beowulf*, these fen-and-bog inhabitants are troubled in their ancestral
homeland and habitats by the Danes, who are the settler colonists in the
poem, and, with their lives disrupted, wreak revenge on the Danish king,
Hrothgar, and his retainers at the royal hall, Heorot, the symbolic heart of
the territorial incursions. The presumptive heroism of the young titular
protagonist, Beowulf, and his later presumptive tragedy as an aged king,
assume an altogether-different cast when this epic is taught as a narrative of
displacement and land theft.

Finally, a decolonizing curriculum would be incomplete without
a substantial component on anti-Semitism, and Europe's treatment of an
internal minority of raced aliens ensconced for centuries in the heartlands
of the Latin West in all the major cities and towns: medieval Jews.

Medieval Jews were racialized for their putative somatic differences as
well as religiocultural differences. Somatically, Jews were said to give off
a special stench from their bodies, to possess a peculiar facial physiology,
even to have horns and a tail. Jewish men were said to bleed congenitally
from their nether parts, like menstruating women: a fictional blood loss
that conveniently fed another fiction, the popular lie that Jews needed the

blood of Christian children, whom they putatively mutilated and crucified in reenactments of the deicide of Christ (*Invention of Race*, chapter 2).

Simultaneously, Jews were also racialized by Christian political theology representing them as God killers, as tormentors of the consecrated host or the Virgin Mary, and as coconspirators of Satan and the Antichrist. At best, they were to be allowed to exist conditionally, according to the Augustinian tradition of relative tolerance, till the last days, at which point they would transform into Christians via conversion and cease to exist as Jews, in a mass extinction of their religioracial identity.

In England, Jews were forced to wear a badge on their chest to set them apart from the rest of the local population; forced to live in cities with a registry by which their livelihoods and economic endeavors could be monitored; forced to hew to a panoply of laws that circumscribed their movements, from the ability to walk in public during Holy Week and the ability to socialize in the homes of Christian neighbors, to the ability to pray at a permissible volume in synagogues.

Imprisoned disproportionately for coinage offenses, periodically slaughtered by mobs, and judicially executed by the state for trumped-up charges of child murder, Jews also had conversionist sermons preached at them, were taxed to the edge of penury, and, once impoverished, were manipulated in a final exploitation that produced their mass expulsion in 1290.

An extraordinary surveillance system – an economic panopticon – was devised by the state to monitor their livelihoods, a panopticon that ramified into sociocultural control well beyond economic rationality, so that by the time of their expulsion, English Jews needed permission to establish or to change their residences and were forbidden to live among Christians, in a segregation of urban geography that suggested the beginnings of the ghetto (*Invention of Race*, chapter 2).

With just one example – medieval Jews – before our eyes, we thus see how racial formation functioned both biopolitically, religioculturally, and socioculturally in the European Middle Ages, essentializing and defining an entire community as fundamentally and absolutely different, in interimplicated ways.

England has the well-earned distinction, I have argued, of constituting the first racial state in the history of the West (*England and the Jews*). Racial politics in England, producing Jews as a raced internal minority through a variety of mechanisms, formal and informal, facilitated the emergence of England as an imagined political community – a medieval-style nation.

As culture, art, literature, architecture, and popular opinion functioned in the service of nation formation, state instruments and apparatuses devised for the surveillance and control of the Jewish population sped the intensification of English state formation. The realization of a totalizing edifice for the intensive sorting, manipulation, and control of Jewish lives and bodies through a panoply of measures thus cumulatively saw the de facto formation of an early racial state in the West.

One skein of English anti-Semitism is summarized in child-murder stories that depict how malignant Jews torture, crucify, stab to death, or nearly behead hapless English children, usually boys at the vulnerable age of seven or eight. The most famous of these child-murder stories is, of course, in Chaucer's *Prioress's Tale* of his *Canterbury Tales*. This tale can be taught as part of a cluster of child-murder stories that include a thirteenth-century Anglo-Norman ballad, *Hugues of Lincoln*, set down soon after the so-called murder of a young boy in Lincoln, and Marian miracle tales such as *The Chorister* (also known as *The Child Slain by Jews*), featuring a beggar boy with a sweet voice who is killed by a Jew when he sings a Marian hymn.

Chaucer's skilled retelling of the child-murder story is extraordinary to teach, in part because the story materializes *all* Jews as Satan's people, while Christians themselves are raced through a shared blood inheritance as Christians-by-descent. In this retelling, Christians are *born*, not just *made* through conversion or baptism, and they share DNA: they are *y-comen of Crysten blode* ("descended from Christian blood"), as Chaucer's *Prioress's Tale* puts it.

Coda: Beyond England and the West, or Decolonizing the Premodern Curriculum by Teaching the World

The teaching of a critical, revisionary canon is best paired with a countercanonical teaching that shunts aside Western literature altogether.

In 2003, I coined the term, the *Global Middle Ages*, in devising a spring 2004 transdisciplinary graduate seminar on early globalism, collaboratively taught by five faculty members at the University of Texas, and two visiting scholars. That pedagogical experiment, now nearly two decades old, birthed the Global Middle Ages Project (G-MAP: www.globalmiddleages.org), an international consortium of scholars engaged in research, pedagogy, digital humanities, workshops, and publications on early globalism, as well as a Cambridge University Press Elements series and an MLA volume called *Teaching the Global Middle Ages.*[10]

That history, and the work undertaken by scholars from several disciplines – archaeology and the sciences/social sciences, literary and cultural studies, the arts and humanities, digital and computational studies – is too long to rehearse here. One skein of the work being accomplished does matter, however, for decolonizing literary curricula in the academy today. In the MLA volume *Teaching the Global Middle Ages*, I argue for teaching an early globalism that uncenters the world through a curriculum of texts wherein every place is the world's center, and that effectively shunts aside the hegemony of Western literature ("The Literatures of the Global Middle Ages").[11]

The guidelines and texts I offer there are not without shortcomings. The sheer variety of texts, gathered from around the world across several centuries, cultures, and languages, means that translations are essential to the project of pedagogy. Such translations, of course, need not be in Western languages – they might be in Arabic, or Chinese, or Malay, or whatever language is apposite for one's classroom, wherever one is located in the world. Nonetheless, translation studies have taught us that the politics, epistemologies, and ethics of translation haunt all projects involving translations and must be addressed.

Moreover, these texts are often authored by sociocultural, political, or religious elites – as is common for premodern texts – and are marked by elite, perhaps imperial, interests and perspectives. They may be concerned with the establishment of key non-Western empires, such as the West African empire of Mali (taught through the epic *Sundiata*), or the Malacca sultanate (taught through the *Sejarah Melayu*, or *Malay Annals*).

We may garner precious knowledge of lives lived in Central Asia and on the Eurasian steppe in Ibn Fadlan's *Mission to the Volga*, but only through the condescending eyes of an envoy from the Abbasid empire, who assumes the superiority of his own civilization over that of the peoples he encounters. Or an ambassador from the Timurid empire of Shah Rukh, grandson of Timur Lenkh (Tamerlane to the West) – Kamaluddin Abdul-Razzak Samarqandi – gazes with disdain on the "Black, naked savages" of India, despite admiration for the empire of Vijayanagar, in the text known as *Mission to Calicut and Vijayanagar*.

A monk of Uighur or Ongut ethnicity from Beijing, Rabban Sauma, travels to the lands of the West, all the way to Rome and France, and discourses on Latin Christianity, but his erstwhile travel companion becomes the Patriarch of the Assyrian Church of the East (the "Nestorian" Church), pointing to the fact that these are not underclass accounts, or histories-from-below, but the narrative accounts of political, intellectual, cultural, and religious elites, like the medieval Western literatures they displace.

Fortunately, there are also more demotic records: for example, mariners' accounts, such as those compiled in Buzurg ibn Shahriyar's *Book of the*

Wonders of India; merchants' accounts, in Abu Zayd al-Sirafi's *Accounts of China and India*; and, of course, the *Thousand and One Nights*, a story compendium accumulated over centuries and featuring the exploits of fisherfolk and farmers, women and slaves, urban citizens and merchants (alongside kings, magistrates, jinn, demons, and the like).

In decolonizing pedagogy, a global premodern curriculum will thus need critical strategies not dissimilar to the teaching of a critical and revisionary canon of Western literature. But its advantage, relative to the English and Western canon, is that it unhinges the grip of the West and its literatures *avant la lettre*.

And today, when students are from everywhere around the world, surely its time has come.

Notes

1. On my campus, where I am the sole premodernist teaching pre-1600 courses that thematize race, class, colonization, empire, Islamophobia, and anti-Semitism, in an English department where students of color have complained there are too few such courses, I was told, before 2020–21 – which brought changes in departmental administrative culture in response to #MeToo, the movement for Black lives, anti-Asian hate, and a post-Trumpian era – that I should teach more traditional "Brit. Lit."

2. A 2003 article by Kate Galbraith reported *The Guardian* quoting Charles Clarke, Great Britain's then-Secretary of Education, declaring unctuously at University College, Worcester: "I don't mind there being some medievalists around for ornamental purposes, but there is no reason for the state to pay for them." Clarke was apparently of the camp that held medieval studies to be a field concerned with obscure interests, comprising academic antiquarians performing custodial functions for archives of little urgency to anyone else. British medievalists were stung by Clarke's condescension and insult but floundered in trying to argue for their work's significance. A Cambridge medievalist was quoted as falling back on an old academic vagueness, when she indignantly defended medievalists as "working on clarity and the pursuit of truth." On medieval studies' entrenched conservatism and urgent need for transformation, see, e.g., Chan, Miyashiro, and Rambaran-Olm.

3. On neoliberal appropriation of the rhetorics of decolonial and progressive movements to further the agendas of late capitalism in academic institutions, see, e.g., Chaganti.

4. Nahir Otaño Gracia, Jonathan Hsy, Adam Miyashiro, and Cord Whitaker are other Medievalists of Color active in undertaking the critical teaching of canons and countercanons. Since it's impossible to list everyone and their teaching, these names merely function as stand-ins for the larger community of scholars who are actively decolonizing the premodern curriculum today.

5. *Invention of Race* substantively expands on the terse descriptions below, in detailed discussions across several chapters.
6. Arabs and Near Easterners who were *Christians* were not called "Saracens" but were flexibly allowed a play of ethnoracial identity. By contrast, Arab and Persian writers did not group all Europeans under a singular collective rubric defined by Christianity but continued to refer to Europeans as Romans, Franks, Greeks, Slavs, and so forth.
7. Since the purview of this volume is English literature, that is the focus in this section of the essay, rather than European literatures in general.
8. In its sly play on phallicism, the romance even deploys a neologism attested only in this one text in Middle English, "cuyle," which alludes to the "fundament" – the body's nether zone, backside, or rear. For the historical Richard's fluid sexuality, see *Empire of Magic*, chapter 2.
9. By contrast, in life on the ground, conversion is impossible to verify, and medieval history is replete with accusations of crypto-conversions on the part of Jews and Muslims, whose conversions to Christianity continued to be disbelieved, often leading to various kinds of persecution (*Invention of Race* 77–80).
10. See Heng, *The Global Middle Ages: An Introduction*. The first eleven titles in the Cambridge Elements in the Global Middle Ages series can be found here: www.cambridge.org/core/publications/elements/global-middle-ages.
11. The literature of early globalism is not the same thing as "world literature." World literature courses amalgamate a miscellany of texts to represent disparate cultures and locales and look for organizational coherence through themes, motifs, and so on, that can suture together a miscellany of texts. By contrast, early global literatures thematize the interconnectivity of the early world. For a detailed argument, see my essay in the MLA volume.

WORKS CITED

Chaganti, Seeta. "Solidarity and the Medieval Invention of Race." *The Cambridge Journal of Postcolonial Literary Inquiry* 9.1 (2022): 122–31.

Chan, J. Clara. "Medievalists, Recoiling from White Supremacy, Try to Diversify the Field." *Chronicle of Higher Education*, July 16, 2017.

Galbraith, Kate. "British 'Medievalists' Draw Their Swords." *Chronicle of Higher Education*, June 6, 2003.

Ghosh, Amitav and Dipesh Chakrabarty. "A Correspondence on *Provincializing Europe*." *Radical History Review* 83 (2002): 146–72.

Heng, Geraldine. "Before *Race*, After *Race*: A Response to the Forum on *The Invention of Race in the European Middle Ages*." *Cambridge Journal of Postcolonial Literary Inquiry* 9.1 (2022): 159–72.

Empire of Magic: Medieval Romance and the Politics of Cultural Fantasy. New York: Columbia University Press, 2003.

England and the Jews: How Religion and Violence Created the First Racial State in the West. Cambridge: Cambridge University Press, 2018.

"On Not Reading, Writing, or Listening to Poetry in a Pandemic: A Critical Reflection." *PMLA* 136.2 (2021): 290–96.

The Global Middle Ages: An Introduction. Cambridge: Cambridge University Press, 2021.

The Invention of Race in the European Middle Ages. New York: Cambridge University Press, 2018.

"The Literatures of the Global Middle Ages." In Geraldine Heng, ed., *Teaching the Global Middle Ages.* New York: Modern Language Association of America, 2022, 27–47.

"Why the Hate? *The Invention of Race in the European Middle Ages,* and Race, Racism, and Premodern Critical Race Studies Today." *In the Middle,* December 21, 2020. www.inthemedievalmiddle.com/2020/12/why-hate-invention-of-race-in-european.html?m=0.

Kim, Dorothy. "White Supremacists Have Weaponized an Imaginary Viking Past. It's Time to Reclaim the Real History." *Time,* April 15, 2019. https://time.com/5569399/viking-history-white-nationalists/.

Medievalists of Color. https://medievalistsofcolor.com.

Miyashiro, Adam. "Decolonizing Anglo-Saxon Studies: A Response to ISAS in Honolulu." *In the Middle,* July 29, 1019. www.inthemedievalmiddle.com/2017/07/decolonizing-anglo-saxon-studies.html.

Perry, David. "White Supremacists Love Vikings. But They've Got the History All Wrong." *The Washington Post,* May 31, 2017. www.washingtonpost.com/posteverything/wp/2017/05/31/white-supremacists-love-vikings-but-theyve-got-history-all-wrong/.

Qitsualik-Tinsley, Rachel and Sean Qitsualik-Tinsley. *Skraelings.* Chicago: Inhabit Media, 2014.

Rambaran-Olm, Mary. "Anglo-Saxon Studies [Early English Studies], Academia and White Supremacy." *Medium,* June 27, 2018. https://mrambaranolm.medium.com/anglo-saxon-studies-academia-and-white-supremacy-17c87b360bf3.

Redfern, Rebecca and Joseph T. Hefner. "'Officially Absent, but Actually Present': Bioarcheological Evidence for Population Diversity in London during the Black Death, AD 1348–50." In Madeleine L. Mant and Alyson Jaagumägi Holland, eds., *Bioarcheology of Marginalized People.* Academic Press, 2019, 69–114.

CHAPTER 19

The Decolonial Imaginary of Borderlands Shakespeare

Katherine Gillen

Undergoing Spanish colonization and then forcibly incorporated into the United States following the 1848 Treaty of Guadalupe-Hidalgo, the United States–Mexico Borderlands have been shaped by colonial and anticolonial struggles. As Gloria E. Anzaldúa writes of the Texas–Mexico Borderlands, "this land has survived possession and ill-use by five countries: Spain, Mexico, the Republic of Texas, the U.S., the Confederacy, and the U.S. again. It has survived Anglo-Mexican blood feuds, lynchings, burnings, rapes, pillage" (112). These waves of colonization in La Frontera – a space encompassing northern Mexico and parts of Texas, New Mexico, Arizona, and California – were driven by the White, settler-colonial desire to appropriate Indigenous land, labor, and resources and by concomitant efforts to maintain the power to enslave diasporic Africans living in the Americas. The effects of this colonial history continue to reverberate in the Borderlands, evident in the deaths, detention, and family separation of migrants and in racial inequality, labor exploitation, and environmental destruction. Colonial power continues to meet resistance in the region, however, as activists work to protect human rights and fight for the sovereignty of Native nations and the self-determination of communities populated predominantly by Black, Indigenous, and Latinx residents.

Borderlands arts and culture contribute to these collective projects by disrupting colonial logics and sustaining the region's communities, often performing restorative, healing work.[1] In this essay, I explore the decolonial power of two Shakespeare appropriations – Edit Villarreal's *The Language of Flowers* (1991), an appropriation of *Romeo and Juliet* set in Los Angeles during Día de los Muertos, and Herbert Siguenza's *El Henry* (2014), an appropriation of *Henry IV, Part I* set in postapocalyptic San Diego. Both of these plays fit into the category of Borderlands Shakespeare, a term used to encapsulate a growing body of translations, adaptations, and appropriations that situate Shakespeare within the unique context of La Frontera.[2]

Written primarily by Chicanx and Indigenous playwrights, Borderlands Shakespeare plays engage with Shakespeare's treatment of issues such as migration, exile, family, sexuality, childbirth, and nature to reflect local concerns. Rather than ceding cultural, linguistic, artistic, or epistemological authority to Shakespeare, though, Borderlands plays such as *The Language of Flowers* and *El Henry* interpolate Shakespeare into a web of Indigenous, Chicanx, and Latinx narratives, rituals, languages, and frameworks. They take what they need from Shakespeare, embracing the Chicanx spirit of rasquachismo, defined by Tomás Ybarra-Frausto as an "underdog perspective" of "making do," a spirit often seen in recycled yard art, adorned low riders, and funky gardens, which "engenders hybridization, juxtaposition, and integration" and favors "communion over purity" (156). In *The Language of Flowers* and *El Henry*, Shakespeare becomes part of this repurposed mixture, his plays reimagined to disrupt colonial narratives and to envision decolonial alternatives.

The United States–Mexico Borderlands may initially seem like an unlikely place to find Shakespeare. However, as in many places around the world, Shakespeare's works have been employed as tools of colonial power in the region, used in schools and theaters to buttress the supremacy of White, Anglo language and culture.[3] In the Borderlands, Shakespeare remains associated not only with the English literary canon but also with the US settler state. His works and image seem ever present, but also in some ways alien and alienating. As Ruben Espinosa argues:

> Because of Shakespeare's deep interconnection with English, and with Englishness, he is often perceived to be less accessible to certain users, such as Latinxs. While apprehension surrounding the knotty nature of Shakespearean verse might partially guide these perceptions, attitudes about Shakespeare's place in the establishment of English linguistic and cultural identity certainly drive these views. ("Beyond *The Tempest*" 45)

Given Shakespeare's prominence, Borderlands residents have no choice but to interact with his plays, which often supplant Black, Indigenous, and Latinx texts in "English" classrooms. Shakespeare thus proves to be a site of contestation, functioning as a representative of European, Anglo, and/or White hegemony but also as a familiar and malleable set of texts, ideas, and characters that can be incorporated into the region's mestizaje, a term Rafael Pérez-Torres defines as "an affirmative recognition of the mixed racial, social, linguistic, national, cultural, and ethnic legacies inherent to Latino/a cultures and identities" (25).

As scholars of postcolonial Shakespeare have demonstrated, Shakespeare remains imbricated within colonial histories and structures even as his provocative engagements with questions of power, identity, and language offer generative material through which to interrogate colonial dynamics. As Espinosa contends, "one can scrutinize Shakespeare as being a tool of colonial oppression while simultaneously recognizing that the colonial, postcolonial or neocolonial subject can appropriate that tool for themselves to offer anticolonial perspectives" ("Postcolonial Studies" 162). Enacting this principle, plays such as Aimé Césaire's *Une Tempête* and Toni Morrison's *Desdemona* "write back" to Shakespeare, contesting the racism within *The Tempest* and *Othello*. Other works such as Vishal Bhardwaj's *Omkara, Maqbool,* and *Haider* decenter both Shakespeare and his English origin by emphasizing local cultures, languages, and conflicts. As Craig Dionne and Parmita Kapadia suggest, such productions *"repossess"* Shakespeare (3), "shattering the notion of the universalist interpretation that privileges Western experience as primary" (6). Postcolonial and decolonial interpretations, as Jyotsna G. Singh and Gitanjali G. Shahani contend, open Shakespeare's plays "to competing histories and a plurality of sociopolitical contexts – the marks of the postcolonial condition" (127). While reproducing Shakespeare runs the risk of reaffirming his centrality, colonized subjects continue to do so both because his plays, at times, invite anticolonial readings and also because they offer opportunities to negotiate, possess, or transform the White Western canon and, by extension, the forms of power that it represents.

Borderlands playwrights participate in this global phenomenon of Shakespeare appropriation, and their approach is influenced by their specific geographic and cultural position in a region shaped by Spanish and US colonialism and by the modes of decolonial and anticolonial thought arising from it. As Ato Quayson reminds us, "the return to Shakespeare is never only about the Elizabethan contexts in which his plays were first produced. It is also about the familiarity of Shakespeare in terms set by the worlds in which he is being reread" (45). In the Borderlands, Shakespeare's resonance is shaped not only by the ubiquity of Shakespeare in schools and theaters, but also by the contemporaneity of the plays with Spanish colonialism in the region and by their use within US colonial projects (as for example, when US troops performed *Othello* in Corpus Christi during the invasion of Mexico, with Ulysses S. Grant playing Desdemona).[4] Plays such as *The Language of Flowers* and *El Henry* contend with these legacies as they reimagine Shakespeare to empower local communities and to address resonant issues related to Indigenous and Chicanx culture, politics, and relationships.

Theorists, writers, and artists in the United States–Mexico Borderlands have long emphasized the need to survive, to resist, and to think outside of the coloniality that has been imposed on the Americas since Spanish contact. As Anzaldúa writes, "This land was Mexican once / was Indian always / and is / And will be again" (113). Because of the encompassing nature of coloniality, theorists from this region emphasize the interrelated aspects of decolonialization, which, as Marco Antonio Cervantes and Lilliana Patricia Saldaña write, is a "political, epistemological, and spiritual project" that disrupts ongoing and systemic colonial operations of power (86). This project involves advocating for the sovereignty of Indigenous nations and working to return stolen land, while also creating new modes of knowledge and sociality for those who lack direct contact with their Indigenous ancestries. The work of Borderlands thinkers and activists dovetails with that of decolonial theorists such as Anibal Quijano, Walter Mignolo, and Catherine Walsh, whose writings focus mainly on Mexico and Latin America. They share with these theorists a critique of colonial modernity as well as a commitment to multiplicity and to creating pluriversal and interversal avenues that challenge Western universals and create space for alternate ways of knowing and being. As Walsh explains, "from its beginning in the Americas, decoloniality has been a component part of (trans)local struggles, movements, and actions to resist and refuse the legacies and ongoing relations and patterns of power established by external and internal colonialism" (17). Having experienced waves of both external and internal colonialism, Borderlands residents are an important part of this decolonial tradition, and their contributions to it are informed by Chicana feminism and by the knowledge systems of the Indigenous peoples of Mexico and what is now the Southwestern United States.

In addition to Anzaldúa's well-known discussion of Borderlands consciousness, Emma Pérez's articulation of the decolonial imaginary is particularly useful for understanding the power of Borderlands cultural production, including Borderlands Shakespeare. For Pérez, the decolonial imaginary is a space of active negotiation, creating a "time lag between the colonial and postcolonial, interstitial space where differential politics and social dilemmas are negotiated" (6). As Pérez contends, Borderlands culture makers resist ongoing coloniality, forging this "rupturing space, the alternative to that which is written in history" (6). This space accommodates a plurality of people and cultures, many of whom are oppressed and marginalized within dominant, White institutions. In this way,

Borderlands cultural production aligns with the Zapatistas' decolonial imperative to create "un mundo donde quepan mucho mundos" (a world where many worlds fit). In many cases, it also instantiates what Cathryn Josefina Merla-Watson calls "altermundos," alternate speculative worlds that, even if dystopian, rewrite the past, present, and future to remind us that "un otro mundo es posible" (another world is possible) (355).

In this essay, I situate Edit Villarreal's *The Language of Flowers* and Herbert Siguenza's *El Henry* within this body of Borderlands cultural production and decolonial thought. Like other Borderlands Shakespeare plays, these works interrogate Shakespeare's position – as a writer, a set of texts, and a cultural phenomenon – within intersecting colonial histories. Borderlands adapters of Shakespeare rarely lose sight of the fact that the dates of his plays align loosely with those of the Spanish conquests in the sixteenth century, a marker that Latin American decolonial theorists identify as the origin of coloniality/modernity. In addition to its material violence, coloniality imposed new regimes of knowledge. As Quijano explains, the Spanish "repressed as much as possible the colonized forms of knowledge production" while imposing European religion, language, and philosophy (541). European literature plays a role in this process, not only because discrete texts express White, colonial perspectives but also because the very idea of national literatures originates from colonial aspirations, functioning as a means of showcasing European cultural supremacy. Shakespeare, of course, has played an outsized role in this colonial project, as his plays have been employed in efforts to assert European experiences and epistemologies as universal. As Pérez writes, the work of decolonization involves rereading and retelling Western narratives, "to shift meanings and read against the grain, to negotiate Eurocentrity" (xvii). Borderlands Shakespeare plays perform this vital work.

Both *The Language of Flowers* and *El Henry* are set in Southern California, a center of El Movimiento, the movement for Chicano liberation begun in the 1960s that advocated for civil rights, labor rights, and political sovereignty. Both plays critique persisting structures of coloniality, seek to recover Indigenous genealogies, and express decolonial ways of knowing and being in the world. *The Language of Flowers* emphasizes the material violence of colonization and its linguistic, epistemological, and spiritual consequences. Indigenous languages, mythologies, and rituals persist into the present and future, Villarreal suggests, and they hold the potential to heal colonial wounds if they can be more fully integrated into Chicanx communities. By contrast, *El Henry* employs dystopian frameworks to trace neocolonial practices that continue to devastate Indigenous and Latinx communities in the United States and throughout Latin America. Siguenza invokes the political construct of Aztlán, the mythical homeland of Chicanxs as well as a potential revolutionary space of reclaimed sovereignty, to assess the limitations and potential of El Movimiento and to chart pathways forward. Both plays thus perform transtemporal and transhistorical work, bringing Shakespeare together with Borderlands art forms, both past and present, to contest colonial histories and to pry open space through which to imagine decolonized futures.

Colonial Violence and Indigenous Futurity in *The Language of Flowers*

Edit Villarreal's *The Language of Flowers* is set in a Mexican American community during Día de los Muertos, or Day of the Dead, a ritual commemoration with deep roots in Mexica spiritual practices in which the deceased return to visit the living. As Jorge Huerta writes, Chicanx drama often "shows a fascination with and respect for the Chicanos' Indigenous roots" and "affirm[s] the Chicano as Native American" (182). Participating in this tradition, *The Language of Flowers* validates Chicanxs' Indigenous heritage and draws on Mexica epistemologies, practices, and languages to negotiate and resist structures of coloniality and White supremacy. In *The Language of Flowers*, Mexica beliefs transform the *Romeo and Juliet* story, as the belief system infusing Día de los Muertos disrupts binary divisions between life and death and permits Romeo and Juliet's love to endure in the afterlife. Furthermore, Villarreal brings both Mexica belief systems and Shakespeare's play into contact with the technologies of the colonial state that has imposed militarized borders on Indigenous land and which inflicts harm on Chicanx communities. Through this triangulation, *The Language of Flowers* explores how myths from earlier periods, both Indigenous and European, might shape the present and provide a means of mitigating its violence.

Villarreal situates Los Angeles within a Pan-American Indigenous history, calling attention to the original inhabitants of the Americas, as well as to broader patterns of voluntary and involuntary migration. In the play's opening scene, Romeo's friend Benny, a combination of Shakespeare's Benvolio and Mercutio, responds to the accusation that he is a "wetback" (1.1), saying:

We're all wetbacks from somewhere. Some of us walked over here. Like the
Indians. Across Alaska, mano. In winter. Red-brown indio mules, they
walked all the way to Patagonia. Later, some of these same indios changed
their minds and came back. They flew out of the valles of Mexico, the
barrios of Central America, the favelas and barrancas of South America like
hungry birds. . . . Everybody in the whole world found themselves right here
in the middle of pinche L.A. Hungry. Tired. Sweaty. And pissed off at
everybody. Eventually somebody said, "Why can't we all get along?" But
nobody listened. (1.1)

Benny critiques colonial borders, which deem some people "citizens" and
others "illegal." Whereas the earlier migration of Indigenous people is
depicted as peaceful, the play exposes the colonial violence that influences
modern migrations. The corridista, a singer of Mexican ballads who
replaces Shakespeare's Chorus, calls attention to these dynamics, explaining that the city is full of "Nicaragüenses y salvadoreños / Guatemaltecos all
fleeing from war / Pobres cubanos, también mexicanos / Searching for
work for themselves / Bringing their families here to stay" (1.2). While Los
Angeles has become a refuge for immigrants, the city can also be harsh and
dangerous. As the corridista sings, "But El Lay is not for loving / El Lay is
not for love / El Lay is not for dreaming / And El Lay is not for luck" (1.2).
This experience is not limited to Latinxs, moreover, and Benny's closing
question, "why can't we all get along?" references one posed by Rodney
King, whose beating by two White police officers and their subsequent
acquittal, sparked a series of uprisings. With this line, Villarreal calls
attention to experiences of Black residents of Los Angeles, who are subjected to state-sanctioned terror. The violence that pervades the city in *The
Language of Flowers* is thus shown to be a result of intersecting histories of
enslavement, settler colonialism, and neoliberal economic policy.

In this play, Romeo and Juliet's love is doomed not by a feud between
their families but by endemic colonial violence and its aftershocks.
Interpersonal conflicts do exist, though, between Mexican Americans
who assimilate to White norms and those who embrace their Indigenous
roots and look toward decolonial futures. Juliet's father, Julian, is committed to upward mobility, and he hopes to marry his daughter to a young
lawyer with "the right credentials" and "the right friends" (2.8) – a stark
contrast to Romeo, who is an undocumented immigrant from Michoacán.
Contending that "the movimiento is over" (1.2), Julian wants undocumented Mexicans to be jailed or deported. Hypocritically, he has divorced
Juliet's mother because she "had an accent," and "was pretty but not light
enough" (1.13), and he has coerced his Mexican housekeeper Maria into

a sexual relationship. He and his associates reject Spanish, seeking to speak without a Mexican accent and objecting when their names are given Spanish pronunciations.

Romeo and Juliet transcend these divisions, however, largely through their embrace of Mexica traditions and the Nahuatl language. When Romeo first meets Juliet, he says in Spanish, "Encantado de conocerle," to which Juliet responds, "You shouldn't speak like that. I mean in Spanish" (1.6), explaining later that her father doesn't want her to learn Spanish. Even as Juliet begins to learn Spanish, however, Romeo and Juliet find a more fundamental connection in "the language of flowers," a phrase that encapsulates a Nahuatl linguistic genealogy and which signifies a more embodied language of love. Romeo and Juliet meet near a magnolia tree, which prompts Romeo to note, "in México, we call magnolias 'yoloxo-chitl.' Flowers of the heart," and he later refers to Juliet herself as a yoloxochitl, explaining that "it's Nahuatl, the language they spoke in Mexico before it was Mexico" (1.13). Romeo's use of Nahuatl aligns with Villarreal's emphasis on the Indigenous roots of Día de los Muertos, and the play's imagery of flowers includes the marigolds, or cempasuchitl, which were sacred to the Mexica and which are traditionally placed on graves during Día de los Muertos to entice souls to return from the dead.

The tragic arc of Romeo and Juliet's love story is shaped by the sequence of Día de los Muertos celebrations, from Día de los Chicos, commemorating the lives of dead children, to Día de los Difuntos, which commemorates the lives of all the dead but, in this play especially, with added emphasis on adults. The servant Manuel – who is a calavera, or skeleton, but who is seldom recognized as such – comments on Romeo and Juliet's unusual decision to marry on Día de los Chicos, but notes that the calaveras "have two days to celebrate with them" before they "must die. Again" (1.18). Later, after Romeo has killed Tommy (the Tybalt figure), he bumps into a calavera who notes that it is now el Día de los Difuntos and says, "Yesterday we honored dead children. Today we honor adults. Which one are you?" (2.7). The question resonates, as Romeo and Juliet marry and die on the cusp of adulthood. In keeping with the core belief of Día de los Muertos, the dead are not excised from the play but rather continue to advise and in some cases torment the living, and Benny holds a special place as a spiritual guide to Romeo and Juliet after his death.

Romeo frequently thinks about his experiences in relation to Mexica mythology, and he feels especially connected to Tezcatlipoca, the god of the Great Bear constellation whose name translates as Smoking Mirror and whose worship was important in sacrificial traditions. Romeo invokes

Tezcatlipoca's smoke as a sign of the death and violence that surrounds Los Angeles but also as part of a broader, rejuvenating spiritual cycle. The city, he says, is full of "nothing but hate. You can smell it. The barrio on fire with uzis light as feathers. Tezcatlipoca's dark smoke burning bright. Brighter than the sun. And nobody sleeps. Even at night" (1.4). He also notes, however, that Tezcatlipoca's smoke "burns in the eyes of those in love" (1.4), and he imagines his reunion with Juliet as occurring in Tezcatlipoca's palace. Read in relation to Mexica myth, Romeo, Juliet, and Benny function as sacrifices, but they also live on in the afterlife. While this Indigenous worldview is dismissed by some of the play's characters, it is fundamental to Villarreal's appropriation of *Romeo and Juliet*, compelling an ending in which the lovers are united in the Mexica afterlife.

Indigenous healing practices promise to facilitate Romeo and Juliet's reunion after Romeo is deported to Mexico, but this happy ending is thwarted by state repression. The drugs that Juliet takes to feign sleep are special medicine "used by curanderos . . . to cleanse the body and calm the mind" (2.11). As Juliet chews the leaves, Benny's calavera encourages her to sleep and "dream of justice" (2.15). Although Romeo purchases fatal poison from a curandera, or healer, in Mexico, he has no need for it, as he is killed by gunfire symbolizing the violence of both the militarized border and the streets of Los Angeles, twin forces that are conflated in a rapid succession of images at the end of Villarreal's play. Upon hearing that Juliet has died, Romeo finds a trafficker to take him across the border, where he sees many calaveras also trying to catch a "ride going north" with "no tickets, no seats, no snacks, no water, no toilets, no cops" (2.21). As they begin to cross into the United States, they are ambushed by a huge figure of Uncle Sam who shoots at them. Romeo explains that he is an American, who speaks English and "has a wife there now," but Uncle Sam rejects him, shouting, "COWARD! BEGGAR! YOU THINK AMERICA WANTS YOUR KIND?" (2.22). Soon after the ambush, Romeo finds himself in the crypt with Juliet and discovers that he has been shot. Against this backdrop, a calavera laments that "El Lay is dying" and "bleeding from knives, bullets, and rage!" (2.26). This scene suggests that bloodshed in Los Angeles itself results from ongoing colonial repression and cannot be disconnected from the racist violence that Romeo and his fellow migrants face at the border.

Although Romeo cannot reunite with Juliet in life, death brings them peace within the play's Indigenous worldview, and the calaveras help to facilitate this passage, encouraging Juliet to kill herself and then ushering the lovers into the thirteen heavens of the Mexica afterlife. Romeo and Juliet, "children of Mexico," are ready to begin their next journey and "become what [they've] always been. Flowers and song" (2.26). Amidst Tezcatlipoca's rising smoke, Romeo and Juliet pledge not to be separated, with Romeo using Spanish and Juliet using English. Beyond merging Spanish and English, though, Romeo and Juliet end the play speaking the language of flowers, the language of the heart and of their Indigenous ancestry. With everyone walking in the direction of the sun, sacred to the Mexica, the calaveras welcome Romeo and Juliet, "Earth flowers, spirits, niños," into their "Divina casa de flores" (2.26). Although the colonized Borderlands prove too oppressive to sustain Romeo and Juliet's love, Indigenous frameworks provide a space of union and possibility. By staging this possibility, *The Language of Flowers* opens decolonial imaginaries that sustain such lifeways, ensuring that they exist not only in the afterlife but in life itself.

As it brings together Shakespeare's *Romeo and Juliet* with the colonial histories shaping the lives of Chicanxs in Los Angeles and with Mexica rituals and epistemologies, Villarreal's play reconfigures colonial chronologies, geographies, and hierarchies. It thus participates in a Chicanx speculative tradition that, as Merla-Watson contends, "unearths objects, images, symbols, and mythos associated with the primitive and the past and recombines them with those associated with the present and the future, thereby re-seeing colonial distinctions between the past and the future, the human and the nonhuman, the technologically advanced and the primitive" (353). *The Language of Flowers* does not depict Mexica spiritual and linguistic practices as preceding colonial Spanish and Anglo practices but rather as coexisting with them and even superseding them, thus coding Indigenous epistemologies not as premodern or primitive but rather as contemporary and necessary for Chicanx survival. If Shakespeare's sixteenth-century play remains in circulation, frequently taught in classrooms and performed in theaters, then so too must the Indigenous and Chicanx ways of knowing that colonial power structures seek to suppress. Shakespeare's plays, Villarreal suggests, can be part of this decolonial project, particularly if – as with all aspects of settler colonial life – they are amenable to critique, revision, and reinterpretation from Indigenous and Chicanx perspectives.

Shakespeare in Aztlán: The Decolonial Politics and Poetics of *El Henry*

Whereas *The Language of Flowers* dramatizes the healing powers of Indigenous spirituality, Herbert Siguenza's *El Henry* emphasizes the political aspects of decolonization. In this appropriation of *Henry IV, Part I,*

Henry is the son of Chicano gang "king" El Hank. Rather than assuming his role as heir, though, Henry prefers to hang out with Fausto, the play's Falstaff figure, and his other friends in a local bar. Set in Aztlan City, a postapocalyptic San Diego, California, *El Henry* explores the successes and limitations of the Chicano Movimiento and reconfigures histories of colonial oppression and political activism to imagine decolonized futures. Aztlán was a key signifier in El Movimiento, a political imaginary encompassing much of what was once northern Mexico and promising a unified homeland for Chicanxs. As Rudolfo Anaya and Francisco Lomelí write, "Aztlán brought together a culture that had been somewhat disjointed and dispersed, allowing it, for the first time, a framework within which to understand itself" (ii). In contrast to the aspirations of El Movimiento, the Aztlan City of *El Henry* has been established not through political revolution or cultural reclamation, but rather through the exodus of White people from regions increasingly populated by Mexican Americans and other Latinxs. Those inhabiting this failed revolutionary space, however, find ways to maintain their cultures, languages, and livelihoods, and their lives bear a resemblance to those of Chicanxs living in barrios that have been abandoned within White-centric neoliberal economies. Similarly, Siguenza infuses Shakespeare with this resilient energy, reimagining *Henry IV, Part I*'s exploration of political power and intergenerational tension from Chicanx perspectives.

Part of La Jolla Playhouse's Without Walls series and performed in San Diego's gentrifying but still largely Mexican American East Village, *El Henry* incorporates Shakespeare into Chicanx space and into Chicanx political, linguistic, and theatrical lineages. Siguenza explicitly aligns *El Henry* with Chicanx teatro, a tradition to which *The Language of Flowers* also belongs. Teatro traces its lineage to El Teatro Campesino, which arose from within the movement of the United Farm Workers (UFW), led by César Chávez and Dolores Huerta, for better pay and working conditions. Founded by Luis Valdez in 1965 on the picket lines of the Delano Grape Strike in Delano, CA, El Teatro Campesino performed scenes, or actos, that used humor and political satire to advocate for the rights of immigrant laborers. Teatro evolved to address a range of political and social concerns and to validate Chicanx identities. Singuenza himself was a founding member of Culture Clash, a theater troupe that adapted teatro to urban Los Angeles and sought to create "theatre of the moment, written and performed first for the people and communities on which it is based, and secondly for a broader audience" (quoted in Zingle 57). This tradition, as Matthieu Chapman observes, shapes *El Henry* and is strikingly evident in Siguenza's decision to cast Kinan Valdez and Lakin Valdez, sons of El Teatro Campesino founder Luis Valdez, in the key roles of El Henry of Barrio Eastcheap and El Bravo of Barrio Hotspur (61–62).

Just as *El Henry* replaces El Movimiento's liberatory nationalist image of Aztlán with a more dystopian version, it also updates teatro both for the twenty-first century and for a future potentially characterized by intensifying poverty, disenfranchisement, and environmental disaster. In particular, Siguenza infuses teatro with a cyberpunk ethos, participating in an artistic movement that Catherine S. Ramírez terms Chicanafuturism, a speculative aesthetic that brings "the high-tech and rasquache together" to envision alternate futures (x). As Lisa Rivera suggests, Chicanx cyberpunk art "often flew in the face of the nationalist logics of *el movimiento*, whose writers and artists largely aimed to recover and preserve a core, essential, and pre-Columbian cultural identity erased by centuries of colonial oppression and exploitation" (96). Chicanx cyberpunk and Chicana futurism are less con-cerned with essential identities than with the ways in which global capitalism has damaged and transformed Indigenous cultures and people. As Rivera writes, cyberpunk illuminates challenges "that are more unique to the new millennium, including the rise of globalization and information technologies and the new hybrid identities made possible by both" (96). With its reconfiguration of Aztlán – and its light critiques of the machismo embedded not only within Chicano politics but also within gang culture and in Shakespeare's *Henry IV – El Henry* participates in this Chicanx dystopian project. It moves beyond the essentialist, nationalist politics of El Movimiento and envisions modes of Chicanx survival even in the most hostile of circumstances.

While *El Henry* emphasizes ongoing structures of coloniality, it also celebrates the vibrancy of working-class Chicanx life and art and celebrates the rasquache ethic of "making do" in contexts in which wealth has been hoarded by White elites. As the play begins, audiences learn that White people have, predictably, taken the most valuable resources with them. Channeling the resourcefulness of teatro, which was often performed in union halls and on flatbed trucks, *El Henry*'s set is comprised of "a collection of trash, old signage, tires and old television sets" with "trash and graffiti along the brick walls" (Prologue). As Fausto welcomes the audience, he emerges from a pile of trash and explains how this situation came about:

> Welcome to Aztlan City, formerly known as San Diego, capital of Aztlan. Now Aztlan is basically California after the Gringo Exodus. Yeah, you heard

me right, I said Gringo Exodus! See back in 2032, there was a worldwide pandemic and all the banks collapsed and Mexico went completely bankrupt and fifty million Mexicans fled north, crossing the border into Califas. No fence, no laws, no drones could keep them out. Raza everywheres! La Jolla started looking like Chula Vista, and Chula Vista, well, kept looking like Chula Vista! In 2035, the Gringos, the Negros, the Chinos, even the Ethiopian cab drivers said, "Chale! Screw this! Too many Mexicans! We're out of here!" So they packed their bags and split, and formed their own country east of the Rockies. It was "White flight" on a big scale, tu sabes! (Prologue)

El Henry's Aztlan has arisen through the collapse of the neoliberal, neocolonial order, a collapse that the United States–Mexico border could not withstand, thus allowing Mexicans to join longtime residents of former San Diego. Preceding this collapse, racial capitalism had only become more violent, with its effects felt most acutely in Indigenous communities. For example, audiences learn about a generation of Mexiclops, "one eyed Mexican cowboys" who were born after a nuclear explosion in Oaxaca in 2020. Despite these violent colonial legacies, though, Chicanxs have their own space in Aztlan City, one in which, as Chapman contends, "rasquache becomes a way of life," with people "repurpos[ing] the garbage left behind into what they need to survive" (64). Chapman points out, moreover, that Siguenza's decision to stage Aztlan in a gentrifying neighborhood in San Diego works to "decolonize the land in the colonizers' minds" by gesturing to both a precolonial past and a postcolonial future, thus exposing the erasures effected by the United States' colonial land claims (67). Land often considered by White residents to be simply part of the United States is reframed to highlight ongoing Indigenous presence. *El Henry* thus challenges the historical processes that colonized the land of the Kumeyaay People and that have displaced many Mexicans and Central Americans, causing them to migrate to the region. Furthermore, through its invocation of Aztlán, the play reveals that this land may not remain in colonial possession forever.

Colonial power structures persist in *El Henry*'s Aztlan, however, even in the absence of White people. The revolution has been thwarted by respectable "Hispanics" who have taken over the violent apparatuses of the colonial state and make liberal use of its police force. This situation leaves a network of street gangs as the only viable avenue through which Chicanxs can attain power. As Fausto explains:

They left us California to live and to rule. We renamed it Aztlan, and it was cool for a whiles, you know. Everybody was happy and got along. "Viva la

Raza," "De Colores," and all that shit, but then it all went to hell. Corrupt
Hispanic politicians who think and look and act like they're white took the
political and civic power, but the people, los Chicanos, we took the streets.
(Prologue)

The Hispanic state has appropriated the Indigenous and activist imagery of
El Movimiento: their dollars are called Cesar Chavezes; their city seal looks
like a Mayan calendar with the UFW eagle over it; and their slogan is
"Gracias, De Colores, Viva La Raza, and God Bless Aztlan" (1.1). However,
the Hispanics employ the rhetoric and political strategies of conservative
Anglo politicians. When El Henry's rival El Bravo kills a member of the
Hispanic Police, the Mayor declares war on the Chicano gangs. The
Mayor's political philosophy is revealed by her quotation of "the great
Anglo leader Ronald Reagan, on whom we Hispanics base our political
ideals," in her statement, "when you can't make them see the light, make
them feel the heat" (1.1).

The Hispanic state seeks to punish El Hank not because he is responsible for killing the policeman, but because he has begun distributing water
to the barrios. As El Hank explains, "the Hispanics don't care if I'm dealing
drugs and guns, but once I got into legit water they had to get me on
something to put me away" (1.2). Amidst Aztlan's economic and environmental catastrophe, water has become a prized commodity, horded by
elites and replacing "guns and coca" (1.2) in illicit trafficking circuits. In
this violent, underresourced world, El Hank facilitates a network in which
Chicano gangs profit from prostitution, gunrunning, and drug dealing.
But the gangs also play an important role in the community, attaining
resources for people who would otherwise be left destitute by the state,
lacking access even to clean drinking water. As El Hank explains:

> The Hispanics drink clean water they buy from the Gringos while we drink
> "toilet to tap" chingadera, if we can even get it. The Hispanics would rather
> have us die of overdoses, kill ourselves, than to thrive and live. Chavalillos in
> the barrio die every day, of dehydration, of disease. Well not anymore. I'm
> buying fresh water from North Aztlan, and I'm distributing it at no cost to
> the barrio. (2.1)

For these reasons, El Henry finally assumes his role in the familia, seeing it
as his responsibility to resist colonial power and to ensure Chicanx survival
in this postapocalyptic world. He embraces his destined role, fashioning
himself as an Indigenous cyberpunk hero, described as both "an Aztec
warrior ready for battle" (2.3) and "a brave Cholo warrior of the
future!" (2.4).

El Henry's victory against El Bravo, however, brings not revolution but only a détente, with structural oppression inhibiting true decolonial politics. Henry and his father are able to avoid prison and to vanquish their enemies, but to do so, El Hank must fund the Mayor's reelection campaign. It initially seems as though El Henry's reign will be more compassionate than his father's, but his promise to pardon all the rebels is quickly shown to be a lie as he takes them outside and shoots them instead. El Henry might succeed in establishing water-distribution centers for the barrios, but this work is contingent upon his family's support for the Reaganite mayor, who polices and impoverishes Chicanx communities. Poverty, Siguenza suggests, engenders violence among Chicanxs, who must compete for the meager resources left to them and who are seduced into colluding with oppressive state power. Such structures of coloniality, *El Henry* reminds audiences, were also enforced both by the English monarchy rendered in its Shakespearean source and by the governments of Spain, Mexico, and the United States that so greatly influenced the history of California.

Despite its pessimistic ending, though, *El Henry* offers a hopeful decolonial vision, rewriting a canonical Anglo story within Chicanx contexts to imagine alternate realities. This decolonial project is evident not only in *El Henry*'s plot and its repurposing of gentrified space but also in the language practices it employs and implicitly validates. Caló, which blends urban Spanish and English, is the dominant language of the play, and this Chicanx vernacular is used throughout *El Henry* without translation for monolingual Anglos or for Spanish speakers accustomed to more state-sanctioned linguistic registers. Glancing humorously at the play's deviation from its Shakespearean source, Fausto jokes that the Mexiclops, who primarily speak Spanish, "don't understand the Queen's Spanglish!" (1.5). The Anglo theatrical tradition is also satirized in the play, and Fausto is compared to histrionic Shakespearean actors, "those putos that used to do theatre in Balboa park, the Old ... English players or something" (1.7). In keeping with the rasquache ethos of Chicanx speculative fiction, *El Henry* repurposes existing narratives, languages, and practices – those of Shakespeare as well as those of El Movimiento – to write Chicanxs into the future and to inspire humor and joy, even amidst ongoing structures of coloniality.

Toward a Culturally Sustaining Shakespeare Pedagogy

Both *The Language of Flowers* and *El Henry* contribute to the decolonial project of the Chicanx speculative arts, which, as Merla-Watson and Ben Olguín demonstrate, "project a utopian spirit through the genre's capacity for incisive social critique that cuts to the bone of shared pasts and presents" (6). As they write, "the Latin@ speculative arts remind us that we cannot imagine our collective futures without reckoning with the hoary ghosts of colonialism and modernity that continue to exert force through globalization and neoliberal capitalism" (4). Shakespeare is one such ghost, as his works continue to be mobilized in the interests of coloniality and White supremacy in the United States–Mexico Borderlands. Rather than treating Shakespeare as sacrosanct, Villarreal, Siguenza, and their fellow Borderlands playwrights take what is of use from Shakespeare's plays, recycling them to meet the needs of their communities. They actively confront colonial power, simultaneously engaging with Shakespeare's nuanced explorations of political power and "delinking" from colonial canons in order to "build decolonial histories" (Mignolo x). In this way, Borderlands Shakespeare ultimately decenters Shakespeare, incorporating his plays into the hybrid histories, cultures, and languages of the region to create space in which to tell stories of and for La Frontera.

Because of its complex negotiation of – and resistance to – coloniality, Borderlands Shakespeare, like other postcolonial and decolonial appropriations, offers generative approaches from which we might learn as we seek to make English literary studies less colonial. Teaching Borderlands Shakespeare productions has become central to my own work at Texas A&M University–San Antonio, a Hispanic Serving Institution on the Southside of San Antonio, situated near the former Mission Espada on land that was home to the Payaya, Coahuilteca, Lipan Apache, and Comanche Peoples. Many A&M–SA students share these heritages, although their ancestral ties have in many cases been attenuated by the region's sequential occupations. On our campus, colonial histories are omnipresent, palpable in the lived experiences of students and in the curricula that we teach – particularly when White settlers like me teach Shakespeare, an author often viewed as the pinnacle of the White colonial canon.

Teaching Borderlands Shakespeare – and other Shakespeare appropriations by BIPOC artists – can contribute to our efforts to employ culturally sustaining pedagogy, described by Django Paris as an approach that honors students' languages, traditions, and experiences as vital funds of knowledge. Borderlands Shakespeare is rooted in the communities to which many of our students belong, and it prioritizes place-based Indigenous and Chicanx epistemologies, languages, and practices. Reading Borderlands Shakespeare empowers students to do the same and to bring their own cultural, racial, and linguistic knowledges to bear on material often considered White property. Such culturally sustaining practices mitigate the epistemic violence so often perpetrated in English classes, which often implicitly devalue students' ways of knowing, speaking, and reading. Borderlands Shakespeare plays, moreover, offer methods – for both students and instructors – of engaging with canonical texts and colonial traditions. Guided by the rasquachismo of Borderlands Shakespeare, readers are empowered to decide which aspects of the colonial canon they wish to reject entirely and which they wish to repurpose for their own ends. Shakespeare becomes not an arbiter of personal taste or cultural value, but rather a potential interlocutor, one of many authors whose work may be revised and reconfigured in the interests of articulating decolonial futures.

Notes

1. For the community work performed by Borderlands, Chicanx, and Latinx literature, see Aldama, Sandoval, and Garcia; López; and Santos, "Surviving the Alamo."
2. For a fuller description of Borderlands Shakespeare, see Gillen, Santos, and Santos, "Tracing the Traditions of Borderlands Shakespeare."
3. For the role of Shakespeare in colonial education in India, see Viswanathan. For Shakespeare in the American Indian boarding school system, see Stevens.
4. See Grier; Yim; and Weaver on the colonial uses of Shakespeare to mediate encounters with Indigenous people in the territories now known as the United States.

WORKS CITED

Aldama, Arturo J., Chela Sandoval, and Peter J. Garcia. *Performing the US Latina and Latino Borderlands*. Bloomington: Indiana University Press, 2012.

Anaya, Rudolfo and Francisco Lomelí. "Introduction." In Rudolfo Anaya and Francisco Lomelí, eds., *Aztlán: Essays on the Chicano Homeland*. Albuquerque: University of New Mexico Press, 1997, ii–iv.

Anzaldúa, Gloria E. *Borderlands/La Frontera: The New Mestiza*. 3rd ed. San Francisco: Aunt Lute Press, 2007.

Cervantes, Marco Antonio and Lilliana Patricia Saldaña. "Hip Hop and Nueva Canción as Decolonial Pedagogies of Epistemic Justice." *Decolonization: Indigeneity, Education, & Society* 4.1 (2015): 84–108.

Chapman, Matthieu. "Chicano Signifyin': Appropriating Space and Culture in *El Henry.*" *Theatre Topics* 27.1 (2017): 61–69.

Dionne, Craig and Parmita Kapadia. *Native Shakespeare: Indigenous Appropriations on a Global Stage.* London: Routledge, 2016.

Espinosa, Ruben. "Beyond *The Tempest*: Language, Legitimacy, and La Frontera." In Valerie M. Fazel and Louise Geddes, eds., *The Shakespeare User.* Cham: Palgrave, 2017, 41–61.

"Postcolonial Studies." In Evelyn Gajowski, ed., *The Arden Handbook of Contemporary Shakespeare Criticism.* London: Bloomsbury, 2020, 159–72.

Gillen, Katherine, Adrianna M. Santos, and Kathryn Vomero Santos. "Tracing the Traditions of Borderlands Shakespeare." In Katherine Gillen, Adrianna M. Santos, and Kathryn Vomero Santos, eds., *The Bard in the Borderlands: An Anthology of Shakespeare Appropriations en la Frontera,* Vol. 1. Tempe, AZ: ACMRS Press, 2023, xv–xxiii.

Grier, Miles P. "Staging the Cherokee *Othello*: An Imperial Economy of Indian Watching." *The William and Mary Quarterly* 73.1 (2016): 73–106.

Huerta, Jorge. "Images of the Indigenous Americans in Chicano Drama." In S. E. Wilmer, ed., *Native American Performance and Representation.* Tucson: University of Arizona Press, 2009, 182–92.

López, Tiffany Ana. "Violent Inscriptions: Writing the Body and Making Community in Four Plays by Migdalia Cruz." *Theatre Journal* 52.1 (2000): 51–66.

Merla-Watson, Cathryn Josefina. "(Trans)Mission Possible: The Coloniality of Gender, Speculative Rasquachismo and Altermundos in Luis Valderas's Chican@futurist Visual Art." In Cathryn Josefina Merla-Watson and B. V. Olguín, eds., *Altermundos: Latin@ Speculative Literature, Film, and Popular Culture.* Los Angeles: UCLA Chicano Studies Research Center, 2017, 352–70.

Merla-Watson, Cathryn Josefina and B. V. Olguín, eds. *Altermundos: Latin@ Speculative Literature, Film, and Popular Culture.* Los Angeles: UCLA Chicano Studies Research Center, 2017.

Mignolo, Walter. *Local Histories/Global Designs: Coloniality, Subaltern Knowledges, and Border Thinking,* 2nd ed. Princeton, NJ: Princeton University Press, 2012.

Paris, Django. "Culturally Sustaining Pedagogy: A Needed Change in Stance, Terminology, and Practice." *Educational Researcher* 41.3 (2012): 93–97.

Pérez, Emma. *The Decolonial Imaginary: Writing Chicanas into History.* Bloomington: Indiana University Press, 1999.

Pérez-Torres, Rafael. "Mestizaje." In Suzanne Bost and Francis R. Aparicio, eds., *The Routledge Companion to Latino/a Literature.* London: Routledge, 2013.

Quayson, Ato. *Tragedy and Postcolonial Literature.* Cambridge: Cambridge University Press, 2021.

Quijano, Anibal. "Coloniality of Power, Eurocentrism, and Latin America." *Nepantla: Views from South* 1.3 (2000): 533–80.

Ramírez, Catherine S. "The Time Machine: From Afrofuturism to Chicanafuturism and Beyond." In Cathryn Josefina Merla-Watson and B. V. Olguín, eds.,

Altermundos: Latin@ Speculative Literature, Film, and Popular Culture. Los Angeles:UCLA Chicano Studies Research Center, 2017, ix–xii.

Rivera, Lisa. "Chicana/o Cyberpunk after el Movimiento." In Cathryn Josefina Merla-Watson and B. V. Olguín, eds., *Altermundos: Latin@ Speculative Literature, Film, and Popular Culture.* Los Angeles: UCLA Chicano Studies Research Center, 2017, 93–108.

Santos, Adrianna M. "Surviving the Alamo, Violence Vengeance, and Women's Solidarity in Emma Pérez's *Forgetting the Alamo, Or, Blood Memory.*" *The Journal of Latina Critical Feminism* 2.1 (2019): 37–49.

Siguenza, Herbert. *El Henry.* In Katherine Gillen, Adrianna M. Santos, and Kathryn Vomero Santos, eds., *The Bard in the Borderlands: An Anthology of Shakespeare Appropriations en la Frontera*, Vol. 3. Tempe, AZ: ACMRS Press, forthcoming.

Singh, Jyotsna G. and Gitanjali G. Shahani. "Postcolonial Shakespeare Revisited." *Shakespeare* 6 (2010): 127–38.

Stevens, Scott Manning. "Shakespeare and the Indigenous Turn." In Carla Mazzio, ed., *Histories of the Future: On Shakespeare and Thinking Ahead.* Philadelphia: University of Pennsylvania Press, forthcoming.

Villarreal, Edit. *The Language of Flowers.* In Katherine Gillen, Adrianna M. Santos, and Kathryn Vomero Santos, eds., *The Bard in the Borderlands: An Anthology of Shakespeare Appropriations en la Frontera*, Vol. 1. Tempe, AZ: ACMRS Press, 2023, 7–131.

Viswanathan, Guari. *Masks of Conquest: Literary Study and British Rule in India.* New York: Columbia University Press, 2014.

Walsh, Catherine. "The Decolonial *For*: Resurgences, Shifts, and Movements." In Walter D. Mignolo and Catherine Walsh, eds., *On Decoloniality: Concepts, Analytics, Praxis.* Durham, NC: Duke University Press, 2018, 16–32.

Weaver, Jace. "Shakespeare Among the 'Salvages': The Bard in Red Atlantic Performance." *Theater Journal* 67.3 (2015): 433–43.

Ybarra-Frausto, Tomás. "Rasquachismo: A Chicano Sensibility." In Richard Griswold del Castillo, Teresa McKenna, and Yvonne Yarbro-Bejarano, eds., *Chicano Art: Resistance and Affirmation, 1965–1985.* Los Angeles: Wright Art Gallery, University of California, 1991, 155–62.

Yim, Laura Lehua. "Reading Hawaiian Shakespeare: Indigenous Residue Haunting Settler Colonialism." *Journal of American Studies* 54 (2020): 36–41.

Zingle, Laura. "El Henry: Herbert Siguenza's Epic Chicano Version of Shakespeare's 1 Henry IV." *TheatreForum* 46 (2014): 56–61.

CHAPTER 20

Decolonizing Romantic Studies

Nigel Leask

Black Lives Matter, Rhodes Must Fall, and other movements have reinvigorated the demand to "decolonize" universities across the world. BLM may
have originated in the USA in response to the toxic legacy of racial slavery,
but the targeting of Black lives that saw the murder of George Floyd is
endemic elsewhere. Even here in Scotland, where according to the 2011
census only just over 1 percent of the population is of African or Caribbean
descent (compared to 2.7 percent Asian), Shako Bayoh was killed by police
in 2015 in depressingly similar circumstances. BLM has shone new light on
the ongoing racial oppression of African Americans, Latinx, and other
ethnic minorities in "the land of the free." Of course, the United Kingdom
shares a slavery legacy with her former American colonies, even if, as Simon
Gikandi has argued, slavery tends to feature as "the political unconscious-
ness of Britishness" rather than a manifest presence, geographically located
as it was "yonder awa" in her American or Caribbean colonies (Gikandi,
Slavery; Morris, "Yonder Awa"). The most intensive phase of this crime
against humanity coincided with the literary period known as romanticism, although the coincidence was only belatedly acknowledged by
scholars of the period.

Britain's "imperial meridian" (1780–1830) saw the colonial and economic power base shifted from the West to the East Indies, partly in
response to abolitionism, as well as the meteoric transformation of an
English trading company into the expansionist "Company State" in
South Asia (Bayly). Beyond the enslavement of Africans, Britain is also
historically accountable for crimes perpetrated in other parts of its global
empire, much of it only formally decolonized in my own lifetime. It's
conveniently forgotten that in early nineteenth-century Britain, "everybody has an Indian uncle," in the words of that archimperialist Thomas De
Quincey, "the English opium-eater" (De Quincey 7:22). Resources
extracted from "the East and the West Indies," as well as southern Africa,
southeast Asia, and the settler colonies of Canada, Australia, and Aotearoa
New Zealand, underpinned the rise of industry, commerce, and civic

institutions and enabled Britain's rise to paramount global power in the Victorian and Edwardian eras. At a high price not only for colonized peoples, but also for the planet as a whole – as eco-historians Jason Moore and Andreas Malm have argued, the "Capitalocene" (a better designation for our current environmental crisis than the "Anthropocene") was based on the colonialist "world-praxis" of "Cheap Nature," the "fossil-imperial metabolism that undergirded the post 1825 development of [the British] empire" (Moore 600; Malm 236). The effects of colonialism and postcolonialism transformed every aspect of life in the UK – including mass migration to the metropolis from the former colonies in the wake of independence, and more recently the ever-more urgent refugee crisis, with accompanying reactionary backlash.

Nonetheless, UK cultural and educational institutions have been slow to address the role of global empire (benignly repackaged as "the Commonwealth") in the history of "our island nation," in anything other than nostalgic or even triumphalist terms. Even in more progressive versions of the curriculum, schooling in the UK tends to focus on the American Civil Rights movement rather than historical events nearer at home: leading to David Olusoga's criticism of "our obsession with American racism . . . as a diversionary tactic from looking at our own history." Olusoga recalls history lessons on the Industrial Revolution in his own school in northwest England, which simply ignored "the 1.8 million African Americans who produced the cotton which went into the 4,500 mills of Lancashire. We miss out the linkages between what we think of as mainstream history and what we've ghettoised as 'black history' – and yet it is just British history" (Olusoga). The same applies here in Scotland – visitors to the UNESCO World Heritage Site at the New Lanark Cotton Mills, for example, learn that millowner Robert Owen was a pioneer of "progressive education, factory reform, humane working practices, international cooperation, etc.," proving that "the creation of wealth does not automatically imply the degradation of its producers." Hardly any mention is made of the "cheap nature" that undergirded this industrial miracle, namely that the raw cotton spun in New Lanark was picked by enslaved Africans in Georgia, New Orleans, Trinidad, Jamaica, Grenada, and Guadeloupe. Nor the fact that Owen "consistently endorsed the arguments of slave masters and specifically opposed emancipation in the late 1820's . . . repeatedly employ[ing] the time-honoured anti-abolitionist rhetoric that 'white slaves' in Britain had it worse than black slaves in the colonies" (Morris, "Problem" 120). The first step in *decolonizing* the curriculum must be to uncover and square up to the past and continuing legacy of colonialism upon our culture.

Institutional and National Reflections

Priyamvada Gopal has argued that "the university cannot be decolonised independently of society and economy, but it can be a site where these questions are frontally addressed towards wider change, not least in habits of mind . . . [this] should not be conceived of as a sop to ethnic minorities or a concession to pluralism but as fundamentally reparative of the institution and its constituent fields of inquiry" (Gopal 11, 8). As university teachers of literature, we have an ethical responsibility to address these issues in our own areas of practice: institutionally through promoting diversity, equality, and antiracism; and pedagogically, by reflecting on our discipline's history and future direction, as well as our positionality. In most of Britain's older universities, the connection with empire is never far from the surface. My own Glasgow "Regius Chair of English Language and Literature" was established by Queen Victoria in 1862 in response to the introduction of competitive examinations for the Indian Civil Service (ICS), in which one-quarter of possible marks were awarded to candidates for proficiency in English language and literature. Thomas Macaulay, the architect of the ICS reforms, believed that English literary education would support "men who represent the best part of our English nation" in the colonies, disseminating "that literature before the light of which impious and cruel superstitions are fast taking flight on the banks of the Ganges . . . wherever British literature spreads, may it be attended by British virtue and British freedom" (quoted in Baldick 71). It was feared that young Scottish men lacking the opportunities of an "English" literary education (as well as any of the sense of the "Englishness" that Macaulay confidently promoted) would lose out in the stakes of becoming imperial Britons, given that an ICS career was a jewel in the imperial crown.

The history of Glasgow's Regius Chair exposes how the birth of our own university discipline of English was underpinned by imperial concerns. Initiated in 1762 with Edinburgh's Chair of Rhetoric, the rise of university English followed a transperipheral trajectory, crossing the Atlantic from Scotland to the American colonies in the eighteenth century, spreading over the red parts of the world map in the century to come, although only making a late footfall in Oxford in 1892 and Cambridge in 1922. In one sense, the discipline of English literature could be said to be coterminous with the rise (and fall) of the British Empire itself (Crawford). That is why, writing in 1968 in postcolonial Kenya, Ngũgĩ wa Thiong'o hit the central target when he advocated the "abolition of the English Department." Ngũgĩ questioned the "role and situation of an English department in an

African situation and environment . . . just because we have kept English as our official language, there is no need to substitute a study of English culture for our own. We reject the primacy of English literature and culture" (Ashcroft 439). That was back in 1968: as the editors of the present volume ask: "Why has the discourse on decolonization come *after* postcolonial thought and theory sprang fully formed from the brow of imperial history in the 1980s and 1990s? . . . It seems strange to return to the time of decolonization in what, strictly speaking, is the postcolonial era."

Glasgow University has an overwhelming preponderance of White staff and students, like the city itself, and much remains to be done to improve diversity in a university that aspires to be a global institution. However, to its credit, it has taken a proactive lead in slavery reparation among UK universities. In 2017, it commissioned a report, the findings of which acknowledged that the university historically benefited from wealth derived from chattel slavery estimated to be between £16 and £198 million (2016 values), although this was only a fraction of monies derived from colonial capital *in toto*, much of it deriving from South and East Asia (University of Glasgow, "Slavery"). The Atlantic port city of Glasgow held a virtual monopoly on the late eighteenth-century tobacco trade, and subsequent commerce in cotton and sugar: and "of all British universities with antecedents in the period of British slavery (c.1600–1838), only [Glasgow] Old College was located in a city that was rapidly transformed whilst closely connected with Atlantic slave economies."[1] Although it petitioned against the slave trade in 1792, report author Stephen Mullen argued that "the institution was pro-slavery in practice" (Mullen 229). Accordingly, Glasgow has committed £20 million to bursaries and studentships in a historic agreement with the University of the West Indies, reported as a reparative justice initiative. These initiatives (following Oxford's All-Souls Codrington project) were inspired by Brown and Georgetown Universities in the USA, as well as by the Rhodes Must Fall movement in South Africa, driven by the student-led decolonization protests. In turn, they have inspired similar initiatives at Cambridge, Nottingham, Bristol, and Aberdeen universities.[2]

As part of the new campus development, Glasgow University's new Learning and Teaching Hub has been named in honor of James McCune Smith (students have already dubbed it "the Jimmy Mac"), an emancipated enslaved person from the USA, who graduated in medicine from the University of Glasgow in 1837. In so doing, he became the first African American to receive a medical degree, an opportunity not open to him in his native country. In 2021, the university launched a "James McCune

Smith" doctoral scholarship to provide full funding for Black UK students to conduct research. Welcome as this is, it is only the tip of the iceberg: in 2019, the University's "Understanding Racism, Transforming University Culture" report uncovered disturbing evidence that half of all ethnic minority students had been racially harassed since beginning their studies at the university, eliciting an apology from the Principal (VC) and a comprehensive action plan to address racial inequality on campus.

Gopal writes pertinently on the importance of attending to historical context in decolonizing universities across the world: "there is no one-size-fits-all formula, no laundry list of action points for universities to table ... posing the right question for each context is itself part of the work of intellectual decolonization" (Gopal 9). The cultural location of my university is complicated by the current crisis of the British Union: Glasgow's role as Scotland's biggest city places it at the heart of the urgent constitutional debate concerning Scotland's independence from the UK. Now supported by a slim majority of the Scottish population in the wake of the Brexit agreement (62 percent of Scots voted Remain), the "Indy 2 movement" has gathered further strength in response to the current UK government's curtailment of devolved powers to the Scottish government and the rise of English ethnonationalism and imperial nostalgia. Many of its supporters see Scottish independence as a significant chapter in the ongoing decolonization of the British state: although dominated by a nationalist paradigm, it interprets Scotland as a "civic" rather than an "ethnic" community and is orientated toward independence within the European Union.

The argument that Scots were also "colonized" by England is now discredited, except among a few fringe nationalists: recent work by Scottish historians underline the fact that many Scottish individuals and institutions did extremely well out of the British (never "English") empire (Mackillop). Historically, the 1707 Act of Union between the two nations opened England's colonies to Scottish agents and capital, enabling Scotland's proactive role in the transatlantic slave trade, as well as other forms of colonial exploitation in the Caribbean and South/East Asia. Even if only twenty-seven recorded slave ships sailed from Scottish ports between 1706 and 1766 (compared to 1,500 from Bristol alone), the Atlantic trade, as well as personal fortunes made by Scots merchants, planters, and "sojourners," had a transformative effect on the Scottish economy and society. The economic benefits were felt more strongly in Scotland than England, Ireland, or Wales, in part because Scotland was poorer than England, with a small but well-educated population well fitted to provide "human capital" for empire (Devine).[3] As Sir Walter Scott wrote in 1821, "India is the corn chest for Scotland, where we poor gentry must send our younger sons as we send our black cattle to the south" (quoted in Caine 7). "Deprovincializing" Scotland and embracing independence means accepting historical responsibility for empire, not blaming it on England. So how, I wonder, can Ngũgĩ's question about the "role and situation of an English Department" apply in an ancient Scottish university, when in stark contrast to Ngũgĩ's Kenyan students, Scots were beneficiaries rather than victims of British imperialism? The question is especially pertinent to me as a socially privileged Scot, born in Glasgow, whose privilege largely accrued from the profits of "Scotland's empire." My grandfather's ascent into the British middle classes from the ranks of the Orcadian peasantry was enabled by a career in the Imperial Bank of India: my father was born in Tamil Nadu, as well as seeing war service in the Indian army. Many friends and colleagues in Scotland as well as England can trace similarly colonial family backgrounds.

For the last decade and a half, my research has focused on Scottish romanticism (*Ossian*, Robert Burns, Sir Walter Scott, etc.), on "domestic" travel writing, and more recently on Gaelic literature in the same period, largely unstudied outside Celtic departments.[4] Until recently, Scottish romanticism was itself marginalized within the English literary canon, despite the central importance of Scottish publishing, critical reviews, novels, and poetry in the period 1750–1850. Therefore, I have my own institutional issues as a professor of "English Language and Literature," teaching Scottish as well as English romantic writing in an English department, located in a university that also boasts (uniquely) a Scottish Literature department. Scottish language and literature are also taught and studied in Glasgow's department of English Language and Linguistics, as well as in the Celtic and Gaelic department, but despite some excellent collaborative projects, there is limited traffic between the four departments. Ngũgĩ's proposal concerning the "English Department" has a distinctive inflection in an institution specializing in Scotland's literary culture, which spans three Indigenous languages, Scots, Gaelic, and English. A similar story could doubtless be told about other UK universities in Wales, as well as in Ireland, undermining the notion of any unified "English" curriculum on these islands, which postcolonialists often set against an equally monolithic colonial "other," largely based on the experience of the North American "English Department."

In the romantic period, the multinational British state was an assemblage of diverse national cultures, in the case of Ireland recently yoked to

Britain by military force, after a major uprising in 1798, the year of Wordsworth's *Lyrical Ballads*. Saree Makdisi has argued for a program of "Occidentalism" in the case of Georgian England, still too internally heterogeneous to represent a civilizational ideal, which worked by "locating and clearing a space for a white, Western self who could be more effectively counterposed to the Orient out there" (Makdisi 26). Studying this kind of internal "uneven development" during the romantic period is perhaps even more urgent in the case of Scotland, Ireland, and Wales, where large segments of the populations couldn't speak English and identified in widely variable degrees with the British crown and the established churches. It should remind us of the importance of the critical study of "Whiteness" – hardly a normative category in this or any period – in any plan to decolonize the romantic curriculum. One of the great possibilities of postcolonial study is its power to break open silos based on oversimplified national canons, as in the potential for collaborative work in my own university with colleagues in Gaelic, as well as modern language departments engaging with Francophone and Hispanic postcolonial literatures. I regret that in my case this opportunity does not extend to non-European languages such as Persian, Bengali, Hindi, and Swahili, because I have no doubt the future direction of postcolonialism will increasingly challenge the monoglot regime of "global English."

Rethinking the Romantic Curriculum

After these reflections on positionality, the rest of my essay hazards some proposals for decolonizing romanticism, in terms of canon, cultural geography, and genre. I stress that these are based on my personal research interests, and my experience of teaching romanticism students in Glasgow: other colleagues with other interests and in other locations will have different priorities. They are, first, to "trouble the universalising function" of the White canon by considering "black romanticism" (meaning more than "just add black writer and stir") (Youngquist 5); second, to remap the cultural geography of British and European romanticism in relation to global empire; third, to include the genre of travel writing alongside poetry, drama, and the novel, given its role in establishing what Mary Louise Pratt calls the "planetary consciousness" of European romanticism. My 1992 book *British Romantic Writers and the East: Anxieties of Empire* sought to rethink romanticism in the light of the pioneering work by the first postcolonial generation of Said, Bhabha, Spivak, Parry, and so on. Engaging with Said's compelling narrative of the relations between orientalism and colonial power, the book proposed a more anxious, unstable, and contradictory representation of the oriental "other" than Said would allow, in the works of a group of canonical male romantics: Byron, Shelley, Coleridge, and De Quincey.[5] In the introduction, I wrote that "the internal decolonization of our culture, ethnically heterogeneous and multiracial, *as well as* European, must proceed by brushing our imperial history against the grain, to adapt Benjamin's aphorism" (Leask, *British Romantic Writers* 12). My focus on Asia excluded considerations of slavery: along with other studies, Simon Gikandi's *Slavery and the Culture of Taste* (2014) has more recently offered a powerful conceptual framework for placing racial slavery at the heart of literary studies in this period, exposing how the brutality and ugliness of enslavement actively shaped theories of taste, beauty, and practices of high culture, fundamental to European enlightenment and romanticism. Excerpts from Gikandi and other critics would frame seminar readings, as well as offering a revisionist angle on traditional topics such as the romantic imagination.

Despite the impressive body of work on romantic orientalism, colonialism, and slavery published since *British Romantic Writers and the East* thirty years ago, it is arguable how much that sort of critique has changed the way in which romanticism is taught at university level. One problem is that the voices of BME and other colonized peoples were marginalized in my own book, even as I acknowledge their "subversions" of the imperialist project. I now reflect with interest on my parenthetical statement in the book's introduction, referring to anticolonial resistance: "(this was largely the work of the colonized peoples who, with the exception of the remarkable Rammohun Roy, are a *silent*, but informing presence throughout my book)" (2). Maybe the colonized were silent in my 1992 book, but certainly not in history, even in English *literary* history. In rethinking my romantic canon, I draw inspiration from Aravamudan's notion of "tropicopolitans" (a term I prefer to "subaltern" in discussing writer/activists), defined as "the residents of the tropics, the bearers of its marks, and the shadow images of more visible metropolitans [who] challenge the developing privileges of Enlightenment cosmopolitans" (Aravamudan 4).

At the same time, I would argue that "Black romanticism" exists as more than just a Derridean "trace" (or "shadow image") in the literary archive. For instance, Olaudah Equiano's *Interesting Narrative* (1789) has proved one of the most popular and engaging texts that I have taught, a generically hybrid work, part-slave narrative, part-conversion narrative, part-autobiographical memoir, and part-travel account. An instructive dialogue can be set up between Equiano and the Scottish-Jamaican radical Robert Wedderburn's *The Axe Laid to the Root* (1817) and *The Horrors of Slavery* (1824): this also exposes an interesting Scottish connection, given that Wedderburn was only two years younger than Robert Burns, whose coronation as "Scotia's Bard" saved him from taking employment as a "negro driver" in Jamaica in 1786. Wedderburn's radicalism also exposes the connections with the Haitian revolution of 1791, which in the annals of *colonial* romanticism takes on equivalent importance to the role of the French Revolution in canonical romanticism: "*Jamaica will be in the hands of the blacks within twenty years,*" Wedderburn wrote, "*Prepare for flight, ye planters,* for the fate of St Domingo awaits you" (McCalman 86). As Joel Pace has suggested, another way of combating the "double consciousness" of conventional literary studies would be to read, for example, West African-born, formerly enslaved Phyllis Wheatley's *Poems on Various Subjects* (1773) in relation to verse by canonical romantics, given their concerns with subjectivity, spirituality, and the powers of nature (Pace 116–18). An equally productive comparison might be with the poetry of White woman abolitionists such as Helen Maria Williams, Hannah More, and Anne Yearsley, all of them aware of Wheatley's verse in promoting their sentimentalized critique of chattel slavery. Finally, a product of the later years of romanticism, *The History of Mary Prince* (1831) is a more conventional but equally disturbing narrative, and the first biography (albeit partially ghostwritten) of a Black enslaved woman published in Britain (Salih).

Moving to "the East Indies" is to engage with a very different form of cultural encounter, following the East India Company's annexation of much of the former Mughal empire, aptly described by William Dalrymple as "the supreme act of corporate violence in world history" (xxxiii). British orientalists such as Warren Hastings and Sir William Jones established hegemonic power in the subcontinent by interpreting and translating Sanskrit culture as (a lesser) equivalent to the legacies of Graeco-Roman civilization in Europe. For all their (relative) cultural sympathy, Jones and his ilk sought to mummify modern India in a timeless Brahminical past, largely ignoring its more recent Mughal history: by contrast, South Asian writers of the romantic period experienced colonial education and institutions as the shock of modernity, stimulating them to reinterpret their own rich cultural traditions. First on my list would be the Indo-Muslim munshi and poet Mirza Abu Talib Khan, whose Persian-language account of his travels in Europe and Britain in 1799–1803 were translated by the Irish scholar Charles Stewart and published in London in 1810, representing one of the first "reverse travelogues" descriptive of Europe written by an Indian author.[6] Next I would return to the Bengali religious reformer and social theorist Rajah Ram Mohan Roy (as mentioned above, the single colonized voice discussed in *British Romantic Writers and the East*) and explore the influence of, say, his *Translations of an Abridgement of the Vedant* (London, 1817) on the ethics and metaphysics of British romantic writers such as Shelley and Bentham. Finally, to explore another cultural exchange, the anglophone poetry of the Eurasian Calcutta teacher Henry Derozio represents an explosive reinterpretation of the "bardic nationalism" of *Ossian*, Walter Scott, and Tom Moore in the Bengali context, evident in a poem such as "The Harp of India" (1827). Rosinka Chaudhuri's excellent edition of Derozio's poetry makes his work readily available for the seminar room.

These represent merely a sample of possible Black or colonized writers of the romantic period to question the notion of "silent subjection." But just as important is to reappraise the contribution of *White* writers who were relegated to secondary status in the traditional canon precisely *because* of their concern with the colonial world, which came to seem ephemeral and meretricious compared to timeless Wordsworthian themes of imagination, nature, and selfhood. As Marilyn Butler indicated many years ago, the best example is Poet Laureate Robert Southey, whose whole literary career was dedicated to reforming and fortifying Britain's imperial ideology, borrowing largely from the literature of the prior Spanish and Portuguese empires that he had studied so assiduously. In addition to his oriental epics *Thalaba* and *Kehama*, I teach sections from his "Mexican" romance *Madoc* (1805), in which medieval Welsh colonists are pitted against orientalized Aztecs as a blueprint for the colonial annexation of Indigenous peoples. Earlier drafts of *Madoc* are also connected to the young and radical Southey's project, shared with the abolitionist Coleridge, of establishing a "pantisocratic" colony in Pennsylvania, subsequently an important influence on contemporary colonial schemes with links to abolition, such as the Sierra Leone settlement (Leask, "Southey's *Madoc*"). Of all the major romantics, Wordsworth seems most resistant to postcolonial reading, as the poet of normative Englishness, organic selfhood, and consolatory nature. Yet as Alan Bewell and David Simpson have argued, his reflective poems of encounter (with discharged soldiers, dying Indian women, old leech gatherers, solitary reapers) can be seen as paradigms of colonial encounter when "the anthropological other begins at home, indeed right outside one's front door" (Simpson 192). Wordsworth was also a pioneer of ecological thinking, exemplified in a poem like "Nutting," which provides an opening to considering the massive environmental damage effected by British imperialists from the sugar islands of the Caribbean to the teak forests of Burma. As environmental historian E. A. Wrigley has demonstrated, colonial "ghost acres" rescued metropolitan Britain from the ecological bottleneck of increasing population and dwindling resources, powering the industrial revolution (39).

Colonial remapping also shines a light on areas of the traditional canon that have seemed secondary or unimportant, connecting gothic and orientalist tropes: Byron's *Turkish Tales*, for example, or the orientalist poems of Shelley and Keats, as addressed in my 1992 study. This could be extended in relation to excellent scholarship on other canonical figures. Sara Suleri's elegant critique of Burke's rhetoric in the impeachment of Warren Hastings offers a new Indian context for thinking about the aesthetics of the sublime and Burke's seminal *Reflections on the Revolution in France* (1790). Saree Makdisi's work has shown the orientalist and imperialist concerns of William Blake and the radical culture of the 1790s, engaging with modernity's uneven development, and the "occidentalizing" of Britain itself. When teaching Blake, I explore visionary poems of revolution such as *America*, *Europe*, and the *Song of Los*, but also *Visions of the Daughters of Albion*, its fable derived from James Macpherson's "Oithona: A Poem" (1762), one of his highly "foreignized" "translations" from ancient Gaelic ballads attributed to the blind bard Ossian but now applied to the modern conditions of transatlantic slavery and Wollstonecraftian feminism. (For all his dissident Jacobite roots in the Highlands, Macpherson himself made a fortune as the London agent of the Nabob of Arcot, and his later career was devoted to theorizing British imperial supremacy [McElroy].) Said's *Culture and Imperialism* (1993) pioneered the "contrapuntal" postcolonial reading of Jane Austen's *Mansfield Park*, which along with Austen's other novels has inspired a spate of excellent criticism of the period's greatest novelist; meanwhile, Mary Shelley's *Frankenstein*, now one of the most widely studied novels in the curriculum, has been opened to incisive postcolonial readings by Gayatri Chakravorty Spivak, Elizabeth Bohls, and others. The verse romances and novels of Walter Scott have tended to be overlooked by postcolonial critics, although closer scrutiny reveals essential links between Scotland and India in *Guy Mannering* (1815) or *The Surgeon's Daughter* (1827), as well as his influential portrait of multiethnic England in *Ivanhoe* (1819), or his historical romance of the crusades in *The Talisman* (1825), with its strangely sympathetic portrait of Saladin. Ian Duncan has proposed that Rob Roy's primitivism (in Scott's 1817 novel of the same name), and the comparison of Scottish Gaels to tribal Afghans, represents a key facet of British imperial ideology that promoted a patriarchal primitivism "still structurally present within modernity," and one that also could account for the brutalities of slavery (128).

Finally, my third and final proposal would see the consolidation of the genre of travel writing firmly at the center of a decolonized romantic curriculum, alongside poetry, drama, and the novel. I commented above on "tropicopolitan" travel writers such as Equiano, Wedderburn, and Abu Talib Khan, but of course the majority of romantic-period travel books described European journeys to the colonial peripheries.[7] Here, I draw largely on research published in my 2002 *Curiosity and the Aesthetics of Travel Writing*, a sequel to *Romantic Writers and the East.*[8] The popularity of books of voyages and travels during the "long romantic" decades was second only to that of novels and romances, coterminous with Europe's colonial expansion in the same period. Travel writing is a form of colonial knowledge: as Linda Tuhiwai Smith writes, "travellers' stories were generally the experiences and observations of white men whose interactions with indigenous 'societies' or 'peoples' were constructed around their own cultural views of gender and sexuality" (Tuhiwai Smith 41). But although the "objectivity" of colonial travel writing is mediated by orientalist and imperialist (as well as gendered) paradigms, in the period the genre was to some extent regulated by empirical protocols: as Antony Pagden writes, "however much we may . . . fabricate rather than find our counter-image, we do not fabricate it out of nothing" (184). Rather than reading accounts of travelers' encounters with "the other" as a Manichaean opposition of power and innocence, I prefer Nicholas Thomas's stress on the contingency (and sometimes confusion) determining the "cultural entanglements" of European travelers in diverse times and places. This was especially the case on the colonial frontier, or beyond the boundaries of colonial rule, where European travelers were in a "weaker" position than the Indigenous people they encountered, often challenging myths of European triumphalism and reminding us that its global paramountcy was never an historical inevitability. At its best, travel writing in this period has a heteroglossic quality that allows the otherwise-silenced voices of Indigenous people to be heard, however mediated: take for example Gikandi's moving account of the fate of "Nealee," an enslaved African woman who formed part of a coffle traveling through West Africa to the slave forts on the Gambian coast in 1797. Unlike millions of African slaves, "Nealee's" testimony survives in the travel narrative of the Scottish explorer and botanist Mungo Park, *Travels in the Interior District of Africa* (1799), "the sole scriptural witness to this event," albeit as "a mere trace in the archive of modern identity" (Gikandi, *Slavery*, ch. 2, "Taste, Slavery and the Modern Self").

By focusing on the "antique lands" of Egypt, India, and Mexico, my 2002 book sought to shift the cultural focus of romanticism from the classical topography of Rome or Athens, or the gothic ruins of medieval Europe, to the pyramids and temples of tropical high cultures in the colonial zone, which both fascinated and threatened Western travelers. These journeys themselves constitute a variety of romantic historicism, as well as orientalism: as J.-M. Degerando wrote in 1799, "the philosophical traveller, sailing to the ends of the earth, is in fact travelling in time; he is exploring the past; every step he takes is the passage of an age" (quoted in Leask, *Curiosity* 46). At the same time, "antique" easily collapses into "antic," as the material conditions of modernity constantly reassert themselves, exposing the travelers' anxiety and dependence upon native peoples who mock (and sometimes take advantage of) their sublime obsessions. Thus, the Scottish explorer James Bruce's hyperbolic account of his discovery of the source of the Nile collapses into bathos as (in a passage of Shandyean irony) he likens himself to Don Quixote, and his toasting George III in Nile water leads the local Agow people to speculate that he has been bitten by a mad dog (quoted in ibid. 79). Italian circus strongman Giovanni Belzoni's role in the "rape of the Nile," extracting Egyptian antiquities for his British employers as described in his *Narrative of the Operations* (1820), is literalized as material engorgement as he tumbles into a mummy pit at Qurna: "I could not pass without putting my face in contact with that of a decayed Egyptian . . . I could not avoid being covered with bones, legs, arms, and heads rolling from above" (quoted in ibid. 141). Sometimes, oriental ruins elicit a more critical note, as when, visiting the Elephanta Cave temples near Mumbai, Maria Graham notes a hidden ledge behind the statue of Siva "where a Brahmin might have hidden himself for any purpose of priestly imposition" (quoted in ibid. 216). But the enduring *antic-olonial* power of Indigenous antiquities is evidenced in Humboldt's account of the massive Aztec statue of Coatlicue ("snake-belt"), which he had persuaded the Spanish authorities to disinter for him in 1803. Previously displayed in Mexico City's university cloisters after its excavation in the late eighteenth century, an Indigenous cult had begun to form around it which threatened colonial authority, remarkable enough considering that Mexicans has been nominally converted to Catholicism for two and half centuries. The Spanish authorities promptly had it reburied (ibid. 278).

Such episodes inspired works of romantic poetry and prose, which can usefully be set on reading lists alongside passages from the travel accounts, providing a new colonial context for romantic lyrics. Examples are Coleridge's response to Bruce's *Travels* in "Kubla Khan," or Felicia Hemans's 1820 poem on "The Traveller at the Source of the Nile," or Shelley's sonnet "Ozymandias" (1818), inspired by the seven-ton statue of Ramesses II brought by Belzoni from Thebes to London that same year (Leask, "Kubla Khan"; *Curiosity* 81–83, 102–28). Another celebrated instance is De Quincey's orientalist nightmare of immolation in *Confessions of an English Opium Eater*, inspired by Belzoni's misadventure at Qurna: "I was buried, for a thousand years, in stone coffins, with mummies and sphinxes, in narrow chambers at the heart of eternal pyramids" (Leask, *British Romantic Writers* 227).

Such narratives of travelers' transactions in the colonial contact zone give life and immediacy to the erased presence of colonial realities in the conventional romantic canon. Although the length and sometimes inaccessibility of romantic travel accounts does raise practical problems for classroom purposes, Elizabeth Bohls and Ian Duncan's excellent anthology *Travel Writing 1700–1830* makes many of the texts mentioned above easily available, as does their increasing digital accessibility. Properly selected and edited, these often-long and digressive texts are now increasingly accessible to students of colonial culture and literature. As with my first two proposals for decolonizing the romantic curriculum, travel texts restore a sense of the global interconnectivity of Britain's colonial and imperial history, allowing citizens of our multicultural society (whether in Scotland or elsewhere in the UK) to recognize themselves in that history and literature and enabling them to better challenge the continuing racial and cultural inequities of the present. Decolonizing the romantic curriculum must be at best a tinkering round the margins, but it's a start. As Gopal indicates, decolonization remains "a meaningless piety without an extensive enactment of material reparations . . . to peoples, communities and countries that still struggle with the consequences of very material losses." But (she paraphrases Jamaica Kincaid), at least it promotes "a more demanding relationship with history and with the world" (Gopal 12, 25).

Notes

1. Anderson 12, quoted in Mullen 211. This article describes the research methodology, conducted largely by Stephen Mullen and Simon Newman in Glasgow's School of Humanities.

2. Mullen 219. The university's external advisory group included three distinguished Afro-Caribbean scholar/activists, Glasgow City Councillor Graham Campbell, Professor Geoffrey Palmer, and Sir Hilary Beckles, Vice-Chancellor of the University of the West Indies. But for criticisms of the selectivity of the university's consultation, see Mullen 219.

3. It is also noteworthy that the University College London research project *Legacies of British Slave-Ownership* quantified the disproportionate Scottish role in Caribbean slaveownership (Mullen 212).

4. Although now a minoritized language, Gaelic was spoken by a quarter of Scotland's population up to the early nineteenth century. In some respects, the fate of Scottish Gaels in the expansion of the British Empire resembles that of a colonized people, especially their racialization and "clearance" in the eighteenth and nineteenth centuries. See Stroh and Leask, *Stepping Westward* 281–99.

5. *Romantic Writers and the East* participated in a postcolonial reassessment of romantic orientalism with distinguished contributions by Saree Makdisi, Srinivas Aravamudan, Javed Majeed, Tim Fulford, John Barrell, Gauri Viswanathan, Mary-Ellis Gibson, Dan White, and Rosinka Chaudhuri, continuing up to the present with new studies by Gerard Cohen-Vrignaud and James Watt.

6. For a revisionary reading of Abu Talib and his kin, see Garcia.

7. For an up-to-date overview of the genre, including Arabic, Indian, and Chinese travel writing, see the essays in Das and Youngs.

8. My recent *Stepping Westward: Writing the Highland Tour* examines travel accounts about a much more proximate "antique land," the Scottish *Gàidhealtachd*.

WORKS CITED

Anderson, Robert. *British Universities: Past and Present*. London: Bloomsbury, 2006.

Aravamudan, Srinivas. *Tropicopolitans: Colonialism and Agency, 1688–1804*. Durham, NC: Duke University Press, 1999.

Ashcroft, Bill. "On the Abolition of the English Department." In Bill Ashcroft, Gareth Griffiths, and Helen Tiffin, eds., *The Post-Colonial Studies Reader*. London: Taylor & Francis, 1994, 438–42.

Baldick, Chris. *The Social Mission of English Criticism, 1848–1932*. Oxford: Clarendon Press, 1987.

Bayly, C. A. *Imperial Meridian: The British Empire and the World, 1780–1830*. London: Longman, 1989.

Bewell, Allen. *Wordsworth and the Enlightenment*. New Haven, CT: Yale University Press, 1989.

Bohls, Elizabeth A. and Ian Duncan. *Travel Writing 1700–1830: An Anthology*. Oxford: Oxford University Press, 2005.

Butler, Marilyn. "Repossessing the Past: The Case for a Particularised Historical Method." In M. Levinson, ed., *Rethinking Historicism: Critical Readings in Romantic History*. Oxford: Oxford University Press, 1989, 244–49.

Caine, Alex M. *The Cornchest for Scotland: Scots in India*. Edinburgh: National Library of Scotland, 1986.

Chaudhuri, Rosinka. *Derozio, Poet of India: The Definitive Edition*. New Delhi: Oxford University Press, 2008.

Crawford, Robert. *The Scottish Invention of English Literature*. Cambridge: Cambridge University Press, 1998.

Dalrymple, William. *The Anarchy: The Relentless Rise of the East India Company*. London: Bloomsbury, 2019.

Das, Nandini and Tim Youngs. *The Cambridge History of Travel Writing*. Cambridge: Cambridge University Press, 2019.

De Quincey, Thomas. "The Casuistry of Roman Meals." In David Masson, ed., *Collected Works*, 14 vols. Edinburgh: Black, 1890, vol. 7, 11–43.

Devine, T. M. "Did Slavery Make Scotland Great? A Question Revisited." In T. M. Devine, *Revisiting Scotland's Slavery Past*. Edinburgh: Edinburgh University Press, 2015, 225–45.

Duncan, Ian. *Scott's Shadow: The Novel in Romantic Edinburgh*. Princeton, NJ: Princeton University Press, 2007.

Equiano, Olaudah. *The Interesting Narrative and Other Writings*, ed. Vincent Caretta. New York: Penguin, 2003.

Garcia, Humberto. *England Re-Orientated: How Central and South Asian Travellers Imagined the West, 1750–1857*. Cambridge: Cambridge University Press, 2020.

Gikandi, Simon. *Slavery and the Culture of Taste*. Princeton, NJ: Princeton University Press, 2011.

Gopal, Priyamvada. "On Decolonisation and the University." *Textual Practice* 35.6 (2021): 873–99. www.doi.org/10.1080/0950236X.2021.1929561.

Leask, Nigel. *British Romantic Writers and the East: Anxieties of Empire*. Cambridge: Cambridge University Press, 1992.

Curiosity and the Aesthetics of Travel Writing: From an Antique Land. Oxford: Oxford University Press, 2002.

"Kubla Khan and Orientalism: The Road to Xanadu Revisited." *Romanticism* 4.1 (1998): 1–21.

"Southey's *Madoc*: Reimagining the Conquest of America." In Linda Pratt, ed., *Robert Southey and the Contexts of English Romanticism*. Aldershot: Ashgate, 2006, 133–50.

Stepping Westward: Writing the Highland Tour, 1720–1830. Oxford: Oxford University Press, 2020.

Mackillop, Andrew. *Human Capital and Empire: Scotland, Ireland, Wales and British Imperialism in South Asia c.1690–1820*. Manchester: Manchester University Press, 2021.

Makdisi, Saree. *Making England Western: Occidentalism, Race, and Imperial Culture*. Chicago: University of Chicago Press, 2013.

William Blake and the Impossible History of the 1790s. Chicago: Chicago University Press, 2003.

Malm, Andreas. "Who Lit the Fire? Approaching the History of the Fossil Economy." *Critical Historical Studies* 3.2 (2016): 215–48.

McCalman, Iain. *"The Axe Laid to the Root." The Horrors of Slavery and Other Writings by Robert Wedderburn.* Edinburgh: Edinburgh University Press, 1991.

McElroy, George. "Ossianic Imagination and the History of India: James and John Macpherson as Propagandists and Intriguers." In Jennifer Carter and Joan Pittock, eds., *Aberdeen and the Enlightenment.* Aberdeen: Aberdeen University Press, 1987, 363–74.

Moore, Jason. "The Capitalocene, Part 1: On the Nature and Origins of Our Current Crisis." *Journal of Peasant Studies* 44.3 (2017): 594–630.

Morris, Michael. "The Problem of Slavery in the Age of Improvement: David Dale, Robert Owen, and New Lanark Cotton." In Alex Benchimol and Gerard Lee McKeever, eds., *Cultures of Improvement in Scottish Romanticism 1707–1840.* London: Routledge, 2018, 111–31.

"Yonder Awa: Slavery and Distancing Strategies in Scottish Literature." In Michael Morris, *Recovering Scotland's Slavery Past: The Caribbean Connection.* Edinburgh: Edinburgh University Press, 2015, 1–21.

Mullen, Stephen. "British Universities and Transatlantic Slavery." *History Workshop Journal* 91 (2021): 210–33.

Pace, Joel. "Afterthoughts: Romanticism, the Black Atlantic, and Self-Mapping." *Studies in Romanticism* 56.1 (2017): 113–23.

Pagden, Antony. *European Encounters with the New World.* New Haven, CT: Yale University Press, 1993.

Pratt, Mary Louise. *Imperial Eyes: Travel Writing and Transculturation.* London: Routledge, 1992.

Salih, Sarah. *The History of Mary Prince, A West Indian Slave.* London: Penguin, 2000.

Simpson, David. "Wordsworth and Empire – Just Joking." In Peter De Bolla, Nigel Leask, and David Simpson, eds., *Land, Nation and Culture 1740–1840.* Basingstoke: Macmillan, 2005, 188–201.

Stewart, Charles. *The Travels of Abu Talib Khan.* Peterborough: Broadview Press, 2007.

Stroh, Silke. *Gaelic Scotland and the Colonial Imagination: Anglophone Writing from 1600–1900.* Evanston, IL: Northwestern University Press, 2017.

Suleri, Sara. *The Rhetoric of English India.* Chicago: Chicago University Press, 1992.

Thomas, Nicholas. *Entangled Objects: Exchange, Material Culture, and Colonialism in the Pacific.* Cambridge, MA: Harvard University Press, 1991.

Tuhiwai Smith, Linda. *Decolonizing Methodologies: Research and Indigenous Peoples.* Zed Books, 2012.

UNESCO World Heritage Convention. New Lanark. n.d. https://whc.unesco.org/en/list/429/.

University of Glasgow. "Slavery, Abolition, and the University of Glasgow." 2018. www.gla.ac.uk/research/az/slavery/report2018/.

"Understanding Racism, Transforming University Culture." 2019. www.gla.ac.uk /myglasgow/humanresources/equalitydiversity/understandingracism.

Wrigley, E. A. *Energy and the English Industrial Revolution*. Cambridge: Cambridge University Press, 2010.

Youngquist, Paul. "Black Romanticism: A Manifesto." *Studies in Romanticism* 56.1 (2017): 3–14.

CHAPTER 21

Victorian Studies and Decolonization

Nasser Mufti

From Decolonization to "Decolonize"

A short essay published in 1963 by literary critic Ruth M. Adams and historian Henry R. Winkler reflects on a course on Victorian England they cotaught at Rutgers University. The course, they tell us, was in direct conversation with the interdisciplinary mission of the newly founded journal *Victorian Studies*, which in its inaugural issue defined itself as having a "concentration on the English culture of a particular age; and openness to critical and scholarly studies from all the relevant disciplines" ("Prefatory Note" 3). "We wanted to test," Adams and Winkler write, "how far the literary materials could be used in seeking a balanced and reasonably accurate picture of the era, to investigate what were the possibilities and the limitations of such an approach" (100). The syllabus they go on to describe covers topics that are still commonplace in Victorian studies: Chartism, the rise of the middle classes, the critique of utilitarianism, religion, Darwinism, and the tensions between rural and urban life.

Unsurprisingly, no mention is made of the British Empire. What should give one pause is how a course on Victorian England offered in the early 1960s, the heyday of decolonization, *could* ignore British imperialism. Vast swaths of the world had just, often quite violently, liberated themselves from European colonization, and others were actively struggling for independence. And yet Adams and Winkler appear to have made no connection between events in the Third World and the Victorian century's most significant achievement: empire. How is it that in the United States in 1962 one could teach Mrs. Jellyby's "telescopic philanthropy" in the Niger delta and not discuss Nigerian independence? Or teach the casual ellipsis of Pip's time in Egypt in the conclusion of *Great Expectations* and somehow not talk about the Suez crisis? How can one talk about Jos Sedley and not discuss the plunder of British India? How does one read *Tono Bungay* in 1962 and not talk about Kwame Nkrumah?

And yet a course on Victorian England offered at a prestigious American university in the early 1960s, amidst the intensification of American interventionism in places like Vietnam, *could* be absolutely and effortlessly blind to the simple fact of decolonization and its condition of possibility, imperialism. Such oversights are centuries in the making and remained the norm in Victorianist scholarship until the quasi-institutionalization of postcolonial studies in the anglophone academy in the 1980s and 1990s. In 1985, Gayatri Chakravorty Spivak declared that "it should not be possible to read nineteenth-century British literature without remembering that imperialism . . . was a crucial part of the cultural representation of England to the English" (243). Even in the aftermath of Spivak's essay, Victorian studies made the impossible possible by routinely ignoring the relationship between culture and imperialism. More scandalous has been the field's complete avoidance of the Subaltern Studies Collective, which was anchored in nineteenth-century British historiography, sociology, and political thought.[1] For decades, it was not only possible but the norm to research what the young Friedrich Engels called "the commercial capital of the world" without talking about where all the money came from (36).

In stark contrast to the early decades of Victorian studies, and particularly since the "undisciplining" turn in the field's American circles, today it is entirely uncontroversial to "decolonize" Victorian studies. The slogan "decolonize" and its cognate "decolonizing" have recently proliferated at major conferences, workshops, reading groups, and essay prizes in the American academy. Both generally serve as umbrella terms for antiracist pedagogy, reflections on the Whiteness of the Victorian corpus, and attention to the history of imperialism.[2] "Decolonize," no doubt, builds on the gradual increase of scholarship on nineteenth-century British imperialism from the 1990s onward, especially in the last ten years (typically in the key of empire studies, very rarely in the mode of postcolonial studies). But "decolonize" also names an institutional shift in research on empire, one that I would say departs from empire studies and especially postcolonial studies. For Victorian studies is not alone in its embrace of "decolonize." Over the last decade, there has been an efflorescence of the verb in the American academy and beyond. Surprisingly versatile, "decolonize" and "decolonizing" can be found across a range of discourses, from scholarship on education and literary studies to self-help to social justice to graffiti to TED Talks, and can be applied to a vast array of contexts, including education, ethnography, literature, anthropology, urbanism, the vote, Christianity, mindfulness, everything.[3] A category like "postcolonial" could have never dreamed of such popularity.

The wholesale institutional embrace of "decolonize" should give one pause. As I am sure many chapters in this book note, and as has been noted by others, it would be a gross misunderstanding to mistake the verb "decolonize" for the noun "decolonization."[4] The verb is new and emerges out of a middle-class encounter with the complicity between culture and imperialism. This is why it is seemingly possible to "decolonize" everything. The noun, however, is much older, has a closer relationship to the "postcolonial," and primarily describes anticolonial nationalism and Third Worldist self-determination of the mid-century (though it remains a salient concept for contemporary Indigenous activism and scholarship). If the bourgeois revolutions of the nineteenth century sought to "create a world after its own image" through empire, then decolonization sought (and seeks) to recreate what this image looked like. As Frantz Fanon famously characterizes it in *The Wretched of the Earth*, decolonization "sets out to change the order of the world," is an "agenda for total disorder," and "is an historical process" that "reeks of red-hot cannonballs and bloody knives" (2, 3). So ambitious is its scope that decolonization reintroduces "man into the world, man in his totality," not better peda-gogical practices or more inclusive syllabi (62). Fanon, in fact, almost never uses the verb "decolonize" in *The Wretched of the Earth*, and when he does, he actually uses it to describe the tactics of neocolonialism.[5] "Decolonizing" is entirely absent in his text. Ngũgĩ wa Thiong'o's classic *Decolonising the Mind*, to which this volume owes a great debt, also never uses "decolonize" or "decolonizing" other than in the title. Ngũgĩ's inter-est, as he states in the conclusion, is in the project of Third Worldist universalism: "This is what this book on the politics of language in African literature has really been about: national, democratic, and human liber-ation," and then echoing Fanon's humanism, "It is a call for the rediscovery of the real language of humankind: the language of struggle" (108). Contemporary calls to "decolonize" Victorian studies have little interest in such rediscoveries, much less the abolition of English departments or conducting research in the languages of the Global South.[6] To put it perhaps too starkly: while decolonization "reeks of red-hot cannonballs and bloody knives," "decolonize" reeks of stale conference hotels and online workshops organized by Dean's initiatives.

I highlight this difference not to trivialize recent calls to decolonize Victorian studies or to downplay the recent increase in Victorianist schol-arship on the British Empire, but to emphasize how "decolonize" and decolonization are products of radically different historical conjunctures and should not be run through one another. Their difference is thrown into even sharper relief when one considers how not only were the leaders of decolonization bourgeois intellectuals trained in the Western academy, but they were also complete Anglophiles and Francophiles. As I illustrate in the next section, the leaders and intellectuals of anticolonial thought in the British colonial world never had a problem with Victorianism. They freely utilized, quoted, and valorized the White, conservative patriarchs of nineteenth-century British literature and culture. From the perspective of W. E. B. Du Bois, B. R. Ambedkar, and C. L. R James, "decolonizing" the Victorian canon would be absurd, as it is this very canon – formed with and alongside colonization – that they loved *and relied on* to theorize the project of decolonization.[7] They might tirelessly work for the liberation of the colonial world, but they do so oftentimes by way of the writings of Victorians like Thomas Carlyle, Charles Dickens, and Alfred Tennyson. From this perspective, it becomes possible to adapt Spivak's maxim: it should not be possible to research Victorian studies without remembering that Victorianism was integral to decolonization. The relation between anticolonial thought and Victorianism remains underresearched, even amidst the popularity of "decolonize."

Indian in Blood, English in Taste

A testament to the successes of Macaulayism, anticolonial intellectuals across the anglophone imperium were well versed in the British canon. In a famous speech in 1941, Rabindranath Tagore discusses the impact of British literature on the early intellectuals of colonial India: "Their days and nights were eloquent with the stately declamations of Burke, with Macaulay's long-rolling sentences; discussions centered on Shakespeare's drama and Byron's poetry add above all upon the large-hearted liberalism of the nineteenth century English politics" (2). Reflecting on his own formation, Tagore recalls listening to the speeches of John Bright in his youth, "overflowing all narrow national bonds, had made so deep an impression on my mind that something of it lingers to-day, even in these days of graceless disillusionment" (3). When Jawaharlal Nehru writes (while imprisoned by the British, it is worth remembering) of his education, he praises his teacher Ferdinand T. Brooks, a late Victorian theosophist teacher and follower of Annie Besant. Nehru gives credit to Brooks for his taste in reading: "the Lewis Carroll books were great favorites, and *The Jungle Books* and *Kim* . . . I remember reading many of the novels of Scott, Dickens, and Thackeray, H. G. Wells's romances, Mark Twain, and the Sherlock Holmes stories, I was thrilled by the *Prisoner of Zenda*, and

Jerome K. Jerome's *Three Men in a Boat* was for me the last word in humor. Another book stands out still in my memory; it was Du Maurier's *Trilby*; also *Peter Ibbetson*" (28).

In a totally different context, but to a similar end, no anticolonial thinker was more devoted to British literature than C. L. R. James. And in *Beyond a Boundary*, it is Britain's nineteenth century that James privileges in his reflections on national culture. The conclusion famously narrates what James describes as the West Indies' entry into the "comity of nations," but this cannot be done without a detour to those who James describes as the founders of Victorianism: Thomas Arnold, the famous headmaster of Rugby, Thomas Hughes, author of *Tom Brown's Schooldays*, and W. G. Grace, the preeminent Victorian cricketer. Indeed, James devotes two chapters of *Beyond a Boundary* to these figures and digresses toward the Victorians countless times in his text. Rather than his teachers, James credits his parents for his devotion to the English canon, one rather densely populated by nineteenth-century writers. James's mother "was a reader, one of the most tireless I have ever known. Usually it was novels, any novel. Scott, Thackeray, Dickens, Hall Caine, Stevenson, Mrs. Henry Wood, Charlotte Brontë, Charlotte Breame, Shakespeare ... Balzac, Nathaniel Hawthorne, a woman called E.D.E.N. Southworth, Fenimore Cooper, Nat Gould, Charles Garvice, anything and everything, and as she put them down I picked them up."[8] His father: "a man of some education he knew who, if not what, the classics were ... 'The Pickwick Papers,' my father would say, taking up the book. 'By Charles Dickens. A great book, my boy. Read it.' And I would buy it" (*Beyond a Boundary* 16). One book in particular made an impression on the young James: "Thackeray's *Vanity Fair*. My mother had an old copy with a red cover. I had read it when I was about eight, and of all the books that passed through that house this one became my Homer and my bible" (17).[9] Reflecting on his formal education, *in the early days of West Indian independence*, it is worth highlighting, James writes:

> Our principal, Mr. W Burslem, M.A., formerly, if I remember rightly, of Clare College, Cambridge, part Pickwick, part Dr. Johnson, part Samuel Smiles, was an Englishman of the nineteenth century ... No more devoted, conscientious and self-sacrificing official ever worked in the colonies ... He was a man with a belief in the rod which he combined with a choleric and autocratic disposition. But he was beloved by generations of boys and was held in respectful admiration throughout the colony ... How not to look up to the England of Shakespeare and Milton, of Thackeray and Dickens, of Hobbs and Rhodes, in the daily presence of such an Englishman and in the

absence of any nationalist agitation outside? . . . What I think of him now is not very different from what I thought then. (29)

How is one supposed to "decolonize" such a statement? Or this one: "*everything* began from the basis that Britain was the source of all light and leading . . . it was the beacon that beckoned me on" (30)? In the 1930s, James followed this beacon to England, where he researched and published *The Black Jacobins*, arguably the founding text of anticolonial historiography.

For someone like James, the Victorian canon was entirely compatible with, indeed necessary for, the project of decolonization. More than being biographically significant, nineteenth-century British literature and culture offered anticolonial thinkers analytical frameworks to conceive the project of decolonization. B. R. Ambedkar begins his lengthy pamphlet on the partition of India by turning to Thomas Carlyle's *The Letters and Speeches of Oliver Cromwell.* In the passage Ambedkar quotes, Carlyle is concerned that class conflict in England would erupt in a civil war and laments that the England of the 1840s lacks a heroic figure like Cromwell to lead it to political and social unity: "Awake before it comes to that! Gods and men bid us awake! The Voices of our Fathers, with thousandfold stern monition to one and all, bid us awake!" (ii). "This warning" of impending civil war, Ambedkar explains, "applies to Indians in their present circumstances [at the cusp of independence] as it once did to Englishmen and Indians, if they pay no heed to it, will do so at their peril" (ii). If the Victorian Sage helps Ambedkar frame his problematic, late Victorian jurists provide him the theoretical backbone for his argument. "No one," writes Ambedkar, "is more competent to answer [the question of the national unity] than James Bryce" (187). Ambedkar's ultimate, and rather worrying, advocacy for the partitioning of India along religious lines at Independence comes through, not in small part, the writings of Henry Sidgwick and James Bryce, to whom he turns in discussions of the role of constitutional law, the history of empires, and the impact of secession on the nation state.[10] For these thinkers, political unity, be it nation or imperium, was tantamount, and if it required partitioning off a portion of the body politic, then so be it.

Pan-Africanists from the United States and the Caribbean also turned to nineteenth-century British writers as a field of intelligibility into the project of decolonization and transnational affiliation.[11] Marcus Garvey's writings are indebted to Carlylean hero worship, and Tennyson looms large in the slogan for the Black Star Line: "One God, One Aim, One Destiny" (Garvey 206–14). Similarly, Victorianism, especially Macaulay and Carlyle, saturates the nonfictional writings of Du Bois (Lewis 75). *Souls of Black Folk* opens each chapter with quotations from nineteenth-century poets, including Tennyson, Byron, Swinburne, and Browning, and Du Bois's language echoes Carlyle's ornamentalism and what J. Hillis Miller calls "Carlylese" (304). For Du Bois, the condition of England question illuminates the condition of the African American working class during Reconstruction. Not unlike Ambedkar's turn to the "hungry forties" of Victorian England, Du Bois argues that "the economic system of the South" is "a copy of that England of the early nineteenth century, before the factory acts, – the England that wrung pity from thinkers and fired the wrath of Carlyle" (138). Rather than the English bourgeoisie, it is "the sons of poor whites fired with a new thirst for wealth and power, thrifty and avaricious Yankees, shrewd and unscrupulous Jews" who have emerged as the new "captains of industry" (138). The sensibility of this industrial bourgeoisie, like that of the England that Carlyle reflected upon, is anchored in "neither love nor hate, neither sympathy nor romance; it is a cold question of dollars and dividends," or what Du Bois, directly quoting Carlyle refers to as "the Gospel of Mammonism" (138). Eric Williams's understudied *British Historians and the West Indies* traces the invention of the Caribbean in colonial historiography. A precursor to Edward Said's *Orientalism*, Williams tracks the ways in which historians like Macaulay, J. R. Seeley, Lord Acton, J. A. Froude, and many others invented the Caribbean in their writings. As he sums up, "a century and a half of denigration of the West Indies in British universities have . . . left their mark on British attitudes to the West Indies . . . The historical field therefore provides the battleground on which imperialist politics struggle against nationalist politics" (182). For Williams, a critique of colonial historiography such as the kind undertaken in his text is central to the anticolonial project.

Victorian studies, and nineteenth-century British literary studies more generally, has had no time for the simple fact that its archive resonates in the history of decolonization. Even amidst recent calls for the field to better address the demographic homogeneity of its canon and its practitioners, Victorianists have primarily looked to contemporary critical race theory (which typically takes the United States as its site of analysis), not critical race theory's antecedents in Pan-Africanism and anticolonialism – movements that are proper to the colonized world. Everyone in the field appears to have read Christina Sharpe, while everyone says, countless times and with nervous energy, that they "own *The Black Jacobins* and have been meaning to read it for years." What is the basis for this resistance to decolonization – *a world-historical process that impacted the majority of the globe* – in Victorian studies?

To begin thinking about this oversight and find a way forward, it is important to repeat a fundamental disparity: while anticolonial thinkers *could not do without* Victorian thought, Victorianist scholarship has easily *done without* anticolonial thought.[12] For a field so rigorously historicist, it is quite odd that the connections between the archive of Victorian culture and the great thinkers of decolonization have never been substantially pursued. Depending on the audience, such realizations can evoke a sense of moral failure, at which point slogans like "decolonize" and "undisciplining" are always near at hand. In contrast, I want to suggest that these historical oversights have to do with the institutional (and therefore ideological) conception of Victorian studies as a field and its own implication in the culture of American imperialism, both of which must be understood as emerging and developing alongside decolonization in Asia, Africa, and the Caribbean. In what follows, I offer a concise history of the birth of Victorian studies in the United States so as to better understand why it is that a field, perfectly poised to encounter the intimate links between nineteenth-century culture and decolonization, did not do so.

The Invention of Victorian Studies and the Age of American Imperialism

Although the term "Victorian" dates back to G. M. Young's *Victorian Poets* (1875), and its usage became increasingly common in the early twentieth century (perhaps most significantly in the title of Lytton Strachey's *Eminent Victorians* [1917]), it was only in 1933, with the publication of the annual "Victorian Bibliography" in *Modern Philology*, that "Victorian" began to take shape as an academic field. In 1940, an important survey by Charles Frederick Harrold observes that "we are, of course, passing through a 'Victorian' vogue'" and that "Victorian scholarship is achieving maturity. It will be found that scholarly advance has been irregular. In a field so new, and relatively so recent, as the years between 1830–1900, we must expect much that is tentative, or incomplete, or unsuccessful" (668). In 1952, the field gained further delineation with the establishment of *Victorian Newsletter*, which included scholarly articles, book reviews, and bibliographies ("Editorial" 1). But it was in 1957 that the field fully arrived with the formation of the journal *Victorian Studies* at Indiana University. The Modern Language Association endorsed *Victorian Studies* and anointed it the home journal for the field when they recommended

"Victorian Bibliography" be published there ("Prefatory Note" 3). During
these years, Victorian studies groups formed at Cambridge University and
the University of Leicester, both of which hailed the journal for galvanizing
a range of scholars from numerous disciplines around the Victorian (Best;
Collins). From all evidence, the founding of *Victorian Studies* was a truly
generative event in the anglophone academy.

Victorian studies emerged amidst the efflorescence of area studies fields
in the United States after the World War II.[13] Populated by experts in
foreign languages, area studies fields were often Cold War knowledge
factories of the Soviet Union and the Third World. As Spivak puts it,
"Area Studies exhibit quality and rigor (those elusive traits), combined
with openly conservative or 'no' politics" (7). Though all scholarly fields
are ideological state apparatuses in Louis Althusser's sense of the term, not
all such apparatuses are the same or have the same function, and area
studies offered the American state a specific tool for its imperial project.
Paul A Bové explains: "Area studies has existed to provide authoritative
knowledge to the state, specifically the government and its policy-makers,
to enable the state to expand its power and to defend its interests geopolitically" (207). Cynically, one might think that the Victorian period would
be fertile ground for American foreign policy during the Cold War.
Nathan Hensley reminds us that "there were at least 228 separate armed
conflicts during the [Victorian] period," and the proliferation of imperial
violence during what is commonly referred to as the "age of Equipoise"
"suggests that the images we take to characterize the world's first liberal
empire should include not just the middle-class hearth or the democratic
ballot box but the war zones and boneyards of England's global periphery,
where mutiny, and its suppression, were all but universal" (2).[14] It would
therefore be reasonable to think that the study of British imperialism in the
nineteenth century might prove useful for the United States' postwar
geopolitical interests. But it doesn't take an insider to Victorian studies
to know that research on the Corn Laws, *Middlemarch*, and Ruskin's
aesthetics have never been especially useful for assassinating democratically
elected leaders, staging coups, installing dictators, or obliterating economies, landscapes, and entire societies in the Global South. Rather, the
usefulness of Victorian studies for the state might be better understood as
complimenting area studies by naturalizing the insularity of metropolitan
national culture – the isolation of the domestic from the international – of,
as Hensley put it, valorizing the "middle-class hearth" over "extrajudicial
killing as everyday life" – a facet of any successful empire. If area studies
encouraged expertise in seemingly far-off places, Victorian studies helped

naturalize the idea that the study of metropolitan culture could take place without any knowledge of those "far-off" places.

In the United States, for example, the National Endowment for the Humanities (NEH) was instrumental in producing such a body of provincial knowledge. A rather remarkable essay by Russell Wyland, Deputy Director of the NEH, is straightforward about the US government's Arnoldian relationship to humanistic inquiry: "Like postwar scholars, Congress had come to regard the civilizing effect of the humanities as protection against anti-democratic forces," and therefore justified public funding projects like the NEH in the mid-1960s (11).[15] Wyland notes how Barnaby C. Keeney's (the first chairman of the NEH) "vision for the Endowment's ideals of scholarly research could just as easily have been a description of the intellectual project pursued by [Walter] Houghton, [Michael] Wolff, and the early editors" of *Victorian Studies* (13). During its first eight years, the NEH funded forty-four fellowships and summer stipends in the field of Victorian studies (only one of which engages with British imperialism). By funding such projects, the NEH provided Victorianists working in the United States the financial resources to organize the field's archive in the form of bibliographies, nineteenth-century periodicals, editions of primary texts, and the publication of letters and diaries. After proudly mentioning that Lynne Cheney was the NEH's first Victorianist chairman (in the very years her husband directed wars in Panama and Iraq), Wyland declares that the "NEH can rightly claim credit for building the infrastructure of modern Victorian studies." Having funded collations such as the diaries of Elizabeth Barrett Browning into one volume, five volumes of Thomas Hardy's poetry, a volume of Thackeray's correspondence, and many others, the NEH had effectively produced and made accessible the very archive that was to prove fundamental to scholarship in Victorian studies. This is, of course, what public funding *should* do. But when done in a metropolitan center like the United States, the implication of such cultural production in the imperial milieu in which it is set is unavoidable. The reproductive quality of such institutional support (again, in the Althusserian sense) is evinced by how, as Wyland celebrates, "Victorian studies can rightly claim credit for the success of the Endowment. The rigor of funded Victorian studies scholars helped set standards for funding, not only for other Victorianists but also for scholars in other emerging disciplines" (23). Such is "sweetness and light" in the age of American imperialism.

Why, one might ask again, would the collected letters of Thomas Carlyle and Jane Welsh Carlyle be useful to postwar American imperialism? Why would Dickens's working notebooks ward off the barbarism that threatened American "democratic values"? Is it conceivable that Lynne Cheney's admiration for Matthew Arnold, who believed in the civilizing effects of culture, impacted Dick Cheney's decision to bomb Iraq? No, they wouldn't, and it isn't conceivable. Wyland's account suggests instead that it was precisely the field's *avoidance* of theorizing the link between culture and imperial politics that rendered it so compatible with an institution like the NEH. Bové notes something similar in the ideological function of American studies: "there was no sense in which the state needed the knowledge produced by American studies for its own executive purposes," but "rather, it was an instrument of the state" (211, 212). He goes on to argue that while American studies attended to the cultural heterogeneity of the United States, its resistance to comparative research meant its domain remained thoroughly domestic, rather than the international scope of the culture and politics of postwar America. Victorian studies too seems to have been such an apparatus in the United States, for, by naturalizing the nation state as the privileged domain of humanistic inquiry, the field foreclosed any connection between its object of study and the liberationist struggles of the Third World, both of which are connected rather well by the history of imperialism. As such, it positioned itself as a complement to the interventionist impulses of area studies fields. What is instead produced is scholarship on culture and society, not culture and imperialism (Said, *Culture and Imperialism* 14). The field's usefulness to the state, one might hypothesize, was precisely in *not* making the connection between civil society and imperialism, thereby offering a vision of a world in which it is possible to read a novel like *Daniel Deronda* and not think about Palestine.[16]

Epilogue for a Preface to Post-Postcolonial Criticism

Four decades after the publication of Adams and Winkler's "An Inter-Departmental Course on Victorian England," *Victorian Studies* published Erin O'Connor's infamous "Preface for a Post-Postcolonial Criticism." The essay accuses postcolonial criticism (mostly just Spivak) of appropriating the Victorian novel for the critique of empire, and for having "silenced" and "colonized the critical imagination of the Victorianist," who otherwise pursued the "unapologetic study of literature as a viable, worthwhile, eminently respectable end in itself" (228, 240). Sarcastic though it is in its characterization, when placed in relation to the early days of Victorian studies, the essay reads as longing to go back to a simpler time, when *Jane Eyre* was "just" a novel, before the advent of poststructuralism and postcolonial theory. For an essay that looks forward, "Preface" has a strange affinity for the past. It is not especially fruitful to revisit O'Connor's argument, or the debates the followed, or to show that postcolonial criticism was in fact the exception in Victorianist scholarship and not the overwhelming force she paints it as, or to recount how a "genre's thematic subtleties, structural indeterminacies, and genuine intellectual rigor" and ideology critique can, in fact, go hand in hand.[17]

But it is worth revisiting O'Connor's essay if only to register how her premise is that the field of Victorian studies existed in isolation from decolonization, and that talk of empire was an artificial insertion into the Victorian art-object by outsiders/theoreticians to the field. My argument in this chapter has been the opposite. Not only was Victorian literature and culture formative to the great theorists of decolonization, but it was also central to how they conceived of and articulated postcolonial liberation. Even the most superficial historicist would have to recognize the salience of this conjuncture. Furthermore, there is good evidence that the very idea of Victorian culture, "English culture of a particular age," was invented in the United States *in negative relation to* decolonization. The art-objects that O'Connor is so interested in saving from postcolonial ideology critique were invented as such amidst the Cold War milieu of American imperialism and produced as "civilizing" forces in the crusade against the Third World socialisms ("anti-democratic forces," as Wyland puts it). Attending to the history of decolonization-as-noun and its rather intimate relation to Victorian culture and society seems to be one way to recover "English culture of a particular age" without isolating culture from imperialism.

Notes

1. Ranajit Guha has even published on Charles Dickens but remains obscure to the field ("Colonial City").
2. This is to say nothing of the term "decolonial," which stands in sharp contrast to (how I represent) decolonization below. The former, Walter Mignolo tells us, "emerged at the very foundation of modern/coloniality, as its counterpoint" and is invested in a "thinking that de-links and opens ... to the possibilities of hidden ... by the modern rationality that is mounted and enclosed by categories of Greek, Latin and six modern imperial European languages" (46). Decolonization, as I argue below, is a determinate negation of modern rationality.
3. For, as I see it, symptomatic examples, see Bejarano, Juárez, García, and Goldstein (2019); Eckhardt. And for critical reflections on "decolonizing," see Thomas; Allen and Jobson; Mbembe.

4. Eve Tuck and K. Wayne Yang put it bluntly: "The easy adoption of decolonization as a metaphor (and nothing else) is a form of this [settler] anxiety, because it
is a premature attempt at reconciliation. "The absorption of decolonization by
settler social justice frameworks is one way the settler, disturbed by her own
settler status, tries to escape or contain the unbearable searchlight of complicity,
of having harmed others just by being oneself." The desire to reconcile is just as
relentless as the desire to disappear the Native; it is a desire to not have to deal
with this (Indian) problem anymore" (9). Being a literary critic, I am unsure of
Tuck and Yang's dismissal of metaphor as such (even in the context of decolonization) and concerned by their ontological framing of colonial discourse. But
I echo their main claim: the verb "decolonize" can, in fact, be a technology of
empire because of its disavowal of the continuing effects of imperialism, and the
ways in which empire continues to structure, amongst many things, the discourse
of social justice.

5. In one of few such instances, Fanon considers the contagiousness of anticolonial rebellion from the standpoint of the colonizer: "The great victory of the
Vietnamese people at Dien Bien Phu is no longer strictly speaking
a Vietnamese victory ... A Dien Bien Phu was now within reach of every
colonized subject ... This pervading atmosphere of violence affects not just the
colonized but also the colonizers who realize the number of latent Dien Bien
Phu's. The colonial governments are therefore gripped in a genuine wholesale
panic. Their plan is to make the first move, to turn the liberation movement to
the right and disarm the people. Quick, let's decolonize. Let's decolonize the
Congo before it turns into another Algeria" (31). Faced with the potential
domino effect of anticolonial rebellions in one colony, the colonizer uses the
slogan "decolonize" to end formal colonialism and continue it by the other
means of economic dependency.

6. Anecdotally, but perhaps tellingly, when I approached one of the organizers of
the annual North American Victorian Studies Association conference about
encouraging crosslingual research by requiring all participants to engage with
a language other than English in order to present at future conferences, the idea
was dismissed because it would mean the end of the conference altogether.
Such is the (perceived) incompatibility of Victorian studies and comparative
literature.

7. The same is true of anticolonial thought in the Francophone world. Gary
Wilder notes Negritude's "contradictory character," at once complicit with the
colonial order of things and simultaneously contesting it, at once Francophilic
and anticolonial. See especially chapters 6 and 7.

8. It is worth pointing out that none of the writers discussed above make much of
a distinction between, say, late eighteenth- or early nineteenth-century writers,
or between romanticism and Victorianism, and slippages between British and
American literature are common. This is in part because, as I suggest below, the
"Victorian period" as an analytical category was itself invented in the mid-
twentieth century.

9. See also Gikandi, "Embarrassment" and "Afro-Victorian."

10. Partha Chatterjee makes the persuasive claim that Ambedkar's advocacy of partition had the ultimate aim of forging solidarity between those of lower caste and Muslims in the name of equal rights (21–22).
11. For an analysis of the importance of Victorian literature and culture for figures like Du Bois, see Dickerson.
12. A notable exception is Banerjee.
13. The National Defense Education Act of 1958 was instrumental in this regard.
14. See also Gopal.
15. I am grateful to Devin Griffiths to pointing me to this essay.
16. This is, of course, precisely Said's intervention in *The Question of Palestine*, which usefully constellates Victorian culture, Zionism, and Palestinian self-determination – but which remains a less-than-minor text in the history of Victorian studies (56–114).
17. For the debates the followed O'Connor's essay, see Brantlinger and David.

WORKS CITED

Adams, Ruth M. and Henry R. Winkler. "An Inter-Departmental Course on Victorian England." *Victorian Studies* 7.1 (1963): 100–102.

Allen, Jafari Sinclaire and Ryan Cecil Jobson. "The Decolonizing Generation: (Race and) Theory in Anthropology since the Eighties." *Current Anthropology* 57.2 (2016): 129–48.

Ambedkar, B. R. *Pakistan, or the Partition of India*. Bombay: Thacker, 1941.

Bannerjee, Sukanya. *Becoming Imperial Citizens*. Durham, NC: Duke University Press, 2010.

Bejarano Alonso, Carolina, Juárez Lucia Lopez, García, Mirian A. Mijangos, Daniel Goldstein, . *Decolonizing Ethnography: Undocumented Immigrants and New Directions in Social Science*. Durham, NC: Duke University Press, 2019.

Best, G. F. A. "The Cambridge University 19th-Century Group." *Victorian Studies* 1.3 (1958): 267–68.

Bové, Paul A. "Can American Studies Be Area Studies." In Masao Miyoshi and H. D. Harootunian, eds., *Learning Places: The Afterlives of Area Studies*. Durham, NC: Duke University Press, 2002, 206–30.

Brantlinger, Patrick. "Let's Post-Post 'Victorientalism': A Response to Erin O'Connor." *Victorian Studies* 46.1 (2003): 97–105.

Chatterjee, Partha. *The Politics of the Governed*. New York: Columbia University Press, 2004.

Collins, Philip. *Death of a Discipline*. New York: Columbia University Press, 2003.

"The University of Leicester Victorian Studies Group," *Victorian Studies* 6.3 (1963): 281–82.

David, Deirdre. "She Who Must Be Obeyed: A Response to Erin O'Connor." *Victorian Studies* 46.1 (2003): 106–10.

Dickerson, Vanessa D. *Dark Victorians*. Champagne-Urbana: University of Illinois Press, 2008.

Du Bois, W. E. B. *Black Reconstruction in America: 1860–1880*. New York: The Free Press, 1992.

Eckhardt, Giana M., Russell Belk, Tonya Williams Bradford, et al. "Decolonizing Marketing." *Consumption, Markets, Culture* 25.2 (2022): 176–89.

"Editorial," *Victorian Newsletter* 1 (1952): 1–11.

Engels, Friedrich. *The Conditions of the Working Class in England*. London: Oxford University Press, 1993.

Fanon, Frantz. *The Wretched of the Earth*, translated by Richard Philcox. New York: Grove, 2004.

Garvey, Marcis. *Marcus Garvey: Life and Lessons*, ed. Robert A. Hill. Berkeley: University of California Press, 1987.

Gikandi, Simon. "Afro-Victorian Worlds." In Martin Hewitt, ed., *The Victorian World*. New York: Routledge, 2012, 671–90.

"The Embarrassment of Victorianism: Colonial Subjects and the Lure of Englishness." In John Kucich and Dianne F. Sadoff, eds., *Victorian Afterlife: Postmodern Culture Rewrites the Nineteenth Century*. Minneapolis: University of Minnesota Press, 2000.

Gopal, Priyamvada. *Insurgent Empire: Anticolonial Resistance and British Dissent*. New York: Verso, 2019.

Guha, Ranajit. "The Colonial City and Its Time(s)." *Indian Economic Social History Review* 45.3 (2008): 329–51.

Harrold, Charles Frederick. "Recent Trends in Victorian Studies: 1932–1939." *Studies in Philology* 37.4 (1940): 667–97.

Hensley, Nathan K. *Forms of Empire: The Poetics of Victorian Sovereignty*. Oxford: Oxford University Press, 2017.

James, C. L. R. *Beyond a Boundary*. Durham: Duke University Press, 2013.

Lewis, David Levering. *W.E.B. Du Bois: Biography of a Race, 1868–1919*. New York: Henry Holt, 1993.

Mbembe, Achille Joseph. "Decolonizing the University." *Arts and Humanities in Higher Education* 15.1 (2016): 29–45.

Mignolo, Walter D. "Epistemic Disobedience and the Decolonial Question: A Manifesto." *Transmodernity* 1.2 (2011): 44–66.

Miller, J. Hillis. *Victorian Subjects*. Durham, NC: Duke University Press, 1991.

Nehru, Jawaharlal. *Toward Freedom: The Autobiography of Jawaharlal Nehru*. New York: The John Day Company, 1941.

Ngũgĩ wa Thiong'o. *Decolonising the Mind: The Politics of Language and African Literature*. Oxford: James Curry, 1986.

O'Connor, Erin. "Preface for a Post-Postcolonial Criticism." *Victorian Studies* 45.2 (2003): 217–46.

"Prefatory Note." *Victorian Studies* 1.1 (1957): 3.

Said, Edward W. *Culture and Imperialism*. New York: Vintage, 1993.

The Question of Palestine. New York: Vintage, 1992.

Spivak, Gayatri Chakravorty. "Three Women's Texts and a Critique of Imperialism." *Critical Inquiry* 12.1 (1985): 243–61.

Tagore, Rabindranath. *Crisis in Civilization*. Calcutta: Vivsa A-Bharati, 1957.

Thomas, Deborah A. "Decolonizing Disciplines: From the Editor." *American Anthropologist* 120.3 (2018): 393–97.

Tuck, Eve and K. Wayne Yang. "Decolonization Is Not a Metaphor." *Decolonization: Indigeneity, Education and Society* 1.1 (2012): 1–40.

Wilder, Gary. *The French Imperial Nation-State: Negritude and Colonial Humanism Between the Two World Wars*. Chicago: University of Chicago Press, 2005.

Williams, Eric. *British Historians and the West Indies*. New York: Charles Scribner's Sons, 1966.

Wyland, Russell M. "Public Funding and the Untamed Wilderness." *Victorian Studies and Its Publics* 55 (2009). www.erudit.org/en/journals/ravon/1900-v1-n1-ravon3697/039554ar/.

CHAPTER 22

Decolonizing World Literature

Debjani Ganguly

In the wake of a spectacular resurgence in racial violence and ethnonationalisms in hitherto-thriving democracies around the world, the project of decolonization has never been more urgent. How might we as teachers of English and world literatures come to terms with the chasm between our decades-long experience of training students in postcolonial and comparative modes of engagement with the world's literary riches, and the staggering racial divides, unspeakable tribalism, and broken psychic regimes that we witness in the wider world? Given the long history of English literary studies as an inextricable part of imperial governance and as a cultural touchstone until World War II, and its continuing flourishing well into the twenty-first century, the stakes of our intellectual and pedagogical engagement in English departments have scarcely been higher.

Ecumenical perspectives on literature have often emerged in the wake of revolutionary or catastrophic world events. The Napoleonic Wars for Goethe, 1848 for Marx, the colonial partition of Bengal for Rabindranath Tagore, the Russian Revolution for Maxim Gorky and Zheng Zhenduo, the Spanish Civil War for Pablo Neruda and W. H. Auden, Nazi-era Europe for Eric Auerbach and Victor Klemperer, the 1968 uprisings for René Etiemble, and the Israel–Palestine conflict for Edward Said, are well-known historical thresholds. Our turbulent global era after 1989 is no less responsible for the contemporary revival of world literature. The field's geopolitical backdrop is a series of catastrophes: the proliferation of global conflicts and civil wars with the end of the Cold War, genocides in Bosnia and Rwanda, the spectacular implosion of 9/11, the wars in Afghanistan and Iraq, and the violent ravaging of the Middle East by the conjoined interests of the global power elites and fundamentalisms of various hues. In the past decade, a wealth of world anglophone literary scholarship has emerged on classic twenty-first crises such as global terrorism, refugee displacement, environmental degradation, populist authoritarianisms, and climate change (Nixon; Cheah; Ganguly, *This Thing*; DeLoughrey; Goyal).

Who and what the *world* is to which world literature refers and is constituted by is a question of deep import to scholars in the field. Theories of world literature have struggled to keep pace with the dramatic reconfiguration of the world since the end of European colonialism, the fall of the Soviet Union, and the resurgence of multipolar ethnonationalisms around the world. One can scarcely miss the disjunction between some recent influential theories of world literature that perpetuate a universalist narrative of European expansion and diffusion and the diversity of global comparatist work that illuminates cartographies of literary world-making across various scales and linguistic zones, and within temporal frames irreducible to European literary history or the capitalist world system. With the global turn in the English curriculum since the rise of postcolonialism in the 1970s and 1980s and the prominence of English as a world language and a translating medium (signposted by the term "global anglophone"), debates about world literature have gained substantial traction in English literary studies.[1]

This essay explores the entangled histories of world literature, postcolonial studies, and global anglophone literatures as they shape English studies today. Drawing on my scholarly and pedagogical work, I offer a decolonial understanding of world literature along three axes: historical, cartographic, and linguistic. The historical axis illuminates the imperial backstory of current iterations of world literature in the rise of comparative philology and orientalist scholarship in the late eighteenth and early nineteenth centuries. It also pluralizes the temporal framing of world literature by reaching back to medieval and early modern instances of literary worlding in Arabic, Chinese, Latin, Persian, and Sanskrit and situates the current valence of English in a literary *longue durée*. The cartographic axis highlights literary world-making athwart transregional zones such as the oceanic, the hemispheric, the archipelagic, and multilocal. These crosscut the binaries of Global North and South and resist being situated within a single world system in which non-European worlds invariably appear as belated or derivative or minor. Finally, along the linguistic axis, I explore how the contemporary resonance of world literature and its counterpart, global anglophone, cannot be grasped unless we disaggregate English from imperial models of the past. This paradoxical claim does not disavow the history of English under the British Empire and the rise of America in the post-War era. But it shifts the ground of discourse from under this Anglo-imperial shadow and illuminates new zones of multilingual transculturation.

Historicizing World Literature

Bound by neither a finite and continuous periodicity nor a specific textual object, nor even any consensus about its theoretical ground, world literature poses a challenge for a literary historian of a magnitude scarcely encountered in fields such as romanticism or postcolonialism. One cannot but be struck by the dizzyingly heterogeneous range of scholarly articulations of it. Literary world-making as the travel and diffusion of forms, genres, and textual patterns; as elliptical movement and reception of works in different regions of the globe; as a site of global competitiveness over literary value; as born-translated works that echo other literary imaginaries; as bibliomigrancy and a global pact with books; as intermediate regional constellations between the nation and the globe; as a normative apprehension of the singularity of literary textuality that resists the technomaterialist coordinates of globalization; as an aesthetic and formalist response to globalization, catastrophic global events, and digital hyperconnectivity; as literature of the capitalist world system – there is no dearth of such substantial and compelling accounts of contemporary approaches to world literature. The reemergence of world literature as an ideal in our global era has unsurprisingly also generated contentious and skeptical accounts: world literature as a handmaiden of the forces of globalization; as a posthistorical triumphal narrative of an enforced unification of the world; as an alibi for an appropriative anglophone dominance; and as a translational scandal.

While one is not in doubt about the significance of *world* as a powerful constellating force in literary studies today, an historian is confronted with the monumental task of "weighing, comparing, analyzing, and discriminating" among this vast array of articulations, to paraphrase Rene Wellek. In what follows, I offer some insights on a decolonial approach to the history of world literature based on a two-volume editorial project I have recently completed. I also briefly discuss the outlines of a graduate course I teach on world literature and the British Empire.

Having undertaken my graduate studies in English, South Asian literatures, and postcolonial studies in Australia under the mentorship of the *Subaltern Studies* collective and having since published books in caste and dalit studies, postcolonialism, global anglophone literatures, and world literature in academic presses across the United Kingdom, the United States, and Australia, I am acutely aware of the complexity of navigating multilingual worlds within an anglophone academy. I have recently edited a two-volume *Cambridge History of World Literature* with forty-eight contributors working across twenty-nine literary traditions (2021). Bound by neither a single market nor a single world history of capitalist unification, world literature, in these volumes, is perceived as a transversal and comparative framework for studying myriad literary worlds across history. The project bears little resemblance to the lamentable picture of world literature as "one-world talk" that projects Anglo-global dominance. Prior eras generated republics of letters across vast continental swathes. English, Arabic, Persian, Chinese, Hindi, French, Spanish, Portuguese, Swahili, and Tamil are large transregional literary-linguistic worlds today, albeit each with very different cultural capital. Collectively, *The Cambridge History of World Literature* offers an account of world literature that is informed by decades of excavation of the origins of modern disciplinary formations in histories of European encounter with civilizations across Asia, the Mediterranean, Latin America, and Africa. It situates the modern origins of "world literature" within a *longue durée* optic. Arab mapmakers from the tenth century onward were among the first to visualize the globe's spatial expansiveness as a concept. European mapmakers in fifteenth century built on these cartographic practices. Ancient and medieval trade routes, like the Silk Route, the Mediterranean, and the Indian Ocean, spanned continents and generated corridors of intense linguistic and cultural mixing. The rise of Sanskrit, Arabic, and Persian republics of letters long preceded that of the European Renaissance. The vernacularization of languages and their proliferation through the modern era began toward the end of the first millennium in Asia and Europe. The vernacular languages existed in a robust ecosystem alongside classical tongues – Latin, Sanskrit, Arabic – and generated long periods of multilingual creativity. Oral, graphic, visual, and performative forms marked aesthetic engagement in much of Africa, Latin America, the Caribbean, and the Pacific before European colonization. Such a long historical view of world literature offers a corrective to the historiographical distortion one finds in influential works such as Pascale Casanova's *The World Republic of Letters*, where the entire literary history of humankind is annexed to the rise of Europe in the sixteenth century. The myriad linguistic resonances of the term "world" – *orbis* in Latin, *kosmos* in Greek, *Welt* in German, *vishwa* in Sanskrit, *duniya* in Hindi/Urdu, *jahan* in Persian, *monde* in French – are a measure of its philological shaping as an aesthetic and a normative category, one that resists the homogenizing power of the global as it reckons with the plenitude and singularity of literatures from around the world.

World literature in the twenty-first century, the *Cambridge History* contends, is primed to explore genealogies of world literary formations that not only predate the rise of Europe but are also critically coextensive with it *and* demonstrably foundational to the very conception of the modern idea of world literature. The *adab* literary tradition, or *belle-lettres* in Arabic, with its beginnings in the late Ummayad caliphal court in the eighth century and its consolidation in the early Abbasid period from 750–1256 CE is one such example. A chapter in volume I of the *Cambridge History* traces the influence of Middle Persian translations of Sanskrit on *adab* and follows a trail of translations until the sixteenth century of key texts from the Indo-Persianate and Arabic literary worlds into Hebrew, Greek, Latin, and the European vernaculars, including German, Danish, Dutch, Spanish, Italian, and English. One cannot conceive of world literature without calibrating the influence of such medieval and early modern philological endeavors, and their recovery and reconceptualization by European philologists in the nineteenth century (Al Rahim). Another chapter tracks the role of East India Company orientalists such as William Jones since the eighteenth century and those of German philologists who mined centuries of literary riches in Sanskrit, Arabic, Persian, and Chinese across a vast swathe of Asia in the company of native scholars. How could Goethe's idea of world literature have emerged, the author asks, without these colonial philological endeavors that reached him via Fredrich Schlegel and other Weimar philologists (Bhattacharya)? Such complex genealogical accounts illuminate pathways toward theories and method-ologies of doing world literature that are not invariably circumscribed by the modern nation state, an international competition for global prestige, the capitalist world system, and the European diffusionist model.

How might one bring these insights into the English curriculum? Typically, students in English departments fall back on canonical works by Damrosch, Casanova, and Moretti without being aware of the genea-logical ground of world literature in the history of empires, and especially the British Empire. In a graduate course I teach on "World Literature, Orientalism, and Empire," the students explore how the bureaucratic machinery of the British Empire was instrumental in the emergence of key conceptual shifts that became foundational to the nineteenth century idea of world literature promoted by Goethe, Marx, and Engels. The shifts include orientalist scholarship, the rise of philology, the comparatist method, and translational endeavors. The course module covers vast ground spanning early orientalist scholarship between 1757 and 1789 to the towering influence of Sir William Jones's historical philology on the Indo-European family of languages. We read about the role of the East India Company in generating global circuits of print publication and the promotion of English Literature in colonial education systems across South Asia and Africa. We trace what Srinivas Aravamudan has called "Enlightenment Orientalism" – a swathe of translational endeavors in European languages of magisterial premodern works in Sanskrit, Chinese, Arabic, Persian, and Tamil. The students begin to see the cross-cutting impact of these developments across India, Britain, and Germany as an exciting chapter in the history of world literature (Aravamudan).

Moving away from stock understandings of translation as contamin-ation or devaluation, or merely a device to exoticize non-European worlds, the students also begin to appreciate the historic role of translation in world literary studies. Scholarly traditions across history have felt the influence of other traditions mainly through acts of translation. The European Renaissance is unthinkable without the discovery of medieval-era Arabic translations of the Greek philosophers Plato and Aristotle. As is the emergence of modern comparative and world literatures without the massive translation enterprises of colonial-era orientalists such as Jones, Schlegel, and Humboldt. The conception of world literature as a global network of intersecting influences has led to a reevaluation of the stature of translation as a foundational practice in the history of literary dissemin-ation. Translation is now widely perceived as a perturbation of the settled economy of two linguistic systems and not a practice of distortion or deformation (Bassnett; Venuti).

The global reach of English appears in a different light when seen through a comparative and translational lens. Just as we are deliberating today about the global reach of English and its imperial foundations, scholars of ancient and early modern worlds have deliberated on the impact of other world languages such as Greek, Latin, Chinese, Sanskrit, Persian, and Arabic. Conquests, commerce, migration, imperial adventures, and cultural influence have allowed languages such as English, French, Spanish, Arabic, Persian, Sanskrit, Russian, Tamil, and Chinese to have a disproportionate historical influence on literatures around the globe. Ancient and medieval trade routes like the Silk Route and the Indian Ocean spanned continents and generated corridors of intense linguistic and cultural mixing. Sheldon Pollock's work on the rise of the Sanskrit cosmopolis from Afghanistan to Java in Southeast Asia from 300 to 1300 CE traces this phenomenon. Muhsin al-Musawi traces the emergence of an Arabic republic of letters at the confluence of vernacular languages that flourished between the twelfth and eighteenth centuries, and which stretched across southern Europe, the Mediterranean, North Africa, West Asia, and Southeast Asia (Pollock; al-Musawi). Today, the influence

of English outstrips all others, and the forces of modern history – mercantile capitalism, colonialism, industrialization, the information technology
revolution – have played a monumental role in its elevation as a world
language and a global medium of translation. Currently, English also exists
in a vast ecosystem with eleven other supercentral languages that boast
more than 100 million speakers. These comprise Arabic, Chinese, French,
German, Hindi, Japanese, Malay, Portuguese, Russian, Spanish, and
Swahili.

While acknowledging the unification of the world under a capitalist
world system that hoists English as its dominant tongue, world literary
approaches allow us to ask generative questions about literary globalism.
How have these languages shaped diverse literary cultures in their inter-
mixing with local and regional traditions? How have they been transformed in turn? How does a perspective that engages with older histories
and other overlapping linguistic geographies produce a different account of
literary evolution? What happens when we explore the use of English as
a medium of literary translation instead of as a source language? Questions
such as these urge us to pluralize the history of culture-power beyond
primordialism, imperial absolutism, language sentiment, and linguistic
monism. Comparative and *longue durée* perspectives on the emergence of
literary worlds enable us to grasp the valence of English and anglophone
literatures within a multilingual realm of expressive elaboration and spatial
dissemination.

Decolonial Cartographies

The question of spatial scale in world literature is as urgent as questions of
temporality and historicity. What constitutes viable units of analysis in
world literature? How do we conceive of median scales larger than the
nation but smaller than the globe that push against notions of
a freewheeling globality and that better reflect the multi-scalar and spatially
dispersed nature of contemporary literary world-making? What about
multilingual nations whose literary worlds cross borders in ways that defy
the classic polarization between the Global North and Global South or
between the local and the global? An exciting development in world
literature is the emergence of literary cartographies such as the oceanic,
the hemispheric, the transregional, the archipelagic, and the multilingual-
local. Works by Isabel Hofmeyr and Gaurav Desai on the Indian Ocean,
Konstantina Zanou on the Mediterranean, Allison Donnell on the
Caribbean, Teresia Teiawa on the Pacific, Anna Brickhouse on

hemispheric American studies, and Dan Ringgard on Nordic studies are good examples. Francesca Orsini, Karima Laachir, and Sara Marzagora's comparative project on "significant geographies" and "multilingual locals," with literatures from northern India, the Horn of Africa, and Maghreb, is another example of decolonial cartographic experimentation. Hemispheric and oceanic approaches have brought literary worlds from the Americas and Europe into meaningful conversation with those from Africa and Asia.

In an advanced-year undergraduate course that I developed a few years ago, entitled "Oceanic Connections: Black Atlantic and Indian Ocean Worlds," students explore the emergence of the "oceanic" as a powerful paradigm in world literary studies. The fluidity of the ocean as against terrestrial borders gives new meaning to categories such as empire, diaspora, postcolonialism, slavery, settler colonialism, and labor history. Through novels, philosophical tracts, and theories of history, we study the import of the transatlantic slave trade and its entanglement with global histories of modern maritime colonialism found in Indian Ocean worlds. We trace these entanglements through the novels of Barry Unsworth, Fred D'Aguiar, Amitav Ghosh, and Abdul Razak Gurnah. In engaging with the *Ibis* trilogy of Ghosh and the Zanzibari novels of Gurnah – works traversing the Indian Ocean world from East Africa, the Arabian Peninsula, and the Indian archipelago to the bays and estuaries in the South China Sea – the students become aware of the critical role played by this maritime route in the consolidation of British Empire. Both Ghosh and Gurnah stretch this historiography back to the preimperial phase and write about the centuries-old trading diasporas of Arabia, India, and China that intersected with the history of European maritime imperialism, and also of histories of slavery that precede the transatlantic slave trade.

In teaching oceanic novels such as the *Sea of Poppies*, *River of Smoke*, *Sacred Hunger*, and *By the Sea*, I invite students to think about the genres these works embed: the classic historical novel and other sea-inspired novelistic and poetic genres, but also thalassography, a branch of oceanic writing that focuses on smaller bodies of water that are populated with habitations intimately connected with oceanic routes; bays, estuaries, rivers, gulfs, and deltas.[2] After all, much of the action in Ghosh's *Ibis* novels, for instance, has aqueous bodies as its backdrop: the Hooghly river, the Bay of Bengal, the Arabian Sea, the Pearl River Delta, and the Hong Kong Bay. The ocean has featured as a setting in any number of classic literary texts from Coleridge's *The Rime of the Ancient Mariner*, Melville's *Moby-Dick*, and Verne's *Vingt mille lieues sous les mers* to Hemingway's *The Old Man and the Sea*, Conrad's *Lord Jim*, and

Walcott's *Omeros*. These works are often familiar to advanced-year under-graduates in the United States, and we spend a few minutes in the first seminar sharing perceptions about them. We also discuss the implications of moving from the thematic of the ocean in literature to conceiving the ocean as both a material force in, and a conceptual frame for, literary history. This we realize is a challenge of a different order and scale. The novels of Ghosh and Gurnah, and the vast scholarship on Afro-Asian oceanic histories, for instance, illuminate conceptual frames that can be deployed retroactively to better understand how past systems of globalism have impacted on the making and refashioning of modern literary worlds, such as the late eighteenth to nineteenth-century Franco-British maritime world system.

The relationship between cartography, cognitive mapping, and aesthetic representation is particularly complex in oceanic literary studies. Since the nineteenth century, the Atlantic has featured as the oceanic zone around which modern literary histories have coalesced. English and French litera-tures led the way and constituted a kind of universal gold standard in the field, or the literary Greenwich meridian, as Pascale Casanova puts it. The consolidation of British and French empires across much of the globe from the 1830s to the 1930s coincided with the rise of literary studies as a discipline, first in the colonies, and then in Europe and America. English literature, with its riches from the era of *Beowulf* to the Victorian period, became the pedagogical norm and was aggressively promoted as a force for cultural transformation in the colonies of Asia and Africa. A vast philological enterprise to master the linguistic and literary riches of Asia, East Africa, and the Arab world (the history of which I briefly revisited above) ran parallel with these developments. Not surprisingly, the North Atlantic, and especially Anglo-French literary historiography, did not intersect with this colonial philological history. And so it remained well into the twentieth century with the rise of America. The victory of the Allies in World War II consolidated a North Atlantic world view as the new universal. This was initiated during the war by the Joint Declaration of Winston Churchill and Franklin D. Roosevelt in Newfoundland on August 14, 1941. The declaration, soon dubbed as the Atlantic Charter, envisioned an Anglo-American alliance that would lay the foundation for a post-War world era of peace based on principles of "sovereign rights and self-government" and the rights of "all the men in all lands." This declar-ation subsequently became the legal basis for the Charter of the United Nations in 1945 (Slaughter and Bystrom). These developments channeled the Atlantic imaginary toward imperial and national histories with a triumphalist narrative from "encounter to emancipation between the late fifteenth and early nineteenth centuries" (Armitage 95).

The rise of Atlantic *world* histories toward the end of the twentieth century complicated this triumphalist political and literary history by drawing attention both to the transatlantic slave trade across the north and south of the ocean and to crosscutting networks of slave and indentured labor across the Indian Ocean after the abolition of slavery. The Atlantic world has featured as a major paradigm in oceanic literary studies since the publication of Paul Gilroy's path-breaking *The Black Atlantic*. The making of Euro-America on the back of the slave trade provides a powerful and sobering counterpoint to the triumphant theatricality of Franco-British maritime domination in the same era, while simultaneously connecting literary discourses and literary themes previously understood as territorially and culturally distinct. Black Atlantic studies has revolutionized the way we study the emergence of modern French, British, and American literatures today. In postcolonial and world literary studies, the phrase Black Atlantic has reconceptualized the Atlantic seaboard as the site of the emergence of capitalist modernity as a transnational system. The African slave trade, the American plantation economies, and the industrial world of Europe are seen as inextricably linked, a phenomenon that the students are historically attuned to.

The students in my course are less aware of an equally resonant oceanic world – the Indian Ocean – that lies at the heart of the European maritime expansion from Africa and the Middle East to South and Southeast Asia, a world that Ghosh's and Gurnah's novels bring powerfully to the fore. Indian Ocean literary worlds have been disconcertingly absent in conceptions of modern European and world literatures. The history of the slave trade was followed by the history of indentured labor (commonly known as the *coolie trade*) from India and Malaya to outposts of the British and French Empires, primarily to the Mascarenhas archipelago, the Pacific islands, and the Caribbean. The Indian Ocean trade routes served as the primary conduit for this transportation. Indians, Chinese, Africans, and Arabs commingled in zones that continued to experience the dark memories of the slave trade. Frederic Douglass, the author of the novella *The Heroic Slave*, wrote in 1871 about his distress at the grim reality of the coolie trade. A century later, the Mauritian poet Khal Torabully articulated a transnational poetics of "coolitude," drawing on the pan-African "négritude" movement of the 1930s and arguing for the centrality of the sea voyage – as both destructive and creative force – in the recovering of the coolie's identity and story (Torabully and Carter). The opium trade between British India and China is equally crucial to foregrounding the importance of the Indian Ocean in the making of capitalist modernity. Opium was Britain's solution to the imbalance of trade with China. The British import of Chinese tea, silks, and porcelain in exchange for silver had vastly drained British resources. Aware of the Chinese addiction to opium, the East India Company forced peasants in eastern India to turn to the cultivation of opium. By the beginning of the nineteenth century, the British used the port of Calcutta and the waters of the eastern Indian Ocean to send more than 4,000 crates of opium via third-party traders to Canton. This consignment quadrupled in the years leading up to the Chinese crackdown on the trade in the 1830s and the decade leading up to the First Opium War. The war led to the victory of the British imperial military forces in 1842 and the handover of Hong Kong to the Crown.

The interconnectedness between the Atlantic slave trade and the movement of labor on Indian Ocean trade routes, and the consequent entanglement of literatures of slavery and indenture, are brought to the fore in the early weeks of our coursework. The students read excerpts from works by Gaurav Desai, Isabel Hofmeyr, Enseng Ho, Sanjay Subramanyam, Sunil Amrith, and Nile Green, among others. They become aware of the need for a renewed attentiveness to interconnected print and literary public spheres of the Indian Ocean world from the eighteenth to the mid-twentieth centuries. European imperial incursions in this region can be seen as generating renewed cultural mixing with pre-European worlds. Literature during this period is broadly understood to cover diverse genres in multiple languages including Gujarati, Hindi, Swahili, Arabic, English, and French. Itinerant travelers such as pilgrims, sailors, soldiers, traders, merchants, and administrators have left records of their experiences. Records also exist of prisoners in the penal settlements of Robben Island and the Andamans. The genres range from travel writing, folktales, and letters to poems, testimonies, short stories, and novels. Many of these exist in special collections primarily in South Africa, the United States, the United Kingdom, India, Mauritius, and Madagascar. Extant texts on the Zanzibari Gujaratis such as Gunvantrai's *Dariyalal* exist alongside Mia Couto's *Voices Made Night* and Zuleikha Mayat's weekly columns from Durban in *Indian Views*. Cynthia Salvadori's three-volume publication, *We Came in Dhows*, records the movement of Indian traders across the Indian Ocean between the west coast of India and Kenya, and their eventual settlement in East Africa during the colonial era. Memorabilia, photographs, travel narratives, diaries, and memoirs feature in this collection and offer a powerful tableau of Indo-British-African cultural connections. A not-insignificant proportion of this literature finds inflection in the works of contemporary novelists such as Abdul Razak Gurnah, M. G. Vassanji, J. M. G. Le Clézio, and Shenaz Patel.

Much like Deeti in *Sea of Poppies*, who sees an apparition of the ship *Ibis* from her landlocked hut in Ghazipur and is filled with fear about what it entails, the students experience considerable trepidation as they dip their feet into the Indian Ocean world and especially the world of Ghosh's *Ibis* novels. Despite their readiness to learn about a world from a relatively unknown past, a world they have not encountered in their English Literature classes in the United States, their disorientation is quite serious. They encounter a facet of the global that resists easy translation. The hybrid languages of oceanic mobility in the early nineteenth century, we realize, is lost to generations who have grown up in the age of air travel.

This becomes an opportune moment in our seminar to turn to linguistic experimentation in the novels and their revival of the many lost idiolects of nineteenth-century Asian maritime worlds. The language weave in Ghosh's *Ibis* trilogy is truly astonishing, ranging from sea-trading argot like *laskari* and Cantonese pidgin to Baboo English and Butler English, not to mention the generous sprinkling of various regional Indian tongues such as Hindi, Gujarati, Bhojpuri, and Bengali. The students are especially intrigued by Ghosh's use of *laskari*, the extinct idiolect of the lascars, the laboring Afro-Asian underclass on board these ships, and of Cantonese pidgin spoken only by those involved in the Canton trading system in southern China in the first half of the nineteenth century. The entanglement of these tongues with specific bodies of water is brought to the fore through characters like Jodu, Serang Ali, Ah Fatt, Bahram Modi, and his Cantonese mistress. We spend a few minutes in class reading aloud excerpts where exchanges occur in Cantonese pidgin. I share with my students the story of Ghosh's discovery of a Laskari Dictionary in a library in Harvard that provided him with the impetus to make generous use of this now-extinct vocabulary in his trilogy. Compiled by Lt. Thomas Roebuck in 1811, *A Laskari Dictionary of Anglo-Indian Vocabulary of Nautical Terms and Phrases in English and Hindustani* was a major inspiration for the novelist, as was Yule and Burnell's *Hobson-Jobson: A Glossary of Colloquial Anglo-Indian Words and Phrases*. The students also research the chrestomathy developed by Ghosh as an appendix to the novels. This philological appendix has a narrative about Neel Rattan Haldar, the disgraced Raja of Raskhali, as the reborn lexicographer who makes it his mission to document every possible word used by girmityas, lascars, and their Anglo-Indian masters during their oceanic journeys. This vocabulary,

Neel predicts, would make its way into the first major lexicographic project undertaken on behalf of the English Language, namely the *Oxford English Dictionary*, but which Neel calls the "Oracle." In the 1840s, the *OED* was nowhere on the horizon. We see this new Neel as the painstaking lexicographer of a global English before the era of globalization in the final novel of the trilogy *Flood of Fire*. Ghosh's brilliant lexicographic excavation bears significant purchase on contemporary debates about English as a world language in the era of globalization.

In brief, the students not only begin to see the Indian Ocean as a powerful archive through which to understand modern literary world making, but also learn to trace lines of intersection with Atlantic perspectives to which they are much more attuned. They also begin to appreciate how the ocean might function as an exciting cartographic frame for a decolonial understanding of world literature. Significantly, they begin to appreciate the embedding of the English language in vast multilingual realms. It is to this multilingual realm of global anglophone worlds that I turn to in the final part of this essay.

Multilingualism and Global Anglophone Worlds

"Decolonizing (the) English," notes Peter Hitchcock, "is . . . an allegory of abnegation in which the power to decolonize does not exhaust the power that English confers, but [it] . . . confounds the process of selving that globalization demands" (751). Just as we need to rethink the language of endings and death in relation to postcolonialism, we might also consider the possibility that global anglophone is much more than an intractable literary monoculture out to extinguish the multilingual provenance of world literature. In recent years, many scholarly works have illuminated the multilingual face of anglophone worlding at different scales. Jeanne-Marie Jackson's *South African Literature's Russian Soul: Narrative Forms of Global Isolation* (2015) is an outstanding example. What might two regions at a vast geographical, geopolitical, and temporal remove have in common? A literary imaginary, it appears, one shaped by oppressive political circumstances, distance from Western centers of influence, and a lag in participating in transformative world historical events. If the Tsarist reign of terror in nineteenth-century Russia prevented the radical social reforms that transformed Europe, apartheid delayed South Africa's entry into the history of decolonization. The former produced Tolstoy, Dostoevsky, Turgenev, and Chekhov, the latter Nadine Gordimer, J. M. Coetzee, Njabulo Ndebele, Van Nierkerk, Janet Suzman, and Reza De Wet.

Having established a plausible template for comparison, Jackson proceeds to parse the legacy of realism of the Russian masters and its influence on apartheid-era novelists. In the process, Jackson brings to the fore a transcontinental history of literary realism that rarely features in standard scholarly works on realism in the Anglo-American sphere. Her knowledge of realism's Anglo-American history, combined with her expertise in Russian literature and South African writing (both in English and Afrikaans), enables Jackson to undertake a rich comparative study of this modern narrative form. Multilingual anglophone comparativism can often emanate from places far removed from hegemonic centers of influence.

Equally resonant are works that explore anglophone worlds at the juncture of multilingual cultures in Asia. A recent essay by B. Venkat Mani compares Mauritian Hindi writer, Abhimanyu Unnuth's novel *Lal Pasina* (Crimson sweat, 1977) with Amitav Ghosh's *Sea of Poppies* (2008). Mani situates Ghosh's global *tour de force* alongside an ultraminor literary work written in Mauritian Hindi within an Indian Ocean frame (Mani). Both novels bring to life the British empire's infamous opium trade and the intricacies of forced labor migration in the Indian Ocean after the abolition of slavery. In neither novel is the narrative weight borne by a standard language. Unnuth's novel is written in Mauritian Hindi that is inflected with Bhojpuri, a demotic version of Hindi spoken by agricultural laborers in eastern India who were transported as indentured laborers to work on British plantations in Mauritius, Fiji, and the Caribbean. French and Mauritian creole also feature in the linguistic weave of this work. Mani uses the term "ultraminor" to describe Unnuth's novel, for it has only been translated into French nearly three decades after its publication, and no English version exists yet. Ghosh's novel, while occupying pride of place in the pantheon of anglophone literatures, dethrones standard English, as we saw, and compels the latter to share the stage with fragments from languages such as Hindi, Bhojpuri, Bengali, Gujarati, Tamil, Malayalam, Arabic, Persian, Malay, Cantonese, Mandarin, Portuguese, and French. Patois of seaborne Afro-Asian worlds such as *Laskari* and Cantonese pidgin feature alongside Anglo-Indian colloquial lingo derived from the *Hobson-Jobson*. Mani's comparative approach capitalizes on the obvious disparity of status between the two novels not to mourn the global invisibility of Unnuth's work, but to make visible its multilingual energy that is on par with Ghosh's. Mani's essay channels multilingualism as a structuring and generative force in world literature, while situating English in the realm of the subaltern and the vernacular.

A similar intent informs Akshya Saxena's book *Vernacular English* (2022). Saxena traces the movement of English in postcolonial India across a range of media – print, visual, and sonic – and offers a theory of anglophone vernacular aesthetics that is legible across the nation. English in her reading is woven into the nation's multilingual and multiregional weave through films, music, billboards, literary festivals, and digital media. Lower castes and neglected regions of the country such as the Northeast deliberately seek out English to counter the political domination of the Hindi. As a medium of desire and empowerment for the nation's under-privileged, as also a language of upward mobility for the Indian middle class, English in Saxena's work breathes as a heteronymic language. Ashley Cohen's project on the Global Indies that crosscuts Atlantic and Indian Ocean worlds, Roanne Kantor's excavation of Latin American influence on modern South Asian anglophone and Hindi-Urdu literatures, and Duncan Yoon's project on the aesthetics of speculation in anglophone and franco-phone African literatures that trace the cultural texture of Chinese capital-ist incursion on the continent are other examples of exciting decolonial work in global anglophone studies. Each project situates its anglophone corpus alongside a multilingual spectrum and navigates translational worlds in multiple languages: French, Hindi, Urdu, Spanish, Chinese, Zulu, Swahili, and Igbo.

A less dramatic and more effective means of demystifying the colonial horrors of English – to dispel the anglophone imperial specter so to speak – may be to attend to the ways in which its contemporary manifestation does the work of decolonization as it adapts to and is transformed by diverse literary traditions and cultural worlds, even those that have never been under its thrall. Where our disciplinary field is concerned, English does not invariably erase but is rather woven into myriad literary and linguistic cultures around the globe. In the process, the language itself has been transformed beyond measure. These manifest a logic of culture-power not reducible to English's colonial history. A recent survey notes that, apart from its 400 million native speakers, more than a billion people know English as a second language, and that it is an official language in more than sixty countries. For most of its life, English was an unabashed importer of words. As the twentieth century came to a close, it became the largest net exporter of words (Mikanowski). The multiple cultural contexts of English in South Asia, East Asia, Southeast and Northeast Asia, the non-francophone Africa and the Caribbean, the Russo-Slavic region, Scandinavia, the Indian Ocean Rim, and the Pacific; the emergence of multilingual diasporic enclaves in the advanced capitalist world; the circulation and reception of translated multilingual literary texts in a world radically transformed by information technology; and more generally, a loosening of the isomorphic fit between a nation and its literary culture, all constitute exciting points of entry for a decolonial approach to English literary studies and the curriculum at large in the twenty-first century.

Notes

1. A clarification about my use of the term "global anglophone" may be in order here. World Literature and English Literature are two distinct fields with some overlaps. In the essay, I explore points of intersection between them. The late twentieth-century iteration of world literature originated in departments of Comparative Literature in the United States and Europe that sought to enlarge their focus beyond European literatures by engaging seriously with non-European literatures from the ancient to the modern. Global anglophone (a term that has gained substantial traction in the US academy) is the primary point of intersection between English Studies and World Literature. The term is understood in two ways: (1) literatures published in English from around the world including sites that have no history of British colonialism; (2) texts translated into English that often feature in both world-lit and Eng-lit curricula. Debates about multilingualism and translation in world literature routinely reckon with the dynamics of English as a world language and a major translational medium.
2. See Miller, a recent work on it.

WORKS CITED

Al-Musawi, Muhsin. *The Medieval Islamic Republic of Letters: Arabic Knowledge Construction.* Notre Dame, IN: University of Notre Dame Press, 2015.

Al Rahim, Ahmed. "Arabic Literary Prose, Adab Literature, and the Formation of Islamicate Imperial Culture." In Debjani Ganguly, ed., *The Cambridge History of World Literature, Volume I.* Cambridge: Cambridge University Press, 2021, 80–108.

Apter, Emily. *Against World Literature: On the Politics of Untranslatability.* London: Verso, 2013.

Aravamudan, Srinivas. *Enlightenment Orientalism: Resisting the Rise of the Novel.* Chicago: University of Chicago Press, 2011.

Armitage, David. "The Atlantic Ocean." In David Armitage, Alison Bashford, and Sujit Sivasundaram, eds., *Oceanic Histories.* Cambridge: Cambridge University Press, 2018, 85–110.

Bassnett, Susan. "From Cultural Turn to Translational Turn." In David Damrosch, ed., *World Literature in Theory.* Oxford: Wiley Blackwell, 2014, 234–45.

Bhattacharya, Baidik. "Colonial Philology and the Origins of World Literature." In Debjani Ganguly, ed., *The Cambridge History of World Literature, Volume I*. Cambridge: Cambridge University Press, 2021, 132–47.

Casanova, Pascale. *The World Republic of Letters*. Cambridge, MA: Harvard University Press, 2004.

Cheah, Pheng. *What Is a World: On Postcolonial Literature as World Literature*. Durham, NC: Duke University Press, 2016.

Cohen, Ashley. "The Global Indies: Historicising Oceanic Metageographies." *Comparative Literature* 69.1 (2017): 7–15.

DeLoughrey, Elizabeth. *Allegories of the Anthropocene*. Durham, NC: Duke University Press, 2019.

Desai, Gaurav. *Commerce with the Universe: Africa, India and the Afrasian Imagination*. New York: Columbia University Press, 2013.

Ganguly, Debjani. *This Thing Called the World: The Contemporary Novel as Global Form*. Durham, NC: Duke University Press, 2016.

Ganguly, Debjani, ed. *The Cambridge History of World Literature*, 2 vols. Cambridge: Cambridge University Press, 2021.

Goyal, Yogita. *Runaway Genres: The Global Afterlives of Slavery*. New York: New York University Press, 2019.

Hitchcock, Peter. "Decolonizing [the] English." *South Atlantic Quarterly* 100.3 (2001): 749–71.

Jackson, Jeanne-Marie. *South African Literature's Russian Soul: Narrative Forms of Global Isolation*. London: Bloomsbury, 2015.

Kantor, Roanne. *South Asian Authors, Latin American Texts, and the Unexpected Journey of Global English*. Cambridge: Cambridge University Press, 2022.

Mani, B. Venkat. "Multilingual Code-Stitching in Ultraminor World Literatures: Reading Abhimanyu Unnuth's *Lal Pasina* (1977) with Amitav Ghosh's *Sea of Poppies* (2008)." *Journal of World Literature* 3 (2018): 373–99.

Miller, Peter, ed. *The Sea: Thalassography and Historiography*. Ann Arbor: University of Michigan Press, 2013.

Mikanowski, Jacob. "Behemoth, Bully, Thief: How the English Language Is Taking Over the Planet," *The Guardian*, July 27, 2018. www .theguardian.com/news/2018/jul/27/english-language-global-dominance.

Nixon, Rob. *Slow Violence and the Environmentalism of the Poor*. Cambridge, MA: Harvard University Press, 2011.

Orsini, Francesca. "The Multilingual Local in World Literature." *Comparative Literature* 67.4 (2015): 345–74.

Pollock, Sheldon. *The Language of Gods in the World of Men: Sanskrit, Culture and Power in Premodern India*. Berkeley: University of California Press, 2006.

Saxena, Akshya. *Vernacular English: Reading the Anglophone in Postcolonial India*. Princeton, NJ: Princeton University Press, 2022.

Slaughter, Joseph and Kerry Bystrom, eds. *The Global South Atlantic*. New York: Fordham University Press, 2017.

Torabully, Khal and Marina Carter. *Coolitude: An Anthology of the Indian Labour Diaspora*. London: Anthem Press, 2002.

Venuti, Lawrence. "Hijacking Translation: How Com Lit Continues to Suppress Translated Texts." *boundary 2* 43.2 (2016): 179–204.

Wellek, Rene. "The Crisis of Comparative Literature." 1959. In David Damrosch, Natalie Melas, and Mbongiseni Buthelezi, eds., *The Princeton Sourcebook in Comparative Literature: From the European Enlightenment to the Global Present*. Princeton, NJ: Princeton University Press, 2009, 161–72.

Yoon, Duncan. *China in Twentieth and Twenty-First Century African Literatures*. Cambridge: Cambridge University Press, 2023.

CHAPTER 23

Decolonizing the English Lyric through Diasporic Women's Poetry

Sandeep Parmar

British poetry has cohered, and perhaps always will cohere, around a singular expressive lyric subject – aesthetic values associated with universal experience read as White – as well as with the canonicity of the lyric tradition: its form, fields of reference, poetic craft. Although mainstream, mostly lyric, British poetry has become increasingly racially diverse in the past decades, a lyric mode predicated on Whiteness remains largely unchallenged. British poets of color all too often rely on an aesthetic of self-foreignizing, for example by voicing of outsiderness or by deploying exoticizing markers of "authenticity." Their poetry thereby leaves the premise of a White lyric universality intact by pointing always to the specific, the local, the personal as other. As I have written elsewhere "a mostly white poetic establishment prevails over a patronising culture that reflects minority poets as exceptional cases – to be held at arms' length like colonial curiosities in an otherwise uninterrupted tradition extending back through a pure and rarefied language" (Parmar, "Not a British Subject"). More recently, I have argued that "to speak of transcending the self is to engage with the complex problem of the lyric. Lyric forms a zone of contact or conflict. The body of the poet of colour is made visible in the space of the poem; their voice becomes a lyric phenomenon inseparable from their social and racial positioning" (Parmar, "Still Not a British Subject"). Where does the dominant poetic mode in Britain leave the poet of color? What violence might it do to their voice when set against a reader's expectations? What shapes the way a reader approaches the lyric "I"? From a pedagogical standpoint, rooted in tertiary education, specifically an English Literature degree, these questions are essential for any teacher of poetry to address both in the classroom and, I would argue, for their own reading practices, their own sense of literary value. One significant sticking point for university teachers like myself is the lack of scholarship on contemporary British poetry and race, a dearth that has only very recently been addressed in any significant way.[1] This absence of capacious critical frameworks – from academic criticism to representative anthologies – puts considerable obstacles in the path of everything from course design and delivery to wider issues that come to bear on reading practices around the lyric, namely the perception of an authentic speaker and the expectations of form.

A postcolonial reading of British poetry by non-White authors cannot be prevented from the marginalizing force of an imperial, and therefore inherited, bestowed, or enforced language. And yet it is likely that many contemporary British poets whose ethnic relations to former colonies are at a second- or third-generation remove from British subjects of empire do not consider themselves postcolonial subjects. There are complex differences between poets who migrated to Britain and those who were born in the UK, whose ties are perhaps more tenuous, limited to intergenerational memories at a remove, shared bloodline, cultures, or surnames. Where critical studies of poetry by non-White British writers sometimes shows its failures is in a flattening of discourse about race, abetted by terms like postcolonial or transnational or even "world literature."[2] Each term makes little room for the industrious – indeed, the market and material culture are never far away from literary production – interconnectivity of poets in the present. A backward-looking glance over the previous century marks the rootedness of scholars in inceptive moments but does not account for a rapidly changing landscape, mostly because criticism is most comfortable where it is cumulative and stable. Nor are there enough studies of contemporary poetry and race as they intersect with the UK in ways markedly different from the USA, where such studies abound.[3] Critical framing of UK poetry often ignores the pressures of racism or xenophobia (even when the work at hand responds to it), the shaping of a reader's perceptions of the poet and her text as one and of the same and from where this cultural construction emerges, as well as the poet's own determination of themselves as a subject. It is my intention here to interrogate the readerly gesture, its lyric premise of expression and authenticity, in order to reproach national canons and traditions that privilege the well-crafted lyric poem and its supposed universality. Mobilizing a decolonized reading of the lyric – one that dismantles formal features and a reader's expectations of an expressive and authentic voice – I will offer finally two examples from my own experience teaching the works of Sarah Howe and Bhanu Kapil. To decolonize the lyric form, one that in its contemporary usage relies on a transposition of the reader onto the "I," is to acknowledge that at its heart lyric and its assumptions of universality and authentic emotional expression can often be a site of violence and objectification for poets of color. To read lyric poems by non-White poets without an awareness of lyric's tacit agreement of universality is to ignore the ruptures – and reconciliations – that the form allows.

The Problem of Lyric

The primacy of late twentieth-century British lyric as an expressive mode, offering experience – and from experience some meaningful truth – naturally makes the poem a vehicle for the poet's life. But what objective reality can the lyric provide? Jonathan Culler's analysis of the problem of lyric speech acts viewed as fictions might be recounted thus: if New Critical approaches define the lyric "I" as a fictional speaker rather than the poet speaking, then the design of lyric as assimilated truth, too, becomes the realm of fiction. The privileging of the text over the utterance, in Culler's view, predisposes the reader to a false self, one constructed by language in the moment of lyric's expression (Culler 105–109):

> Modern criticism, increasingly cognizant of the problems of treating lyric as the direct and sincere expression of the experience and affect of the poet, has moved toward something of a compromise position, treating lyric as expression of a persona rather than the poet and thus as mimesis of the thought or speech of such a persona created by the poet. (Culler 109)

The dissociation of the poet from the speaker, the primacy of the text over intention by a New Critical model, empties lyric from its formal inception. Culler's investment in the lyric "I" as determined by form, meaning, and address resists the postures of linguistic determination. But what he returns to the lyric – the intimacy of song, of lyric's ritual function as a subjective experience both in its own time and in time immemorial – is poetry's conspicuous dialectic function. A poem needs a reader to give it the force of speech, and the reader is in turn creator of that speaking subject in her listening. It is a mutually constitutive project, more so than in, say, in fiction. But the problem of overidentification between poet and speaker rests lightly on whoever is least conspicuous to a reader. Where there is a disconnect between a perceived reality presented by the lyric subject and its reader, that distance constructs dissonance. This is especially true when the experience conveyed is one that positions itself as other by way of deviating from a transcendent universal subject, which is so often White, middle class, male, even when student readers themselves may not identify as such. Bridging the distance between the speaker's voiced consciousness and the reader's own inner consciousness is where lyric does its work. But particularities of identity obstruct this connection, complicate a reading that might otherwise be transposition, and turn it into a perception of that distance between, say, the White reader and the non-White body making itself visible in the lyric space. And yet all lyric reading, regardless of the perceived identity of the "I," requires the reader to be aware of the constructedness of the speaker's voice and its seeing (or being seen). Such failed transpositions in the readerly act are among the most challenging to overcome in a teaching context. Before I consider lyric as a poetic mode – the dominant mode, in fact, of poetry taught throughout education for all ages – it is necessary to think more deeply about how British poetry by non-White poets is often framed within critical and educational contexts.

Admittance to the canon of contemporary British poetry for poets of color often comes at a price: legibility, a racial markedness that, for incorporation in an invariably White curriculum, singles itself out as deviating from universality, coded as White. University undergraduate students most often arrive with reading strategies shaped by school and exam syllabi. It is therefore worth briefly noting how inclusive these exams, particularly A-levels, are – and on what terms poets of color are included. Whilst generally in the UK context A-levels are crucial for admittance into undergraduate degrees, there is considerable latitude in options provided by teachers at secondary schools and colleges, and the variations between exam boards mean that there is no one set syllabus. However, what is striking and not altogether surprising is that exam boards' suggested contemporary poems by poets of color tend to foreground racial otherness, longing, thematic concerns presumably taken for granted as the preserve of non-White writers. One example, "The Wedding" by British Pakistani poet Moniza Alvi, dramatizes a metaphorical mismatch between bride and groom as exile from one's homeland, a failed romance with the country of arrival which is in this case England. "I expected a quiet wedding / high above a lost city / a marriage to balance on my head / like a forest of sticks, a pot of water" (Alvi 74–75). The bride's innocence, and indeed ignorance of her betrothed, naturally plays into a cultural stereotype of arranged marriages, one no doubt as familiar to British readers as a rural woman carrying a water jug on her head. The poem's existence, alongside so many others like it on an A-level syllabus, raises the difficult question of what is edifying about lyric's claim to authenticity: to present a genuine voice from a White reader's (and teacher's) perspective that speaks to the longing of the migrant. An even more thorny question might be what does the lyric poem create in its space of personal expression – transmuted through landscape, sensory detail, experience – that allows for this poem to be written in this way where the poet might be seen to be speaking about the self at a distant remove, a moment of double consciousness? No doubt the poem's place in the classroom is to exemplify the poet's own biographical situation and its wider appeal for those in a similar racial positioning as the poet's presumed cultural background.

A simplistic reading would identify the poet with the speaker, and yet a simplified (what Veronica Forrest-Thomson called in *Poetic Artifice* "bad naturalisation") reading is what is called for in the rooting out of the marriage metaphor and unbelonging. The three "I" statements in the poem – "I expected," "I insisted," "I wanted" – correspond with silent desire, unrealized hope, and disappointment. This disempowered speaker capitulates to the plural "we," and the lyric subject is lost, finally, to interpretations of their situation inscribed on racial tropes that translate in a British context as foreign: bathing buffalo, hennaed hands like "roadmaps." Alvi, who was born in Pakistan but left for Britain as an infant, has spoken about her projected fantasies of a lost homeland standing in for lived experiences (Shamsie). The complexity of her relationship, as a poet, to her own history does not match the rootedness of the lyric subject who is from elsewhere – for Alvi, the marriage here is perhaps an embodiment of duality, of selves married into one, rather than a migrant's dashed hopes. But in the context of teaching this poem, it would be neither right nor possible to draw the author's biography into our reading. The lyric stands alone in its educational purpose as a vehicle for meaning – a meaning predetermined by its being chosen. And the poem's use of language – a heavily crafted translation of faux naïf sentiments into English that mimics a nonnative speaker, as in for example the lines "The time was not ripe / for us to view each other" – confirms such a reading. The British-Cypriot poet Anthony Anaxagorou describes his own experience learning poetry in sixth form as presupposing an ideal (White, middle-class) reader: "To suggest certain poetries are better aligned with certain readers is to reinstate a conservative and violent rhetoric which assumes there is either a singular/correct way to navigate a poem, or that one must first be trained in knowing how to think about the mechanisms central to poetic logic" ("Accessibility"). Yet the constructing of an ideal reader – one whose sensibilities and interactions with the world mimic those of a universal experience coded by a privileged majority – underlies the way we teach poetic value, especially in the well-crafted lyric.

In and outside of an educational context, it is hard to divorce our expectations of "I" statements from the voice that formulates this speech act. To do so requires recognizing that the lyric poem inscribes itself into a tradition where the "I" may have no referent in the real world; it necessitates a leap toward fictionalizing that genre that we have inherited wholesale as a vehicle for personal experience and emotion. Unless a lyric situates itself within an imagined persona, through dramatic monologue, a reader will, as Fred D'Aguiar writes of Irish Nigerian poet Gabriel Gbadamosi's typically English poetry, seek the "burying [of] feeling into sensuous detail which collectively should stand for what the poet thinks and feels" (D'Aguiar 67). D'Aguiar's foundational essay on Black British poetry, "Have You Been Here Long?," tellingly never offers critical distance between the speaking subject and the poet. Perhaps this is largely because the poets he discusses directly reference experiences of discrimination and migration in a time (his essay focuses on poets of the 1970s and 1980s) when the political marginalization of Black people and racialized poets within the wider canon required a direct speaking back to White readers. There is something beguiling and satisfying about this clear identification of the "I" with the poet – it makes use of the full force of expression that lyric has to offer. His readings of Jackie Kay, Linton Kwesi Johnson, James Berry, Grace Nichols, and Kamau Brathwaite, among others, are distinguished by their deeply knowledgeable, attentive ear for dub, reggae, and dialect-inflected poetics. But, as I have explained above, the danger remains, as D'Aguiar alludes to in the conclusion of his essay, that the centering of racial experience in reading these poets categorizes and marginalizes them, as if to suggest that the English language and English-language poetry had not been changed irrevocably in ways to which we do not often enough attend by the cultural imports of writers from across the world. A fuller understanding of lyric's ability to communicate difference requires a grounding of lyric's function of address in a social and historical space. As Culler also writes, "a socially oriented criticism can treat the work as its recurrent coming into being in a social space, which is itself in part the effect of that work and always to be constructed by a reading of one's own relation to it" (301). In other words, the deferral of a text's objectivity, a return to the lyric's force of speech and utterance around a speaker and the society it addresses, opens up political possibilities for the text that are crucial to a decolonized reading of lyric poetry.

Reshaping the Syllabus

The common practice of a slow incorporation of "diverse" poetic voices into reading lists, we can agree, is wholly inadequate. When I began teaching in higher education, as one of two people of color teaching literature in my department, the task of filling the contemporary poetry course's "Black British Poetry" week fell to me. The course, which I have recently taken on and remade entirely, covered British poetry from 1930 to the present, an odd departure point that scooped up late modernists like Auden, Gascoyne, or Bunting or (American-born) H. D.'s Blitz poems in with fellow poets Ted Hughes, Philip Larkin, and Dylan Thomas. Looking back over that first reading list, I see that one mooted version sandwiched Linton Kwesi Johnson between weeks dedicated to Jeremy Prynne and Geoffrey Hill. A few clear pedagogical problems emerge from the course design I inherited, such as the single-author focus, the absence of national, regional, and historical contexts, a disregard for aesthetic, political, and social factors, and, most obviously, the lack of non-White poets (and indeed the few women poets). What such a course offers is an exemplary list, not just examples of British poets, but those who are either seen as unrivaled or broadly representative of the four nations (and linguistic differences) of Britain across twelve weeks of teaching. Where lyric is concerned, attention on one poet and their work – detached from an understanding of, say, the broadly antimodernist strain of twentieth-century British poetry from Georgian poets to the New Generation Poets – reinforces the voice of the poet against the biographical limitations of an author-focused discussion. Anecdotally, it was my experience that students saw "Black British Poetry" week or a week devoted to a seemingly marginalized poet as optional, unnecessary, and even unfairly imposed on a largely White student body. They were less likely to attend lectures they felt were noncanonical. But surely the very structure of a course that would tokenize writers in this way is sending a subliminal signal already, one that undermines their inclusion on merit alone.

How best to reflect the complexity and variations across the UK as well as aesthetic/poetic modes and complex questions of identity? Structuring a course that takes two main presumptions to task – that British poetry can be spoken of as a national tradition in the present and that this it is distinct from other anglophone poetic cultures – was one solution to this conundrum devised by me and a fellow tutor.[4] Moving away from the use of anthologies, many of which are entirely White or include limited selections of poets of color, was another crucial step. In fact, an opening gambit I enjoyed as part of an introductory lecture was to haul a stack of UK poetry anthologies to class and to scrutinize their tables of contents with students. That, coupled with a selection of poetry magazines from 1930 to the present (and statistical analysis of poetry publishing and poetry reviewing, which remains largely White), prepared our discussions for a critical approach to what had otherwise seemed stable realities.[5] Practically speaking, lectures and seminars were not apportioned to single authors or groups of authors but divided into three main strands – "nation," "theory," and "poetics." These thematic strands exposed students to issues particular to place, voice, style, and sociohistorical contexts and included race, class, lyric, and antilyric poetics as well as climate crisis and landscape poetry. A natural denaturing of these "strands" occurred: for example, national traditions were exposed as fluid and varied, and race theory supplanted postcolonial approaches and the pedagogical obstacles this analysis presents. Jahan Ramazani acknowledges that postcolonial readings have been seen as "homogenising" and "victim-centred, too colonially-fixated" but maintains that the term postcolonial "continues to be a powerful tool for revealing linkages across regions emerging from colonial rule, even as it avoids dissolving all writers in an undifferentiated globality, heedless of the differentials of power, history, and language" (Ramazani, "Introduction" 2). In the wider project of anglophone poetry written across national borders, diasporas, and former colonies, the rootedness of power, of English-language educational systems as "producing and sustaining structures of domination" (Viswanathan 4), this particular lens is useful. But at the heart of empire, in its hostile environment and its unrelenting Whiteness, an argument could be made that postcolonial literary readings invert the ongoing, persistent domination of linguistic violence. In his book, *A Transnational Poetics*, Ramazani offers a more fluid paradigm for reading poets whose ties to multiple places cannot be easily resolved through national canons but must be seen as in constant relation and, at times, opposition. Considering poetry by Black British writers from McKay to Evaristo, he offers a utopic vision of variety, in-betweenness, of movement that enables "their creolization of Britain and Britain's creolization of themselves" (Ramazani, *Transnational* 180). Standing in for hybridity, creolization is a cross-cultural term used here to imply a kind of mixing that makes little space for differentials of power (or that, as Ramazani will know, White modernist poets often creolized to shore up that aesthetic dominance). No mode of reading is satisfactory that does not vigorously bring itself up to date – poetry is a fast-changing genre – or face up to present-day social and political realities that shape the contexts in which poetry is produced. The crystallization of critical frameworks and the stasis of the poetry culture they promote can only be avoided by being attentive to change, by seeing the poem not as an isolated event (as the lyric often purports to be) but a line of thinking that points in several directions at once. Would it be possible to teach Linton Kwesi Johnson's work without the long lens of radical Black activism that stretches to Jay Bernard's recent book, partly concerning the New Cross Fire, taking into account the archiving of events and of continued experiences of racism, state violence, and police brutality that sit between the two? Yes, but in my view it would not be advisable.

Decolonizing the Lyric

In the T.S. Eliot Prize's near thirty-year history, only two women of color have won it, Sarah Howe in 2015 for her debut *Loop of Jade* and Bhanu Kapil in 2020 for her sixth full-length collection *How to Wash a Heart*. Prize culture's complex relationship with poetry canons does not in any way guarantee longevity to a book or its author, even if the prize is the most coveted of all, but, like a weather vane, prizes are a useful gauge of present conditions: the direction of public opinion on literary value and its relationship to the empowerment of a (sometimes conservative, sometimes progressive, depending on your sympathies) judging panel. Awarding a prize is never an apolitical gesture. And for teachers of poetry, the visibility of prize-winning books and their sometimes-direct link to educational contexts – with, say, the Forward Prizes for Poetry, which through its foundation disseminates prize poems directly to schools to develop its audiences – makes a critical analysis of their reception in context all the more necessary. It would be foolhardy to offer a rejoinder to lyric reading that ignores its reception in public life and critical culture; such a reading would only reinforce the text's primacy and the subject's assumed universality or marginalization based on the poet's race. Since its publication, I have taught Howe's book as a way to think through lyric and antilyric poetics on undergraduate and postgraduate poetry courses. Her book as well as Kapil's employ lyric subjects but in doing so undermine assumptions innate to dominant forms of lyricism, namely authenticity, personal expression, a suspended just-past moment detailed through anecdote and leading to an epiphanic meaningfulness. Both books also introduce a linguistic difficulty either by introducing extratextual reference and allusion or through formal and syntactical complexity. My reading of Kapil's most recent book is informed by many years of teaching her previous works primarily at postgraduate level. Howe and Kapil offer alternatives to lyric poems that appear to unquestioningly inscribe themselves onto an "I" that coheres around the performance of an "authentic" racial otherness.

In keeping with reading poets in light of their reception as well as their aesthetics, I turn back to Howe's Eliot Prize win. As I have discussed elsewhere and as Mary Jean Chan details in her essay "Journeying Is Hard," Howe's book was almost immediately beset by controversy in the press.[6] Newspaper reviews and interviews – as well as parodies in *Private Eye* and the *TLS* – highlighted Howe's youth, beauty, Oxbridge pedigree, and her foreignness (she is mixed race, born in Hong Kong but raised in England). The furor over her win and the disquiet from mostly White men that ensued quickly overshadowed the enormous range (subject and style) of Howe's collection, reducing it to poems about her and her mother's ethnic background.[7] The book's many poems that fall outside of perceived biographical reference were mostly ignored by these critics. Where might the interstices lie between a lyric self that constructs a legible racial experience and an ironic subject that elsewhere takes apart chinoiserie and race in the literary imagination? How might these impulses be read as mutually constitutive of a rejoinder to lyric violence? I read and teach *Loop of Jade* in light of its determination to decategorize and defamiliarize forms of knowledge, linguistic and material function – where objects and people as much as languages and places disrupt lyric's arrival at meaning, discarding such an impulse as colluding with the very hierarchies of domination that she seeks to dismantle. Radically rethinking lyric from the inside – in poems that look as though they are driven by personal expression and "I" statements – Howe's work opens onto categories foundational to how we think of race, nation, and empire.

A critique of taxonomy in language shapes Howe's book, not least by her quotation and further parody of Jorge Luis Borges's own parodic "certain Chinese encyclopaedia," in which animals are divided into fourteen arbitrary categories. Howe takes each category – from "those that belong to the Emperor" to "that from a long way off look like flies" – and skewers their fabulist definitiveness. In doing so, she calls to mind Foucault's own fascination with Borges's invented text – set within a wider critique of a universal language – and inevitably questions the relation between the self and other in the space of lyric coherence and unity of voice. Purposefully set among these forgeries of sincerity, Howe's "autobiographical" poems must be read similarly as constructions of, and thereby an undermining of, lyric authenticity. In the sonnet "(n) that from a long way off look like flies," the smudge of a dead midge in the binding of an edition of Shakespeare opens onto a father–daughter relationship. The speaker identifies herself as the owner of the book "my undergrad Shakespeare," and queries whether the fly's blood is her own, but the lyric "I" does not appear until the end of the poem:

> At empathy's darkening pane we see
> our own reflected face: how, if that fly
> had a father and mother? On the heath, Lear
> assumes all ragged madmen share
> ungrateful daughters. The way my father,
> in his affable moods, always thinks you
> want a gin and tonic too. I wonder
> if I should scrape her off with a tissue.

(Howe 51)

Its sudden wondering, emphasized by the enjambed line – tellingly rhyming "wonder" with "father," "share" and "Lear" – solidifies the poem's voice both inconclusively and after much melding. The fly, its blood, the "we" and "our" gives way to an addressee "you" who may be general or yet another way for the "I" to escape being pinned down in the pages of tragedy.[8] The "affable" father drinks gin and feels his daughter is ungrateful, suggesting of course that the speaker's father has less affable moments too. This lyric returns at the end of the sonnet, the silent "you" in "tissue" and its thrum in "too" midway through the penultimate line rhythmically separates the fly from the speaker finally in the moment of subject–object distance. But the speaker isn't "a long way off" from this fly, in all ways she assembles herself and the reader into the same category of animal. Howe is fulfilling Foucault's own sense here of threatening "with collapse our age-old distinction between the Same and the Other" (Foucault xv). Authenticity, too, is under threat with the constant fluidity of positioning, accomplished by the fast-paced move through pronouns, and the fly is finally gendered as female, removable but not removed. The speaker pauses inconclusively as if scraping her own face from its canonical aberration. This is empathy's "darkening pane," the mirror made possible by the dim light of lyric's intimate situation, the half-light of self-recognition in others. But, as Ruth Ling observes, "in all its opacity, *Loop of Jade* thoroughly denies that any sense of enlightenment or epiphany can be reached through lyric" (Ling 81).

Readers familiar with British-Indian-American poet Bhanu Kapil's back catalogue, namely her five previous full-length collections, her performances and pamphlets, will note immediately that her sixth book (the first to be published in the UK) looks very dissimilar to anything she has written before. *How to Wash a Heart* is a lyric sequence of five interrelated parts, written in very short lines; the main action is concerned with a tense and at times hostile imagined guest–host relationship. "It's exhausting to be a guest / In somebody else's house / Forever" (Kapil, *Heart* 4). Conversations between the two women (the host is White, the guest is Brown) are interspersed with recollections or narratives that reveal the guest's past history of migration from the Partition of India onward to the UK (and the USA). *How to Wash a Heart*, as Kapil noted in an interview I conducted last year, is intended to be read quickly – in just enough time for a cup of tea to go cold (Parmar, Interview). Kapil and I have coauthored an essay/poem text on the legacy of Partition and lyricism that was published first as a standalone piece in *Poetry London* (a special issue edited by Sarah Howe) and then as part of *Threads*, a conversation between me, Kapil, and the British Indian avant-garde poet Nisha Ramayya. In *Threads*, Kapil and I imagine a fourth space, a radical site of undoing and becoming, beyond our shared three countries of origin and migration, where the nomadic self as lyric subject can untangle themselves from personal and shared histories: "In the fourth space, the memorised pattern has been tugged loose, the yarn or wool or radical fibres on the floor like water."[9] Kapil is an expert user of personae: her book *Ban en Banlieue* is the apex of lyric entanglement with another named figure, Ban, who is a character invoked by the speaker to stand in for a self. Recounting her creation of Ban, Kapil writes that a dream "requires me to acknowledge that my creature (Ban) is over-written by a psychic history that is lucid, astringent, witty. No longer purely mine" (*Ban* 27). A hybrid text written in mainly prose fragments, *Ban* is a site of generic experiment – first a failed novel then a series of autosacrifices, performances, narrations where the speaker and Ban meet and diverge in a history of racist violence. One that is "no longer purely mine," the text navigates the readership it addresses and one that it is addressed by the very same readers. By comparison with this book and Kapil's others, *How to Wash a Heart* seems beguilingly straightforward. It begins:

> Like this?
> It's inky-early outside and I'm wearing my knitted scarf, like
> John Betjeman, poet of the British past.
> I like to go outside straight away and stand in the brisk air.
> Yesterday you vanished into those snowflakes like the ragged beast
> You are.
>
> (*Heart* 1)

The half-question that sets the poem in motion may be "Do you like this?" or "Is it done like this?" It may indeed be "Is this how you wash a heart?"

Whichever way we read it, the answer depends on external guidance, knowledge, approval from what I imagine is the host, whether this is the nation state or its native population to whom the immigrant is always cautiously beholden. The invocation of John Betjeman, laureate whom my mother's generation read in school, sets up this lyric moment of address – asking if the speaker is starting off in the right way. The heart is both metaphor and a physical object appearing in the poem and in the performance (at the ICA in London) that inspires the book, a melting heart of red ice. Emotively, lyric is a kind of cleansing, a purgatory expression that is momentary and complete. It is a washing of one's heart, a private act made public for an unknown audience. Kapil explains her formal decisions and her use of short lines as a kind of controlled energy. "I'm curious about the forward movement of the sentence when it is curtailed ... how do you build emotion in a work? The non-verbal elements of the poem are the place where emotion resides. In this book, it is less about commas or semicolons but the ways the lines are cut. I understand that as syntax" (Parmar, Interview).

As lyric goes, Kapil's use of the "I" subject position is not straightforwardly demarcated in the poem's sections describing host–guest interactions. Very often the "I" shifts between the two women so that the acts of violence are reciprocal, and the victim/ aggressor dynamic is unified by a desire so intimate that it feels shared, almost erotic. "I want you to touch / my cervix. / I want my dress / Shredded / And my life / Too. [...] Whatever you want to do / to me do it" (*Heart* 38). To consider the violence that the lyric space creates for an "I" who does not stand in for universality is to invite intimacy leading to obliteration. What "I want" and "you want" are bound together by an unspoken agreement not to disrupt the balance of power: to want what the host wants is the guest's only hope of fulfillment.

> The host–guest chemistry
> Is inclusive, complex, molecular,
> Dainty.
> Google it.
> Does the host envelop
> The guest or does the guest
> Attract diminished forms
> Of love, like the love
> A parent has for a child
> In September

And January, when the child
Is at its most vulnerable?
Are these questions enough
To violate
Your desire for art
That comes from a foreign
Place?
What are the limits
Of this welcome?
After all, I don't feel anything
For you.

(*Heart* 40)

To reconcile the lyric subject in this lengthy passage with the former quotation is to always question who is speaking and what truth is being expressed. Truth, after all, is a preoccupation of the expressive post-Romantic lyric poem. Is it that the "I" feels nothing for the host, or is this the host speaking? More interestingly perhaps, "I don't feel anything" as a standalone line points us back to the host's assumptions that her guest is subhuman, a kind of animal. Or maybe this is the guest's refusal to feel emotion for the "you," for the reader who voyeuristically awaits the emotional payload. Kapil mimics lyric form but undermines its unspoken contract with this reader who, like the host, transposes its desire on the speaking subject who "comes from a foreign place."

It is certainly possible to reclaim the lyric from textual, political, and social spaces of Whiteness and violence without denaturing its intended purpose. One need not, as a teacher, bury the student in a textual analysis that shuts out a poem's context, nor should they use a biographical lens to interpret the poem's meanings. Rather, by choosing poets who challenge the primacy and expectations of lyric, we stand to gain strategies of thinking through poetic language on its own terms, to listen afresh for the multiplicity of the self in all forms of speech.

Notes

1. I was invited to edit a special issue on race and British poetry for the *Journal of British and Irish Innovative Poetry*, which appeared in 2020, the first of its kind in the UK.
2. I have in mind here critics such as Jahan Ramazani, Deirdre Osborne, Kwame Dawes, Elleke Boehmer, and Gemma Robinson, whose critical writing is informed by the lenses of "world literature," "transnational," and "postcolonial" poetry, among others.

3. For a few examples, see Wang; Yu; Shockley; Nielsen and Ramey.
4. I am grateful to my colleague Dr. Sam Solnick for his imaginative pedagogical leaps.
5. For data on poetry publishing and poets of color see Coates; Kean; Teitler 2.
6. See "Still Not a British Subject" and Chan 22.
7. When Sarah Howe's debut collection, *Loop of Jade*, won the 2015 T.S. Eliot Prize, a troubling set of reviews, satire, and interviews appeared in British newspapers and magazines. Kate Kellaway's 2015 *Observer* round-up predated this but unwittingly set the tone. Kellaway praised the "oriental poise" of Howe's volume, which had "slipped through [her] net." After Howe also won the *Sunday Times* Writer of the Year, an interview in the *Times* ran under the headline "Born in the rubbish tip, the greatest poetry today." The interviewer, Oliver Thring, situates Howe's book within an extraneous fact (or myth) of her mother's abandonment as a baby. Howe's "racial fluidity" as both Chinese and White English is unpicked in the most severe terms, all of which has little bearing on the poems themselves, expressing instead a discomfort with Howe's unprecedented success. Perhaps not surprisingly, *Private Eye* and the *TLS* both ran conspiracy-ridden pieces expressing shock and sensing a political motivation for awarding Howe the prize.
8. Certainly, one might also hear an echo of Gloucester's words here on the heath, "As flies to wanton boys, are we to the gods. / They kill us for their sport" (Act IV, scene 1). This may well be the image that suggested Lear to the poet rather than some actual situation.
9. This line is written by Bhanu Kapil but part of our jointly authored piece in *Threads* (20).

WORKS CITED

Alvi, Moniza. *Carrying My Wife*. Newcastle-upon-Tyne: Bloodaxe Books, 2000.

Anaxagorou, Anthony. "On Accessibility and Permission." 2020. *The Sunday Times Young Writer of the Year Award*. www.youngwriteraward.com/poetry-accessibility-permission/.

Chan, Mary Jean. "Journeying Is Hard: Difficulty, Race and Poetics in Sarah Howe's Loop of Jade." *Journal of British and Irish Innovative Poetry* 12.1 (2020): 1–29. https://doi.org/10.16995/bip.745.

Coates, Dave. "The State of Poetry and Poetry Criticism in the UK," commissioned report, 2019. www.liverpool.ac.uk/new-and-international-writing/emerging-critics/.

Culler, Jonathan. *Theory of the Lyric*. Cambridge, MA: Harvard University Press, 2015.

D'Aguiar, Fred. "Have You Been Here Long?" In Robert Hampson and Peter Barry, eds., *New British Poetries: The Scope of the Possible*. Manchester: Manchester University Press, 1993, 51–71.

Foucault, Michel. "Preface." In Michel Foucault, *The Order of Things*. New York: Pantheon, 1970, xv.

Howe, Sarah. *Loop of Jade*. London: Chatto & Windus, 2015.

Kapil, Bhanu. *Ban en Banlieue*. New York: Nightboat Books, 2015.

How to Wash a Heart. Liverpool: Pavilion Press, 2020.

Kapil, Bhanu, Nishya Ramayya, and Sandeep Parmar. *Threads*. London: Clinic Publishing, 2018.

Kean, Danuta. "Publishing Opportunities for Black and Asian Poets." Free Verse Report, 2005. www.spreadtheword.org.uk/wp-content/uploads/2016/11/Free-Verse-Report.pdf.

Ling, Ruth. Review of Sarah Howe's Loop of Jade. *The Wolf* 33 (2016): 78–82.

Nielsen, Aldon Lynn and Lauri Ramey. *What I Say: Innovative Poetry by Black Writers in America*. Tuscaloosa: University of Alabama Press, 2015.

Parmar, Sandeep. Interview with Bhanu Kapil. February 17, 2021. *The Guardian*. www.theguardian.com/books/2021/feb/17/ts-eliot-winner-bhanu-kapil-its-hard-to-study-something-by-standing-in-front-of-it.

"Not a British Subject: Race and UK Poetry." December 6, 2015. *Los Angeles Review of Books*. https://lareviewofbooks.org/article/not-a-british-subject-race-and-poetry-in-the-uk/.

"Still Not a British Subject: Race and UK Poetry." *Journal of British and Irish Innovative Poetry* 12.1 (2020). https://doi.org/10.16995/bip.3384.

Ramazani, Jahan. *A Transnational Poetics*. Chicago: University of Chicago Press, 2009.

"Introduction." In Jahan Ramazani, ed., *The Cambridge Companion to Postcolonial Poetry*. Cambridge: Cambridge University Press, 2017, 1–15.

Shamsie, Muneeza. "Exploring Dualities: An Interview with Moniza Alvi." *Journal of Postcolonial Writing* 47.2 (2011): 192–98.

Shockley, Evie. *Renegade Poetics: Black Aesthetics and Formal Innovation in African American Poetry*. Iowa City: University of Iowa Press, 2011.

Teitler, Nathalie. "Diversity in British Poetry 2005–2017." Freed Verse Report 2017: Diversity in British Poetry 2005–2017. n.p.

Viswanathan, Gauri. *Masks of Conquest: Literary Study and British Rule in India*. New York: Columbia University Press, 2015.

Wang, Dorothy. *Thinking Its Presence: Form, Race, and Subjectivity in Contemporary Asian American Poetry*. Stanford, CA: Stanford University Press, 2014.

Yu, Timothy. *Race and the Avant-Garde: Experimental and Asian American Poetry Since 1965*. Stanford, CA: Stanford University Press, 2009.

CHAPTER 24

Postcolonial Poetry and the Decolonization of the English Literary Curriculum

Nathan Suhr-Sytsma

"In 2190, Albion's Civil Conflicts Finally Divided Along Norman–Saxon Lines," states the title of a speculative poem by Trinidadian-British writer Vahni Capildeo (b. 1973), published in their Forward Prize-winning collection *Measures of Expatriation* (2016). Implicitly identified as a Norman invader, "with superior weaponry," the poem's first-person speaker addresses a second person interpellated as Saxon: "Soon, you stopped sounding wrong" (Capildeo 85). Is this a reference to the historical evolution of Old English into Middle English, with manifold borrowings from Anglo-Norman, or to the tuning of the arrivant's ear to the addressee's vernacular? The Norman–Saxon division between "I" and "you" maps onto other distinctions of body type ("thin" and "thick") and gender ("So far as I was woman," muses the poet, not quite claiming that identity while addressing their interlocutor as "Young man") (Capildeo 85). Capildeo has noted, too, that "'2190' encodes '1290', which was the year of the Jewish expulsion from England; a forced migration not enough remembered" (Parmar, "*The Wolf* Interview" 59).[1] Such divisions – linguistic, embodied, gendered, and religious – both displace and evoke another, unspoken distinction between non-White and White. As Vidyan Ravinthiran observes of Capildeo's writing, "this is poetry which enters phenomenologically, with heartbreaking and case-making fidelity, into racial travails" ("Myriad Minded" 169). The final stanza of this poem suggests how ideas of "home" and habits of speech are deployed against racialized immigrants, a long-standing current of British political discourse that would gain force in the run-up to the Brexit referendum over the months following the February 2016 publication of Capildeo's collection:

> Let's start a conversation. Ask me where I'm from.
> Where is home, really home. Where my parents were born.
> What to do if I sound more like you than you do.
> Every word an exhalation, a driving-out.

> (Capildeo 85)

Anticipating the script of this "conversation," the poet satirizes it by deploying imperatives and turning racist clichés into declarative fragments. By the final sentence, it is ambiguous whose words are driving out whom. At once memorable and oblique, the poem conveys how the identities of "Albion" (or Britain) and the English language depend on the presence of outsiders over the past millennium and more.

A selection of Capildeo's poems were among the final readings I assigned for an upper-level undergraduate course in 2020 on Contemporary Literature, with the theme "Multicultural Britain." This course attempts to introduce students to the contours of postwar British literature, involving both fiction and poetry, while challenging dominant ways of charting that literary history by centering themes of decolonization, migration, and race. Thus, we read novels by Sam Selvon, Kazuo Ishiguro, and Bernardine Evaristo alongside a range of poetry: Louise Bennett's "Colonization in Reverse" on her fellow Jamaicans migrating to Britain; Philip Larkin's "The Importance of Elsewhere," which relies on a contrast between Ireland and England; poetry written in Northern Ireland during the Troubles by Seamus Heaney, Michael Longley, Ciaran Carson, and Medbh McGuckian, who hardly identified as British despite their passports; Carol Ann Duffy's "Comprehensive," a dramatic polylogue of immigrant and xenophobic students in an East London school; Linton Kwesi Johnson's poems, from "Sonny's Lettah" to "Liesense fi Kill," protesting decades of anti-Black violence by police; Daljit Nagra's metapoetic "Kabba Questions the Ontology of Representation, the Catch 22 for 'Black' Writers ... " and "Hadrian's Wall," commissioned in 2016 by the Mansio project, which moves from the Roman wall constructed "to keep out the barbarous" to ask "Where will our walls finally end?" ("Mansio"; Nagra 15). Following on from Evaristo's Booker Prize-winning *Girl, Woman, Other*, a polyphonic novel in free verse or what Evaristo terms "fusion fiction" (Donnell 101), we considered Capildeo along with Sandeep Parmar's 2015 essay "Not a British Subject: Race and Poetry in the UK," in order to reflect on how readers' assumptions about race and aesthetic experimentation might lead to misjudging, or outright excluding, poets of color. Even as my students struggled with Capildeo's work, they grasped Parmar's dissatisfaction with the paths laid down by Larkin but also by Nagra's earlier poetry "voiced in ... 'Punglish,' a faux parodic mix of English and Punjabi." According to Parmar, "the singular lyric voice should not merely reproduce poetic sameness through a universal 'I' or self-fetishizing difference through a poetic diction of otherness." Capildeo's writing, I added, was doing the difficult work of making something new; it warranted the same quality of close, appreciative reading as the now-canonical early twentieth-century modernists. And in a literary field other than that of twenty-first-century Britain, less recognizably modernist poetic procedures, even the cultivation of a seemingly stable "I," may produce a different force or meaning equally deserving of close reading.

In an editorial in the venerable *Journal of Commonwealth Literature* entitled "Decolonizing English," Ruvani Ranasinha writes that her students want to see writers of color "included in canonical courses on Poetry or Modernism" (120), not relegated to the optional edges of the curriculum, and she herself emphasizes that "Britain was always 'multicultural'" (121). For Ranasinha, "it remains equally important to consider the *poetics* as well as the *politics* of postcolonial or minority writings in our teaching" (121). While *poetics* refers here to writers' "artistic strategies" across genres (Ranasinha 121), what better way to become attentive to poetics than by studying and writing about poetry? Postcolonial poetry, as both a body of poems and a field of critical discourse, furnishes opportunities to foreground anticolonial and antiracist work, whether in "canonical courses" or those devoted to postcolonial literature, without disregarding the aesthetic dimensions of such work. Would it be possible, Ravinthiran wonders, for postcolonial poetry criticism to live with a poem "intensively, combining appreciation – such as world poets rarely receive – with a susceptibility to the cognitions of form, the thinking that is uniquely done in poems and that outgoes simplistic frameworks of mimesis or subversion?" ("(Indian) Verse" 647). To elaborate some of the thinking that is done in Capildeo's "In 2190, Albion's Civil Conflicts Finally Divided Along Norman–Saxon Lines," for instance, I propose that their poem enacts a decolonizing practice in at least three ways that ramify throughout postcolonial poetry more broadly: (i) it questions the politicized distinctions between outsiders and insiders, (ii) it makes available for poetry undervalued forms of language and definitions of home, and (iii) it embarks on a project of world-unmaking and world-remaking. Highlighting these three modes of practice, this chapter reflects on how university-level aesthetic education and pedagogy might elucidate the decolonizing work of poets and poems. At the same time, it tests the limits of the term "postcolonial poetry" for such decolonizing work.

"Always with a House There Is an Inside and an Outside": Constructing Postcolonial Poetry

Postcolonial poetry has gained recognition over the past two decades, following the publication of Jahan Ramazani's *The Hybrid Muse: Postcolonial Poetry in English* (2001). Although poets had been studied in the contexts of fields demarcated according to national borders (e.g. Nigerian literature), geographic regions (e.g. African literature), or transnational affiliations (e.g. Black literature), Ramazani's book was the first to name "postcolonial poetry" as a coherent field in its own right. The term tends to adhere to poets of the former British Empire following World War II. As a scholar of postcolonial poetry based in an English department, I follow the primarily anglophone focus of Ramazani's book and of Rajeev S. Patke's wide-ranging *Postcolonial Poetry in English* (2006). However, the appearance of two articles on "postcolonial poetry" in a 2007 special issue of *Research in African Literatures* on Lusophone African and Afro-Brazilian literatures, both translated from Portuguese, suggests genealogies for the field beyond English and possibilities for comparative research (Mata; Secco). From the start, "postcolonial" embeds tensions between emphasizing "peoples from regions of the so-called global South or Third World" and including those oppressed by settler colonialism in the Global North, whether peoples of the Celtic fringe or Indigenous peoples in North America (Ramazani, "Introduction" 1). As Ramazani acknowledges, "the term 'postcolonial' has been criticized for being too political, too homogenizing, too victim-centered, too colonially-fixated, or just premature amid persisting neocolonialisms" (2). Objecting in the early 1990s that "the term" both "lures us into a false sense of security, a seeming pastness of a past that is still painfully present" and "endows its principal morpheme 'colonial' with an originary privilege," Nigerian poet and intellectual Niyi Osundare (b. 1947) asked derisively, "When you meet me in the corridors tomorrow, will you congratulate me on my 'post-colonial' poetry?" (Osundare 208). While some scholars find "postcolonial poetry" a valuable framework for building institutional spaces that recognize underrepresented bodies of poetry, some poets wonder whether truly decolonizing the curriculum may entail dispensing with the term.

Having grown up in Canada but moved to the United States for college, I first read postcolonial poetry, marked as such, in a multigenre course in Twentieth-Century British and Postcolonial Literature. There I encountered Derek Walcott's lyric poems, taught by a scholar who was completing a book, begun as a dissertation advised by Ramazani, about Caribbean poets as the creators of "new world modernisms" (Pollard). Eventually, in my first book (Suhr-Sytsma), I attempted to recast the literary history of the mid-twentieth-century era of decolonization by focusing on anglophone poets from nonmetropolitan sites: Walcott (1930–2017), the tragically short-lived Nigerian/Biafran poet Christopher Okigbo (1930–67), and Seamus Heaney (1939–2013), along with their nationally eminent but internationally underappreciated contemporaries such as Louise Bennett (1919–2006), J. P. Clark (1935–2020), and Michael Longley (b. 1939), many of them linked to each other by other cultural gatekeepers and itinerant intellectuals who had been mostly lost to literary history.

To decolonize the literary curriculum, however, it is not enough to elevate a handful of "great" postcolonial poets, nearly all of them male, to the canon. In an essay published two months after Walcott's death in March 2017, Jamaican writer Kei Miller (b. 1978) responds to the Trinidadian writer Earl Lovelace (b. 1935) – and through him to Walcott – by reflecting that "his generation of writers, they created a house. And always with a house there is an inside and an outside. We are interested in the outside – in the people you left out. . . . What of the Syrian-Caribbean writer who could never chant 'Black Power'? What of the queer Caribbean writer who never felt the freedom of independence?" ("In the Shadow of Derek Walcott" 9). Miller suggests a kind of agonism between different generations of Caribbean poets, yet he implies that Caribbean poetry cannot be circumscribed by agonism with British colonialism or the English lyric tradition. Rather, contemporary poets whom we might identify as postcolonial probe how inequity and injustice remain embedded in localized norms of race, gender, and sexuality – and the language in which these norms are expressed.[2]

Nor should the United States be exempt from this inquiry. Within the United States, the study of postcolonial literature is still too often understood as the study of the rest of the world. When US-based scholars began to teach and discuss "British Commonwealth Literature" during the 1940s through 1960s, they conceived of it as wholly separate from American literature, even as the CIA was secretly funding the Congress of Cultural Freedom to promote literary initiatives across the Commonwealth as part of the United States' postwar rivalry with both the waning British Empire and the ascendant Soviet Union (Raja and Bahri 1156–57; Kalliney). There are, of course, alternate genealogies for postcolonial literary studies in African Diaspora-focused institutions such as the journal *Callaloo* (est. 1976) (Raja and Bahri 1166–67). By the time postcolonial studies was finally recognized as a Division of the Modern Language Association, in 2007, "the designation 'postcolonial,' initially intended as a largely geographic or geohistorical designation, had grown into a full-fledged *approach* to all manner of literary, language and cultural studies" (Raja and Bahri 1179). Yet a risk remains that English departments treat the postcolonial as a catchall term for issues related to canonicity, empire, otherness, and race without engaging squarely with settler colonialism or US empire.[3]

Poet Natalie Diaz (b. 1978), who "is Mojave, Akimel O'otham and an enrolled member of the Gila River Indian Community" and also identifies as Latinx and queer, notes in an interview that genocidal language about Native people "is still present in our Declaration of Independence" (Diaz, "Natalie Diaz"; Rodriguez). Her Pulitzer Prize-winning collection *Postcolonial Love Poem* (2020) challenges readers to ask if or how poetry in the United States might be postcolonial. An epigraph precedes each section of the collection; the first, preceding the title poem, is from Joy Harjo (Muscogee Nation): "I am singing a song that can only be born after losing a country" (Diaz, *Postcolonial* n.p.; Harjo 7). Also featured as part of "Living Nations, Living Words: A Map of First Peoples Poetry," Harjo's signature project as US Poet Laureate (2019–22), "Postcolonial Love Poem" locates itself in the Mojave Desert. Every line unexpected, the poem unfurls images of war, wounding, and erotic desire:

> I was built by wage. So I wage love and worse –
> always another campaign to march across
> a desert night for the cannon flash of your pale skin
> settling in a silver lagoon of smoke at your breast.
>
> (Diaz, *Postcolonial* 1)

As in Capildeo's poem above, the first-person speaker addresses a second person, but here the "you" is less adversary than lover. The poem's final lines emphasize the possibility for a shared first-person "we":

> The rain will eventually come, or not.
> Until then, we touch our bodies like wounds –
> the war never ended and somehow begins again.
>
> (2)

As scholar and novelist Daniel Heath Justice (Cherokee Nation) maintains, "in the Americas, colonialism continues; if anything, it has become an assumed part of the sociopolitical fabric that marks any claims to Indigenous political, social, economic, or intellectual sovereignty as being 'special' rather than Indigenous rights" (492).[4] In a prose poem – or lyric essay – later in *Postcolonial Love Poem*, "The First Water Is the Body," Diaz writes, "What threatens white people is often dismissed as myth. I have never been true in America. America is my myth" (47). If Diaz's poetry is postcolonial, it is so in the sense that it grapples with ongoing American colonialism, even as it turns away from the myth of the

United States to the life-giving elements of land and water, the Mojave language, and queer desire.

Postcolonial poetry criticism need not, then, cordon off histories of European empire from those of genocide, slavery, resistance, and survivance in North America. Indeed, the history of the university where I work, a private, predominantly White institution located on land that the Muscogee people were forced to relinquish, involves Indigenous dispossession and slave labor ("Land Acknowledgment"). For those of us in North America, there is no necessary contradiction between advocating for our institutions to reckon with such histories, including pursuing reparative actions toward the descendants of those harmed, and holding space in the curriculum for perspectives from outside North America. Writers have often been ahead of scholars in noticing parallel oppressions and possibilities for solidarity. For instance, poets and novelists from northeast India, who may identify India less as their home than as a colonial state, have found inspiration in Indigenous American and African American writing, as well as anglophone African and Latin American writing (Kashyap).

A matter of departmental decisions about what is required to major in English and which courses are offered, as well as school-wide decisions about degree requirements, the curriculum is also a matter of syllabus design. As I develop syllabi, I want my students to encounter the full breadth of poetry in English – to find poems to which they feel drawn and poets with whom they identify, to develop an informed appreciation for the craft of postcolonial as well as canonical poets, and to grasp the aesthetic, conceptual, and political stakes of these poets' projects. "We are confronted," write Ben Etherington and Jarad Zimbler of precedents for decolonizing practical criticism, "with the problem of deciding not only what or whom to read, but also *how* to read (or listen) . . . in a way that responds to the distinctive dimensions of verbal arts" (229). Confronting this problem involves different approaches both at different levels of the curriculum and in multigenre courses in Contemporary Literature or Postcolonial Literature as compared with single-genre courses in poetry. Even so, the most inclusive syllabus or incisive reading practice will not address the fundamental issue that John Guillory identifies in *Cultural Capital* as "access to the means of literary production" (ix), including literacy, higher education, and publication. Or as Ranasinha puts it, "access to English remains classed" (120). As a scholar and teacher, I look for ways to acknowledge *both* how poetry functions as cultural capital within inequitable systems *and* how poets strive to practice liberation in language.

"This Little Boat / of the Language": Revaluing Languages, Defining Home

The introductory poetry course I teach involves three movements: it begins with the fundamentals of how poems work, with examples from "Caedmon's Hymn" to Cathy Park Hong's "Ballad in O," moves to how to interpret poems, including through encounters with the drafts of published poems, and culminates with a unit examining postcolonial poetry in global Englishes and in translation from other languages into English. In this third unit, we read poems by Louise Bennett, whose satirical ballads in Jamaican Creole or patois the poetry establishment was slow to recognize *as* poetry (Innes 230–31; Suhr-Sytsma 91–92), in conjunction with her radio monologue about "Jamaica Language." Bennett's "Bans a Killin" takes to task a fellow Jamaican, "Mas Charlie," who has sworn to "kill dialec!" (Bennett 4). Playing dumb before humorously demolishing his classed linguistic snobbery, the speaker inquires, "Yuy gwine kill all English dialec / Or just Jamaica one?" (4). She goes on to point out that if he is against all dialects, he will have to "kill" numerous English, Irish, and Scottish modes of speech, not to mention swathes of the literary canon:

> Yuh wi haffi get de Oxford Book
> A English verse, an tear
> Out Chaucer, Burns, Lady Grizelle
> An plenty a Shakespeare!

> (5)

Each era, the poet implies, has witnessed the forging of new, nonstandard idioms for poetry, an experimental tradition that she extends. Having demonstrated her superior learning and logic through the medium of patois, Miss Lou's final blow is to caution Mas Charlie against dropping his "h" lest he become the victim of his own linguicide. As Janet Neigh observes of a recorded version of "Bans a Killin," Bennett "draws attention to how everyone (even Mas Charlie) speaks an accented version of English that does not correspond with its written representation" (169). English does not belong exclusively to any class, nationality, or race – and crafting written renditions of its spoken varieties has long been a productive challenge for poets now considered canonical as much as for those identified as postcolonial.

From questioning how English is defined and valued, we move to reading an English-language collection that draws on another language, such as *The Half-Inch Himalayas* (1987) by Kashmiri-American poet Agha

Shahid Ali (1949–2001), whose poems repeatedly allude to the Urdu ghazals of Ghalib (1797–1869) and Faiz (1911–84), or *The January Children* (2017) by Sudanese-American poet Safia Elhillo (b. 1990), whose poems incorporate lines in Arabic from the songs of Abdelhalim Hafez (1929–77). Each of these collections meditates, moreover, on experiences of migration accessed through dream and fantasy as well as personal and familial memory. In a riveting conversation with the class in spring 2021, Elhillo explained that the term *asmarani*, the "dark-skinned" or "brown-skinned" beloved of some of Abdelhalim's songs with whom the speaker of many of her poems identifies (v), helped her to name the intersection of Black and Arab. Her choice almost entirely to eschew capitalization owed something to the absence of capitalization in Arabic. At the same time, Elhillo's "self-portrait with lake nasser," in which the speaker declares, "there once was a world / & then there was only water," relates the damming of the Nile to the unmourned loss of the Nubian language: "i call arabic my mother tongue / & mourn only that orphaning" (Elhillo 44). Having read a pair of recent poems in the form of the ghazal, Elhillo shared that Patricia Smith's "Hip-Hop Ghazal" and Fatima Asghar's "WWE" had won her over to this form about obsession and sound even before she encountered Agha Shahid Ali's ghazals.

Finally, we read translation theory, and I invite students, in preparation for becoming poet-translators themselves, to think critically about the dual-language format of Irish-language poet Nuala Ní Dhomhnaill's *Pharaoh's Daughter* (1990) and the varied approaches of its thirteen translators. The collection's title is drawn from its closing poem, "Ceist na Teangan," translated by Paul Muldoon as "The Language Issue":

Cuirim mo dhóchas ar snámh	I place my hope on the water
i mbáidín teangan	in this little boat
[. . .]	of the language, [. . .]
féachaint n'fheadaraís	only to have it borne hither and thither,
cá dtabharfaidh an sruth é,	not knowing where it might end up;
féachaint, dála Mhaoise,	in the lap, perhaps,
an bhfóirfidh iníon Fhorainn?	of some Pharaoh's daughter. (154, 155)

Ní Dhomhnaill, who has referred to this poem as her "final answer to why I write in Irish" ("Why I Choose to Write" 22), taps into the biblical book of Exodus, in which Moses's mother places her son in a basket in the river to avoid Pharaoh's death sentence on Israelite boys, and Pharaoh's daughter, finding Moses, decides to foster him rather than obey her father's edict.

Even without reading Irish competently or comparing Muldoon's translation with Ní Dhomhnaill's own English-language crib of the poem as "The
Language Question" (*"Dánta Úra"* 45), sharp-eyed students notice the
absence of Moses ("Mhaoise") and the final question mark from the right
side of the page, leading to a discussion of Muldoon's translation strategy.
They also notice the layered metaphor, in which the Irish language is
likened not to Moses but to the basket. Are those of us who speak
English as a primary language being interpellated as Pharaoh's daughter,
the scion of the oppressor in the biblical story, and if so, what kind of
responsibility do we bear to Irish and other endangered languages? I try to
emphasize, in sum, that as poems revalue denigrated, non-Western, and
endangered languages through which their speakers inhabit or pursue
a sense of home, poems engage in a decolonizing practice. That such
poems may unsettle those of us who feel secure in English as a home
tongue might lead us, rather than engaging with texts only in English as is
habitual for English departments, to advocate for and contribute to programs that center the study of nondominant languages.

"Maps That Break / Eggs": Unmaking and Remaking Worlds

Poems can be portals to understanding the world; they can also enact the
unmaking of a world tainted by colonialism in order to make new worlds
in language. In an undergraduate senior seminar entitled Poetry Worlds
that I led a few years ago, students investigated the world-making capacity
of poetry in tandem with actual social worlds in which poets have lived and
written, from London, England, to Lagos, Nigeria, and from Belfast,
Northern Ireland, to Kingston, Jamaica. Having read Una Marson,
Bennett, Walcott, and Kamau Brathwaite – poets who grew up, studied,
or taught in Jamaica – early in the semester, we read two full collections by
poets from Kingston during its second half: Lorna Goodison's *Guinea
Woman* (2000) and Kei Miller's *The Cartographer Tries to Map a Way to
Zion* (2014). In the title poem of *Guinea Woman*, Goodison (b. 1947),
Jamaica's Poet Laureate from 2017 to 2020, pays homage to her great-
grandmother as a dark-skinned African woman. The very next poem,
"Nanny," in the voice of Queen Nanny or Nanny of the Maroons, to
whom Goodison referred at a 2018 reading not only as a national hero but
as "original Wonder Woman," "could be seen as paradigmatic of the
decolonizing struggle in postcolonial poetry" in that it honors one who
literally fought colonial authority (Goodison, "Poetry Reading";
Ramazani, "Introduction" 8). Even more than these historical poems,

though, my students gravitated toward poems in which Goodison seems to theorize her own experiences with poetry as a decolonizing practice.

"The Mango of Poetry" begins in the lyric present: "I read a book / about the meaning of poetry" (*Guinea* 103). The poet confesses, "I'm still not sure what poetry is. // But now I think of a ripe mango," specifically "one from the tree / planted by my father / three years before / the sickness made him fall prematurely" (103). Together with the mango, the word "fall" alludes to the biblical account of Eden, in which the first humans bring death into the world by eating from a fruit tree, an association emphasized when the poet returns to "the shortfall // of my father's truncated years" (103). After this line, the poem shifts to the conditional mood, as the poet details how exactly she would enjoy this mango "while wearing a bombay-coloured blouse" to allow its juices to "fall freely" on her (104). The numerous "I'd" and "I would" constructions accentuate the capacity of poems to make a world that does not yet exist, in which the "fall" signifies vitality rather than mortality. The poet then joins the lyric present and conditional in the final stanza:

> And I say that this too would be
> powerful and overflowing
> and a fitting definition
> of what is poetry.

> (104)

"Poetry is the spontaneous overflow of powerful feelings," asserted William Wordsworth in his preface to *Lyrical Ballads* (1800) (xxxiii). Referring to the mango's juices as "overflowing," Goodison both literalizes and tropi- calizes Wordsworth's definition, while radicalizing his emphasis, elsewhere in the preface, on poetry as pleasure.[5] Her quatrain stanzas evoke the ballad stanza, of which Wordsworth made occasional use, but are not fixed to its customary rhyme and rhythmic pattern. Her final line echoes the poem's eighth line but subtly shifts away from Standard English ("what poetry is") along the Creole continuum ("what is poetry") (103, 104). For Goodison, the mango tree becomes an apt figure for English-language poetry, which, though not indigenous to the Caribbean, metaphorically grows out of Jamaican soil, thanks to a previous generation of Jamaicans, and furnishes sensuous experiences that exceed colonial designs.

It is possible to appreciate Goodison's "The Mango of Poetry" and also Capildeo's satire, in their prose poem "Too Solid Flesh," of the mango as a trope that plays into the mainstream British reception of postcolonial poetry as exotic: "I opened a book and a mango fell out. I opened another,

and another mango fell out. .... Woman doth not live by mango alone"
(24). One of the last poems in Goodison's collection, "Was It Legba She
Met outside the Coronation Market?", presents the ingestion not of
a mango but of an eyeball as an image for poetry as a decolonizing practice.
The name Coronation Market, like that of Kingston, in which it is located,
refers to the British monarchy and thus to colonial history, but Goodison's
poem seeks Afro-Caribbean rather than British precedents for poetic
vision. Composed in three free-verse stanzas and the third person, the
poem is focalized through a child (a figure of the poet as a young person?)
who meets "a crooked man" or "bush doctor" (Goodison, *Guinea* 127). In
a trance,

> he removes his eye's white ball
> and swallows it. It reappears in her palm, she returns
> the white sphere, he swallows it and speaks prophecy.
>
> (127)

This enigmatic exchange leaves the child "at the crossroads" between
human and spirit worlds, which Legba is thought to guard. One of my
students queried why this figure from Haitian Vodou would be in Jamaica.
One possibility is that Legba authorizes a pan-Caribbean and – through his
association with the Yorùbá òrìṣà Èṣù – pan-African lineage for poetry
which, crossing colonial borders between former British and French colonies, may be cognizant of the colonial library but does not rely on it. The
poem's final lines offer a finely balanced image: "The child is silent as the
ball's / white weight levitates on the tip of her tongue" (128). The child's
silence and restraint are all the more potent, given that Goodison's poetry
notably celebrates the liberating potential of Afro-Caribbean women's
speech and taste.

Miller, who disavows Walcott's influence, names Goodison as one of
"the poets whose shadows I'd actually been writing in" ("In the Shadow of
Derek Walcott" 8). Miller's Forward Prize-winning *The Cartographer Tries
to Map a Way to Zion* is not dedicated but "livicate[d]" to "the bredrens and
sistrens of 'Occupy Pinnacle', still fighting for Zion, still fighting for
a rightful portion of land" (4). Formed in late 2013, Occupy Pinnacle
sought to preserve the site of a Rastafarian community founded in 1940 by
Leonard P. Howell and repeatedly raided by colonial police. Activists
"argued that Pinnacle stood as an example of decolonisation many years
prior to the 1962 declaration of independence from British rule" (Dunkley
37). Amplifying the associations among anticolonial, antiracist, and spiritual struggles, the collection juxtaposes Miller's livication with a pair of

epigraphs on the facing page: two stanzas from Bennett's "Independence" about newly independent Jamaica's position on the "worl-map" – Miller has recalled that his mother "was a brilliant reciter of poems by Louise Bennett, a dialect poet who stands in Jamaica's consciousness as our most national of poets" (Wachtel 28) – and two stanzas from a Rastafari chant contrasting the wearisome ever-presence of "Babylon" with the transcendence of "Holy Mount Zion" (Miller, *The Cartographer* 5).

Early in the collection, "Quashie's Verse" stands out as a postcolonial *ars poetica*, like "The Mango of Poetry," and as a concrete poem resembling a jar. Miller's poem asks what "measure," a recurring term in the collection that is relevant for both cartography and prosody, is available for the Afro-Caribbean poet "who can no longer / measure by *kend* or by / *chamma* or by *ermijja*" – measurements from Ethiopia based on individual human bodies rather than standardized units (Miller, *The Cartographer* 12; Berhane). "As emblematic Jamaican Everyman, Quashie is the guttersnipe offspring of slaves and slavery," explains British-Jamaican poet Karen McCarthy Woolf (93).[6] Salvaging this archetype, Miller's poem treats Quashie sympathetically as a figure of the postcolonial poet, alienated by colonization from his ability to shape poems to "earthenware," formed by his hands with "no two jars" identical (12). The poem concludes:

> So what now shall Quashie do – his old
> measures outlawed, and him instructed
> now in universal forms, perfected by
> universal men who look nothing
> and sound nothing
> like Quashie?
>
> (12)

The repetition of "nothing" at the line endings casts doubt on the neutrality of the repeated adjective "universal," which should be heard in scare quotes.

Such questioning – of whose experiences are included in or excluded from definitions of poetry, who is authorized to speak or expected to listen, what kinds of language are considered acceptable, and how worlds are cognitively mapped – is deepened by the twenty-seven-poem title sequence, "The Cartographer Tries to Map a Way to Zion." Jamaican scholar Carol Bailey describes the sequence this way: "Miller's poems capture the postcolonial challenge to the colonial-era land grab in a back-and-forth between a mapmaker who feigns innocence and objectivity and a rastaman who is grounded in folk wisdom, fully aware of colonial dispossessions, and equally well versed in the vernacular strategies available for rethinking the relationship to land." The students in my Poetry Worlds seminar noticed that the rastaman's voice is rendered in what Brathwaite named "nation language" – Bailey, following Velma Pollard, specifies that "dread talk is a form of nation language" – as well as that the title sequence is intercut both with individual poems and with another, "Place Name" sequence. I pointed out, in turn, how Miller's poems develop the relationship between rastaman and cartographer as dialectical rather than dichotomous. Compare, for example the openings of poems "vi" and "xiv": "For the rastaman – it is true – dismisses / too easily the cartographic view" and "But the cartographer, it is true, / dismisses too easily the rastaman's view" (Miller, *Cartographer* 21, 34). Far from offering a false balance between colonial and postcolonial points of view, however, the poems examine what is at stake in the inevitable process of trying to know the world and recreate it in language.

Referring in an interview to cartography as a "way of knowing" like language, Miller contends that "every language is partial" (Wachtel 24). He confides, "it was easy for people to think I was the Rastaman in the book, but in my mind I was clearly the cartographer. . . . How does my education make me see the world, and how do I challenge myself to see other things?" (Wachtel 24). The poems search for ways of knowing that would redress colonial misrepresentation without rejecting mapping wholesale. Inspired by Kai Krause's "The True Size of Africa," critiquing Mercator's projection (Miller, *Cartographer* 71), poem "vi" amplifies the rastaman's belief that such European-made maps "have gripped like girdles / to make his people smaller than they were" (21). The next poem, "vii," submits a more planetary perspective:

> And what are turtles born with
> if not maps that break
> eggs and pull them up from sand
> guide them towards ocean instead of land?

(22)

This rhetorical question leads, tellingly, from the unmaking of the creatures' first worlds into a watery world. Here, postcolonial poetry imaginatively models noncoercive forms of belonging that are not defined by the colonial-turned-national borders into the service of which maps are so often pressed.

If the rastaman may underestimate the prospects for decolonizing cartography, poem "xiv" suggests, tongue in cheek, that the cartographer

certainly underestimates the rastaman's ease with institutionally accredited
ways of knowing,

> has never read his provocative dissertation –
> *"Kepture Land" as Identity Reclamation*
> *in Postcolonial Jamaica.* Hell!
> the cartographer did not even know
> the rastaman had a PhD (from Glasgow
> no less) in which, amongst other things, he sites
> Sylvia Wynter's most cryptic essay: *On How*
> *We Mistook the Map for the Territory,*
> *and Reimprisoned Ourselves in*
> *An Unbearable Wrongness of Being.* . .

(34)

Miller, too, has a PhD from Glasgow, although his dissertation focused on
Jamaican epistolary practices ("Jamaica to the World"), including verse
epistles by Bennett and Goodison, whose "Heartease I" (*Guinea* 32–33)
Miller quotes in poem "xix" (*Cartographer* 44). In "xiv," the rastaman sites
(positions) rather than cites (summons) Wynter, the Jamaican writer and
critical theorist, whose essay argues "that the systematic devalorization of
racial blackness [is], in itself, *only* a function of another and more deeply
rooted phenomenon – in effect, only the map of the real territory, the
symptom of the real cause, the real issue" (115), which is a constrained
imagination of "*genres* or *kinds* of being human" (119). Ultimately, the
poet's vocation is to make not just a new map, but a new territory.

The relation between map and territory, concept and material world,
becomes an especially acute subject for inquiry at the graduate level. In
graduate seminars on poetry, I structure readings around notable poets, but
also around what alternative frameworks to the nation – postcolonial,
transnational, cosmopolitan, diasporic, global, and/or planetary – might
be adequate to twentieth- and twenty-first-century poetry that registers the
violence of the Atlantic slave trade, European colonialism, and contemporary migration while inventively refashioning poetic form. A recent
multigenre graduate seminar on African Writing and Futurity – the course
posed the question, how have African writers imagined not only their place
but their time in the world? – concluded with a virtual visit by Motswana
poet Tjawangwa Dema. Her collection *The Careless Seamstress* (2019),
which bears cover artwork by the South African artist Mary Sibande,
features a number of seamstress figures. Responding to a question about
these figures and women's labor, Dema reflected that sewing was historically gendered, with women being assigned the role of home-makers, men

that of heroes or world-makers. As the speaker of the title poem, dealing with her husband's sexism, declares, "A woman knows the way things puncture and hold" (*Careless* 21). For Dema, poetry poses the challenge of "world-building" in an economical or brief form, and her experience of "trying to stitch together an entire collection" opened up "entire worlds" (Dema, African Writing).

While poets exert some agency over their language and labor, institutional issues with editing and publishing differentially afflict both poets in the Global South and poets of color in the Global North, affecting which poets are included in anthologies aimed at the classroom as well as which individual collections can be assigned. Those of us engaged in university teaching can support presses in the Global North that keep crucial poets in print while also assigning poets whose work is not being promoted or published in the Global North. The digital is no panacea, but the digitization of archival or out-of-print materials and the efflorescence of digital publications across the Global South offer possibilities for our pedagogy beyond what the campus bookstore can order.

Decolonization is a perpetually unfinished business. Even as I have tried here to present the postcolonial less as geography or identity than as critical practice, many geographies and identities vital to the decolonizing work of poetry have gone unmentioned. Whether or not "postcolonial poetry" remains the most efficacious framework, poems and poets will continue to enact decolonizing practices, at least until the thorough reimagining and reordering of "*genres* or *kinds* of being human" is effected (Wynter 119).

Notes

I am grateful to Omaar Hena, Mandy Suhr-Sytsma, Jarad Zimbler, and the editors, Ankhi Mukherjee and Ato Quayson, for their valuable comments on drafts of this chapter. I also acknowledge Tjawangwa Dema's kind permission to quote her remarks.

1. The poet adds, "The (non-Jewish) narrator in that poem is transhistorical, inhabiting one after another 'foreign' body that arrives or invades as Other but eventually may be absorbed into the story of 'Englishness'" (Parmar, "*The Wolf* Interview" 60).
2. For an overview of gender and sexuality in postcolonial poetry, focusing on the trope of motherhood, see Innes.
3. Although there is no chapter on US poetry in *The Cambridge Companion to Postcolonial Poetry*, edited by Ramazani, he makes the case, in his introduction to a subsequent special issue on poetry and race, for the need "to bridge Americanist with transnational or postcolonial perspectives" ("Poetry and Race" xiii).

4. Writing in a Canadian context, Heath Justice "offer[s] 'paracolonialism' (coined by Ashinaabe theorist Gerald Vizenor) as a term more suited to the material and intellectual struggles of the Indigenous peoples of this land" than "the term 'postcolonialism'" (485).

5. Wordsworth's daffodils, which often stand in for postcolonial poets' jarring encounters with the colonial curriculum, appear in the following poem, "To Mr William Wordsworth, Distributor of Stamps for Westmoreland," which plays on the shared name of the historic county in northwest England where Wordsworth lived and the parish in southwest Jamaica where Goodison's great-grandmother "wrote her lyrical ballads on air / scripted them with her tongue" (Goodison, *Guinea* 104).

6. Derived from the Akan name Kwasi, "Quashie" is defined by the *Oxford English Dictionary*, which identifies the word as "*Caribbean* (chiefly *derogatory*)," as a "generic name for: a black person, esp. one considered as credulous or insignificant" and by the online *Jamaican Patwah* dictionary as a "vulgar" synonym for "low class." See also McCarthy Woolf (101 n. 4).

WORKS CITED

Bailey, Carol. "Voicing the Reclamation in Kei Miller's *The Cartographer Tries to Map a Way to Zion*." *sx salon* 32 (Oct. 2019). http://smallaxe.net/sxsalon/discussions/voicing-reclamation-kei-millers-cartographer-tries-map-way-zion.

Bennett, Louise. *Selected Poems*, ed. Mervyn Morris. Kingston: Sangster's Book Stores, 1983.

Berhane, Yared. "Systems of Measure in Ethiopia." *Abyssinia Gateway*. http://abyssiniagateway.net/info/measure.html.

Brathwaite, Edward Kamau. *History of the Voice: The Development of Nation Language in Anglophone Caribbean Poetry*. London: New Beacon Books, 1984.

Capildeo, Vahni. *Measures of Expatriation*. Manchester: Carcanet, 2016.

Dema, Tjawangwa. African Writing and Futurity Seminar. 23 Nov. 2020. Emory University, Zoom.

———. *The Careless Seamstress*. Lincoln: University of Nebraska Press, 2019.

Diaz, Natalie. "Natalie Diaz Reads and Discusses Postcolonial Love Poem on August 4, 2020." *Library of Congress*. www.loc.gov/item/2020785237/.

———. *Postcolonial Love Poem*. Minneapolis: Graywolf, 2020.

Donnell, Alison. "Writing of and for Our Time: Bernardine Evaristo Talks to Alison Donnell." *Wasafiri* 43.4 (2019): 99–104.

Dunkley, D. A. "Occupy Pinnacle and the Rastafari's Struggle for Land in Jamaica." *Jamaica Journal* 35.1–2 (2014): 36–43.

Elhillo, Safia. *The January Children*. Lincoln: University of Nebraska Press, 2017.

Etherington, Ben and Jarad Zimbler. "Decolonize Practical Criticism?" *English* 70.270 (2021): 227–36.

Goodison, Lorna. *Guinea Woman: New and Selected Poems*. Manchester: Carcanet, 2000.

"Poetry Reading and Reflections." YouTube, August 6, 2019. www .youtube.com/watch?v=4-JozFtaK7o [University of Virginia, "Poetry and Race" Symposium, Oct. 5, 2018].

Guillory, John. *Cultural Capital: The Problem of Literary Canon Formation.* Chicago: University of Chicago Press, 1993.

Harjo, Joy. *Conflict Resolution for Holy Beings: Poems.* New York: W. W. Norton, 2015.

Heath Justice, Daniel. "Indigenous Peoples' Writing in Canada." In Ato Quayson, ed., *The Cambridge History of Postcolonial Literature*, vol. 1. Cambridge: Cambridge University Press, 2012, 484–510.

Innes, Lyn. "Gender and Sexuality in Postcolonial Poetry." In Jahan Ramazani, ed., *The Cambridge Companion to Postcolonial Poetry.* Cambridge: Cambridge University Press, 2017, 222–36.

Kalliney, Peter J. *The Aesthetic Cold War: Decolonization and Global Literature.* Princeton, NJ: Princeton University Press, 2022.

Kashyap, Aruni. "What the Poet Can Do in the Face of the Modern Colonial State." *Literary Hub*, Sep. 20, 2021. https://lithub.com/what-the-poet-can-do-in-the-face-of-the-modern-colonial-state/.

"Land Acknowledgment Statement." Emory University, www.emory.edu/home/ explore/history/land-acknowledgment/index.html.

"Mansio / Matthew Butcher, Kieran Wardle and Owain Williams." *ArchDaily*, May 27, 2016. www.archdaily.com/788252/mansio-matthew-butcher-kieran-wardle-and-owain-williams.

Mata, Inocência. "Under the Sign of a Projective Nostalgia: Agostinho Neto and Angolan Postcolonial Poetry," trans. Vicky Hartnack. *Research in African Literatures* 38.1 (2007): 54–67.

McCarthy Woolf, Karen. "Hybrid Hierophanies: Where Rastafari Meets Religious Ecology in Kei Miller's *The Cartographer Tries to Map a Way to Zion." Journal of Foreign Languages and Cultures* 3.1 (2019): 91–102.

Miller, Kei. *The Cartographer Tries to Map a Way to Zion.* Manchester: Carcanet, 2014.

"In the Shadow of Derek Walcott: 1930–2017." *PN Review* 43.5 (2017): 7–10.

"Jamaica to the World: A Study of Jamaican (and West Indian) Epistolary Practices." Diss., University of Glasgow, 2012.

Nagra, Daljit. *British Museum.* London: Faber & Faber, 2017.

Neigh, Janet. "Orality, Creoles, and Postcolonial Poetry in Performance." In Jahan Ramazani, ed., *The Cambridge Companion to Postcolonial Poetry.* Cambridge: Cambridge University Press, 2017, 167–79.

Ní Dhomhnaill, Nuala. "*Dánta Úra*: New Poems." *Éire-Ireland* 25.3 (1990): 38–45.

Pharaoh's Daughter. Winston-Salem, NC: Wake Forest University Press, 1993.

"Why I Choose to Write in Irish, the Corpse That Sits Up and Talks Back." In Oona Frawley, ed., *Selected Essays.* Dublin: New Island, 2005, 10–24.

Osundare, Niyi. "How Post-Colonial Is African Literature?" In Marlies Glaser and Marion Pausch, eds., *Caribbean Writers: Between Orality & Writing / Les Auteurs Caribéens: Entre L'Oralité et L'Écriture.* Amsterdam: Rodopi, 1994, 203–16.

Parmar, Sandeep. "Not a British Subject: Race and Poetry in the UK." *Los Angeles Review of Books*, Dec. 6, 2015. https://lareviewofbooks.org/article/not-a-brit ish-subject-race-and-poetry-in-the-uk/.

"*The Wolf* Interview: Vahni Capildeo." *The Wolf* 34 (2016): 54–61.

Patke, Rajeev S. *Postcolonial Poetry in English*. Oxford: Oxford University Press, 2006.

Pollard, Charles W. *New World Modernisms: T. S. Eliot, Derek Walcott, and Kamau Brathwaite*. Charlottesville: University of Virginia Press, 2004.

Raja, Ira, and Deepika Bahri. "Key Journals and Organizations." In Ato Quayson, ed., *The Cambridge History of Postcolonial Literature*, vol. 2, Cambridge: Cambridge University Press, 2011, 1155–88.

Ramazani, Jahan, ed. *The Cambridge Companion to Postcolonial Poetry*. Cambridge: Cambridge University Press, 2017.

"Introduction." In Jahan Ramazani, ed., *The Cambridge Companion to Postcolonial Poetry*. Cambridge: Cambridge University Press, 2017, 1–15.

"Poetry and Race: An Introduction." *New Literary History* 50.4 (2019): vii–xxxviii.

Ranasinha, Ruvani. "Guest Editorial: Decolonizing English." *Journal of Commonwealth Literature* 54.2 (2019): 119–23.

Ravinthiran, Vidyan. "(Indian) Verse and the Question of Aesthetics." *New Literary History* 50.4 (2019): 647–70.

"Myriad Minded." *Poetry* 216.2 (2020): 169–82.

Rodriguez, Janet. "Ways to Become Unpinnable: Talking with Natalie Diaz." *Rumpus*, Mar. 14, 2020. therumpus.net/2020/03/the-rumpus-interview-with -natalie-diaz/.

Secco, Carmen Lúcia Tindó. "Postcolonial Poetry in Cape Verde, Angola, and Mozambique: Some Contemporary Considerations," trans. Russell G. Hamilton. *Research in African Literatures* 38.1 (2007): 119–33.

Suhr-Sytsma, Nathan. *Poetry, Print, and the Making of Postcolonial Literature*. Cambridge: Cambridge University Press, 2017.

Wachtel, Eleanor. "An Interview with Kei Miller." *Brick* 101 (2018): 23–36.

Wordsworth, William. *Lyrical Ballads, with Other Poems*. 2nd ed., vol. 1. London: T. N. Longman and O. Rees, 1800. https://archive.org/details/lyricalballads wi04word/page/n3/mode/2up.

Wynter, Sylvia. "On How We Mistook the Map for the Territory, and Re-Imprisoned Ourselves in Our Unbearable Wrongness of Being, of *Désetre*: Black Studies Toward the Human Project." In Lewis R. Gordon and Jane Anna Gordon, eds., *Not Only the Master's Tools: African-American Studies in Theory and Practice*. Boulder, CO: Paradigm, 2006, 107–69.

CHAPTER 25

Decolonizing English Literary Study in the Anglophone Caribbean

William Ghosh

How have scholars and teachers of literature in the anglophone Caribbean understood the task of decolonizing the English literary curriculum? What lessons might this hold for those working both within and – as in my case – very far distant from the Caribbean today? This chapter provides an account first of the nature of English literary study in the colonial Caribbean, and then of Caribbean attempts to decolonize the practice in the later twentieth century. My aim is to analyze the evolving ways scholars and teachers have understood the "coloniality" of the practices they inherited, and the different means by which they have attempted to change them.

English Literary Study in the Colonial Caribbean

Toward the beginning of Erna Brodber's 1988 novel *Myal*, the child protagonist recites Rudyard Kipling's "Big Steamers" to a visiting Anglican parson at her school in St. Thomas Parish, Jamaica. "The words were the words of Kipling," we are told, "but the voice was that of Ella O'Grady, aged 13" (Brodber 5). Ella is a mixed-race child, the daughter of an Irish policeman and his Jamaican housekeeper. Growing up in a rural area, she is bullied by her classmates for her light skin and fair hair. Finding comfort in her studies, she learns from the maps and books her school provides. "When they brought out the maps and showed Europe, it rose from the paper in three dimensions, grew big, came right down to her seat and allowed her to walk on it, feel its snow" (Brodber 11). Asked to recite "Big Steamers" to the parson, she is undaunted. "She had already been to England several times" in her imagination, and "all she was doing at Teacher's rehearsals was to open her mouth and let what was already in her heart and in her head come out" (Brodber 11–12).

Scenes like this give a picture of the colonial nature of literary education in the early to mid-century colonial Caribbean. The set text here, Kipling's "Big Steamers," was first published in *A School History of England*, a 1911 textbook written, as the authors claimed, "for all boys and girls who are interested in the story of Great Britain and her Empire" (Fletcher and Kipling 2). "Big Steamers" is a didactic, question-and-answer poem in which the child questioner learns from the adult respondent about the work of the British merchant navy, crossing the Empire and Dominions. Its message is of a vast world made tame and safe for the child by the bravery and skill of the imperial merchants. The significance of the scene in *Myal* turns not just on what Ella is reading but on how she is reading it. She has learned it verbatim and is reciting it from memory, such that by a process of "osmosis" Kipling's words have become her own (Brodber 11).

British materials, imperial values, rote learning: these are the characteristics many Caribbean writers describe when recalling the colonial literary classroom. Ella O'Grady, attending school in 1913, reads from generic textbooks produced for readers across Britain and its colonies and dominions. Alongside Kipling, she might have encountered Nelson's series of *Royal Readers* or the Mcdougall Readers series. Slightly later, from the mid-1920s onward, Nelson's began to produce their successful *West Indian Readers* series, written by the colonial schoolmaster Captain J. O. Cutteridge. These later textbooks include more material specific to the West Indies, including lessons on Caribbean flora and fauna, regional agriculture, and local crops. But they also contained extracts and retellings of English literary classics and lessons in art history focused on paintings by British and European artists (Low, "Empire of Print" 117). Moreover, as Gail Low has shown, the West Indian history they did tell was framed in Eurocentric terms: celebrating Columbus's "discovery" of the islands and skating over the history of slavery in their celebratory story about the region's agricultural development (Low, "Read" 107).

In the work of many Caribbean writers (as for Ella O'Grady above), the *Readers* become unwitting objects of fantasy, longing, and projection (Fraser 99). It is clear, however, that these authors, and their characters, read against the grain. In many primary schools, as Carl C. Campbell notes, English classes consisted simply of grammatical drilling and the recitation of poetry (Campbell, *Young Colonials* 89). In Naipaul's *A House for Mr Biswas*, a novel about literary formation in the late colonial West Indies, literature is studied by copying and repetition, as a route to better comportment, social capital, and exam success. In Jamaica Kincaid's *Annie John*, the disciplinary undertone to English literary education is made explicit when the protagonist, Annie, is "ordered to copy Books I and II of *Paradise Lost* by John Milton" as a punishment for writing satirical comments below a picture of Christopher Columbus (Kincaid 82). As Simon Gikandi has argued, colonial schooling understood the ideal student of literature to be someone who easily absorbed and replicated the insights and values of the foreign text: "A powerful mythology among young colonials was that while they could become accomplished readers, writing was alien to their experiences" (Gikandi xvii). Repetition and inculcation were valorized and tested, not creativity, response, or critique.

For most people in the colonial West Indies, secondary education was the exception not the rule. Despite receiving substantial public funding, the best schools in the British West Indies – including Queen's Royal College (QRC) in Port-of-Spain, Jamaica College in Kingston, and Harrison College in Bridgetown – were accessible to the general public only through a small and exceptionally competitive scholarship program, and then, only for boys. These were grammar schools in the old British tradition with a deep commitment to a European humanistic and literary education. C. L. R. James's 1963 memoir *Beyond a Boundary* gives a portrait. At QRC, he writes, "I mastered thoroughly the principles of cricket and of English literature, and attained a mastery over my own character" (James, *Beyond* 31). Among his reading, he lists Virgil, Caesar, and Horace (in Latin), Euripides and Thucydides (in Greek), all thirty-seven volumes of Thackeray held in the school library, Dickens, George Eliot, Shelley, Keats, and Byron, Milton and Spenser. "As schools go, it was a very good school, though it would have been more suitable to Portsmouth than Port of Spain," he writes (James, *Beyond* 37). Associating literary study with "mastery" over "character," James alludes to the idea that studying English literature might instill a British-derived, masculine-coded form of rectitude. From the later nineteenth century, school certificates were administered by the Cambridge University Local Examinations Syndicates, who adapted to allow West Indian topics and texts only slowly through the mid-twentieth century (Low, "Empire of Print" 118–19). The Caribbean Examinations Council was finally established only in 1973 (see Low, "Read" 108). This, at last, allowed syllabi and examinations to be governed solely from the Caribbean.

The University College of the West Indies was founded in 1948 in a "special relationship" with the University of London. Upon graduation, students received "External" London degrees ("UWI Timeline"). The Department of English was established two years later, in 1950, offering courses for the General degree program and offering its own Honours (or "Special") degree in English. As a colonial institution, the department offered four papers for the general degree: "Middle English and Early Tudor Literature," "English Literature 1550–1700," "English Literature 1800 to the present day" (in practice, this meant "to 1900"), and "Exercises in Critical Appreciation." In 1963, as an autonomous university in a newly independent region, practical criticism was scrapped, and five new papers were offered. These were: "English Literature, Chaucer to Wyatt," "Donne to Pope," "Johnson to Byron," "The Victorian Period," and "Shakespeare." In other words, very little changed. With some minor rearrangements ("Chaucer to Wyatt" became "Chaucer to Spenser"), this structure remained through the 1960s, and the Special Degree syllabus, whilst having a little more variation, followed the same pattern. "We still live under a compulsion," Edward Baugh wrote in 1970, "to make sure that the students get a comprehensive course in the literature of England, as if we must first seek the heaven of that kingdom" (Baugh 58). A full course in West Indian Literature was made compulsory for the first time for Special Degree students in 1970.[1] The University of the West Indies (UWI) was significant because it was the key institution in which future teachers and professors of English in the West Indies were educated. One common view, discussed below (pp. 479–480), is that it provided institutional continuity or memory, enforcing colonial disciplinary norms and practices well into the postcolonial period. But at the same time, as Glyne Griffith has argued, it provided an institutional site for methodological reflection and critique (Griffith 295). Most of the scholars discussed in this chapter passed through the University of the West Indies as either students, professors, or both. Many published in forums housed at the UWI.

What defined English literary study in the preindependence Caribbean as colonial in nature? I would point first to the limited franchise. For social groups outside the colonial elite, primary education was not universal, secondary education was rare, and university education exceptionally so. Most of the best schools, as we have seen, were reserved for men. Literary education, at primary level, was very limited, and, despite the efforts of some reformers, emphasized the inculcation of exemplary texts at the expense of critique. At both primary and secondary level, literary study was seen to be a conduit of "conduct" (to quote C. L. R. James). At all levels, the texts studied were overwhelmingly English and European, some championing overtly imperialist views, and some containing racist representations. At university level, the rationale of the syllabus was to tell the story of a nation's – England's – literary development through time. All of these characteristics would be the subject of the evolving critique I will now trace from the 1960s to the present. All would have stubborn afterlives in the institutions in which these critics worked, the syllabi that they attempted to reform, and even in their own minds and assumptions.

From Enfranchisement to Critique

Two of the larger British Caribbean colonies, Jamaica and Trinidad achieved independence in 1962; Barbados and Guyana followed in 1966. As is well known, the last years of formal colonialism and the first years of independence saw a flourishing of Caribbean letters. The twenty years between the publication of George Lamming's *In the Castle of My Skin* (1953) and Derek Walcott's *Another Life* (1973) saw the publication of Selvon's *The Lonely Londoners* (1956); V. S. Naipaul's *House for Mr Biswas* (1961) and *Mimic Men* (1967); Jean Rhys's *Wide Sargasso Sea* (1966); Merle Hodge's *Crick Crack, Monkey* (1970); Kamau Brathwaite's *Arrivants* trilogy (1967–9); and Walcott's *In a Green Night* (1962) and *Dream on Monkey Mountain* (1970). How did this literary flourishing influence the development of literary criticism and pedagogy in the region? One simplistic but conceptually useful distinction would distinguish nationalist approaches that aimed to enfranchise Caribbean writers within existing models of literary value from more radical forms of critique that used Caribbean experience, and Caribbean texts, to query those values. The tension between these two approaches, sometimes in the work of the same critic, and the gradual shift in critical fashion from enfranchisement to critique through the long 1960s, is a helpful map for understanding Caribbean critical trends in the period.

"Take the whole line of them," C. L. R. James wrote in a *Trinidad Guardian* magazine feature in 1965, "Jane Austen, Henry Fielding, Samuel Richardson ... even Charles Dickens. None of them at twenty-three was so much a master of the novelist's business as this young man, George Lamming, who has grown up in the West Indies" (James, "Home" 4). Just as "half-a-dozen West Indian cricketers" were now "acknowledged as people who could hold their own in any department of the game with the greatest historical figures who have ever been," so it was no longer "unduly nationalistic" to make this claim for the region's novelists. James's thoughts about literature and culture were complex and changed through his life, but this article clearly instantiates the "enfranchisement" model. James takes for granted existing understandings of what great literature is and argues that West Indian writers, though historically neglected, meet this standard and deserve attention. James's argument is that the West

Indian literature of the 1950s and 1960s constituted a major new branch in the long tradition of "Western" literature ("we are a Western people," he bluntly states), one of singular relevance to the contemporary decolonizing world, and to the Caribbean region in particular (James, "Home" 5).[2] Just as "Aeschylus wrote at home in his native language for the illiterate people around him," so writers such as Lamming ought (James believed) to express the West Indian experience authentically, that is – in Lamming's own phrase – "from the inside" (James, "Home" 5; Lamming 37–38). Many critics of James's generation localized the correct topic of West Indian literature onto the Romantic concept of the "folk." The standard was international, the subject matter local, giving the West Indian (James was a federalist, after all) a national literature by which to understand themselves and present their experience to the world. At the university and in schools, this approach called for the dedicated study of West Indian literature as such. "Each nation is interested first and foremost in its own literature," Edward Baugh wrote, quoting from Louis Dudek; at the University of the West Indies, "the study of West Indian literature should naturally have a central and increasingly important place" (Baugh 56, 59).

Even as Baugh was making this relatively modest proposal however – this essay was first given as a lecture at the P.E.N. Club, Jamaica, in April 1970 – he acknowledged that the demands of student activists on the UWI campus far outstripped the nationalist politics of a generation of scholars now viewed as part of the establishment. Speaking of the "upsurge of questioning and self-examination" now manifesting itself "in all aspects of the university's life," he describes the local manifestation of a wider shift (Baugh 49). The historian Kate Quinn has described the "crisis of failed expectations" that developed in postindependence Caribbean states through the 1960s. "Flag independence," it was felt, had done little to redress the deeper legacies of the colonial era: dependence on foreign countries; racial hierarchies that still valorized White or lighter-skinned people; cultural hierarchies that valorized European norms; and social and economic divisions that continued to disenfranchise the Black poor (Quinn 2). In this climate, a more radical vision of culture and politics was offered by the Black Power movement, which called for a break with colonial patterns of government and administration, economic redress in favor of the poor, and – to quote from Walter Rodney's famous manifesto – "the cultural reconstruction of the society in the image of the blacks" (quoted in Quinn 2).

The Mona campus of the University of the West Indies, east of downtown Kingston, played an important role in the Black Power protests.

A Black Power group had been formed on campus in 1967. When Rodney, a UWI lecturer, was denied reentry to Jamaica by Hugh Shearer's centrist government in October 1968, students marched toward the office of the Minister of Home Affairs. Although the students, in all likelihood, were not responsible for organizing or inciting the larger protests and riots that spread through Kingston, the campus was seen as a symbolic center and was surrounded by the military during the protests (see Lewis 61–67). This was the context in which the university finally moved to increase the representation of West Indian literature on the English syllabus. It also, in Rupert Lewis's words, led to "the Afrocentric reorientation of performance poetry and dance, and, most obviously, in the black-consciousness messages of the popular music of its day" (Lewis 70). These formal and thematic developments in the popular arts, including poetry, did not much impinge on the initially moderate reforms in the UWI English department. Later on, as we shall see, they would.

"The imperial way of seeing has not disappeared with the imperial flag," wrote Sylvia Wynter, then a lecturer in Hispanic literatures at UWI Mona. "Its manifestations are more subtle; because more subtle, they are more dangerous. It was easier to fight 'manifest unfreedom' in 1938 . . . than to grapple with 'seeming freedom' as we must do now" (Wynter, "We Must 1" 30). Wynter's essay "We Must Learn to Sit Down Together and Talk about a Little Culture" was published in the *Jamaica Journal* in two parts, in December 1968 and March 1969. A crucial expression of, and reflection upon, its cultural moment, it rejected moderate nationalist ideas in favor of a systematic critique of the definition and function of literature and criticism.[3] The essay is a review of *The Islands in Between* (1968), a collection of critical essays on Caribbean literature edited by the English critic Louis James, who had previously taught at UWI Mona. But as its subtitle "Reflections on West Indian Writing and Criticism" suggests, Wynter's essay extends into a larger meditation. The target of Wynter's criticism is what she calls the "branch plant" perspective on Caribbean literature, one which "adjusts new experience to fit an imported model" (Wynter, "We Must 1" 26). Despite its still-tiny presence in the main undergraduate curriculums, Wynter had noticed that by this point most critical writing in the English-speaking Caribbean, and specifically most criticism of Caribbean literature, was "centred at and diffused from the university" (Wynter "We Must 1" 24). In her view, the model of criticism practiced by Louis James, and modeled as exemplary to new scholars at the UWI (she uses the example of Wayne Brown) had imported wholesale from England fundamental assumptions about what literature was, and what constituted literary value, without interrogating them, or their contemporary relevance in the Caribbean.

Wynter's essay made a distinction between what she called "acquiescent" writers and critics and "challenging" or "revolutionary" ones. In her view, the key error made by "acquiescent" critics was to view "literature" as a "fetish object," a special category of language-use to be understood and assessed by special, universal "artistic" standards (Wynter, "We Must 1" 24). The corollary of this attitude for critics was to view critical activity as disinterested in the Arnoldian sense: dispassionately evaluating literary work against a quasi-objective standard, and without acknowledging one's own stakes or investments in the judgment formed. For Wynter, this was an error that found its source in European dualist philosophies (the separation of mind and body, intellect and activity) and in the imperial-capitalist commodification of the work of art. Against this, Wynter offered a vision of literature that was purposive rather than aestheticist: literary texts, including critical essays, are means to an end, "not ends in themselves" (Wynter, "We Must 1" 24). Their purpose is fundamentally social: literary texts exist for living audiences. And the social purpose that Wynter emphasized was interpretive and epistemic. She called for literature which "*reinterpret*[ed]" Caribbean life by drawing attention to the economic inequalities and the spurious social and racial hierarchies that permeated the region. To reinterpret the social world in this way, she says, "is to commit oneself to a constant revolutionary assault against it" (Wynter, "We Must 1" 24). In this sense, it is important that the two literary forms that most interest Wynter in this essay are the novel and the critical essay: both are seen to share a common critical and interpretive function.

A key word for Wynter in this essay is "awareness." If literary texts are social performances, speaking from person to person in specific social contexts, then it was important to ask: who is speaking, and why? "I am a Jamaican, a West Indian, an American," she wrote, "I write not to fulfil a category, fill an order, supply a consumer, but to attempt to define what is this thing to *be* – a Jamaican, a West Indian, an American" (Wynter, "We Must 1" 24). Where you were speaking from, your social position, background, and investments, fundamentally shaped the meaning of what you said. Her objection to Louis James or W. I. Carr was not that they were English but that their writing did not – in her view – reflect on and acknowledge the position from which they spoke. They replicated colonial ideas about literature and literary value unconsciously and attempted to shape readers and students in their image. Instead of this, Wynter argued, writers and critics should understand their own writing, and the writing of others, in their total social and historical context: "Challenging criticism seems to me to relate the books discussed to the greatest possible 'whole' to which they belong" (Wynter, "We Must 2" 34–35). The "whole" to which both Caribbean and English writers belonged was a world shaped by imperial capitalism and Atlantic slavery. Like Rodney, Wynter saw imperialism as an evolutionary phase in the history of capitalism – "in effect the extended capitalist system" – in which divisions between capital and labor, "exploiters and ... the exploited," had through recent centuries been organized geographically: capital in London; labor drawn from West and Central Africa, and later India and China; the site of production in the West Indies (Rodney, loc. 584).

"With Hawkins's first raid on Africa, his first Middle passage to the West Indies," Wynter wrote, "the nature of being an African, the nature of Englishness had changed. In the place of African and Englishman there was now only a relation" (Wynter, "We Must 2" 30). For this reason, English, West Indian, and West African literature could only be understood in relation to one another. These observations prefigure a number of the most influential anticolonial theories of the later twentieth century, including Edward Said's model of "contrapuntal" reading or Paul Gilroy's writings on Black Atlantic culture. Equally important, when considering the legacy of this essay, was her focus on criticism itself as an interpretive activity on a par with the novel and sharing a common social function. This was evident in what she wrote about, moving seamlessly from novels to critical texts and assessing them both by the same standard of "acquiescent" versus "challenging"; it was evident in how she defined the tasks of writing and criticism; and it was evident in her own style. "I am a Jamaican, a West Indian, an American," she wrote, making clear both where she was writing from, who she was writing to, and why.

New Forms, New Constituencies

Radical though it was, "We Must Learn" was nonetheless an unfinished project. In that essay, Wynter championed work that, eschewing middle-class enchantment with a European myth of high art, addressed and spoke from within the living culture of the West Indian people. Yet the actual texts she studies are largely novels and essays – prestigious and accepted literary forms. Moreover, they were all by men. This need be no criticism of Wynter – her essay broadly tracks the writers discussed in *The Islands in Between* – but it does tell us something about West Indian literary culture of the period. Most of the writers to whom literary critics – acquiescent or critical – paid attention in the 1960s were men, working in recognizable "literary" genres. One of the key developments in Caribbean literary study in subsequent decades would be to expand the object of study beyond the traditional literary genres, and to foreground the work of different constituencies of writers.

Moving beyond traditional literary genres, the work of Guyanese critic and UWI professor Gordon Rohlehr was of fundamental importance. On April 7, 1967, whilst completing a PhD on Joseph Conrad at the University of Birmingham, he had given a talk at the West Indian Student Centre in London on "Sparrow and the Language of Calypso."[4] It would be published as an essay in the second volume of *Savacou* in September 1970, and the project it begins would broaden into a series of essays published over the next three decades, culminating in *Calypso and Society in Pre-Independence Trinidad* (1990) and *A Scuffling of Islands: Essays on Calypso* (2004). One way of articulating the originality of Rohlehr's approach is to compare "Sparrow and the Language of Calypso" with Mervyn Morris's "On Reading Louise Bennett Seriously," published in the *Jamaica Journal* in 1967. Both essays are attempts to extend the purview of West Indian literary criticism to popular forms that had hitherto been seen as subliterary: the lyrics of calypsonian Sparrow and the popular performance poetry of Louise Bennett. Morris was one of the critics Wynter had called "acquiescent," and his argument for the literary significance of Louise Bennett rests on the claim that she wrote what were in fact recognized poetic genres in the English tradition. He compares her work to the satirists of the eighteenth century (72), to the comic librettos of W. S. Gilbert (72), and – most extensively – to the dramatic monologues of Robert Browning (70–71). "I believe Louise Bennett to be a poet," Morris had written, "and the purpose of this essay is to suggest literary reasons for doing so" (69). By contrast, Rohlehr's essay, though noting occasional literary parallels, is not fundamentally concerned with making a claim for the literariness or otherwise of Sparrow's lyrics, but rather with discerning the kinds of "intelligence" and verbal play that characterized Sparrow's lyrics (89). He describes, for instance, the "essential directionless irony" in Sparrow's lyrics, "the gift of a normless world" (91). Where Morris had positioned Bennett's poetry in a lineage with British satirists, Rohlehr emphasizes the contrast between the "merciless invective" of "calypsos of abuse" and the "metropolitan tradition of complaint" (92). Finally, he notes that the ease with which Sparrow's unforced, idiomatic lines realized the syncopated calypso rhythm might offer a model for a relationship between idiomatic

West Indian verse and the demands of poetic meter. Whereas Morris persuades his readers that Bennett's writing is "poetry" according to a preexisting definition, Rohlehr sees the relation between calypso and poetry as different but overlapping, and mutually porous.

A second key expansion of the object of literary study in the Caribbean has been an increased focus on constituencies of Caribbean writers under-represented in the Caribbean canon of the 1950s and 1960s, and a new attention to the intersections of gender, race, sexuality, and class in colonial and postcolonial experience. As in earlier decades, critical trends and literary developments reinforced one another. Increased attention to writing by Caribbean women, for instance, emerged at a time when writers such as Jamaica Kincaid, Michelle Cliff, and Lorna Goodison were beginning to gain international prominence. The work of Carolyn Cooper, who was a student of Morris at UWI Mona, combined an enlarged sense of what constituted literature with an enlarged understanding of who wrote it or performed it. Indeed, her work consistently makes the point that elite defin-itions of what constitutes literature and literary value are commonly predicated on assumptions about the class, race, and gender of readers, writers, and critics.

Cooper had written her PhD on the poetry of Derek Walcott at UWI in the mid-1970s. Yet in a series of essays written through the 1980s, many of which were published in the *Jamaica Journal*, Cooper wrote what she would retrospectively see as a both a development from and an inversion of the work she had done as a doctoral student (Cooper 13–14). Published as a book in 1993 called *Noises in the Blood*, these essays both build a connected historical argument and can be read as a record and index of an emerging critical method. Beginning with the observation that "one culture's 'knowledge' is another's 'noise,'" Cooper – as Rohlehr did with Trinidadian calypso – examines a range of Jamaican popular texts for the intelligence or "know-ledge" therein (4). Beginning with transcriptions (by White historians) of bawdy songs or dramatic monologues, supposedly sung by enslaved women, *Noises in the Blood* analyzes the performance poetry of Louise Bennett, Jean "Binta" Breeze, and Mikey Smith, the oral histories of the Sistren collective, the lyrics of Bob Marley, and the dancehall lyrics of Josey Wales, Lovindeer, and Shelly Thunder. One of Cooper's most important ideas is that opposi-tions between "high" and "low" cultural forms, "scribal" and "oral" texts, "culture" and "slackness" (the vulgarity or indecency associated with dance-hall and bacchanal) are better understood as mutually constitutive relation-ships. In Josey Wales's "Culture a lick," a parodic morality song calling for the deportation of "Slackness" from Jamaica, the chorus figures "Slackness in di backyard hidin', hidin' from Culture" (quoted in Cooper 147). What is

suggested by the metaphor, and the song, is that "Slackness" and its traditional spaces (the carnival, the dancehall) exist in a parodic, fugitive relationship with "Culture," and that "Culture" in Jamaica is itself an invention of
those anxious not to be associated with what was vulgar or slack. For Cooper,
oral texts "contaminate" the valorized scribal texts of Jamaican literature
either by drawing them closer to the verbal habits of vernacular speech,
or – conversely – by inciting them to veer away, protesting too much (3).

The subtitle of *Noises in the Blood* is *Orality, Gender, and the "Vulgar"
Body of Jamaican Popular Culture*. Looking at oral texts, Cooper suggests,
forces us to engage with their embodied contexts, and the racialized and
gendered contexts in which they are performed. "Vulgar," for Cooper, is
a complex word. It can mean common or ordinary; it can denote vernacular
speech, the spoken language of the people; it can denote impoliteness; and it
has connotations of sexual flagrancy or crudeness. Uses of the word "vulgar"
in the Jamaican context show how poverty, vernacular speech, and sexuality
have become associated with one another, as much for those who celebrate
as for those who criticize cultural expressions perceived as vulgar or slack.
Throughout the book, Cooper focuses on the pragmatic meaning of vulgar
expression, both in the sense of nonvalorized and vernacular, and in the
sense of self-expression that foregrounds crude or sexual topics. Louise
Bennett's poetry, for example, unashamedly foregrounds "the amplitude
of the speaker's body," which in turn acts as a "figure for the verbal
expansiveness that is often the only weapon of the politically powerless"
(41). "The raw sexism of some DJs," Cooper writes in her chapter on
dancehall, "can … be seen as an expression of diminished masculinity
seeking to assert itself at the most basic, and often only level where it is
allowed free play" (165). Cooper repeatedly emphasizes the vernacular
eloquence of invective or derisory speech, "throwing words" (6) or "trac-
ings" (41), as an index of racial, gendered, and economic disenfranchisement. The eloquence of the vernacular and its impropriety and crudeness
cannot be understood separately from one another, she suggests. In this
way, Cooper's criticism, by broadening its object of study, critiques the
colonial association of literary study with rectitude and good conduct and
shows the assumptions about class and gender that were implicit in it.

Conclusion

Writing in 1993, at a time of growing interest in the literatures of the
formerly colonized world, Carolyn Cooper warned of the danger that "our
literatures can become appropriated by totalising literary theories that

reduce all 'post-colonial' literatures to the common bond(age) of the great – however deconstructed – European tradition" (15). Taking my prompt from this, this chapter has looked at the history of literary scholarship in the Caribbean itself as it addressed itself to the task of decolonization. I have shown how innovations in literary scholarship arose in response to concrete colonial legacies in the region's educational institutions. In the process, I have offered a more detailed analysis of a number of texts that had a key influence on the process of literary decolonization, and which I have found particularly illuminating in my own reading. The story I tell is of course selective – though not, I hope, arbitrary – and readers may find much that they would add or argue about. My hope is that it offers a useful map for how the complex concept of decolonization has been parsed by scholars and teachers in practice.

While researching this chapter, three larger methodological trends became apparent that – for me, at least – seem helpful for thinking about research and teaching today. First, this chapter has shown the decolonization of English literary study in the Caribbean as a project that unfurled in conversation, through time. Asking students to compare the different and evolving critical approaches of three committed anticolonialists, such as Mervyn Morris (in "On Reading Louise Bennett, Seriously"), Gordon Rohlehr (in "Sparrow and the Language of Calypso"), and Carolyn Cooper (in "Slackness Hiding from Culture") reframes the task of decolonization not as a series of doctrines to be learned, but as practice of critique. Knowing, for example, that Morris, one of Wynter's "acquiescent" critics, was also a valued teacher and influence for Cooper, laying the groundwork for her studies of Bennett and others, is to frame the conversation as one of collaboration. It is to foster an attitude of critical scrutiny and openness toward different viewpoints, including one's own.

Secondly, Sylvia Wynter's work poses a series of questions that we might ask of ourselves and ask students to reflect on. What are the largest systems or "wholes" of which the text I am reading forms a part? Where do I stand within that whole, and in relation to the text I am studying? How does attending to Caribbean literature and history inflect, alter, or expand the larger literary-historical or theoretical stories implicit (or explicit) in my research and study?

The final methodological point I would draw attention to is related to this. Through this chapter we have seen the symbiotic evolution of literature and criticism: how reading practices respond to new works, or genres, and how critical ideas feed back into literary development. Sensitive readers are always in principle attentive to how texts, readers, and genres invite us to engage with and handle them. Yet whatever our literary background, there will always be times when, encountering new types of text, we are pulled up short. Why does this text not fit the model I was expecting or meet the expectations I unconsciously carry with me from elsewhere? As Wynter says, practices of reading and evaluation are never objective, nor universally applicable. In a literary classroom, whether we are reading the allusive metrical inventions of Walcott, or the lyrics of Josey Wales, we might ask ourselves, or our students, to make explicit the tacit expectations we have of specific authors, texts, or genres in order to understand, situate, and provincialize them. Reading the work of Rohlehr and Cooper, we see a model of a dynamic critical intelligence at work, asking itself constantly, "How is this text inviting me to engage with it?" and stretching, adapting, expanding to account for the different pragmatic worlds, the different types of verbal invention or "intelligence" (Rohlehr's word) at play. Of course, some texts will still disappoint. Cooper's work has great fun with the subpar performance poets who, consciously or unconsciously, "exploit the low expectations and ignorance of . . . the perversely 'liberal,' patronising art establishment" in the UK (71). Nonetheless, the practice of reading these critics model – flexible and responsive to the texts themselves, alive to its own assumptions and expectations – seems to me worth studying, imitating, and passing on.

Notes

1. See Baugh 56–8 for a detailed description of syllabus changes in the period 1950–70.
2. James had offered a more detailed reflection on these issues in "From Touissant L'Ouverture to Fidel Castro," the essay appended to the 1963 edition of *The Black Jacobins*. Here, he argues that to enfranchise West Indian literature, and historical experiences, into the narrative of Western Europe and its cultures is fundamentally to *change* that narrative, and to understand it more critically. See James, *Jacobins* 305–26.
3. A brilliantly entertaining and informative account of Wynter's life, education, and career, her role in the founding of the *Jamaica Journal*, her relationship with the New World Group, and the prompts and ambitions of this essay can be found in a long-form interview with David Scott (see Scott 123–33, 145–48, 151–54).
4. On the context and contemporary influence of Rohlehr's talk, see Walmsley (68–71).

WORKS CITED

Baugh, Edward. "English Studies in the University of the West Indies: Retrospect and Prospect." *Caribbean Quarterly* 16.4 (1970): 48–60.

Brodber, Erna. *Myal*. London: New Beacon Books, 1988.

Campbell, Carl C. *The Young Colonials: A Social History of Education in Trinidad and Tobago 1834–1939*. Cave Hill: University of the West Indies Press, 1996.

Cooper, Carolyn. *Noises in the Blood: Orality, Gender, and the "Vulgar" Body of Jamaican Popular Culture*. Durham, NC: Duke University Press, 1995.

Edwards, Norval. "The Foundational Generation." In Michael A Bucknor and Alison Donnell, eds., *The Routledge Companion to Anglophone Caribbean Literature*. Abingdon: Routledge, 2011, 111–23.

Fletcher, C. R. L. and Rudyard Kipling. *A School History of England*. Oxford: Clarendon Press, 1911.

Fraser, Robert. "School Readers in the Empire and the Creation of Postcolonial Taste." In Robert Fraser and Mary Hammond, eds., *Books without Borders*, vol. 1. Basingstoke: Palgrave Macmillan, 2008, 89–106.

Gikandi, Simon. "Introduction." In Simon Gikandi, ed., *The Novel in Africa and the Caribbean Since 1950*. Oxford: Oxford University Press, 2016, xv–xxviii.

Girvan, Norman. "New World and Its Critics." In Brian Meeks and Norman Girvan, eds., *Caribbean Reasonings: The Thought of New World*. Kingston: Ian Randle, 2010. Kindle ed.

Griffith, Glyne. "Forging the Critical Canon." In Raphael Dalleo and Curdella Forbes, eds., *Caribbean Literature in Transition, 1920–1970*. Cambridge: Cambridge University Press, 2020, 293–307.

James, C. L. R. *Beyond a Boundary*. London: Yellow Jersey, 2005.

The Black Jacobins. London: Penguin, 2001.

"Home Is Where They Want to Be." *The Trinidad Guardian Magazine* February 14, 1965: 4–5.

Kincaid, Jamaica. *Annie John*. 1985. London: Vintage, 1997.

Lamming, George. *The Pleasures of Exile*. London: Pluto, 2005.

Lewis, Rupert. "Jamaican Black Power in the 1960s." In Kate Quinn, ed., *Black Power in the Caribbean*. Gainesville: University of Florida Press, 2014, 53–74.

Low, Gail. "An Educational Empire of Print: Thomas Nelson and 'Localisation' in the *West Indian Readers*." In Theo van Heijnsbergen and Carla Sassi, eds., *Within and without Empire: Scotland across the (Post)colonial Borderline*. Newcastle-upon-Tyne: Cambridge Scholars Press, 2013, 108–22.

"'Read! Learn!': Grobalisation and (G)localisation in Caribbean Textbook Publishing." In Elleke Boehmer, Rouven Kunstmann, Priyasha Mukhopadhyay and Asha Rogers, eds., *The Global Histories of Books: Methods and Practices*. Cham: Palgrave Macmillan, 2017, 99–127.

Morris, Mervyn. "On Reading Louise Bennett, Seriously." *Jamaica Journal* 1.1 (1967): 69–74.

Naipaul, V. S. *A House for Mr Biswas*. 1961. London: Picador, 2003.

Quinn, Kate. "Introduction: New Perspectives on Black Power in the Caribbean." In Kate Quinn, ed., *Black Power in the Caribbean*. Gainesville: University of Florida Press, 2014, 1–24.

Rodney, Walter. *How Europe Underdeveloped Africa*. London: Verso, 2018. Kindle ed.

Rohlehr, Gordon. "Sparrow and the Language of Calypso." *Savacou* 2 (1970): 87–99.

Scott, David. "The Re-Enchantment of Humanism: An Interview with Sylvia Wynter." *Small Axe* 8 (2000). 119-207.

"UCWI/UWI Timeline." University of the West Indies. September 22, 2021. www.uwi.edu/timeline/.

Walmsley, Anne. *The Caribbean Artists Movement 1966–1972: A Literary and Cultural History*. London: New Beacon, 1992.

Wynter, Sylvia. "We Need to Sit Down Together and Talk about a Little Culture: Part One." *Jamaica Journal* 2.4 (1968): 23–32.

"We Need to Sit Down Together and Talk about a Little Culture: Part Two." *Jamaica Journal* 3.1 (1969): 27–42.

CHAPTER 26

#RhodesMustFall and the Reform
of the Literature Curriculum

James Ogude

The #RhodesMustFall movement that preoccupied the public imagination
at universities in South Africa foregrounded not only the legacy of British
colonialism in South Africa and especially the Cape, but also the place of
Imperial statues in former British colonies. The protests, which took place
between 2015 and 2017 crystallized around the statue of Cecil Rhodes, which
continued to loom large in one of Africa's foremost institutions, the
University of Cape Town (UCT). The protests brought back not just
memories, but also a lingering presence of the Empire through its architecture and, in this instance, its monuments, and with it a discursive culture or
a colonial discourse that continues to pervade educational institutions such
as the University of Cape Town. Cecil Rhodes statue worked like a semiotic
system, with layered meanings. In its more basic form, it signified
a celebration of a historical figure from a specific historical moment with
its entire troubled legacy. It signified a specific understanding of the past
whose traces could be seen in the present, while drawing attention to that
connection between these two zones of history as if they were inseparable.
However, there was also a much deeper meaning, more insidious than what
we could readily glean from the surface symbol itself. The statue clearly
signified a great deal more, and that is not to suggest that the literal
signification was less significant. The point is that a closer and deeper reading
of the statue revealed a complex network of spatial and ideological codes of
signification, which pointed to what is clearly a system of a surreptitious
authority and power that we can only feel and experience in our daily
encounters. A closer look at the statue pointed to subtle layers of power at
work – a stark reminder of an imperial authority that we cannot ignore. For
example, its location at the university, the center of intellectual knowledge,
but one whose history speaks to a historical network of imperial patronage
and a production of an exclusionary discursive knowledge, was not lost on
many, especially its Black students. With its towering figure and a sweeping
imperial gaze over the city of Cape Town, one could not help but notice the

positioning of this imperial authority, the architect of British imperialism at the southern tip of Africa.

Monuments, Stephen Slemon has reminded us, are not just historical, they are monuments to history (Slemon 4). There is no doubt that the architects of Cecil Rhodes's statue intended it to be an important signpost in South Africa's imperial history. It was deliberately positioned "to construct the category of 'history' as the self-privileging inscription of the coloniser, but also to legitimate a particular concept of history" (4–5). Like most monuments, "it signified history as the record of major events, the inscriptions of great men upon the groundwork of time and space" (5). Cecil Rhodes was "a gift" to South Africa, cast in both bronze and stone, for posterity, but one that also signaled the banishment of colonized cultures. Thus, to inscribe Rhodes into history meant that the colonized history and cultures – their everyday practices – had to remain silenced. The point is that the semiotic system that the colonizer imposes through monuments such as that of Cecil Rhodes sets the terms of engagement and the ultimate limits of expression that the colonized are allowed to possess. And this has very little to do with the agency of the colonized or the lack thereof, it is just that the terms of speaking have already been predetermined by a discursive system that the colonized have been hailed into. As Slemon observes, "there is no gaze outside that of the coloniser, no angle of vision that opens to a future other than that which the statue, as a monument to History, inscribes – unless, of course, it is that of the viewers" (5–6).

What does it mean to say that there is no gaze outside that of the colonizer, unless it is that of the viewers? A response to this question requires an understanding of the limits of complicity by the colonized when they are drawn into a semiotic field triggered by a monument like that of Rhodes. It is to understand that this complicity is neither benign nor absolute in the sense of it being facile or totalizing. In the first instance, the viewers have to be part of the colonizer's gaze to understand it, and to participate in it actively. Secondly, it is their knowledge of Western modes of representation that enables them to grasp the hidden meanings of the statue, in the way that the students of UCT did. In other words, it takes an understanding of how the discourse of colonialism works to understand both its more obvious ideological enactment and its deeper signification processes.[1] I am suggesting here that those who have been hailed into the discourse of colonialism understand its violence most. As Foucault puts it, discourse is "a violence we do to things"; it is a "diffuse and hidden conglomerate of power"; and as a social formation, it works to constitute "reality" not only for the objects it appears passively to represent but also for the subjects who form the coherent interpretive community upon which it depends (Young 48). According to Foucault then, discourse, and this would apply to colonial discourse too, designates those discursive practices that work to produce and naturalize the hierarchical power structures of the imperial enterprise. Hulme complicates this further by suggesting that discourse also serves, "to mobilise those power structures in the management of both colonial and neo-colonial cross-cultural relationships" (Hulme 2).

The nature of contestation by students at UCT revolved around what Foucault refers to as "violence we inflict on things." Foucault's reference to violence inflicted on "things" is instructive here, especially in the context of the Empire, where violence was not only directed at humans, but also the totality of the colonized environment. In Africa, it was violence directed at its total ecological system and a devious separation of the human from nature through a Cartesian logic. If Rhodes's statue at the University of Cape Town was offensive to most students, it was because it represented what Rob Nixon, in a different context, refers to as "slow violence" – a systemic annihilation of colonized subjects and their spaces – their institutions and their systems of knowledge. It is not because they were incapable of a nuanced translation of this symbol of imperialism, or simply unable to grasp what Anne Coombes has characterized as supplementary meanings that monuments often bring to the fore with the passage of time – as they travel across history.[2] As one listened to the narratives of students, it became evident that the statue was a trigger, if not an eloquent reminder, of an institutional culture that several generations of Black students have endured in silence, with occasional outbursts, since 1994, when the university truly opened its doors to Black students. It was also a reminder of forms of subliminal racism that have continued to inform not just the neoliberal universities, but also the world of work – especially the corporate world – which this new generation of students, who had all along assumed that they had been hailed into a modern system that their parents could only dream about, would soon discover was a façade. Perhaps more importantly, it was a deliberate attempt to subvert those codes of recognition that had been normalized over the years in their institution and to establish the presence of cultural heterogeneity and difference as a push against a dominant discourse and epistemic unilateralism in knowledge production. It was the struggle to reclaim representational strategies and to create the conditions for their possibilities – for their realization.

Here are post-Uhuru or postapartheid youth, the born frees as we call them in South Africa, staging their pain and rage around a monument, but in a manner that even their liberators like Mandela could not bring themselves to do. What the monument uncovered for these students was painful traces of the colonial, apartheid, and a dreadful postcolonial moment, all rolled into one political nightmare – urgently in need of change. In a sense, the #Rhodes Must Fall movement pointed to a radical reconstruction of memory as a site upon which the intractable traces of the past are felt on people's bodies, in their landscapes, landmarks, and souvenirs. Indeed, it uncovered how it is felt in their everyday lives and routines, in their daily encounters and entanglement, in their lecture halls – a tough moral fabric of their social relations – whether at institutions of learning or at work. The movement redirected our attention to the urgent need to rethink our understanding of the force of memory, its official and unofficial forms, its moves between the personal and the social postcolonial transformations.

How else would we be able to explain this most improbable irony, that a hundred or so years ago Rhodes, in being buried in the Matopos hills in Zimbabwe, was "twinned" with Mzilikazi, the founder of the Ndebele kingdom that Rhodes's British South African Company conquered. Almost exactly a hundred years later, Rhodes is now "twinned" with Nelson Mandela, with the creation of the Mandela–Rhodes Foundation, a partnership between the Rhodes Trust and the Mandela Foundation. Reflecting on the irony, Paul Maylam remarks during Rhodes memorial lecture at Rhodes University in 2002:

> Another Paradox? A coalition of two very different men – or perhaps a combination of Rhodes' financial might and Mandela's generosity of spirit. It is certainly a combination that would have delighted Rhodes because it gives legitimacy to his name and ensures its perpetuation at a time when his reputation is at a low. (146)

Daniel Herwitz, writing on "Monument, Ruin, and Redress in South African Heritage," has suggested that controversies around heritage symbols, such as Rhodes's statue, "are often responses to a world of ruin" (232) – perhaps the pain and despair, poverty and squalor in the townships and squatter camps – often juxtaposed in close proximity to the townships – the gigantic malls of South Africa, that have become the new monuments of power and opulence. Herwitz is drawing attention here to the persistence of apartheid spatial arrangements – its ruins – in which squalor, depravation, and extreme poverty are placed in stark juxtaposition to opulence. If Rhodes's statue was a marker of imperial power and capital, the gigantic malls that have come to define the face of South Africa are the new monuments – markers of a neoliberal market economy that serves as a trigger for resistance to old colonial monuments and all that they stand for in the new South Africa.

If I have lingered on the controversy around the #Rhodes Must Fall movement, it is because it allows us, as a layered semiotic figure of meaning, to understand the insidious nature of the imperial master code and how complicated the challenges to its authority are, and that they are likely to take multiple paths across history. It offers an important window into various institutional structures, political and cultural, that colonial discourse authorized, and I want to argue that one such important institution was the English syllabus within the British colonies. The debate around the Rhodes statue opens up a range of issues that are pertinent to our engagement with the English curriculum in South Africa. Like the Rhodes monument, the English Literature syllabus in South Africa has stood as a colossus – a cultural edifice that has been so central in shaping what canonical literature really is in the imagination of many, within and outside the academy. It was always the bedrock of imperial values and history – a purveyor of norms and values against which the colonized other had to be judged. The English Literature syllabus, more than any other discipline, was so central to the definition of what it meant to be or not to be an enlightened colonized subject, and this understanding would continue to hold sway within the academy for several years to come. To be a learned person, at least within the colony, one had to show not only a mastery of the English language, but also a mastery of the great English writers.[3] Outside the English tradition, there was no literature, and there was no culture. What this implied was a persistent attempt to silence Indigenous narratives and voices, right into the independence period. The irony of course is that even as colonialism was having a huge impact on its idea of Englishness internally in England, as Simon Gikandi has demonstrated in *Maps of Englishness*, the variables within British colonies remained largely constant. On a recent anniversary of Shakespeare, the BBC reported that the English writer was more widely known among high-school children in India and South Africa as in the United Kingdom itself.[4]

One can therefore understand and sympathize with the passion of resentment that the statue of Rhodes unleashed among the students at the University of Cape Town. After all, what Rhodes figured at both a literal and an allegorical level found expression in what was taught in the lecture halls. Rhodes's gaze found its most eloquent performance in the lecture rooms and in the discursive knowledge formations that continued to frame everyday meanings and relationships of students and their lecturers. Significantly, a close examination of the Literature syllabus at the University of Cape Town at the height of #Rhodes Must Fall in 2015 showed nothing close to what one would regard as a transformed curriculum, carrying, as it should, the weight of African literature. Up until 2018, the pace of change had been so slow that one could hardly claim that a student would graduate in the department of English with a sound grasp of African literature. For example, before 2018, African Literature and Language Studies I and II and English Literary Studies I and II, taught in the first and second years, were often paired, and students had to choose between African or English streams. Given the dominant history of the English-language syllabus at high school, in which the canonical texts were privileged, the African-language stream had very little chance of succeeding. Students understandably flocked to the English stream because that is what they had been exposed to.[5]

When change eventually came, it was neither a thoroughgoing study of African literature nor a centering of African literature at the heartbeat of its curriculum. It was cloaked behind some esoteric and some undifferentiated course titles that served to diffuse any situational and contextual approach that should enable a better understanding of a literary province or culture. Instead, one came across courses such as "Image, Voice, Word"; "Cultures of Empire, Resistance and Postcoloniality"; "Literature and the Work of Memory"; "Movements, Manifestos and Modernities." Running through all these courses was an attempt to provide a world scope in terms of the texts studied, at times with authors and texts sitting so uneasily that one wondered what the motivation or the endgame was. I can understand the idea behind all these attempts to "deprovincialize" the curriculum and push for a comparative approach that is less driven by context of production, but more by theoretical considerations and conceptual approach. The danger with this approach is that it continues to center the West, since various modes of reading some of the issues signaled in the course titles are underpinned by Western notions of genre, and Western-derived critical-theoretical models, which are often deployed indiscriminately when talking about concepts such as memory, postcoloniality, and image, among others. Postcolonialism, a popular rubric in framing a number of literature courses here in South Africa, is not without its flaws, as critics such as Ato Quayson and McLeod have pointed out (Quayson; McLeod). It ends up, as McLeod writes, "[creating] a ghetto for literature from once-colonised countries within English departments and degree schemes" (249). The courses become readings into ideas as opposed to a sustained grasp of texts and how these help us to voyage into specific contexts of production and how literature really works in Africa to colonize meaning – to offer us a window into those competing cultural and political facets of Africa. Instead of students having a sustained experience of African literature, the literature itself is driven underground, and a smattering of texts are eclectically thrown into courses that are largely thematically or conceptually driven. Take for example the University of Cape Town's senior undergraduate course titled "Movements, Manifestos and Modernities," which brings together Steve Biko's *I Write What I Like*, Alice Walker's *Meridian*, Maryse Conde's *Land of Many Colours and Nanna-Ya*, and Virginia Woolf's *A Room of One's Own*. Although the course works through the broad rubric of what it calls "the history of literary and cultural studies," it is nevertheless difficult to understand what motivates the choice of these writers and texts, which are random and eclectic, even when one appreciates the political and cultural capital of these texts independent of each other.

To be fair, the English Department at the University of Cape Town, unlike many in the region, has moved away from a conservative structure, which ensured that African literature courses were ghettoized. Next door at the University of the Western Cape, allegedly leftist leaning and closely associated with the antiapartheid struggle, African literature only appears in a course called "Africa and the World" at second-year level. The English-language syllabus remains at the core of the courses taught from second year through to third year. At the center of its syllabus, it continues to retain courses such as "Romanticism and 19th Century Fiction"; "Renaissance Studies," which privileges the English and European Renaissance; "Post-Colonial Literature and Postmodern Fiction," the latter largely driven by theory and again with J. M. Coetzee's *Foe* as the only text from the continent of Africa taught in the course. With a few exceptions, a schizophrenic character runs through a number of courses taught in most of the English departments in South Africa that are seeking to disavow the colonial tradition, while continuing to cling to the core aspects of the same tradition. Of these, it is the Literary Studies in English at Rhodes University that offers one of the most radical departures from the English canon, and perhaps the most comprehensive study of what would pass as strong streams of African literature. The syllabus is evenly balanced, with courses on African and English traditions at undergraduate level and distinct courses at postgraduate level that focus on early modern to Romantic literature, world literature, and African literature. Thus, throughout undergraduate and postgraduate levels, African literature remains one of the core streams that constitute literary studies at Rhodes University. With the exception of Fort Hare University, with courses organized around genre and regional and Black diasporic movements such as the Harlem Renaissance, most departments of English remain highly schizophrenic in their content and choice of texts. In their anxiety to placate the authorities and to signal a specific gesture toward curriculum diversity, they display contradictory literary poles without being mindful of coherence. A decolonized curriculum amounted to a facile tokenism, in which a syllabus gets sprinkled with Black or Brown writers, women writers, and gay writers – a deeply flawed nod at diversity, which at times lacked the intellectual principles that undergird a coherent and serious curriculum design.

The schizophrenic impulse behind curricula innovation could be explained in terms of the mixed constituencies that that these departments continue to serve. On the one hand, we have a traditional cohort of students, who are predominantly White, but who also include a section of the Black elite for whom English without Shakespeare and the Great Tradition is incomplete – they push back at any attempts to bring about curriculum transformation. On the other hand, we have a cohort of Black students who are insisting on asserting a new identity through the literatures they read and are demanding change now. Both groups are not hegemonic and quite often are not certain about the nature of what ought to be retained in the old order and what needs to be introduced in the new order. The push-and-pull situation has proved to be counterproductive for genuine curriculum reform, as curriculum creators strive to please these competing constituencies. The end result is what can hardly be described as a decolonized English curriculum, but the result of competing interests ranging from the interests of those senior faculty who are not prepared to let go of their old practices, and a new but energetic cohort of scholars who are seeking change but remain at the mercy of the senior scholars who see transformation as a threat to their own careers. That they also minister to a divided constituency of students and parents, often split along racial and class lines, does not help the situation.

What the above scenario points to in relation to the movement of ideas is compelling: that, although it is important to register an awareness of the lingering presence of a colonial discourse, it is equally important to understand that the authority of the imperial culture could only find force within the limits of those shifting boundaries of accommodation and resistance that the Empire generated. It is in that sense that I seek to argue that, important as the "Fallist" movement was in the imagination of many South Africans, and in spite of the ripples it caused within the continent and beyond, it was never the inaugural moment of the decolonial turn.[6] We have to understand decoloniality as a process and perhaps a much more protracted one when it comes to curriculum change in a discipline such as English with so many competing interests. If one wants to see glimmers of change and challenges to the English Literature syllabus, then one has to look elsewhere – far from the mainstream sites of scholarship and the academy.

A number of important issues are worth flagging here in relation to my observation above. The struggle for a distinct voice within the broad terrain of culture and specifically with reference to the English Literature syllabus has a long history in South Africa as it does in the rest of the continent. These struggles took different routes, ranging from a basic reactivation of the traditional resource base, as Ato Quayson reminds us (*Strategic Transformations*) or simply in the preservation of oral forms. It also took the route of translating received stories and inventing new narratives that are different, even if sometimes mimicking those received templates linked to colonial tutelage, or simply insisting on writing in Indigenous languages, not English. What distinguished these initiatives was that common goal to restore agency to the colonized subjects in a cultural domain dominated by the English language and literature. My point is that the struggle to have control over what constitutes the content of literature in South Africa and the broader cultural terrain has captured the imagination of colonized subjects for decades, especially among the Black intelligentsia. The English dominance was always challenged from the margins of the academy even when it continued to hold sway in a number of English departments in South Africa.

One of the main challenges to the unassailed position of English language and literature in South African universities and high schools was a notable presence of African Languages departments in most universities, which offered not just basic language teaching of isiZulu, isiXhosa, and Sesotho, among others, but also taught literatures in these languages. And although most of these departments were underresourced and often ghettoized, with no substantive lecturer-track positions other than that of tutors, it was a tacit admission – even if grudgingly – that Indigenous cultural streams needed to be acknowledged in their own right. As a result, South Africa remains one of the very few countries on the continent of Africa where Indigenous languages have a long history of presence within the academy. So in its eagerness to perpetuate some form of "tribal nativism," the Apartheid regime, by encouraging the teaching of African languages literatures, ended up establishing a visible presence of cultural heterogeneity and difference against the backdrop of a dominant colonial discourse. It was an act of "nibbling" at resilient English dominance in South Africa, as Francis Nyamnjoh, would have it in a different context.

One of the ways in which African writers in general and a number of South African writers in particular engaged in this process of decolonizing English was through the act of translating canonical texts and Western classics. In *The Translator's Invisibility*, the critic Venuti decries the hegemony of the English language and Anglo-American cultural values and advocates a translation practice of foreignization, namely "resisting dominant values in the receiving cultures so as to signify the linguistic and cultural differences in the foreign text" (18). What Venuti is challenging here is the Anglo-American idea of translation as domestication, in which a foreign work is assimilated into the values and hierarchies of the receiving culture and made to read as if it were an "original" in the target language, effectively rendering the act of translation and the translator invisible. For Venuti, translation is a political act, and in translation practice, one has to see the potential to destabilize cultural hierarchies and interrogate cultural norms in the receiving culture.

Foundational South African writers such as Sol Plaatje, Oscar Dhlomo, and AC Jordan, among others, were adept at the kind of translation that Venuti describes here but often pushed a line that combined a strong reliance on European genres with a powerful and assertive attitude on issues of race and culture. They were also able to placate the authorities, whose power alone allowed them access to a voice in print, even as they asserted their differences from that power. Their texts were not simply working to resist and dismantle, mimic and assimilate Western modes of self-writing without any intervention or aesthetic agency, but rather they set out very deliberately, and regardless of whether they were writing in English or Indigenous African languages, to develop a new language. It was a new grammar of writing that was neither strictly Western nor traditional. It was something new in which a creative evocation of an Indigenous resource base played a part as much as received modes of self-inscription did. These writers were also deeply concerned with the project of translation, not simply of the African world to Europe, but equally a translation of the Western world and their classics. As I have argued elsewhere, "part of it was to demonstrate that the European classics they were keen to translate could travel and inhabit spaces that had been designated as the other, because the assumption was that the European classics could not be carried and processed (that is, not assimilated) by receiving cultures and local languages" (Ogude, "Foundational Writers" 30). Significantly, in their endeavor to appropriate these texts into local contexts, they went for the Western canon, especially plays of Shakespeare such as *Julius Caesar*, *Othello*, and *Macbeth*, among others – subjecting them to the tyranny of local languages and idioms. These forms of translation that I outline here marked important moments of subversion and intrusive challenge to the supremacy of English-language culture.

A gradual "nibbling" at the resilience of English in South Africa also started from within English departments in South Africa among the leftist-leaning and feminist scholars who could not articulate their ideas with any form of coherence and ideological certainty without taking recourse to some form of African literature in their syllabus. This shift took different forms at different universities. In some, it found expression within an omnibus course going under the title of "World Literature" that drew its content from a cross section of continents and subcontinents, such as India, the Caribbean, and African American literatures, but without abandoning some of the core English texts. In others, it took a selective focus on some of the canonical writers in Africa, such as Chinua Achebe and Ngũgĩ wa Thiong'o. As early as the late 1970s to the 1980s, one could come across a sprinkling of African literary texts, largely those from the leftist-leaning writers such as Ngũgĩ wa Thiong'o. When I arrived in the South African academy in 1991, Ngũgĩ's texts such as *A Grain of Wheat* and some of his collection of essays such as *Decolonizing the Mind* were already present in the syllabus of many English departments.[7] In a rare gesture of recognition, as early as 1989, one of the leading South African journals of literature, *English in Africa*, had dedicated a special issue to Ngũgĩ's works. Of course, the White liberal left within the South African academy were much more comfortable with Ngũgĩ's Marxist and class approach to issues than with, say, Chinua Achebe, whose works often drew attention to the lingering presence of Whiteness and race issues.[8] This shift would grow into full-fledged courses in African literature in a number of English departments in South African universities. This acknowledgment was nevertheless undermined by the fact that African literature was never a core elective and was often paired with English courses such as Shakespeare and the Victorian Novels, much to the detriment of African literature courses that remained totally unknown to the students. For students, Black and White, who had never encountered African literature at high school, the introduction of African literature at university level was an anomaly, and, without deliberate coaxing, the courses never stood a chance of enlisting high numbers.

The students went for what they knew and what they had been told counted in the study of English over the years. As a result, the incremental introduction of African literature was stillborn right from the start, and it would never take off because there were no incentives for choosing it as a course. It continued to carry little to no premium within the academy and in the inherited intellectual horizons of the students. The usual rejoinder that "students, including African students, never liked African literature" has been used to sustain an exclusionary system that continued to privilege the English syllabus way into the third decade of South Africa's democratic dispensation.

This discussion would be incomplete without the mention of one exceptional example in which a nibbling at the English curriculum would decidedly assume the form of centering African literature and related streams of Black diaspora literatures and local narratives drawn from its oral and popular cultural traditions. The African Literature department at the University of the Witwatersrand started as a division of the Comparative and African Literature Department. The South African writer and critic Es'kia Mphahlele in 1983 founded the division that soon grew into a fully established department just a few years after his return from exile. It now stands as one of the very few departments that is singularly focused on the teaching of African literature and other related streams that speak to those literatures produced by peoples of African descent in North America and the Caribbean. Significantly, the department emerged at one of the leading liberal institutions in South Africa – the University of the Witwatersrand – an institution that boasted a strong English department, but one that until recently hardly taught African literature except for a few texts by White South Africans such as Alan Paton, Olive Schreiner, and more recently, J. M. Coetzee. I recall that in 1988 when I applied to do my PhD at the department, the head of department politely informed me that they did not teach African literature and that they had referred my application to the African Literature Department, then headed by the founding professor, Es'kia Mphahlele.

I single out the African Literature department here for three reasons. First, for the creative and bold approach that it took in implementing a syllabus that was grounded in a rich staple of modern African literature. It covered novels, plays, and limited poetry, starting with foundational writers right through to contemporary writers. Secondly, it was unapologetic in seeking to provide a panoramic view of African literature, while at the same time drilling into regional trends and a rich mix of thematic clusters. It touched on topics such as "Gender and Writing in Africa,"

"Performing Power in Post-Independence Africa," "Love in Africa," "Memory, Violence and Representation in Africa," and "Contemporary Trends in African Literature," among others. It also focused on regions, especially on "Literatures of the Black Diaspora." Finally, the department was one of the first to take full advantage of a cultural studies approach[9] as an interdisciplinary, transdisciplinary, and sometimes counterdiscursive field that allowed for content that moved beyond the narrowly conceived disciplinary boundaries and their dominant ideologies. In the process, the department was able to extend the province of imagination and to encourage a deliberate engagement with other zones, adjacent to literature, such as popular music, media, and other oral sources akin to the Indigenous resource base. The department would argue for the need to study African literature in relation to its hinterlands and to pay attention to grassroots intellectual traditions, in a context where African literature continued to be annexed by international trends. The idea was to foreground unknown or hidden intellectual patterns in the broad area of African literature and cultures. The study of popular literature and cultures offered a challenge to postcolonial literary theory, in its multiple variants, which until recently was the prism through which scholars both here and abroad encountered the literature and intellectual history of the continent. Postcolonial theory, for example, tended to homogenize the literature of the continent or reduced it simply to one of the binary logics of opposition and resistance. Significantly, in privileging the imaginative capacity of literature and the creative arts broadly, the department also foregrounded the social and moral function of literature and related forms of cultural production, which Ato Quayson has termed "calibrations" to denote a kind of reading that draws links between the literary-aesthetic, social, cultural, and political domains (Quayson, *Calibrations*, xii). The true impact of the African Literature department at the University of the Witwatersrand has to be measured against its excellent tradition of mentorship at the postgraduate level. It has produced some of the finest scholars of African literature and cultures, who continue to be dispersed across a number of English departments here in South Africa and beyond, playing that role of challenging Englishness through some of the most striking subversive maneuvers and political interventions in the ongoing reconstitution of the English literature syllabus.

The lesson to be drawn from this continuing experiment at the African Literature department is not so much that Englishness was constantly being reconfigured. That the English syllabus was unstable and its boundaries of control shifting is now obvious. My point is that the colonized cannot continue to be seen as victims of Englishness and imperial poetics as certain strands of #Rhodes Must Fall implied. Rather, through a constant struggle and as Simon Gikandi reminds us, "in inventing itself, the colonial space would also reinvent the structure and meaning of the core terms of Englishness" (*Maps* XVIII), including ways in which the English canon are read, even if we think these are not radical enough. It is a case of change in permanence, very similar to the readings of the Rhodes statue as a semiotic figure, whose meanings were contingent not simply on those ascribed to it by the colonizer, but also the colonized subject's disruptive readings. The privileging of African literature is therefore a challenge to the very supremacy of English. The second lesson that we glean from the African literature experiment is that a certain amount of African literature content is needed to register its overlapping territories and rich diversity. It is not enough to use African literature texts as some *deus ex machina*, for a conceptually driven course, which fails to embed it in a curriculum as a serious subject in its own right. Third, it is not enough to teach African literature, important as content is, if method and theoretical protocols in themselves are not decolonized, because there is always the danger of sliding into a nativist approach that valorizes anything African and Black, while closing off other streams of literary and cultural knowledge. The flipside of this argument is of course the persistent trend to want to teach African literature but do so through the lenses of Northern theories as if these are neutral implements for cutting knowledge, and as if African literatures in themselves do not have the force of offering theoretical insights. A productive reading of African literature, especially if it has to offer a formidable challenge to Englishness, must see it as a site of reflection and praxis. I believe the one thing that the African Literature department at the University of the Witwatersrand has done so well over the years is to posit African literature as a site of reflection and struggle, and always in an ongoing tension with other cultural streams emanating from within and outside our borders. In conclusion, one has to agree that #Rhodes Must Fall, with all its fault lines,[10] has been important in forcing the institutions of higher learning to take curriculum transformation in all disciplines in the humanities and social sciences seriously. The effects of challenging colonial discourse may be slow and painful along the way, but acts of formidable refusal like the one enacted by the #Rhodes Must Fall have been critical in destabilizing the canonical position of English literature here in South Africa and beyond.

Notes

1. For further discussions of the discourse of colonialism, see Hulme; Brown.
2. Annie E. Coombes in her book *History of Apartheid* discusses the shifting meanings attached to apartheid monuments, especially Voortrekker Monument. She argues that over time, "the Monument has in fact accrued significance, supplemental to and in some cases, of course, directly at odds with, its intended symbolic presence. I see this as not simply a symptom of the passing of time and the necessary sedimenting of meanings that accumulate as part of that process of historical change" (175). Similarly, one has to acknowledge how Cecil Rhodes had grown to become a symbol of benevolence and financial patronage directed at universities such as Oxford through his Trust. Later on, Rhodes would twin with Mandela in what is now dubbed the Rhodes–Mandela Scholarship.
3. See Ngũgĩ wa Thiong'o 12. Ngũgĩ draws attention to how English was highly privileged in colonial education and generously rewarded. It was "the ticket to higher realms. English became the measure of intelligence and ability in the arts, the sciences, and all the other branches of learning. English became the main determinant of a child's progress up the ladder of formal education." It was so primed that failing English meant failing the entire set of exams even if you had passed other subjects.
4. My observation is based on a report by BBC survey on UK students' awareness of Shakespeare on Shakespeare Day in the UK on April 23, 2019. The survey was also conducted among Indian and South African students, with the result that Shakespeare was more widely known among South African and Indian students than their UK counterparts.
5. Compared to University of Kwazulu Natal, another liberal university, University of Cape Town English Department had made relatively major interventions in their English syllabus. At the University of Kwazulu Natal, the English Department remained steeped in the mainstream English syllabus: The English Novel, Understanding Poetry, Romanticism, and so on, with only one major elective at Year Three with a course titled "African Experience in Drama and Performance," with special focus on the continent's drama.
6. See Mamdani for a history of decolonization on the continent.
7. See my engagement with this issue in "Location and History."
8. I have in mind here Chinua Achebe's foundational texts such as *Things Fall Apart* (1958) and *Arrow of God* (1964), texts that grapple with issues of race and racism in the colonial enterprise, while equally drawing compelling attention to the destruction of traditional authority by colonial statecraft. For more on the destruction of traditional authority, see Olaniyan 27.
9. It is difficult to tell when Stuart Hall's pioneering work on cultural studies began to shape the debate in South Africa. What is clear is that in the early to mid-1990s, the debate on the place of cultural studies was already raging in South Africa. In September 1993, the Centre for African Studies at the University of Cape Town convened a conference called "Appropriations: New Directions in African Cultural Studies?". The conference led to

a publication of the proceedings titled *Transgressing Boundaries: New Directions in the Study of Culture in Africa* (Cooper and Steyn). Significantly, Isabel Hofmyr, who was the Chair and Head of the African Literature department at the time, was an important interlocutor in these debates and in the publication called on the scholars to look beyond southern Africa to the rest of the continent if they wanted to enrich cultural studies.

10. For a compelling discussion on some of the fault lines of #Rhodes Must Fall and their contexts of articulation, see Kasembeli. See also Ahmed.

WORKS CITED

Achebe, Chinua. *Things Fall Apart*. London: Heinemann, 1958.

Arrow of God. London: Heinemann, 1964.

Ahmed, Kayun A. "#Rhodes Must Fall: How a Decolonial Student Movement in Global South Inspired Epistemic Disobedience at the University of Oxford." *African Studies Review* 63.2 (2020): 281–303. https://doi.org/10.1017/asr.2019.49.

Brown, Paul. "'This Thing of Darkness I Acknowledge Mine': The Tempest and the Discourse of Colonialism." In Jonathan Dollimore and Alan Sinfield, eds., *Political Shakespeare: New Essays in Cultural Materialism*. Ithaca, NY: Cornell University Press, 1985, 48–71.

Coombes, Anne E. *History of Apartheid: Visual Culture and Public Memory in a Democratic South Africa*. Johannesburg: Wits University Press, 2004.

Cooper, Brenda and Andrew Steyn, eds. *Transgressing Boundaries: New Directions in the Study of Culture in Africa*. Cape Town: University of Cape Town Press, 1996.

Gikandi, Simon. *Maps of Englishness: Writing Identity in the Culture of Colonialism*. New York: Columbia University Press, 1996.

Herwitz, Daniel. "Monuments, Ruin, and Redress in South African Heritage." *The German Review: Literature, Culture, Theory* 86.4 (2011): 232–48.

Hulme, Peter. *Colonial Encounters: Europe and the Native Caribbean, 1492–1797*. London: Methuen, 1986.

Kasembeli, Serah Namulisa. "The South African Student #Fallist Movement: Xenophobia and the Impossibility of Including the African 'Other'." *Journal of African Cultural Studies*. 32.3 (2020): 316–31.

Mamdani, Mahmood. "Between the Public Intellectual and the Scholar: Decolonization and Some Post-Independence Initiatives in African Higher Education." *Inter-Asia Cultural Studies* 17.1(2016): 68–83.

Maylam, Paul. "Monuments, Memorials and the Mystique of Empire: The Immortalisation of Cecil Rhodes in the Twentieth Century." *African Sociological Review* 6.1 (2002): 138–47.

McLeod, John. *Beginning Postcolonialism*. Manchester: Manchester University Press, 2000.

Ngũgĩ wa Thiong'o. *A Grain of Wheat*. London: Heinemann, 1967.

Decolonising the Mind. London: James Currey, 1986.

Nixon, Rob. "Slow Violence, Gender, and Environmentalism of the Poor." *Journal of Commonwealth and Postcolonial Studies* 13.2/14.1 (Fall 2006– Spring 2007): 3–12.

Nyamnjoh, Francis B. *#Rhodes MustFall: Nibbling at Resilient Colonialism in South Africa*. Bamenda: Langas Research and Publishing, 2016.

Ogude, James. "Foundational Writers and the Making of African Literary Genealogy: Es'kia Mphahlele and Peter Abrahams." In Bhekizizwe Peterson, Khwezi Mkhize, and Makhosazana Xaba, eds., *Foundational Writers: Peter Abrahams, Noni Jabavu, Sibusiso Nyembezi and Es'Kia Mphahlele*. Johannesburg: Wits University Press, 2022, 27–51.

"Location and History: Salient Issues in Teaching Ngugi to Black South African Students." In Oliver Lovesey, ed., *Approaches to Teaching the Works of Ngugi Wa Thiong'o*. New York: Modern Languages Association, 2012, 315–37.

Olaniyan, Tejumola. "Chinua Achebe and an Archaeology of the Postcolonial African State." *Research in African Literatures* 32.3 (2003): 22–29.

Quayson, Ato. *Strategic Transformations in Nigerian Writing*. Oxford: James Currey, 1997.

Calibrations: Reading for the Social. Minneapolis: University of Minnesota Press, 2003.

Young, Robert. Preface to Michel Foucault, "The Order of Discourse." Trans. Ian McLeod, in Robert Young, ed., *Untying the Text: A Post-Structuralist Reader*. Boston: Routledge & Kegan Paul, 1981.

Slemon, Stephen. "Monuments of Empire: Allegory/Counter-Discourse/Post-Colonial Writing." *Kunapipi* 9.3 (1987): 1–16.

Venuti, Lawrence. *The Translator's Invisibility: A History of Translation*. 2nd ed. New York: Routledge, 2008.

Index